SPLASH!
LEARN ABOUT WATER

BY NADIA HIGGINS

The Child's World

Published by The Child's World®
1980 Lookout Drive • Mankato, MN 56003-1705
800-599-READ • www.childsworld.com

ACKNOWLEDGMENTS
The Child's World®: Mary Berendes, Publishing Director
Content Consultant: Raymond Hozalski, PhD
    Associate Professor of Environmental Engineering
    University of Minnesota
The Design Lab: Design and production
Red Line Editorial: Editorial direction

PHOTO CREDITS: iStockphoto, cover, 1, 2, 3, 4, 6, 8, 10, 12, 14, 16, 18, 20, 22; Lee
Pettet/iStockphoto, 5; Stephan Hoerold/iStockphoto, 7 (top); Peter Wey/iStockphoto, 7
(bottom); Robert Churchill/iStockphoto, 9; Stasys Eidiejus/Fotolia, 10; Paul Yates/iStockphoto,
11; Sebastien Cote/iStockphoto, 13; Mikael Damkier/iStockphoto, 15; Tony Tremblay/
iStockphoto, 17; Peter Zelei/iStockphoto, 19; Jiri Vaclavek/iStockphoto, 21; Jane Yamada, 23

LIBRARY OF CONGRESS CATALOGING-IN-PUBLICATION DATA
Higgins, Nadia.
  Splash! Learn about water / by Nadia Higgins ; illustrated by Jane Yamada.
      p. cm.
  ISBN 978-1-60253-514-5 (lib. bd. : alk. paper)
  1. Water—Juvenile literature. I. Yamada, Jane, ill. II. Title.
  QD169.W3H54 2010
  546'.22—dc22   2010010982

Printed in the United States of America in Mankato, Minnesota.
July 2010
F11538

CONTENTS

Wet Water

Drink it.

Spill it.

Splash it.

Spray it.

Water is wet.

It is a **liquid**.

It is fun to splash in water on a hot summer day. ▶

4

Liquid water rains down from clouds.

It rushes in rivers and fills lakes.

It soaks deep into the ground.

It swirls in the ocean
and crashes on the shore.

Water can be found deep underground. ▶

Water is also found above ground. ▶

Cold, Hard Ice

But liquid water changes.

It gets cold.

It freezes.

It becomes hard ice.

Ice chunks float on a lake. ▶

A snowflake is made of ice.

It is full of holes, like lace.

When snowflakes pile up,
they make white, fluffy snow.

Snow blankets the ground on a calm winter day. ▶

A snowflake usually has six sides. ◀

The coldest parts of Earth are covered in sheets of ice.

Glaciers creep over land.

Giant ice chunks float on the Arctic Ocean.

A glacier is a slow-moving river of ice. ▶

But ice changes.

It warms up.

It melts back into liquid water.

The warm
sun melts
an icicle. ▶

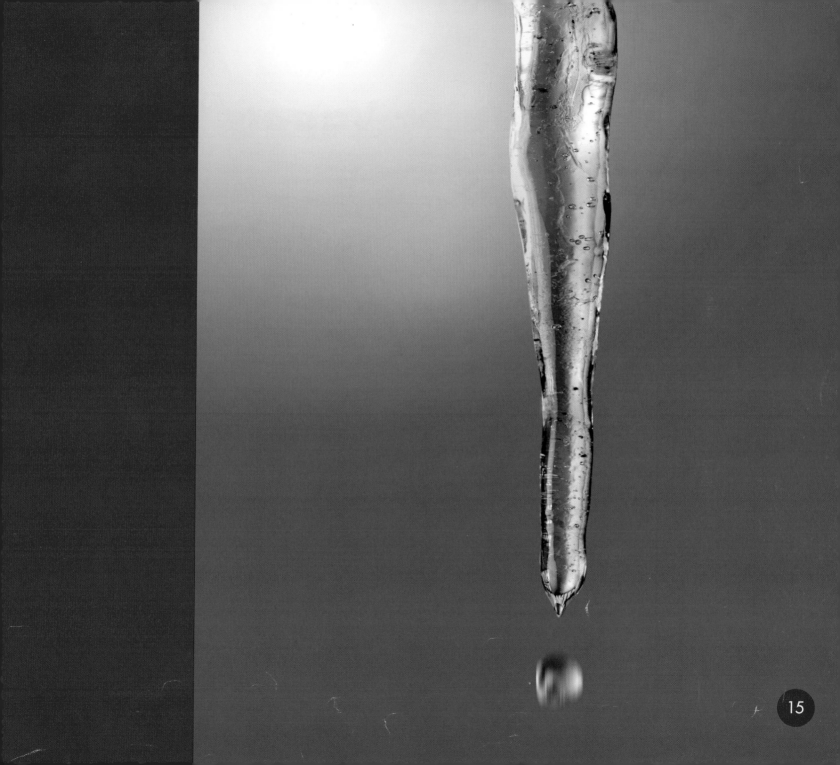

Invisible Water Vapor

If water warms up enough,
it changes another way.

It breaks up into bits too tiny to see.
They float away. They become
water vapor.

Water vapor is part of invisible air.

Clothes dry because water has turned into water vapor. ▶

But then water vapor changes.

It cools down.

It forms tiny drops of liquid water.

The drops may form clouds in the sky, or **fog** over land, or **dew** that coats the grass in the morning.

Fog is like a cloud that is close to the ground. ▶

Amazing Water

Most of Earth is covered by water. And it's a good thing, too.

Plants suck up water with their thirsty roots. People and animals slurp it up, too. Every living thing needs water to stay alive.

A tree's roots seek water deep under the ground. ▶

Think of all the ways you use water:
    for drinking
    for cooking
    for washing
    for flushing.

And water never runs out!
It just keeps changing between
its three forms.

The Three Forms of Water

Water vapor is a gas.
It is part of invisible air.

Water is a liquid.
It is wet.

Ice is a solid.
It is cold and hard.

Words to Know

dew (DOO): Dew is tiny drops of water. Dew covers grass, cars, and other outdoor things on cool mornings.

fog (FOG): Fog is like a cloud that is near to the ground. Fog is a mass of tiny water droplets.

glaciers (GLAY-shurz): Glaciers are huge, frozen rivers of ice. Glaciers creep along land on Earth's coldest places.

liquid (LIH-kwid): A liquid is something wet that you can pour. Water is a liquid.

water vapor (WAH-tur VAY-pur): Water vapor is made of tiny, floating bits of water. Water vapor is part of invisible air.

The Irwin Series in Marketing

Gilbert A. Churchill, Jr., Consulting Editor
University of Wisconsin, Madison

PROMOTIONAL
STRATEGY

Managing the Marketing Communications I

PROMOTIONAL STRATEGY

Managing the Marketing Communications Process

James F. Engel
Eastern College

Martin R. Warshaw
The University of Michigan

Thomas C. Kinnear
The University of Michigan

Eighth Edition

IRWIN

Chicago • Bogotá • Boston • Buenos Aires • Caracas
London • Madrid • Mexico City • Sydney • Toronto

Cover Illustration: Rick Smith © 1994

Executive editor: Rob Zwettler
Senior developmental editor: Andy Winston
Project editor: Denise Santor-Mitzit
Production manager: Bob Lange
Designer: David Lansdon
Art manager: Kim Meriwether
Compositor: Bi-Comp, Inc.
Typeface: 10/12 Cheltenham Light
Printer: R. R. Donnelley & Sons Company

Library of Congress Cataloging-in-Publication Data

Engel, James F.
    Promotional strategy : managing the marketing communications
process / James F. Engel, Martin R. Warshaw, Thomas C. Kinnear.
    p.   cm.—(The Irwin series in marketing)
    Includes bibliographical references and index.
    ISBN 0–256–08204–9
    1. Marketing.   2. Advertising.   3. Marketing—Management.
    I. Warshaw, Martin R.   II. Kinnear, Thomas C., 1943–.
    III. Title.   IV. Series.
HF5415.E65   1991
658.8′2—dc20
                                                                        90-44246

Printed in the United States of America

2 3 4 5 6 7 8 9 0 DO 1 0 9 8 7 6 5

Preface

This book had its beginning in the fall of 1961 when Jim Engel, then an assistant professor of marketing at The University of Michigan, was assigned to teach the promotion course. Available texts proved to be unsatisfactory, thus leading him to contact his graduate school mentor, Hugh Wales, at the University of Illinois. Both agreed to try their hand at an innovative approach that would focus on the entire promotion mix, not just advertising, and build from a solid behavioral foundation.

As they prepared preliminary outlines, they realized that another person was needed to shore up the material on sales management and reseller strategies. The logical candidate was Marty Warshaw, Jim Engel's colleague at Michigan. And so the book was launched. Hugh Wales retired after the third edition, and another Michigan colleague, Tom Kinnear, joined the team.

Our purposes have changed little since the first edition. Our basic conviction is that advertising, sales promotion, personal selling, direct marketing, public relations and publicity, and corporate advertising are all component parts of *one integrated promotional mix*. There is no way that an individual activity, say advertising, can be managed without fully considering these strategic interrelationships. We are pleased to note that in the 1990s, many other authors and marketing practitioners are also beginning to advocate this integrated marketing communications approach.

We are also convinced that marketing strategy must be grounded in realistic research that clearly documents the opportunities and problems to be faced. This requires knowledge of consumer motivation and behavior, the competitive climate, the legal climate, and so on. While this is not a book on research per se, it will help students identify and glean the information needed and teach them how to think strategically once it is in hand.

Since the outset, we have provided the reader a thorough grounding in consumer behavior. Initially we felt, with justification, that few students would have course work in that field. Hence, we tried as much as we could to include a summary of Engel, Kollat, and Blackwell, *Consumer Behavior* (now Engel, Blackwell, and Miniard, *Consumer Behavior*, 7th ed). We now are aware that most readers have had a basic exposure to consumer behavior, so in this edition we concentrate on stressing its unique implications for promotional strategy. Our coverage of consumer behavior remains extensive, however, and is foundational to everything else.

We also have always written from the perspective of those who must conceive and execute promotional strategy. Our intent is to mold and shape effective strategic thinking rather than to provide cookbook lists of answers. We avoid simple answers to problems that defy rule-of-thumb solutions. We make no attempt to imply certainty when it does not exist in the real world.

Finally, our goal—and our greatest challenge over the years—has been to make this book both theoretically sound and highly practical. As we have gained experience ourselves both in teaching and in practical marketing strategy, our perspectives understandably have become modified. Certainly a comparison of this edition with the 1967 version would reveal a marked shift toward consistent use of the criterion, *what does this all mean on the firing line?*

Some schools still retain separate courses in advertising and sales management. Although we take an integrated approach, our material is readily adaptable to a more limited course in advertising by skipping the sections that do not directly apply. We strongly recommend the broader integrated approach, however, because of the trend in that direction in business practice.

Changes to this Edition

Long-time users will quickly see that we have retained our traditional focus which has given this text a leading position in the field. But, *this is an altogether new book throughout.* The following are the greatest changes:

1. The book has an even expanded number of examples and illustrations over the extensive number from the last edition. Most of the short examples, the more extensive promotion-in-actions illustrations, and the chapter opening profiles have been updated to the 1990s. We continue to use the Carnival Cruise Lines example from the previous edition throughout the book, but have updated it to the present.

2. Data on media audiences, costs, effectiveness, etc., all reflect the latest numbers available right up to the publication date of the book.

3. At the request of our professor and student users, we have moved the cornerstone material on communications forward to Chapters 2 and 3.

4. We have expanded the presentation on the measurement of promotional effectiveness well beyond our previous coverage in measuring advertising effectiveness to include coverage of the measurement of sales promotion and sales-force effectiveness. This material has all be integrated into Chapter 21, in a section of the book covering coordination and control of promotion. This change, along with the shifting of the communications material noted above, have resulted in slight changes in chapter numbering. The major logical flow of material in the book has been maintained.

5. We maintain our strong grounding in consumer behavior relevant to promotion. As always, the latest research findings on consumer behavior that are relevant to promotion are included in the book, along with the latest practical and theoretical developments in promotional mangement.

6. We continue to put emphasis on the socioeconomic and ethical dimensions of promotion, and updated this coverage to reflect the issues of the 1990s.

Teaching Aids

In order to provide a more complete and integrated teaching experience, we have expanded the package of available teaching aids with this edition. Now, in addition to the traditional Instructor's Manual and Test Bank, we offer a set of 75 color acetates and a cassette containing video cases that complement many of the concepts in the book.

ACKNOWLEDGMENTS

Over the 26 years of our existence, we have been the beneficiaries of widespread input from colleagues literally throughout the world. This has proved invaluable. They are far too numerous to acknowledge by name here, but we do want to thank those who have specifically contributed their insights to this edition:

Cathy Cole, *University of Iowa*

Eleonora Curlo, *University of Maryland*

Patricia Kennedy, *University of Nebraska–Lincoln*

Alan G. Sawyer, *University of Florida*

Brian van der Westhuizen, *California State University–Northridge*

We have always thanked our families over the years for their forbearance through the tyranny of eight revisions. Jim and Marty are empty nesters, but we still join Tom in expressing appreciation to our wives and kids who always have been partners with us. And, in keeping with our tradition, each of us continues to blame the other guys for errors and omissions in the manuscript.

James F. Engel
Martin R. Warshaw
Thomas C. Kinnear

Contents

ANALYZING THE MARKET   95

Section 5

SALES PROMOTION STRATEGY   343

Chapter 13
Working with Resellers: The Struggle for Channel Control   345

Section 8
COORDINATION AND CONTROL 487

Section

9

EPILOGUE   587

Chapter 22
**Economic and
Social Dimensions   589**

FUNDAMENTALS OF MARKETING COMMUNICATIONS

Section 1 of this book introduces concepts that provide a foundation and framework for the chapters that follow, including communication, information processing, and decision making within a promotional-strategy framework.

Chapter 1 stresses the importance of promotional strategy in the success of businesses and nonprofit organizations of all types, and ties the promotional activity directly to the marketing concept and to the practice of marketing management. This relationship is presented through a discusion of promotion as the communications activity of marketing and through the demonstration of how other parts of the marketing mix—price, distribution, and product—also have communication power.

Chapter 2 is a review of interpersonal and mass communication, examining the persuasive effectiveness of these two differing approaches. We develop a model of communications processes, drawing on contemporary thinking in the field.

Chapter 3 answers this critical question: How does the consumer process the information he or she receives? Market researchers and consumer psychologists have made great strides in understanding this issue. This chapter covers the subject of information processing from a practical marketing point of view.

Chapter 4 describes a framework for analyzing, planning, and implementing decisions that confront the promotion manager. Examples drawn from the advertising, sales force, and consumer and trade promotion of Carnival Cruise Lines are used to illustrate this framework in depth.

1

Promotional Strategy: An Overview

RISING FROM THE ASHES

In 1860, the Edouard Heuer watch factory was founded in St. Imier, in the heart of the Swiss Jura. Heuer chose an unusual path when he chose to concentrate on the manufacture of chronographs and sports watches. The company rose to dominance in the world market, only to fall into crisis in the early 1980s along with other Swiss watch manufacturers. It was then taken over by TAG (Techniques d'Avant-Garde).

The launch of a new brand name—TAG-Heuer—catapulted the company into the top seven of the Swiss watch industry within just a few years. TAG-Heuer has now achieved particular dominance on the Asian market and in Britain and Spain.

TAG-Heuer's chief executive officer, Christian R. Viros, a French citizen, has been the architect of this remarkable comeback. In his words,

> Until three years ago, TAG-Heuer sold sports watches without much of a marketing strategy. There were no clear market and distribution policies. We had to redefine the role of TAG-Heuer as the ultimate sports watch in the top price bracket. Are you a Yuppie, 20–40 years old, upper class, high income? Do you want a sports watch? Then you need a TAG-Heuer!
>
> If you examine watch advertising today, you'll see it consists primarily of product advertising. TAG-Heuer, however, advertises an image. This resulted in the creation of our slogan "Don't Crack under Pressure," which connotes a relationship between the resilience and reliability of our watches with the physical and mental qualities of high-performance athletes.

Much of the company's success is due to its $6 million public relations investment in sponsorship of the Formula One three-time champion team McLaren-Honda and the reigning two-time world champion, Ayrton Senna. TAG-Heuer also sponsors three World Cup ski racing champions, and the TAG-Heuer watch serves as the official timepiece of the famous Indy 500.

The company's product and marketing concept is supported by an annual advertising budget of $30 million. There is a selective distribution network with offices in the United States, Spain, France, and Italy. Only first-class watch retailers are found among the 10,000 sales locations, and TAG-Heuer products are not found in department stores or discount outlets.

Viros explains the company's turnaround in this way: "We have a clear strategy. One day we want to be right next to Rolex, with an identity that is just as strong as theirs. Most important, we regard ourselves as a highly professional enterprise and not as heirs of a watch baron."

Source: "TAG-Heuer—Great Timing," *Swiss Business*, November-December 1991, pp. 28–32.

WHAT PROMOTIONAL STRATEGY IS ALL ABOUT

The remarkable success of a "reborn" TAG-Heuer has a simple explanation—*skillful marketing strategy*. Meeting customer needs became the company's driving focus under the guidance of chief executive officer Christian R. Viros. TAG-Heuer found a niche among the emerging yuppie market worldwide, and all activities of the company (its products, pricing, distribution, and promotion) were integrated in a consistent and coherent way.

It was only a decade ago that the once-dominant company, plus nearly the entire Swiss watch industry, almost toppled. What had gone wrong? The answer is that a comatose management had been ignoring a vitally changing market. Before TAG-Heuer knew what was happening, competitors throughout the world had introduced new technology and mass-marketing methods. Suddenly the game changed, and traditional Swiss dominance was dealt a nearly fatal blow.

Fortunately, a new breed of managers such as TAG-Heuer's Viros moved to the forefront and revolutionized the industry through application of the marketing concept. *Marketing* is "the process of planning and executing the conception, pricing, promotion, and distribution of ideas, goods, and services to create exchanges that satisfy individual and organizational goals."[1] Together, these activities are referred to as the *marketing mix*, which represents the front line of business activity as the enterprise adapts its offerings to a changing world.

The Marketing Mix Communicates

Much of TAG-Heuer's success, of course, is due to promotion, but each of the other elements in its marketing strategy puts forth a clear message:

1. *The product communicates.* The entire TAG-Heuer product line, especially its flagship, Series 2000, far exceeds industry standards for wear and tear under demanding conditions. Furthermore, a TAG-Heuer watch is made easily recognizable by its unidirectional turning bezel, its two screw-in crowns (which ensure water resistance), and its luminous markings.

2. *The price communicates.* Potential buyers use price as a cue to define the product and to help direct their choice. TAG-Heuer prices range from about $375 to $2,700, depending upon exchange rates. A significantly lower price would likely signify lower quality and would detract from TAG-Heuer's image as a technical trendsetter.

3. *The distribution location communicates.* What if TAG-Heuer products were sold at Kmart or Macy's? The message would be that this brand is just one of many mass-market alternatives. Therefore, it is wise for TAG-Heuer to confine distribution of its product to fine jewelers whose atmosphere and personal attention complement the TAG-Heuer image.

Promotional Strategy

The word *promotion* comes from a Latin word meaning "to move forward." The meaning has narrowed so that *promotion* refers to communication undertaken to persuade others to accept ideas, concepts, or things.

As used in this book, the term *promotional strategy* refers to a controlled, integrated program of communication methods designed to present an organization and its products or services to prospective customers; to communicate need-satisfying attributes to facilitate sales; and thus to contribute to long-run profit performance. Promotional tools include advertising, personal selling, sales promotion, reseller support (trade promotion), publicity, and public relations and corporate advertising.

Advertising   *Advertising* represents all forms of paid non-face-to-face communication of ideas, goods, or services by an identified sponsor transmitted to a target audience. Although historically advertising has predominantly used various mass media, other means, such as direct advertising and telephone solicitation, have become increasingly common.

TAG-Heuer's $30 million media investment has been instrumental in publicly positioning the company's products as the ultimate in sports watches (see Figure 1–1). The unique product-design features and the slogan "Don't crack under pressure" are always prominent in TAG-Heuer ads. While sports stars often appear in the ads, their faces are never used to divert attention away from the products themselves.

Personal Selling   In contrast to advertising, *personal selling* is the process of persuading and assisting a prospect to buy a good or service or to act on an idea through the use of person-to-person communication. Buyers of fine watches and other technically sophisticated products often require demonstration and information before they are willing to make a choice. TAG-Heuer management wisely recognized this fact and made exclusive use of top-of-the-line jewelry retailers, which offer point-of-sale expertise.

Sales Promotion   *Sales promotion* is a set of paid marketing activities (other than advertising and personal selling) undertaken to stimulate buyer action. It includes such inducements as point-of-sale displays and coupons. Sales promo-

FIGURE 1-1

The Ultimate in Sports Watches

31

TAG-Heuer's sports watch collection

At TAG-Heuer design is the answer to a required function. When the designer creates a new model, the first question he asks himself is how he will incorporate the technical specifications. Not a single watch series leaves the TAG-Heuer workshop without undergoing 26 different tests. Thanks to the latest electronic developments, tests simulating extreme pressure, temperature, humidity, impact and wear-and-tear far exceeding normal conditions can be performed. A TAG-Heuer watch is easy to recognise: There is a uni-directional turning bezel and two screw-in crowns which ensure water resistance, a band with two lengths, plus luminous markings.

The collection consists of the following main lines:

Series Formula One

The Series Formula One includes chronographs and watches which are modern and affordable. The Formula One casings are of finest quality stainless steel and resistant, synthetic material. They are light-weight and comfortable to wear.

Series 1500

The Series 1500 was introduced by TAG-Heuer in 1990 and is considered the new classic. The collection combines high-tech timing functions with modern design in several different versions. An extremely resistant and reliable watch, the Series 1500 is especially suitable for professional atheletes. Its success can be attributed not least to its remarkable precision. There is a large selection of faces, turning bezels and leather watch bands. An authentic

TAG-Heuer
Series 2000 Chronograph

TAG-Heuer can be purchased from the Series 1500 at a very attractive price.

Series 2000

The flagship of TAG-Heuer – the Series 2000 – is the pièce de la résistance of the TAG-Heuer collection, exemplifying the firm's form and function philosophy. For the client with high demands, this line combines unique sport styling with traditional Swiss craftsmanship and excellent manufacturing. The large selection of watches and chronographs is available with mechanical movements and self-winding mechanisms, as well as quartz. Every model is water and pressure resistant to 200 meters.

All Series 2000 chronographs contain typical TAG-Heuer characteristics as do the wrist watches. They are equipped with the most precise time-keeping functions required by professional athletes. The Super 2000 chronograph also features a tachometer scale that monitors speeds in kilometers or miles per hour.

TAG-Heuer
Series 4000

Series 4000

The Series 4000 uncompromisingly elegant: clear, fluid lines from the casing to the band. The divisible TAG-Heuer logo on the turning bezel and housing characterises the Series 4000. The Series 4000 combines precision, top functions and strength to satisfy the demands of the professional athlete and the challenges of everyday life.

TAG-Heuer
Chronometer S/el

Series S/el

S/el stands for Sports Elegance. An appropriate description for a watch collection, which combines the advanced technology and specifications of a TAG-Heuer sports watch with a very original design. Whether worn at a candlelight dinner, on the ski slope or while exploring a coral reef, the S/el is the suitable watch. It is also very comfortable to wear. The band and casing are stylish and technically superior. The outstanding characteristics of the S/el make it an indispensable accessory for everyday wear and sporting activities.

The prices for these TAG-Heuer watches range from Sfr. 500 to Sfr 2,500. In addition, TAG-Heuer produces three professional watches: The "Pilot", a computer watch for flight navigation, the "GMT" with two time zones and a diving watch which is water resistant to the depths of 1000 meters! In 1992 the new "Series 6000" will be launched. With the introduction of this series, TAG-Heuer will be driven into the Sfr 3500 price bracket for the first time. For enthusiasts, an 18-carat gold model will be available in the "Series 6000".

Contact:
TAG-Heuer SA
Professional Sports Watches
14a, Avenue des Champs-Montants
2074 Marin
Switzerland
Phone: 038/356 356
Fax: 038/356 400

swissBusiness November/December 1992

tion assumes a much greater role with low-priced mass-market products than with specialty products such as sports watches. Yet no manufacturer, including TAG-Heuer, can ignore package design, displays, and other means to make the product attractive and visible at the point of sale.

Reseller Support   Often referred to as trade promotion, *reseller support* encompasses incentives given to distributors to build their allegiance to the company and its products and to encourage their promotion and sale. Displays, high profit margins, cooperative advertising funds, and sales training are some of the incentives manufacturers use to build alliances.

Publicity   *Publicity* includes all forms of nonpaid communication of information about a company or its products. Think of the publicity generated when Formula One racers such as Jean Alesi, Ayrton Senna, or Carl Lewis proudly wear and display a TAG-Heuer watch when they are featured on TV or in person. The communication value generated by publicity often can exceed that of any kind of paid promotion.

Public Relations and Corporate Advertising   *Public relations and corporate advertising* form a broad category of activities designed to build corporate name recognition and establish a favorable public image. TAG-Heuer regularly sponsors hospitality events for VIPs and journalists featuring its Formula One racers. The company also has publicly associated itself with the promotion and development of automobile racing as well as downhill ski racing.

The Dangers of a Sales Orientation

TAG-Heuer's current management has avoided the costly lessons learned in the late 1980s by the Seven-Up Company, which tried unsuccessfully to extend its famous brand name past its traditional 7UP brand.[2] Management initially was misled by the early success of Cherry 7UP, a cherry-flavored version introduced in 1986. Although Cherry 7UP initially captured over a 2 percent share of the total beverage industry, which was impressive, it soon fell back to an unacceptable 1.2 percent share.

Problems were compounded when 7UP Gold, a spicy citrus soft drink containing caffeine, was introduced in April 1988. It was positioned as the "Wild Side of 7UP" and aimed at cola drinkers aged 18 to 34. But 7UP Gold missed its mark because consumers did not like the taste.

Seven-Up's president and CEO, John Albers, believes that "perhaps in our zeal and in our euphoria over Cherry 7UP we underestimated the trade's growing impatience with new brands . . . and pressure for shelf space." Despite a $10 million media campaign, 7UP Gold failed to attain its objective of 20 percent of the company's sales volume.

During this period, the two new products were allocated promotional dollars at the expense of 7UP and Diet 7UP. As a result, the market position of these two flagship brands deteriorated. In all, Seven-Up experienced a market-share decline in the lemon-lime product category of over nine percentage points in five years. The 1990s find the company struggling to reverse its decline.

What went wrong here? No doubt there were many considerations, but one dominant factor is that management lapsed into a *selling,* or a promotional *orientation.* As Philip Kotler puts it:

> The selling concept is a management orientation that assumes that consumers will either not buy or not buy enough of the organization's product unless the organization makes a substantial effort to stimulate their interest in its products.[3]

The selling concept is based on the assumption that a high level of advertising or sales firepower will somehow work to move the product. It almost endows promotion with a kind of magic through which the consumer can be maneuvered in almost any direction management desires.

No one denies the potential impact of skillful use of media, but a selling concept tends to ignore an absolute fact of business life often referred to as *consumer sovereignty.* The fact is that consumers see and hear what they want to see and hear, and the firm can do little to overcome this basic human characteristic! If the consumer does not want what is offered, the firm is powerless to do anything except to change what it offers to the market.

The essential point is this: Promotion is only one part, albeit an important one, of a total marketing mix. Promotion cannot move an unwanted or overpriced product. Seven-Up's lessons were painful ones. It had simply gotten out of touch with its current customers, failed to understand the needs and desires of those in its new market target, and fell short of the expectations of distributors and retail outlets.

PROMOTIONAL STRATEGY IN ACTION: WE'VE COME A LONG WAY!

What does it take to conceive and execute a successful promotional strategy in this last decade of the 20th century? One thing is sure—the competitive challenges of today are unique in economic history.

It is important to give you a broad panorama of these challenges before jumping into the details of this subject. One of the best ways to do this is to contrast the competitive realities of the 1960s with those of today. Therefore, we drop back to the first edition of this book, which appeared in 1967, to resurrect a case you will find interesting if for no other reason than it is so different from what you will see today.

First, we return once again to the watch industry, this time to discuss a company that mass-marketed the first expansion watchband—the Speidel Corporation.[4] Then, when we show you the dramatic contrasts that exist in promotional strategy today, it will be unmistakable that we've come a long way.

A Quieter and Gentler Time

The challenges of promotional strategy in the 1960s were vastly different from those of today. Television then loomed as the great selling force of its day. Mass markets existed for nearly all products, and competitors were fewer in number. In short, it was a quieter and gentler time.

The Speidel Corporation revolutionized the watchband industry in 1945 by introducing the first metal expansion band. Soon Speidel became a household name. Its market dominance was ensured when it introduced the Twist-O-Flex band in 1959.

The Twist-O-Flex band represented a significant improvement over the older scissors-action watchbands in that the Twist-O-Flex band could be stretched and twisted into virtually any shape. As a result, the Speidel band possessed a degree of comfort and durability no one else could match. In 1965, Speidel's prices ranged between $6.95 and $12.95, somewhat above the competitive norm for that time.

In the fall of 1964, Speidel executives and the account team at their advertising agency, the Marschalk Company, Inc., were developing the 1965 campaign. By this time, competitors had rebounded and were beginning to make some new inroads.

Competition   In the early 1960s, the most widely distributed brands of watchbands were Brite and Topps, which both sold at lower prices than Speidel. The only competitors in the jewelry store, however, were Kriesler, Gemex, and J.B., none of which offered national advertising or dealer support programs.

Distribution   Speidel products were distributed through 11 exclusive wholesalers, which employed a total of 77 salespeople. The wholesalers sold, in turn, to retail jewelry stores, department stores, some discount stores (which were just making their appearance), and other outlets.

Jewelers were dominant because Speidel bands required some adjustment to fit the wrist. Most mass-merchandising outlets found this difficult to do, although growing numbers distributed the line.

To ensure reseller support, Speidel provided window streamers, display pieces, and counter displays. Also, in 1964 Monte Carlo Sweepstakes advertisements were featured in *Life* magazine. Readers were encouraged to fill out a contest application at their jeweler to take a chance on winning a free Speidel band. The grand prize was an all-expenses-paid trip to Monte Carlo. Over 12,000 Speidel bands were given away, and most jewelers reported strong sales increases. Therefore, another sweepstakes was scheduled for 1965.

Dealer loyalty was further ensured by distribution of the "Speidel Times," a newsletter that served to "merchandise the advertising" (i.e., build enthusiasm for company efforts) and encourage dealer display and cooperation.

Advertising   Since 1950, Speidel had placed nearly all of its advertising in network television. In 1964, the company sponsored such shows as "Peyton Place," "Alfred Hitchcock Presents," "The Tonight Show with Jack Paar," and the "Huntley-Brinkley Evening News" on NBC.

Since the early days of TV, the company and its agency had agreed that a strong sales personality could do more to help a commercial succeed than could the best copy. Commercials during 1964 featured Warren Hull, a well-known announcer, and Pat Harrington, Jr., as commercial spokesmen. (Unfortunately, no one used the term *spokesperson* in those days.)

Figure 1–2 contains examples of these commercials, including one script and one storyboard. Of the five commercials used in 1964, three were well above average in terms of consumer recall of brand name and major selling points.

The Rationale for This Strategy   Speidel's strategy was well conceived for its time, for the following reasons:

1. *The early 1960s were the heyday of mass media.* The market for products such as watchbands was relatively large and homogeneous. Furthermore, most prospects could be reached through mass media, especially television. Therefore, TV ads were ideal to attract a large audience at very low costs per contact.

2. *The consumer had far fewer alternatives.* The watchband buyer of 1964 did not have many options to choose from. Therefore, a strong name such as Speidel could make a real difference when it came to making a decision. As a result, brand preferences developed and endured, thus permitting relative freedom from price competition.

3. *Hypermarts, super discounters, and megamalls were unheard of.* Discount outlets had only just begun to make any notable impact, and shopping malls were in their infancy.

4. *Manufacturers had greater opportunity and power to "command" distribution channels.* Mass advertising served to "pull" demand through the distribution channel, meaning that consumers were attracted and expected an advertised product to be at the point of sale. What options did retailers have if they wanted to survive competitively? Speidel, to a large degree, was in the drivers seat, which is contrary to the situation many companies are facing today.

The "Good Old Days" Are Long Gone

The competitive arena we have just described bears little resemblance to that of the mid-1990s. Many factors have emerged and now interact in such a way that the environment for promotional strategy is radically different.

The Consumer Has a Cornucopia of Options   In most developed countries today, there is a neverending deluge of new products. What this means, of course, is that the buyer has an incredible range of choice compared with 30 years ago. Today, the Speidel Company would find itself in a large pack of competitors and would face an uphill struggle in establishing brand preference.

For example, the number of new cereal brands that sell at least $1 million annually in the United States grew from 84 in 1979 to 150 in 1989. Furthermore,

FIGURE 1–2

Speidel Commercials

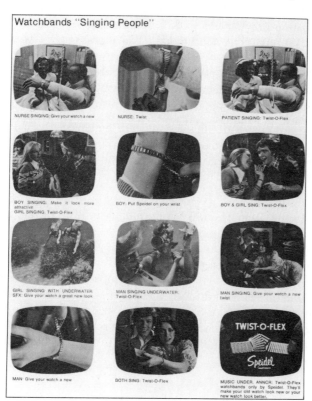

Video

OPEN MS FATHER AND SON IN BATHROOM IN MORNING, FATHER IS SHAVING, BOY IS WATCHING, AND THEY ARE CARRYING ON A CONVERSATION.

FATHER TWISTS AND TURNS BAND FOR SON.

DISS: WARREN HULL ON CAMERA. REVOLVE OF TWIST-O-FLEX JR.

CU WRIST
TEMPEST REVOLVE

CU WRIST
SUPER TRADEMARK "THE SPEIDEL CORPORATION"

Audio

SON: Dad? Why do you take your watch off when you shave? Is it uncomfortable?

FATHER: No, son, just the opposite. My Speidel Twist-O-Flex is the most comfortable watchband I've ever worn.

SON: Then why do you take it off?

FATHER: Because it's so easy to slip on and off. I do it automatically . . . when I wash or shave or do anything that could damage my watch.

SON: Well, what makes it so comfortable?

FATHER: The way it's made, Johnny. It's so flexible. Look how I can twist and turn it.

SON: Gee . . . and it's a beauty, too.

FATHER: It sure is. It's the newest Twist-O-Flex watchband Speidel makes . . . the Tempest.

SON: Boy, I wish they made a Twist-O-Flex in my size.

HULL: They do now, son. I'm Warren Hull for Speidel, announcing . . . The new Twist-O-Flex Jr. The perfect gift for graduation. What boy wouldn't be thrilled to own a watchband like this? It's just like dad's but made to fit any boy's wrist. And it's only $2.95. And in time for Father's Day, here's the new Twist-O-Flex, only $9.95.

A small price to pay for a thoughtful gift that dad will appreciate and use for years to come.

over 10,000 new food and nonfood products are introduced into supermarkets each year at costs averaging $15 to $20 million apiece.[5] In fact, the number of items carried by the typical supermarket has increased by nearly 50 percent since 1985.

Unfortunately, many product categories are characterized by brands that offer little differentiation. As Marylin Silverman, executive vice president of Backer Spielvogel Bates points out, this trend has serious outcomes for the marketer:

> The relationship of a brand with a consumer in the 1960s was usually as a problem solver. [Now] we have a marketplace that's overglutted with brands that are undifferentiated—brands that have not really identified themselves to the consumer as products that can't be substituted.[6]

Mass Distribution Outlets Abound   A dominant trend in developed economies is toward mass merchandising, especially the deep-discount chains. It is most unlikely today that Speidel could survive with a policy of selective distribution confined largely to jewelry stores.

Speidel could not ignore Wal-Mart, for example, which had a total of nearly 2,000 stores by the end of 1991 and sales in excess of $40 billion. Newly emerging warehouse clubs accounted for $32 billion in 1992, nearly double the $17 billion in 1989.[7] And on it goes. Many of these distributors, in turn, are making their own private, or store, brands available, thus adding to the glut of product options in the marketplace.

Consumer Motivation and Buying Behavior Have Changed   The last three decades have seen pronounced shifts in the nature of the exchange between marketer and buyer. These have been brought about largely by the burgeoning growth in the available alternatives.

Consumers show less "involvement"   *Involvement* is defined as "the degree of perceived personal importance and relevance accompanying product and brand choice within a specific situation or context."[8] As you will learn in later chapters, high involvement leads to a carefully reasoned decision in which information is sought and evaluated. Low involvement, on the other hand, is quite a different story.

How much personal importance, for example, do most people place on the purchase of toilet tissue? Few will take the time to do extensive alternative evaluation. Most of the time, almost any brand will do. Certainly, most people are unlikely to go elsewhere if a particular brand is out of stock when so many other acceptable options are available.

The majority of watchband purchases today fall into the category of replacement bands for inexpensive, throwaway watches. Appearance and features are pretty common across the widely distributed low-price options.

Watchbands thus tend to rate much lower in personal importance than they once did. While involvement no doubt would be higher in the premium watch segment, Speidel bands would have to be marketed differently if the company wanted to make inroads into this segment.

Products increasingly are viewed as "commodities"   When the alternatives are all pretty much alike, consumers perceive them as *commodities* and follow a "Buy the cheapest" decision rule. The disposable razor market, for example, degenerated to this status in the 1970s and mid-1980s as Gillette and Bic fought the battle on the basis of price. Gillette, in particular, saw its fortunes dim as its once lustrous brand name dwindled in importance to the buyer. Only the introduction in 1990 of its radically new shaving concept, the high-tech, premium-priced Sensor, saved this company from a likely takeover.[9]

One product after another has succumbed to becoming a commodity,[10] including non-premium-priced watchbands. Compaq, for example, dropped its personal computer prices 32 percent and rolled out a new line of under-$1,000 computers. Others quickly followed suit, and prices plummeted. Now choices in the PC market are increasingly being made on the basis of features and price, not brand preference.

Once brands descend to commodity status in the buyer's eyes, there is little that marketers can do. This can have disastrous effects, as Andrew Kupfer graphically indicates:

> The pessimists fear that because PCs are virtually a commodity, sold by units of speed or memory like so many pounds of oats, the business will come to resemble the airline industry—profits minimal or nil, price wars and bankruptcies the order of the day, stocks in a death spiral.[11]

Brand loyalty has eroded   Yes, commoditization is becoming widespread, with the result that brand loyalty is crumbling. Promotion in Action 1–1 paints a vivid picture of the dynamics of this central fact of life throughout a broad range of product/service categories.

As Brand Loyalty Crumbles, Marketers Look for New Answers

Promotion in Action

1-1

Brands are under siege—and are losing the battle. Once the foundation of the marketing world, package-goods companies are being buffeted by internal and external forces threatening the future of their brands.

For a decade, the Roper Organization has measured brand loyalty to a broad group of package goods. Three years ago, 56 percent of those polled by Roper said they know what brand they want to buy when they enter a store. That figure fell to 53 percent in April 1990 and plunged to 46 percent by mid-1991.

"Just the sheer proliferation of brand names has led to consumers viewing them as parity," says DDB Needham's Martin Horn. But experts also blame advertising. The erosion of ad dollars has exacerbated the problem, says Richard Furash, national director of consumer products for Deloitte & Touche's consultancy group.

"The problem with branding today is that consumer goods marketers aren't investing in their brands. Then it becomes a self-fulfilling prophecy. Manufacturers decreasing the amount of advertising behind their brand is one big reason people don't have the same brand loyalties they used to," Mr. Furash says.

Source: Julie Liesse, "Brands in Trouble," *Advertising Age*, December 2, 1991, p. 16. Reproduced by special permission.

We now have a much clearer picture of consumer behavior at the point of sale because of the growing use of electronic scanner technology. Recent research by Leo Burnett, a Chicago-based advertising agency, shows four different patterns of brand loyalty and buying strategies:[12]

1. *Long loyals* are committed to one brand regardless of price or any other factor. These numbers are declining and are seen mostly when the purchase is highly involving. Top-of-the-line cosmetics are a good example.
2. *Rotators* show regular patterns of shifting between preferred brands motivated by variety rather than price.
3. *Dealer sensitives* show a pattern of shifting between preferred brands determined by availability of special offers or incentives.
4. *Price sensitives* follow a decision rule to purchase the cheapest option, regardless of brand.

The percentages of buyers falling into these categories vary widely from one product/service category to the next, and we will learn more of these dynamics in Section 2 of this book. But one central fact of life is clear: Brand loyalty, if it exists at all, is confined mostly to a *set of brands* regarded as essentially equivalent. Speidel would have an uphill struggle today to hold its market-share dominance.

Changing Power Relationships in Distribution Channels   Speidel had the enviable position in 1964 of being channel commander; retailers had little choice but to stock the dominant Speidel brand. Today Speidel would face a different situation, because *retailers are assuming channel command.*

This should come as no surprise in light of the new product glut, the growing product commoditization, and the dominance of mass merchandisers. Distributors have limited space for the flood of new products and now are in the position of determining which ones will be accepted.

Even such strong mass marketers as Procter & Gamble now have to pay what are known as *slotting fees,* which total as much as $10,000 *per store,* just to have the product put on the shelves. As we have pointed out earlier, it is becoming increasingly difficult for a manufacturer to build sufficient brand loyalty to buck this trend in channel power.

If it were to survive today, Speidel would have to put much more emphasis on reseller support programs (trade promotion) to "push the product through the channel." Moreover, it would have little power to maintain its price structure in such a situation. The ball now is in a different court.

Changed Priorities in the Promotion Mix   The growing significance of trade promotion is not the only change in promotional strategy today's marketers face. NBC researcher Horst Stipp has pointed out that "there is a *crisis of confidence* in advertising."[13]

Television and general consumer magazines, the traditional kings of mass media, have been hit especially hard. Few companies today would follow the strategy of Speidel with its focus on *Life* magazine and network TV buys. There are several reasons why this is the case.

Markets have become increasingly segmented   Nondifferentiated mass markets rarely exist today. As a case in point, heavy users of Coors Light beer are heads of households aged 21–34, middle to upper income, primarily suburban and urban. They are much more likely to rent videos than to view television, other than TV sports shows.[14] No truly mass medium would be appropriate. Rather, Coors must use media that allow greater precision targeting, such as cable TV and *Sports Illustrated* magazine.

The power of consumer sovereignty   There has been a raging war among three major long-distance telephone carriers in the United States. As one analyst observed, "Never before have consumers been bombarded by so many TV campaigns about telephone use, using tactics that range from warmth and humor to seriousness, direct comparison, and downright intimidation."[15] Yet there has been little discernible impact of all this on market shares.

The long-distance carriers' war provides yet another illustration of consumer sovereignty. The consumer is not a pawn to be manipulated by the persuader. It is amazing to consider that a viewer who watches 30 hours of TV a week will be inundated by more than 35,000 commercials per year.[16] Yet, as we will demonstrate in Chapter 3, viewers regularly use electronic remote controls to "zap" everything they do not want to see.[17] In short, consumers are increasingly screening out unwanted advertising.

The battle has shifted to point-of-sale promotion   What can be done to move a product such as Coors Light beer? Advertising plays some role in maintaining brand awareness, or "share of mind." Yet Coors is only one of dozens of brands at the supermarket or other convenience outlets. Also, it is most likely just one of several equally satisfactory options in the minds of many buyers. Now everything possible must be done to catch the shopper's eye through distinctive packaging, display, and so on. Coupons and price incentives also can make a big difference.

In the long run, the frontline battle in many product categories will be fought more in the sales promotion trenches than with the advertising artillery. Because distributors now act as channel commanders, we now have quite a different competitive war from that of the 1960s.

DOMINANT ISSUES IN CONTEMPORARY PROMOTIONAL STRATEGY

You have a good feel for the realities of promotional strategy today. Tom Peters summarizes the situation well:

> No company's edge is commanding anymore. No transformation, no matter how dramatic, provides safety against the wildly gyrating forces at work. In today's fast-changing world, where we don't even know the names of next month's competitors, let alone their cost structure, no one has a safe lead. For the foreseeable

future, organizations must learn to cherish change and to take advantage of constant tumult as much as they have resisted change in the past.[18]

Survival demands *entrepreneurship*—risk taking and innovation. During the next decade, seven major factors will differentiate success from failure in promotional strategy: (1) a philosophy of individualized marketing; (2) building brand equity; (3) an integrated promotion mix; (4) a rebirth of retail selling and service; (5) thinking globally, acting locally; (6) a new emphasis on accountability; and (7) a bottom-line commitment to consumer rights. Each of these is discussed below and will be mentioned frequently throughout this book.

Individualized Marketing

Appealing to unidentified individuals in a mass market is increasingly becoming a dead end. Many marketers are taking Stan Rapp and Tom Collins seriously in their challenge to embrace a strategy of *individualized marketing*, which they define as follows:

> a very personal form of marketing that recognizes, acknowledges, appreciates, and serves the interests and needs of selected groups of consumers whose individual identities are or become known to the advertiser.[19]

This philosophy is most commonly expressed in the form of *database marketing*.[20] Names of customers are acquired through various means, and each person then becomes a *microsegment*. The enterprise then can initiate *direct marketing*, whereby advertising and promotion are aimed at an identified individual and adapted where necessary to meet that person's needs.

When Nissan introduced its new Altima in the fall of 1992, many of its ads were heavily oriented toward inducing prospects either to phone an 800 number or send a response card if they wished to receive "The Luxury Sedan Road Report" (see Figure 1–3.) No doubt the information provided helped many potential buyers, but the greatest gain was to Nissan, which acquired names of potential customers.

Direct marketing will experience continued growth for yet another reason. It allows an enterprise to gain independence from the retail arena, which increasingly is under reseller command.

Direct marketing, however, is only a stepping stone toward *customized marketing*,[21] an individualized marketing mix based on direct dialogue beween buyer and seller. This strategy will become increasingly feasible when interactive television (two-way response between source and sender) takes off, as it is expected to do in 1993.[22]

Building Brand Equity: A Challenge to Short-Range Thinking

Many product categories either have reached or are well on their way toward commodity status. What this means, of course, is that brand ceases to be a factor in choice, and competition degenerates to sales promotion and price. The distributor becomes channel commander, of course, and the manufacturer no longer has much power to influence the situation.

The blame for this to a high degree can be laid at the feet of shoddy marketing thinking. As one commentator points out:

> Under pressure to make big short-run gains in sales, many brand managers are cavalier about the long-term commercial health of their products. Increasingly they are abandoning brand-building activities, such as advertising, in favor of tactics, especially price promotions, which aim to increase market share quickly.[23]

The consequences of this kind of short-range thinking can be serious indeed:

1. Price promotions can increase sales sharply for a brief period, but evidence increasingly shows that almost all consumers who switch ultimately revert to their previous buying patterns.[24]

2. A consistent policy of reductions quickly can erode image. This happened to a once-great brand name, Gillette, as you recall. One formerly loyal customer put it this way: "When I think 'Gillette,' I think 'hollow, plastic, and blue.'"[25]

FIGURE 1–3

Nissan Captures Names for Individualized Marketing

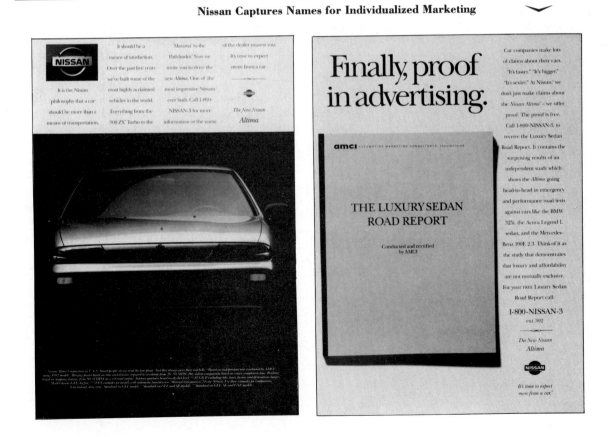

3. A strong brand name can provide a measure of competitive invulnerability. In 19 of 22 standard brand categories, today's market leader also was the favorite in 1925.[26] For example, Clorox Company management painfully discovered the power of Procter & Gamble's Tide brand name when Clorox tried to launch a laundry detergent containing bleach. A short-run competitive advantage was neutralized when P&G immediately retaliated with Tide with Bleach. P&G wound up increasing the market share of its well-known flagship brand, while Clorox failed to gain a foothold.[27]

Existing brands are under siege, especially from private labels such as Sam's Choice, offered by Wal-Mart, which projects that private-label sales could jump from $825 million in 1992 to 2.6 billion by 1995.[28] For this reason, David Aaker argues in an influential recent book that maintaining and increasing brand equity (awareness, acceptance, and loyalty) will be a central front in the competitive battle of the 1990s.[29]

One tried-and-true way to maintain (or regain) brand equity is through constant product innovation. As mentioned earlier, the Gillette Company risked its survival in a bold strategy to reestablish its brand name through its all-new shaving concept, the Sensor. See Promotion in Action 1–2 for details of this stunning example.

Promotion in Action

1-2

The Resurgence of Gillette

In April 1990, Gillette's Bruce Cleverly made one of the hardest decisions a marketing boss can ever face: to pull an expensive television advertising campaign off the air. Hard, but in this case, enviable. Mr. Cleverly was forced to stop advertising his company's newest product, Sensor, because demand for the high-tech razors was so intense that the company could not produce them fast enough to merit it.

Sensor was the company's attempt to buck a decade-long trend in Europe and America toward disposable razors. As more consumers turned to cheap throwaway models in the late 1970s and early 1980s, the shaving-products market looked set to turn into a commodity market. Most consumers could not tell one disposable razor from another and simply bought the cheapest available. This, in turn, had made Gillette vulnerable to takeover.

Sensor is that rarity in today's supermarket: a product that is demonstrably better than its competitors. Its twin blades are mounted on tiny springs, so they hug the contours of the face and give a closer shave. Gillette's research shows that 80 percent of men who try Sensor keep on using it.

Sensor's position has proved easy to defend for much the same reason that the razor's launch was so successful: the new strength of the Gillette brand name. Sensor was a giant hit because of Gillette's willingness to spend heavily on its own brand name—and its ability to deliver a product good enough to keep up with it.

Source: "The Best a Plan Can Get," *The Economist,* August 15, 1992, pp. 59–60. Reproduced by special permission.

It is rare for a company to produce a true innovation such as the Sensor; most product changes are more minor. Hence it is unlikely that we will see a wisespread return to the kind of advertising-dominated promotional strategy that prevailed in 1964. But a new interest in brand equity also is leading to revamped promotional thinking in other ways.

One possible option, especially for large firms, is to follow the lead of Procter & Gamble in reducing sales promotion expenditures, especially slotting fees.[30] Reductions in reseller support programs can be dangerously shortsighted, however, unless they are made to regain a measure of channel control by maintaining brand equity through such conventional means as media advertising.

Therefore, there is good reason to resist the trend toward cutting media advertising to the bone. Without name recognition, no brand can hope to achieve and retain a foothold at the point of sale. For example, Van den Bergh Foods is wise to advertise its brand I Can't Believe It's Not Butter in food and beverage magazines (see Figure 1–4). Without ongoing advertising, a company cannot

FIGURE 1–4

Ongoing Advertising Is a Key to Brand Equity

assure that distributor support will be provided, especially with the growth of distributor private brands.

Media advertising will experience some resurgence in the next decade because of the brand equity crisis. However, the new advertising strategy will not resemble the mass market strategy of the Speidel Company in 1964, because markets have become highly fragmented. For example, cable TV and other options now exist to reach a much narrower market segment.

An Integrated Promotion Mix

Ever since the first edition of this book, we have advocated an organized, integrated promotion mix—a seemingly commonsense, yet often ignored, recommendation. A carefully orchestrated strategy is all the more crucial in today's turbulent atmosphere, where one misstep can have serious consequences.

Part of the Gillette renaissance (see again Promotion in Action 1–2) is due to skillful promotional integration. The first stage was an $80 million investment in corporate image advertising in 1989 to build brand awareness and set the stage for the Sensor launch in January 1990. The slogan "Gillette—the best a man can get" achieved high awareness through a single commercial that ran throughout Europe and America. The same ad, with the addition of computer animation showing how the spring-loaded shaving blades worked, launched the Sensor.

In addition to the $175 million budgeted for advertising, $75 million was spent on public relations. The Sensor was mentioned favorably on the "CBS Evening News," "The Johnny Carson Show," and in many other places.

Packaging was designed to fit with the ads, the futuristic name, and the high-tech design of the handle. The name dominated the package and could not be missed in a display. The price also was set low for promotional reasons. At $3.75, the razor was cheaper than many other nondisposables and well within the range of nearly everyone.

Another important facet of integrated strategy is the development of a *flexible response system*, which makes use of an information system linking manufacturer and distributor to minimize the lag time between customer request and distributor response. Kao Corporation, Japan's largest soap and cosmetics company, has just such a system, which comes close to synchronizing production in proportion to customer demand (see Promotion in Action 1–3). Many other companies—such as VF Corporation, makers of Lee and Wrangler jeans and Jantzen sportswear—have also implemented similar quick-response inventory control systems.

A Rebirth of Retail Selling and Service

If you go back to the first marketing courses in 1906, you will find strong emphasis on sales expertise and service. But sales expertise and service became eclipsed in the mass marketing of recent decades and have been considered by many as a lost art. However, this is rapidly changing, because the public has lost its patience with indifferent and often rude salespeople.

David Woodruff has described how radical the change has been at General

Motors Corporation's Saturn division, where sales training has been introduced that sounds remarkably old-fashioned: "The new way of selling involves—hold on to your warranty—listening to customers and actually treating them like human beings."[31]

Yes, we are beginning to realize anew that old-fashioned courtesy and concern still have a part in marketing and can go a long way toward building customer loyalty.[32] It's amazing what hard economic times, an uphill battle for market share, and a shortage of jobs will do to change how people relate to each other.

Thinking Globally, Acting Locally

A growing number of Western firms are being forced to *think globally* because of a rapid increase in the percentage of sales beyond home country boundaries. Japan is the number three market for Procter & Gamble, for example.[33] In fact, the greatest profit opportunities often are overseas.

A deceptively simple strategy is to engage in what has become known, unfortunately, as *global marketing.* This term was popularized by Theodore Levitt, who argued that standardized promotional strategies can and should be used worldwide.[34] Many companies have discovered, however, that this is a quick road to disaster.[35]

The key to successful marketing anywhere in the world is *adaptation to a changing environment.*[36] Procter & Gamble entered the Japanese market in 1973 and lost money until 1987. It started with American advertising, sales, and promotional methods. Finally, it discovered through marketing research that some major changes were warranted if inroads were to be made.

Synchronizing Production with Demand: "Kao's Koup"

Promotion in Action

1-3

Check out Kao Corporation, Japan's biggest soap and cosmetics company and the sixth largest such company in the world. No other company can match the flexibility of Kao's distribution. It derives from a stunning information system that allows the company and its wholly owned wholesalers to deliver goods within 24 hours to any of 280,000 shops, whose average order is for just seven items.

Brand managers see daily sales, stock, and production figures. Within a day, they can learn if a competitor is running a sale and can adjust accordingly. When Kao brings out a new product, it melds point-of-sale information from 216 retailers with a test-marketing operation called the Echo System, which uses focus groups and consumers' calls and letters to gauge public response and is faster than market surveys.

Says William Best of A. T. Kearney's Tokyo office: "Kao can know if a product will be successful within two weeks of launch. They know who's buying it, whether the packaging works, whether to change anything." That helps explain how Kao stormed into the highly profitable cosmetics business, going from nowhere to number two in Japanese market share in less than 10 years.

Source: Thomas A. Stewart, "Brace for Japan's Hot New Strategy," *Fortune,* September 21, 1992, p. 6. Reproduced by special permission.

The key, then, is to *think globally* but *act locally*. A standardized advertising campaign is an especially dangerous lure. Even Coca-Cola has 21 versions world-wide of its TV spot featuring children singing the praises of Coke.[37]

A New Emphasis on Accountability

"I know that half of my advertising is wasted, but I don't know which half." This quote has been attributed to at least a dozen turn-of-the-century industrial leaders. It's a good line, no matter who said it, and unfortunately it has been, until recently, all too true.

Few managers would settle for this kind of thinking today, however, because profit pressures have become too great. Fortunately, retail scanning methodology has come along at just the right time. As you will discover later in this book, we now have the technology to isolate the sales and profit impact of individual elements of the promotion mix. This is bound to challenge many long-standing assumptions and practices, and it opens a new era of accountability.

A Bottom-Line Commitment to Consumer Rights

It is important to recognize at the outset that there is a growing consumer backlash against business actions that go against social consensus. G. Heilman Brewing Company, for example, was forced to withdraw Powermaster, its new high-potency malt liquor aimed at inner-city consumers. Similarly, R. J. Reynolds did not proceed with introduction of Uptown, a menthol cigarette aimed at blacks.

The impact of the consumerism movement, which began in the 1950s, has continued to grow. A high-water mark came in 1960 when President John F. Kennedy broke new ground by issuing a Bill of Consumer Rights, which appears in Figure 1–5.[38]

The Bill of Consumer Rights establishes that such actions as outright deception, distribution of unsafe products, and nonresponse to legitimate complaints are unviable and nonnegotiable. Consumer protection in these terms must be part of the bottom line of any responsible marketer.

FIGURE 1–5

John F. Kennedy's Consumer Bill of Rights

1. *The Right to Safety*—protection against products or services that are hazardous to health and life.
2. *The Right to Be Informed*—provision of facts necessary for an informed choice; protection against fraudulent, deceitful, or misleading claims.
3. The Right to Choose—assured access to a variety of products and services at competitive prices.
4. *The Right to Be Heard (Redress)*—assurance that consumer interests receive full and sympathetic consideration in formulation and implementation of regulatory policy; prompt and fair restitution.
5. *The Right to Enjoy a Clean and Healthful Environment.*
6. *The Right of the Poor and Other Minorities to Have Their Interests Protected.*

Faith Popcorn has called the 1990s the *decency decade* and has argued convincingly that "corporate soul" be expressed in four distinctive ways:[39]

- *Acknowledgment:* Our industry hasn't always done everything possible to make the world a better place.
- *Disclosure:* This is who we were, and this is the company we are trying to become with your help.
- *Accountability:* Here is how we define our area of responsibility and the ways in which we can be held accountable.
- *Presentation:* Here is what we pledge to you, our consumer: You will find our corporate soul in all our products.

We will address these issues throughout this book. Also, Chapter 22 goes more deeply into the social and ethical issues that should be the concern of everyone.

STRUCTURE OF THIS BOOK

This chapter gives you a broad picture of promotional strategy and the many environmental considerations shaping its expression in the mid-1990s. It shows how effective promotion can help a consumer-driven marketing program to succeed. It also shows that promotional strategy cannot move a marketing concept that does not satisfy real consumer needs.

This book is concerned with analyzing, planning, and implementing effective promotional programs. Section 1 focuses on persuasive communication. Chapters 2 and 3 provide a solid foundation for promotional decisions by covering the nature of communication and the ways in which consumers process information. In Chapter 4, we introduce a decision-making framework that will be elaborated on in subsequent chapters. It is here that the term *consumer sovereignty* will take on new meaning as you discover the ways in which people process and respond to persuasive communication.

The three chapters in Section 2 proceed to focus on market analysis. You will discover in Chapters 5 and 6 how the nature of consumer decision processes shape promotional strategy. From this foundation, we then discuss the ways in which markets are segmented and audience targets are chosen (Chapter 7).

Section 3 covers two cornerstone concepts in promotional strategy: promotional objectives (Chapter 8) and allocation of funds (Chapter 9). We then will have the background necessary to begin discussion of the management of the major elements in the promotional mix.

Section 4 focuses on advertising strategy. Chapter 10 discusses how ads are designed and created. Chapters 11 and 12 introduce you to the characteristics of advertising media and the considerations that shape media selection and scheduling decisions.

Section 5 tackles the related issue of sales promotion strategy. Here we will look first at working with distributors and the issue of channel control (Chapter 13) and management of consumer sales promotion (Chapter 14).

Our attention turns to the sales force in Section 6. Chapter 15 covers principles of effective personal selling. Chapter 16 goes on to discuss management of the sales force, including selection, training, and compensation.

Section 7 concludes the emphasis on elements of the promotion mix by centering on direct marketing (Chapter 17) and public relations, publicity, and corporate advertising (Chapter 18).

If we stopped at this point, we would neglect important issues of coordination and control (Section 8). Of particular importance are adaptation to the legal environment (Chapter 19), working with promotional resources (Chapter 20), and measurement of effectiveness (Chapter 21).

Section 9 concludes the book by focusing on the too-often-neglected issues of social effects of advertising and ethical considerations. Of special concern, as you saw in this chapter, are consumer rights, yet another bottom-line consideration in promotional strategy.

In summary, this book provides a complete view of promotional strategy from a managerial standpoint. It is based on realistic analysis of consumer behavior and is strongly tied to the real world of strategic thinking. It is our hope that the examples presented in this chapter have given you a taste of the excitement and challenge faced by those who are on the front lines in marketing warfare.

REVIEW AND DISCUSSION QUESTIONS

1. For each of the major examples used in this chapter (Gillette, Seven-Up, TAG-Heuer, and Speidel):
   a. Relate how the marketing concept applies.
   b. Identify the elements of the promotional mix.
   c. Identify the fundamental role promotion was forced to play within the marketing mix.

2. Visit a supermarket or convenience store where soft drinks are sold. Based on what you observe, which manufacturers, if any, have achieved sufficient power to be designated as channel commanders? Why do you say this?

3. For years, the United Dairy Industry Association, which represents 95 percent of all American dairy farmers, has been trying to stem a continuing decline in fluid milk consumption. This decline is especially pronounced among adults. Serious consideration is being given to introduction of a carbonated milk product positioned between milk and soft drinks.

   It is your task to design a preliminary promotional strategy. What is your estimate of the odds for success? What are some things that you might do?

4. Refer back to the text example of the Nissan Altima, a 1992 product introduction. If Nissan is effective in attracting names of prospective customers, how would it capitalize upon this through individualized marketing?

5. Do you agree with many industry analysts that inexpensive personal computers are becoming commodity products? IBM has been fighting this trend. Visit a computer outlet and compare IBM products with others. Do you think the company has been successful in reversing commoditization? Is there anything else it could do?

6. Management expert Tom Peters is reported to have said that we have reached a great

turning point in business history, equivalent in many ways to the impact of the industrial revolution 200 years ago. Based on your interpretation of the environment today, would you agree? What do you feel would lead Peters to make such a dramatic observation?

7. Consumerists often point out that aspirin is aspirin. No matter what price is charged, the government requires that all brands of aspirin contain the same chemical formulation. Higher-priced brands have no more therapeutic benefit than lower-priced options. Yet such brand names as Bayer draw a substantial price premium and have attained marketing success. Based on your understanding at this point, would this be a violation of consumer rights? Why or why not? What recommendation would you make?

NOTES

1. Peter D. Bennett, ed., *Dictionary of Marketing Terms* (Chicago: American Marketing Association, 1988), p. 54.

2. Based on "Seven-Up Concentrates on 7UP," *Advertising Age,* February 20, 1989, p. 62; "Seven-Up Stays Close to Home," *Advertising Age,* August 15, 1988, p. S-10; "Seven-Up Rallies," *Beverage World,* October 1988, pp. 51–54; and "Seven-Up Puts New Fizzle in Ads," *Advertising Age,* October 17, 1989, p. 34.

3. Philip Kotler, *Principles of Marketing,* 4th ed. (Englewood Cliffs, N.J.: Prentice Hall, 1989), p. 22.

4. James F. Engel, Hugh G. Wales, and Martin R. Warshaw, *Promotional Strategy* (Homewood, Ill.: Irwin, 1967), pp. 553–64.

5. Stan Rapp and Tom Collins, *The Great Marketing Turnaround—The Age of the Individual and How to Profit from It* (Englewood Cliffs, N.J.: Prentice Hall, 1990), p. 16.

6. Julie Liesse, "Brands in Trouble," *Advertising Age,* December 2, 1991, p. 16.

7. Liesse, "Brands in Trouble," p. 18.

8. See Giles Laurent and Jean-Noel Kapferer, "Measuring Consumer Involvement Profiles," *Journal of Marketing Research* 12 (February 1985), pp. 41–53.

9. "The Best a Plan Can Get," *The Economist,* August 15, 1992, pp. 59–60.

10. Bill Saporito, "Why the Price Wars Never End," *Fortune,* March 23, 1992, pp. 68–78.

11. Andrew Kupfer, "Who's Winning the PC Price Wars?" *Fortune,* September 21, 1992, p. 80.

12. "Strategic Shopping," *The Economist,* September 26, 1992, pp. 82–83.

13. Horst Stipp, "Crisis in Advertising?" *Marketing Research* 4 (March 1992), p. 39.

14. Michael J. McCarthy, "Marketers Zero In on Their Customers," *The Wall Street Journal,* March 18, 1991, p. 10.

15. Kate Fitzgerald, "Hello? Is Anybody Listening?" *Advertising Age,* October 22, 1990, p. 34.

16. "Getting inside Their Heads," *American Demographics,* August 1989, p. 20.

17. Joanne Lipman, "Ads on TV: Out of Sight, Out of Mind?" *The Wall Street Journal,* May 14, 1991, p. 81.

18. Tom Peters, "There Are No Excellent Companies," *Fortune,* April 27, 1987, p. 382.

19. Rapp and Collins, *The Great Marketing Turnaround,* p. 37.

20. Susan Krafft, "The Big Merge," *American Demographics,* June 1991, pp. 44–48.

21. For an interesting discussion see Regis McKenna, *Relationship Marketing* (Reading, Mass.: Addison-Wesley, 1991).

22. Rebecca Piirio, "Battle for the Black Box," *American Demographics,* November 1992, p. 6.

23. "The Purest Treasure," *The Economist,* September 27, 1991, p. 67.

24. A. S. C. Ehrenberg, Kathy Hammond, and C. J. Goodhardt, "The After-Effects of Consumer Promotions" (preliminary report of a study conducted at the London Business School, 1991).

25. "The Best a Plan Can Get," p. 59.

26. "The Purest Treasure," p. 67.

27. Bradley Johnson, "Clorox's Identity Crisis," *Advertising Age,* May 6, 1991, pp. 1, 54.

28. Cyndee Miller, "Better Quality, Packaging Boost Popularity of Private Label Goods," *Marketing News* 26 (November 9, 1992), p. 14.

29. David A. Aaker, *Managing Brand Equity* (New York: Free Press, 1991).

30. Cyndee Miller, "Moves by P&G, Heinz Rekindle Fears that Brands Are in Danger," *Advertising Age,* June 8, 1992, p. 1.

31. David Woodruff, "May We Help You Kick the Tires?" *Business Week,* August 3, 1992, p. 49.

32. See Ruth N. Bolton and James H. Drew, "A Longitudinal Analysis of the Impact of Service Changes on Customer Attitudes," *Journal of Marketing* 55 (January 1991), pp. 1–9.

33. Laurie Freeman, "Japan Rises to P&G's No. 3 Market," *Advertising Age,* December 10, 1990, p. 42.

34. Theodore Levitt, "The Globilization of Markets," *Harvard Business Review,* May-June 1976, pp. 106–18.

35. Two studies have documented the dangers of standardized global marketing. See Saeed Samiee and Kendall Roth, "The Influence of Global Marketing Standardization on Performance," *Journal of Marketing* 56 (April 1992), pp. 1–17; and Alan Shao, Lawrence P. Shao, and Dale H. Shao, "Are Global Markets with Standardized Advertising Campaigns Feasible?" *Journal of International Consumer Marketing* 4, no. 3 (1992), pp. 5–16.

36. See George S. Yip, *Total Global Strategy* (New York: Prentice Hall, 1992).

37. Julie Skurr Hill and Joseph Winski, "Goodbye Global Ads," *Advertising Age,* November 16, 1987, pp. 16ff.

38. See Robert J. Lampman, "JFK's Four Consumer Rights, a Retrospective View," in *The Frontier of Research in the Consumer Interest,* ed E. Scott Maynes (Columbia, Mo.: University of Missouri and the American Council on Consumer Interests, 1988), pp. 19–33.

39. Faith Popcorn, *The Popcorn Report* (New York: Doubleday, 1991).

C h a p t e r

2

The Nature of Communication

ADVERTISING COMMUNICATES IN UNEXPECTED WAYS

Few advertising images have achieved greater instant recognition than the Marlboro Man. Pause for a moment and reflect on the kind of man he is represented as being. How does his image transfer to the Marlboro brand? Now consider this interpretation by Barry Vacker, who sees in the Marlboro Man remarkable resemblances to Michelangelo's famous statue of David (Figure 2–1):

> First commissioned in 1954 by Philip Morris, 450 years after the *David,* the Marlboro Man was created to give value to an objective, a failing cigarette brand, where little value had existed before. . . . There are striking executional emphases and similarities in both the *David* and the Marlboro Man: the emphasis on the strong square-jawed "Western" profile, the oversized masculine hands grasping a sling or a cigarette, the Aristotelian man of action.
>
> However, the greatest similarity between the *David* and the Marlboro Man is the philosophical ideas they symbolize. . . . The Marlboro Man symbolizes the universal in man: reason, independence, efficacy, and egoism. Like *David,* the Marlboro Man controls and is at home in an intelligible universe, comprehending reality and acting in accordance with it.
>
> . . . The Marlboro Man stands tall on the billboards of the world as the Aristotelian aesthetic ideal, symbolizing reason, independence, efficacy, egoism and explicitly or implicitly, republican liberty.

Source: Barry Vacker, "The Marlboro Man as a Twentieth Century *David:* A Philosophical Inquiry into the Aristotelian "Aesthetic of Advertising," in *Advances in Consumer Research,* vol. 19, eds. John F. Sherry, Jr., and Brian Sternthal (Provo, Utah: Association for Consumer Research, 1992), pp. 753–54.

The Marlboro Man as a modern *David?* Seem a bit farfetched? Maybe, but the point is that communication is one of the most complex of all human processes. Look closely at the root meaning of the word *communication:* commonness. We communicate only when meaning is transferred from one person to another and common understanding is achieved.[1]

It is the purpose of this chapter to introduce you to what takes place as people struggle to understand one another. As we have stressed earlier, *all* elements of the marketing mix communicate—the product, its price, the distribution methods, and promotion. We will introduce insights from traditional communication theory as well as from the newer field of *semiotics,* which centers on how meaning is generated in communication messages.[2]

We begin by focusing on models of communication. The most crucial issue is how meaning is established and transferred between two or more parties. Theories abound, ranging from those in semiotics and semantics, discussed in this chapter, to human information processing, covered in Chapter 3.

Then we turn to interpersonal versus mass communication in a marketing context and highlight general principles that shape promotional strategy. You will discover that the key to successful communication lies in understanding your target audience and adapting your message and media strategy accordingly. People see and hear what they want to see and hear. In short, the audience is sovereign.

FIGURE 2–1

Michelangelo's *David*

WHAT COMMUNICATION IS ALL ABOUT

Defined precisely, *communication* is a transactional process between two or more parties whereby meaning is exchanged through the intentional use of symbols. Notice these important elements:

> Communication is *intentional*—A deliberate effort is made to bring about an intended response.[3] This is especially true when the purpose is to persuade.
>
> Communication is a *transaction*—Messages are exchanged based on the motivations of all participants in expectation of mutual response.
>
> Communication is *symbolic*—Symbols (words, pictures, etc.) are deliberately created and used to cause another party to focus on the object or person represented by that symbol.[4]

A Model of the Process

It is helpful to visualize the communication process through the use of the descriptive model in Figure 2–2. This model is a composite of perspectives and theories that have appeared in the vast literature on this subject.[5]

FIGURE 2–2

A Model of the Communication Process

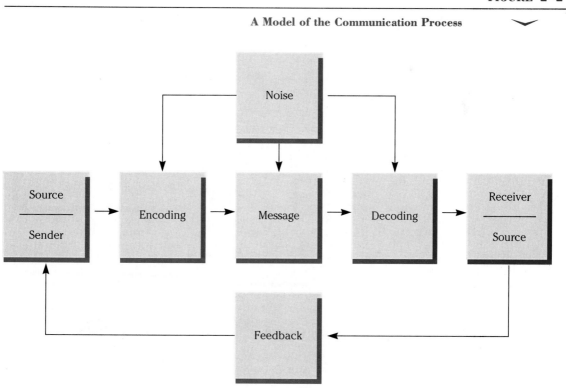

Although writers may differ on details, most agree on the essence of what occurs when communication takes place. But it must be recognized that no simple diagram can reflect all of the nuances.[6] First of all, it must be recognized that receivers become senders and senders become receivers through a continuing process of feedback. Also, the sender may be an organizational entity sending a message to multiple receivers who can interact with one another, in which case the communication process becomes more complex (see Figure 2–3).

Communication begins when symbols are selected and arranged in a sequence to be transmitted. This is referred to as *encoding.* The encoded message then is transmitted through one of the various media, ranging from face-to-face interaction to mass media.

The receiver then attempts to *decode* these symbols and uncover their meaning. To complete the process, the receiver becomes a sender by transmitting feedback. As this transaction takes place, meaning is transferred and clarified.

The fidelity or accuracy of communication can be negatively influenced by noise that enters into the message itself, the communication channel, or the encoding and decoding process. *Noise* refers to any extraneous factors that can interfere with reception of the message and distort the intended meaning. Examples include the use of contradictory words or inappropriate illustrations, poor printing quality or fuzzy audio reception, a clamor of others for attention while a television show is watched, and so on.

Bringing About Common Meaning

Turn once again to the Marlboro ad in the chapter opener photo and study it for a few moments. We may now look to the field of semiotics for some insights into how two or more people can observe this stimulus and arrive at common meanings.

FIGURE 2–3

A Model of the Mass Communication Process

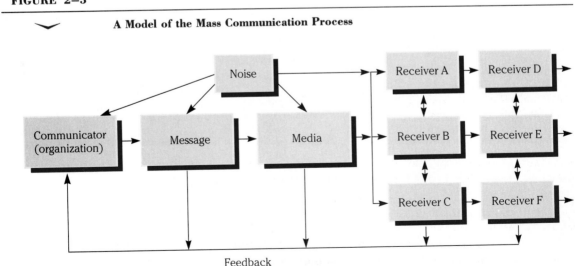

All communication takes place through *signs*. According to eminent semiologist C. S. Peirce, a sign is "anything that stands for something (its object), to somebody (its interpreter), in some respect (its context)."[7]

Broadly speaking, signs fall into three general categories:

1. *Icon*—a sign that visually resembles and signifies the object. In Figure 2–1, the presence of snow and the woods in the background are icons representing the harsh realities of a wilderness setting in winter. Few people, if any, would attribute any other meaning to these signs.

2. *Index*—a sign that relates to its object by a causal connection. The lariat in the hand of the rider is an index that he has roped another animal, presumably a calf or a wild horse, although we can only infer this. The body positioning of his horse also signifies that the other animal was roped only moments before.

3. *Symbol*—an artificial or conventional sign created for the purpose of providing meaning once people have agreed on the sign's form and on what it represents. As we pointed out earlier, the Marlboro Man provides a rich symbol of independence and maleness. This same symbolism is intended to carry over to the product itself.

Using Symbols Effectively   Icon, index, and symbol combine in a complex way in Figure 2–1 to create meaning. It is the symbols, however, that create the greatest difficulty in transferring meaning from one party to another. Don Fabun puts it this way:

> Most of our present day failures in communication can be traced either to misunderstandings of the role that symbols play in inter-human communication, or to inadequacies in the way we create, transfer and perceive symbols—whether they are spoken or written.[8]

Always remember that symbols, especially words, are something we create and therefore do not have meaning in and of themselves. Words do not have meanings—only people have meanings.

Given this fact, how can people ever hope to understand each other using symbols that have no meaning in and of themselves? Part of the answer lies in the way in which languages are learned from birth. Newborn children are initially incapable of symbolic communication. Although they notice people and phenomena of various types, babies can interact with others only nonverbally, using an apparently disorganized system of sounds. These sounds, which may serve as signs of their physical state, can be roughly understood only in terms of intensity, pitch, and duration.

Soon infants begin to imitate some of the sounds they hear, with the result that they come to associate specific words with specific objects. When the word reaches a point that it calls forth the same response as the object itself, it is said to have attained *denotative meaning*. Given the fact that everyone in a society goes through the same process, these meanings are conventionalized and shared in common; thus transfer of meaning is greatly facilitated.

On the other hand, the meaning that is unique to the individual is referred to as *connotative meaning*. For example, a prospective customer who associates the Marlboro Man with the cigarette of the same name will attribute a different meaning to this symbol than someone who does not have this association.

Connotative meanings reflect differences in backgrounds and motivations, thus posing a challenge to the communicator. For this reason, it is necessary to learn *empathy*—the ability to put ourselves in another's shoes. Empathy requires a sensing of needs, background, experiences, and so on. The communicator's goal is to use symbols that are relevant and have shared meaning.

Communication is also facilitated when all parties are as similar as possible in background and outlook. In other words, they should experience an *overlap in psychological fields*. This is especially critical when people have cultural differences, as we will see later in the chapter.

Often two people attempting to communicate are subject to common influences. Perhaps both are from the same Philadelphia suburb, belong to the same church, are graduates of the same college, and are members of the same tennis club. Because of similar environmental influences, they should be able to empathize and transfer meaning with relative ease.

Practical Uses of Semiotics   As you can readily understand, the meaning of any kind of stimulus in marketing communication can be rich and complex, moving beyond that which is easily verbalized. As Sidney J. Levy said in an influential paper more than two decades ago:

> The things people buy are seen to have personal and social meanings in addition to their functions. Modern goods are recognized as psychological things, as symbolic of personal attributes and goals, as symbolic of social patterns and strivings.[9]

Product symbolism is an especially potent way people give a clear message about self-esteem, values, expectations, and lifestyle.[10] Not surprisingly, marketers are beginning to turn to semiotics for new insights.

Semiotics provides research tools that augment the direct questions of conventional marketing research and include play, drama, projective techniques, and so on. Also, as Morris Holbrook has noted, semiotics accepts as legitimate a researcher's personal, subjective, and introspective inputs as an important part of the analysis.[11] You will enjoy the report in Promotion in Action 2–1 on how all of this is carried out.

Now, let's try our hand at doing semiological analysis with another advertising stimulus. What is the meaning conveyed by the ad in Figure 2–4? Why would a baby ever be featured in ads for tires? An attempt has been made over the years to symbolize Michelin comfort and safety by featuring a baby located comfortably within the tire. The baby, then, is intended to symbolize Michelin quality. There is no question that this well-conceived advertising has done much to establish dominant market position for this company.

Some Insights into Strategy

Semiotics and its related fields of syntactics and semantics have developed an extensive repertoire of methods that can be used to help ensure that intended

Symbols, Icons, and Semantics

In just a few years, Lever Brothers Co. built a $300 million fabric softener brand through the charms of a huggable teddy bear named Snuggle. Most marketers only dream of creating such a powerful advertising symbol, and Lever didn't want to do anything to jeopardize this little gold mine. It believed it needed to know more about why Snuggle was so successful and how the bear should be used in ads. So Snuggle got psychoanalyzed.

Carol Moog, a psychologist turned advertising consultant, did an analysis of Snuggle that went way beyond cuddliness. "The bear is an ancient symbol of aggression, but when you create a teddy bear, you provide a softer, nurturant side to that aggression," she says. "As a symbol of tamed aggression, the teddy bear is the perfect image for a fabric softener that tames the rough texture of clothing."

Lever had other questions about Snuggle: Should the bear be a boy or girl? Should it interact with humans in the ads? How about blinking its eyes, wiggling its ears, and sniffling the laundry? Blinking, wiggling,and sniffling were all deemed suitable behavior, but Ms. Moog recommended that Snuggle remain genderless and that people not be included in ads."To keep the magic, it has to be just Snuggle and the viewer communicating," she says. "The teddy bear acts as a bridge between the consumer's rational and more instinctual, emotional side."

Ms. Moog calls her analysis of signs and symbols in advertising *psychological semiotics.* Some people refer to it simply as semiotics; others prefer *iconology* or *image decoding.* Whatever academic jargon they use to describe it, more marketers are turning to social scientists to help them understand the many messages their advertising is transmitting to consumers on both conscious and subconscious levels. Ads have always been rich with psychological imagery, but advertisers now are trying harder to control and manipulate the symbols. Even the penguins in a new Diet Coke commercial aren't there just for humorous effect. SSC&B, an ad agency that practices semiotics, notes that the birds symbolize coolness, refreshment, and friendliness.

"It's mind boggling to try to control all the nonverbal symbols in our creative work," says Elissa Moses, a research executive at the BBDO ad agency. "But if advertisers aren't aware of subtleties, they may inadvertently communicate the wrong message." Consider an ad for Grey Flannel cologne. The marketer was startled to learn from a psychologist that the ad showing only a man's back could be perceived as "rudely giving the consumer the cold shoulder."

Some ad agencies, though, are skeptical of semiotics. They question whether social scientists read too much into commercials, and they chafe at efforts to transform the creative process from an art to a science. "These psychologists tend to be overly intellectual and a little tutti-frutti," says George Lois, chairman of Lois Pitts Gershon Pon/GGK, an ad agency.

Even companies that do semiotic research sometimes take it with a grain of salt. That was the case with executives at American Cyanamid Co., when Ms. Moog, the psychologist, studied a commercial for a Pierre Cardin men's fragrance. The ad was designed to show men who are aggressive and in control, but Ms. Moog saw a conflict in an image of the cologne gushing out of a phallic-shaped bottle. She said it symbolized male ejaculation and lack of control. "We recognized that she probably was right," says a marketing official who worked with Ms. Moog, "but we kept the shot of the exploding cologne in the commercial anyway. It's a beautiful product shot, plus it encourages men to use our fragrance liberally."

Source: Adapted from Ronald Alsop, "Agencies Scrutinize Their Ads for Psychological Symbolism" *The Wall Street Journal,* June 11, 1987, p. 25. Used by special permission.

meaning is attributed to symbols.[12] We will mention only two: *metaphor* and *contiguity*.

Metaphor   By invoking imagination, it is possible to transfer through analogy or implied comparison the qualities of one object to another, dissimilar object. You don't have to read Thai to understand the message in the first of the two ads in Figure 2–5. The goose is well-known for its flexible neck and thus is a good metaphor for Johnson Wax's new flexible-necked toilet bowl cleaner. We are less certain, however, about the metaphorical meaning conveyed in the Löwenbräu ad also in Figure 2–5, which, incidentally, was taken from a German-language magazine. What qualities are transferred from the lion to the product? Use your imagination.

Contiguity   Contiguity, on the other hand, brings other objects, activities, or people into association with an object in order to transfer the qualities of one to

---

FIGURE 2–4

The Michelin Baby as an Advertising Symbol

the other. Contiguity is used almost universally in cigarette advertising, as well as in ads for other products. The Swatch ad in Figure 2–6 unmistakably conveys a clear message about the lifestyle associated with use of the product.

Such tactics have been challenged, however, from an ethical perspective.[13] Some ethical considerations will be discussed in the last section of Chapter 3.

The Multiple Ways We Communicate

Although we pay greatest conscious attention to the use of visual and audio symbols, we communicate in many other nonverbal and nonsymbolic ways through the languages of smell, touch, numbers, space, optics (light and color), artifacts, time, and kinetics. Some of these "languages" are consciously used by marketing communicators, while others are often ignored. It is these "silent languages" that require further elaboration.

Using Metaphors to Create Meaning

The Language of Numbers   Alberto VO5. WD-40. Colt 45 Malt Liquor. Porsche 911. What connotations are given by these brand names? The answer, perhaps not surprisingly, is that it all depends upon the culture. This is because a number is not just a number—it is a complex symbol. Promotion in Action 2–2 provides vivid illustrations of how numerical meanings vary worldwide. Be careful in your use of numerical symbols!

The Language of Space   In this society, we maintain a sense of private space or territoriality. When this space is somehow violated, say, in a crowded elevator, people can react with discomfort or even hostility. On the other hand, space can be used consciously to deliver a clear message. Is there much doubt about the nature of the relationship conveyed in Figure 2–7?

The Language of Artifacts   Look at the ad in Figure 2–8 announcing a new cola "Thai style." Without ever having been in Thailand you learn a great deal about

---

FIGURE 2–6

The Product Takes on Meaning by Contiguity

Numbers Carry Meaning

In the context of brand names that contain numbers, it is important to recognize that a number is not just a number. Like other symbols, a number evokes thoughts and connotations beyond mere quantity, a fact that has been documented in many societies.

In the United States, for example, 3 is a sacred number connoting Christianity and the triple Godhead; strength and power (FBI, CIA are three-letter acronyms); and business acumen or quality (IBM, RCA). Euroamericans agree that 7 and 13 are lucky and unlucky, respectively. In Chinese culture, 8 signifies good fortune. In many Native American societies, 4 is a special number related to the four directions. But in Japan, this number is to be avoided since the word associated with it is also the word for death.

Finally, Americans feel that odd numbers are lucky and powerful, whereas even numbers are thought to be smooth and feminine. Small numbers are simple and weak, whereas larger numbers (those above 3) are powerful and masculine.

Source: Adapted from Jamneen Arnold Costa and Teresa M. Pavia, "What It All Adds Up To: Culture and Alpha-Numeric Brand Names," in *Advances in Consumer Research* vol. 19, eds. John F. Sherry, Jr., and Brian Sternthal (Provo, Utah: Association for Consumer Research, 1992), p. 40.

FIGURE 2–7

The Space between People Says It All

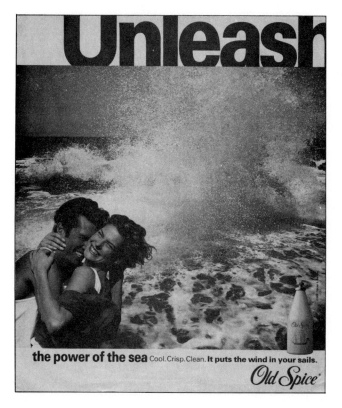

the target market by the artifacts featured here (clothing and the upscale outdoor surroundings connoting the rising young professional class). In other words, what we own and display can convey meaning.

The Language of Time   The ways in which we use and express time can be quite revealing, and these expressions vary widely from culture to culture. North Americans can be perplexing for Africans and Latins, who might well disapprove of the businesspeople in Figure 2–9 as "too busy for others," even though the image is perfectly suited to North Americans, who will likely associate the same figures with energy, momentum, and success. In short, time is also a language and should be used consciously in the development of advertising images.

The Language of Kinetics   *Kinetics* refers to gestures and movements. The couple in the ad shown in Figure 2–10 send a clear message, supported by artifacts of clothing, that they are busy career people on the move. Their facial expressions convey a real sense of joie de vivre.

FIGURE 2–8

The Artifacts Tell a Story

FIGURE 2—9

Busy People on the Move

Never stop at our counter again.

When you're a member of Hertz #1 Club Gold, there's no stopping at counters, no paperwork, nothing to slow you down. At 28 major airports, "Gold" is the fastest, easiest way ever to rent. It's another way #1 has more going for you.

Hertz rents Fords and other fine cars.   **AMERICA'S WHEELS**   ® REG. U.S. PAT. OFF. © HERTZ SYSTEM INC. 1990.

Courtesy The Hertz Corporation.

The Importance of the "Silent Languages" These and other nonverbal signals often are used unconsciously. Think of the harm that can be done by inappropriately moving in on someone else's space, violating time expectations, using a wrong gesture (don't wave your hand to call someone in most parts of Asia; you might be surprised what will happen), or using an artifact that conveys the wrong impression (wearing an open-collared shirt when making a sales call on a Wall Street lawyer). Such actions can adversely affect credibility. The solution, of course, is to be conscious of the multiple languages and use them purposefully.

COMMUNICATION IN MARKETING

Marketing communication does not differ in essence from communication in any other field. The challenge is to make appropriate use of all options, ranging from personal selling to wide-scale mass advertising.

FIGURE 2–10

Many Messages Are Conveyed by "Nonstop Legs"

Le 1er pot-au-feu qui donne envie de rentrer à la maison.

Knorr
TRADITION DU JOUR
Pot au Feu
3 bonnes assiettes

TRADITION DU JOUR   KNORR, TOUT SIMPLEMENT.

Knorr

Personal Selling

Personal selling is a widely used promotional strategy, especially in industrial goods marketing. Although self-service retailing is becoming increasingly commonplace in the consumer goods field, the demands for effective personal selling still exist in high-service product fields.

Personal selling offers some real strategic advantages:

1. The communication is face to face. Therefore, *dyadic interaction* can take place—it is possible for each party to learn all that is necessary about the other party to bring about empathy and meaningful exchange.

2. Feedback is instant. If the first efforts are off target, the skillful use of feedback offers the opportunity to try again and ultimately establish common ground.

3. Exposure is usually voluntary. This means that the customer (receiver) is actively seeking information or help and hence will be receptive to what is said.

The marketing challenge lies in answering this question: Where can I find a good salesperson? This is a common lament, especially at the retail level. Three chapters in Part 6 will look in detail at the issues related to this problem.

Mass Communication

The economic requirements of reaching a large audience place distinct limits on the use of interpersonal communication in marketing. Therefore, the mass media contain widespread use of advertising and public relations.[14]

As you saw earlier in Figure 2–4, the source of a mass communication is usually a commercial, governmental, or educational organization. Its purpose is to persuade audience members to accept a particular point of view or to inform and educate them with respect to a particular topic.

The U.S. Army, for example, ran a very effective recruiting campaign in the late 1980s featuring the upbeat slogan, "The Army—Be All You Can Be!" Visualize what must have taken place as this campaign passed through various levels of review, reaching into the highest levels of the Pentagon. Organizational theorists long have recognized what happens—compromises are made and the outcome is institutionally safe and often mediocre. The fact that this was not the case with the army recruiting campaign underscores the political savvy that must have been exercised to keep the cutting edge intact.

Mass Media and the Promotional Mix   The major reason for the wide use of mass communication is that it can reach a large audience quickly and inexpensively when viewed in terms of cost per individual contacted. Indeed, often no other practical way is available to reach a large and widely dispersed audience.

Although the benefits of mass media are significant, a downside must be recognized. Audiences turn to the mass media for the gratifications offered by entertainment, news, and education. When that is the case, exposure to advertising is usually *involuntary*. As a result, the probability is high that such advertising will be ignored or disregarded through selective information processing (discussed in Chapter 3).[15] This dilemma is compounded further by the deluge of competing ads in most media.

The only exception is when the consumer is engaged in active extended problem solving (see Chapter 5) and is interested in scanning ads for information. Now exposure becomes *voluntary*, and the individual actively processes the information that is presented.

An additional difficulty is that effective and timely feedback from mass media communication is difficult and expensive to obtain because the parties are physically separated. At the very least, feedback, usually in the form of an audience survey, is delayed. A survey used to generate feedback cannot adjust its content on the spot as a salesperson can do, with the result that the communication opportunity often is lost. An audience's reading and viewing can be determined only by asking people what they have read or seen. Standardized techniques for this purpose are discussed in Chapter 21.

Making the Most of the Mass Media   From the perspective of the effective transfer of meaning, the mass media present formidable challenges. But it is possible to use these media with considerable effectiveness if some necessary steps are taken. The following is a brief discussion of these steps.

Isolation of market segments   You will learn in Chapter 7 how to isolate specific groups or segments within the total market that offer the greatest receptivity and to avoid those that are unreceptive.

The General Motors Corporation, for example, tried unsuccessfully to broaden the appeal of its Cadillac Eldorado and Seville models to the younger import-oriented buyers. At the same time, GM hoped that the loyal market core of people in their 50s and 60s would not be alienated by the changed advertising strategy. In reality, the only results were the alienation of the loyal core and the failure to attract import buyers. In the end, sales were less than half of expectations.[16]

This situation could have been prevented if a more careful analysis of buyer motivations and behavior had been undertaken. First, did evidence indicate that younger buyers were wavering in their beliefs regarding the superiority of imported luxury cars? We doubt seriously that this was the situation, in which case the advertising seed was wasted by being sown on nonfertile soil.

Even if the opportunity had existed to make inroads with this approach, a different campaign should have been used for each market segment. Some companies that must reach 10 or more segments use different campaigns designed for each. The chances of getting the message across are significantly greater when this segmentation is done skillfully.

Careful media selection   Advertising strategists make every effort to match target audience characteristics with media audience characteristics. The goal is to minimize waste coverage to the maximum extent possible. This is a demanding task, but you will see in Chapter 12 that dollar productivity is increased when this task is accomplished.

Avoidance of ethnocentrism   Anthropologists use the word *ethnocentrism* to refer to the very common practice of assuming that others think and act as we do. Nothing could be farther from the truth. Naive lack of awareness of cross-cultural differences has led to any number of cross-cultural communication misfires. Some interesting examples appear in Promotion in Action 2–3.

Examples of Cross-Cultural Communication Misfires

Promotion in Action

2-3

- In the United States, the Marlboro Man (Figure 2–1) sells a lot of cigarettes; but in Hong Kong, the appeal failed. Hong Kong consumers are urbane and increasingly affluent buyers; they saw little charm in riding around on a horse in the hot sun all day.

- In a Nigerian ad, a platinum blonde sitting next to the driver of a Renault was intended to enhance the image of the product, but she was perceived as not exactly respectable.

- The concept of cooling and heating the body is important in Chinese thinking; malted milk is considered heating, while fresh milk is cooling; brandy is sustaining, while whiskey is harmful.

- A perfume was presented against a backdrop of rain, which for Europeans symbolizes a clean, cool, refreshing image, but to Africans is a symbol of fertility. The ad prompted many viewers to ask if the perfume was effective against infertility.

Source: Philip R. Cateora, *International Marketing,* 8th ed. (Homewood, Ill.: Richard D. Irwin, 1992), pp. 509, 522–23.

Pretesting appeals   There is no chance to try again if an appeal is off target. Therefore, every effort must be made in advance to determine the extent to which an appeal will attract and hold attention and to which the objectives of the message will be achieved. Determining these factors requires pretesting exposure of the message on smaller groups. Pretesting can provide enough information to minimize the probabilities of a communication misfire (see Chapter 21).

Analysis of feedback   Feedback, of course, is either delayed or absent altogether when mass media are used, whereas the salesperson has the advantage of instantaneous feedback. The advertiser must resort to after-the-fact measures of readership or viewership, comprehension, and response. Although it is too late to change what already has happened, this so-called *postmortem analysis* can prove invaluable in sharpening the impact of future efforts (see Chapter 21).

A Summary Comparison

Table 2–1 enables you to grasp quickly the comparative features of interpersonal and mass media. You can readily understand the benefits of using both in combination whenever possible.

TABLE 2–1

The Comparative Advantages and Limitations of Interpersonal and Mass Communication

Factors	Interpersonal	Mass
Reaching a large audience		
Speed	Slow	Fast
Cost per individual reached	High	Low
Influence on the individual		
Attraction of attention	High	Low
Probability of interest and response	High	Low
Accuracy of comprehension	High	Relatively low
Feedback		
Direction of message flow	Two-way	One-way
Speed of feedback	High	Low
Accuracy of feedback	High	Low

SUMMARY

This chapter introduces the fundamentals of *communication,* which is defined as a transactional process between two or more parties in which meaning is exchanged through intentional use of symbols. Meaning does not lie in words themselves but in individuals.

Communication makes use of symbols—signs designed and used to convey meaning about an object or person. The chapter presents a semiological analysis to explain how symbols are transmitted and are given meaning in the communication process.

Communication goes far beyond the use of verbal and pictorial symbols. As discussed in the chapter, people also use, perhaps unconsciously, such "silent" languages as time, kinetics, artifacts, and space. It is in this realm that communicators make some of the most serious mistakes that undermine their credibility.

The differences between interpersonal communication and mass communication in a marketing context are discussed in detail. As noted, interpersonal communication offers the benefits of face-to-face interaction, thus providing a greater opportunity to bring about changes in the other party.

Mass communication, on the other hand, has the advantages of speed and low cost per contact, but it poses real challenges caused by lack of flexibility and feedback. From this base of understanding, an overview presents the steps required to use communication effectively in marketing strategy.

REVIEW AND DISCUSSION QUESTIONS

1. Answer the following questions about the interaction between customer and salesperson presented at the top of page 47.
   a. How would you describe the dynamics of what has taken place here?
   b. You are assigned to train this salesperson on how to be more effective. What would you stress in this training?

	Thoughts	Words
Salesperson	(Oh boy, another one! Won't 9 o'clock ever come?)	(Cheerily). May I help you?
Customer		Yeah, I think I might be interested in a computer.
Salesperson	(Maybe I can get this over with quickly.)	Our Packard Bell Hard Drive System Model PB8810H is on sale. It comes with a Packard Bell 14-inch color RGB monitor for $888.83. This is $200 off list price.
Customer	(What did she say? I'd better not show my ignorance.)	I'm not quite sure what I want.
Salesperson	(I've got to sell one more of these today.)	Well, you'll never find a better system at this price
Customer	(How do I get out of here?)	I don't know. . . .
Salesperson	(I had better push harder.)	(interrupting) Look, this is a real deal. It's got a 30 meg hard disk and a floppy drive plus 640K RAM.
Customer	(What in the name of common sense is she saying? Can't she even speak English?)	(hesitating). That's interesting, but. . . .
Salesperson	(OK, I'll clinch this thing right now.)	Tell you what I'll do. I'll also throw in MS DOS 3.3 and GW Basic at no extra price.
Customer	(For crying out loud, I'm out of here.)	I think I'll look a little more. I own the drapery shop around the corner. My partner and I think it's time we got a computer, and this is the first time I've looked.
Salesperson	(Just a neophyte who's looking, huh? Thanks for wasting my time, buddy!)	Sure, here's my card.
Customer	(Fat chance you'll see me again, lady.)	I may be back.

2. Describe what kinds of connotative meaning most people have for these terms: *affection, love, fondness, tenderness, attachment, endearment, liking, devotion, Republican,* and *Democrat.* How do the connotative meanings differ from denotative meanings?

3. Turn to the ad in Figure 2–6 (p. 38). Carefully examine this picture and indicate which signs are icons, indexes, and symbols. Compare your analysis with that of others and see what differences you note. What conclusion can you draw about the uses of semiological analysis?

4. Turn now to the Hertz ad in Figure 2–9 (p. 41). Was any use made of metaphor or contiguity? If so, was the use effective in your opinion?

5. A salesperson is busy selling a wedding gown to a bride-to-be. Given the many languages of communication that we all use, to what specific kinds of feedback should the salesperson be sensitive?

6. A regional soft drink manufacturer has marketed under one brand name since 1904 and still has the original product line consisting of root beer and orange soda. The CEO is being pressed by her board to consider market segmentation. You are asked to comment on this request. How would you define market segmentation? Under what conditions would you recommend it?

NOTES

1. This is the heart of contemporary definitions of communication. See especially Em Griffin, *A First Look at Communication Theory* (New York: McGraw-Hill, 1990); Dominic A. Infante, Andrew S. Rancer, and Deanna F. Womack, *Building Communication Theory* (Prospect Heights, Ill.: Waveland Press, 1990), Chapter 1; Don Fabun, *Communications: The Transfer of Meaning* (San Francisco, Calif.: International Society for General Semantics, 1987); and Wilbur Schramm, "The Unique Perspective of Communication: A Retrospective View," *Journal of Communication* 33 (Summer 1983), pp. 14–15.

2. This is a difficult and challenging field that involves many theories and conceptualizations. For a good introduction, see Arthur A. Berger, *Signs in Contemporary Culture: An Introduction to Semiotics* (New York: Longman, 1984); John Fisk, *Introduction to Communication Studies* (New York: Methuen, 1982); Arthur A. Berger, *Media Analysis Techniques* (Beverly Hills, Calif.: Sage Publications, 1982), Chapter 1; and David G. Mick, "Consumer Research and Semiotics: Exploring the Morphology of Signs, Symbols, and Significance," *Journal of Consumer Research* 13 (September 1986), pp. 196–213.

3. Infante et al., *Building Communication Theory*, p. 9.

4. Symbols have long been accepted as being at the very heart of the communication process. See, for example, Kenneth Boulding, *The Image* (Ann Arbor, Mich.: University of Michigan Press, 1956); and Sidney J. Levy, "Symbols for Sale," *Harvard Business Review* 37 (July-August, 1959), pp.117–24. For a more contemporary statement, see G. Cronkhite, "On the Focus, Scope, and Coherence of the Study of Symbolic Activity," *Quarterly Journal of Speech* 73 (1986), pp. 231–46. Also, see Mick, "Consumer Research and Semiotics," pp. 196–213.

5. For an important discussion on changes in the ways in which communication is described and conceptualized, see "Ferment in the Field," an entire issue of *Journal of Communication* 33 (Summer 1983).

6. For a helpful summary of descriptive models, see Infante et al., *Building Communication Theory*, pp. 24–32.

7. Quoted in Mick, "Consumer Research and Semiotics," p. 198.

8. Fabun, *Communications: The Transfer of Meaning*, p. 16.

9. Sidney J. Levy, "Symbols by Which We Buy," in *Advancing Marketing Efficiency*, ed. Lynn H. Stockman (Chicago: American Marketing Association, 1959), p. 410.

10. See, for example, Eva M. Hyatt, "Consumer Stereotyping: The Cognitive Bases of the Social Symbolism of Products," in *Advances in Consumer Research,* vol. 19, eds. John F. Sherry Jr., and Brian Sternthal (Provo, Utah: Association for Consumer Research, 1992), pp. 299–303; and Newell D. Wright, C. B. Claiborne, and M. Joseph Sirgy, "The Effects of Product Symbolism on Consumer Self-Concept," in *Advances in Consumer Research,* vol. 19, eds. John F. Sherry, Jr., and Brian Sternthal (Provo, Utah: Association for Consumer Research, 1992), pp. 311–18.

11. Morris B. Holbrook, "Seven Routes to Facilitating the Semiological Interpretation of Consumption Symbolism and Marketing Imagery in Works of Art: Some Tips for Wildcats," in *Advances in Consumer Research,* vol. 16, ed. Thomas K. Srull (Provo, Utah: Association for Consumer Research, 1989), p. 420.

12. To discover more about how semiotics has been applied in marketing, see Morris B. Holbrook, "Aims, Concepts, and Methods for the Representation of Individual Differences in Esthetic Responses to Design Features," *Journal of Consumer Research* 13 (December 1986), pp. 337–447.

13. Grant McCracken and Richard W. Pollay, "Anthropology and the Study of Advertising" (Working Paper No. 815, Faculty of Commerce and Business Administration, University of British Columbia, 1981).

14. For an excellent introduction to mass communication, see Denis McQuail, *Mass Communication Theory* (Beverly Hills, Calif.: Sage, 1984).

15. See Blaine Goss, *The Psychology of Human Communication* (Prospect Heights, Ill.: Waveland Press, 1989), especially Chapter 4.

16. Russell Mitchell, "GM's New Luxury Cars: Why They're Not Selling," *Business Week,* January 19, 1987, pp. 94ff.

3

Consumer Response to Persuasive Communication

MOSCOW: NOT THE DREAMLAND ADVERTISERS EXPECTED

In theory, it is an advertiser's dream: 288 million product-starved consumers whose main experience of television commercials has been a lifetime of crude pitches for heavy machinery. In practice, Russians may not turn out to be such pushovers. A study commissioned by J. Walter Thompson (JWT) shows that Muscovites are far less gullible—and more discriminating—than Western marketers might have hoped.

In one recent study, Russia's biggest television channel, Gostelradio, broadcast five hours of typical British programming and, with it, a series of JWT's adverts (British lingo for *ad*. Afterward, CRAM International, a research company, replayed the ads to small groups of young, well-educated, and affluent (hence more readily targeted) Muscovites to test their reactions.

Unlike naive Westerners of 25 years ago, the Russians—weaned on propaganda and deeply distrustful of the media—were skeptical of the adverts' messages. Their interpretations were often quite sophisticated. A spot for Listerine mouthwash was seen as a morality play where evil (bad breath) was conquered by good (the product). And sensible: a harried car-phone-toting yuppie was derided as unstable, hyperactive, and frivolous.

Source: "The Hidden Persuaders," *The Economist,* March 23, 1991, p. 79.

As our opening example so vividly reveals, the consumer worldwide is not a pawn on the marketer's board. Apparently, Western marketers believed that they could capture the emerging affluent market in Moscow by sheer persuasive power. They discovered anew the cornerstone principle of *consumer sovereignty:* Consumers have full power to see and hear what they want to see and hear.

This all comes down to the basic proposition (discussed in Chapter 2) that, if we are not careful, a marked difference can exist between meaning intended by the sender and the meaning attributed by the receiver. Why does this happen? To find the answers, we turn to the study of information processing.

Our first purpose is to clarify what happens in the consumer's mind from the initial exposure to a message to the ultimate response. You will learn quickly that the study of information processing is providing a rich yield of marketing insights. Then we turn more specifically to an exploration of how persuasive communication works to bring about changes in attitudes and behavior.

INFORMATION PROCESSING: FUNDAMENTAL CONCEPTS

The Coca-Cola Company developed a TV spot in 1992 designed to communicate the message that "new" Coke (introduced during the 1980s) is now being called Coke II. The commercial featured a can of Coke II with a voice-over informing the viewer that new Coke had changed its name and that it now had a genuine cola taste and the sweetness of Pepsi-Cola. The goal, of course, was to stimulate trial of Coke II among Pepsi users.

Did this commercial have its intended effect? If Coke's objectives were to be achieved, viewers would have had to go through the following stages:[1]

1. *Exposure*—The consumer must have proximity to the message so that one or more senses may be activated.
2. *Attention*—Information-processing capacity must be allocated to the stimulus.
3. *Comprehension*—The message must be interpreted, and meaning must be attributed to it.
4. *Acceptance*—The message must be accepted into the structure of existing knowledge and/or beliefs and attitudes. Persuasion is said to occur if there also is *yielding*—modification of existing beliefs and attitudes or creation of new ones.
5. *Retention*—The interpreted stimulus is transferred into long-term memory.

What this all means is that a message must survive five different stages before it is retained in memory. This explodes the folklore that says, "You can win them if you just get the message to them." Exposure does *not* guarantee the desired response.

Now, how well did the Coke II commercial perform? Figure 3–1 provides a useful scorecard based on persuasion tests undertaken by Research Systems Corporation (RSC).[2] From its previous experience, RSC provided this benchmark: If 23% of those who are exposed recall seeing the commercial and 16% can state the main selling points, an ad has a 41% chance of achieving superior selling power. The Coke II ad scored as follows:

The ad did very well in attention attraction. Of those who were exposed to the commercial in this test, 57 percent recalled seeing it when contacted 72 hours later by telephone. This exceeded the benchmark level by 34 percent.

Twenty-four percent correctly recalled the main selling points, surpassing the benchmark by 8 percent.

The commercial fell short, however, of the average commercial in this product category in persuasion. RSC computes an index of persuasion based on changes in brand preference, and this commercial scored +2.2 versus a +3.0 average.

The Central Role of Involvement

Motivation to process a promotional message varies directly with the extent to which the consumer experiences involvement in the purchase process. *Involvement* is defined as the degree of perceived personal importance and relevance accompanying product and brand choice within a specific situation or context.[3]

Involvement and relevance are personalized issues with some diverse roots:[4]

1. *Perceived risk of negative outcomes.* From time to time, everyone has doubts or fears that purchase expectations will not be met. As an example, Americans have been found to distrust Wall Street to the extent that only 11 percent would turn to a stockbroker for advice on investing a $10,000 windfall.[5] Who could blame the public in view of the sense of powerlessness the average investor felt during the unpredictable stock fluctuations in the most recent economic recession?

2. *Social sanctions.* To the extent that peer group influence defines the "right choice" and becomes an important determinant of choice, involvement correspondingly increases.

3. *Ego relatedness.* Involvement increases to the extent that consumer actions are seen as enhancing or affecting self-image.

When involvement is high, *message relevance* is the key to breaking through and communicating as intended. In other words, the individual is motivated to receive pertinent information and his or her filters are open.

Another outcome of high involvement is *selective perception,* in which unwanted or nondesired communication is actively tuned out. In other words, perceptual defenses can be erected that lead to selective exposure (if there is forewarning that an unwanted message is coming), lack of attention, imperfect comprehension, or outright rejection.

FIGURE 3–1

Coke II Spot Goes Flat on Persuasion

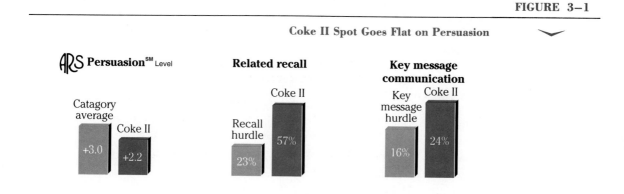

Information Overload

There is no question that people living in developed countries face an overload of commercial persuasion. Not surprisingly, defenses are erected against its influence. Be certain to read Ellen Goodman's lament, "The American Cornucopia Has Become a Landscape of Too Many Choices" (Promotion in Action 3–1).

THE STAGES IN INFORMATION PROCESSING

In the previous section, we defined *consumer sovereignty*. Now we will see how it works in practice. In the discussion that follows, we will explain what takes place at each of the five stages of information processing outlined above.

Exposure

Information processing among target audience members begins when the message activates at least one of the five senses. To ensure exposure, advertisers must select communication media (interpersonal or mass) that reach people where they are. This is the great challenge of media selection (and will be more fully discussed in Chapter 12).

Selective Exposure   Consumers worldwide have become adept at finding ways to avoid exposure to unwanted messages. It has been known for decades that this can happen when involvement is high in order to protect beliefs and practices

---

Promotion in Action

3-1

The American Cornucopia Has Become a Landscape of Too Many Choices

I arrive at the supermarket for my weekly round of speed shopping. It occurs to me that I do not anymore regard the choices in this consumer hall of fame as emblems of my freedom but as demands on my time and attention. I have become less interested in widening my options than in narrowing them.

At some point, the exploding number of decisions to be made between Brand X and Y and Z, the options in the ice cream and cable channels squeezes too much time from the day. I buy shaving cream indiscriminately and cannot for the life of me make a distinction between or among toilet tissues. I doubt that a new, improved product is truly new or improved.

I doubt that this is my own middle-aged hardening of the consumer arteries. Rather, like many Americans, I am reacting to a choice overload. . . . The consumer world still expands and so much our defenses. Against too many choices that make too little difference. Against the time that must be paid for a life of informed consuming. Against the need to decide. And decide.

Source: Ellen Goodman, "Consumers Have Too Many Choices, © 1993, The Boston Globe Company. Reprinted with permission. Reproduced by special permission.

from attack. When involvement is high, the consumer seeks supportive information but actively avoids contradictory information.

Most products and services, however, do not attain the degree of importance and relevance necessary to incur selective exposure. They do not attain it because low involvement is a fact of life. Does it really matter which brand of toilet paper or motor oil a consumer purchases? Are brand preferences established that must be shielded from attack? In the majority of situations, no.

As was pointed out earlier, consumers also avoid exposure because they are inundated. Howard Shimmel, vice president for audience research at MTV Networks, estimates that a person watching 30 hours of TV per week is bombarded by 37,822 commercials a year.[6] We cannot help wondering how Mr. Shimmel managed to arrive at such a precise number, but we believe that he is not far off.

The fact is that consumers have become active *zappers* (actively switching channels during commercials or using the mute button),[7] *zippers* (using the fast-forward button on a VCR),[8] and *grazers* (wandering through various channels).[9] But as Abernethy and Rotfield tell us in Promotion in Action 3–2, there is nothing much new here. Consumers always have been adept at avoiding the advertiser.

In one study, over half of those sampled indicated that they regularly take action to avoid unwanted commercials, and this is becoming increasingly common,[10] especially when commercials are grouped or clustered into one time period, referred to as a *pod*.[11] Further, men are more likely to do this than women.[12]

What can be done about the zappers? One suggested strategy is to ignore them. George Garrick, executive vice president of Information Resources, Inc., put it this way:

> If these people are sitting around changing channels all day and night, maybe they're not the kind of people we want to reach anyway. If you bear in mind that the average household is exposed to about 140 commercials per day, it is easy to have a viewer do what he considers to be "a lot" of zapping when, as a percentage of all commercials, he really is doing relatively little.[13]

Accepting Garrick's advice, however, may be a bit like putting your head in the sand. Such a practice could lead to loss of major market segments, especially that of baby boomers, who lead the "zapping pack."

On the other hand, some methods have proved helpful in holding the viewer and inhibiting zapping. First of all, since most zapping seems to occur during the first and last five minutes of programs, it might be wise to move ads into the interior of the program whenever possible.

Research also indicates that people often see a few seconds of a spot before zapping. As a result, major attempts are made to build drama and interest into spots by making them look like a real production before centering on the product (a medieval battle scene selling a computer, for example). Other spots follow quite an opposite strategy and hope to beat the zapping button by hitting the brand name and benefit in less than five seconds.[14]

Finally, programming that holds viewer interest decreases zapping. For example, zapping drops sharply when viewers become embroiled in the legal and

Promotion
in Action

3-2

Zipping through TV Ads Is an Old Tradition

"We'll be right back after these messages"

Illustration by Richard Westgard for Marketing News.

News stories increasingly discuss how TV viewers avoid commercials, but the news is misleading. The problem is no more a modern innovation than broadcasting advertising itself.

Even when stations were switched by hand and VCRs were rare, people could always avoid commercials simply by leaving the room. And they still can. Technology did not create the problem of physical avoidance of commercials, though it might have made it greater.

A variety of studies conducted since 1965 that directly assessed TV viewing behavior all found high rates of sets in use with no audience and commercials that played to an empty room. They consistently agreed that commercial audiences are lower than program audiences.

The unique environment of British political commercials purported to allow a surrogate measure of advertising avoidance by use of electrical load data around 5- to 10-minute political ads shown simultaneously on all TV channels. Electricity use significantly increased during these breaks, a finding the researcher suggested was caused by tens of thousands of viewers turning on lights, opening refrigerator doors, and so on.

More directly, several studies took pictures or videotaped anyone in the viewing area of the TV set in sample homes. Even during the program time, the set would often be on with no one in the room. However, viewership of commercials averaged 20 to 24 points lower than viewership of the actual program.

Source: Avery Abernethy and Herbert Rotfield, "Zipping through TV Ads Is Old Tradition—But Viewers Are Getting Better at It," *Marketing News,* January 17, 1991, p. 6. Reproduced by special permission.

sexual maneuvers on "L.A. Law."[15] To the extent that this is true, ads should be placed accordingly, but such programs are hard to find.

Attention

Attention is defined as allocation of processing capacity to the incoming stimulus. Capacity is a limited resource at best. Therefore, a person's cognitive system must constantly be active in monitoring sensory inputs, Selecting only a subset for further processing. This selection occurs at a preconscious level and is referred to as *preattentive processing.*

What this means is that some stimuli will receive attention and others will be ignored. Test for yourself the limits of your attention span. How long does it take for you to concentrate on a thought in this book before your mind begins to wander? Not very long? Consider the challenge to marketing communicators in a world of information overload. It is small wonder that there has been a trend toward commercials that air for 15 seconds or less.[16]

The Role of Individual Characteristics   There is a vast literature documenting the extent to which needs, motivations, attitudes, and other individual characteristics and dispositions affect the degree to which information processing capacity will be allocated. We will give you a few highlights.

Needs and motivations   Think of the last time you were in a shopping mall around mealtime. Did you find yourself paying more attention to the vendors selling pizza, frozen yogurt, or cinnamon buns? Almost everyone will respond affirmatively.

This is a simple example of the consistent outcome from hundreds of studies dating back to the 1930s: Needs affect attention by enhancing the likelihood that need-relevant stimuli will be noticed. Marketers have long capitalized on this fact to promote goods at moments or places of high consumer receptivity (e.g., beer and soft drinks at a baseball game on a hot summer day).

Beliefs and attitudes   A large percentage of people under the age of 40 have refused to even consider purchasing American cars for nearly two decades. It is a matter of record that domestic manufacturers across the board lost touch with this market in the 1970s and 1980s by offering cars of inferior quality.

But now Detroit is experiencing a comeback. In 1993, the Chrysler Corporation, for example, introduced the technologically advanced "cab forward" Chrysler Concorde and Dodge Integra models. Trade reports are unanimous that Chrysler has at least matched the higher-priced imports and surpassed them in significant ways.

Take a moment to read the Chrysler ad in Figure 3–2. Do you think it has a chance of attracting and holding the attention of the hard-core market that has sworn off American cars? It will be an uphill struggle, but Chrysler has a good chance of changing the attitudes of many potential customers.

There is no question that some people who hold an anti-American-car value quite strongly will be unreceptive to what Chrysler is trying to do. This is because all of us strive to maintain a consistent system of beliefs and attitudes, and this is especially true when involvement is high and preferences are strongly held. When this is the case, we maintain cognitive consistency by paying attention to reinforcing messages and screening out (avoiding) opposing ones.[17]

What this means is that selective attention is most likely to occur when involvement is high. One way cognitive consistency is maintained is though *perceptual defense*—a filtering process that prevents a message from being processed. Many who have strong negative attitudes toward Detroit will pass right over this ad because their defenses are activated at a subconscious level.

Perceptual vigilance, on the other hand, maintains or enhances consistency by stimulating attention to belief-relevant messages. For example, preferred brand names are often processed more readily than are nonpreferred names.[18] Given this fact, Chrysler could attract the attention of a substantial segment of those who are willing to give Detroit another chance.

Adaptation level   Have you ever noticed how you can become so habituated to an always-present stimulus, such as a smell or a noise, that you scarcely notice

---

FIGURE 3–2

Will This Ad Change Attitudes?

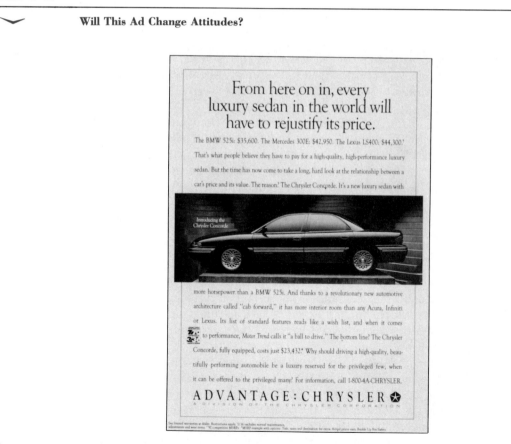

From here on in, every luxury sedan in the world will have to rejustify its price.

The BMW 525i: $35,600. The Mercedes 300E: $42,950. The Lexus LS400: $44,300.* That's what people believe they have to pay for a high-quality, high-performance luxury sedan. But the time has now come to take a long, hard look at the relationship between a car's price and its value. The reason? The Chrysler Concorde. It's a new luxury sedan with

Introducing the Chrysler Concorde

more horsepower than a BMW 525i. And thanks to a revolutionary new automotive architecture called "cab forward," it has more interior room than any Acura, Infiniti or Lexus. Its list of standard features reads like a wish list, and when it comes to performance, Motor Trend calls it "a ball to drive." The bottom line? The Chrysler Concorde, fully equipped, costs just $23,432.* Why should driving a high-quality, beautifully performing automobile be a luxury reserved for the privileged few, when it can be offered to the privileged many? For information, call 1-800-4A-CHRYSLER.

ADVANTAGE: CHRYSLER
A DIVISION OF THE CHRYSLER CORPORATION

it at all? What happens is that you develop an *adaptation level* for that stimulus so that it rarely, if ever, attracts your attention. Advertising is susceptible to this process, especially when the product or service is low in involvement.

Burger King introduced a $30 million campaign to announce that the weight of its flagship Whopper hamburger had been increased by 20 percent. Such television personalities as Mr. T and Bruce Weitz were the spokespersons. During the first month, there was a 3.6 percent increase in the mention of Burger King when consumers were asked to name the first fast-food ads that came to mind. After just one month, however, this awareness dropped 5.6 percent, placing it at one of the lowest levels in that chain's history.[19] Another ad fell victim to "commercial wearout."

Advertising, in reality, has become part of the cultural background noise and is therefore scarcely noticed, especially when involvement is low. It is small wonder, then, that advertisers resort to sometimes dramatic and frequently controversial gimmicks to overcome habituation and break through the noise. Can you blame Hiram Walker & Sons, Inc., for turning to the unexpected in its Christmas ads for Kahlúa (Figure 3–3)?

FIGURE 3–3

The "Unexpected" Attracts Attention

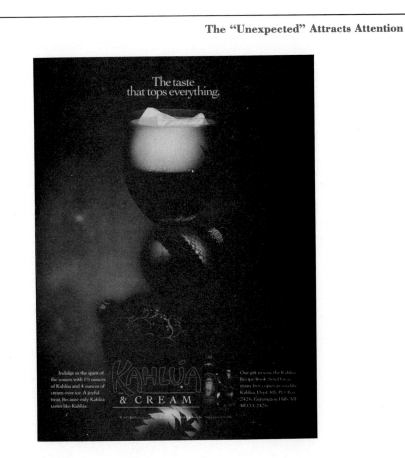

The trend toward television and print "spectaculars" is likely to continue, but this is not without its risks. Attention is commonly attracted to secondary stimulus factors, while the main message is completely missed. Unless the brand name and selling proposition are reinforced, the promotional investment can be wasted.

The Role of Stimulus Characteristics   Try paging through a magazine and notice what makes some ads stand out more than others. Advertisers use many devices to attract attention, one of which is novelty.

Most readers of the widely read German magazine *Stern* are likely at least to notice the ad for Bols Blue Curaçao appearing in Figure 3–4. The reason, of course, is the unusually dominant position of the ship. Whether or not the brand name will be seen is another matter.

Another attention-attracting device is color. One study demonstrated, for example, that four-color, two-page ads scored 53 percent higher in readership than black-and-white ads.[20] Also, it was found that the addition of one color to an otherwise black-and-white newspaper ads produced 41 percent more sales.[21]

FIGURE 3–4

Novelty Attracts Attention

Directionality—the use of visual design to direct a viewer's attention—also can be an effective strategy. Look at the ad for Jeep Cherokee on the left-hand page of Figure 3–5. Where does your eye move? Right off the page and away from the Jeep name. Notice the very different pattern of directionality for the Pentax ad. Your eye is pulled to the product and its brand name.

Finally, some stimuli are more noticeble than others because of their location or position. Retailers are well aware of this fact and try to put the fast-moving and high-profit items at the customer's eye level whenever possible.

Position also is important in print media. Greater attention is attracted by ads located in the front part of a magazine, on right-hand pages, and on the inside front, inside back, and outside back covers.[22] Similarly, broadcast advertisers are well aware that commercials do better when they are separated from the clutter of other commercials at the beginning and end of programs.

Can Consumers Be Influenced without Awareness?   In the 1950s, a great deal of interest was stimulated by a widely publicized report that consumers apparently

FIGURE   3–5

How Does the Eye Move in These Ads?

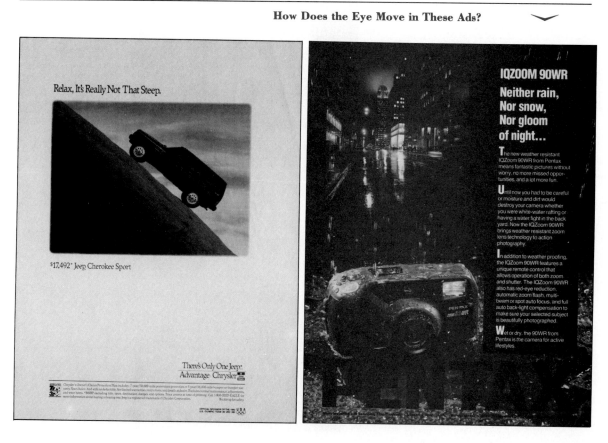

can be induced to react to a certain type of advertising without knowing that they have been influenced.[23] This is known as *subliminal perception,* a phenomenon that has been demonstrated many times in the literature of experimental psychology.[24]

A virtual firestorm erupted when this issue went public. Cries from all quarters raised the specter of "Big Brother" influence and thought control. But matters subsided when the researcher in question admitted that everything he had done was a hoax.

Meanwhile, marketers began to experiment with subliminal stimuli, and no one seemed to notice or to care. Consumers spend millions of dollars

---

FIGURE 3–6

Sexy Ice Cubes?

Courtesy Thomas J. Lipton Co.

each year on self-help tapes with imbedded subliminal messages. Retailers have placed subliminal messages designed to curb shoplifting within their in-store music.

The issue was largely dormant until Wilson Bryan Key wrote a popular book arguing that erotic subliminal clues are planted in ads to stimulate subconscious sex drives for the purpose of increasing sales.[25] Key's original book revived fears of thought control, which have been further enhanced by his latest book.[26]

Key has always focused his attention on liquor ads, many of which feature a closeup of a tantalizing drink poured over ice cubes. He claims that sexually oriented subliminal symbols are embedded in the ice cubes to increase the persuasive power of the ads.

Although most people scoff at such an allegation, research has verified that this tactic might have the alleged effect, at least in experimental settings.[27] Figure 3–6 contains an "ice cube" ad, not for liquor but for ice tea. Study this ad carefully from the perspective of Key's comments. The issue is this: Do you see any sexual stimuli embedded in the ice cubes?

Frankly, we do not believe that advertisers ever were guilty as charged. Key may discern sexual symbols, but he is open to the charge that these are entirely a product of his own imagination. Here is an instance in which subjective semiology can run amok.

Despite their occasional use, there is real doubt that subliminal messages have much persuasive impact.[28] Our assessment is that, to date, the effects of subliminal stimulation do not warrant its use in promotional strategy. We agree with Moore's conclusion:

> A century of psychological research substantiates the general principle that more intense stimuli have a greater effect on people's behavior than weak ones. . . . Subliminal stimuli are usually so weak that the recipient is not just unaware of the stimuli but is also oblivious to the fact that he/she is being stimulated. As a result, the potential effects of subliminal stimuli are easily nullified by other ongoing stimulation in the same sensory channel whereby attention is being focused on another modality.[29]

In short, it is difficult enough to create understanding through persuasive communication without adding an inferior, although exotic, strategy.

Comprehension

"Warning: This Story Will Be Miscomprehended." So read the headline of a *Marketing News* report on the results of a study designed to measure comprehension/miscomprehension of editorial and ad copy in 18 magazines.[30] This research undertaken by Jacoby and Hoyer found that more than one third of the people surveyed could not correctly state what they had read.[31] But, surprising to some, the readers comprehended ad content slightly better than editorial features.

What this says, of course, is that exposure and attention do not guarantee that correct meaning is attributed to the message. At least one third of the time, understanding is not created and communication thus misfires.

The Creation of Meaning   Meaning depends to a large degree on how a person categorizes and elaborates a stimulus through the use of existing knowledge and beliefs.[32]

Categorization   Categorization involves comparing a stimulus with memory content so that it can be classified as to its physical properties and assigned meaning. In other words, the stimulus undergoes something analogous to an unconscious filing process.

It is here where brand equity (mentioned in Chapter 1) becomes especially important. Stressing a familiar brand or model name is a major step in helping the receiver to attribute correct meaning to the message. An unfamiliar name, on the other hand, may be incorrectly categorized or not categorized at all. Keith Crain gives all advertisers an important warning not to neglect this principle (see Promotion in Action 3–3).

Elaboration   In addition to categorization, the extent of elaboration that takes place also affects comprehension. *Elaboration* is the process by which the new information received is compared with existing knowledge stored in memory. It is here that personal connections are made between the stimulus and the individual's life experiences or goals.[33] Elaboration typically is conceived as a continuum ranging from low to high (or shallow to deep)[34] and is detected by analysis of thoughts during exposure.

The Role of Individual Characteristics   We discussed earlier how involvement, motivation, and attitudes can influence the attention process; they have a similar

---

Promotion in Action

3–3

Brand Equity Is an Asset—Do Not Neglect It

I have never understood how a manufacturer can blithely abandon the goodwill and name recognition built up over decades and then launch a new brand name from scratch. It seems to be a way of spending an unnecessary few zillion dollars that could be spent more wisely.

The greatest value of any brand is the name itself. When Cadillac introduced its newest and most exciting cars in a decade, it did not rename them. The Seville and Eldorado may be General Motors' most successful new model launches in a long time. They are building on the brand names that GM has already spent millions of dollars to develop.

By contrast, look at the newest Oldsmobile, the Achieva. It will take an extra pile of dollars to create any consumer awareness for that name. And this comes at a time when Oldsmobile can ill afford to squander its limited resources. Obviously, Oldsmobile officials felt they had little risk with the name of the predecessor model, the Cutlass Calais. But they are adding confusion to an already overwhelmed dealer and customer base.

All names are valuable; protect them.

Source: Keith Crain, "Detroit's Brand Values," *Advertising Age*, April 20, 1992, p. 24. Reproduced by special permission.

effect on comprehension.[35] Deeper and more elaborate information processing is likely when an important need is activated by emotional and complex message symbolism.

A good example is the Waterman ad in Figure 3–7. Notice how the rich meaning surrounding a long and valued friendship now becomes associated with the Waterman pen. If the ad had shown only the pen and listed its features, the potential attributed meaning would have been more barren.

A person's expectations or perceptual set will affect the attribution of meaning. For example, it is common to discover that people perceive the taste of a food or beverage product quite differently when a familiar brand name is used than when it is not. The management at the Coca-Cola Company learned this lesson when its new Coke was blind-tested. The taste-testing edge given the formulation of the new Coke without identification of brand name did not hold up once the product was introduced to the market.[36] Consumers may have liked the new Coke formula, but this no longer represented the Coca-Cola they had come to know and love.

FIGURE 3–7

A Pen Is More Than Just a Pen

The Role of Stimulus Characteristics   Message elements such as words, graphics, and design also affect comprehension, as the following two examples show.

When Apple Computer introduced the Apple IIc, a trimmer but more powerful version of earlier models, many prospects refused to accept that smaller size and greater power were compatible attributes. To counteract this perception, the Apple IIc advertising used the slogan "It's a lot bigger than it looks."

Color also makes a difference because of the rich connotations of each hue. Green and blue connote security to many U.S. customers; therefore, IBM may have benefited for years from its nickname, Big Blue. Another manufacturer found greater acceptance of its line of cat litter products by introducing green granules to reinforce its message of deodorizing power.

Acceptance

Exposure, attention, and comprehension do not necessarily lead to acceptance. *Acceptance,* as you recall, refers to the degree to which a stimulus influences a person's knowledge and/or beliefs and attitudes.

Turn to the fur coat ad in Figure 3–8. Do you think that this ad will be effective? By this we mean, will it result in sufficient modification or change in existing beliefs and attitudes to lead to appropriate buying action?

The answer depends to a high degree on how you feel about animal rights. Growing numbers of people have decided that fur is out, and the industry has been adversely affected.[37] Animal rights activists' negative attitudes can serve as a potent barrier, resulting in this ad never being accepted into their memory.

Three degrees of acceptance are possible as information is being categorized. First, the information can be filtered out with no effect on existing dispositions. This response is especially likely when both involvement and the contradiction with existing outlooks are high. A more favorable outcome is *assimilation*—integration into existing cognitive structures. The best outcome of all is *accommodation,* in which existing beliefs and attitudes are changed or new categories are created to handle the new concept.[38]

Cognitive Responses   Growing evidence suggests that *cognitive responses* (mental reactions that occur as information is processed) are indicators of the degree to which acceptance and yielding actually happen, especially when involvement is high[39] and the consumer is actively engaging in brand evaluation.[40] These responses are classified as follows:

1. *Counterarguments*—Disagreement with message claims.
2. *Support arguments*—Agreement with and support of message claims.
3. *Source derogations*—Negative response to the source of the message.

Evidence to date indicates the following:

1. The greater the extent of counterargumentation, the less the probability of change in beliefs, attitudes, and behavior.
2. Support arguments and probability of acceptance are positively related.

FIGURE 3–8

The Fur Flies

3. Source derogation may entirely rule out acceptance and yielding.

4. When involvement is low, acceptance is determined more by cognitive responses to the executional elements of the message than by the content.[41]

Back once again to our fur coat ad (Figure 3–8). If a person is not sympathetic to the animal rights cause and also has an active need for this product, the person would be expected to offer support arguments: "Great-looking coat," "An interesting color."

The opponent, on the other hand, could counterargue: "What a bunch of baloney. Anybody who wears this thing is commiting a crime." You also would expect to hear source derogations, such as "You'll never catch me anywhere near a fur store."

The marketer often can anticipate counterarguments and try to refute them but should not underestimate the potency of the acceptance barrier. Many have tried to change beliefs and attitudes only to experience economic frustration. For example, Sears created a major marketing blunder by ignoring its changing customer market and letting Wal-Mart and Kmart encroach on its market share. Consumer indifference indicates that Sears's "everyday low prices" ad theme is falling mostly on deaf ears. As a result, this once venerable company is facing a monumental uphill battle to survive in the 1990s.

Affective Responses   The term *affective responses* refers to emotions and feelings induced by a stimulus.[42] These feelings can be quite varied, encompassing fear, surprise, sadness, disgust, anger, anticipation, joy, and acceptance.[43] They also play an important role in mediating the process of acceptance.

Retention

As we have seen, messages are often transformed as information processing progresses so that they become quite different from what the sender intended. Now we reach the last step, *retention*, in which information is transferred into long-term memory. Marketers are increasingly turning to cognitive psychology to learn more about what happens during retention.

The human brain is divided into left and right hemispheres, which play different roles. Evidence consistently indicates that the left hemisphere processes information sequentially, verbally, and logically, whereas the right functions spatially, intuitively, and wholistically.[44] This would suggest that advertising copy is processed more in the left hemisphere than in the right, and visual and other executional elements more in the right.

Theories on memory structure abound. One currently popular theory holds that three different memory storage systems work as follows:[45]

1. A stimulus is first processed in *sensory memory*, at which time information is extracted about physical characteristics. Meaning is not attributed at this stage.

2. The input then goes to *short-term memory*, where it is temporarily held and analyzed for meaning. It is held there for no more than 3 to 10 seconds

and then is transferred into long-term memory. The content that is *re-hearsed* (i.e., the subject of silent, inner speech that analyzes and elaborates it) is transferred and vice versa. We referred to rehearsal earlier but used the term *cognitive responses.*

3. If the input survives the filtering in short-term memory, it enters *long-term memory* either intact or in modified form.

Much more could be said about various memory control processes, such as retrieval and coding. Although additional information might be useful for general understanding, the background provided in this section is sufficient to help you think more strategically about the stages of information processing.

ETHICAL CONSIDERATIONS: THE RIGHT TO BE INFORMED

The second plank in Kennedy's original Bill of Consumer Rights (refer back to Figure 1–8 in Chapter 1) is the right to be informed:

> [The consumer has the right] to be protected against fraudulent, deceitful, or grossly misleading information, advertising, labeling, or other practices, and to be given the facts that he [or she] needs to make an informed choice.[46]

This statement brings clarity to the often-ignored issue of ethics in persuasion. It affirms loudly that the consumer has legitimate expectations that cannot be violated by anyone who takes consumer sovereignty seriously. Several important issues emerge: informed choice, information overload, truth in advertising, and manipulation.

What Is an Informed Choice?

We will soon discover that this question is not a simple one to answer. It involves other questions, such as: How much information does the consumer want and need? Can we provide too much information?

When Is a Message Informative?   To help answer this question, consider the two ads in Figure 3–9. The main selling points for the Du Pont SilverStone ad, which appeared in a Thai general interest magazine, may be translated as follows:

> Food won't stick, because of the SilverStone premium no-stick surface. You can cook better becauase food doesn't stick. The utensil cleans easily and you don't need to use oil. The product is guaranteed, because Du Pont is a trusted name around the world.

Now, which ad is most informative? Most readers probably will nominate the Du Pont appeal because of its explicit selling copy. If this is the criterion you are using, however, you will find that only half of all ads are informative in the sense that they focus on objective features.[47]

Does this mean, therefore, that the Chivas Regal ad is *not* informative because of its more subjective, emotional appeal? Do not ignore the fact that consumers can draw a rich yield of information and meaning as they elaborate the symbols they see—tradition, warmth, hospitality, and so on.

What this means is that information can be provided in many ways. In the final analysis only the consumer can decide whether useful information has been communicated. A factual, objective appeal is just one way to be informative.

How Much Is Enough?   Earlier in the chapter we raised the issue of *information overload.* Many well-meaning consumer advocates assume that "more is better." But this certainly is not the case when information overload impairs decision making. We feel that Ralph Day provides the most helpful perspective on this issue:

> What is clear . . . is that it is not enough to simply provide consumers with more information. That is simply the first step in a major educational task of getting consumers to understand the information, and persuading them to use it.[48]

FIGURE 3–9

Which Ad Is the Most Informative?

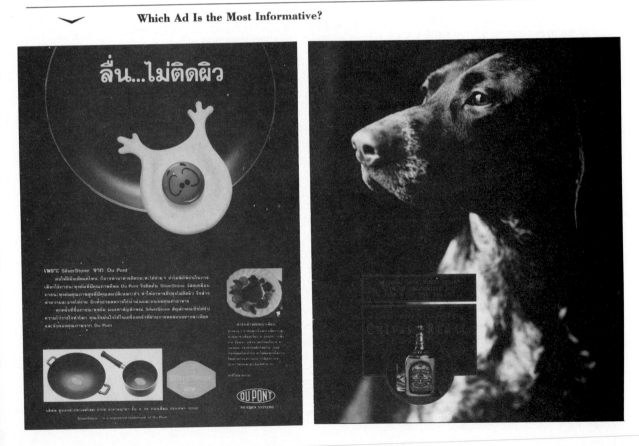

Truth in Advertising

An ad for Tropicana orange juice featured Olympic decathlon winner Bruce Jenner squeezing orange juice directly into the carton. But this is not how Tropicana is made—it is pasteurized and frozen first. Is this an example of deception? What do you think?

The Federal Trade Commission (FTC) has legal jurisdiction over the issue of truth in advertising, and you will learn about FTC standards and processes in Chapter 19. Its practice has been to declare a promotional claim to be false and misleading if the representation, omission, or practice affects consumer decision-making processes adversely.[49]

Terence Shimp and Ivan Preston give us useful guidelines in deciding whether Tropicana is guilty of a violation.[50] A promotional claim may be considered false if each of the following occurs:

1. The claim is *attended to* by the consumer.
2. The claim (or its implication) *affects* beliefs.
3. The (claim or its implication) is *important* to the consumer.
4. The claim (or its implication) becomes *represented in long-term memory.*
5. The claim (or its implication) is *objectively false.*
6. Either the claim itself or an implication that can reasonably be derived from it influences *behavior.*

Unless each of these six consequences occurs, we have no cause for remedial action. In the Tropicana case, however, the FTC did put forward a "guilty" charge and dealt a severe blow to this company.

Manipulation

We have demonstrated how the consumer retains sovereignty through selective information processing, which can erect formidable defenses against unwanted persuasion. Yet there always is the danger of *manipulation,* defined by Em Griffin as the use of strategies that inhibit an individual's freedom of action and induce a response that otherwise would not be made if opportunity had been provided for more thoughtful reflection.[51]

False and misleading appeals are manipulative, of course, in that the consumer may be induced to act in a manner against her or his best interests. Another type of manipulation is the use of various forms of message execution that dominate content and stimulate a response just because they were used. Examples include appeals to strong but irrelevant emotions, the use of distractions such as music or loud sounds, and so on. Consumers catch on to such gimmicks and rarely become repeat customers if they feel that they have "been had."

The following is an especially offensive manipulative sales tactic:

"If you buy tonight, we have a special offer that is guaranteed to help your child do better in school."

"Well, I don't know. . ."

"You must buy tonight, because you don't want Tommy to look back and say you failed him. You never will get this low price again."

Notice how consumer logic is overwhelmed. Many people have immediately regretted making purchases in such a context. Fortunately, "cooling off" laws, which allow cancellation and rebate within the first few days after a sale, are an effective deterrent.

SUMMARY

This chapter picks up on an important principle from Chapter 3: Significant differences can exist between the meaning of a message intended by the sender and the meaning attributed by the receiver. The message is molded and shaped by the recipient through a sequence of stages in information processing.

Information processing has five basic stages: (1) exposure, (2) attention, (3) comprehension, (4) acceptance, and (5) retention. What takes place, however, is profoundly shaped by the degree of perceived involvement (perceived risk, social sanctions, or ego relatedness). High involvement leads consumers to actively process relevant stimuli and avoid the unwanted ones.

Exposure to stimuli occurs when one or more of the five senses are activated. The message is said to attract attention when information processing capabilities are focused and activated. As the stimulus is processed for its sensory and content characteristics, it then is given meaning through comprehension.

Persuasion does not occur, however, until the stimulus is accepted into existing cognitive structures (beliefs and attitudes). When this happens, existing beliefs and attitudes are modified or altogether new ones are formed. Processing terminates once this new information is transferred into long-term memory and is retained.

Information processing is highly selective in that people are free to see and hear what they want to see and hear. Unwanted exposure can be avoided. Selective attention can filter out nonrelevant information and facilitate entry of that which is viewed more positively. Needs, attitudes, and other cognitive factors strongly affect this process.

At other times, the consumer's attention can be attracted and held without accurate comprehension. This is because our existing biases can cause us to distort the content and miss the point. Finally, inconsistent or unwanted information can be short-circuited when the consumer refuses to accept it into cognitive structures, whereas the opposite occurs when the input is seen as credible and relevant.

Even though consumer sovereignty is underscored, there always is concern about manipulation—interfering with a person's freedom of choice. This chapter showed that, short of outright deception, the consumer is quite capable of resisting manipulation and that the marketer has no magic power to bypass defenses.

REVIEW AND DISCUSSION QUESTIONS

1. Assume that a teenager cannot remember seeing ads for any brand of deodorant other than her preferred brand, even though she has finished paging through a consumer magazine replete with competitive ads, one of which was a two-page, four-color spread. How can you explain her response?

2. Try, if you can stand it, to pay close attention to a series of TV ads. Write down your own thoughts (cognitive responses), noting which ads induce counterarguments, sup-

port arguments, and source derogation. When do source derogation and counterargumentation occur most often? And when are you most likely to find support arguments?

3. Up to 20 percent of all TV viewers "zap" ads. You have been asked by Sears to design a series of TV ads stressing the everyday low appliance prices at Sears Brand Central. What strategies could you follow to minimize zapping?

4. Many critics today object to the amount of creative "gimmickry" and flashy attention-attracting devices used by advertisers. The point is, the critics contend, that good advertising should sell, not entertain. How would you respond to this point of view?

5. According to a leading critic, advertising has the power to influence people to buy unwisely—that is, to induce them to act in a manner inconsistent with normal behavior. Do you agree? Why or why not?

6. Subliminal messages have been found to have persuasive power when they are embedded in either audio- or videotapes. You are the owner of a resort in a Caribbean country and have the opportunity to advertise your resort at subliminal levels in videotapes distributed by the government vacation bureau. Is this strategy likely to be effective? Are there ethical concerns that you should consider?

7. Volvo Cars of North America reinforced the cars used in a series of ads to demonstrate how the Volvo withstands unusual crushing because of its strength. The Adolph Coors Company improperly claimed that it uses Rocky Mountain spring water as a source for its popular beers (and was sued for doing so). Are these examples of deception? Of manipulation? Why or why not?

NOTES

1. These stages are modeled after the information-processing model developed by William McGuire. See William J. McGuire, "Some Internal Psychological Factors Influencing Consumer Choice," *Journal of Consumer Research* 2 (March 1976), pp. 302–19.

2. "Coke II Spot Goes Flat on Persuasion," *Advertising Age,* September 7, 1992, p. 9.

3. John Antil, "Conceptualization and Operationalization of Involvement," in *Advances in Consumer Research,* vol. 11, ed. Thomas Kinnear (Provo, Utah: Association for Consumer Research, 1984), p. 204.

4. See Giles Laurent and Jean-Noel Kapferer, "Measuring Consumer Involvement Profiles," *Journal of Marketing Research* 12 (February 1985), pp. 41–53.

5. Gary Putka, "People Invest Little Faith in Wall Street, *The Wall Street Journal,* September 25, 1989, p. B1.

6. *American Demographics* 11 (August 1989), p. 20.

7. Dennis Kneale, "'Zapping' of TV Ads Appears Pervasive," *The Wall Street Journal,* April 25, 1988, p. 21.

8. Phillip J. Kitchen, "Zipping, Zapping, and Nipping," *International Journal of Advertising* 5 (1986), pp. 343–53.

9. Jim Bounden, "Trouble Corralling the Grazers," *Advertising Age,* November 28, 1988, p. S-4.

10. Kitchen, "Zipping, Zapping, and Nipping," pp. 343–52.

11. John J. Cronin and Nancy E. Menelly, "Discrimination vs. Avoidance: "Zipping" of Television Commercials," *Journal of Advertising* 21 (June 1992), pp. 1–8.

12. "Clutter Suffers Zap attacks," *Advertising Age,* March 30, 1992, p. 38.

13. "War against Zapping," *Marketing News,* September 14, 1984, p. 1.

14. Patricia A. Stout and Benedicta L. Burda, "Zipped Commercials: Are They Effective?" *Journal of Advertising* 18 (1989), pp. 23–32.

15. R. D. Percy, as quoted in Kneale, "Zapping of TV Ads," p. 21.

16. Scott Ward, David Reibstein, Terence A. Oliva, and Victoria Taylor, "Commercial Clutter: Effects of 15-Second Television Ads on Consumer Recall," in *Advances in Consumer Research*, vol. 16, ed. Thomas K. Srull (Provo, Utah: Association for Consumer Research, 1989), pp. 473–78; and Wayne Walley, "Have :15s Hit Their Peak?" *Advertising Age,* November 13, 1989, p. 16.

17. For a good introduction to cognitive consistency theories, see Richard E. Petty and John T. Cacioppo, *Attitudes and Persuasion: Classic and Contemporary Approaches* (Dubuque, Iowa: Wm. C. Brown, 1981), Chapter 5.

18. Homer E. Spence and James F. Engel, "The Impact of Brand Preferences on the Perception of Brand Names: A Laboratory Analysis," in *Marketing Involvement in Society and the Economy*, ed. P. R. McDonald (Chicago: American Marketing Association, 1970), pp. 267–71.

19. Scott Hume, "BK Sees Ad Awareness Slipping Away," *Advertising Age,* September 30, 1985, p. 12.

20. "How Important Is Color to an Ad? It's Not Just a Black and White Issue," *Tested Copy,* February 1989.

21. Larry Percy, *Ways in Which the People, Words, and Pictures in Advertising Influence Its Effectiveness* (Chicago: Financial Institutions Marketing Association, July 1984), p. 19.

22. Adam Finn, "Print Recognition Readership Scores: An Information Processing Perspective," *Journal of Marketing Research* 25 (May 1988), pp. 168–77.

23. For a helpful review, see J. V. McConnell, R. L. Cutler, and E. B. McNeill, "Subliminal Stimulation: An Overview," *American Psychologist* 11 (1958), pp. 230ff.

24. For excellent reviews of the evidence, see Norman F. Dixon, *Subliminal Perception: The Nature of the Controversy* (Maidenhead-Berkshire, England: McGraw-Hill, 1971).

25. Wilson B. Key, *Subliminal Seduction: Ad Media's Manipulation of a Not-So-Innocent America* (Englewood Cliffs, N.J.: Prentice Hall, 1972).

26. Wilson B. Key, *The Age of Manipulation* (New York: Henry Holt, 1987).

27. Sharon E. Beatty and Del I. Hawkins, "Subliminal Stimulation: Some New Data and Interpretation," *Journal of Advertising* 18 (1989), pp. 4–8; and Nicolas E. Synodinos, "Subliminal Stimulation: What Does the Public Think about It?" in *Current Issues & Research in Advertising*, vol. 11, ed. James R. Leigh and Claude R. Martin, (Ann Arbor, Mich.: University of Michigan Business School, Division of Research, 1988), pp. 157–88.

28. See especially Beatty and Hawkins, "Subliminal Stimulation."

29. Timothy Moore, "Subliminal Advertising: What You See Is What You Get," *Journal of Marketing* 46 (Spring 1982), p. 45.

30. "Warning: This Story Will Be Miscomprehended," *Marketing News* March 27, 1987, pp. 1ff.

31. Jacob Jacoby and Wayne D. Hoyer, "The Comprehension/Miscomprehension of Print Communication," *Journal of Consumer Research* 15 (March 1989), pp. 434–43.

32. For a helpful discussion of the categorization process, see Joseph W. Alba and J. Wesley Hutchinson, "Dimensions of Consumer Expertise," *Journal of Consumer Research* 13 (March 1987), pp. 411–54; and Joel B. Cohen and Kunal Basu, "Alternative Models of Categorization: Toward a Contingent Processing Framework," *Journal of Consumer Research* 13 (March 1987), pp. 455–72.

33. Herbert Krugman, "The Measurement of Advertising Involvement," *Public Opinion Quarterly* 30 (March 1966), pp. 583–96.

34. For an excellent discussion, see Deborah J. MacInnis and Bernard J. Jaworski, "Information Processing from Advertisements: Toward an Integrative Framework," *Journal of Marketing* 53 (October 1989), pp. 1–23.

35. See Richard L. Celsi and Jerry C. Olson, "The Role of Invovement in Attention and Comprehension Processes," *Journal of Consumer Research,* 15 (September 1988), pp. 210–24.

36. See Jack Honomichl, "Missing Ingredients in 'New' Coke's Research," *Advertising Age,* July 22, 1985, p. 1.

37. Cyndee Miller, "The Fur Flies as Fashion Foes Pelt It Out over Animal Rights," *Marketing News,* December 4, 1989, pp. 2ff.

38. Mita Sujan and James F. Bettman, "The Effects of Brand Positioning Strategies on Consumers' Brand and Category Perceptions: Some Insights from Schema Research," *Journal of Marketing Research* 26 (November 1989), pp. 454–67.

39. The literature is extensive. For a description and review, see James F. Engel, Roger D. Blackwell, and Paul W. Miniard, *Consumer Behavior,* 8th ed. (Fort Worth, Tex.: Dryden Press, 1993), pp. 412–14.

40. Manoj Hastak and Jerry C. Olson, "Assessing the Role of Brand-Related Cognitive Responses as Mediators of Communication Effects on Cognitive Structure," *Journal of Consumer Research* 15 (March 1989), pp. 444–56.

41. Scott B. MacKenzie, Richard J. Lutz, and George E. Belch, "The Role of Attitude toward the Ad as a Mediator of Advertising Effectiveness: A Test of Competing Explanations," *Journal of Marketing Research* 23 (May 1986), pp. 130–43.

42. Julie A. Edell and Marian C. Burke, "The Power of Feelings in Understanding Advertising Effectiveness," *Journal of Consumer Research* 14 (December 1987), pp. 421–33.

43. David M. Zeitlin and Richard A. Westwood, "Measuring Emotion Response to Advertising," *Journal of Advertising Research* 26 (October/November 1986), pp. 34–44.

44. Susan E. Heckler and Terry L. Childers, "Hemispheric Lateralization: The Relationship of Processing Orientation with Judgment and Recall Measures for Print Advertisements," in *Advances in Consumer Research,* vol. 15, ed. Melanie Wallendorf and Paul Anderson (Provo, Utah: Association for Consumer Research, 1987), pp. 46–50.

45. See, for example, Lyle E. Bourne, Roger L. Dominowski, and Elizabeth F. Loftus, *Cognitive Processes* (Englewood Cliffs, N.J.: Prentice Hall, 1979).

46. "The Consumer Bill of Rights," in *Consumer Advisory Council, First Report* (Washington, D.C.: U.S. Government Printing Office, 1963).

47. Edward Russo, Barbara Metcalfe, and Debra Stephens, "Identifying Misleading Advertising," *Journal of Consumer Research* 7 (September 1981), p. 125.

48. George S. Day, "Assessing the Effects of Information Disclosure Requirements," *Journal of Marketing* (April 1956), pp. 42–52.

49. Dorothy Cohen, "Legal Interpretations of Deception Are Deceiving," *Marketing News,* September 26, 1986, p. 12.

50. Terence A. Shimp and Ivan L. Preston, "Deceptive and Nondeceptive Consequences of Evaluative Advertising," *Journal of Marketing* (Winter 1981), pp. 22–32.

51. Em Griffin, *The Mind Changers* (Wheaton, Ill.: Tyndale, 1976).

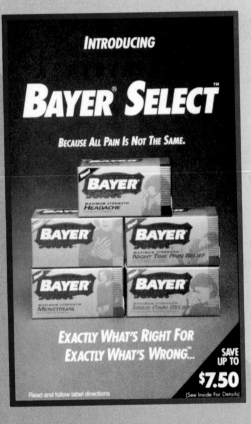

Chapter

4

Promotional Strategy: A Decision-Making Framework

BAYER SELECT IS INTRODUCED WITH A $116 MILLION INTEGRATED MARKETING COMMUNICATION STRATEGY

Sterling Health USA is using integrated marketing communication in spades—everything from ads in doctors' waiting rooms to a program with Emergency Medical Services (EMS)—in the $116 million introduction of Bayer Select nonaspirin pain reliever. Going beyond the $70 million ad campaign that broke November 13, Sterling said it wants to blanket the United States with the message that the Bayer name isn't just for aspirin anymore.

The program is Sterling's largest product introduction ever. It uses the ad theme "Put the help where it hurts" and explains the concept that "all pain is not the same." Bayer Select includes five symptom-specific pain relievers: for nighttime, sinus, menstrual, headache, and general pain relief. All are either ibuprofen-based, like competitive brands Advil or Motrin, or acetaminophen-based, like the market leading brand, Tylenol. Examples of Bayer Select ads are presented in the opening photo for this chapter.

The company approach to the introduction reflects that "we can't reach the world by traditional TV alone—there are women working and men who don't watch much TV," said Jay Kolpon, group product manager for Bayer analgesics. Sterling said it will drop more than 1 billion coupons in the first 12 months of the introduction, including a Carol Wright (promotion mailing company) direct-mail piece that offers $1.50 off each product. Bayer select is also being advertised on Whittle Communications' "Special Report TV" (a cable system program). Also, Sterling is using ActMedia's instant coupon machines on store shelves to further stimulate trial.

In addition, Sterling broke in December a national education program with EMS that includes financial contributions to EMS volunteers and distribution of literature explaining when to dial for an emergency. Actor William Shatner, host of the TV program "Rescue 911," kicked off the program at a news conference. This cause-related marketing effort provides free publicity for EMS and uses public relations to promote the Bayer Select brand to consumers and professionals.

Sterling is also running its first ethnically targeted advertising using Hispanic print and broadcast media, with ads developed for these audiences. In addition, Sterling is providing special advertising and free samples of Bayer Select for physicians.

To accomplish all of this, Sterling is utilizing five different support companies for the standard advertising, Hispanic advertising, coupon mailings, in-store coupons, and advertising and sampling to doctors. Sterling is combining the activities of all these firms to create an integrated marketing communications strategy. Also, the Sterling sales force was trained about the launch and presented the trade promotion aspects of it to retailers.

Despite all of these promotional communications, capturing market share will still be difficult for Bayer. The Bayer name is virtually totally associated with aspirin and has been losing share to nonaspirin products like Tylenol and Advil for years. These products are expected to defend their market share in the nonaspirin pain-relief market very aggressively. In addition, the FDA is expected to allow a prescription-only nonaspirin pain-relief brand, Naprosyn, to be marketed over the counter soon. Procter & Gamble, a highly competent marketer, will market this product under license from Syntec Laboratories.

If Bayer Select is to obtain significant market share and be profitable for Sterling, its integrated marketing communication program must be superior to the current and possible new competitors' promotional programs.

Source: Adapted from Patricia Winters, "$116M Intro for Bayer Select Isn't Just Ads," *Advertising Age,* November 22, 1992, p. 37.

The fortunes of the competitors in the hot pain-reliever market are not an accident. Rather, they are the result of carefully conceived and executed integrated promotional strategies that are part of broader marketing plans—plans that include all the elements of the marketing mix. In this book, we are concerned primarily with decision making for the promotional aspect of the marketing mix only.

In Chapters 1, 2, and 3 of this book, we presented a general overview of promotional strategy and examined the nature of communications and consumer response to persuasive communications. We now turn our attention to a decision-making framework that ties our understanding of communications to an approach to making decisions about advertising, sales force, and consumer and trade promotions. We address this question: What is involved in promotional decision making? After a brief general discussion of the stages involved in the process, we will illustrate the procedure with a detailed example. The stages in promotional planning and strategy described here provide an ordering of the topics in the rest of this book.

THE STAGES IN PROMOTIONAL PLANNING AND STRATEGY

Table 4–1 provides a summary of a systematic integrated marketing communications approach to promotional planning and strategy. This approach encompasses the following stages: (1) situation analysis, (2) establishment of objectives, (3) determination of dollar appropriation, (4) management of program elements, (5) coordination and integration of efforts, (6) measurement of effectiveness, and (7) evaluation and follow-up.

This decision-making approach is presented in this chapter only in overview. The remaining chapters in this book develop each of the steps in the process in detail. As already mentioned, this decision-making process provides a structural

TABLE 4–1

Stages in Promotional Planning and Strategy

Step 1. Situation analysis
- A. Demand
  1. Consumer needs assessment
  2. Cultural and social influences
  3. Product category and brand attitudes
  4. Individual differences
  5. Consumer decision-making processes
- B. Definition and identification of target markets
  1. Segmentation
  2. Targeting of selected segments
  3. Positioning
- C. Competitive assessment
- D. Legal considerations
- E. Internal organizational considerations: strengths and weaknesses
  1. Personnel skill levels
  2. Monetary resources and priorities
  3. Established policies and procedures
  4. Implementation skills

Step 2. Establishment of objectives
- A. Relationship to market targets
- B. Communication of message objectives
- C. Sales objectives

Step 3. Determination of dollar appropriation: in total and to various promotional elements

Step 4. Management of program elements
- A. Advertising
  1. Analysis of media resources
  2. Selection of advertising media
  3. Message determination
- B. Personal selling
  1. Analysis of resources
  2. Selection, motivation, deployment, compensation, and evaluation
- C. Stimulation of reseller support: trade promotion
  1. Analysis of reseller resources
  2. Stimulation of performance
  3. Improvement and augmentation of performance
- D. Consumer sales promotion
  1. Choice of types
  2. Packaging as promotion
- E. Supplemental communications (public relations/publicity)
  1. Assessment of relevant publics
  2. Determination of media and message

Step 5. Coordination and integration of efforts
- A. Achievement of proper balance between program elements
- B. Scheduling of execution
- C. Utilization of personnel and outside services
- D. Dollar-appropriation revision

Step 6. Measurement of effectiveness for the program as a whole and for each program element

Step 7. Evaluation and follow-up

guide to this book. In addition, in order to bring life to this structure, we will utilize an extended example, involving Carnival Cruise Lines, in this chapter and throughout the book. As you read later chapters in this book and thus develop a better understanding of each step in this decision-making process, you should look back to this Carnival Cruise Lines example to develop additional insights that will not be evident in your first reading. For now, just use this example to get a general sense of the process.

Figure 4–1 graphically presents the same sequence outlined in Table 4–1. Note, however, that Figure 4–1 depicts the sequence as an "adaptive" process in that it specifically includes systematic procedures for gathering information that can then lead to needed program adaptations. For example, advertising message and media decisions are interrelated. The decisions in one area can lead to modifications in another, as the two-way arrows indicate. Furthermore, a feedback loop represents the fact that the initial budget may have to be modified as planning proceeds. Evaluation and follow-up are shown as providing vital new input to the situation analysis for succeeding planning periods. Thus, Figure 4–1 portrays the continual and ongoing nature of integrated promotional planning.

The profile of Bayer Select in the chapter opener illustrates the outcome of the decision-making process outlined in Figure 4–1. That outcome is a totally integrated promotional plan. What is not presented in that profile, however, is any of the detailed analysis that underpins each stage of the decision-making process. In order to examine this level of analysis at each stage of the process, we now turn to the extended example using Carnival Cruise Lines.

UTILIZING THE FRAMEWORK: CARNIVAL CRUISES TO THE TOP AND STAYS THERE[1]

It is not often that a company is able simultaneously to climb to the top of its industry and lift the entire fortunes of the whole industry. In addition, it is not often that a company is able to maintain its number one position in the context of intensifying competition. This is exactly what Carnival Cruise Lines was able to do. The success of Carnival, of course, was not an accident. Rather, it was the outcome of a carefully conceived promotional strategy. The story of Carnival's success, which follows here, is designed to illustrate the use of the framework presented in Figure 4–1. Carnival's strength in implementing an integrated promotional strategy also has allowed it to continue to be the number one cruise company even with the growing competition that has characterized the cruise business in the 1990s. In addition, its position in the industry has allowed Carnival to be more resistant than competitors against the price discount pressures that the increased competition has brought.

SITUATION ANALYSIS

The starting point is always an analysis of the environment. In the presentation that follows, we will discuss demand and competition as the key elements of this

© 1992 Great Waters of France, Inc.

They tell a story around

Whitefish, Montana about the friends who

stopped by for a drink and didn't leave

until the April thaw.

Perrier. Part of the local color.

Following its public relations problems with benzene contamination, Perrier voluntarily removed its product from stores and turned to ads that promoted its broad appeal to all classes of beverage drinkers.

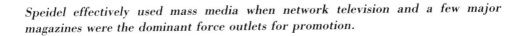

Speidel effectively used mass media when network television and a few major magazines were the dominant force outlets for promotion.

Speidel-A Textron Company

Idents "Beach"

SONG: Let your

Feelings show

wherever you go

Let somebody know

How you

Really feel

ANNCR V.O.: If you can put your feelings into words...

Speidel gives you the place to put them.

Speidel Idents are beautiful jewelry

that let you say anything you want to say

SONG: Let your feelings show. Wherever you go.

V.O.: Speidel Idents

SPEIDEL TIME MODULATOR® DIGITAL WATCHES

SPEIDEL CHRONOGRAPH

TITLE: LEONARDO & MONA - FALL

LENGTH: 30 SECONDS

ANN. V.O.: Leonardo da Vinci for Speidel Watches.

LEONARDO: They call me the greatest inventor ever, next to Tom Edison.

But even I never dreamed of this beautiful!

Speidel Chronograph. It gives me the time and date of course,

but also four stopwatch functions.

Great gift, Mona. Very inventive. Say... you have a beautiful Speidel Digital too.

MONA: Edison gave it to me.

ANN. V.O.: Speidel's beautiful new digitals. Very inventive gifts.

Off-beat images are used to sell "fun" snacks in all countries, as this example from Israel shows.

FIGURE 4–1

Decision Sequence Analysis of Promotional Planning and Strategy

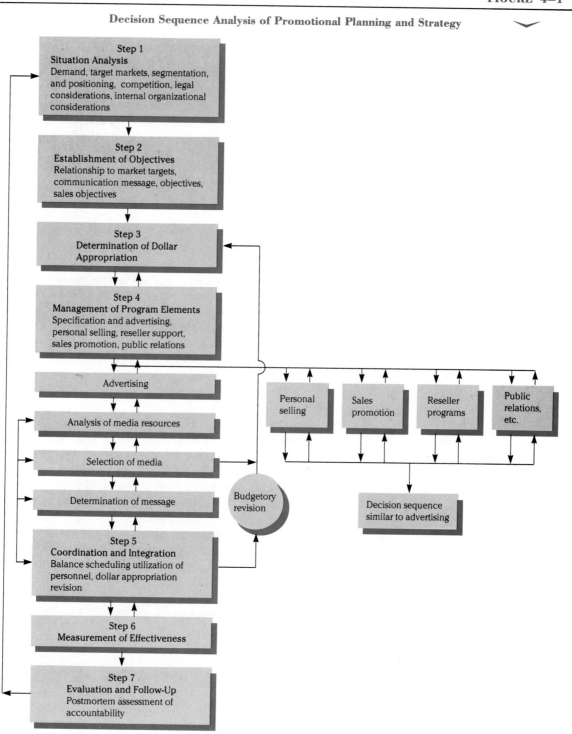

analysis. Although space limitation prevents us from presenting all aspects of Carnival's situation analysis, we will present a brief history of Carnival Cruise Lines.

History

Ted Arison started Carnival Cruise Lines in 1974 with one used ship (the *Mardi Gras*). The company sought to open the formerly exclusive cruise business to budget-conscious travelers. Through intensive promotion of its moderately priced four- and seven-day cruises, Carnival won the patronage of people who had never dreamed that they could afford a vacation at sea.

In its first three years, Carnival constantly battled to stay afloat, but the company's fortunes turned around in 1975 after Arison assumed full ownership of the company. Carnival's marketing department capitalized on the positive reaction to the *Mardi Gras* cruise program, which destroyed traditional class distinctions and pretensions of formality. The cruise line turned the shipboard experience into total recreation rather than a sedate mode of travel, and the Fun Ship concept, which has since become a hallmark of Carnival's success, was born.

Carnival had acquired two other ships by 1978 when Arison made the first of many announcements that shocked and then changed the industry. In the midst of record-high shipbuilding costs, skyrocketing fuel prices, and an industry of medium-sized vessels, Carnival built a new passenger ship, *Tropicale,* with significantly increased capacity. The popularity of this new ship's spaciousness and efficiency sparked more than $1 billion worth of new passenger construction in the 1980s. Encouraged by Tropicale's success, Carnival defied the industry again and built three superliners over the next four years. The critics were skeptical, but the passengers loved them!

After building up its capacity, Carnival decided to diversify its product line. After 14 years of offering seven-day cruises, the company capitalized on the American trend toward shorter and more frequent vacations by adding three- and four-day trips to the Bahamas to its schedule in May 1984. Carnival has since become the leader in the short cruise segment of the market. In December 1985, Carnival began offering Thursday and Sunday departures, another new concept in the industry. In November 1986, the company began service from San Juan, giving Carnival a presence in every North American warm-water cruise region.

The success of its superliners and the popularity of these line extensions made Carnival the largest cruise line in the world. By 1987, the company held over 45 percent of the total North American market and carried almost twice as many passengers as its nearest competitor. To strengthen this position, Carnival added three more state-of-the-art passenger ships by the early 1990s: the *Fantasy,* the *Ecstacy,* and the *Sensation.* The *Fantasy* will be the first ship in the industry ever intended for year-round trips in the Bahamas market. The new ships offer additional three- and four-day trips.

Carnival has continued to expand its vacation/travel market through acquisitions. It acquired Holland America Line (HAL) for $645 million in January 1989.

Holland America has four ships that sail to Alaska in the summer and to the eastern Caribbean in the winter. HAL operates in the premium cruise segment. The acquisition furthered Carnival's goal of carving a niche in every segment of the cruise industry. Carnival has chosen to maintain two distinct positioning strategies for its two entities. The Carnival line is still targeted at the mass market, while HAL targets the more upscale traveler. HAL is also priced about 47 percent above Carnival on comparable routes. Chief Executive Officer Micky Arison believes that as Carnival passengers become more affluent and more sophisticated, they will be ready to graduate to Holland America cruises.

Carnival is also constructing three vessels of its own for the luxury market as part of Project Tiffany. The three luxury liners of Project Tiffany will be equipped with suites instead of individual cabins and will carry only 700 passengers to increase spaciousness, comfort, and individual service. According to Karine Armstrong, vice president of marketing for Carnival Cruise Lines, "We have such a humongous repeat factor that there are some people who have traveled on all of our ships. The natural evolution is to move up." Carnival plans to sell this upscale product at a midlevel price.

Demand and Target Markets

Carnival caters to two market segments: the Type A cruise market and the Type B cruise market. Type A is the contemporary cruise market that features cruises lasting from two to seven days, a casual on-board atmosphere, and an average per diem of $200 or less. These cruises, which represent the volume end of the cruise market, appeal to all age groups with annual household incomes of at least $25,000. This market targets the first-time cruiser, and statistics indicate that 240 million North Americans are in this target audience.

The Type B market is the traditional cruise segment, which offers cruises lasting at least 10 days, a more formal on-board atmosphere, and an average brochure per diem of at least $250. These cruises are designed to appeal to the over-50 age market with annual household incomes of at least $40,000. This market targets the repeat cruiser, and statistics indicate that approximately 13 million people in North America are in this target audience.

Carnival has built its strength on the contemporary market. Although approximately 30 percent of its passengers are in the 55 and over segment, another 30 percent are under the age of 35. Carnival targets this younger group by using younger personalities in its advertisements. Working from the company's premise that "the average age [of a cruiser] used to be deceased," Kathie Lee Gifford's long-running "Ain't We Got Fun" commercials are a prime example of Carnival's efforts to lower the average age of its passengers. According to Robert Dickinson, Carnival's senior vice president, sales and marketing, "We're marketing to a younger clientele than the cruise industry." The acquisition of HAL is designed to allow better tapping of the Type B consumer segment.

A detailed discussion related to understanding consumers, market segmentation, and positioning is presented in Chapters 5, 6, and 7.

Competition

A total of 37 cruise lines operate in North America. The largest of these are Norwegian Caribbean, Princess Cruises, Sitmar, Cunard, American Hawaii, Holland America, Royal Caribbean, Royal Viking, and Admiral. These lines compete on the basis of image, target market, destinations, price, and promotions. In a poll of 700 travel agents, no agent could name the slogan of even four cruise lines, indicating a low degree of brand identity in the industry. Carnival scored well in this poll in terms of name recognition. A few of the large lines enjoy economies of scale that create cost, product, price, and branding advantages. The smaller lines must carve out market niches to survive. Long-term forecasts predict significant industry consolidation.

Despite this plethora of seagoing competitors, Carnival considers land-based vacation packages, such as an excursion to Hawaii, to be its main competition. Based on this premise, Carnival markets the total cruise ship experience, in which the actual trip is more than half the fun and the ports of call are "mere" bonuses. Carnival capitalizes on its Fun Ships theme and stresses the value of its all-inclusive, up-front prices, which cover transportation, meals, and endless activities.

We now present a summary of the promotional strategies of the main competitors of Carnival Cruise Lines.[2] This summary presents the competitive environment in which Carnival's promotion decisions are being made and provides background for the discussion of Carnival presented throughout the book. In addition, it illustrates the dynamic and competitive world of promotion. As you read, imagine being responsible for the promotional activities of Carnival or one of its competitors.

Norwegian Caribbean   Norwegian targets adults between the ages of 35 and 49 with no children at home. Most are married, have had at least some college education, and have annual household incomes of at least $35,000. Norwegian Caribbean spends about $15 million on media advertising. Network television accounts for 60 percent of this budget, magazines for 30 percent, and newspapers for the remaining 10 percent. The company uses both 15- and 30-second television spots to reach viewers. Norwegian mainly uses mass audience magazines such as *People, Travel & Leisure, Time,* and *Newsweek.* Newspaper promotions have been deemphasized, decreasing from 70 percent of the total media budget to about 10 percent. Norwegian buys space in the top 20 markets and goes for a newspaper's first section instead of limiting its campaign to the Sunday travel section. Ric Widmer, Norwegian's senior vice president, marketing and sales, notes that "newspapers' own research" has found that 45 to 90 percent of all readers never get to the travel sections.

Norweigan uses consumer promotions, such as a direct-mail drop to several million households offering dollars-off coupons worth $200 to $250 savings on selected cruises. As long as cruise demand holds steady, Norwegian does not discount prices. It also offers trade promotions to its travel agents, who book 100 percent of the company's trips. Depending on available space, agents are offered familiarization cruises, seminars at sea, and "walk-through for the weekend" deals in which agents eat on board a docked ship but stay in a local hotel.

Princess Cruises   Princess, which sails to worldwide destinations, classifies its product as upscale and targets passengers 35 and over with household incomes of at least $40,000. Michael Hannan, senior vice president, marketing services, notes that since many of the company's offerings are two-week trips, Princess cruises tend to appeal to the 50 and older group who have the time and disposable income for longer excursions.

The "Love Boat" television series increased the popularity of cruises. Princess capitalizes on the "Love Boat" image by using Gavin McLeod, who played the ship's captain on the program, as its spokesperson in all consumer and trade advertisements. Princess spends about $10 million in advertising, the majority of which goes to newspapers. The company advertises mainly in the travel section of Sunday newspapers in the larger market areas, and uses some limited local (spot) television. Princess invests over half of its media budget in the western United States since half of its business originates in that region. Princess also advertises in regional lifestyle magazines, such as *Sunset, Southern Living, Los Angeles,* and *The New Yorker;* national magazines, such as *Architectural Digest, National Geographic, Gourmet,* and *Signature;* and several consumer travel magazines, including *Travel & Leisure, Travel-Holiday,* and *Cruise Travel.*

Trade promotions are not popular at Princess. Free cruises are not offered to travel agents despite the fact that these agents book 100 percent of the company's trips. According to Hannan, "We prefer to work with travel agents by helping them with sending out brochures, doing presentations, and cooperative advertising on a local basis."

Sitmar   From its humble beginnings as an immigrant transport ship between England and Australia, Sitmar has developed into one of the leading North American cruise lines. Although Australian cruisers still account for 25 percent of its business, most of Sitmar's cruises go to the Caribbean, Alaska, and Mexico. The average age of Sitmar's passengers is 54, and the average household income is $35,000. Sitmar wants to attract "retired older couples, middle-aged working couples, or more mature singles in their 50s." According to William Smith, senior vice president, marketing and sales, "The reason is cruises are longer, so we need to get to that segment with more disposable time or leisure to take a longer cruise."

Sitmar spends about $15 million on media advertising: 25 percent for broadcast ads, 25 percent for trade magazines, and the remaining 50 percent for newspapers. Smith asserted, "We feel it's very important to position ourselves to the consumer and trade. Sitmar is a quality product for the experienced cruiser. Our past advertising was a lot less targeted and specific." TV spots are used mainly for image building. "You can visually depict the setting you're trying to create. Radio or print ads are more effective at driving a price." Based on this premise, Sitmar runs ads with more pricing and details in newspapers, primarily Sunday travel sections and cruise sections of approximately 70 papers in the top 26 markets. The cruise line also advertises in consumer magazines including *Smithsonian, National Geo-*

graphic, and *Travel & Leisure* and in trade publications including *Travel Weekly, Travel Age West, Travel Age East, Travel Agent, Travel Trade,* and *Tours & Travel News.*

Consumer and trade promotions are prevalent at Sitmar. Supersaver programs, advance-purchase discounts, and group rates are among the consumer offerings. Travel agents, who book almost 100 percent of Sitmar's trips, are eligible for familiarization trips, reduced rates, and incentive programs. A partnership program is available for smaller travel agencies; it allows them to pool their sales in order to compete with the larger agencies for bonus commissions and cooperative dollars. Sitmar also advertises in trade publications.

Cunard   Cunard, famous for its *Queen Elizabeth* luxury liner, targets the more affluent segment of the population. The income of its passengers falls in the $40,000 to $200,000 range. This cruise line sails around the world in addition to its transatlantic trips.

Cunard spends about $12 million on its media advertising. According to Ron Santangelo, vice president, marketing communications, Cunard is "so targeted that television is not an appropriate medium." Newspapers and magazines get the bulk of Cunard's advertising business. Because the majority of its business comes from New York, California, and Florida, the company places ads only in the travel section of Sunday newspapers in the top 15 markets for those regions. Cunard also runs ads in upscale magazines such as *Gourmet, Vogue, Town & Country, Travel & Leisure, Smithsonian,* and *Architectural Digest.*

Cunard also utilizes consumer and trade promotions. Through direct-mail marketing, passengers can get discounts for selected dates or a companion's ticket for half the price of the first ticket. Travel agents book 96 percent of Cunard's cruises, and they can earn a compact disc player for selling a few cabins on Cunard's less luxurious ships. Agents who sell five cabins win a large-screen color television set.

American Hawaii   American Hawaii targets adults 35 and over with annual household incomes of at least $30,000. This Pacific cruise line sails to Hawaii and Tahiti. American Hawaii spends about $5.7 million on advertising: $4.5 million for magazines, $651,000 for Sunday magazines, $1.98 million for newspapers, $36,000 for spot television, $434,000 for outdoor ads, and $144,00 for spot radio. American Hawaii runs ads for its Hawaii cruises in 25 newspaper markets nationwide and emphasizes the West Coast markets for the Tahitian cruises.

The cruise line also offers consumer and trade promotions. Passengers can earn discounts by booking six months in advance, or they can earn free hotel accommodations before or after a cruise if they want an extended vacation in the islands. American Hawaii also promotes its services through trade books such as *Travel Age West, Travel Weekly,* and *Travel Agent.* Trade publications such as *Sunset, Travel & Leisure, Signature,* and *Islands* are used as well.

Holland America   Holland America offers Caribbean and Alaskan leisure cruises. Although its passengers have traditionally been in the 45 and older age group,

Rich Skinner, corporate director of public relations and sales promotion, acknowledged that this is changing: "There has been a trend toward skewing into a younger group in the last few years, especially in the Caribbean. Even Alaska seems to have a downward trend." Jan Edmonston, vice president, management supervisor at the company's advertising agency, asserts that Holland America wants "balanced" advertising: "We haven't segmented like other cruises. We don't think we can because demand is so small."

Holland America spends about $4.6 million on media advertising. Most of the budget goes to newspapers, with the remainder going to magazines. Skinner explained that print advertising is used because cruises are a complex product that require study. Because 60 percent of its business comes from the West Coast, most of Holland America's advertising is in the Sunday travel section of daily newspapers in 15 markets on the East and West Coasts. The Alaskan cruises are targeted to a bit older crowd in upscale consumer magazines such as *Smithsonian, Travel & Leisure, National Geographic, Gourmet,* and *Modern Maturity.*

Holland America targets its consumer promotions. A direct-mail program sends newsletters and special discounts to the cruise line's "alumni." When a cruise is not filled near its departure date, Holland America uses local newspapers to advertise special discount rates to selected secondary markets. Travel agents book 99 percent of Holland America's trips. Trade promotions include lottery sweepstakes for free cruises and various contests and trivia puzzles.

As noted previously, in 1989, Carnival purchased the Holland America Line for $645 million. Currently, Carnival manages Holland America separately in terms of customer targets, branding, and promotional strategy.

Royal Caribbean   Concentrated in the Caribbean and based in Miami, Royal Caribbean targets first-time cruisers. Most of its passengers are between the ages of 35 and 54 with annual household incomes over $50,000. Royal Caribbean is well known for its *Sovereign of the Seas,* "the largest cruise ship in the world."

Royal Caribbean spends about $22.2 million on advertising: $3.8 million for magazines, $6.3 million for network TV, $4.5 million for spot TV, $478,400 for network cable, $1.3 million for national syndications, $15,500 for newspapers, and $15,500 for Sunday magazines. Newspaper advertising is conducted in 45 local markets. According to Mike Petty, director of marketing, this target marketing is intentional. "Ten years ago, 60 to 70 percent of our business came out of the top 20 markets. Now those markets account for 40 percent of Royal Caribbean business."

Royal Caribbean does not use special promotions. Petty noted, "Royal Caribbean is unique in the cruise industry in that we do our best not to price promote." He believes that this policy gives the passengers "more for the money they are paying."

Royal Viking   Royal Viking offers worldwide destinations, including Leif Ericsson's path to Newfoundland and World War II Pacific battlegrounds. Royal Viking targets 50-year-olds with annual incomes over $50,000 who have sailed before and have taken an international vacation within the past three years. Most of its passengers have incomes around $100,000 and more than 50 percent have sailed with Royal Viking before.

Royal Viking spends about $6 million each year on media advertising and direct marketing. The media budget is split about evenly between magazine and newspaper advertising, with the exception of the 5 percent that goes to cable television's Arts & Entertainment Network. According to John B. Richards, vice president, marketing and planning, "It's done rather well for us. It's the most targeted electronic media available to us. We just can't use broadcast media as effectively."

Royal Viking's print advertising includes a variety of literary, travel, and special-interest magazines such as *Travel & Leisure, Harper's, Signature, The New Yorker, The Atlantic, Food & Wine, Gourmet, Bon Appetit, Architectural Digest, Better Homes and Gardens, Sunset,* and *Golfer's Digest.* Theater publications such as *Opera News* are also used. Newspaper ads are run only in the travel section of 35 to 40 Sunday papers in the top 40 markets including the *Christian Science Monitor, New York Times, Los Angeles Times,* and *San Francisco Chronicle.*

Consumer promotions include a direct marketing campaign offering tips on discounts and special-interest programs. This program targets past Royal Viking passengers. Travel agents book 98 percent of Royal Viking's cruises. Trade promotions include familiarization trips at attractive rates and special commission rates for large-volume producers.

Admiral   Admiral Cruises, Inc., was formed in 1986 by the merger of Eastern Cruise Lines, Western Cruise Lines, and Sundance Cruises. Admiral targets passengers between the ages of 37 and 55 with annual household incomes of $30,000 to $35,000.

Although cruises are often associated with couples on romantic getaways, Robert R. Mahmarian, senior vice president, sales and marketing, portrays Admiral's atmosphere as one in which "people alone chaperone each other and have a ball." Mahmarian believes that Admiral is most attractive to women and families because the third or fourth passenger in the group sometimes gets a free cruise as a special promotion. Admiral is also using a shotgun approach with consumers by emphasizing the relative value of cruising as a vacation alternative.

Admiral spends about $11 million on advertising. Approximately 70 percent of the budget goes to newspapers. Ads appear in the Sunday travel section in about 82 markets. The remaining media dollars go to magazine and television advertising. Admiral uses magazines such as *McCall's, Southern Living,* and *Sunset.* Mahmarian notes that the cruise line also advertises in *USA Today* because "about 60 percent of cruises are being decided by men, so a newspaper like *USA Today* is a good opportunity to advertise because it has that kind of mixed reader." He also emphasized that TV commercials are used merely as a veneer for the line's other advertising. "When you're buying a cruise, you need to inspect more. A 30-second commercial can get you interested but can't sell you a cruise."

Travel agents book 100 percent of Admiral's trips. Trade promotions include incentive programs that provide override commissions for large revenue producers.

Cooperative advertising programs also allow travel agencies to share ad costs with Admiral.

Figure 4–2 presents examples of advertisements for some of these competitors. Note the competitive thrust in the statements in these ads.

Internal Organizational Considerations

As indicated in the history section above, Carnival's management is willing to innovate in terms of products, promotion, and taking risks. Managers developed skills in promotion and spent aggressively to take market share and to expand the entire market. Carnival's market share dominance generates a cash flow large enough to support the acquisition of new ships and to support even more promotion.

ESTABLISHMENT OF OBJECTIVES

Carnival's corporate goal is to be the market-share leader in the cruise industry. Its promotional objectives are to be the number one name in terms of consumer recognition and to be the preferred booking line by travel agents. Its promotional program is designed to reach these promotional objectives as part of an overall marketing program to reach the corporate goal. Note that these objectives are quantifiable or measurable.

A more detailed discussion of developing and implementing promotional objectives is presented in Chapter 8. A detailed description of Carnival's promotional program is presented below.

FIGURE 4–2

Advertisements of Competitive Cruise Lines

DETERMINATION OF DOLLAR APPROPRIATION

Once objectives have been established, a preliminary promotional budget should be determined. This budget both sets the total promotion budget and specifies the amount for each component of the promotional budget: advertising, sales force, consumer promotion, and trade promotion. This is a difficult task. A detailed discussion related to establishing the promotional budget is presented in Chapter 9. The initial estimate usually can be only tentative, and modifications generally are required as the planning proceeds. Carnival spends more than $30 million per year to promote itself to consumers and to travel agents through its advertising, sales force, and trade promotions.

MANAGEMENT OF PROGRAM ELEMENTS

Among the various communication resources available to the firm are advertising, trade promotion (directed at and through wholesalers and retailers); sales force actions; consumer promotion (certain types of packaging, price offers, coupons, rebates, etc.); and supplemental communication support such as public relations programs and publicity. The promotional planner works to get the best promotional mix, making use of these elements as appropriate. In the rest of this book, details on how to approach planning and implementing these promotional elements is presented as follows: advertising—Chapters 10, 11, and 12; trade promotion—Chapter 13; consumer promotion—Chapter 14; sales force actions—Chapters 15 and 16; and supplemental promotion—Chapters 17 and 18. Listed below are some elements of Carnival's activities in these areas.

Advertising

Message　The Fun Ships theme of Carnival's ads was described in the history section above. This approach, as well as the appearance of Kathie Lee Gifford, the central presenter in Carnival's television ads, has been constant over many years. Recent Carnival ads have also featured Frank Gifford, Kathie's spouse and ABC football broadcaster, and Regis Philbin, Kathie's cohost on the syndicated television show "Live with Regis and Kathie Lee." Figure 4–3 presents examples of Carnival ads and other promotional materials.

Media　In addition to its large investment in television advertising, Carnival runs newspaper ads in over 200 markets. Most of these ads are in the Sunday travel section of newspapers primarily in the United States and Canada. The company places much less emphasis on magazines but does advertise in a few such as *Cruise Travel, Travel-Holiday,* and the cruise section of *Modern Bride.* Dickinson noted, "We have done some *Sunset* or *Southern Living,* but it takes a real effort to get noticed. They're pretty thick publications."

Carnival leads the industry in media spending with expenditures of about $26 million: $67,600 for magazines, $49,600 for national Sunday magazines, $11.5 million for newspapers, $13.4 million for network television, $1.25 million for spot TV, $489,900 for network cable, and $1,900 for outdoor advertising.

Distribution Channel Support

In 1973, 75 percent of Carnival Cruise Line's business came from wholesalers and tour operators. Carnival continued to develop its own sales force, and by 1975 the company had shifted its focus to direct sales to travel agents. By 1978, 95 percent of Carnival's sales were conducted through travel agents; this number reached 99 percent by 1990. Carnival employs a direct sales force of about 70 representatives. In addition, Holland America has about 40 representatives of its own. The current system allows each Carnival representative to serve 500 to 550 travel agents effectively.

Incentives for the sales force are developed based on both past figures and future goals. Sales representatives have no caps on their earnings, and they have direct input into their sales quotas. Travel agents receive a base commission of 10 percent, but this figure can increase based on an agent's commitment to Carnival and sales volume achieved. Carnival also offers several trade incentives, including free cruises, an agency-of-the-year competition, and mystery vacation contests. In these contests, a Carnival employee posing as a confused traveler visits a travel agent and asks about vacations. Travel agents are awarded $10 if their first suggestion is a cruise, and $1,000 if their suggestion is a Carnival cruise.

FIGURE   4–3

Example Carnival Advertisements and Other Promotional Materials

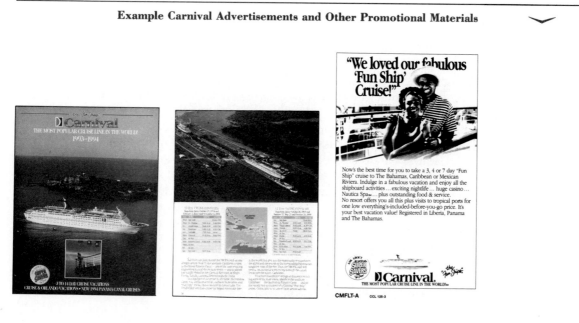

Supplemental Communications: Public Relations and Publicity

In general, Carnival's public relations (PR) tasks involve communication with three external publics: the trade press, travel editors and free-lance travel writers, and the financial community. Carnival's PR also targets various internal publics, such as the company employees. PR vehicles include in-house newsletters, such as *Carnival Capers* and *Carnivalgrams,* information releases for travel agents' in-house newsletters, daily discussions with the trade press, video news releases, and use of the PR Newswire to communicate any changes in the company's financial status.

For example, Carnival launched a major PR program after it purchased HAL. The program's main purpose was to assure the trade and the public that the union would not lower HAL's quality, that the acquisition would not "turn a Cadillac into a Chevrolet." Public relations also kept the employees of both Carnival and HAL informed about the developments and implications of the acquisition. Special video news releases providing both local and national coverage were developed around the announcement.

Carnival's publicity efforts take the form of working with travel magazine writers and newspaper travel editors to feature Carnival in their stories about cruising.

A more detailed discussion of public relations and publicity is presented in Chapter 18.

COORDINATION AND INTEGRATION OF EFFORTS

Coordinated management of various components of the promotion mix obviously is essential. Advertising, for example, should not be overemphasized relative to other types of communication unless the problem calls for dominant use of mass media. Too often, one phase is allowed to get out of balance, with the result that profit opportunities are lost.

Coordination also requires skillful use of managerial talent. Decisions must be made regarding the necessity of using outside services such as advertising agencies, research suppliers, and media-buying services. Because the advertising agency is in such widespread use, the decision may focus on division of responsibilities between management within the firm and the agency personnel. Internal staff coordination from the legal department and across the sales force is also critical. Chapter 20 discusses coordination issues in more detail.

Carnival carefully coordinates all aspects of its promotional activities. The advertising is consistent with presentations to travel agents by the sales force, and the advertisements and presentations are timed to support each other.

MEASUREMENT OF EFFECTIVENESS

Occupancy rates are one measure of a cruise line's marketing effectiveness. Since 1980, Carnival has achieved occupancy rates between 108 and 110 percent. (Cabins occupied by two people equal 100 percent occupancy.) Capacity is another major cruise line statistic. Carnival has about 12,800 berths.

As we have seen, Carnival also excels when measured by market share, controlling about 45 percent of the domestic market. Cruise Line International Association (CLIA) compiles market-share data by monitoring the sales of 40 cruise lines worldwide. Any Carnival territory with average or lower-than-average market share warrants immediate attention and corrective action. Patterns are identified and examined.

Another indication of success is repeat business. For Carnival, repeats generally account for about 30 percent of its sales. Repeats have increased over the years, which also indicates success. Perhaps at this point, this trend indicates that the company should concentrate more effort on expanding its markets than on pursuing current customers.

Carnival also evaluates specific parts of its promotional program by answering such questions as the following: Did the advertisements communicate the desired message? Did the target number of consumer and/or travel agents respond to a specific consumer or trade promotion, respectively? Did the sales force obtain the target number of new travel agents who designate Carnival as their preferred cruise line? Chapter 21 discusses approaches to measuring the effectiveness of promotional activity.

EVALUATION AND FOLLOW-UP

Every effort should be made to assess the strengths and weaknesses of the promotional plan with the objective of cataloging experience for use in future planning. Given that management turnover is a way of life in many organizations, it is not surprising that past mistakes are repeated continually. Part of the problem lies in the fact that records are not kept, perhaps because managers are avoiding accountability for performance. Whatever the reason, failure to use the results of experience in future planning is inexcusable, and a formal postmortem analysis should be a routine part of the management process.

In the case of Carnival, we see a management that constantly monitors its situation and responds accordingly. This monitoring has been very effective for the company to this point. However, management will have to stay alert to maintain its dominant position because the environment is constantly changing.

THE MARKETING MANAGER'S PROBLEM

It should be stressed that the issues faced in the management of promotion are too complex to allow pat answers. Certain decision routines are developed later, but they are intended only to discipline thinking and to guarantee systematic and rigorous analysis. It is human nature to give way to a "quest for certainty," that is, a search for concrete and definite answers where none exist. The proper attitude of inquiry, however, calls for an awareness of the state of knowledge and an appreciation of the need for research in areas where knowledge is scanty or missing. A keen appreciation for research and a certain sophistication in its use are central to promotional success.

This book is intended to provide the marketing decision maker with a guide to the dynamic, complex, and exciting world of promotional strategy. In doing so, we recommend that you return to the discussion of Carnival Cruise Lines presented here to reinforce the in-depth presentation in the later chapters. We will also continue with more specific parts of the Carnival promotional program throughout the book.

REVIEW AND DISCUSSION QUESTIONS

1. In what ways can the external and internal environments of the business firm affect promotional planning and strategy in general? In the case of Bayer Select?

2. What reasons can you give for the fact that preselling through advertising has largely precluded the need for personal selling at the retail level? Will this trend continue? In what areas does a role for personal selling remain? Why?

3. What role will advertising, personal selling to the trade, consumer promotion, and trade promotion have in Bayer Select's market entry? How will competitors likely use these promotional elements to counter Bayer Select's market entry?

4. Analyze the Carnival case history in terms of the outline given in Table 4–1 and the sequence in Figure 4–1, and then answer the following questions:
    a. Was the situation analysis sufficiently complete to permit realistic planning?
    b. Were the objectives for the campaign reasonable?
    c. Did the emphasis of the television campaign seem appropriate in view of the demand analysis?
    d. Would it be reasonable to use local newspapers, spot radio, Sunday supplements, or other forms of local media rather than spot television?
    e. What role does the sales force play in Carnival's promotion mix?
    f. How does trade promotion affect Carnival's approach to the marketplace?

NOTES

1. Based on "Carnival Tries Sailing Upstream," *Business Week*, September 25, 1989, pp. 82–86; "Liner Notes," *Marketing and Media Decisions*, January 1987, pp. 63–72; "How Carnival Stacks the Decks," *Fortune*, January 16, 1989, pp. 108–16; "Ain't We Got Fun!" *Marketing and Media Decisions*, March 1988, pp. 101–6; "Batten Down the Hatches and Rev Up the Jacuzzis," *Business Week*, February 15, 1991; "Cruise Lines Deep into Discounts," *Advertising Age*, February 3, 1992, p. 16; *Wall Street Journal*, February 10, 1992, p. B4; internal documents of Carnival Cruise Lines; and interviews with experts in the industry.

2. The specific promotional programs presented for these competitors and for Carnival are not exact for any given year, but are typical of the promotional programs implemented by these cruise lines.

ANALYZING THE MARKET

Defining and researching the target market is the first step in forming a promotional strategy. The three chapters in this section review the steps in determining the critical aspects of markets. Of particular interest is practical guidance in diagnosing behavior and thinking strategically.

Chapter 5 stresses the importance grounding promotional strategy in a proper diagnosis of the motivation and behavior of prospective buyers. The chapter frames this discussion with a focus on the differences between extended and limited problem solving, and the real importance that these variances have for the development of promotional strategy.

Chapter 6 continues the discussion of consumer behavior begun in chapter 5, but focuses on moving the promotional activity from diagnosis to strategy. Specifically, the chapter discusses the powerful role of need recognition, and the ways in which different sources of information influence promotional strategies.

In Chapter 7, we address competitive considerations and wrestle with definitions of the consumer segments (or market targets) where the opportunity is greatest, plus key issues in the positioning of products relative to consumer needs and competitive products. This chapter lays the foundation for much of what follows in the book.

C h a p t e r

5

Diagnosing Target Markets

TWO SCENARIOS

Two examples of comprehensive promotional campaigns are presented below. As you will quickly discover, the strategies are very different. Read the two cases carefully, putting yourself into the shoes of a potential buyer. In what ways would your motivation and buying behavior differ in considering a Saturn versus Baking Soda Crest? Based on this reflection, can you see clues that explain why the promotional strategies differ to such a great extent?

THE SATURN: ONE OF THE MOST SUCCESSFUL NEW BRANDS IN MARKETING HISTORY

There is one bright star in the otherwise tarnished decade of the 1980s at General Motors Corporation—development of the Saturn. A partnership was built between management, labor, and suppliers to produce a car that would excel in so many respects that it would almost single-handedly reverse America's seemingly unending love for imports.

Despite severe limitations on production output, Saturn achieved a 2.1 percent share of the American car market in 1991 and ranked a proud third in the J. D. Powers Customer Satisfaction ratings. At a starting price of $9,195, it was exceeded in satisfaction only by Lexus and Infiniti, costing three times more.

The promotional mission was to position Saturn as the friendliest, best-liked car company in America. Its competitively low $100 million ad effort was limited to 35 magazines and to such innovative television initiatives as a documentary infomercial, "Spring in Spring Hill," aired on Arts & Entertainment and Video Hits One cable networks. "Spring in Spring Hill" (the site of the Saturn plant) featured employees and team members talking, often emotionally, about the Saturn concept and what it means to them.

"A different kind of company, a different kind of car" became the advertising theme line. Every effort was made to build trust by depicting a satisfied customer, a caring employee, and a bond between them. (For an example of a Saturn print ad, see Figure 5–1).

Sources: Adapted from Raymond Serafin, "The Saturn Story," *Advertising Age*, November 16, 1992, pp. 1, 13, and 14; and adapted from Jennifer Lawrence and Riccardo A. Davis, "P&G Enters New Toothpaste War," *Advertising Age*, July 13, 1992, pp. 1 and 34.

Dealers were carefully chosen and specially trained to carry this partnership theme forward. No price haggling or high pressure was permitted—just straightforward informative sales presentations showing the Saturn at its best.

P&G ENTERS A NEW TOOTHPASTE WAR

Larger competitors were stunned by Church & Dwight Company's Arm & Hammer success in capturing an 8.4 percent share of the total toothpaste market in 1991, an 87 percent increase over 1990. Arm & Hammer made these inroads through network TV commercials stressing the "fresh-from-the-dentist-clean" formulation of its baking soda–based Dental Care and Tartar Control Dental Care products. Colgate countered with Colgate Baking Soda toothpaste, as did Unilever with Mentadent, a baking soda and hydrogen peroxide toothpaste.

Uncharacteristically, Procter & Gamble was fourth to respond, with Baking Soda Crest toothpaste. It launched heavy introductory ads to communicate the toothpaste's "clean, mint flavor" and the money-back guarantee if not fully satisfied.

FIGURE 5–1

In Choosing a Saturn, You Buy Far More Than a New Car

The money-back guarantee was the focus of point-of-sale material including displays and in-store demonstrations. Members of the trade were offered enhanced cooperative marketing funds, trade allowances, and preassembled displays. In addition, samples were heavily promoted and distributed through dentists.

THE IMPORTANCE OF RESEARCH-BASED STRATEGIC THINKING

In the preceding two examples, the promotional strategy was grounded in a proper diagnosis of the motivation and behavior of prospective buyers. Notice, first of all, that both companies made a major effort to establish their brand name and build brand equity. This was done in full recognition of the obvious fact that there would be no buying action at all if this basic information were not communicated. But the two strategies sharply diverge from this point on.

The Saturn strategy reflects awareness that most prospective car buyers are motivated to take action to assure that the "right decision" is made. Therefore, they will engage in *extended problem solving (EPS)*, which may be defined as "detailed and rigorous decision-making behavior, including need recognition, search for information, alternative evaluation, purchase, and outcomes."[1]

Automobile shoppers are likely to undertake a motivated search for meaningful information through multiple sources and then to consciously weigh and evaluate that information to be sure their needs are met. Knowing this, Saturn management made use of magazine and TV ads that positioned the Saturn as "something altogether new and trustworthy." Saturn ads assured potential buyers that their expectations for quality, performance, and service would be met—attributes taken very lightly by most American manufacturers in the previous decade. These ads, in turn, generated substantial dealer traffic, further point-of-sale information search and evaluation, and subsequent sales.

Toothpaste buyers, on the other hand, are far less likely to undertake such lengthy consideration, and most will engage in *limited problem solving (LPS)*, which may be defined as "restricted decision-making behavior using a reduced number and variety of information sources, alternatives, and evaluation criteria."[2] After all, choosing a brand of toothpaste is hardly a momentous issue with potent ramifications if a wrong decision is made.

While toothpaste buyers often prefer an existing brand, many are open to brand shifting without information search and conscious deliberation. Everything that P&G did was designed to stimulate *trial*. Heavy advertising was undertaken so that the new Crest brand would be recognized at the point of sale. Special displays and incentives, in turn, were designed to activate a "Why not try it?" response. The typical buyer is quite content to evaluate the brand after purchase, not before.

It is apparent that proper thinking about the consumer lies at the heart of strategic promotion. Take time to read Promotion in Action 5–1, which documents how General Foods used properly done consumer research as the foundation for its highly successful International Coffees promotional campaign.

AN OVERVIEW OF CONSUMER DECISION PROCESSES

Decades ago, John Dewey conceptualized decision-process behavior as *problem solving*—thoughtful, reasoned action focused on need satisfaction.[3] In general terms, consumer decision making follows the sequence shown in Table 5–1. The sequence and the actions at each stage vary sharply, however, depending on the extent to which the consumer engages in extended problem solving (EPS) as opposed to limited problem solving (LPS).

Factors that Shape Problem-Solving Behavior

Two basic factors shape the nature of buyer decision-making behavior: (1) the degree of involvement accompanying the action and (2) the extent to which individuals perceive differences between alternatives. If involvement is high and alternatives are significantly different, EPS is the most probable outcome, and vice versa.

Promotion in Action

5-1

The Secret Life of the Female Consumer

Women who drink General Foods International Coffees (GFIC) take their ads light and sweet. Scenes that show best friends chatting do well. So do images of women relaxing with their husbands and kids. And women respond favorably when soft, relaxing music plays in the background.

GFIC isn't like other coffees. It's presweetened and positioned as a specialty product, not a commodity. "GFIC is the closest coffee comes to the fashion or perfume business," says Tom Pirko, president of Bevmark Inc., a Los Angeles consultancy firm. "It's selling the sizzle as much as the steak."

As one of the largest consumer-products companies in the world, General Foods has long depended on consumer research to market its brands. To determine what women want from the brand, management stages hundreds of focus groups each year and mails out thousands of questionnaires. From that research, the team has determined that the typical GFIC consumer is a baby boomer or younger, earns a middle income, is warm, friendly, and drinks coffee on a regular basis. And although she works, research reports that she's not obsessed with her career.

But as the roles of American women have changed, it has become more difficult to peg female consumers. Today it is important for marketers to define not only who consumers are but also who they would like to be. Increasingly, women, like men, buy products because they identify—or strive to identify—with the kind of people who use them.

GFIC's marketers stress an emotional benefit—"more the feeling than the function," says Nancy Wong, director of marketing for General Foods' Maxwell House division. And that feeling? When it comes to GFIC, it's self-indulgence and traditional values represented by a series of emotional moments in commercials and ads. (See Figure 5–2 for an example of GFIC advertising.)

Source: Bernice Kanner, "The Secret Life of the Female Consumer," *Working Woman*, December 1990, pp. 69–70. Reproduced by special permission.

TABLE 5–1

The Five Stages in Consumer Decision Making

1. *Need recognition*—The consumer perceives a difference between the desired state of affairs and the current situation. This arouses and activates problem-solving action.
2. *Search for information*—The consumer acquires relevant information either from memory or from external sources.
3. *Alternative evaluation*—The consumer evaluates need-satisfying options from the perspective of expected benefits. The outcome narrows choice to the preferred alternative.
4. *Purchase*—The consumer acquires the preferred alternative (or substitute).
5. *Outcomes*—The consumer evaluates the chosen alternative after using it against the criteria of whether the product meets needs and expectations.

FIGURE 5–2

General Foods International Coffee: It's the Feeling that Counts

Courtesy General Foods Corp.

EPS will not take place, however, unless the buyer has sufficient time for deliberation. What if an unexpected ice storm leads to a freeway accident in which your only car is totaled as you start on a long-awaited vacation? Time pressure no doubt will truncate your decision process and rule out some options you might otherwise have considered.

Involvement   Of the two determining factors in the decision process, the degree of involvement has the greatest ramifications. This is because there is usually little motivation to engage in EPS unless there is a high degree of perceived personal importance and relevance accompanying product and brand choice within a specific situation or context.[4]

Strong personal relevance reflected in high involvement has several underlying determinants:[5]

1. *Perceived risk of negative outcomes.* From time to time everyone has doubts or fears that their purchase expectations will not be met. Perceived risk is especially likely when the price is high. In the car buying example, this factor alone could have triggered high involvement and motivated the prospective buyer to learn a great deal about the Saturn as well as other options. On the other hand, would you expect the person replacing his or her toothpaste supply to experience high perceived risk when trying new Crest? If it doesn't live up to expectations, so what?

2. Social sanctions. For many who are looking for a new car, the level of involvement could be influenced strongly by the brands considered to be "in" by friends and associates. In this case, baby boomers choosing a Saturn would go against the grain given the strongly held views against American cars by many of their peers. The fact that most Saturn buyers previously owned an import underscores the careful reasoning required before they would "buy American" and experience skepticism among friends. Social sanctions, however, rarely extend to the level of toothpaste purchases. Who else cares what brand you buy?

3. *Ego relatedness.* Involvement increases to the extent that consumer actions are seen as enhancing or affecting self-image. Most people would agree that the choice of Crest, Colgate, or Arm & Hammer probably has little connection with self-esteem. Therefore, choice can be made without deliberation. Selecting an automobile, on the other hand, is an entirely different matter. What you drive makes a public statement about what is important to you. Certainly the Saturn buyer is proclaiming that he or she is willing to buck the import mystique and to take risks. Also, the widespread public acclaim and interest surrounding this product introduction could support the image that the "pioneer buyer" is savvy and wise.

Yes, the extent of involvement affects behavior, but it is important to make clear that there is no such thing as a high-involvement or low-involvement product. It all depends upon the individual—high involvement for one may be low involvement for another. Also, involvement can be transient or enduring.

The inventory reproduced in Table 5–2 will help you to understand the dynamics of involvement. Think of the product or brand choices you have made in the past few weeks and rate them using these 10 factors. To the extent that you

TABLE 5–2

A Personal Involvement Checklist

For each of the 10 statements, circle the extent to which you agree or disagree. The scale ranges from (1) strongly agree to (6) strongly disagree.

1. I would be interested in reading about this product.	1	2	3	4	5	6
2. I would read a *Consumer Reports* article about this product.	1	2	3	4	5	6
3. I have compared product characteristics among brands.	1	2	3	4	5	6
4. I think there are a great deal of differences among brands.	1	2	3	4	5	6
5. I have a most preferred brand of this product.	1	2	3	4	5	6
6. I usually pay attention to ads for this product.	1	2	3	4	5	6
7. I usually talk about this product with other people.	1	2	3	4	5	6
8. I usually seek advice from other people prior to purchasing this product.	1	2	3	4	5	6
9. I usually take many factors into account before purchasing this product.	1	2	3	4	5	6
10. I usually spend a lot of time choosing what kind to buy.	1	2	3	4	5	6

Source: Adapted from Edward F. McQuarrie and J. Michael Munson, "A Revised Product Involvement Inventory: Improved Usability and Validity," in *Advances in Consumer Research,* vol. 19, eds. John F. Sherry, Jr., and Brian Sternthal (Provo, Utah: Association for Consumer Research, 1992), p. 111. Used by special permission.

find yourself saying, "Yes, I agree," the greater the level of involvement you have experienced.

As you might expect, involvement is a factor motivating consumers worldwide, but, not surprisingly, its expression and impact can vary from one culture to the next. You will enjoy the research findings presented in Promotion in Action 5–2.

Perceived Differences between Alternatives   Buyers make use of *evaluative criteria*—"the standards and specifications which are used to compare different products and brands."[6] Often referred to as *attributes,* these criteria can be objective (lowest price, quality which exceeds industry standards) or subjective (a company I can trust, a brand name respected by others). And, as you would expect, certain attributes will be more important or salient than others.

The buyer faces a real challenge when various brands or makes differ with regard to such salient attributes as price and guarantee. The number of automobile options is overwhelming. How can the buyer make the best choice? EPS becomes a necessity.

If there are no essential differences between salient attributes, however, there will be little motivation to invest the time and energy EPS requires. Therefore, LPS becomes the appropriate decision-process strategy. While someone who has run out of toothpaste also has many options, the differences are pretty minor. When it comes down to the essentials, Arm & Hammer, Colgate, Crest, and Mentadent are essentially alike.

DIAGNOSING CONSUMER BEHAVIOR

At a major petroleum refinery, the manager responsible for marketing motor oil had a completely erroneous understanding of how consumers make their brand choices at the pump island. He based his strategy on the assumption that most decisions would be based on EPS and made use of advertising giving strong "reason why" copy. Later he learned that nearly every customer believed that "motor oil is motor oil" and used a very common LPS decision-making criterion: Buy the cheapest.[7] The manager's misunderstanding resulted in a serious waste of marketing funds.

This mistake could have been avoided if the manager and his staff had been more accurate in diagnosing consumer behavior. Table 5–3 provides specific diagnostic questions to be used for this purpose.

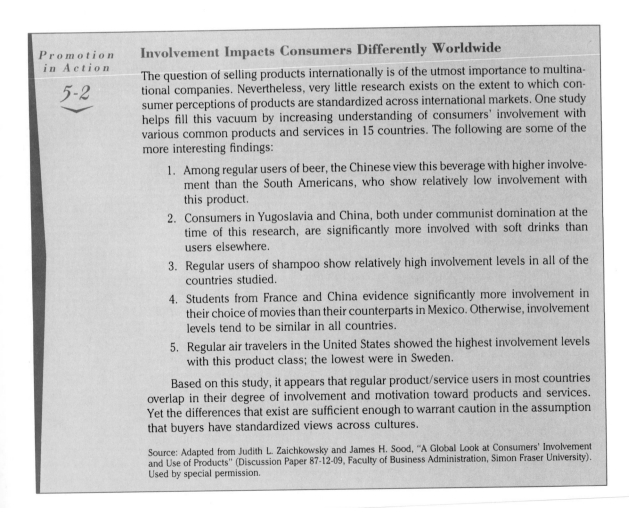

Promotion in Action

5-2

Involvement Impacts Consumers Differently Worldwide

The question of selling products internationally is of the utmost importance to multinational companies. Nevertheless, very little research exists on the extent to which consumer perceptions of products are standardized across international markets. One study helps fill this vacuum by increasing understanding of consumers' involvement with various common products and services in 15 countries. The following are some of the more interesting findings:

1. Among regular users of beer, the Chinese view this beverage with higher involvement than the South Americans, who show relatively low involvement with this product.

2. Consumers in Yugoslavia and China, both under communist domination at the time of this research, are significantly more involved with soft drinks than users elsewhere.

3. Regular users of shampoo show relatively high involvement levels in all of the countries studied.

4. Students from France and China evidence significantly more involvement in their choice of movies than their counterparts in Mexico. Otherwise, involvement levels tend to be similar in all countries.

5. Regular air travelers in the United States showed the highest involvement levels with this product class; the lowest were in Sweden.

Based on this study, it appears that regular product/service users in most countries overlap in their degree of involvement and motivation toward products and services. Yet the differences that exist are sufficient enough to warrant caution in the assumption that buyers have standardized views across cultures.

Source: Adapted from Judith L. Zaichkowsky and James H. Sood, "A Global Look at Consumers' Involvement and Use of Products" (Discussion Paper 87-12-09, Faculty of Business Administration, Simon Fraser University). Used by special permission.

TABLE 5–3

A Research Outline to Diagnose the Nature of Consumer Decision-Process Behavior

Motivation and Need Recognition

1. What needs and motivations are satisfied by product purchase and usage (i.e., what benefits are consumers seeking)?
2. Are these needs dormant or are they presently perceived as felt needs by prospective buyers?
3. How involved with the product are most prospective buyers in the target market segment?

Search for Information

1. What product- and brand-related information is stored in memory?
2. Is the consumer motivated to turn to external sources to find information about available alternatives and their characteristics?
3. What specific information sources are used most frequently when search is undertaken?
4. What product features or attributes are the focus of search when it is undertaken?

Alternative Evaluation

1. To what extent do consumers engage in alternative evaluation and comparison?
2. Which product and/or brand alternatives are included in the evaluation process?
3. Which evaluative criteria (product attributes) are used to compare various alternatives?
   a. Which are most salient in the evaluation?
   b. How complex is the evaluation (i.e., using a single attribute as opposed to several in combination)?
4. How important are perceived social actions in shaping the outcomes?
5. What are the outcomes of evaluation regarding each of the candidate purchase alternatives?
   a. What is believed to be true about the characteristics and features of each alternative?
   b. Are the alternatives perceived to be different in important ways, or are they seen as essentially the same?
   c. What attitudes are held regarding the purchase and use of each alternative?
   d. What purchasing intentions are expressed, and when will these intentions most likely be consummated by purchase and use?

Purchase

1. Will the consumer spend time and energy to shop until finding the preferred alternative?
2. Is additional decision-process behavior needed to discover the preferred outlet for purchase?
3. What are the preferred modes of purchase (i.e., retail store, in the home, or in other ways)?

Outcomes

1. What degree of satisfaction or dissatisfaction is expressed with respect to previously used alternatives in the product or service category?
2. What reasons are given for satisfaction or dissatisfaction?
3. Has perceived satisfaction or dissatisfaction been shared with other people to help them in their buying behavior?
4. Have consumers made attempts to achieve redress for dissatisfaction?
5. Is there an intention to repurchase any of the alternatives?

You will soon discover that it is a real marketing research challenge to provide information about consumer behavior. Yet, if it is done properly through survey and skilled observation, it will soon be apparent whether the majority of a target market segment undertake EPS, LPS, or some pattern between these two extremes. Then the options for promotional strategy will emerge with greater clarity, as you will discover in Chapter 6.

Ways in Which EPS and LPS Differ

Table 5–4 gives you a summary of the essential ways in which EPS and LPS differ based on the questions outlined in Table 5–3. Take time to grasp these distinctions.

There are a few statements in Table 5–4 that require further explanation. First of all, we have not yet explained differences in the ways in which persuasion takes place in EPS versus LPS. Therefore, it is necessary to delve further into how information is processed and used.

TABLE 5–4

An Overview of the Differences between Extended Problem Solving (EPS) and Limited Problem Solving (LPS)

	Extended Problem Solving (EPS)	Limited Problem Solving (LPS)
Motivation and need recognition	High involvement.	Low involvement.
Search for information	Strong motivation to search.	Low motivation to search.
	Information processed actively and rigorously.	Information processing not deep.
	Buying action influenced by brand recall.	Buying action influenced by brand recognition.
Alternative evaluation	Rigorous evaluation before purchase.	Nonrigorous evaluation mostly after purchase.
	Multiple evaluative criteria used.	Limited number of criteria used.
	Alternatives perceived as significantly different.	Alternatives perceived as essentially similar.
	Social compliance often an important motivator.	Social compliance not important.
Purchase	Will shop many outlets if needed.	Not motivated to shop extensively.
	Personal selling influences choice.	Choice often prompted by display and point-of-sale incentives.
Outcomes	Satisfaction improves brand loyalty.	Satisfaction motivates repurchase because of inertia, not loyalty.

In addition, brand preference and repeat purchasing behavior, important outcomes of the buying decision, also differ in significant respects. As you will discover, these two issues have important implications for promotional strategy.

Information Processing and Use   Following the definition of Richard Petty and John Cacioppo, persuasion is "any instance in which an active attempt is made to change a person's mind."[8] The goal is to influence both thinking and behavior, and this is most frequently accomplished by changing a person's attitude or overall evaluation, pro or con, toward an object or person.

The Process of Persuasion   The ways in which persuasion takes place differ depending on the degree of involvement and the type of information processing it stimulates in the consumer. Marketing thinking has been influenced by the *elaboration likelihood model* developed by Richard Petty and John Cacioppo.[9] In this model, communication is said to be persuasive to the extent that it stimulates *elaboration*—"the amount of integration between new information and existing knowledge stored in memory (or, the number of personal connections made between the stimulus and one's life experience or goals."[10]

When consumer involvement is high, the *central route* to persuasion is the primary path the commercial persuader should use. What this means is that the strength of message arguments becomes the primary determinant of attitude change. Put differently, arguments induce elaboration and lead to a reasoned response associating a brand object with desirable outcomes.[11]

The *peripheral route,* on the other hand, should be used under LPS, when consumer involvement is low or nonexistent. The means that there will be little or no elaboration in the mind of the consumer. Therefore, responses to secondary or peripheral factors, especially message execution, play a more important role in affecting brand attitude than the arguments themselves.

Research thus far has largely confirmed the validity of the elaboration likelihood model,[12] and Figure 5–3 offers a simple diagram showing how these two paths affect attitude toward the brand (A_B).

1. The central and peripheral routes appear to be polar opposites, but they are best considered as ends on a continuum. Notice in Figure 5–3 that all of the variables (involvement, attention, and so on) are separated by a dashed line designed to indicate this fact. Therefore it is important to think of varying degrees between extremes.[13]

2. The involved person, of course, is most likely engaging in EPS and is actively seeking information; thus attention is *voluntary*. Low involvement leads to *involuntary* attention, which means that any kind of attention to a commercial message happens incidentally while the person is using the medium for other purposes.

3. High involvement generates deeper information processing and greater elaboration. Therefore, the intended cognitive responses (changes in information and belief) and affective responses (liking or disliking) are generated more by what you say than how you say it.

4. Under low involvement, how you say it tends to be more important than

what you say. This is because attention is directed toward editorial or program elements, not the commercial message. If attention is attracted at all, this is a tribute to marketing creativity. We think that the Kahlúa ad in Figure 5–4 is a good example of this point.

It is a mistake to assume, however, that the central route to persuasion boils down to an either/or issue of using a cognitive (informational) approach versus creative message execution. Common sense argues that good message execution always makes a difference. There is growing evidence that *likability*, frequently designated as attitude toward the ad (A_{ad}),[14] also affects brand attitude and behavior—it's all a matter of relative emphasis.

FIGURE 5–3

How Information is Processed and Used to Simulate Attitude Change

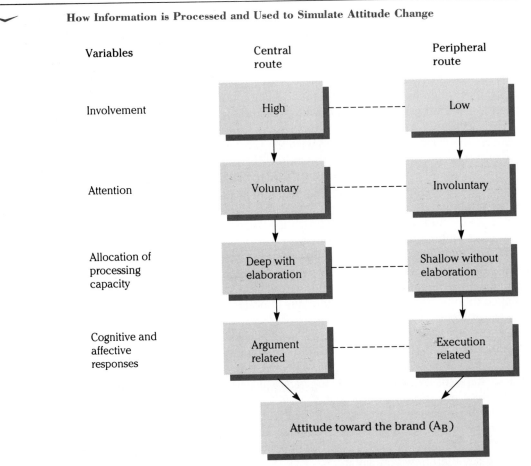

Source: Adapted from Deborah J. MacInnes and Bernard J. Jaworski, "Information Processing from Advertisements: Toward an Integrative Framework," *Journal of Marketing* 53 (October 1989), pp. 1–23.

Establishing Brand Awareness and Equity   What is Avia International Ltd.? Give up? Don't feel bad if you did, because Promotion in Action 5–3 documents that lack of familiarity with a brand or company name is quite common. This serves to reinforce one of the most basic principles of promotional strategy: The greatest asset a company can gain is brand awareness and understanding.

One of the greatest problems any company faces is finding a product stumbling toward *commoditization*—a state in which brand names no longer matter and competition degenerates to the level of price. In fact, as mentioned in Chapter 1, consumer brand shifting has become a way of life. Furthermore, the distributor now is in position to assume channel control and largely dictate the destiny of the brand.

Recall from Chapter 1 the discussion of the Gillette Company. In the late 1980s, Gillette discovered that its once illustrious brand name in shaving products had come to mean very little in its life-and-death struggle against the Schick and Bic brands. To the consumer, one brand was equivalent of the others—therefore, buy the cheapest. Profits plunged, and it appeared that Gillette was ripe for a takeover. Only the last-ditch introduction of its innovative, high-tech razor, the Sensor, saved the day. Through the Sensor's successful introduction and promotion Gillette had a basis to reestablish brand equity.[15] In other words, Gillette regained a much-needed competitive advantage.

Brand equity has yet another advantage. Consider the fact that Coca-Cola's

---

Name of the Game: Brand Awareness

Promotion in Action

5-3

Is Avia International Ltd:

   a. a small Italian commuter airline?

   b. an up-and-coming courier service?

   c. a map exporter specializing in exotic spots?

None of the above. But if you're still stumped, you have plenty of company. Only 4 percent of U.S. consumers know that Avia makes sneakers and sports aparel—a dismally low percentage that Avia hopes to increase with a new advertising campaign poking fun at its low name recognition.

Given today's market clutter, name recognition is almost priceless. Selling a product that's not a household word "is like rowing a boat upstream," notes Frank Delano, chairman of Delano Goldman & Young, a corporate—and brand—image consultant in New York. "Movement is almost backwards."

Approximately 90 percent of new products are pulled from the market within two to three years, according to Robert McMath, director of New Products Showcase and Learning Center, an Ithaca, New York museum of 75,000 products that failed. "In most cases, failures were the result of a lack of product recognition," he says.

Source: Joseph Pereira, "Name of the Game: Brand Awareness," *The Wall Street Journal,* February 14, 1991, p. B1. Reproduced by special permission.

promotional spending is only about 4 percent of its total sales, whereas promotional spending approaches 40 percent at lesser-known Royal Crown Cola.[16] As Philip Dudek, Royal Crown's director of promotion points out, "There's no question Coke and Pepsi are better known names than Royal Crown, and there's no question that brand name is important in the Cola Wars."[17]

Given the importance of brand awareness and equity, we come to a crucial question: Are there differing impacts on buying behavior from brand information communicated through the central route as opposed to the peripheral route? In other words, how does establishment of awareness and equity work itself out in practice when these two very different approches to consumer persuasion are undertaken?

First of all, remember that serious prepurchase alternative evaluation is more prevalent under EPS than under LPS. When this is the case, the goal of advertising and personal selling is to communicate relevant brand information in such a way that it is (1) noticed, (2) processed deeply and elaborated as connections are

---

FIGURE 5–4

Kahlúa Says It Well without Words

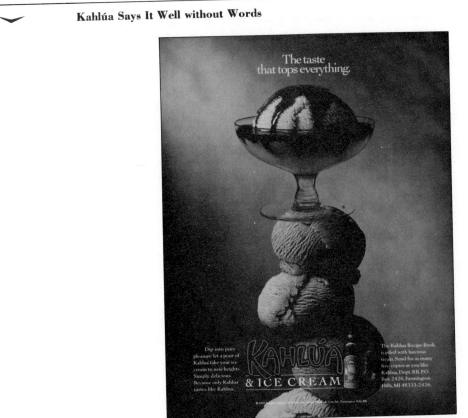

Courtesy Hiram Walker & Sons, Inc.

made with previous knowledge and attitudes, and (3) stored in memory in such a way that it may be recalled and used in alternative evaluation. *Recall,* then, is the basic promotional objective.

The marketing staff at General Motors' Saturn division is not the least bit interested in having prospective buyers read the story of Cheryl Silas (see again Fig. 5–1) if they fail to recall the basic message highlighting the unusual safety and damage resistance attributes of the Saturn. Persuasion has misfired if recall does not take place.

Detailed recall is not the objective, however, of P&G's product advertising for its new Baking Soda Crest. Few will consciously remember seeing print or TV ads for this product because of the involuntary, shallow information processing so common in LPS. The objective of P&G's advertising is brand name *recognition* at the point of sale.

Why is recognition such an important outcome of peripheral route persuasion? If advertising has done its job, the consumer has included the brand in his or her acceptable set of alternatives. When the brand name is recognized by the buyer as he or she scans the shelves, there is a very good chance that a price offer or other form of incentive will trigger a "Why not try it?" response.

Remember these two promotional objectives—brand recognition and brand recall. Everything depends on the extent to which advertising and other forms of promotion have succeeded in building brand awareness and equity.

FIGURE 5–5

The Consumer—Faithful or Fickle?

Percentage of respondents saying, "I usually know the brand I will buy and get that brand." Figures represent percentage of product buyers and other respondents offering an answer to the question, from a nationwide survey of 2,000 adults by the Roper Organization.

Brand Category	April 1990	April 1991
Mayonnaise	62%	55%
Coffee	63	53
Beer	62	52
Canned soup	55	47
Tea bags	51	43
Liquor	55	43
Cold cereal	47	42
Ice cream	46	37
Orange juice	39	36
Dry soup mix	39	32
Plastic wrap	31	26

Source: Julie Liesse, "Brands in Trouble," *Advertising Age,* December 2,1992, p. 16. Reproduced by special permission.

Stimulating Repeat Purchase Behavior   The goal of every promotional campaign is to build customer satisfaction and brand loyalty. And it is in the best interest of consumers to establish buying habits that truncate the need for repeated problem solving.

Yet the data in Figure 5–5 show that the percentages who stay loyal to a preferred brand differ from one product category to the next. Furthermore, it is apparent that brand loyalty levels are dipping sharply.

Why brand switching takes place   Research by the Leo Burnett Company, a Chicago-based advertising agency, reveals that repeat purchasers in many product classes fall into four distinct categories:[18]

1. *Long loyals*—those committed to one brand regardless of price or competition.
2. *Rotators*—regular switchers within a handful of favorite brands largely on the basis of variety seeking.
3. *Deal sensitives*—regular switchers within a set of acceptable brands on the basis of a special offer or incentive.
4. *Price sensitives*—regular switchers who consistently purchase the brand within the lowest price.

What emerges are three essentially different groups: (1) the truly brand loyal, (2) the switchers wihin a preferred brand set, and (3) the consistent switchers. Each of these groups has a different set of reasons.

First of all, true brand loyalty usually emerges when the initial purchase is motivated by a relatively high degree of involvement accompanied by perceived differences between alternatives. One of the best indicators of enduring brand loyalty is the response given to this question: "What brand would you choose if your favorite is not available?" The answer "None—I'll shop further" indicates strong brand commitment.

When product use leads to satisfaction under these conditions, there will be natural resistance to further problem-solving behavior when repurchase is called for. But, how many people are motivated to be brand loyal with dry soup mixes or plastic wrap? Apparently not many.

The second segment includes those who evidence a degree of loyalty within a group of acceptable brands. But is this true loyalty? We think not. If they repurchase the most recently bought brand, it is mostly because of inertia. A routine is established that can be overcome, however, through some sort of incentive or a desire for variety.[19]

At the other extreme are the regular brand switchers. In their eyes, the alternatives have become nothing more than commodities. Therefore, the decision-making criterion is "Buy the cheapest."

Maintaining brand preference and loyalty   Even true or enduring loyalty is by no means a guaranteed company asset. It can be lost quickly if it is taken for granted. The key to maintenance of market share is an all-out commitment to continued innovation and customer satisfaction. Consider these prophetic words:

> Marketers have made it easy for consumers to trade down and tune out presumably venerable brand names—by siphoning ad dollars to fund trade promotions, by producing all too similar ad messages, by losing the edge in product innovation.[20]

It is difficult to dislodge an entrenched competitor with a loyal core. As a result, many companies concentrate on increasing the loyalty of their own customers. Tony Adams, vice president of marketing research at the Campbell Soup Company explains his company's strategy in this way:

> The probability of converting a nonuser to your brand is about 3 in 1,000. The best odds are with your own core franchise. Our heavy users consume two or three cans of soup a week, and we'd like to increase that.[21]

Finally, it is advisable to at least maintain advertising levels in relation to competition. Many in the trade refer to this practice as *maintaining share of mind.* Consider the words of Clayt Wilhite, president of D'Arcy Massius Advertising Agency: "Every time 24 hours pass without any advertising reinforcement, brand loyalty will diminish ever so slightly—even for a powerful brand like Budweiser."[22]

To maintain share of mind, Kraft General Foods stepped up advertising for its Maxwell House brand after stopping for a year in 1987. Dick Mayer, president of the General Foods U.S.A. division noted, "Even though brand loyalty is rather strong for coffee, we need advertising to maintain and strengthen it."[23]

SUMMARY

This is the first of two chapters designed to help you understand the dynamics of consumer behavior. This chapter views the consumer from a problem-solving pespective and points out the five basic steps in the decision process: (1) need recognition, (2) search for information, (3) alternative evaluation, (4) purchase, and (5) outcomes of purchase, especially satisfaction or dissatisfaction.

The rigor with which these decision-process steps will be followed, especially on an initial purchase, will vary from one situation to the next depending upon (1) the degree of involvement (personal relevance), (2) the extent to which individuals perceive meaningful differences between alternatives.

When involvement is high and the alternatives differ significantly, the decision process takes the form of extended problem solving (EPS). At the opposite end on the continuum is limited problem solving (LPS), in which decisions are made with far less deliberation.

The varying dynamics between EPS and LPS have real significance for promotional strategy. In the first place, persuasive strategies for EPS-motivated buyers make use of the central route to persuasion, which places primary emphasis on the message and its selling appeals, as opposed to its creative execution. On the other hand, the peripheral route to persuasion (in which "how you say it" takes precedence over "what you say") has greater impact when LPS is dominant.

Furthermore, a consistent theme throughout the chapter is the central importance of creating and maintaining brand awareness and equity. Many examples are given of the perils of either not establishing brand equity initially or allowing it to slump.

REVIEW AND DISCUSSION QUESTIONS

1. What are the essential distinctions between extended problem solving and limited problem solving? What type of decision process would you expect most people to follow in the initial purchase of a new product or brand in these categories: electric shavers, gold jewelry, soft drinks, stereo equipment, men's underwear, women's lingerie, and flashlight batteries?

2. You have been asked to prepare an advertising campaign for Panasonic's new "flatter picture" television models, which offer greater brightness and intensity. Would you use the central route to persuasion or the peripheral route? Why? What would be the distinctions if you were to follow one as opposed to the other?

3. "Low-priced Personal Computers Are Rapidly Degenerating to the Commodity Level." So read the headline in a recent trade news story. What does it mean to say that a product is becoming a commodity?

4. What are the implications of the commoditization of personal computers for manufacturers such as IBM and Compaq, which have until now relied heavily on their brand name only to find their market share diminishing in the face of blistering price competition? Is it fair to speculate that personal computers now are being bought on the basis of limited problem solving? Why or why not?

5. Advertising analyst Harry W. McMahan always contended that "the name of the game is the name. . . . Here is where all advertising starts and where so much of television advertising misses." What is the rationale behind this statement?

6. In September 1991, H. J. Heinz executives announced that all advertising support was being removed from many of Heinz's old-line products, including tomato paste and vinegar. The reason given was that they had become commodities that consumers choose by price, not by brand image. Was this a wise decision? Why or why not?

7. Many consumers have a set of preferred brands and engage in brand switching within that set. This, of course, undermines the exclusive brand loyalty that manufacturers want. Why is brand loyalty dwindling so seriously? Do you see any signs that this will change based on your own purchasing experience?

8. Your task is to design an advertising campaign to promote the sales of the Nintendo video games line. Would you be likely to use the central route to persuasion or the peripheral route? Why?

NOTES

1. James F. Engel, Roger D. Blackwell, and Paul W. Miniard, *Consumer Behavior*, 8th ed. (Fort Worth, Tex.: Dryden Press, 1993), p. G-5.

2. Ibid., p. G-7.

3. John Dewey, *How We Think* (New York: Heath, 1910).

4. John Antil, "Conceptualization and Operationalization of Involvement," in *Advances in Consumer Research*, vol. 11, ed. Thomas Kinnear (Provo, Utah: Association for Consumer Research, 1984), p. 204.

5. See Giles Laurent and Jean Noel Kapferer, "Measuring Consumer Involvement Profiles," *Journal of Marketing Research* 12 (February 1985), pp. 41–53.

6. Engel et al., *Consumer Behavior,* p. G-5.

7. Wayne D. Hoyer, "Variations and Choice Strategies Across Decision Contexts: An Examination of Contingent Factors," in *Advances in Consumer Research*, vol. 11, ed. Richard J. Lutz (Provo, Utah: Association for Consumer Research, 1986), pp. 23–26.

8. Richard E. Petty and John T. Cacioppo, *Attitudes and Persuasion: Classic and Contemporary Approaches* (Dubuque, Iowa: Wm. C. Brown, 1981), p. 4.

9. Ibid. See also Richard E. Petty and John T. Cacioppo, *Communication and Persuasion: Central and Peripheral Routes to Attitude Change* (New York: Springer-Verlag, 1986).

10. Engel et al., *Consumer Behavior,* p. G-4.

11. Charles S. Areni and Richard J. Lutz, "The Role of Argument Quality in the Elaboration Likelihood Model," in *Advances in Consumer Research*, vol. 15, ed. Michael J. Houston (Provo, Utah: Association for Consumer Research, 1988), pp. 197–201.

12. The confirming research is extensive. See, for example Ibid.; Paul W. Miniard, Sunil Bhatla, Kenneth R. Lord, Peter R. Dickson, and H. Rao Unnava, "Picture-Based Persuasion Processes and the Moderating Role of Involvement," *Journal of Consumer Research* 18 (June 1991), pp. 92–107; and Paul W. Miniard, Peter R. Dickson, and Kenneth R. Lord, "Some Central and Peripheral Thoughts on the Routes to Persuasion," in *Advances in Consumer Research*, vol. 15, ed. Michael J. Houston (Provo, Utah: Association for Consumer Research, 1988), pp. 209–12.

13. For a helpful argument on the continuum between extremes, see Deborah J. MacInnis and Bernard J. Jaworski, "Information Processing from Advertisements: Toward an Integrative Framework," *Journal of Marketing* 53 (October 1989), pp. 1–23.

14. See, for example, Gabriel Biehal, Debra Stephens, and Eleonara Curlo, "Attitude toward the Ad and Brand Choice," *Journal of Advertising* 21 (September 1992), pp. 19–36.

15. "The Best a Plan Can Get," *The Economist,* August 15, 1992, pp. 59–60.

16. Joseph Pereira, "Name of the Game: Brand Awareness," *The Wall Street Journal,* February 14, 1991, p. B1.

17. Ibid., p. B1.

18. "Strategic Shopping," *The Economist,* September 26, 1992, pp. 82–83.

19. See Leigh McAlister and Edgar Pessemier, "Variety Seeking Behavior: An Interdisciplinary Review," *Journal of Consumer Research* 9 (December 1982), pp. 311–22.

20. Julie Liesse, "Brands in Trouble," *Advertising Age,* December 2, 1991, p. 16.

21. Ronald Alsop, "Brand Loyalty Is Rarely Blind Loyalty," *The Wall Street Journal,* October 18, 1989, p. B8.

22. "Rediscovering the Corporation," Forum Corporation, 1988.

23. Alsop, "Brand Loyalty Is Rarely Blind Loyalty," p. B8.

Chapter

6

Moving from Diagnosis to Strategy

A GLIMPSE AT CONSUMER BEHAVIOR WORLDWIDE

- On a recent Thursday afternoon before a holiday weekend at a Colra hypermarket northwest of Paris, shoppers loaded up on Coke and Coke Light (the French name for Diet Coke) in quantities that would stun some Americans—10, 15, or even 20 large plastic bottles. Women dressed in bright red-and-white outfits passed out coupons in the aisles, and near the store entrance a display of 31,941 Coke bottles—a world record—advertised low, low prices.

- Ad agency Saatchi & Saatchi found unexpected resistance when it tried to market Pampers disposable nappies (diapers) in Thailand by stressing their convenience. Market research showed that Thai women were worried that using disposable nappies might mark them out as bad mothers, interested more in their own comfort than that of their babies. Saatchi has now developed a nighttime use theme for Pampers. The idea is to convince mothers that disposable nappies stay drier than cloth ones, thus making their little darlings more comfortable at night. Consciences assuaged, Thai moms are buying Pampers in droves.

- Europeans are changing their eating and shopping habits. As the population ages, many consumers are becoming more concerned about health and nutrition, which is leading them away from heavy eggs-and-meat breakfasts to ready-to-eat cereals.

- Asian yuppies crave big-name brands. A cruise through Sunrise Department Store in Taipei finds Ungaro, Boss, Ermene-guildo Zegna, and Gianni Versace, to mention a few high-fashion names. Plus: Timberland deck shoes for $172; Ralph Lauren shorts for $90; Allen Edmonds shoes for $306; and a Giorgio Armani sports jacket for $1,280. all this on the same floor as a movie theater that sells popcorn and boiled chicken feet.

Sources: Patricia Sellers, "Coke Gets Off Its Can in Europe, *Fortune,* August 13, 1990, p. 70; "Advertising in Asia, Full of Western Promise," *The Economist,* November 14, 1992, p. 85; Christopher Knowlton, "New Weapons in Europe Cooks Up a Cereal Brawl," *Fortune,* June 3, 1991, p. 176; and Ford S. Worthy, "Asia's New Yuppies," *Fortune,* June 4, 1990, p. 226.

Interesting reading, isn't it? Take away the geographic references and you would never know that you were looking in on Asians and Europeans:

Coke mass-merchandised in France to capitalize on impulse buying motivated by limited problem solving.

Mothers make a choice of disposable nappies in Thailand, insisting that the brand purchased must feature the attributes *they* want and resisting the "American model."

Europeans turning to the American custom of eating prepared breakfast cereals, largely for the same reasons as their American counterparts.

Highly brand-conscious young adults (yuppies) in Taiwan.

And, as we saw in Chapter 5, consumers worldwide experiencing both high and low involvement as they make purchases.

Despite some similarities, however, do not conclude that buyer behavior is standardized worldwide. Anything but! Listen to the words of Tina Ma, aged 29, a public relations specialist living stylishly in Taiwan: "We're so confused by all of the influences from the West. I don't want to be Western. I want to be Chinese."[1]

But we can say with some certainty that common decision-making processes emerge when there is a sufficient disposable personal income to allow a wide range of choice. In other words, French, American, Nigerian, or Peruvian consumers with comparable economic backgrounds all will make use of limited problem solving (LPS), extended problem solving (EPS), brand loyalty, brand switching, and so on.

The ways in which decision processes are worked out in the marketplace, of course, can be radically different from one culture to the next. But we find the same kinds of differences between segments in North America also. Therefore, promotional strategy decisions worldwide must be based on a careful diagnosis of consumer motivation and behavior. Once this basis is in place, strategic options emerge with greater clarity.

It is the purpose of this chapter to help you move from diagnosis to strategy. The discussion will be oriented around the five stages in the consumer decision-making process: (1) need recognition; (2) search for information; (3) alternative evaluation; (4) purchase; and (5) outcomes (refer back to Table 5–1 in Chapter 5). A number of helpful research findings will be reviewed, and you will discover an abundance of practical insights into strategic thinking.

NEED RECOGNITION

All decision-process behavior begins with *need recognition,* defined as "perception of a difference between the desired state of affairs and the actual situation sufficient to arouse and activate the decision process."[2] For example, you may experience need recognition because you feel hungry (actual state) and desire to relieve those hunger pangs (ideal state).

One of the many factors that can precipitate need recognition is *motive activation.* By *motive,* we mean a lasting disposition to strive to attain a specified goal or desired state.

For example, you have been under a pile of work for a long period of time and desire some rest and relaxation. The sense of deprivation you feel triggers a state of discomfort known as *drive,* which, in turn, energizes goal-oriented behavior. A logical outcome here might be taking a few days off or even taking a cruise if you can afford it.

At other times, previous buying actions define an all-new sense of the "ideal," which makes the present situation seem inadequate. For example, new wallpaper can make existing carpeting look pretty shabby. Once the carpet is replaced, in turn, something else may have to go.

Need recognition is also triggered by something that causes your present situation to be unsatisfactory. This can happen through changed circumstances such as suddenly realizing that you have no diet cola anywhere in your house or room, or finding that your washing machine has failed to complete its full cycle and that the repair will require some major financial outlays.

Targeting the Receptive

The following principle should come as no surprise: Promotional strategy has its greatest payoff when need recognition already exists—in other words, when consumers are open and receptive to potential solutions. When there is no felt need, however, promoting a product can be an uphill struggle. For example, if you have an inclination to be a life insurance salesperson among yuppies in Asia, Promotion in Action 6–1 should convince you to reconsider your plans.

The initial goal, then, is always to isolate the *receptive* market segments, in which the probability of response is greatest and in which the marketer has a competitive edge. Parents of young babies, for example, have a pet peeve—leaky diapers. Kimberly-Clark Corporation's product designers responded quickly to this need by adding a raised strip of padding to its Huggies brand of disposable diapers to effectively stop leaks around the leg openings. This product redesign helped the company to maintain its 30 percent share in a very competitive market.

Insurance Salespeople Are Dead Meat among Asia's Yuppies

Promotion in Action

6-1

No matter how finely tuned the marketing pitch, some products and services aren't likely to appeal to Asia's yuppies for a long time. Insurance is a prime example. Few young people could image insuring their homes against loss from fire or theft. As Seoul accountant Choi Yil-Hwan put it, "We don't like to think about the worst things that can happen."

Life insurance, commonly viewed as "death insurance" by most Chinese, is only slightly more popular. James Wong, senior vice president for American International Assurance in Hong Kong, believes life insurance will eventually appeal to the yuppie generation only if they can be made to see it as a way to save.

Source: Fred S. Worthy, "Asia's New Yuppies," *Fortune*, June 4, 1990, p. 235. Reproduced by special permission.

Strategies to Stimulate Need Recognition

As you will recall, during the late 1980s, manufacturers of women's fashions found to their dismay that their efforts to win acceptance for shorter skirts were a costly failure. Working women, in particular, let it be known loud and clear that they were not going to be manipulated into an unwanted wardrobe change. No amount of marketing firepower could reverse this resounding negative vote.

Nevertheless, skillful promotion can stimulate need recognition by bringing the ideal state into sharper focus. Do you find yourself feeling thirsty as you contemplate the natural taste of Belgium's Stella Artois beer in Figure 6–1? This need stimulation approach is commonly used and serves to change perceptions of the ideal state by highlighting a need that might be latent at a given point in time.

Another strategy to stimulate need recognition is to take aim at a prospect's present choice or action and stress its inadequacies. Consider the following appeal for the full-sized Chevy pickup:

FIGURE 6–1

The Natural Taste of Stella Artois Beer

Go forward with Chevy or backward with Ford. The key is Insta-Trac.™ It lets you shift into four-wheel drive High and back to freewheeling two-wheel drive without slowing down, stopping or backing up. With Ford's Touch Drive you still have to shift the transfer case, come to a complete stop, shift into reverse and back up *at least* 10 feet to get from four-wheel drive into free-wheeling two-wheel drive.

The key to success lies in a product change that offers a unique product benefit that is perceived as significant and relevant. The benefit of instant shifting into or out of four-wheel drive has a chance of convincing at least some truck owners that it's time to replace their old truck.

SEARCH FOR INFORMATION

Once a problem is recognized, the next stage in the decision process is to search for additional information. At times, a scan of the information presently stored in memory (*internal search*) provides that additional information. When that is the case, the consumer switches out of EPS into LPS or habitual, routinized behavior.

Internal search will prove to be inadequate and will lead to *external search* when:

1. The person has had little or no previous experience to draw on.
2. Previous choices have resulted in dissatisfaction.
3. A lengthy time period has passed since the last purchase.
4. The benefits offered by available alternatives clearly have changed.
5. The person has little confidence in his or her ability to make the right choice in a given situation.
6. There is a high level of involvement, which reflects strong enduring interest and motivation to avoid risk.[3]
7. Consumer beliefs and attitudes trigger a felt need for additional information.

In particular, "consumers engage in more search to the extent that their attitudes toward shopping are favorable,"[4] and "more effort will be devoted to search when the benefits are seen to be high and the costs (outlay, time, and energy) are low."[5]

You can readily discern that external search usually is not needed when involvement is low, alternatives are comparable, and LPS is the appropriate strategy. External information still is processed, of course, but it is done *involuntarily,* taking place through the *peripheral route,* with little or no conscious recall. But, as you recall, such information still plays the important role of stimulating recognition at the point of sale.

Degree of External Search

Consumers commonly engage in less external search than one might expect, even for such major purchases as furniture, appliances, and automobiles. For example, automobile buyers exhibit six levels of search behavior.[6] About 25 percent do not search at all, and only 5 percent use all the sources they can find. In another example, only about 50 percent of all men seek information when they are buying clothing.[7]

Research also indicates that search behavior varies from one demographic segment to the next.[8] Age is negatively correlated with search because older consumers are often brand loyal. Also, they can make use of experience gained over the years. Similarly, those with high incomes value their time greatly and are less prone to invest it in search activities.[9]

As you would expect, the degree of external search directly relates to the type of decision-process strategy. Table 6–1 provides a good summary of research on this topic.

At times, stimulation of search is a legitimate promotional objective. Certainly it would not be surprising if a large number of potential travelers returned a coupon to Lufthansa requesting the Winter Value Guides to Germany (see Figure 6–2).

Sequence of Search

When consumers need and acquire more facts on the attributes offered by various brands, they process and use this information in two ways.[10] One way is *processing by brand*, in which each brand is examined according to its various attributes before proceeding to the next brand. The other option is *processing by attribute*, in which all brand information is collected and compared on an attribute-by-attribute basis.

Processing by brand is most common in EPS, when the buyer has a high level of present knowledge or previous purchasing experience. Processing by attribute, however, is most often seen when LPS is the decision-making strategy.

TABLE 6–1

Differences in the Degree of Search as a Function of the Decision-Making Process

	Decision-Making Process		
Nature of Search	Extended Problem Solving	Limited Problem Solving	Habitual
Number of brands	Greater	Fewer	One
Number of stores	Greater	Fewer	Unknown
Number of attributes	Greater	Fewer	One
Number of external information sources	Greater	Fewer	None
Amount of time	Larger	Smaller	Minimal

Source: James F. Engel, Roger D. Blackwell, and Paul W. Miniard, *Consumer Behavior*, 7th ed. (Forth Worth, Tex.: Dryden Press, 1993), p. 516. Reproduced by special permission.

When processing by brand is expected, the best promotional strategy is to place heavy emphasis on brand features and distinctions to be certain that the consumer doesn't miss any. Certainly this is the advertising tactic used by the 3M Company in promoting Scotch-Brite to the middle-class Thai homemaker (see Fig. 6–3). With pictures and words, the message is delivered that Scotch-Brite can work through grease and fat to produce a shiny finish where needed throughout your home. Don't forget the important principle that the effect of this type of advertising is measured by recall of brand name as well as product features and attributes.

But it is entirely possible that processing by attribute will be used in both EPS and LPS, especially in the early stages of decision making. Now the essential question is, "Which brands offer the features that are important to me?" For example, insurance companies generally offer discounts on homeowners insurance to retirees. A couple about to retire could be strongly influenced by an Allstate ad that ran several years ago claiming, "John Haight is 55 and retired and busy earning a discount on his homeowners insurance."

FIGURE 6–2

Who Can Resist Knowing More about Germany's "Enchanting Alternatives"?

Use of Information Sources

Broadly speaking, information sources can be placed into two categories: *commercial* and *general.* In each category, we find the use of both one-on-one communication and the mass media. An overview of the various options appears in Table 6–2, and each source will be discussed in more detail below.

The impact of any given source varies according to the person and the nature of the decision. The following is a helpful typology to use when assessing media influence:

1. *Decisive effectiveness*—The information source has a major influence on choice.

2. *Contributory effectiveness*—The information source plays some role such as stimulating awareness or interest, but not a decisive one.

3. *Ineffective*—The information source creates exposure but no particular impact on outcome.

FIGURE 6–3

Stressing Product Attributes

Media influence has been the subject of decades of research, and the studies are too numerous to detail here.[11] But we can give the following major generalizations regarding media influence in the context of extended problem solving:

1. The various media are *complementary,* not competitive. People generally do not rely exclusively on one source of information.

2. The mass media, whether marketer dominated or not, most frequently have been found to perform a *contributory* role by providing such information as brand features and product availability. As we will see later, however, advertising properly conceived also can be *decisive* in many situations.

3. The general content media tend to be perceived as more credible than advertising and other commercial (marketer-dominated) sources. As a result, they tend to have a greater contributory influence.

4. Personal selling often will have a decisive role when it is available.

5. Word-of-mouth communication from friends or relatives usually will have decisive impact and greatest total overall effectiveness in shaping consumer behavior. The primary reason is that information provided by a peer is often regarded as more credible and truthworthy than anything the mass media can provide.

Personal Selling   Even in an age of mass merchandising, situations still exist in which point-of-sale negotiation or information exchange is needed. For example, the inclusion of energy-use ratings on appliances has proved to be of little value without additional explanation by a salesperson.[12]

It should come as no surprise to you that personal selling can be decisive in its impact. You will recall from Chapter 3 that interpersonal communication offers the significant benefits of instant feedback and opportunity to use various nonverbal signals.

What makes for effectiveness in personal selling? This is the subject of Chapter 18, but a study on the automobile salesperson is worth noting here.[13] In the 1970s, flamboyant sales methods, not genuine concern for the buyer, were the norm. By the 1980s, just the reverse was found to be true. Now, as you will discover in

TABLE 6–2

The Information Sources Used by Consumers

Source	One-on-One Communication	Mass Media
Commercial	Personal selling In-home selling Direct marketing	Advertising Sales promotion Publicity Public relations
General	Word-of-mouth influence	General content media

Promotion in Action 6–2, the pendulum has swung, forcing a real focus on the consumer's expectations and satisfaction.

In-Home Selling   At a much earlier stage in marketing development, in-home personal selling was the norm. The legendary "Yankee peddler" carried a variety of household goods either on his back or by horse and carriage to people who were totally isolated from any type of central shopping area.

Today in-home personal selling is experiencing something of a revival. The Lincoln-Mercury division of Ford Motor Co., for example, is considering selling its Mark VIII models through house calls and making it possible for the buyer to avoid visiting a dealer during the period he or she owns the car.[14] And the Avon Company is finding great success in selling cosmetics door-to-door in China, a strategy it has largely been forced to abandon in the United States.[15]

Direct Marketing   More than half of all U.S. households now do some purchasing at home during a typical month through direct marketing (direct mail, telemarketing, etc.). As you will discover in Chapter 17, those who respond to this type of selling prefer to avoid the costs, loss of time, and inconvenience of shopping at retail stores.

Promotion in Action

6-2

Smart Selling: Winning Over Today's Tough Customers

Thanks to years of devoted service to its customers, Sears, Roebuck & Co. was once nothing less than where America shopped. It commanded, in the words of writer Donald R. Katz, "the sort of fealty normally reserved for nations and churches." Unfortunately, nations can betray their citizens, and churches can alienate their worshipers.

At Sears and elsewhere, selling once meant knowing your customers and knowing how your products could meet their needs. Hard as it may now be to believe, department stores were once filled with knowledgeable, courteous salespeople.

In recent years, however, that kind of selling has become a relic of a more leisurely, genteel age. But something is happening. Call it the death of a certain kind of salesman. Many companies are starting to focus on the way they present themselves to that most precious of resources, the customer. They're changing the way they sell, and that means rethinking everything from how salespeople are trained and compensated to the way a corporation is organized and how the chief executive spends his or her time.

With their customers ever more value-conscious, companies are realizing that sales must join the rest of marketing—from product development to pricing and advertising—in delivering perceived benefits.

Now, no company can afford to alienate a single customer with its selling approach. They are now recognizing selling and service as the latest and best arena for capturing customers. Smart selling means building relationships with customers, not just slam-dunking them on a single sale. And it means using salespeople to solve customers' problems, not just take their orders.

Source: Christopher Power and Lisa Driscoll, "Smart Selling: How Companies Are Winning Over Today's Tougher Customer," *Business Week,* August 3, 1992, pp. 46–48. Reproduced by special permission.

Advertising   As you know, the role and nature of advertising differs between EPS-motivated buying and LPS-motivated buying.

EPS-motivated buying   Once a need is recognized, customers generally become more receptive to advertising that they might previously have ignored. Consumers often consult ads for information, although the informative role of advertising can vary. Consider the following examples:

1. Print and TV ads were found to be the primary information sources used by purchasers of small electrical appliances and outdoor products.[16]

2. Nearly half of those interviewed in one study reported purchasing a product after exposure to a commercial or magazine ad. What were they looking for? Information on price reductions.[17]

3. Those who rely most heavily on advertising are likely to be male, young, single, and employed.[18]

Does advertising play a contributory role or a decisive role in EPS-motivated decision processes? One can argue either way on this issue, but we believe the insights of Jack Trout and Al Ries are worthy of note:

> Apologists for advertising are fond of claiming that advertising doesn't sell anything. It only creates awareness. Other functions are responsible for sales. The facts suggest otherwise. For most products, awareness is not the issue, perception is. Brands like Coke, Pepsi, Chevy, Ford, Burger King and McDonald's already have awareness ratings in the 90th percentile.
>
> To increase sales, a high-awareness brand must sharpen its perception in the mind. With the right name, the right positioning strategy and the right execution, advertising alone is the most powerful force in marketing. With other factors approximately equal, as they usually are in the real world, advertising alone can determine who will win the marketing way.[19]

LPS-motivated buying   Bear in mind that in LPS-motivated buying, information processing is involuntary, largely through the peripheral route (i.e., how you say it may be more important than what you say). Brand recognition at the point of sale becomes the marketer's central objective. If advertising has done its job, the consumer previously included the brand in his or her acceptable set of alternatives. This sets the stage for product trial, especially if promotional incentives are provided.

Notice the strong focus on brand and benefits in the ads in Figures 6–4 and 6–5. You cannot miss the fact that the French mineral water, Badoit, claims to offer refreshment and "lift" (Figure 6–4) and that Campbell's (Figure 6–5) offers two ways to make broccoli a "part of your dinner."

Remember that information processing in this context is largely involuntary, relying on execution factors to capture attention. But many ads, if not most, simply get lost in the "noise" in an overcommunicative society. Therefore, memorability becomes necessary—creative ways must be found to make the brand name and benefit stand out.

How can advertisers achieve memorability? This question will plague us later in the book because there are no formulas to follow in designing effective ads. This problem becomes especially acute when involvement is low and brands are similar, because there really isn't much difference to emphasize.

Look at the ad for Maalox Plus in Figure 6–6. Let's face it; ads for self-medication products often head the list of consumers' most disliked advertising and thus fail to accomplish their intended purposes. Although the point of advertising is to be effective, not to be liked, there is no reason why brand name and benefit cannot be communicated in an enjoyable way. Most people can identify with the guy in the Maalox ad, and the product benefit stands out.

Memorability can be misused, however, if the execution gets in the way of the message. Many readers will remember the much talked about ads for Burger King a few years ago featuring "Herb the Nerd." The theme was "Where's Herb?" Rather than thinking that poor old Herb had never been to Burger King, consumers associated his negative characteristics with the chain itself.[20]

FIGURE 6–4

Badoit Delivers an Uplifting Benefit

Badoit. Il y a une vie après le repas.   BADOIT

Repetition of brand name and benefit can be a fruitful strategy when LPS is the predominant decision-making strategy. Breaking through the competitive noise barrier always has low odds and may take many exposures. Therefore, repetition of brand name and benefit becomes important. More will be said about this in later chapters.

Sales Promotion (In-Store Information)   Many buying decisions are made at the point of purchase based on displays, labels, price reductions, and other types of information. While sales promotion assumes greatest importance when LPS prevails, it also plays a role in EPS.

The role of package labels is worthy of noting here. Information provided through this source can be decisive. A problem occurs when labels that provide crucial information—such as nutrition and safety facts—are misperceived, used only in part, or disregarded. Numerous studies over the years have shown that this can take place, which suggests that manufacturers should use advertising to highlight the importance of label information.

Publicity and Public Relations   Publicity and public relations both involve information that is marketer controlled but normally disseminated through the mass

---

FIGURE 6—5

Two Easy Ways to Serve Broccoli

FIGURE 6–6

The Maalox Moment—A Good Registration of Brand Name and Benefit

media. The objective is to influence sales by gaining public acceptance of company policies and products.

Eastman Kodak, for example, flooded the general media with information on its new disk camera in the 1980s long before it began to advertise. This information dissemination proved to be an effective sales tactic, although the product was later withdrawn for other reasons.

Word-of-Mouth Influence   Consumers frequently turn to others for advice about products and services. The transmitter of information is referred to as an *influential.* More than 30 years of research have shown that word of mouth becomes decisive when one or more of the following conditions exists:[21]

1. The product is difficult to evaluate using objective criteria; hence the experience of others becomes a substitute for actual trial and use.
2. The person needing information lacks the ability to evaluate the product or service.
3. The influential person is more accessible than other sources.
5. Strong social ties exist between transmitter and receiver.
6. The receiver has a high need for social approval.

Anyone can serve as an influential if he or she possesses information that others do not have. In fact, most people play this role at some point in their lives simply because they have been a recent purchaser and are willing to share their experience.

The impact of word of mouth   Research consistently demonstrates that personal influence generally plays a more decisive role than any other information source, primarily because word-of-mouth information has greater credibility.[22] This is especially likely to be the case when the receiver initiates the conversation.[23] We also know that more than one third of all word of mouth is negative and usually is given higher priority and assigned a greater weight in decision making.[24]

Some clues for promotional strategy   Positive word of mouth can be one of the greatest marketing assets a company can have. The opposite occurs, of course, when the content is negative. At the very least, monitoring whether or not word of mouth is occurring and what impact it has is essential for advertisers.

Focus group research is often the best way of monitoring word of mouth. A focus group consists of 8 to 12 people who are guided by a monitor to discuss their experiences, motivations, values, and attitudes. If friends and relatives have shaped their decisions at all, this fact usually emerges clearly in discussion.

Sometimes positive word of mouth can be stimulated. One of the most often used advertising themes is "Ask someone who owns one." It is even possible to trigger discussion of ads by using novel and interesting characters. Certainly the two bucolic characters in ads for Bartles & Jaymes wine coolers have become a part of American folklore, and there is little doubt that these spokespersons accelerated product trial.

At other times, the need is to curb word of mouth, especially when it has become negative. The Exxon Corporation triggered much public hostility by its inept handling of the infamous Exxon *Valdez* oil spill in Alaska. After a long period of silence, company spokespersons were perceived to be denying all culpability for this incident. Not surprisingly, large numbers of consumers boycotted Exxon stations. Much of the uproar could have been prevented by a clear and honest statement of responsibility backed by immediate remedial action. Failure to act in such a way has hurt many otherwise credible companies over the past decade. There seems to be an unwillingness to accept the fact that the general public is rapidly losing confidence and is less willing to forgive irresponsible action.

General Content Media   The consumer can often gain valuable information regarding product features and comparisons through the general content media. It is not uncommon for this source to be decisive in its impact. An example of the importance of the general content media is the negative effect on the sales of some running shoe brands and the positive effects on others after publication of shoe comparisons in *Runner's World*.[25]

ALTERNATIVE EVALUATION

Following the search for information, the next stage in decision-process behavior is to weigh potential product/service alternatives against the evaluative criteria (product attributes) that really count. This differs greatly as one moves from LPS to EPS.

Prechoice alternative evaluation under LPS consists, at most, of a quick comparison of competing brands in terms of one dominant attribute: "Gets out the worst dirt and stains." "Lowest price." "Contains no saturated fats." This usually takes place at the point of sale and is a "go, no-go" decision—alternatives are eliminated if they do not fill the bill on the dominant attribute. Therefore, as we have stressed before, the promotional strategy is relatively straightforward: associate brand name with the dominant attribute, and provide some kind of incentive to trigger trial.

EPS presents greater challenges, however, with multiple evaluative criteria, a more complex weighing process, and evaluation of information through the central route. We will illustrate how alternative evaluation takes place under EPS by using the example of four-wheel-drive vehicles (known as 4×4s) designed for off-road performance—a hot growth market in the automotive industry. Because many purchasers are first-time buyers, an EPS decision process is to be expected. What information is needed? How are available options evaluated?

Each buyer must arrive at a decision as to what attributes are really important. Is interior comfort important? Off-road handling? Low price? Ability to switch instantly from two-wheel to four-wheel drive? In other words, *evaluative criteria* must be established to compare various alternatives. Once these criteria are in place, information processing and alternative evaluation begin in earnest.

First of all, *beliefs* are formed or changed reflecting the buyer's conclusions on how each alternative make of 4 × 4 measures up competitively. Then the total rating for each make forms an *attitude* toward the act of purchasing that alternative. Then, all things being equal, the potential buyer forms an *intention* to purchase the preferred make. We also must recognize that intentions can be affected by social influences and conformity pressures.

Evaluative Criteria

Alternative evaluation requires a set of evaluative criteria by which expected product attributes or benefits can be used to compare the alternatives under consideration. These often form a product-specific representation of underlying motives.

Evaluative criteria can take many forms, ranging from subjective to objective. What would be the most important expected benefits to a potential four-wheel-drive truck purchaser who says, "I like to have the best in everything"? Such a customer most likely will make sure that he or she considers only those makes that rate highest mechanically. What would be most important to the person who agrees that "I'm not afraid to take risks when I do the things I enjoy the most"? Now the most salient criterion might be "demonstrated ability to conquer the toughest terrain."

The Alternative Evaluation Process

Now let's assume that marketing research has isolated a segment of prospective 4 × 4 buyers who use the following criteria (the numbers represent an averaged weighting of the importance of each on a scale ranging from very unimportant [−3] to very important [+3]):

Ease of shifting from two-wheel to four-wheel drive	+3
Engineered to handle rough off-road terrain	+3
Interior comfort of a passenger car	+2
Low frequency of repair	+2
Low price relative to competition	+1

Recalling our discussion in Chapter 5, consumers process EPS information via the central route, meaning that belief and attitude change takes place by active processing of the message content itself. Message execution, although always important, is a secondary consideration in processing information. In central route processing, the individual forms cognitive responses reflecting the extent to which the promotional appeals are accepted or rejected.

In addition, product information generally is processed by brand, with the individual making a decision on each evaluative criterion and forming a brand attitude. As a rule, weakness on one attribute may be offset or compensated by strength on others. Attitude toward purchase, then, is a summed total of ratings making use of all evaluative criteria.

Let's show how this attitude formation process could take place. Prospective buyers are asked to rate the five competitive 4 × 4 models making use of the five criteria they indicated were of importance (highly salient) to them. These ratings appear in Table 6–3. A score of +3 indicates the highest score for any given attribute, and −3 is the lowest mark.

You may be wondering how we arrived at the numbers at the bottom of the table labeled Attitude toward Purchase. We used the formula given by Icek Ajzen and Martin Fishbein in their theory of reasoned action.[26] The formula states that the attitude toward the act of purchase is the sum total of belief ratings given for each of the attributes, taking into account their importance rates.

For example, prospective 4 × 4 buyers rated Make A as tops (+3) in terms of ease of shifting from two-wheel to four-wheel drive. Drive shifting itself was rated +3 as an attribute, indicating that it is very important. These two figures were multiplied, giving a sum of +9. The formula was followed for the other four attributes, giving Make A a winning total score of +25.

Although these numbers may seem to be a bit abstract, look at the profile that is revealed:

Make A: Very strong on the attributes that count most: drive shifting and off-road handling. A bit weaker on comfort and price, two factors that were not very important to those in this market segment.

Make B: Also well rated, but a bit weaker on off-road handling. Negative ratings on interior comfort and price do not affect overall evaluaton very much.

Make C: Very weak on off-road handling and drive shifting. The high rating on low price does not offset the weaknesses.

Make D: Strong on interior comfort, but an also-ran in every other sense.

Make E: Strongest in drive shifting but otherwise very weak.

TABLE 6–3

Summary of Consumer Attitudes toward Five Leading 4 × 4 Vehicle Manufacturers

Attribute	Importance	Manufacturer Ratings				
		A	B	C	D	E
Two-wheel to four-wheel drive shifting	+3	+3	+3	−3	−2	+3
Off-road handling	+3	+3	+2	−2	−3	+1
Frequency of repair	+2	+2	+3	+1	−2	−1
Interior comfort	+2	+1	−2	−1	+3	−1
Low price	+1	+1	−1	+3	+1	+1
Attitude toward purchase		+25	+16	−12	−12	+9

Some Clues for Marketing Strategy

Marketers have four strategic options for influencing the alternative evaluation process: (1) Feature the product's salient attributes, (2) minimize the product's weakness by making the most of its strengths, (3) change the product, and (4) change consumers' awareness and perceptions.

Feature the Salient Attributes   In the 4 × 4 example, makes A and B are in the strongest position because of high ratings on the two attributes that count the most: drive shifting and off-road handling. The objective, then, is to reinforce this highly favorable market position by driving home product superiority. This is precisely the strategy followed by Mitsubishi in featuring its Active Trac 4WD™ "shift-on-the-fly" system (see Figure 6–7).

Brand recall, of course, is the overriding objective of marketing strategy. This recall must go far beyond mere name awareness, because the consumer will be influenced only if the brand name is associated with the most important expected

FIGURE   6–7

For Everything from Light Rain to Rocky Stream Beds

product attributes. Accomplishing this association may require repetition; association rarely happens fully with only one or two exposures.

Once a favorable image is achieved, management also faces the challenge of retaining it in a highly competitive market. Market share can erode virtually overnight. First, continual innovation must be used to maintain the competitive edge. Second, it is necessary to retain share of mind (i.e., present awareness and perception). The best strategy for this is to use consistency of message from one ad to the next.

Minimize Weakness   As Table 6–3 indicates, Make D faces a real dilemma because of its poor ratings on the three most salient attributes. If consumer perceptions indeed reflect reality, all this company can do is make the most of its strength (interior comfort) and hope to attract a few customers who consider this quality to be most important.

Another possible option, but a highly risky one, is to feature and promote an all-new benefit not presently offered by others. Perhaps it would be possible for this manufacturer to offer front-and-back-wheel steering, an option limited to a few passenger cars. This might work if front-and-back steering is indeed perceived as a benefit. Marketing experience has shown, however, that promoting an all-new benefit can be an uphill battle.

Change the Product   It is important to assess through further marketing research whether low ratings on salient criteria are, in fact, true. If Makes C and D are indeed weaker than their competitors in off-road handling, it is time for a product redesign. This then becomes a product policy problem, not a promotional problem.

Change Awareness and Perceptions   If Makes C and D are in reality competitive in drive shifting and off-road handling, the poor ratings indicate low consumer awareness. The challenge, then, is to revamp the promotional strategy. Both companies need to tell their stories on these features with much greater impact.

The Role of Social Influence in Shaping Action

All of us, at times, wish to emulate those whom we greatly admire. And certain purchases confer more social status than others. Certainly such social influences could affect a 4 × 4 purchase. When attitudes and behavior are affected in this way, others serve as a *reference group.*

Three factors determine whether reference groups will be important in a given situation: (1) social visibility, (2) public display and use, and (3) the extent to which the product is a public luxury. These three factors are depicted in Figure 6–8, and you will gain interesting insights as you contemplate the four quadrants.

The ultimate form of social influence was labeled in 1899 by economist Thorstein Veblen as *conspicuous consumption*—wealth put on display for esteem and status. For evidence that this motivation looms large today, one only has to turn to the Hermes boutique in Paris, where shoppers paw over $215 Hermes scarves favored by such status symbols as Queen Elizabeth.

There is evidence, however, that luxury goods are beginning to wane as the ultimate symbols of status. If the analysis in Promotion in Action 6–3 proves to be true, conspicuous consumption soon could be taking some very different forms.

PURCHASE AND OUTCOMES

Purchase and its outcomes are the last two stages in the decision process. Point-of-sale influence, of course, plays a dominant, although differing, role in both EPS and LPS.

Research demonstrates that LPS purchasers use the shelves as their shopping list; they plan no more than one third of their buying decisions. The most rigorous alternative evaluation takes after a product has been purchased and used. New Tide with Bleach makes this advertising claim: "You'll have the cleaning power of the best detergent ever *plus* the whitening power of the best liquid bleach." If Tide fulfills these promises, the outcome will be an intention to repurchase, all things being equal.

FIGURE 6–8

The Determinants of Reference Group Influence

Publicly consumed

Product / Brand	Weak reference group influence (−)	Strong reference group influence (+)
Strong reference group influence (+)	*Public necessities* Influence: Weak product and strong brand Examples: Wristwatch, automobile, man's suit	*Public luxuries* Influence: Strong product and brand Examples: Golf clubs, snow skis, sailboat
Weak reference group influence (−)	*Private necessities* Influence: Weak product and brand Examples: Mattress, floor lamp, refrigerator	*Private luxuries* Influence: Strong product and weak brand Examples: TV game, trash compactor, icemaker

Necessity ————————————————————————— Luxury

Privately consumed

Source: William O. Bearden and Michael J. Etzel, "Reference Group Influence on Product and Brand Purchase Decisions," *Journal of Consumer Research* 9 (September 1982), p. 185, Used by permission.

The same process occurs when EPS has been the decision-making strategy, and satisfaction looms even larger as an outcome. The buyer will compare the performance of the chosen product or service against expectations. If he or she concludes that the best action was taken, the response will be satisfaction. If the response is dissatisfaction, on the other hand, additional information is sometimes used to affirm that the initial choice was correct. Owner's manuals can be a real help in this respect.

If it appears that the product or service is defective, on the other hand, the buyer may complain and seek redress. Any failure by the manufacturer or service provider to act responsibly about a customer complaint can have decidedly negative word-of-mouth impact.[27]

British Airways found out that widespread dissatisfaction can lead to heavy losses. The problem was so bad that the initials BA came to stand for "bloody awful."[28] Management turned the situation around, however, with a complete marketing overhaul. The company motto was changed to read, "To Fly, to Serve." The outcome represented a major switch to building maximum customer satisfaction, and both revenue and profits have increased dramatically.

Promotion in Action

6-3

Demise of the Deluxe and Start of the Meat-Loaf Years?

Writing in 1899, Thorstein Veblen thought naive the idea that the purpose of acquisition is consumption. Wealth, he argued, confers honor; it suggests prowess and achievement. But wealth would have no social meaning if it were simply consumed or possessed.

Veblen's argument was that as wealth spreads, what drives consumers' behavior is increasingly neither subsistence nor comfort but the attainment of "the esteem and envy of fellow men." As economies boomed, the *nouveau riches* joined the *vieux riches* in a Veblenian binge. Hermes ties protruded from every striped collar; Rolexes were worn loose on every languid wrist. In the City of London, people watered their plants with Perrier and watered themselves with Dom Perignon. Louis Vuitton became Tokyo's favorite Frenchman.

Then the bottom fell out. There is evidence that the slump is not cyclical but secular; the consumers are abandoning the excess and ostentation of the 1980s in favor of the antisnob appeal of such firms as The Gap. Pundits are proclaiming "the demise of the deluxe" and the start of the "meat-loaf years."

Maybe the pundits are right, and Veblen wrong. It would mark a big change in human behavior; a growing disenchantment with "immaterial goods" and "personal ornaments" whose "chief purpose is to lend eclat to the person or their wearer by comparison with other persons who are compelled to do without."

If so, the trade's answer will be to make ostentation less ostentatious. BMW has shifted from stressing status to stressing safety. Cartier reports that its Tank watches are as popular as ever, but with a nuance: People now prefer leather straps to gleaming gold and silver ones. Though styles may change, snobbery is forever.

Source: "The Luxury-Goods Trade," *The Economist*, December 26, 1992–January 8, 1993, pp. 95–98. Reprinted by special permission.

Advertising and promotion must create realistic expectations that are backed by product performance. If what is promised is actually achieved, the company stands to gain market loyalty. If the product fails, the consumers' negative votes will soon be felt in market share. This point seems to be quite obvious. Why, then, do so many companies ignore it?

SUMMARY

This chapter continues the discussion of consumer behavior begun in Chapter 5, but focuses on moving from diagnosis to strategy. Starting with need recognition, this chapter demonstrates that the greatest promotional payoff comes when a need already is activated. Therefore, the best strategy is to focus on receptive market segments. Where this is not the case, it is possible to trigger response by showing either the benefits to be gained by pursuing the "ideal" state or the deficiencies of present options and situation.

Information search, of course, largely occurs under extended problem solving (EPS). Many sources can be used, some of which are decisive (major impact on attitudes and choice) and others contributory (some impact but not decisive). This can only be discovered from research focusing on information exposure and use.

Noncommercial sources of information, especially word of mouth, are often more decisive than those under the control of marketers. There are various ways in which word of mouth can be stimulated or influenced to the benefit of the organization.

While there are differences in the way alternative evaluation takes place between EPS and LPS, four major promotional strategies should be: (1) feature the dominant or most salient product/service attribute; (2) minimize the product's weaknesses and stress its strengths, even if they are not dominant; (3) use diagnostic information as the key for product change where necessary; and (4) change consumer awareness and preferences where they are not in accord with reality.

Finally, the chapter demonstrates that buyer satisfaction can be influenced by the nature of the expectations created by promotion. If expectations are either unrealistic or are not fulfilled by the product or service, dissatisfaction and loss of future business can be the unfortunate outcomes.

REVIEW AND DISCUSSION QUESTIONS

1. You are called in to serve as a marketing consultant for a soft drink company that is introducing a new line of fruit drinks featuring 25 percent real fruit juice. The brand name is well known. What type of consumer decision process would you expect in this situation? How would that affect promotional strategy?

2. Would you expect purchasers to develop high brand loyalty once they have tried and liked the new fruit-based soft drink in Question 1? Why or why not? What difference would this make in ongoing promotional strategy?

3. A survey entitled "The American Way of Buying" in *The Wall Street Journal* found that 53 percent of today's car buyers switch brands.[29] This has happened because of the explosive growth in the number of competing models and in the number of automobile showrooms. Also, American manufacturers have suffered from serious competitive inroads made by Japanese and European imports.

You are the manager of a large Ford dealership in a major U.S. city and have been mandated by the owner to do all you can to retain a larger percentage of customers who have bought their cars from you. What will your strategy be?

4. Consumers over the age of 50 use a disproportionately large amount of aspirin but have been largely ignored by advertisers. Therefore, the Bristol-Myers Squibb Bufferin brand is being targeted for the over-50 crowd.[30] Bufferin's advertising emphasizes that people over 50 can lead full lives despite occasional aches and pains that come with age. Print ads ran in women's service magazines and other targeted periodicals such as *Modern Maturity*. Design a point-of-sale strategy that will stimulate brand switching and trial to complement this advertising campaign.

5. A product that used a synthetic substance as a substitute for leather failed in test market. Consumers said that it could not possibly have the same properties as leather, especially flexibility and ability to breathe. Could these perceptions be changed through advertising?

6. Sales of the Audi 5000 slumped drastically after an unfavorable exposure on CBS's "60 Minutes." It was alleged, erroneously as it turned out, that the manufacturer was responsible for unpredictable surges in acceleration that resulted in death-causing accidents. Consumer word of mouth became decidedly negative, and consumers blamed management for irresponsibility. What would you do in this situation if you were the North American marketing manager for this German company?

7. For a period of time, Isuzu cars and trucks were advertised in North America featuring a spokesperson, Joe Isuzu. Joe, as you may remember, made outrageous claims for Isuzu vehicles; his claims were always corrected by words shown on the TV screen as he spoke. Although many people loved these ads, their influence on sales appeared to be negative. Why do you think this took place? What implications can you draw for advertising strategy?

8. All evidence indicates that companies totally dedicated to product quality and customer service come out on top. Problems occur, however, in motivating designers and engineers to view the product from the consumer's perspective. As the CEO, you are becoming increasingly aware that consumers are rejecting your room air-conditioning line because the designers and engineers did not consider the consumer. What can you do to bring about a changed orientation at the engineering and factory levels?

NOTES

1. Ford S. Worthy, "Asia's New Yuppies," *Fortune*, June 4, 1990, p. 225.

2. James F. Engel, Roger D. Blackwell, and Paul W. Miniard, *Consumer Behavior*, 7th ed. (Forth Worth, Tex.: Dryden Press, 1993), p. G-8.

3. See Peter H. Bloch, Daniel L. Sherrell, and Nancy M. Ridgeway, "Consumer Search: An Extended Framework," *Journal of Consumer Research* 13 (June 1986), pp.119–26; Sharon E. Beatty and Scott M. Smith, "External Search Effort: An Investigation Across Several Product Categories," *Journal of Consumer Research* 14 (June 1987), pp. 83–95; and Banwari Mittal, "Must Consumer Involvement Always Imply More Information Search?" in *Advances in Consumer Research*, vol. 16, ed. Thomas K. Srull (Provo, Utah: Association for Consumer Research, 1989), pp. 167–72.

4. Beatty and Smith, "External Search," pp. 83–95.

5. Itamar Simonson, Joel Huber, and John Payne, "The Relationship between Prior Brand Knowledge and Information Acquisition Order," *Journal of Consumer Research* 14 (March 1988), pp. 566–78.

6. See, for example, David H. Furse, Girish N. Punj, and David W. Stewart, "A Typology of Individual Search Strategies among Purchasers of New Automobiles," *Journal of Consumer Research* 10 (March 1984), pp. 417–31.

7. David K. Midgley, "Patterns of Interpersonal Information Seeking for the Purchase of a Symbolic Product," *Journal of Marketing Research* 20 (Winter 1983), pp. 174–83.

8. Sharon E. Beatty and Scott M. Smith, "External Search Effort: An Investigation across Several Product Categories," *Journal of Consumer Research* 14 (June 1987), pp. 83–95.

9. Joel E. Urbany, "An Experimental Examination of the Economics of Information," *Journal of Consumer Research* 13 (September 1986), pp. 257–71.

10. Simonson et al., "The Relationship between Prior Brand Knowledge and Information Acquisition Order," pp. 566–78; and James R. Bettman and C. Whan Park, "Effects of Prior Knowledge and Experience and Phase of the Choice Process on Consumer Decision Processes: A Protocol Analysis," *Journal of Consumer Research* 7 (December 1980), pp. 243–48.

11. For more detail, see Engel et al., *Consumer Behavior,* Chapter 16.

12. John D. Claxton and C. Dennis Anderson, "Energy Information at the Point of Sale: A Field Experiment," in *Advances in Consumer Research,* vol. 7, ed. Jerry C. Olson (Ann Arbor, Mich.: Association for Consumer Research, 1980), pp. 277–82.

13. "Unctuous Auto Salespeople May Be a Thing of the Past, Study Suggests," *Marketing News,* November 23, 1984, pp. 1+.

14. John P. Cortez, "New Lincoln May Make House Calls," *Advertising Age,* November 30, 1992, p. 21.

15. Lena H. Sun, "A Cosmetic Change in China, Avon Sales Are Flying in the Face of Socialism," *The Philadelphia Inquirer,* July 3, 1991, p. 8-E.

16. "Study Tracks Housewares Buying, Information Sources," *Marketing News,* October 14, 1983, p. 16.

17. *A Study of Media Involvement* (New York: Magazine Publishers' Association, 1979).

18. "Whirlpool Corporation," in Roger D. Blackwell, James F. Engel, and W. Wayne Talarzyk, *Contemporary Cases in Consumer Behavior,* rev. ed. (Hinsdale, Ill.: Dryden Press, 1984), pp. 365–88.

19. Jack Trout and Al Ries, "The Decline and Fall of Advertising," *Advertising Age,* June 26, 1989, p. 20.

20. "Marketers Blunder Their Way through the 'Herb Decade,'" *Advertising Age,* February 13, 1989, p. 3.

21. See Engel et al., *Consumer Behavior,* Chapter 5.

22. For an extensive review, see Linda L. Price and Lawrence F. Feick, "The Role of Interpersonal Sources and External Search: An Informational Perspective," in *Advances in Consumer Research,* vol. 11, ed. Thomas C. Kinnear (Provo, Utah: Association for Consumer Research, 1984), pp. 250–55.

23. Hubert Gatignon and Thomas S. Robertson, "A Propositional Inventory for New Diffusion Research," *Journal of Consumer Research* 11 (March 1985), pp. 849–67.

24. Marsha L. Richins, "Word of Mouth Communication as Negative Information," in *Advances in Consumer Research,* vol. 11, ed. Thomas C. Kinnear (Provo, Utah: Association for Consumer Research, 1984), pp. 697–702.

25. Sam Harper, "Athletic Shoe Surveys Run into Industry Dispute," *Advertising Age,* September 22, 1980, p. 22.

26. Icek Ajzen and Martin Fishbein, *Understanding Attitudes and Predicting Social Behavior* (Englewood Cliffs, N.J.: Prentice Hall, 1980).

27. For a review of research findings, see Steven P. Brown and Richard F. Beltramini, "Consumer Complaining and Word of Mouth Activities: Field Evidence," *Advances in Consumer Research,* vol. 16, ed. Thomas K. Srull (Provo, Utah: Association for Consumer Research, 1989), pp. 9–16.

28. For the story of BA's woes, see Kenneth Labich, "The Big Comeback at British Airways," *Fortune,* December 5, 1988, pp. 163–64.

29. Paul Ingrassia, "Is Buying a Car a Choice or a Chore?" *The Wall Street Journal,* October 24, 1989, p. B1.

30. Pamela Winters, "Bufferin Aims at 50-Plus," *Advertising Age,* October 23, 1989, p. 4.

Chapter

7

Market Segmentation and Competitive Positioning

PASTA SAUCE MAKERS USE SEGMENTATION AND POSITIONING

Although true Italians still may cringe at the very thought of using pasta sauce from a jar, the $850 million pasta sauce market indicates that many Americans are using it. In an age when health and convenience often rule, pasta and ready-made pasta sauces are increasingly popular. According to Arbitron/SAMI, whereas 1979 sauce production totaled 545 million pounds, 1992 sauce production topped 2 billion pounds, and sales have been increasing at a 5 to 10 percent rate over the last five years. Ragú, Prego, Classico, Hunt's, and Aunt Millie's are the market's top five brands. Sales totals were approximately $520 million for Ragú, $275 million for Prego, $70 million for Classico, $45 million for Hunt's, and $30 million for Aunt Millie's.

The high volume in the sauce segment attracts a lot of promotional dollars. The top five sauce brands spent about $55 million on advertising. TV accounted for $45 million of this media expense. New products and line extensions are prime targets for consumer promotions, with battles for market share and shelf space expected to be heated. Keeping this in mind, the top five brand marketers use segmentation and positioning to enhance their promotional efforts in order to increase their market share and sales.

Market leader Ragú, which holds half of the sauce market, spent about $22 million per year on advertising, with $15.3 million going to network TV. Pursuing a strategy of protecting its market share, Ragú has remained "king of the shelf" through its ability to adapt quickly to a changing market. Until Hunt came out with Prima Salsa in the mid-1970s, Ragú and Chef Boyardee dominated the national market. The new sauce was positioned as "heartier," so Ragú countered with Thick & Zesty Ragú. Prima Salsa was pulled off the market by the early 1980s. The Campbell Soup Company introduced Prego in 1982, stressing its homemade taste. Ragú countered with its Homestyle line. When "chunky" became the rage in spaghetti sauce, Ragú introduced its Chunky Garden Style sauce with chunks of tomatoes and vegetables. "Thick and rich" sauce was the style in 1987, so Ragú premiered its Thick & Hearty line. Ragú's versatility enables the leading sauce maker to execute effectively its strategy of keeping up with the market and maintaining its share.

Since its 1982 entrance into the market, Prego has positioned itself as a high-quality sauce that is "better than Ragú." Executing an image campaign, Prego ads feature a visual comparison with Ragú. Prego and Ragú are simultaneously poured over pasta; Prego is the thicker sauce. Gary Fassak, director of marketing of Italian food products at Campbell, remarked, "We're trying to build long-term added value and get the word out that our sauce, in testing, tastes better than Ragú Old World Style." In marketing Prego, Campbell uses geographic segmentation. The company's regional marketing system tailors promotional programs for each of its 21 marketing areas. According to Fassak, "The idea is to get some attention on what the local marketing needs are, particularly in the area of consumer and trade promotion. We try to tie back to the advertising, with the basic notion of Prego being a high-quality sauce."

Positioned as a line of authentic regional Italian pasta sauces, Classico stands apart from the other market leaders. Priced 40 to 50 cents above the other major brands, Classico is out to prove that class sells. Classico's promotional campaign centers on its regional Italian recipes, which are part of the sauces' packaging. The jars are shaped differently than those of other sauces, and the label is designed for "old-world appeal." Classico targets the slightly upscale, 25- to 54-year-old segment that is willing to pay more for a premium product. TV ads are shot in Italy to further stress the product's authenticity. Maxine Houghton, marketing director for Prince Foods Canning Division of Borden, describes the brand's strategy as a "pretty simple program of television and couponing to get trial and create awareness." Classico has also used ads in upscale magazines such as *Bon Appetit, Southern Living,* and *Sunset.*

Positioning itself as a traditional name in tomato products, Hunt-Wesson Foods, Inc., uses couponing and promotions to retain its number four position. Hunt-Wesson considers print an important advertising medium since recipes using its sauces can be featured to stimulate consumers' interest. *Good Housekeeping, Redbook,* and *Ladies Home Journal* are perennial favorites. In an attempt to distinguish its market position, Hunt-Wesson is targeting the "busy family" market with Minute Gourmet, its new line of specialized sauces for the microwave. Each package includes one of six sauces and a cooking bag—consumers just add their choice of meat. The target segment includes busy singles, couples, and working parents.

Aunt Millie's, a 42-year-old regional brand also owned by Prince Foods, captured the number five spot due to its solid base of loyal regional users. Sold in only 12 markets. Aunt Millie's sauce generated about $30 million in sales in 1992 with less than $100,000 in ad expenditures, all of which went into newspapers. Positioning itself as the leading brand with "no sugar or starch added," Aunt Millie's original sauce has long attracted the health-conscious segment of one- and two-person households. Targeting "the sweet tooth of American children," Aunt Millie's has developed a family-style sauce that is sweeter and chunkier. According to Prince's Houghton, "Kids love sweet things and sweet sauces, so we brought Aunt Millie's Family Style out to attract the larger families that eat a ton of spaghetti sauce." This new product should increase family volume usage.

Source: "Mangia! Mangia!" *Marketing & Media Decisions,* June 1989, pp. 83–93; updated to 1993 with industry advertising and market reports, and information provided by industry experts.

THE CONCEPT OF MARKET SEGMENTATION

The pasta sauce marketers discussed in the chapter opener are following a deliberate policy of market segmentation. *Market segmentation* is defined as:

> The process of dividing large heterogeneous markets into smaller, homogeneous subsets of people or businesses with similar needs and/or responsiveness to marketing mix offerings.[1]

In a sense, each of us is a distinct market segment because no two people are exactly alike in their motivations, needs, decision processes, and buying behavior. Obviously, it is not feasible to tailor a specific marketing mix to every individual. Thus, the objective is to identify groups within the broader market that are sufficiently similar in needs and responses to promotional and other marketing mix actions to warrant separate marketing treatment. The marketer then seeks to correlate the groups defined by their needs and responsiveness to other characteristics such as demographics or geographic location.

More specifically, effective market segmentation requires five steps, which are listed below.

1. *Identify the needs structure of the consumer population at the individual level.* This is usually done by selecting a sample from the overall population and measuring individual consumer needs as they relate to the product or service of interest. Thus, the promotional manager at this point will have many needs profiles that represent the diverse needs of the whole group of consumers.

2. *Group the consumers into homogeneous subgroups or segments based on their needs profile.* The intention in this step is to form groups of consumers that are very homogeneous within the groups in terms of needs and very heterogeneous across the groups. This is usually done with the use of some sort of clustering computer program that can quickly do the calculations on the sample of consumers that are necessary to form the homogeneous needs profile groups. For example, in the car market, this might yield one segment whose primary need is large people and cargo capacity, while another segment's primary needs might be for fuel economy.

3. *The identification of factors that are correlated with the needs-based subgroups or segments of the market.* These correlates include such variables as demographic, lifestyle, geography, and consumption patterns. Note in the pasta sauce example that began this chapter that the Classico brand is said to be targeted at the "25- to 54-year-old segment." What is really happening here is that this age profile is correlated in a useful fashion to the need for higher quality sauce that this segment manifests. Be careful with this issue, because many marketers often loosely discuss segments in terms of the variables that correlate with the needs and not with the real needs themselves. It is the needs that form the segment and the correlates that allow one to access the segment with promotional effort.

4. *The selection of target markets.* This is the selection of the segment or group of segments for which a specific promotional program or programs and other elements of the marketing mix will be developed. The selected target segment or segments are those that offer the greatest opportunity for profitability under a given set of market and competitive conditions.

5. *The development of a "positioning" for the product or service offering within the selected segment or segments.* Positioning addresses the issue of how consumers in the targeted segment or segments are supposed to perceive the marketer's product or service offering as compared to those of competitors. Positioning is discussed in detail later in this chapter.

These five steps require a careful analysis of buyer motivation and behavior as discussed in the previous chapters. The first three steps are designed to identify usable market segments. In a sense, the identification of usable market segments is one of the most practical payoffs in marketing research. In this chapter, we will discuss the first three steps together in the next section and steps 4 and 5 in the following two sections, but first we will discuss the issue of usable market segments.

Criteria of Usable Segments

Sometimes segmentation identification produces results that are not of much use in promotional planning. For a market segment to be usable, five criteria should be met: (1) The segment should be of sufficient size and market potential to warrant expenditure of marketing funds; (2) the segment's market potential must be measurable; (3) it must be possible to reach or access the segment through available media; (4) the segment should show clear variations in market behavior in comparison with other segments (i.e., the response of the segment to promotional variables must be different); and (5) the existence of the segment must be durable.

Sufficient Size   If a total market consisted of 1 million persons, it probably has 1 million segments. Obviously, such a conclusion is of no use, because a segment must offer sufficient size and market potential to be of any significance. A leading manufacturer of paper products was confronted by this problem when it introduced a new and demonstrably different crayon in 11 test markets. Although the product appealed to a certain segment of users more than to others, it appeared that only 2 percent of a $30 million market could be captured. The possible sales revenue did not warrant the expenditures necessary to produce and market the product.

Measurability   A key to assessing the size of a segment is the degree to which its purchase potential can be measured. For example, the market potential for machine vision systems in factory automation of circuit boards in the electronics industry is unknown. The size of paint inspection systems in the auto industry for the same machine vision technology is accurately known. The latter target is a more useful one for promotional planning because some sense of the likely payback is possible.

Reachability or Accessibility   It is also critical that the marketer design a promotional program that can be delivered to the identified segment. For example, the marketers of Sunkist lemons found little or no demographic correlation with the heavy consumption of lemons. This made targeting heavy lemon users with demographic-based media such as magazines very inefficient.

Market Response Differences   For any segmentation scheme to be useful, the consumers in the segments must in general respond differently to variations in promotional activity directed at the segment. Thus, we have Coke using various versions—country, rock, blues, and so on—of its basic musical theme. The country music–oriented radio audience responds well to a country theme but not as well to some general theme or to a rock version. Without this variation between segments, the market segmentation has no point at all.

Durability It is also imperative that the identified and targeted segments exist over a long enough period of time to warrant the cost and effort of developing specific promotional activities and other marketing mix dimensions to meet the needs of the consumers in the segment.

BASES FOR REACHING MARKET SEGMENTS

Once the market segments have been formed based on the clustering of similar consumer needs structures, a key issue becomes how to reach these consumers. A great variety of factors can be used to aid the promotional manager in reaching the targeted segment. The key is that the selected factor or factors, sometimes called *market descriptors,* must be correlated with the fundamental needs that defined the segments. These descriptors do not define the segments themselves, but serve as a basis to reach the segments. Often marketers refer to these descriptors as "segmentation variables." Again, be careful with this because these descriptors do not in themselves define the segments. Only the basic needs structure defines the segments. The descriptors must (1) be correlated with the needs-defined segments and (2) be associated with particular media or other promotional devices. For example, a needs-based segment might demand "smooth ride" in a car. The question for the promotional manager then becomes how to reach this segment to inform them of how a particular vehicle fits this need. A segment descriptor could be "age." People over 55 might have a high need for smooth ride. Thus, age fulfills the first requirement because it is correlated with the needs structure of the segment. In turn, the over-55 age group is highly associated with certain magazines such as *Modern Maturity.* Thus, age also fulfills the second requirement of being associated with particular media.

Many of these segment descriptors are itemized in Table 7–1. In this table, the bases for reaching segments are classified as being geographic, demographic, psychographic, or behavioral. The first two classes describe the consumer's "state of being," whereas the third and fourth are related to the consumer's "state of mind."

Not all of the bases listed have proved equally useful in developing promotional strategies. Bases of a demographic or geographic type, together with selected psychographic and behavioral bases such as product usage rate, attitude toward brand, and preferred values and benefits, are the most widely used in current practice. Thus, our discussion here of bases for reaching market segments will be limited to these, with particular attention being paid to the problems associated with measurement and analysis. Market segmentation is not difficult to understand conceptually, but real problems may arise when applying the concepts.

Geographic Variables

Very significant differences exist in the usage of many products based on geographic location, both across countries and within the United States. Thus, promotional managers commonly use a geographic basis to form segments. Indeed, one of the significant trends in promotional activity over the last several years has been the development of regionalization of promotional programs. Promotion in

TABLE 7–1

Major Segmentation Variables and Their Typical Breakdowns

Variable	Typical Breakdowns
Geographic	
Region	Pacific, Mountain, West North Central, West South Central, East North Central, East South Central, South Atlantic, Middle Atlantic, New England
County size	A, B, C, D
City or SMSA size	Under 5,000; 5,000–20,000; 20,000–50,000; 50,000–100,000; 100,000–250,000; 250,000–500,000; 500,000–1,000,000; 1,000,000–4,000,000; 4,000,000 or over
Density	Urban, suburban, rural
Climate	Northern, southern
Demographic	
Age	Under 6, 6–11, 12–19, 20–34, 35–49, 50–64, 65+
Sex	Male, female
Family size	1–2, 3–4, 5+
Family life cycle	Young, single; young, married, no children; young married, youngest child under 6; young, married, youngest child 6 or over; older, married, with children; older, married, no children under 18; older, single; other
Income	Under $10,000; $10,000–15,000; $15,000–$20,000; $20,000–25,000; $25,000–$30,000; $30,000–$50,000; $50,000 and over
Occupation	Professional and technical; managers, officials, and proprietors; clerical, sales; craftspeople, foremen; operatives; farmers; retired; students; housewives, unemployed
Education	Grade school or less; some high school; high school graduate; some college; college graduate
Religion	Catholic, Protestant, Jewish, other
Race	White, Black, Oriental
Nationality	American, British, French, German, Scandinavian, Italian, Latin American, Middle Eastern, Japanese
Psychographic	
Social class	Lower lowers, upper lowers, working class, middle class, upper middles, lower uppers, upper uppers
Lifestyle	Straights, swingers, longhairs
Personality	Compulsive, gregarious, authoritarian, ambitious

TABLE 7-1

Concluded

Variable	Typical Breakdowns
Behavioral	
Occasions	Regular occasion, special occasion
Benefits	Quality, service, economy
User status	Nonuser, ex-user, potential user, first-time user, regular user
Usage rate	Light user, medium user, heavy user
Loyalty status	None, medium, strong, absolute
Readiness stage	Unaware, aware, informed, interested, desirous, intending to buy
Attitude toward product	Enthusiastic, positive, indifferent, negative, hostile

Source: Philip Kotler, *Marketing Management: Analysis, Planning, Implementation, & Control,* 7th ed. (Englewood Cliffs, N.J.: Prentice Hall, 1991), p. 269. Reprinted by permission of Prentice Hall, Inc.

Action 7-1 presents an example of this regional approach to segmentation. Since the basic consumer need is correlated with geography and the promotional effort can be directed regionally, this approach satisfies the two reachability criteria.

For geography to be most useful as a basis for reaching segments, the promotional manager must calculate the relative sales possibilities in the various potential geographic segments. For example, if a product is sold nationwide, how much promotional effort should be expended in Chicago relative to Phoenix? This key question can be answered only when market potentials are computed, for effort is generally allocated in proportion to potential, all other things being equal.

Several different potentials might be computed for a given product: (1) volume attainable under ideal conditions (i.e., if all efforts were perfectly adapted to the environment); (2) the relative capacity of a market to absorb the products of an entire industry such as the major appliance industry; (3) the relative size of market for a company's type of product (i.e., sales of color television sets versus stereo sets); and (4) the actual sales a company can expect. The last category, of course, is the equivalent of the sales forecast for a firm, or the sales volume that can be expected if the firm continues on its present course. Potential, on the other hand, refers to sales possibilities rather than expected sales and is of greater significance for purposes of demand analysis. Although forecasting is necessary in determining allocations and budgets, an extended discussion of it is beyond the scope of this book.

This is not to say, however, that potential is the sole basis for allocating resources because potentials for industry sales do not reveal the competitive structure of a market or the firm's ability to make inroads. Boston, for example,

Geographic Segmentation: Frito-Lay Advances with Regional Marketing

Regional marketing is an increasingly popular strategy in our distinctly diverse nation. "Different strokes for different folks" is an old adage worth remembering. A product that does poorly in one area of the country may have great market potential in another. Matching regional interests with the right marketing mix can significantly increase a product's sales volume.

Frito-Lay is a firm believer in the regional marketing approach. After testing the regional idea, the snack food unit of PepsiCo., Inc., decided to proceed full speed at the national level. Frito-Lay allocated 30 percent of its total advertising and promotion budget to regional marketing. Previous allocations had never exceeded 10 percent. Frito-Lay divided the country into seven zones. The marketing managers in charge of each zone were given greater decision-making authority. The company's Dallas headquarters facilitated local marketing decisions by providing more analytical assistance to each manager.

At first glance, Frito-Lay's impressive 50 percent share of the $7 billion salty-snack industry may not seem to demand such a specialized marketing approach. But stiff competition from local and regional snack companies alters this picture. According to Leo Kiely, senior vice president, marketing and sales, Frito-Lay may have a 50 percent share of the potato chip segment on a national basis, but the company's share is 30 percent or less in half of its markets. This is where the regional approach can build sales.

Steve Bryan, vice president, marketing planning, explained Frito-Lay's strategy: "We're approaching regional marketing from an evolutionary rather than revolutionary perspective. Our objective is to do what we need to do to be competitive by geography and to tailor our programs to customer needs."

Although Frito-Lay's initial efforts focused on price and promotion rather than separate regional advertising and product development, the company is very aware of different regional taste preferences. To capitalize on these differences, Frito-Lay is testing new flavors and line extensions in key regional markets.

Dwight Riskey, vice president, marketing research and new business, gave Doritos Salsa Rio as an example. The spicy tomato-flavored chip is being test marketed in the Northwest, where tortilla chips sell well. New Orleans, which has long preferred kettle-cooked chips, is an ideal market for Crunch Tators, Frito-Lay's entry into the "hard-bite" potato chip segment. The company's regional strategy also sent the promotion of its Delta Gold potato chips to the Southeast, where lighter, golden chips are preferred.

Emmanuel Goldman, analyst at Montgomery Securities, thinks Frito-Lay is on to something: "Frito is carving up the country into various segments and targeting programs much finer than ever before. This strategy gives different pricing by region and a different product push. It's great for spot advertising. This is for real, and there's going to be more of it."

Source: "Frito Makes Regional Advances," *Advertising Age,* July 4, 1988, p. 21.

might appear to offer high potential, whereas in reality competitors are so entrenched that inroads would be impossible. Ideally, then, potentials must be augmented with information about the competitive structure as well as the firm's previous experience in the market. The goal, of course, is to make an optimum allocation of resources to alternative markets. This can be done only with great precision with a reliable estimate of the impact of a given level of promotional expenditure on market share. An array of markets in terms of potential provides a workable estimate of probable response to sales efforts. The methods used to compute potentials will be discussed in Chapter 9.

Demographic Characteristics

The market potential for any product is equal to the number of people who want or need that alternative and have the resources to obtain it. Motivation to buy is to some extent both determined and revealed by the demographic life position of the person (age, education, income, sex, and so on), as is ability to pay. Of the many possible demographic bases for segmentation itemized in Table 7–1, the most widely used are age, income, and sex.

Age   A buyer's wants and ability to buy obviously change as he or she ages and passes through various stages in life, and this provides useful clues for marketing strategy. Jergens's Aloe & Lanolin lotion proved to be most appealing to women over 35. This is not surprising, given the preference of younger consumers for a medicated skin conditioner. There would have been little to gain if the younger market had been the target of efforts to change preferences, so the logical strategy was to target the older segment and capitalize on that opportunity. We noted in Chapter 4 that Carnival Cruise Lines targets two distinct consumer segments based on age.

Income   Income segmentation has long been used by marketers with generally favorable results. For example, the Jaguar is targeted to those making about $100,000 per year, and the media used include mostly national magazines and Sunday newspaper supplements appealing to this affluent segment. This effort is confined largely to the two coasts, reflecting the geographic segmentation of the market. One must be cautious in assuming that income is a reflection of the consumer's social class. This obviously is not the case, given the high wages now earned by those in the trades and various blue-collar occupations. Therefore, income by itself usually is not an accurate basis for segmentation.

Sex   It is obvious that some products appeal more to men than to women, and vice versa. With the emergence of the working woman and greater female initiative as a result of the equal rights movement, women have become a target for more products. Almost half of all cars sold in the United States are purchased by women for their own use; this requires major changes in the promotional activities of car companies. In addition, changing sex roles have resulted in the necessity to promote many grocery products to men.

Demographics as a Clue to Lifestyle

Demographic data can provide some interesting insight into lifestyle differences between segments. For example, the heavy buyers of Kentucky Fried Chicken have this demographic profile:

Two working spouses.

More children than average.

Significantly higher family income than average.

Average educational attainment.

Middle-class occupational status.

It is not difficult to conclude that time is at a premium for members of this household. Undoubtedly, they are willing to incur the extra cost of purchasing prepared food in return for the gains in leisure time. Given the relatively high-income status, it is also probable that they would be responsive to buying with a credit card, and so on.

Figure 7–1 presents examples of ads that are demographically based in terms of their target audience and theme. The "no more ouchies" ad uses age, while the Midas ad uses gender as its main descriptor variable.

The usefulness of both geographic and demographic segmentation working together is best illustrated in the description of Claritas's geodemographic target marketing system, PRIZM.[2] Using census and other secondary data on lifestyles, the system develops population clusters based on demographic information and ties these data back to a specific geographic location. The geographic analysis is available at the block group, census tract, minor civil division, postal carrier route, and ZIP code levels. The levels used in any particular case are those consistent with statistical reliability.

Based on this analysis, Claritas has divided the United States into 12 social groups and 40 lifestyle clusters. For example, two of the social groups are "educated, affluent executives and professionals in elite metro suburbs" and "mid-scale, child-raising, blue-collar families in remote suburbs and towns." Within the first social group above, two of the lifestyle clusters are "blue blood estates" and "money and brains." Within the second social group above, two of the lifestyle clusters are "blue-collar nursery" and "middle America." The names of the clusters are short-form descriptors. A detailed description is available of the characteristics of those composing these groups and clusters. In addition, the geographic location of all those assigned to a specific group or cluster is known to the group block, tract, or ZIP code level as noted above. A customer or potential target customer can be assigned to a cluster based on the street address, and then marketing activity can be directed to the relevant cluster's geographic location. For example, in the 77-square-block area of Manhattan's ZIP code 10019, PRIZM can target eight different lifestyle clusters by specific blocks.

The power of PRIZM to aid promotion activity is high. PRIZM can be applied to retail location analysis, direct-mail promotions and catalogs, media planning, and prospect identification. For example, a publisher of a very upscale magazine could mail a subscription promotion to only the relevant block addresses in the 10019 ZIP code of Manhattan mentioned above. A mailing to the other blocks would be a waste of money. The promotion efficiencies of this approach are large. This illustrates the use of an advanced marketing database to reach the desired needs-based segment.

Worldstyle, a new fashion magazine, is convinced that the approach of PRIZM is effective.[3] *Worldstyle* has decided to use demographic data to target "the classiest zip codes" in the top 25 retail markets. The magazine will be distributed strictly as a Sunday newspaper insert and will be zoned exclusively to women with household incomes of $25,000 and higher. If initial estimates prove true, this strategy will provide a circulation of 3.3 million households and total readership of about 7 million, making *Worldstyle* the world's largest circulation fashion magazine. According to data from Simmons Market Research Bureau and Audit Bureau of Circulation, *Worldstyle* will reach 550,000 homes with incomes of over $25,000 in the New York City market alone. *Cosmopolitan* and *Mademoiselle* have circulations of 163,000 and 83,000, respectively, in this category. Subtitled "The

---

FIGURE 7–1

Examples of Demographically Based Advertisements

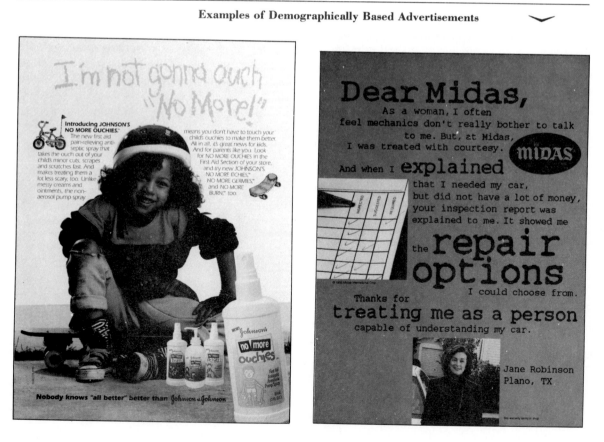

International Fashion Forecast Magazine," *Worldstyle* will target a certain upscale taste level by emphasizing a lasting, classic look and balancing high style with reality. Based on the newspapers' audiences, this target segment will share the following characteristics:

Median age of 36.5 years.

Average income of $41,950.

75 percent employed outside the home.

60 percent with a college education.

Women in this group are likely to fit *Worldstyle*'s image. Many are established career women who have a professional need for classic clothes but do not have time to shop for them. Most appreciate and want both high quality and style, and they have the financial status to afford *Worldstyle*'s fashions.

Psychographic Characteristics

In the psychographic approach to reaching segments, consumers are differentiated on the basis of differences in patterns by which people live and spend time and money. The requirement for this type of segment descriptor is that the segment needs are correlated with these psychographic characteristics. These patterns represent consumer lifestyle. Some analysts include social class as a part of lifestyle (see Table 7–1), whereas others classify it as a demographic variable. For the most part, psychographics or lifestyle refers here to consumer attitudes, interests, and opinions (often referred to as AIO measurements) and the way in which these affect buying activities. For example, consider the heavy users of eye makeup. Demographically, they are younger and better educated than average and are more likely to be employed outside the home. This tells us something, but notice how much is added when users are differentiated from nonusers in psychologically graphic terms:

Highly fashion conscious.

Desire to be attractive.

Oriented to the future.

Interested in art and culture.

Interested in world travel.

Not home centered.

Relative rejection of the traditional.

These data, of course, say nothing about awareness or attitudes toward specific brands or types of eye makeup. Their usefulness in promotional strategy is in providing clues about the type of person the prospects are and the way they should be depicted in the message.

One could use this psychographic profile in a mechanical way and depict an overdressed woman with a man worshipping at her feet as they sit in an art institute in Paris with a letter from mother crumpled on the floor. Needless to say, this example is extreme, but an appeal to the wrong type of person and in contradictory settings will trigger selective screening of the message by the prospect.

Two companies have recently discovered psychographic segments that the cosmetic industry had previously overlooked: women concerned with their sensitivity to cosmetics and women who are unimpressed by sexy models and big names.[4] Bausch & Lomb has introduced a line of fragrance-free cosmetics for women with sensitive eyes. Rubigo Cosmetics has targeted women who have no "covergirl aspirations" but want to look good in their own way.

Sheila Rose, director of marketing and sales for Bausch & Lomb, said that her company estimates that 78 percent of all women have some sensitivity to cosmetics and that this sensitivity influences at least 33 percent of all women when they choose eye cosmetics. With its prominent reputation as a maker of optical products, Bausch & Lomb believes that cosmetics are a natural extension for the company and a good way to leverage the Bausch & Lomb name.

The new line is not limited to women who wear contact lenses. Many firms, including Aziza, have recently launched cosmetic lines exclusively for women who wear contacts, but not all women who wear contacts have problems with their cosmetics. According to Rose, "Obviously women with contact lenses are attracted to us, but there are other women who are concerned with the cosmetics they're wearing." Rose continued by saying that Bausch & Lomb wants to attract "all women who use cosmetics five times a week." The majority of this audience is projected to be between the ages of 25 and 45.

Rose Mary Worthen, executive vice president of Rubigo Cosmetics, remarked that many women look at famous models and say, "Okay, I'm at this age and no matter how hard I try, I'm not going to look like that girl." Worthen was a mother long before she went into cosmetics and believes that she can "fully appreciate what a working woman is looking for." Rubigo does not want to neglect teenagers or older women. Worthen says that the cosmetic industry reaches further than the 18- to 34-year-old range. Older women want to look good, too, and even 11-year-olds have significant buying power.

Both companies sought an upscale and fashionable image. They altered their packaging, displays, and product selection accordingly. Stylish colors took their place next to standard shades. Ad campaigns were designed and distribution channels were selected. Bausch & Lomb went to the "slick" look. Its novel TV commercial shows no women, only the admiring looks of dashing men at a party. Print ads in *Vogue, Cosmopolitan, Glamour, Self,* and *Mademoiselle* feature the new products under the headline, "Introducing Bausch & Lomb cosmetics. The perfect blend of art and science." This embellishes but does not mar the company's "clean" image.

Rubigo went to a more classic look. The company's entrance into the cosmetic market was a great success. Its original product is its now-signature powder blush in an urn. These urns were sold exclusively in department stores and netted $3 million in sales during their first year. The company later reduced the size of the urn and went to mass merchandising. Its strategy was to become more visual and create an aura around the product. Rubigo's print and TV ads revolve around the distinctive urn, capitalizing on its target segment's desire for a unique and classy product.

Figure 7–2 presents examples of lifestyle-based themes. The Mazda Miata ad captures the lifestyle dynamic of its young female target market, and the Ban Clear AP ad gives the flavor of the active lifestyle of its target segment.

The makeup example above is an illustration of *product-specific* AIO analysis. That is, the AIO scales were tailor-made for the product. Another type of AIO scale is based on *general patterns* of lifestyle.

Generalized psychographic segments usually are concerned with such issues as (1) how people take control of their circumstances, (2) how they approach action, and (3) how they make judgments about information. Each of these segment descriptors is then correlated with brand usage, demographics, desired benefits, and other data to aid the selection of the best target market for specific products and services.

Evidence to date indicates that lifestyle segmentation is most appropriate when the following circumstances are present:

FIGURE 7–2

Examples of Lifestyle Themes in Advertisements.

- The product primarily offers psychological gratification.
- Product performance cannot be evaluated objectively.
- High involvement is present with most buyers.
- Advertising is the major tool in the marketing mix.
- Consumers are willing to switch brands when not completely satisfied.
- The product category is not dominated by one or two brands.
- The product is not purchased primarily on the basis of price.

Behavioral Variables

In the behavioral method of reaching needs-based segments, buyers are differentiated on the basis of their knowledge of and attitude toward a product or its attributes, and of their response to and use of the product. It is finding widespread use. Our discussion here is confined to segmentation by benefits sought and by product usage rates.

Benefit Segmentation

Considerable attention was focused in earlier chapters on the attributes used (or benefits desired) by consumers in the process of alternative evaluation. In benefit segmentation, the first step is to determine these desired benefits. The consumer then assesses, from his or her perspective, whether or not available products fill the bill. If not, there may be a market niche that can be filled by careful product design and marketing strategy. In effect, then, the consumer sets the agenda.

Benefit segmentation played a large part in the successful introduction of Bacardi Tropical Fruit Mixers.[5] Market research, which included numerous focus groups, found an unmet consumer need that Bacardi could fill. Over the past five years, people have been drinking more light alcohol (e.g., rum and vodka) and less dark alcohol (e.g., bourbon and scotch), and drinking less alcohol overall. The popularity of tropical drinks has exploded in bars and restaurants. Bacardi saw that an easily accessible, in-home alternative would have vast market potential.

Lacking the specific expertise to develop and distribute the product, Bacardi entered into a partnership with Coca-Cola Foods, Inc. Bacardi brought its well-established name and Caribbean heritage. Coca-Cola brought a highly developed technical department, a well-established sales force, and direct access to the grocery distribution system.

The two companies combined resources to produce a revolutionary new product that tasted homemade and was identical to the drinks purchased at bars and restaurants. In comparison to the powdered-mix alternatives on the market, Bacardi mixers provided superior quality at a lower per-ounce price. Coke and Bacardi chose the slogan "Perfectly simple. Simply perfect." Advertising emphasized taste, convenience, and Caribbean imagery. Packaging stressed that the product was made by Bacardi and was a mixer, not an alcoholic beverage. This positioning communicated the product's superiority and separated it from everything else in its category.

How did these efforts add up? Within one year, Bacardi mixer sales were equal to the entire bottled mixer category. As Caryn McQuilkin, marketing manager for Coca-Cola Foods, Inc., stated, "What we ended up with is perfectly simple and simply perfect—a great product and a great price, with communication in terms of good advertising and beautiful packaging." By determining and fulfilling an unmet consumer need, Bacardi and Coca-Cola revolutionized the bottled mixer industry.

Product Usage Rates

Promotional managers often find consumer usage rates for a specific product category helpful in reaching segments in the market. Different strategies are then required for those in various usage categories. Again, the requirement is that the basic needs of consumers are correlated with the descriptor, product usage rates.

Nonusers of Product Category   It is important to determine whether or not nonusers offer a potential market. Frequently the problem is only lack of awareness. If this is the case, an opportunity may exist to build familiarity through promotion and thereby lay the groundwork for later sales. In other instances, a basically favorable attitude may exist but may be constrained by opposing forces from the environment. For example, if the problem is concern over financing, advertising or personal selling could possibly stimulate sales by promoting the offer of easy credit.

Most likely the analysis of nonusers will document segments that will not respond, regardless of the strategy. There may be a basic conflict between the company offer and evaluative criteria, lifestyles, and so on. Every attempt should be made to avoid such segments if possible, because the probable return would not be worth the expense.

Users of the Product but Not the Company Brand   The purpose of this inquiry is to assess the probability of making inroads into competitors' markets. If their offerings or images are weak in certain respects or fail to satisfy important evaluative criteria, it may be possible to increase market share. On the other hand, competitors may be invulnerable in certain segments, especially if there is brand loyalty based on psychological commitment or centrality. The best strategy always is to appeal to the waverers (those whose commitment is diminishing) rather than to attack an entrenched competitor head-on.

Regardless of competitive market shares, many promotional managers believe that the best strategy is to appeal to heavy users of the product class, often referred to as the heavy half. For example, the so-called heavy half of the beer drinkers' market (in actuality, this is 17 percent of the total market) consumes 88 percent of all beer; the heavy half in the market for canned soup (16 percent of the total) consumes 86 percent of the product sold. The assumption is that the heavy half is the most productive segment, and there probably is some merit in this viewpoint. Certainly the propensity to respond will be higher. Concentration on this segment has been made more feasible through use of data from syndicated research services showing the product consumption by audiences of various advertising media.

Efforts should not be concentrated on the heavy half, however, unless there is evidence that it is not feasible to turn nonusers into users and light users into heavy users. There should be an inquiry into why they buy or do not buy, what the product means to them, and other related questions. The answers to these questions may make it possible to win over buyers.

Users of Product and Company Brand   The greatest asset possessed by any organization is its core of satisfied users, and the present user cannot be overlooked in promotional strategy. It is particularly important to monitor brand image and to clarify that the company offerings are still satisfying salient evaluative criteria better than the perceived offerings of a competitor. Any deficiencies should, of course, be remedied. Frequent buyer programs (airlines, hotels, rental cars, etc.) take this approach as their basic premise. The promotional program is then designed to help establish a lasting relationship with these consumers.

In addition, it is useful to monitor awareness of the company brand and competitive brands. In a highly volatile market, eroding awareness can be followed by a sales decline. A frequent advertising objective is just to maintain "share of mind"—that is, relative awareness via-à-vis competitors.

It also may be possible to assess the potential for increasing brand loyalty among light to moderate users, for stimulating new product uses, for encouraging switching from competitive brands, and for preventing inroads by competitors, to mention only a few of the many possibilities.

Undertaking Segmentation Analysis

Many bases for reaching segments, and associated segment descriptors, have been analyzed in this section; none of these are applicable in every situation. Thus, it is impossible to generalize with respect to the ideal descriptor variables. What emerges is the wide variety possible and the ways in which imaginative research and creative planning can identify groupings that are a part of the total market. Promotional strategy requires a probing analysis to determine if viable segments exist. If these are present and recognized, they offer an opportunity for profit.

There are, however, two general approaches to reaching segments: *a priori* and *post hoc.* In the a priori approach, the marketer has a good reason to define the segmentation description criteria in advance. We might be certain, for example, that the most frequent purchasers of our product category are either women or people with incomes over $50,000. The *Worldstyle* magazine example discussed earlier is an example of the a priori segmentation approach.

In the post hoc approach, the criteria for segmentation are not decided in advance but rather are an outcome of the analysis itself. The first step is to develop a set of AIO questions that define the domain of interest to the marketer. This could be either a generalized or a product-specific list. Second, a large sample of potential consumers is selected and asked to indicate their degree of agreement with the battery of AIO statements. Third, the respondents are clustered into homogeneous groups or segments on the basis of the similarity of their responses across the whole battery of AIO statements. They are clustered using one of a number of multivariate data analysis procedures that are appropriate for this purpose. The needs structure of these AIO groups is then examined for its uniqueness, and other characteristics (demographic, media usage, etc.) are checked for their correlation with the AIO groups. Levi Strauss used the post hoc approach to define five segments in the men's clothing market, including the "utilitarian jeans customer," the "clothes horse," and the "trendy casual" segments.

THE TARGET MARKET DECISION

Once the market has been segmented along the relevant bases or criteria, the marketing manager must make the target market decision. The target market decision relates to the selection of the specific segment or segments toward which promotional activity will be directed. The firm has three basic options in this regard: undifferentiated marketing, differentiated marketing, and concentrated marketing.

Undifferentiated Marketing

If an undifferentiated marketing strategy is followed, segments are in effect ignored and one marketing mix is offered for everyone. All efforts are poured into building a superior image that will overcome these demand variations. Certainly the cost advantages to the approach are undeniable, as Henry Ford found when the Model A Ford was introduced in any color you wanted "as long as it is black." Ford, of course, had a near monopoly on the market, but few firms enjoy that advantage today. As a result, undifferentiated marketing is exceedingly rare.

A more common variation is to target only the largest segment of the market, perhaps using the heavy-half concept. The problem is that this strategy appeals to most competitors—they concentrate in similar fashion and ignore smaller segments. The outcome of using this approach is often that the marketer becomes a sitting duck for competitors who differentiate and provide the desired option ranges.

Differentiated Marketing

In differentiated marketing, a firm operates in two or more segments and offers a unique marketing mix for each. This strategy has become quite common in larger corporations, as is reflected in a trend toward multiple product offerings. It certainly offers the advantage of recognizing the demand variations that exist and capitalizing on them, in contrast with undifferentiated marketing.

Differentiated marketing is not without its disadvantages. For example, national marketers are finding that the latest marketing trend—regionalization—can be a complex way to market their products. Regionalization replaces national mass-marketing strategies with custom-tailored approaches in the hope that such localized targeting can boost market share in a slow-growth environment. By segmenting the market into tightly focused areas, companies can design special advertising and promotional campaigns, and even develop new products (or new versions of existing products) that cater to local tastes. Although the idea seems simple enough, implementing the strategy can be a major undertaking.

Companies experimenting with regionalization have also found that it can carry an expensive price tag. General Foods Corp. promoted its Maxwell House coffee brand by sponsoring a series of regional events, such as rodeos in Dallas and a show at Radio City Music Hall in New York. The company later estimated that sponsoring such varied events had cost two to three times as much as a single national promotion.

Indeed, the cost of running regional advertising can be prohibitive for some companies. Domino's Pizza, Inc., already offers different toppings for its pizzas in different regions of the country but doesn't publicize the fact. According to Douglas J. Dawson, a Domino's vice president, taking a regional approach "would blow our whole advertising budget."

Thomas J. Lipton & Co. agrees. Although Lipton has acquired a great deal of information about the preferences of tea drinkers around the country, the company is resisting regionalization. Instead, Lipton continues using the same tea blends and advertising themes nationwide. Ted Labiner, Lipton's director of creative services, defends the undifferentiated marketing strategy, saying that "the economies of scale you get make it much more efficient to market nationally than regionally."

Concentrated Marketing

In the undifferentiated strategy, marketers target the whole market, while in the differentiated strategy, they target two or more segments. However, it is often wise to concentrate on one segment. The objective is to establish a larger share and focus resources on excellence in a more limited market. Numerous examples could be cited. One of the most notable is the success that Schweppes has had in concentrating on adult mixed-drink users to the exclusion of more youth-oriented segments. Although it has a great many competitors, Schweppes has held a strong position in the soft drink market through continued product innovation, intensive distribution, and effective promotion.

The danger of concentration, of course, is that the target market can be a small segment or can even dry up with amazing rapidity. Therefore, including some diversification may be a wise policy to follow, especially if there is a high rate of product change. For example, Schweppes is essentially an insignificant competitor in the much larger youth-based segment, where Coke and Pepsi dominate.

The Choice of Approach

The fundamental means by which the marketer selects one of these approaches to segmentation is a cost/benefit analysis. The marketer expects to generate additional revenue from a segment by more completely satisfying the needs of that group and by providing promotional activities that better match the segment. In doing so, the marketer incurs additional costs for new ads, new promotions, new sales-force activities, and so forth. In general, a unique program would be developed for a segment if the incremental revenue expected exceeds the incremental costs of serving it. Of course, the promotional manager must also consider other constraints such as financial resources, personnel limitations, and relationships of one segment to others. The Lipton, Campbell Soup, and Domino's examples above illustrate the recognition of the limitations caused by the incremental cost of serving additional segments.

POSITIONING[6]

Once the promotional manager has identified the potential segments and has chosen the segments to be targeted for promotion, he or she must still select a *positioning* for the product or service in the minds of the consumers in the selected segments. *Positioning* is defined as the perception that targeted consumers have of a firm's offering relative to competitors.

Positioning is often the most critical element in a firm's marketing strategy because it defines the perception the firm intends consumers to have of its product or service. In addition, positioning directs the entire marketing mix of the firm. A clear positioning statement is key to the direction of promotional activity.

Positioning strategy may be approached in one of six ways: (1) by attributes, (2) by price and quality, (3) by use or application, (4) by product user, (5) by product class, or (6) by competitor.

Positioning by Attribute

The most commonly used positioning strategy is to associate a product with an identified level of a defined set of attributes such as power, sportiness, caffeine content, or color. Thus, Ivory soap is positioned highly on the attribute "gentleness," an attribute of great salience to a certain segment of consumers, and Volvo takes the high position on the attribute "safety." See Figure 7–3 for ads associated with these products.

Positioning by Price and Quality

Although price and quality may be thought of as attributes, they are so important that they warrant separate treatment. In many product categories, some brands that offer more features, better service, or better performance use a higher price as a cue to the consumer that they have higher quality. Alternatively, other brands emphasize lower price with limited features to drive a value positioning. For example, BMW holds a premium-quality positioning, and Geo holds a value-based positioning.

Positioning by Use or Application

In positioning by use or application, the marketer attempts to position his or her brand as being associated with a particular use or occasion. For example, Gatorade took the "use with strenuous exercise" positioning when it was first introduced, and Hallmark took the positioning of being the card to send "when you care enough to send the very best."

Positioning by Product User

In positioning by product user, the brand is associated with a specific user or class of users. For example, Cover Girl makeup has built a consumer franchise on a succession of well-known models such as Christie Brinkley.

FIGURE 7–3

Advertising Designed to Establish a Competitive Positioning

Positioning by Product Class

It is possible to position one's brand with respect to the product class in which it competes or to some associated product class. For example, the margarine brand "I Can't Believe It's Not Butter" has been positioned with respect to the associated product class "butter" rather than "margarine." Weight Watchers brand foods have been positioned with respect to normal but more caloric foods rather than diet foods.

Positioning by Competitor

In all positioning approaches, an explicit or implicit frame of reference is the competition. This is because an established competitor's image can be used as a reference point for another brand's positioning. In addition, what is most important is how consumers perceive your brand relative to competitive offerings, not how it is absolutely perceived. The relevant question is whether your brand is better than a given competitor in service, cost, or value, or for use at snack time. Note that in the Volvo ad in Figure 7–3, the superior safety positioning is relative to competitors' minivans. Also, the famous Avis rent-a-car campaign, "We're number two, so we try harder," is an example of the competitor as reference point for a positioning. Figure 7–4 presents a brand positioning map for automobiles on the attributes of sportiness and economy relative to the competitors.

It is also helpful to place segment ideal points on these maps to represent the demand structure relative to the product positioning. For example, the ① in

---

FIGURE 7–4

Product Positioning of Automobiles by Two Attributes

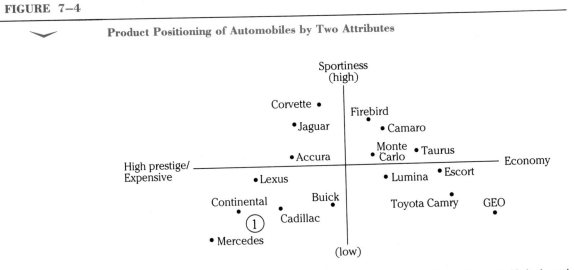

Source: Updated to 1991 brand and adapted from Yoram J. Wind, *Product Policy: Concepts, Methods, and Strategy* (Reading, Mass.: Addison-Wesley Publishing, 1982), p. 84.

Figure 7–4 represents the "luxury sedan" segment of the market. To the marketer, the positioning of the brands within the target segment is the key issue. Clearly, we want our brand to be closer to the ideal of the segment. The physical product, distribution location, package style, and promotion activity all help position a brand.

Developing a Positioning Strategy

The development of a competitive positioning strategy is a seven-step process:

1. Identify the relevant competitors; they may be brands within the product category or substitute products outside the category.
2. Determine how the competitors are perceived and evaluated; this requires marketing research to measure consumer perceptions. It may involve research to determine the relevant attributes for the positioning.
3. Determine the competitors' positions; all competitors, including one's own brand, are placed relative to each other; the use of a perceptual positioning map such as that in Figure 7–4 is a common way to do this.
4. Analyze the consumers relative to their needs; the marketing research is designed to define an open and attainable position for the current product or new product.
5. Select the desired positioning; for example, a firm might desire to offer the highest fiber cereal.
6. Implement a marketing and promotional program to establish the desired positioning.
7. Monitor the consumers' perception of the positioning. The marketer must continuously monitor the marketplace to see the impact of changing consumer tastes and competitors' new products or attempts to reposition themselves.

KEY STRATEGIC CHOICES: SEGMENT TARGETING AND PRODUCT POSITIONING

The success of a promotional strategy depends on many details of media choice, creativity in ads, sales training, and so on. However, all of these depend on two key strategy choices: the choice of segment or segments to be targeted for promotional effort and the designation of the position desired for the organization's product in consumers' minds. The choice of target segment determines where the marketer will fight the promotional battles, and the designation of positioning determines what ammunition the marketer will fight with. Indeed, in any given market, the segment target and the positioning choices will largely determine who the competitors are going to be.

SUMMARY

This chapter is the first of five chapters that lay the foundation for the development of specific aspects of advertising, sales promotion, trade promotion, and sales-force programs. Segmentation and competitive positioning are the cornerstone elements of promotional strategy.

Segmentation is the process of dividing large, heterogeneous markets into smaller, homogeneous subsets of people or businesses with similar needs and/ or responsiveness to marketing mix offerings. Effective segmentation requires the identification of criteria or bases for the formation of the segments, the selection of target markets from the identified segments, and the development of a competitive positioning for the product or service within the selected segments. Usable segments have sufficient size to support a separate promotional program, must be measurable in terms of purchase potential, must be reachable by promotional vehicles, and must have different response functions to different promotional efforts and other marketing activities. Common bases for the description and reaching of segments are geographic variables, demographic variables, psychographic variables, and behavioral variables. Segments can be identified as either a priori or post hoc.

The choice of target markets falls into three general categories: undifferentiated marketing, in which promotional activity does not consider segment differences; differentiated marketing, in which different promotional programs are developed for the different targeted segments; and concentrated marketing, in which all promotional effort is directed at the one segment that is targeted. The choice of which and how many segments to target is based on a cost/benefit analysis of the increase in revenue in the segment against the increased cost of giving the segment a separate promotional program.

Positioning is the perception targeted consumers hold of a firm's offering relative to competitors. It defines the intended perception of the product or service and gives direction to the development of promotional activity. Basic approaches to competitive positioning are by attributes, by price/quality, by use or application, by product user, by product class, and by competitor. Development of competitive positioning requires the use of marketing research to identify relevant competitors, to determine consumer perception of these competitors and their positioning relative to the firm's offering, and to determine consumer needs and possible competitive positionings. The manager can then select a desired positioning and implement a promotional program to establish the desired competitive positioning.

It is critical that segmentation, targeting, and competitive positioning be done well for promotional methods to have their optimal impact.

REVIEW AND DISCUSSION QUESTIONS

1. For Ragú, Prego, and Classico sauces, and for Frito-Lay:
   a. Describe the basic needs of their identified market segments and the basis by which they are reaching these segments.

    b. Describe the target markets selected for a specific promotional program.

    c. Describe the positioning of the product(s).

2. Describe how Avon could undertake a segmentation study of the makeup consumer using a post hoc approach based on AIO measures.

3. Survey data reveal that the market for a line of name-brand stereo units selling for a minimum of $200 is concentrated among unmarried, college-educated males under 35, located on the East and West coasts, with yearly incomes of $13,000 and over. How can these findings be used in promotional strategy?

5. Why are there no specific rules to follow in determining the best descriptors for segmentation?

6. Select five ads from magazines for different product categories. Identify the product positioning taken by the product in these ads; name the relevant attributes and the rating on these attributes.

NOTES

1. This definition is from Thomas C. Kinnear and Kenneth L. Bernhardt, *Principles of Marketing,* 3rd ed. (Glenview, Ill.; Scott Foresman/Little Brown, 1990), p. 103. It is similar to a definition in Peter D. Bennett, *Dictionary of Marketing Terms* (Chicago: American Marketing Association, 1988), p. 114.

2. This section is based on Thomas C. Kinnear and James R. Taylor, *Marketing Research: An Applied Approach* (New York: McGraw-Hill, 1991).

3. "Fashion Magazine Targets Classiest ZIP Codes," *Marketing News,* June 6, 1988, pp. 1–2.

4. Two Companies Find New Faces in Cosmetic Market," *Marketing News,* April 10, 1989, p. 8.

5. Based on "Coke Bacardi Use Segmentation to Develop a 'Tasteful' New Product," *Bank Marketing,* July 1988, p. 12.

6. This section is based on David A. Aaker and Gary Shansby, "Positioning Your Product," *Business Horizons* (May–June 1982), pp. 56–62.

SETTING PROMOTIONAL OBJECTIVES AND APPROPRIATIONS

Having thoroughly explored consumer motivation and buying behavior and having considered market segmentation and competitive positioning, this section turns to two fundamental issues in promotional strategy.

Chapter 8 focuses on the determination of promotional objectives where the challenge is moving from the situation analysis (Figure 2–2) to a statement of objectives that covers the entire promotional mix and gives specific tracks for strategic thinking in each area of the mix.

Chapter 9 considers budgeting and allocation. Traditionally, budgets have been determined using somewhat arbitrary methods. This chapter focuses on ways to be more precise, given the onset of a new generation of measurement tools. Certainly the pressures on financial bottom line are forcing new thinking in this crucial area.

C h a p t e r

8

Establishment of Promotional Objectives

THE BUNNY BATTLES DURACELL

The Eveready Energizer battery "bunny" entertains TV viewers as he parades across their screens with the message "He always keeps going." One time he wears a gas mask while mocking a spot for the fictional Airedale air freshener—complete with animated odors. And he confronts a buoyant youth who's dancing on the ceiling—à la Fred Astaire—in celebration of the fictional Chug-a-Cherry soft drink.

"The bunny has been a tremendous success, from our point of view," says Patrick Farrell, manager of corporate information for Eveready parent Ralston Purina Co. He points to Eveready consumer research showing unaided brand awareness up 33 percent from a year ago, while awareness of Energizer's TV campaign was up 43 percent and recall of the brand's "long-lasting" product message was up 49 percent for the same period.

Mr. Farrell also said Eveready statistics show a 40 percent increase in the past year in the number of displays retailers use to merchandise Energizer batteries. "We view merchandising activity as critical in this category, because batteries are frequently an impulse buy," he said.

Yet the Energizer bunny may find that the one thing he can't interrupt is competitor Duracell's growing success. Duracell maintains that up to 40 percent of consumers who remember the bunny campaign think it's advertising Duracell, not Energizer. In fact, Eveready's share of the replacement battery market has dropped from its precampaign level of 51 percent to 40.5 percent.

In analyzing this communication paradox, Steve Leavitt, president of research company Marketing Evaluations/TVQ, points out, "It just may be that Duracell advertising consistently and for a long period of time has achieved market share and in-store dominance and cumulatively planted itself as the leading battery company in consumers' minds."

Source: Julie Liesse, "Bunny Back to Battle Duracell," *Advertising Age,* September 17, 1990, pp. 4 and 73. Reproduced by special permission.

SETTING PROMOTIONAL OBJECTIVES

You have just had an inside look at one of the most interesting promotional battles of recent years—Energizer versus Duracell. Creative advertising has consistently raised awareness and recognition of the Energizer brand name, a bottom-line objective if product trial, another crucial objective, ever is to be stimulated at the point of sale. And Eveready has had consistent success in meeting its objective of increased numbers of displays at the retail level.

Furthermore, the bunny was recognized in one test by 79 percent of those surveyed, versus the 59 percent average familiarity rating for similar commercial characters.[1] Yet a high level of confusion exists over which product the bunny is advertising—Eveready or Duracell. Once again, we encounter the vagaries of the consumer information process discussed in Chapter 4.

An even worse dilemma is that market share has slumped in spite of apparently successful communication, an outcome that cannot be tolerated for long. What does it mean to have communicated if sales do not respond accordingly?

This example introduces you to what is involved in the process of moving from the analysis of consumer demand and competition to a realistic set of objectives for the promotional mix. In particular, most of the time we are confronted with a hoary issue: What is our objective—to sell or to communicate? It is the purpose of this chapter to help you wrestle with this issue and to arrive at a defensible, integrated set of objectives.

The Components of the Promotional Mix

The challenge is to define the objectives for each component of the promotional mix, taking into account the central fact that none can be considered in isolation. The following is a brief review of what each program element is intended to do:

> *Advertising*—(1) to communicate by building awareness, understanding, and interest; and (2) to motivate trial and repurchase.
>
> *Sales promotion*—to provide a trigger for buying action at the point of sale.
>
> *Personal selling*—to provide needed information and a catalyst to closing the sale through face-to-face communication and negotiation.
>
> *Reseller support (trade promotion)*—to provide displays, personal selling where needed, special incentives, and other forms of point-of-sale support.
>
> *Public relations and publicity*—to build public support and acceptance, generally through nonpaid media.

For example, a major soft drink company is introducing a new line of soft drinks containing at least 10 percent fresh fruit juice. The marketing objective is to attain a 6 percent market share by the end of the introductory campaign. The promotion objectives might look like this:

> *Advertising*—to generate 60 percent brand awareness in the target market of teenagers and families with preteen children.
>
> *Sales promotion*—to stimulate trial by 50 percent of those who are aware of the brand name.

Personal selling—to gain 1,200 new retail accounts.

Trade promotion—to motivate 80 percent of all retailers stocking the brand to make use of end-aisle displays for two 3-week periods during the introduction.

Public relations and publicity—to have 80 percent of stockholders aware and supportive of this new product introduction. Also, to convince 60 percent of school nurses that the brand should be available in soft drink machines on school premises because of health benefits.

Sales versus Communication Objectives: A Continuing Controversy

The analgesic market in the United States is a highly competitive one. The ibuprofen segment (22.8 percent of the overall market) was headed in 1991 by Whitehall Laboratories' Advil brand, with a 50 percent market share. Bristol-Myers Squibb Company's Nuprin brand was far behind, with an 18 percent share.[2]

Bristol-Myers Squibb decided to make market share inroads by launching a new campaign featuring sports stars such as Jimmy Conners treating much-publi-

FIGURE 8–1

Jimmy Connors Helped This Brand Communicate a Strong Message—"Nupe it"

cized injuries with Nuprin: "So Nupe it . . . I did it. You can do it." The 30-second spots were backed by extensive trade promotion.

Now we face an age-old question: What is the unique role of promotion in Bristol-Myers Squibb's overall marketing mix? Many marketers would respond with such statements as "To increase sales by 10 percent" or "To increase market share by one point." But others would counter by pointing out that a sales/market share increase is the outcome of an integrated marketing effort functioning in a unified way. According to this point of view, the role of promotion is to *communicate*—to change awareness and interest and create a frame of mind that stimulates action.[3] In addition, many will contend that it is difficult, if not impossible, to isolate the sales impact of any individual component.

The latter point of view gained strong acceptance after a highly influential statement in 1961 by Russell Colley, speaking on behalf of the National Association of Advertisers, that has since become known as DAGMAR (Defining Advertising Goals, Measuring Advertising Results).[4] DAGMAR is based on the premise that the primary role of promotion, especially advertising, is to communicate. Therefore, concrete and measurable communication objectives must be set.

For years there was an intriguing polarity on this issue. Nevertheless, there has been a significant outcome: Advertisers, in particular, have begun to pay much more serious attention to the communication functions advertising must perform. Specific, measurable outcomes have begun to emerge (awareness, name recognition, and so on), and this, in our opinion, has represented a major step forward.

An Unnecessary Controversy   One unfortunate outcome of DAGMAR is that a legitimate concern about the sales impact of promotional efforts tended to be pushed into the background. This has given rise to an unnecessary controversy that obscures the point that both communication and increased sales/market share are valid promotional objectives.

To return to our example, the Nuprin TV ad campaign was successful in communicating the major selling proposition of the brand while at the same time producing a demonstrable impact on sales. Nuprin's sales rose 23 percent following the debut of the Jimmy Connors campaign, leading to a 1 percent gain in market share. One analyst pointed out, "The [Nuprin] campaign's effective. People remember it. It could have a good impact and give Nuprin more of a brand identity."[5] It is interesting, however, that this brand initiative later faltered, and Nuprin dropped to an 8.8 percent market share by December 1992. The reason given is that the "Nupe it" campaign failed to focus sufficiently on relief of headache pain, the selling proposition of Advil, Motrin IB, and the major private-label brands.[6] This underscores the ever-present fact of rapid change and the need for a continual thumb on the pulse of the market.

A Balanced Perspective   The question, in reality, is not one of communication versus sales. Rather, it is a question of the relative emphasis to be placed on each outcome. The impact of promotion on sales, of course, will be highest when stimulation of immediate buying action is the anticipated outcome. Direct marketing and retail advertising, in particular, can legitimately be assessed by the degree to which sales are influenced. Also, the role of communication versus sales stimulation varies depending on the prevailing consumer decision process. Accurate consumer research is a necessity.

Extended problem solving (EPS)   You will recall that attitude change is a valid promotional objective when EPS is the prevailing consumer decision-making mode. We discovered in Chapter 6 that current research supports this important proposition: All things being equal, a change in belief will lead to a change in preference, a change in buying intention, and a buying action. In other words, the purchasing process follows this general sequence:

1. Brand name awareness
↓
2. Knowledge of benefits
↓
3. Liking, interest, preference
↓
4. Intention to buy
↓
5. Purchase

Notice, first of all, that the act of buying is predicated on successful communication during steps 1 through 4. If this does not take place, no sales or market share objective ever will be met.

On the other hand, successful communication can be barren of sales impact. Let's assume that the Chrysler Company achieves an 80 percent awareness of its radically new Dodge Intrepid and a 65 percent awareness of the improved riding and interior room benefits of its "cab forward" design. If there is no effect on liking, intention, and buying action, then communication has occurred without persuasive impact.

Communication always must be undertaken with the intent of changing behavior. If this doesn't happen, the consequences can be severe. If you were a stockholder of PepsiCo Inc., how would you react to the headline in Promotion in Action 8–1: "Pepsi: Memorable Ads, Forgettable Sales"?

Limited problem solving (LPS)   Limited problem solving, on the other hand, presents quite a different promotional challenge. Most alternative evaluation takes place after trial rather than before. There is now a different flow of influence:

1. Brand and benefit awareness
↓
2. Trial
↓
3. Evaluation

Back to Jimmy Connors's "Nupe it" message. Apparently, this came through loud and clear to many TV viewers, given the effect on sales when the ad first aired. Promotion (advertising in this case) both communicated and stimulated a sales increase.

A Renewed Focus on the Bottom Line   Management has every right to expect both communication and sales results, and few managers are willing to tolerate anything less. Scanner technology has been added to the existing arsenal of research tools, thus greatly increasing our ability to assess bottom-line impacts. The importance of this renewed focus on accountability is vividly stated in Promotion in Action 8–2. Don't miss its main points!

DEFINING PROMOTIONAL OBJECTIVES

As you can readily appreciate, the objectives for promotional strategy always must be viewed in a broad marketing context. Prior decisions on market segmentation, decisions on other areas of marketing strategy (especially the product/service and its attributes), projected increases in sales and/or market share, and financial resources all shape and influence the role of promotion. These factors must be viewed as the givens within which promotion functions. Deficiencies in any of these respects dooms promotion to diminished or negligible impact.

Promotion in Action

8-1

Pepsi: Memorable Ads, Forgettable Sales

By Madison Avenue's reckoning, Pepsi has left Coke in the dust. Pepsi owns the most popular advertising on television. With its slightly goofy arm gesture, the Summer Chill Out campaign caught the imagination of viewers. And the current Diet Pepsi campaign has inspired millions to sing along with Ray Charles and his rendition of "You've Got the Right One Baby, Uh-huh."

While Pepsi ads routinely rank number one in viewer recall, Coke usually ranks fourth or fifth. Yet memorable advertising hasn't saved Pepsi from forgettable sales. James Murren, an analyst at C. J. Lawrence Inc., predicts that the recession and a fierce price war between Coke and Pepsi will reduce third-quarter earnings at Pepsi by 1 percent.

To some Pepsi bottlers, the slow sales point up the limitations of even the best ads. Earl G. Graves, chairman of PepsiCo's Washington, D.C., bottler, says slick pitches can't combat Coke's rampant discounting. Such tactics have helped Coke hold on to a lead over Pepsi in grocery-store sales since 1984.

To be sure, Coke spends millions on image advertising as well. Yet Coke clearly doesn't share Pepsi's yen for the award-winning ad. Says Peter S. Sealey, director of global marketing at Coca-Cola: "Whether or not Coke wins a Gold Lion at Cannes in 1992 is so immaterial as to be inconsequential to me."

Source: Mark Landler, "Pepsi: Memorable Ads, Forgettable Sales," *Business Week*, October 21, 1992, p. 36. Reproduced by special permission.

Begin with the Situation Analysis

In Chapter 2, Figure 2–2 outlined the promotional planning process and clarified the stages in the situation analysis. You are familiar with this material, but it is helpful to review several of the major issues. In the following discussion, we use the term *goal* to refer to the broadest expected outcomes, whereas *objective* focuses on the specific results that must happen for a goal to be achieved.

Corporate and Marketing Goals   Bristol-Myers Squibb must reverse its slide in Nuprin sales, especially given the burgeoning sales increase in the overall ibuprofen market. Let's assume that it is now the end of 1992 and that the marketing goal is to increase sales from a level of $12.8 million to $14.0 million by July 1, 1993. The corresponding projected market share increase is a change from 8.8 percent to 9.4 percent.

Obviously, this will require increased spending levels for advertising and consumer and trade sales promotion. Do sufficient financial resources exist? And how much increase is necessary to achieve these goals? This important question is the subject of Chapter 9, and we will reserve further discussion until then.

An End to Communication Overkill

Promotion in Action

8-2

For many marketers, the 1980s stood for excess. They blitzed the U.S. consumer with sales pitches, collectively spending more than $6 a week on every man, woman, and child in the United States—almost 50 percent more per capita than in any other nation.

In retrospect, too much of it was wasted. Flawed products, inept ad campaigns, misguided gimmicks, poorly monitored promotions—these are the marketing legacies of the decade. Sales receipts often couldn't justify the soaring bills for advertising and promotion.

So, in the dawn of a jittery new decade, a tough tactical and strategic reappraisal got under way. The new resolution: Reap more with less. "I'm telling my people that every dollar they spend has to work 25 percent harder than it did in the good old days of endless supplies of money," says Brian Ruder, vice president for consumer products marketing at H. J. Heinz Co.'s U.S. unit.

For many companies, trade promotion gobbles up far more marketing dollars than does consumer advertising. By one estimate, $25 billion was spent on promotions last year alone. And, as in advertising, promotion is coming under intense scrutiny for potential savings and accountability.

Data from supermarket scanners is helping marketers improve the cost-effectiveness of their promotions. Such information doesn't come cheap, but companies are discovering that paying more up front often means less waste later.

Analysts at Chicago scanner specialist Information Resources Inc. reviewed a big Kraft General Foods promotion in 1989 and concluded that 7 of every 10 boxes of its macaroni and cheese would have been sold even without the promotion. Since promotion campaigns are pricey, such findings can save plenty.

Source: Richard Gibson, "Marketers' Mantra: Reap More with Less," *The Wall Street Journal,* March 22, 1991, pp. B9 and B10. Reproduced by special permission.

Analysis of Consumer Research and Competitive Trends   Measurable objectives are a virtual impossibility without systematic market analysis. This holds true in all areas of the promotional mix, even public relations, as you will discover in Promotion in Action 8–3.

Table 8–1 shows you the dynamics of the ibuprofen segment of the pain relief market. While sales of the total analgesic market were up only 2.6 percent during the period of this analysis, ibuprofen products have increased 13.6 percent.[7] Therefore, the overall market outlook is rosy indeed.

Aspirin's slump is due in part to the Federal Drug Administration's actions in restricting ads that urge aspirin use to reduce the dangers of heart disease. But ibuprofen's growth is due, at least in part, to its relative youth as an over-the-counter remedy. Jeff Needham, vice president for private-label manufacturer Preeigo Co., says, "Ibuprofen enjoys a consumer perception that it provides very strong relief for a variety of pain."[8]

One of the most notable competitive dynamics is the growth of private-label brands, which are sold at a 30 percent to 50 percent discount. The national brand manufacturers could well face further inroads because of this price advantage.

Now, what strategy should Bristol-Myers Squibb use for its Nuprin brand? One thing is for sure—there can be no continuation of reductions in advertising and sales promotion spending initiated during 1992 unless a conscious decision is made to cut expenditures and reap profits while the brand still is viable.

Promotion in Action

8-3

Public Relations by the Numbers

The days of public relations programs designed by hunch and measured by a stack of press clippings are almost gone. Counting the number of clippings doesn't tell you how many people read them or how their perceptions changed. Communications research can do this, and more.

One residential security company based its marketing strategy on its status as a large national company that offered a technologically superior product. The company's PR firm, Pollare/FIscher Communications, suggested a simple telephone survey. The company learned that most of its customers wanted a security company with local roots. Its marketing strategy was wrong.

Based on the research and the demographics of the Southern California target audience, the security company's new PR program boosted company involvement in community groups. the company targeted parents by giving heroism awards to school-children in key communities. Publicity about these awards was arranged in weekly community newspapers rather than metropolitan dailies.

"The client quickly acquired a local presence," says Roger Fischer, a partner in the public relations firm. "Awards were presented on a monthly basis, local radio stations called to request company spokespeople as on-the-air experts, and sales reps went out to speak in community forums."

Source: Eric Stoltz and Jack Torobin, "Public Relations by the Numbers," *American Demographics,* January 1991, p. 42. Reproduced by special permission.

Bristol-Myers Squibb management has opted, however, to be proactive and regain market share. It is clear from all indications that its emphasis on muscle pains rather than headache relief has been off target. This is easily remedied, of course, by a strengthened focus on headache relief—the dominant attribute for most buyers. The message that must be registered is "Nuprin—Stops Any Kind of Pain!"

The challenge now is to do something to increase *share of mind*—to boost the frequency with which Nuprin is mentioned when prospective buyers are asked to name the brands of analgesics they would consider using. This is a concrete, measurable communication objective for advertising.

A price war looks to be inevitable. Therefore, coupons and other incentives must be used to increase *trial*—a measurable sales/market share objective. And, for this to happen, retail cooperation must be recruited through trade promotion (e.g., increased slotting allowances).

Bristol-Myers Squibb also could benefit from stepped-up public relations through doctors and other health practitioners. A worthwhile objective is to increase the distribution of Nuprin samples as well as specific recommendation of Nuprin as a preferred remedy.

Other possible outcomes could be considered, of course. Our intent here has been to give you some insight into how measurable objectives emerge from marketing and competitive research. You can also benefit by reviewing the discussions in Chapters 5 and 6, which laid the basis for what is said here.

Stating the Objectives

This section will draw upon a helpful case study that shows how promotional objectives should be formulated and stated.[9] You will learn that the statement of promotional objectives should include the following:

TABLE 8—1

Ibuprofen Gives Competitors Headaches

Top-Selling Ibuprofen Brands*	Sales (millions)	% Change from Year Earlier	% Share of Category
Advil	$76.1	+ 15.0%	52.3%
Private label	30.3	+ 19.7	20.8
Motrin IB	19.6	+ 13.7	13.5
Nuprin	12.8	− 12.1	8.8
Excedrin IB	1.6	+188.6	1.1

* Based on sales in supermarkets, drugstores, and mass-merchandise outlets during the 12 weeks ended December 13, 1992.

Source: Information Resources Inc.

1. A definition and description of market target.
2. A clear message platform.
3. The expected communications results.
4. The expected outcomes in terms of trial and repurchase.

The National Pork Producers Council (NPPC), headquartered in Des Moines, Iowa, comprises over 100,000 producing members and 45 affiliated state organizations. Its stated mission is to influence pork sales and enhance the producer's opportunity for profit.

There was legitimate concern that pork consumption per capita had slumped. In fact, per capita consumption in 1985 was 62.0 pounds per year, compared with the 1960 level of 60.3. In addition, pork's share of total meat consumption declined from 32 percent in 1960 to 26 percent in 1985. Therefore, a decision was made to pursue extensive market research and to undertake a promotion campaign to reverse these trends.

Definition and Description of the Market Target   Identifying the segment or segments to be targeted is a process that affects all of marketing planning. What we are calling for here is the use of segmentation and positioning analysis (described in Chapter 7). It is important that the target(s) be described in specific demographic terms so that media may be chosen with minimum waste and precise geographic allocation undertaken.

The NPCC and its advertising agency, Bozell, Jacobs, Kenyon & Eckhardt (BJK&E), undertook a survey of pork consumption and were able to differentiate heavy users, moderate users, and light/nonusers. A summary of this analysis appears in Table 8–2. The demographic differences between these three segments are notable.

On the basis of this analysis, the NPCC felt that the greatest potential for increased pork consumption lay in the light-to-moderate user segment. Therefore, it used this definition of the target market: women 25–54 years of age who belonged to 3+ member households with incomes of $30,000+.

Message Platform   The *message platform* (sometimes referred to as the *creative platform* or *unique selling proposition* is an answer to the question "What exactly do you want to communicate to your audience?" It will usually be stated in broad terms, with specific details of execution left to artists and writers.

The basic objective of the "Pork—The Other White Meat" campaign was to create *real* consumer demand via high top-of-mind awareness of the positive attributes and perceived benefits of pork. The research findings summarized in Table 8–3 provided the basis for the following statements about the benefits of pork, which formed the message platform:

Pork fits into today's active lifestyles.

Pork is lean, wholesome, and as high in quality as its principal competitors, beef and chicken.

Pork is a versatile, convenient meat to prepare and has excellent taste.

Pork products are good value, both economically and nutritionally.

Pork products offer excellent substitution appeal as alternatives to other "center of the plate" entrees.

Expected Communication Results   While the message platform does define the content to be communicated, it has two shortcomings as a workable set of objectives:

1. It lacks benchmarks. In other words, we have no precise indication of the present beliefs of those in the target market regarding pork and its role in family diet.

2. There are no indications of the magnitudes of belief change that are expected if the campaign is a success.

The consumer research undertaken by the NPPC gives an excellent foundation for this kind of precision. Read Table 8–4 carefully. It compares pork against chicken (the dominant white meat) along eight important attributes. Also, the

TABLE 8–2

National Pork Producers Council: "Pork—The Other White Meat" Campaign
(Demographic Profile of Three Pork Consumption Levels for those Categories with
Significant Differences)

Category	Pork (Fresh and Processed) Usage Level		
	Heavy Users (15% of Sample)	Moderate Users (36% of Sample)	Light-Nonusers (49% of Sample)
Meals at home per week:			
20 or more	26%	15%	16%
14–19	42	36	27
7–13	23	32	28
Less than 7	9	17	29
Family size:			
One	10%	15%	22%
Two	23	29	36
Three–Four	47	41	32
Five or more	20	15	10
Ethnic background:			
White/Caucasian	42%	58%	72%
Black/Negro	49	32	19
Other	9	10	9
Totals*	100%	100%	100%

* Percentages totaled to 100% vertically for each category.

Source: NPPC Consumer Pork Attitude Study.

Source: "National Pork Producers Council: "Pork—The Other White Meat Campaign," Harvard Business School Case 9-589-055, p. 38. Reproduced by special permission.

TABLE 8–3

Summary Conclusions from a Review of Primary and Secondary Research on Pork Consumption

- Chicken is replacing both pork and beef in the diet.
- The trend in meat consumption is toward leaner, more nutritious cuts of meat that are more versatile and simpler to prepare.
- Pork's major perceived drawbacks involve health-related issues and concerns with its high fat, cholesterol, and calorie content. These concerns may be based on inaccurate or out-of-date information about pork, pointing to a need for educating consumers to some of pork's advantages.
- Pork's actual positive attributes include its true nutritional value and its evolution toward becoming a leaner product. Consumers perceive pork as having a cost advantage, a unique taste, and ready availability in a large variety of cuts. These attributes potentially could form the underpinnings of an advertising message.
- Pork is a highly satisfying meat to its consumers, and it appears that consumers would be responsive to communications providing information about pork's advantages which would allow them to justify eating more pork.
- Though pork lags behind poultry in a number of important areas, pork is at parity or superior in taste appeal.
- In general, pork is considered to be somewhat of a "blue-collar" food.

Source: National Pork Producers Council: 'Pork—The Other White Meat' Campaign," Harvard Business School Case 9-589-055, pp. 8–9. Reproduced by special permission.

mean rating for all meats is given to allow even further comparison of buyer perceptions. The ratings of pork in Table 8–4 could be used as the benchmarks in the NPCC's campaign. The unmistakable conclusion is that pork has a long way to go before it catches up with the number one white meat in terms of consumer beliefs. This also is true in comparison with the mean score for all

TABLE 8–4

The Two "White Meats" Compared with Each Other

Positive Purchase Influence*	Pork	Chicken	Mean for All Meat
Variety of ways it can be served	32	76	59
Taste appeal	52	66	55
Ease of preparation	30	59	52
Appeal to children	15	56	38
Value for the money	25	76	33
Overall wholesomeness	25	73	33
Nutritional value	24	65	33
Cost	22	65	32
How exciting it is to eat	23	47	28

* Positive influences—tip three boxes on a 10-point scale.

Source: The National Pork Producers Council: "Pork—The Other White Meat Campaign," Harvard Business School Case 9-589-055, p. 35. Reproduced by special permission.

meats (ground beef, fresh beef, pork, and chicken), although the differences are not so great.

Pork comes out especially poorly against chicken in terms of value for the money (-51 in comparative ratings), overall wholesomeness (-48), variety of ways it can be served (-44), and cost (-43). The only attribute where pork is competitive is taste appeal, where there is only a 12-point deficiency.

From these data, it is clear that pork can capitalize on its taste appeal. But there is a real need to change beliefs in other areas, especially in variety of ways it can be served, ease of preparation, value for the money, and overall wholesomeness. It could be worthwhile to set the goal of moving the ratings on these dimensions to the average levels across the four meat categories. If this decision is made, the communication objectives would be to increase the positive ratings given pork in terms of:

The variety of ways it can be served from 32 percent to 59 percent.

Ease of preparation from 30 percent to 52 percent.

Value for the money from 25 percent to 33 percent.

Overall wholesomeness from 25 percent to 33 percent.

To this we also might add:

To increase the positive ratings given pork in terms of taste appeal from 52 percent to 66 percent (the current level for chicken).

Notice that we now have a great opportunity for precise measurement of effectiveness. All that is required is to ask the same (or similar) questions *after* exposure to print ads and commercials. This in fact was done, leading to the conclusion that awareness and attitudinal measures showed dramatic improvement from precampaign levels.

Here, for example, is the script from one 30-second TV commercial:

Looking for some new thoughts on food? Look into today's leaner pork. Great tasting pork is more than a change of pace, it can change your outlook on cooking. For instance, how about pork-ka-bobs tonight. Or a juicy pork blade steak smothered in mushroom sauce. Something simple? Zesty pork burgers. There are so many great pork ideas, it's no wonder . . . AMERICA YOU'RE LEANING ON PORK.

Fifty percent or more of those who viewed this commercial gave such answers as, "I learned something new about pork," "I liked the fact that this commercial gave me recipes to make with pork," "The commercial made it clear that pork fits into today's active lifestyle," and "The commercial made me realize that pork is easy to make."

Expected Sales/Market Share Results   Interestingly enough, there is no indication that a sales goal was put in place for this campaign. This certainly could have been done. Here are two examples:

Increase the per capita consumption of pork during the next year from 62.0 pounds to 68 pounds.

Increase the market share of pork in comparison with all other meat products from 26.0 percent to 26.5 percent.

Perhaps it is better for the NPCC and agency management in retrospect that no sales objectives were given, because sales did not increase, despite substantial changes in attitudes and beliefs. We cannot imagine that many producers would be satisfied with no product movement after an expenditure of $9 million on the campaign. Maybe sales will increase next year. Or maybe not. Enough said?

Concluding Comments

In our experience, we have not found many marketers who set objectives in such concrete terms, even though the benefits to be gained are well worth the effort. Sometimes the establishment of specific numerical increases can be arbitrary. But at the minimum, we recommend that benchmarks be in place so that the extent of change, if any, can be measured once the campaign has been carried out.

We can give you no formula to follow in setting objectives that are more than arbitrary guesses or even wishful thinking. It comes down to the fact that there is no substitute for past experience. Over time, we can look back on similar situations and arrive at more reasonable expectations. Probably there is no way to avoid guesswork and some experimentation.

SUMMARY

The purpose of this chapter is to provide guidance for moving from marketing research and other background information to making a statement of realistic advertising and sales promotion objectives.

An important initial issue is whether an increase in sales or market share is a legitimate goal for promotion. It is fair to state that promotion is the communication function of marketing. Yet communication must be related to stimulation of trial and repurchase, even though other elements of the marketing mix also affect sales. Therefore, both communication and sales objectives are important.

A statement of objectives has these components: (1) a definition and description of the target market, (2) a statement of the message (creative) platform, (3) the expected sales outcomes, and (4) the expected communication outcomes. The challenge is to state objectives specifically so that it is possible to measure outcomes unambiguously.

REVIEW AND DISCUSSION QUESTIONS

1. Review the rationale used and the outcomes produced by the NPCC "Pork—The Other White Meat" campaign. Now put yourself in the shoes of the chief marketing executive. How would you answer a memo from the chair of the National Pork Producers Council asking why there were no increases in pork usage in spite of a $9 million campaign?

2. Now you are the advertising manager for a high-fashion women's wear chain and have received a memo identical to that in Question 1. Would your answers be different? Why?

3. The advertising campaign for a leading brand of camping items is based on this statement of objectives: "Our objective is to tell as many people as possible that camping is fun for the whole family and is inexpensive and easy." Is this sufficient? Are changes needed? If so, what would you suggest?

4. The promotion manager for a new brand of cat litter has $30 million to spend. Present levels of awareness for this brand are less than 10 percent in the 30 leading metropolitan markets. She is faced with the challenge of figuring out how much increase in awareness she can generate with this budget. This budget, by the way, is three times larger than in the previous year. What counsel can you give her?

5. One of the major competitors of AT&T in the long-distance market has mounted an aggressive campaign with an emphasis on better service at a lower price per call. The first market share results showed that top-of-mind recall of company name and advertised benefits increased from 35 percent to 48 percent. Management concluded that advertising was a resounding success, although a longtime senior executive expressed a dissenting view. He argued that awareness is not enough. What would your answer be?

6. A leading brand in the highly competitive headache remedy market has dropped in top-of-mind awareness from 31 percent to 20 percent because of competitive product introductions. What does this mean in practical terms? What implications do you see?

NOTES

1. Julie Liesse, "Bunny Back to Battle Duracell," *Advertising Age,* September 17, 1990, p. 4.

2. Pat Sloan, "Nuprin's Smash Hit," *Advertising Age,* October 14, 1991, pp. 3 and 62.

3. See Russell H. Colley, ed., *Defining Advertising Goals* (New York: Association of National Advertisers, 1961), p. 21.

4. Ibid.

5. Sloan, "Nuprin's Smash Hit," p. 62.

6. Kathleen Deveny, "Ibuprofen's Success Pains Aspirin Makers," *The Wall Street Journal,* January 12, 1993, p. B1.

7. Ibid.

8. Ibid.

9. The case in this section is drawn from "National Pork Producers Council: 'Pork—The Other White Meat' Campaign," prepared by John L. Teopaco and Stephen A. Greyser. Harvard Business School Case 9-589-055 (Cambridge, Mass.: Harvard Business School, Publishing Division, 1988). The information is used by special permission.

9

The Promotional
Appropriation

PROMOTIONAL STRATEGY: HOW MUCH TO SPEND
ON SUPER SOFT

Betty Wilson was appointed product manager for Super Soft Skin Lotion (SSSL) in February and was given three months in which to recommend a promotional appropriation for the brand for the next fiscal year. To accomplish this task, she would have to project sales and profits for the coming year, but to do so, she would have to develop a marketing plan that specifies the appropriate level and nature of three types of promotional expenditures: consumer advertising, consumer promotion, and trade promotion. Ms. Wilson decided to begin by analyzing the history and results of SSSL's marketing strategy over the previous five years, with particular emphasis on the nature, effectiveness, and profitability of SSSL's various promotional efforts.

She found that the primary objective of SSSL's past advertising was to increase sales by suggesting new uses for the product. An analysis of bimonthly advertising expenditures showed substantial period-to-period fluctuations. Wilson believed these data indicated the absence of a sustained commitment to consumer advertising, as well as management's tendency to cut advertising expenditures during the fourth quarter to meet annual profit targets.

Media selection was more consistent. Network television was the principal medium and received almost 40 percent of the promotional appropriation. Print media were used to announce special consumer promotions. Historically, SSSL brand management had spent little on trade promotion. However, in the past two years, these expenditures increased rapidly as major retailers demanded more and larger slotting allowances (payments by the manufacturer to provide shelf space). In contrast, less money had been allocated to consumer promotions over the past three years. Two years ago, for example, only two such promotions were run. One offered a cents-off coupon and the other a self-liquidating premium (a premium for which the consumer pays for the wholesale cost of the item).

Gross sales two years previous were approximately $25 million, with total promotional expenditures (excluding personal selling) of $5 million. During the past five years, sales had almost doubled while promotional expenditures had increased 50 percent. Last year, the promotional appropriation was reduced to $4.5 million and sales remained about the same as the previous year. Expenditures to date in the current year were about the same as for the preceding year, and sales were barely up to the levels for the same period in the previous year. Profit contributions averaged about 30 percent of gross sales over the past three years but rose to 34 percent last year.

Ms. Wilson was faced with the problem of recommending not only a level of promotional expenditure but also a complete promotional strategy. Management had given her a free hand but had told her that the brand would be expected to show a profit increase of 10 percent next year.

Her first impression was that management might be "milking" the brand to increase short-run profitability by holding down promotional expenditures. To overcome milking, she knew that she would have to show that the brand had enough growth potential to support investment spending. If she could not build a strong enough case to support this approach, she knew she would be the caretaker of a declining brand rather than the manager of a product with increasing sales.

Determining how much to spend for promotion is one of the most perplexing problems facing management today. Because of the large number of variables that come into play, as the opening example illustrates, finding a solution is not easy. Fortunately for Betty Wilson, she was able to develop a promotional strategy that convinced her superiors that the brand had investment potential, and a budget sufficient to perform the necessary promotional tasks to reach the specified goals was approved.

THEORETICAL FOUNDATIONS OF THE OUTLAY PROBLEM

Before considering various approaches to the problem of determining the promotional appropriation, it is useful first to understand something about the economist's notion of the optimal expenditure. With this background, it is possible to analyze existing appropriation procedures, to grasp the extent to which these methods approximate the ideal, and to analyze the potential of newer methods. This chapter focuses primarily on the problems inherent in determining the amount to be spent on advertising because of its highly visible role in the promotional mix. Of course, most firms spend more on personal selling and, perhaps, sales promotion than on advertising, but the modes of analysis with regard to advertising apply to determining expenditures for the other forms of promotion as well.

Sales Response to Advertising Function

A great deal of research into the relationship between sales response and advertising has indicated that it is a function with decreasing returns. That is, with more and more input, one gets less and less output. Such a relationship is illustrated by Curve A in Figure 9–1.

In many cases, however, the function assumes an **S** shape, as shown by Curve B in Figure 9–1. This function rises slowly at first and then more rapidly before leveling off because most advertising campaigns must overcome a substantial inertia. However, as the impact of repeated messages and resulting consumer learning attracts a larger group of consumers, sales per dollar of input increase rapidly. As time passes, returns to advertising diminish because demand has, to a large extent, been satisfied and more advertising input is necessary to convert a prospect into a customer.

Figure 9–2 indicates that, given an S-shaped response function, the optimal expenditure level is found at Point *b* on the x-axis, where marginal cost equals marginal revenue. Additional inputs of advertising past this point will not produce enough additional sales to pay for their costs.

The Key Question

Is such marginal analysis useful in determining how much should be spent on advertising or other forms of promotion? The answer is that marginal analysis is a useful *theoretical construct* that forces management to evaluate other means of determining the promotional appropriation in terms of whether or not they direct the expenditures of dollars to that point at which incremental profit gains are offset by incremental promotional costs. The value of marginal analysis is that it illustrates that because of the curvilinear shape of the promotion response function, not all dollars of input create the same sales response, and it emphasizes that profitability is the outcome to be maximized. Research has shown that many firms operate in the upper part of the S curve and that spending less on promotion and staying in the lower half of the S curve might result in more profitable sales.

FIGURE 9–1

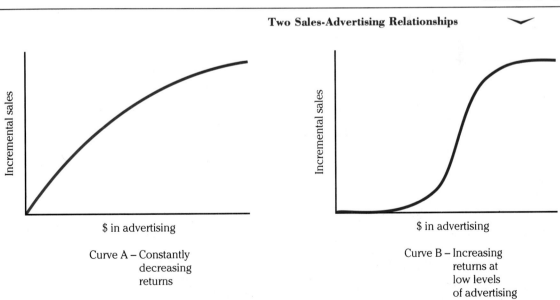

Two Sales-Advertising Relationships

Curve A – Constantly decreasing returns

Curve B – Increasing returns at low levels of advertising

Source: Leonard M. Lodish, *The Advertising & Promotion Challenge* (New York: Oxford University Press, 1986), p. 93.

Unfortunately, marginal analysis has limited direct applicability due to several problems. First, predicting the shape and position of the response function is very difficult because the nature of the function is influenced by managerial decisions relating to type, quality, and amount of promotional input; product characteristics; distribution policies; and pricing levels. Finally, the sensitivity of demand to promotional input for most product or service offerings is affected by environmental factors beyond the control of management such as consumer behavior, competitive pressures, and the general level of economic activity.

We must also understand that the aim of a great deal of promotion is not to maximize short-run profit but to increase consumer awareness, change attitudes, or achieve other communication objectives with longer-run benefits.

TRADITIONAL APPROPRIATION APPROACHES

Methods for determining the promotional appropriation have been classified as either being judgment oriented or data oriented.[1] In the first category are included (1) arbitrary allocation, (2) percentage of sales, and (3) all you can afford. In the data-oriented category are (1) competitive parity, (2) objective and task, (3) experimentation and testing, and (4) modeling and simulation.

FIGURE 9–2

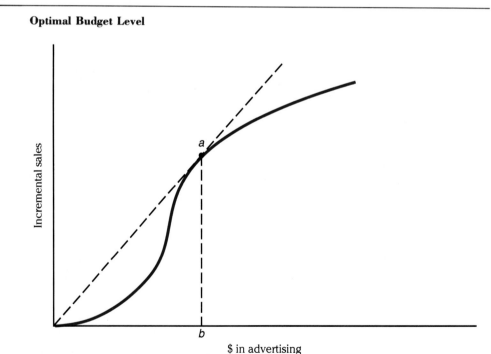

Optimal Budget Level

Source: Leonard M. Lodish, *The Advertising & Promotion Challenge* (New York: Oxford University Press, 1986), p. 93.

Recent empirical research has indicated a growing trend toward the use of the data-based methods with special emphasis on the objective and task method. This is a build-up approach in which the costs of the tasks necessary to achieve the promotional objectives are summed to obtain the promotional appropriation.[2]

Why is it so important that firms appropriate their resources for promotion as efficiently as possible? Of course, at the micro level the firm that does a poor job of setting and/or using an appropriation will suffer the consequences on its bottom line. At the macro level the problem is important because of the magnitude of the expenditures involved. For example, look at Table 9–1, which lists the top 100 national advertisers for 1991. The totals include outlays for measured media including print, TV, radio, and outdoor. They also include an estimate of expenditures for unmeasured media such as sales promotion and direct marketing.

Total ad spending of the top 100 was $33.7 billion (a decline of 5.6 percent from 1990 levels). Top 100 spending for unmeasured media declined only 1.8 percent to $15 billion. This change in promotional emphasis reflected the impact of the Gulf War and the continuing economic recession.[3] Add to the spending of the top 100 what smaller firms are spending, and then consider that many firms spend twice as much for personal selling as they do for advertising, sales promotion, and direct marketing, and you can see that improving the quality of appropriation decisions of individual firms is also important in aggregate. To paraphrase the late Senator Dirksen, tens of billions here and tens of billions there, and before long you're talking about real money.

TABLE 9–1

The 100 Leading National Advertisers of 1991

Rank 1991	Rank 1990	Advertisers	Ad spending in 1991*	Rank 1991	Rank 1990	Advertisers	Ad spending in 1991
1	1	Procter & Gamble Co.	$2,249.0	51	55	SmithKline Beecham	$208.3
2	2	Philip Morris Cos.	2,045.6	52	54	Adolph Coors Co.	206.9
3	4	General Motors Corp.	1,442.1	53	51	American Stores Co.	201.6
4	3	Sears, Roebuck & Co.	1,179.4	54	53	Hasbro Inc.	201.4
5	6	PepsiCo	903.4	55	46	General Electric Co.	198.8
6	5	Grand Metropolitan	744.7	56	52	Schering-Plough Corp.	198.4
7	15	Johnson & Johnson	733.0	57	71	Wal-Mart Stores	189.8
8	8	McDonald's Corp.	694.8	58	62	Clorox Co.	182.6
9	14	Ford Motor Co.	676.6	59	68	Gillette Co.	182.5
10	13	Eastman Kodak Co.	661.4	60	65	Paramount Communications	179.4
11	12	Warner-Lambert Co.	656.5	61	63	S.C. Johnson & Son	174.0
12	16	Toyota Motor Corp.	632.2	62	60	U.S. dairy farmers	167.9
13	7	AT&T Co.	617.3	63	89	Delta Air Lines	164.5

TABLE 9–1

⌣ **Concluded**

Rank 1991	Rank 1990	Advertisers	Ad spending in 1991*	Rank 1991	Rank 1990	Advertisers	Ad spending in 1991
14	10	Nestle SA	600.5	64	61	Campbell Soup Co.	164.1
15	18	Unilever NV	593.7	65	73	Helene Curtis Industries	157.4
16	9	Time Warner	587.5	66	67	Carter Hawley Hale Stores	151.9
17	17	Kellogg Co.	577.7	67	76	AMR Corp.	150.1
18	11	RJR Nabisco	571.0	68	64	ITT Corp.	141.5
19	20	General Mills	555.6	69	78	Marriott Corp.	139.7
20	21	Chrysler Corp.	531.1	70	130	MCI Communications Corp.	139.5
21	19	Kmart Corp.	527.2	71	84	Thompson Medical/Slim-Fast Food Cos.	137.5
22	22	Anheuser-Busch Cos.	508.4				
23	23	Walt Disney Co.	489.1	72	88	News Corp.	135.8
24	25	American Home Products Corp.	447.1	73	59	Phillips NV	133.1
				74	102	Dr Pepper/Seven-Up Cos.	131.4
25	26	Sony Corp.	438.6	75	80	CPC International	131.4
26	36	H.J. Heinz Co.	403.1	76	69	Sprint Corp.	131.4
27	31	Ralston Purina Co.	393.5	77	58	Goodyear Tire & Rubber Co.	130.7
28	29	Coca-Cola Co.	367.4				
29	28	J.C. Penney Co.	362.6	78	66	Levi Strauss & Co.	129.4
30	24	Bristol-Myers Squibb Co.	352.5	79	56	Loews Corp.	129.0
31	34	Honda Motor Co.	333.1	80	74	Revlon Group	128.0
32	38	Hershey Foods Corp.	298.9	81	83	Bell Atlantic Corp.	127.5
33	32	Matsushita Electric Industrial Co.	292.3	82	75	Dow Chemical Co.	127.1
				83	50	Montgomery Ward & Co.	126.7
34	41	R.H. Macy & Co.	289.4	84	133	Reebok International	126.5
35	30	May Department Stores Co.	277.3	85	82	Seagram Co.	126.3
36	35	Sara Lee Corp.	273.0	86	87	Wm. Wrigley Jr. Co.	125.4
37	27	Nissan Motor Co.	268.9	87	95	Wendy's International	124.1
38	40	Mars Inc.	253.9	88	91	Daimler-Benz AG	122.2
39	37	U.S. Government	253.0	89	72	Hallmark Cards	121.8
40	45	ConAgra	249.7	90	77	Mobile Corp.	120.0
41	42	Quaker Oats Co.	237.7	91	81	Hyundai Group	119.5
42	39	Colgate-Palmolive Co.	227.5	92	97	Upjohn Co.	119.3
43	33	Dayton Hudson Corp.	226.5	93	92	UAL Corp.	119.2
44	49	American Express Co.	226.4	94	96	Canon Inc.	117.6
45	57	Nike Inc.	223.3	95	103	Ciba-Geigy	115.4
46	43	Federated Department Stores	222.8	96	94	U.S. Shoe Corp.	113.3
47	48	American Brands	217.5	97	129	B.A.T. Industries	113.0
48	44	Mazda Motor Corp.	215.0	98	104	Kimberly-Clark Corp.	107.7
49	70	Circuit City Stores	213.7	99	156	American Cyanamid Co.	105.2
50	47	Tandy Corp.	213.3	100	99	Monsanto Co.	100.8

* Dollars are in millions.

Source: *Advertising Age*, September 23, 1992, p. 1. Used by permission.

Judgmental Approaches

Arbitrary Allocation   It goes without saying that allocation by arbitrary methods has always been common. The shortcomings of such an approach are numerous. For example, advertising frequently seems to serve as a vent for executive emotion and personality traits. One authority puts it this way:

> Noneconomic, or psychological, criteria by which management evaluates advertising also need to be understood. . . . The function of advertising is highly cathartic, it is the focus of many strong emotional needs and drives relating to "self-expression" or aggressiveness. . . . Executive decisions on advertising philosophy and budget often may reflect as much the executive's psychological profile as they do the familiar economic criteria. The advertising philosophy and budget may be determined as much by personality as by profit maximization. . . . Each type of executive personality has a characteristic mode of feeling toward advertising in the light of this association of advertising with self-assertiveness or aggressive tendencies. Those who have either naturally or compensatorily induced strong self-expressive tendencies clearly tended to budget more for advertising. The latter tended to have wider swings in "intuition" or feelings of satisfaction or dissatisfaction.[4]

Moreover, the appropriation determined by emotions may in no way be relevant for promotion in that it does not consider the task to be performed or the impact of the expenditure on the bottom line. The focus should be on the strategic requirements of the firm rather than on the satisfaction of psychological needs of executives.

Percentage of Sales   A commonly used method of determining an advertising budget is the percentage-of-sales approach. In its simplest application, this technique requires the calculation of the proportion of the sales dollar allocated to promotion in the past and then the application of this percentage to either past or forecasted sales to arrive at the amount to be spent. A fairly common variation is to allocate a fixed amount per unit for promotion, and then to obtain the appropriation by multiplying this amount by the forecasted unit sales.

The percentage of sales invested by advertisers can vary widely. For example, data for 1992 published by Schonfeld & Associates indicated that manufacturers of special cleaning and polishing preparations (SIC 2842) spent 14.7 percent of sales on advertising, while advertising agencies (SIC 7311) spent 0.2 percent.[5] It should not be inferred, however, that the firms noted determined their advertising appropriations through the use of the percentage-of-sales approach.

Two studies of company practices disclosed that many firms use the sales ratio as a fixed guideline for their expenditures.[6] The base figure is the sales volume projected or forecast for the period that the appropriation will cover. Many firms reported that the percentage used remains constant from year to year, and in some cases industry averages are taken as a point of reference. Variable ratios find favor with some companies, especially when new products are to be introduced.

The percentage-of-sales approach is widely used for several basic reasons. It is simple to calculate, and it is almost second nature for management to think of costs in percentage terms. Because the percentage-of-sales approach gives an illusion of definiteness, it is easy to defend to management, to stockholders, and to other interests. In addition, it is a financially safe method because expenditures are keyed to sales revenues, thereby minimizing the risk of nonavailability of funds. Finally, when it is widespread throughout the industry, advertising is proportional to market shares, and competitive warfare is made less probable. This competitive aspect is especially appealing to those who give strong credence to the human inclination to resist change.

It should be clear to the perceptive reader that the advantages of the percentage-of-sales approach are illusory. Most important is the inherent fallacy that appropriating for promotion as a percentage of past sales views advertising as a *result, not a cause, of sales.* This logical deficiency is widely recognized, and forecasted sales rather than past sales are more widely used. The use of forecasted sales, however, is fraught with circular reasoning: How can sales be forecasted without knowing how much is to be invested in sales-generating efforts? Basically, the fundamental and perhaps fatal weakness is that the focus is not on the promotional job to be done; deceptively simple and arbitrary means are substituted for the comprehensive analysis that must, of necessity, be undertaken to reach both promotional and financial goals.

The percentage-of-sales method, then, is seldom an adequate tool unless the environment is almost totally static and the role for promotion is unchanging from period to period—a highly unusual situation. This method should be used only as a starting point to calculate how many dollars would be allocated if conditions remain the same. Then the promotional objectives must be examined to fine-tune the appropriation to the job to be done. More is said later about this use of percentage of sales.

All You Can Afford   Some firms determine their appropriation largely on the basis of available funds. It is not unusual that the need to show satisfactory profits in a given year limits advertising expenditures. Also, upper limits are sometimes based on customary ratios between total advertising expenditure and forecasted sales revenue. When these are exceeded, the appropriation will be pared. In other words, management spends as much as it believes the company can afford without unduly interfering with financial liquidity.

It cannot be denied that liquidity is an important consideration. Assume the situation shown in Table 9–2. With successive deduction of margins and other costs and a planned profit of 6 cents per unit, a residual of 13 cents remains for advertising, taxes, and other expenses. Assume further that it is determined that 10 cents will be allocated to advertising and that forecasted unit sales are 100,000. Then the advertising appropriation cannot exceed $10,000 unless funds are available from other sources. Management may be hard put to counteract financial necessity unless compelling reasons exist for expanding the appropriation by borrowing or other means, although management may, with considerable justification, propose *payout planning,* a procedure to be discussed later in connection with new-product budgeting.

It is apparent that the $10,000 appropriation may in no way be related to objectives in that it may lead to either underspending or overspending. For this reason, it is seldom relied on exclusively, except possibly in the case of new products or in situations in which it is grossly apparent that the firm has underspent in the past and that any amount of funds within reason will still generate a positive marginal return. Regardless of the situation, however, liquidity will always be an important factor, and management must be prepared with convincing arguments to justify requested increases.

Data-Oriented Approaches

Competitive Parity *Competitive parity* occurs when dollars are allocated by emulating competitors and spending approximately the same amount. Data for this approach can be found in advertising periodicals or can be obtained from the U.S. Internal Revenue Service and various trade associations.

Competitive parity offers the advantage that competition, a major component of the environment, is specifically recognized and adaptation to it is sought. In this sense, at least, competitive parity represents a small step past the percentage-of-sales method. It also offers the advantage that competitive relationships are stabilized and aggressive market warfare minimized.

Aside from coping with the variable of competition, however, this technique in no way recognizes other components of the promotion task, and the most gross oversight is the total lack of emphasis on the buyer. Competitive parity also assumes that all competitors have similar objectives and face the same tasks—a most dubious assumption. It further assumes that the competitor or competitors spent dollars with equal effectiveness; however, identical expenditures seldom imply identical effectiveness. Finally, the only data available to management, short of outright collusion or competitive espionage, are past expenditures. These data become useless, however, if the competitor changes its promotional mix. Future spending plans are seldom known, so the ability to match competitor expenditures will always be limited by available information.

TABLE 9–2

Computation of Promotion Cost per Unit

Selling price	$1.00
Retailer margin 30%	−0.30
Wholesalers' selling price	$0.70
Wholesalers' margin	−0.11
Manufacturer's price	$0.59
Manufacturer's production cost	−0.40
Revenue minus costs	$0.19
Specified 6% profit (on retail price)	−0.06
Residual for selling and other costs	$0.13

In all fairness, it must be stated that few companies rely on competitive parity as the sole means of determining their appropriation. It should not be rejected totally as an appropriation approach because competitive efforts can be the dominant variable to be met in the promotional environment. The firm's objectives may by necessity be largely defensive in nature. Although it seldom is practical to match the competitor to the degree implied in competitive parity, this consideration will often weigh heavily in promotional strategy.

Objective and Task   No method discussed thus far stands up under close scrutiny, either because of failure to focus on the job to be done or because of the unavailability of needed data. This leads to the last major method of determining the amount to be spent on promotion—objective and task. In contrast to the methods discussed so far, the objective-and-task approach involves a buildup that aggregates the costs of performing those tasks needed to reach stated objectives to determine the total promotional appropriation. Of all the methods discussed, it has the most merits, and a recent study indicates that its use by leading consumer goods advertisers in the United Kingdom increased from 45 percent in 1982 to 56 percent in 1987.[7] Its use in the United States is at least at this level, if not greater.

This widely used method is simple to describe. It requires only spelling out objectives realistically and in detail, and then calculating the costs necessary to accomplish the objectives. Often, financial liquidity will enter as a constraint on the upper limit of the appropriation. It is assumed that research will have been done to specify the tasks necessary to attain the objectives; all that remains is to put dollar estimates on these efforts.

On the face of it, one cannot argue with this approach. It epitomizes the concept of marginal analysis in that it forces striving for the intersection of marginal cost and marginal return. It avoids the arbitrary decisions and the illusory certainty of other approaches and generates research-oriented analysis consistent with a modern philosophy of promotional strategy.

No matter how compelling the advantages, it must be stated that management frequently has no conclusive idea of how much it will cost to attain the objective or even whether or not the objective is *worth* attaining. What is the best way, for example, to increase brand awareness by 20 percent next year? Should a combination of network television, spot radio, and newspapers be used with hard-sell copy, or should these variables be changed? Obviously, all possible combinations of efforts cannot be evaluated, and it is perhaps impossible to isolate the *best* promotion mix. Nevertheless, what other alternative exists for profit-oriented management? There is no shortcut to experimentation and other forms of research if scientific management is to be implemented.

A realistic goal is to find an approach that seems to work well on the basis of research, estimate the costs, and then accumulate an appropriation by this means. It may not be the best mix of efforts, but it will no doubt exceed the estimate arrived at by percentage-of-sales or other arbitrary means. Measurement of results will then permit the accumulation of data that, over time, should provide an invaluable source of information for future appropriating with the objective-

and-task method. The difficulty of the method cannot continue to be a barrier to its practice. More suggestions for implementation will be given later in this chapter.

Experimentation and Testing   This method involves selecting a set of typical and matched markets. Different "trial" promotional budgets are spent in each market, and the resulting sales results are compared. The budget variant that best meets the objectives of the promotional strategy (sales, market share, profits, and so forth) is generalized and used for the total market. An advantage of this method is that the advertiser can control for several market factors, thus getting a clearer measure of promotion's contribution.

The disadvantages are threefold: (1) the cost of conducting the experiment, (2) the time it takes to get results, and (3) the premature informing of competitors of proposed promotional strategies.

Modeling and Simulation   Modeling and simulation are quantitative approaches that attempt to mathematically describe the past performance of a brand and to simulate what might be its future performance given changes in promotional strategy. Worthy of special note is PROD II, developed by Fred Zufreyden.[8] This is a PC-based system that allows marketing and promotion managers to forecast various market performance measures for consumer products, including awareness levels, sales volume, purchase frequency, and profitability. It can be used to evaluate alternate TV media schedules and can aid in determining the most appropriate level of future promotional expenditures.

Problems associated with modeling and simulation include the cost and the time necessary to construct and validate the model and the lack of sufficient evidence that simulation using the model has meaningful predictive value given the dynamics of the market environment.

There is increasing interest in these quantitative approaches by managers of promotion, but to date they are used generally as supplements to the other data-based methods.

CONCLUSIONS ON DETERMINING THE APPROPRIATION

Of the appropriation methods discussed, the objective-and-task approach most nearly approximates the ideal as provided by marginal analysis. Yet implementation of this approach is fraught with the difficulty of estimating the tasks necessary to accomplish objectives, to say nothing of the costs. This approach requires a great commitment to researching the shape of the response to promotion for individual brands as an indication of interest (awareness, sales, etc.). In general, this response function has been found to exhibit decreasing returns as advertising expenditures are increased.[9]

To monitor the effectiveness of the promotional strategy for selected brands or categories (including the appropriation), specific research is necessary. The primary objective of this research should be to guarantee promotional accountability. That is, how well are the goals being met given the resources expended? Many companies have introduced semiannual, quarterly, or monthly reviews for the purpose of evaluating current promotional strategies and introducing modifications where necessary. Procter & Gamble, Quaker Oats, Bristol-Myers, and North American Philips are all reported to have instituted this type of system.

IMPLEMENTING THE OBJECTIVE-AND-TASK APPROACH

The ideal approach to determining the optimal level of expenditures builds on the concepts inherent in marginal analysis. The logical procedure would be to establish objectives and then to experiment until determining the level of expenditure that most closely approximates the optimum. Larger firms commonly follow this procedure, although it can be time consuming and expensive.

In a three-year test experiment, a major petroleum company divided a large number of cities into three test groups and one control group. One test group received half as much advertising as normal; expenditures were twice the normal rate in another group, and three times the rate in the third. It was found that a 50 percent reduction had no great effect, whereas the greatest sales increases were in the double-expenditure markets. A tripling of the budget led to only minimal increases. Similarly, a six-year research program at the Anheuser-Busch Company comprising advertising variations in 200 geographical areas showed that it was possible to reduce advertising expenditures and still increase sales. Many believe, as a result, that experimentation is the only feasible approach, given management pressures for greater promotional efficiency and accountability.

Experimentation obviously is not feasible for most firms because of time and cost constraints. Therefore, some combination of the procedures mentioned above must usually be employed. A logical approach encompasses the following steps:

1. Isolation of objectives.
2. Determination of expenditures through a "build-up" analysis.
3. Comparison against industry percentage-of-sales guidelines.
4. Comparison against a projected cost figure based on percentage of future sales.
5. Reconciliation of divergences between built-up costs and industry percentage-of-sales guidelines.
6. Establishment of a payout plan where appropriate.
7. Modification of estimates in terms of company policies.
8. Specification of when expenditures will be made.
9. Establishment of built-in flexibility.

Isolation of Objectives

The first step in building a budgetary plan is to estimate the total market for the product category. These figures may be available from governmental sources, trade publications, or from market research firms such as A.C. Nielsen or the Market Research Corporation of America. Then it is necessary to estimate the share of the total market that the firm most likely can attain. Factors underlying this estimate are:

1. Product uniqueness—the advantages relative to competition and the ease with which they can be duplicated.
2. Number of competitors—it is difficult to obtain a large share in a highly fragmented market.
3. The spending pattern of competition—a large share is more feasible when competition has not been aggressive and is unwilling and/or unable to become so in the future.

Estimated market share becomes significant in that it is possible to approximate necessary spending levels based on past industry performance, as is discussed later.

In addition, of course, communication objectives must be specified. These objectives should be combined into a comprehensive and specific statement on which a detailed plan of efforts producing measurable results can be built.

Expenditure Estimation through Build-Up Analysis

Once objectives have been specified, the next question concerns what is required to accomplish these tasks. This analysis, in turn, should encompass mass media expenditures (advertising and public relations), direct selling costs, and costs of stimulating reseller support.

Advertising and Public Relations   If the objective, for example, is to saturate the teenage market through repetitive advertising, it is clear that this objective will require a large budget for continued advertising in media that reach this market segment. In more technical terms, media strategy would be established to achieve *frequency* (the number of exposures, per individual target audience member, in a purchase cycle). On the other hand, the task may call for reaching as large a market as possible, in which case a wide variety of media would be utilized to attain *reach* (the number of target audience individuals exposed to advertising in a purchase cycle). Reach and frequency requirements, therefore, are instrumental in determining the required appropriation. The basic approach is to "build up" or select the necessary media.

The analysis underlying media selection, which is complex, is the subject of Chapter 12. It is recognized that media analysis lies at the heart of the objective-and-task approach; in fact, Roger Barton, a widely quoted authority, does not even mention percentage-of-sales and other approaches in his discussion of budgeting.[10] He contends that the final budgetary figure is based on (1) definition of the types of media to be used, (2) the costs of individual media, (3) the frequency of insertions, (4) the media mix, and (5) other related considerations. This analysis is common to both advertising and public relations, although much publicity is achieved at no direct cost to the firm.

Direct Selling Costs   Next it is necessary to determine the required selling activities and resulting costs to reach wholesalers and retailers and to stimulate their promotional support. Computations are usually made by territory or other subunits of the firm when environmental situations are known to differ. Judgment armed with research data is the only tool available. Recourse must be made to historical records detailing efforts under similar sets of alternatives in the past and the costs that were incurred. In the absence of appropriate records, experimental research may be required.

The cost of efforts raises problems that require some discussion. A first step will always be to determine the total of fixed selling costs because, in all probability, they will change only slightly from period to period. A similar relationship may be found for semivariable costs that, for all intents and purposes, are fixed over large ranges of output. The problem comes in estimating variable costs, and detailed historical records are required for the estimates to have any meaning.

The problem of variable costs is clarified considerably if standard costs can be constructed for each activity. A cost standard is a predetermined norm for an operation intended to represent the costs under usual operating conditions. Standard costs frequently are based on time and duty analysis whereby time intervals required to perform an activity are translated into monetary terms. The availability of standard costs then permits the computation of a sales budget on the basis of estimates of the functions to be performed multiplied by the appropriate cost standard for each function. It might be discovered, for example, that the standard cost per sales call in territories 1, 2, and 3 is $100 and the best estimate of calls required during the coming year is 300, 200, and 150, respectively. The budgeted costs then would be $30,000 in territory 1 (300 × $100), $20,000 in territory 2, and $15,000 in territory 3.

Cost Standards   The two most widely used cost standards are cost per sales call and cost per dollar of net sales. Standards are also established frequently for the salaries and expenses of home office sales administration, the expenses of field supervision, the costs of home office and field office clerical efforts, and other related functions.

Even though standard costs are a significant aid, the applicability of standards depends greatly on the nature of the tasks performed. Clerical activities, of course, are routine, and it is not difficult to establish standards such as cost per invoice line posted. Creative selling, on the other hand, may be far from routine in that a sale may not be made until many preliminary customer contacts are completed. In such instances, it may be impossible to establish reasonable standards.

Stimulating Reseller Support   The point of departure is the history of trade efforts in the product category. What is the ratio of trade expenditures to the advertising of major competitors? What are the demands from the chains for "slotting allowances" to gain retail shelf space? In most situations, it is necessary to be competitive because more manufacturers seek support than can be accommodated by resellers. Additional costs to be considered include product samples, coupons, free goods, cooperative advertising, provision of point-of-sale and other displays, and so forth.

Comparison against Industry Percentage-of-Sales Guidelines

It is frequently found that *share of industry advertising,* sometimes referred to as *share of voice,* is a primary criterion of success, especially in marketing a new product. The share of industry advertising needed for a successful new product introduction in categories such as household goods, food products, and proprietary medicines is generally about 1.5 to 1.6 times the share of industry sales.

For example, if the sales objective for a new product is set at 10 percent of category sales, then the advertising appropriation for that product should be about 15 percent of the total category advertising expenditure.

The exact multiplier to use is a function of the strength of the brand; weaker offerings require higher multipliers such as 2 or 3. In addition, the effectiveness of the advertising campaign can also exert an influence. Exceptionally creative campaigns reduce the multiplier to less than 1.5. Most experienced promotion managers use results of previous product offerings as guidelines in determining the most effective multiplier and thus the advertising appropriation needed to reach the sales objective.

Comparison against Projected Percentage of Future Sales

It was suggested earlier that the percentage of sales devoted to promotion in the past is a useful starting point in setting an appropriation. These figures are readily available in conventional accounting statements, and breakdowns can be provided for sales territories and products.

The application of percentages to forecasted sales involves circular reasoning, to the extent that it is difficult to forecast sales without knowing the investment in promotion. As a result, this is not a sufficient basis for appropriating, but it does provide an estimate, all things being equal, of what would be spent if proportions were not altered to meet changed objectives. Thus it serves as a benchmark against which to compare the built-up budgetary sum.

Reconciliation of Divergence between Built-Up Costs and Industry Percentage-of-Sales Guidelines

Once the projected percentage figures for the industry and the company, as well as those for built-up expenditures, are available, the focus can be on reconciling differences. If a 1.6 to 1 ratio is reasonable, given past industry experience in the product category, and projected spending is far in excess of the ratio, it may be necessary to revise premises, assumptions, and other factors to ascertain whether the projected figure is reasonable. The budgetary analysis is a continuing process of this type because only by accident will a sum be determined that is clearly the optimum appropriation.

Payout Planning

Frequently, extending the budgetary period is desirable, especially when new products are introduced, because one calendar year may not be sufficient to accomplish objectives. Strategy may encompass three to five years, and the appropriation must be viewed in that time perspective. Moreover, profitability may not be realized until the end of the period. In other words, the payout from the expenditures is expected to occur at a later point in time; this extension of the planning period is frequently referred to as *payout planning.* Because it is most frequently used in introducing new products, further discussion of payout planning is reserved for a later section of this chapter.

Modification of Estimates in Terms of Company Policies

It is also pertinent to fine-tune the appropriation figures to make the sums consistent with the overall framework of company policy and dollars invested in the other functions. Financial liquidity must always be considered, for there are bound to be financial constraints that cannot be exceeded, even in payout planning, regardless of logic or compelling necessity. Moreover, *too much can be spent* for promotion in view of the entire company situation. There is the possibility that advertising and selling can easily disturb orderly flows of manpower, inventory, and cash by borrowing sales from the future and introducing unwarranted fluctuation in other flows. The fact that the company is a system of related flows must never be overlooked, and dollars must be invested to maximize the response of the *system,* not the *function* itself. The danger to be avoided is suboptimization, which results when management loses sight of the system in which it operates.

Specification of When Expenditures Will Be Made

A well-developed appropriation plan requires the designation of when, during the budgetary period, dollars will be expended. This determination permits forecasting of cash flow requirements by the company comptroller to ensure that funds are available when needed. The choice of timing patterns for promotional input to the various media is a part of the overall promotional strategy. Whether these patterns will be continuous or pulsing or take some other form will be discussed in some detail in Chapter 12. We are concerned here with the impact of the selected strategy on a company's cash needs.

Building In Flexibility

The appropriation should never be viewed as a perfect map to be followed without variation. The dangers of inflexibility are analyzed at length in the management literature, and there is compelling logic for building in sufficient flexibility to allow for changing conditions. Markets are becoming more volatile, product planning deadlines are shortened, and many possibilities of tactical shifts by competition may occur. This flexibility may be provided by a 10 to 15 percent reserve sum that is not allocated until needed.

Adaptation to change, of course, requires maintenance of detailed records of results. More and more companies are now establishing a new management post—the advertising controller. He or she is appointed to be a watchdog over spending, with the result that performance may be more or less continually reviewed. Records are also useful as guides to future strategy decisions. Unfortunately, this type of record is seldom kept on any systematic basis, and this lack can serve as a real impediment to the application of the philosophy of marginal analysis.

Comments on the Suggested Approach

This section has not been presented with the objective of providing a formula that can be followed automatically. Rather, a step-by-step procedure has been suggested to approximate marginal analysis through the objective-and-task approach, and it must be adapted creatively and analytically to each situation. The final result should never be construed as being ideal because there may always be good reasons for major changes throughout the planning period. Also, the tendency to use the appropriation as a screen to hide inefficiencies must be guarded against. This danger can be avoided if top management insists on measuring results and evaluating the competence of personnel in performance terms.

A decision that management faces once the total appropriation has been determined is how to allocate it to various parts of the country. This so-called *geographic allocation* is an important issue if the best returns for the money expended are to be realized.

GEOGRAPHIC ALLOCATION

Geographic variables often provide a useful basis for allocating promotional expenditures. To use these variables it is necessary to determine the *relative sales possibilities* from one geographic area to the next. For example, if a product is sold nationwide, should twice as much effort be placed in the Chicago market as in Detroit, Michigan? Or should Detroit receive an equivalent allocation of promotional funds? Such questions can be answered only when *market potentials* are computed, for as a general rule, efforts are allocated in proportion to potential, all other things being equal.

Several different categories of potential might be computed for a given product:

1. Volume attainable under ideal conditions (i.e., if all efforts were perfectly adapted to the environment).
2. The relative capacity of a market to absorb the products of an entire industry, such as the major appliance industry.
3. The relative size of market for a company's type of product (i.e., sales of color television sets versus stereo sets).
4. The actual sales a company can expect.

The last category, of course, is the equivalent of the sales forecast for a firm, or the sales volume that can be expected if the firm continues on its present course. Potential, on the other hand, refers to sales possibilities rather than expected sales, and is of greater significance for purposes of demand analysis. Although forecasting is necessary in determining allocations and budgets, it is beyond the scope of this book.

Useful Measures

The measure of potential that is generally found to be most useful is either category 2 or category 3—market strength (capacity) for industry products or for types of products rather than the specific products of a firm. This is not to say, however, that potential is the sole basis for allocation of resources because potentials for industry sales do not reveal the competitive structure of a market or the firm's ability to make inroads. Detroit, for example, might appear to offer high potential, whereas in reality competitors are so entrenched that inroads would be impossible. Ideally, then, potentials must be augmented with information about the competitive structure as well as the firm's previous experience in the market. The goal, of course, is to make an optimum allocation of resources to alternative markets; this can never be done with great precision without a reliable estimate of the impact of a given level of promotional expenditure on market share. Nevertheless, an array of markets in terms of potential provides a workable estimate of the probability of response to sales efforts.

The methods used to compute potentials include (1) a corollary products index, (2) industry sales, (3) general buying power indexes, and (4) custom-made indexes.

Corollary Products Index   At times, it is possible to use the sales of another product as an indication of potential. Presumably the corollary product and the product in question are related in some way. If such a product can be found and its sales data are available, these data may be used as clues of expected variations in sales patterns of one's own product from one market to the next.

Residential building permits, for example, should be a realistic indication of the sales potential for bathroom fixtures. The danger, of course, is that association between one product and another does not mean that the two sell in direct proportion in different areas. As a result, this method should be used with caution, and in many instances it will be found to be inapplicable.

Industry Sales   This method uses sales of the industry or a major portion of it as the measure of potential. It is thus possible to clarify areas where the industry has made maximum penetration. The advantage is that it considers the experience of all competitors and avoids the error of considering only the circumstances peculiar to an individual firm. From the industry sales data, the share of market possessed by the firm can be computed easily, thereby arriving at a measure of sales possibilities.

Assume, for example, that industry sales are available and that a firm is discovered to derive 1.3 percent of its sales revenue from Connecticut, but that the total industry derives 3.4 percent from that state. It is clear that remedial steps are needed, and it is probable that a larger share of promotional dollars should be allocated to this state, all other things being equal. It is thus possible to capitalize on areas where industry products sell strongly and to avoid excessive promotion in the weak markets.

Unavailability of data   One limitation of this method is the frequent lack of availability of industry sales data. For some products (e.g., automobiles and motorboats), license or tax records are a good source of this information. Trade associations such as the National Electrical Manufacturers Association also make such statistics available to their members.

Sales data, however, reflect only *what is,* not *what might be.* In other words, there is no certainty that available data measure untapped market opportunity for both the industry and the firm. Moreover, it is assumed that past experience is a good measure of the future. In some industries producing staple commodities, this may be true. It is doubtful, for example, that total sales of men's shirts vary drastically from year to year. In dynamic markets, however, the probable existence of untapped demand makes this an unsafe assumption. As a result, other types of indexes may be preferable.

General Buying Power Indexes   The index of relative buying power in various localities is a good indication of potential for many products. A number of data sources, including magazine circulation, are used for this purpose. This index is based on the assumption that those reading magazines have money to spend. No doubt this is often true, especially among subscribers to special-purpose periodicals. A manufacturer of fishing reels, for example, might find the circulation of *Sports Afield* to be a reliable criterion; similarly, manufacturers of photographic equipment selling to skilled amateurs could use *Popular Photography* for this purpose.

Total retail sales in various markets are also used for a buying power index. *Census of Business* data are issued periodically and are updated annually by *Sales & Marketing Management* and other publications for this purpose. Buying power should not be used, however, unless it is clear that there is high correlation between variations in total retail sales and variations in sales of the product under analysis.

Accurate indexes   Usually the most accurate indexes are those that are constructed using several factors in combination. The best-known combination index is the *Sales & Marketing Management Survey of Buying Power,* published annually. This index is derived by weighting population by two; effective buying income by five; and total retail sales by three. If the state of Illinois, for instance, were found to have 5 percent of effective buying power, a manufacturer using this index would allocate 5 percent of its promotional dollars to that state. Regardless of absolute sales volume, this state should generate about 5 percent of the total sales. Data are also provided by counties and cities so that a more precise allocation can be made (see Table 9–3).

A buying power index offers several advantages: (1) It is available in published form and can be used directly without additional computations, (2) the indexes are issued frequently and in considerable geographic detail, and (3) they may be used when other data that might be of greater use cannot be procured. A general index of this type, however, is not always appropriate. It is assumed that demand varies directly with this index, but this variance is likely to be correct only for those products whose demand rises or falls with purchasing power, regardless of other considerations. The demand for milk should not vary with buying power, and the use of snow tires is more associated with climatic conditions than anything else.

Custom-Made Indexes   It may be necessary to construct an index unique to a given product. In order to do so, it is necessary to isolate the important factors affecting demand, obtain data on these factors, and combine them into one index, with appropriate weights assigned to those with greatest influence. These factors may include any of the data mentioned previously. Buyer studies may be helpful, but the method usually depends more on informed guess than on scientific procedure.

For example, a large manufacturer of high-style belts, braces, garters, and jewelry found that the *Sales & Marketing Management* buying power index did not reflect the urban concentration of demand for its product. As a result, it used urban population (with a weight of three), retail sales (weight of three), and disposable income (weight of four). The result was a more precise indication of potential. Similarly, a brewery used the *Sales & Marketing Management* index to compute new-product potentials and found that sales in metropolitan areas did not meet expectations based on the index. It was discovered that total retail sales have little relation to the sales of beer, and that the important determinants instead were the number of people over age 18, social class, and per capita consumption of malt beverages.

Such an index is often constructed in somewhat arbitrary fashion by selecting and trying those factors that seem to be relevant. A more sophisticated procedure is to experiment with a greater variety of factors and choose those that are found to have the greatest relationship to sales through use of multiple correlation

TABLE 9–3

Sales & Marketing Management Survey of Effective Buying Power for Selected Areas of Michigan (estimates: 12/31/91)

METRO AREA County City	Total EBI* ($000)	Median Hsld. EBI	% of Hslds. by EBI Group: (A) $10,000–$19,999 (B) $20,000–$34,999 (C) $35,000–$49,999 (D) $50,000 & Over				Buying Power Index
			A	B	C	D	
ANN ARBOR	4,842,662	37,643	14.2	22.3	19.1	34.5	.1272
Washtenaw	4,842,662	37,643	14.2	22.3	19.1	34.5	.1272
● Ann Arbor	1,926,342	34,651	15.9	22.9	16.4	33.1	.0558
SUBURBAN TOTAL	2,916,320	39,310	13.2	21.9	20.7	35.5	.0714
BATTLE CREEK	1,803,234	29,351	19.3	26.3	19.2	21.2	.0527
Calhoun	1,803,234	29,351	19.3	26.3	19.2	21.2	.0527
● Battle Creek	722,827	26,854	21.0	24.8	16.9	20.0	.0219
SUBURBAN TOTAL	1,080,407	30,959	18.0	27.3	20.9	22.1	.0308
BENTON HARBOR	2,142,207	29,671	18.8	26.1	20.4	20.6	.0605
Berrien	2,142,207	29,671	18.8	26.1	20.4	20.6	.0605
● Benton Harbor	76,033	11,320	27.0	16.6	7.3	3.8	.0065
SUBURBAN TOTAL	2,066,174	31,132	18.1	27.0	21.4	21.8	.0540
DETROIT	69,088,249	36,150	14.2	21.3	19.7	31.9	1.8182
Lapeer	1,044,157	37,594	14.6	22.4	22.6	31.5	.0275
Livingston	2,070,225	47,186	8.8	18.7	21.6	46.0	.0461
Macomb	11,637,833	39,838	12.8	22.5	22.8	34.5	.3245
Roseville	707,791	33,303	16.5	27.0	24.3	22.6	.0260
St. Clair Shores	1,142,323	37,951	13.7	24.5	23.7	31.2	.0291
Sterling Heights	2,003,133	47,026	9.0	18.2	22.4	45.3	.0584
Warren	2,221,634	36,992	14.3	24.4	22.5	30.5	.0663
Monroe	1,849,465	36,104	14.9	23.3	22.3	29.4	.0459
Oakland	23,410,841	46,139	10.0	18.7	19.7	45.0	.5835
Farmington Hills	1,923,300	54,014	7.0	15.7	18.0	54.8	.0430
● Pontiac	759,405	24,553	20.5	22.9	17.9	16.6	.0240
Rochester Hills	1,453,417	57,264	6.5	13.6	16.0	59.8	.0299
Royal Oak	1,250,509	39,425	12.0	24.1	23.4	33.8	.0323
Southfield	1,659,603	43,275	10.7	20.1	20.7	41.2	.0554
Troy	1,721,304	57,222	6.3	13.0	17.1	59.2	.0526
St. Clair	2,020,820	32,650	16.3	25.2	20.5	25.6	.0528
● Port Huron	398,704	23,680	21.2	26.1	16.2	15.0	.0156
Wayne	27,054,908	29,239	17.1	22.1	18.1	23.8	.7379
● Dearborn	1,466,605	35,723	15.4	22.9	20.1	30.9	.0497
Dearborn Heights	985,698	37,809	14.3	23.9	22.0	32.4	.0230
● Detroit	9,772,335	20,039	21.2	21.6	14.6	13.9	.2689

TABLE 9–3

			Concluded					

METRO AREA County City	Total EBI* ($000)	Median Hsld. EBI	% of Hslds. by EBI Group: (A) $10,000–$19,999 (B) $20,000–$34,999 (C) $35,000–$49,999 (D) $50,000 & Over				Buying Power Index
			A	B	C	D	
Lincoln Park	557,028	31,525	17.6	27.7	22.6	21.1	.0164
Livonia	1,856,402	49,114	8.0	17.3	21.4	48.7	.0539
Taylor	909,388	33,984	14.4	25.4	22.8	25.5	.0302
Westland	1,266,962	35,909	13.7	26.2	23.6	27.9	.0357
SUBURBAN TOTAL	56,691,200	41,521	11.7	21.2	21.3	38.2	1.4600
DETROIT–ANN ARBOR CONSOLIDATED AREA	73,930,911	36,239	14.3	21.4	19.5	32.1	1.9454

* Effective buying income.

Source: *Sales & Marketing Management*, August 24, 1992, p. C-93. Used with permission.

analysis. Correlation analysis measures the extent to which two or more variables are related by assessing the variation in one variable (say industry sales) that is accounted for by the association between this variable and others (say disposable income and housing starts).

Computing measures   The task of computing measures of multiple correlation once was formidable, but electronic computers have greatly simplified the procedure. Once various combinations have been tried, measures may be readily compared. Assume that five series are tested and found to have coefficients of correlation with sales of 0.66, 0.81, 0.91, 0.84, and 0.87. The third (0.91) obviously is the best of the five, since a correlation of 1.0 is ideal. In reality, however, it is doubtful that a correlation of 0.91 will be found because this is an exceptionally high degree of relationship.

Probably this procedure is the most acceptable of all of those discussed in this section, but it also has its disadvantages. First, the correlation may be spurious—a coincidence rather than a cause-and-effect relationship. Moreover, it is assumed that past industry sales success will hold in the future, and it is obvious that this might not be so in a volatile industry in the early stages of its growth. Finally, the data needed may not be attainable or may be of questionable accurcy. Regardless of the problems, this procedure does focus on finding the combination of factors that offers the best relationship to sales, and as such it is likely to be superior to a more general index under most circumstances.

EXPENDITURES FOR NEW PRODUCTS

Some special considerations enter into the appropriation process for new products, in addition to those that have been mentioned. Payout planning assumes particular importance, and experimentation with quantitative methods is providing some interesting new insights.

Payout Planning[11]

A payout plan is a procedure that extends the planning period for longer than one year, and it has proved especially useful in evaluating the proper course of action in introducing new products. Most often it covers three years, but in the case of slow-maturing products such as proprietary medicines or when large initial expenditures are necessary, the payout plan may be extended to cover four or five years. The stages in payout planning are (1) estimation of market-share objectives, (2) assessment of needed trade inventories, (3) determination of needed expenditures, (4) determination of the payout period, and (5) evaluation.

Estimation of Market-Share Objectives   It was previously mentioned that the first step in appropriating is to estimate the total market for the product category and then to assess the probable share to be captured by the firm. It should be noted that most new products reach their peak share and then decline to a lower level. Share builds slowly as distribution is achieved, promotion pressure is applied, and consumer trial is generated. Usually a brand will hit its peak share approximately 6 to 12 months after its introduction in a new area and will then level off or decline. It is then necessary to recycle the brand through product improvement.

This short life cycle for low-involvement packaged goods makes it important to accelerate trial through heavy advertising expenditures in the first few months after introduction. Products are new only once, and this is the most important period in the life of a brand. The higher the peak share, the greater the probability that the brand will be a success. Of course, for high-involvement products, longer payout periods would be more realistic.

Assessment of Needed Trade Inventories   The company also makes money on what is sold to the trade, so the goods necessary to "fill the pipeline" must be added to consumer sales to get the total volume for this manufacturer. There are two general guidelines to follow:

1. The larger the projected volume, the shorter the number of weeks' supply necessary in trade inventories.
2. Most products lose pipeline sales in the second year through resellers' cutbacks unless share is climbing; this exerts a negative force on sales in that year.

Determination of Needed Expenditures   Several guidelines should be followed in arriving at the proper appropriation level based on experience:

1. The first-year budget should permit a heavy introductory schedule (13 to 26 weeks) followed by a sustaining schedule at least equal to the second-year advertising budget.

2. A good rule of thumb is that expenditures for the introductory schedule should be about twice the rate currently spent by competitors who have shares equal to the company's objective.

3. Carefully check expenditures on a per unit basis against competitors. The brand with the highest shares usually has a lower cost per unit, and vice versa.

Determination of the Payout Period   In today's competitive marketplace, the trend is toward shorter payout periods. Most product development can be duplicated by the competition in a short time. There is also reason to believe that brand loyalty is not as great as it once was. Finally, there is a high rate of new-product failures. Long payouts are justified only when the projected life cycle of the product is very long and the potential rewards are very big.

Two payout plans are shown in Tables 9–4 and 9–5. Notice that the new food product considered in Table 9–4 was projected to return a loss in the first year and pay out in the second year. The drug product considered in Table 9–5, on

TABLE 9–4

Payout Plan for a New Food Product (000s)

	Theoretical Marketing Years		
	First	Second	Third
Total market (units)	50,000	52,000	54,000
Market share (%)	5.0	5.2	5.0
Volume (units)	2,500	2,704	2,700
Pipeline (units)	400	(50)	—
Total volume (units)	2,900	2,654	2,700
Total sales (@ $9)	26,100	23,886	24,300
Gross profit (@ $4)	11,600	10,616	10,800
Advertising ($)	6,500	4,000	4,000
Promotion to the trade ($)	8,000	2,000	2,000
Total advertising & promotion ($)	14,500	6,000	6,000
Gross trading profit ($)	(2,900)	4,616	4,800
Profit (% of sales)		19.3	19.8
Cumulative gross trading profit ($)	(2,900)	1,716	6,516

the other hand, was not expected to pay out until the fourth year. In the former example, the total promotional appropriation was highest in the first year so that maximum impact could be made, whereas the opposite is the case with the drug product, which matures more slowly.

Evaluation   In evaluating the soundness of a payout plan, management usually directs attention to the first year (the year of heavy investment) and to the first year after payout is achieved. This latter year gives management an opportunity to assess the long-term rewards of the investments they have made in the other years. By comparison with other opportunities and with competitive products, it is possible to make an experienced judgment on the wisdom of the investment. Of particular importance are examination of profit margins and the financial implications of an investment of this size. Additionally, the net present value of cash flows may be calculated to determine the investment viability of the expenditures.

Adaptation   It must be emphasized that a payout plan is a theoretical financial plan calling for a national introduction at one specific point in time. Management has the option to make the plan fit overall company fiscal goals more closely by, first of all, picking the most propitious time to introduce a product. For example, introducing at the end of a fiscal year could fatten company profit for that year by accumulating the profits from heavy initial trade sales, while deferring the heavy introductory advertising expenses until the next fiscal year.

TABLE 9–5

Payout Plan for a New Drug Product (000s)

	Theoretical Marketing Years				
	First	Second	Third	Fourth	Fifth
Total market (units)	200,000	211,000	223,500	235,500	246,000
Market share (%)	2.0	3.3	4.4	5.6	6.7
Volume (units)	4,000	6,963	9,834	13.188	16,482
Pipeline (units)	700	750	780	800	800
Gross sales ($)	4,700	7,013	9,864	13,208	16,482
Gross margin (%)	7	7	7	7	7
Gross profit ($)	3,290	4,909	6,905	9,246	11,537
Advertising ($)	4,400	4,200	5,000	5,760	6,000
Promotion to the trade ($)	1,500	700	800	900	1,000
Total advertising and promotion ($)	5,900	4,900	5,800	6,660	7,000
Gross trading profit ($)	(2,610)	9	1,105	2,586	4,537
Profit (% of sales)	—	—	16.0	27.9	39.3
Cumulative gross trading profit ($)		(2,601)	(1,496)	1,090	5,627

Companies frequently choose to introduce in waves. They might introduce in 20 percent of the market to start, then 20 percent in the next two months, and so on. This has the effect of lowering the deficit position at any one point in time. There are other advantages, such as leveling production schedules and correcting errors found in the first regions. The disadvantages are that it may result in shortening lead time over competition and that paying a premium to do regional advertising instead of national advertising might be necessary.

Evaluation of Payout Planning   Payout planning is being followed by an increasing number of firms. An assumption is made, of course, that environmental conditions existing during the first year will not change greatly during the planning period. Competition might enter and drastically change the competitive environment, to mention only one possibility. Also, it is assumed that the effect of promotional expenditures on sales can be estimated with some accuracy. Nevertheless, payout planning encompasses a managerial philosophy that has merit, for it makes a realistic attempt to implement the objective-and-task method without imposing arbitrary restrictions on funds in any given year. We must recognize, however, that given the increasing turbulence of the marketplace, payout periods may be decreasing. Instead of five-year plans, we may now have two- or three-year plans.

SUMMARY

This chapter deals with one of the most complex and important problems in the management of promotion: How much should be spent to achieve planned promotional objectives? The opening feature, a story about a product manager, illustrates the many variables that must be considered in arriving at an optimal solution to the problem. The chapter begins with a look at the marginal or incremental mode of analysis to discover the theoretical underpinnings of a solution aimed at profit maximization in the short run. Such an approach is applicable only under very restrictive conditions, although such conditions may be present in certain classes of promotional situations.

The chapter then reviews the traditional approaches to the problem, most of which do not meet the twin criteria of *promotability* and *profitability.* In other words, the approaches suggest appropriations that are either not large enough to reach promotional goals or so large that profitability was reduced. The objective-and-task approach seems to meet the dual criteria best and thus receives the support of the authors as the most appropriate approach. The chapter spends considerable time discussing the means of developing such an approach and of checking it.

Next comes the problem of geographic allocation of promotional effort. The use of several indexes, including the *S&MM Survey of Buying Power,* is illustrated.

Finally, we give special attention to the determination of the promotional appropriation for new products. We discuss payout planning because it is required by many corporate controllers before funds can be provided for new-product introductions. However, because of the increased uncertainty resulting from rapidly changing market conditions, the payout periods may be getting shorter than they were in the past.

We conclude with the belief that a systematic approach to the problem will provide better results than will using rules of thumb such as percentage of sales. We believe that even the best analysis cannot replace experience and good judgment when it comes to deciding how much to spend on promotion. Thorough analysis, however, can certainly sharpen one's judgment.

REVIEW AND DISCUSSION QUESTIONS

1. Imagine that your task is to determine the advertising appropriation for a new automobile to be introduced this coming fall. You have been impressed by the use of marginal analysis and would like to utilize it in your decision process. How should your thinking proceed with respect to the pros and cons of marginal analysis in the case at hand?

2. You have just received a copy of your advertising budget and have found that your boss has added several items that do not appear to be directly related to advertising and that seriously reduce the amount available to you for purchasing space in the print media and time in the broadcast media. How would you handle this situation?

3. Refer back to the Betty Wilson scenario at the opening of this chapter. Put yourself in her shoes. What could you do to make sure that your career was not damaged by management's insistence on a short-run milking strategy for the brand?

4. Given an annual sales objective of $40 million for a new health and beauty aid product, develop a hypothetical objective and task approach to determine the promotional appropriation. Be sure to illustrate how you would use a build-up analysis as part of the process.

5. Assume that the advertising share of successful products in the soft drink industry exceeds sales share by about 2.1 to 1. You are the advertising manager of Twink, a new dietary soft drink. Would you abide by the customary ratio? What size appropriation would result if first-year sales were estimated at $8 million? What factors might lead you to depart from the customary ratio?

6. You are working for a large pharmaceutical manufacturer that requires payout planning before a new product can be launched. Assume that Table 9–5 is a payout plan that you developed given the company's five-year planning horizon. You are suddenly informed that because of increased market risk, the planning period has been reduced to three years with breakeven in Year 2. Develop a new plan. *Hint:* Set up the old plan on a PC spreadsheet and see what works best for a three-year plan.

NOTES

1. James E. Lynch and Graham J. Hooley, "Increasing Sophistication in Advertising Budget Setting," *Journal of Advertising Research,* February/March 1990, pp. 67–75.

2. Ibid.

3. R. Craig Endicott, "Top 100 Take It on the Chin, Feel Biggest Drop in Four Decades," *Advertising Age,* September 23, 1992, p. 1.

4. Melvin E. Salveson, "Management's Criteria for Advertising Effectiveness," *Proceedings, 5th Annual Conference* (New York: Advertising Research Foundation), p. 25. Quoted with special permission of the Advertising Research Foundation.

5. "Advertising-to-Sales Ratios, 1992," *Advertising Age,* July 13, 1992, p. 16.

6. Kent M. Lancaster and Judith A. Stern, "Computer-Based Advertising Practices of Leading U.S. Advertisers," *Journal of Advertising* 12, no. 4 (1983), p. 6.

7. Lynch and Hooley, "Increasing Sophistication," p. 72.

8. Fred S. Zufryden, "How Much Should Be Spent for Advertising a Brand?" *Journal of Advertising Research* 29, no. 2 (April/May 1989), pp. 24–34.

9. For a review of this literature, see Julian L. Simon and Johan Arndt, "The Shape of the Advertising Response Function," *Journal of Advertising Research* 20, no. 4 (August 1980), pp. 11–28.

10. Roger Barton, *Media in Advertising* (New York: McGraw-Hill, 1964), pp. 15–19.

11. This section was contributed by Robert Sowers, formerly senior vice president, Ogilvy & Mather, Inc.

ADVERTISING

In Section 4, Chapter 10 presents a discussion of the first promotional program element that we will discuss, the advertising message. We review what is referred to in the trade as the creative strategy. The focus is on a logical and pragmatic approach to the key element in the success of an advertising campaign—the message. The advertising message must be placed in selected media for potential exposure to consumers. Thus, Chapter 11 surveys the array of available advertising media, and Chapter 12 considers the basics of how a media plan should be designed.

C h a p t e r

10

The Advertising Message

GETTING DHL MOVING WITH GARY LARSON'S "THE FAR SIDE"

Securing a piece of the air-express business is increasingly difficult in today's crowded skies. Fierce competition in both domestic and international markets makes maintaining market share a feat and increasing market share quite a challenge. DHL Worldwide Express, the world's oldest and largest international air-express company, found itself with a paltry 5 percent share of the U.S. market and a major visibility problem. When competing giants Federal Express and UPS began going after DHL's international market, finding an immediate solution was vital. DHL's answer: humor à la Gary Larson.

Gary Larson, creator of "The Far Side," is possibly the hottest cartoonist in America. "The Far Side" is a wacky cartoon series based on "a warped world of funny and frequently grotesque people and other creatures doing and saying some pretty strange things." Wacky or not, "The Far Side" outgrew its original daily newspaper domain, and Larson's distinctive cartoon characters can now be found in a series of books and on posters, calendars, and coffee mugs—and in DHL ads!

Dick Rossi, DHL's director of marketing services, acknowledged the inherent risks involved in using humor in advertising. "There's always a risk when you use humor. It tends to polarize your audience a little; there are those who get it and those who don't. But our research shows there's a relatively small number of people who don't like it." He equated the risk to doing anything unusual and said that DHL preferred taking the risk to doing what everyone else is doing and getting lost in the crowd.

Rossi explained the company's risky move: "We went to Larson primarily because we needed to get the DHL name out there. We needed a very quick boost in our visibility, to increase awareness and enhance our image. One thing you have to do in advertising, because there's so much out there, is to break through, and Larson does that very well. He has that impact."

DHL adopted a two-pronged approach. Its TV ads were designed for image building, and print ads were designed to deliver a specific message. Thirty-second TV commercials were produced for the nation's eight largest markets. These TV spots build an animated story around a "Far Side" cartoon. One spot features sagging birds laboriously flying across the screen to deliver packages for the other air-express companies. DHL's bird waves as it cruises by all of them in a jet plane.

DHL also placed full-page print ads in eight business and news magazines. Rossi explained that these ads were selected to fit two basic objectives: "One, explain that overseas shipping is different from shipping in the United States. Two, explain that DHL is the best at doing this, because of our experience, network, worldwide scope, and people." One popular ad features a strange-looking doctor searching his medical bag as he leaves a plane. The caption reads: "Suddenly, Dr. Frankenstein realized he had left his brain in San Francisco." The major headline beneath the cartoon reads: "He should have shipped it DHL." The ad copy goes on to humorously explain the relationship between the two statements.

Though revenue results are difficult to prove, the Larson campaign appears to be succeeding. The ads have boosted DHL's image in America. The impact on TV markets is the easiest to measure. Rossi says, "Sales are better, growing faster in areas we're advertising in than in markets where we don't advertise." Since print ads are run in national magazines and the air-express industry is growing, it is harder to attribute increased sales specifically to the advertising. But general sales are up pretty sharply, indicating that DHL must be doing something right.

Source: "Larson's Humor Flies for DHL," *Industry Week*, April 3, 1989, pp. 33–34.

The chapter opener illustrates the impact an advertising message may have on the market success of a firm. The development of advertising messages, called the creative aspect, is usually implemented by a copywriter and an art designer. They do their creative work based on the message strategy prepared by the advertising agency's account management team, which works in conjunction with the client's marketing people. The copywriter and art director may also provide a support role in the meetings where the message strategy is formulated. This chapter is concerned with the development of advertising message strategy and with general approaches to the development of successful advertising messages. We begin with a review of the elements of creative strategy and then present the subject of the actual advertising message.

CREATIVE STRATEGY

The creative strategy, sometimes also called copy strategy or copy platform, is based on (1) the proper definition of the target audience, (2) the objective for the advertising, (3) the advertising strategy to reach the defined objective, (4) the support for the advertising strategy, (5) consideration of other elements belonging in the advertisement, and (6) the tone of the advertisement. The working definitions of these six elements are presented below. In addition, a potential application of these elements to the Simplicity Sewing Patterns Company is presented in Table 10–1.[1]

The creative strategy (copy platform) forms the basis on which the copywriter and the art director work to create the actual advertisement to be used in a campaign. Without having the six elements of the copy platform in place, the creative people lack the necessary guidance to develop advertisements that are effective in the marketplace. The Simplicity copy platform presented in Table 10–1 points out a clear direction for the development of an advertisement. With the creative strategy in place, we can turn our attention to issues of the production of the actual advertisements, called the creative execution.

	Creative Strategy or Copy Platform
Target audience:	This is an outline of who is the most likely candidate to be motivated to do something as a result of the advertising. Most often, it is stated in demographic and psychographic terms.
Objective:	What you want the advertising to do. Usually this starts with the words "to establish. . . ."
Strategy:	How you want the advertising specifically to accomplish the objective above. A good outline for this strategy statement is "to convince the target group to buy [use, prefer, or other verb] the Brand [substitute the name] instead of _____ because _____."
Support:	This is the reason to believe the strategy. It can be either research that supports the strategy or an advertising "reason why."
Considerations:	This is where you would put other things that you would like to have built into the advertising if space or time allows. Usually this is not really pertinent to the discussion but would be nice to include. Quite often this is a client dictate.
Tone:	This is the philosophy of the advertising in tone form.

Source: Professor Lawrence V. Johnson of the University of Kansas.

TABLE 10–1

Application of the Six Elements Approach to Creative Strategy

	Simplicity Copy Platform
Target audience:	Women 18 to 34 with a college education.
Objectives:	To establish Simplicity patterns as the quick and easy way for the target audience to obtain the clothes they want.
Strategy:	To convince the target group to buy Simplicity instead of shopping for clothing in boutiques and stores because Simplicity is the most efficient method of obtaining first-quality clothing with the right color and style.
Support:	Simplicity patterns eliminate the difficulty of searching for the right clothing because the target audience can select the fabric and color and because the patterns are current, durable, and active.
Considerations:	1. Easy-to-follow instructions. 2. Can be made in a few hours. 3. Sewing can avoid frustration.
Tone:	Active, yet fashionable.

Source: Professor Lawrence V. Johnson of the University of Kansas.

CREATIVE EXECUTION

Although a correct strategy is essential to advertising success, the strategy in itself will never be sufficient. The strategy must be executed into the message at some point. It is here that the creative ability of the writer or designer comes to the fore.

What is creativity? According to Webster, something is created when it is produced, formed, or brought into being. True creativity is not undisciplined imagination. Controls and discipline may be highly subjective and personal; they may also be subconscious, almost secret, or covered up with a facade of "absolutely no control," but this does not mean that they do not operate powerfully in the creative personality. Creative work is largely conscious, deliberate, and disciplined. It is disciplined by the objective toward which it is directed and by the information and experience on which it is based. First the creator hunts for new information and details and arranges them into a pattern through discipline of thought processes. The creative process at each step is the same, whether the discovery is made as a contribution to science, music, technology, art, advertising, or some other area of interest. Rules or syntax can be developed, thereby keeping imagination within its most productive bounds.

Real communication does not occur until the message is attended to and correctly comprehended, retained, and acted on by members of the target audience in the manner specified in the statement of advertising objectives (see Chapter 3). Results that fall short of real communication signify that true creativity was not achieved in the execution process.

However, the intuition and skill of the writer and designer do play a significant role. Comprehensive objectives provide the boundaries for creative work; they do not guarantee advertising success any more than staying within the sidelines of a football field guarantees a winning performance. Indeed, intuition and imagination are required, and it is this subjective element that differentiates ordinary advertising from great advertising.

Persuasion through Advertising: Influencing Attitudes and Behavior[2]

The proper understanding of the likely persuasive power of advertising messages requires an understanding of potential impact of advertising on attitudes and behavior. We know from our discussion in Chapter 3 that the influence of any communication depends on what happens at each stage of information processing. An advertisement must capture attention, be accurately understood, be retained in memory, and be yielded to by the target audience in order to have persuasive impact. Yielding represents the persuasive impact of the advertisement. A key question, then, concerns what determines how much, if any, yielding occurs during information processing. Advertisers often focus on the *cognitive response* (i.e., thoughts) that occur during message processing. These thoughts are classified on three dimensions: valence, focus, and abstraction.

Valence represents the favorability of the thoughts. Positive thoughts in response to an advertisement are called *support arguments;* negative thoughts are called *counterarguments. Focus* refers to the content of the thoughts. Advertisers distinguish between thoughts focused on the brand versus those focused on the executional elements of the ad itself (e.g., picture, color, headline). *Abstraction* relates to the amount of elaboration reflected by the thoughts. The lowest level of abstraction would be thoughts that just play back a message. Greater abstraction would be demonstrated by thoughts reflecting the integration of various elements of the ad with each other or with one's own knowledge.

These classifications of thoughts are used as predictors of the attitudes formed following message exposure. The basic notion is that the persuasion impact of ads will be greater (more yielding) as cognitive responses become more favorable. Cognitive responses are certainly part of the persuasive impact of an advertisement, but they do not tell the whole story. We must also be concerned with *affective responses* as they relate to attitude and behavior change in advertising.

Affective responses represent the feelings that are elicited by the advertising. Affective responses are "hot" responses, in contrast to the "cold" cognitive responses, and are important in what is called *transformational* (as opposed to informational) advertising. Transformational ads attempt to "make the experience of using the product richer, warmer, more exciting, and/or more enjoyable, than that obtained solely from an objective description of the advertised brand."[3]

For example, one of the most memorable campaigns to hit the airwaves was the California Raisin Advisory Board's television ads featuring raisins dancing to the sounds of Marvin Gaye's classic song "Heard It through the Grapevine." The original idea behind the campaign was to enhance the product's appeal by emphasizing the nutritional value of raisins. This approach seemed quite sensible given the trend toward greater health consciousness that has swept the country during the past decade or so.

However, research revealed that consumers already appreciated the nutritional properties of raisins. The problem was that consumers viewed raisins as plain and ordinary. As explained by Alan Canton, the board's advertising and promotions manager, "Nutritionally, they were appealing; emotionally, they were not appealing." It was hoped that the feelings evoked by the music and animated raisins would help overcome this limitation.

Did it work? Prior to the campaign, raisin sales had fluctuated between flat and declining. Sales jumped 5 percent after the campaign began and have remained at these higher levels.

Other examples of emotional appeals include AT&T's "Reach Out and Touch Someone," Pepsi's "Get That Pepsi Feeling," and the diamond suppliers' "Tell Her You Would Marry Her Again" campaigns.

The importance of affective responses in persuasion is quite strongly supported by research findings.[4] Affective responses can be measured in advertising studies by asking respondents to write down the feelings they experienced while processing the message, or by asking them how strongly they experienced various feelings on structured rating scales.

Advertising and the Elaboration Likelihood Model of Persuasion

Many advertisers consider both cognitive and emotional responses important in influencing attitudes and behavior. Petty and Cacioppo's *elaboration likelihood model* (ELM) of persuasion is useful in pulling all these elements together. The ELM states that the degree of elaboration in the form of issue-relevant thinking is the key determinant of the influence exerted by various communication elements. When elaboration is high, the central route to persuasion is followed where only those message elements relevant to forming a "reasoned" opinion (called *arguments*) are influential. So-called informational ads would apply in this case. Alternatively, the peripheral route to persuasion occurs under low levels of elaboration as elements irrelevant to developing a reasoned opinion (called *peripheral cues*) become influential. So-called transformational ads would apply here. Both arguments and peripheral cues are operative under moderate levels of elaboration.

Elaboration in turn depends on the person's motivation, ability, and opportunity during message processing. A person who is motivated and able and has the opportunity to elaborate will take the central route; the peripheral route applies when motivation, ability, or opportunity is lacking. Motivation was discussed in Chapter 3. Ability relates to such factors as intelligence, education, and product

FIGURE 10–1

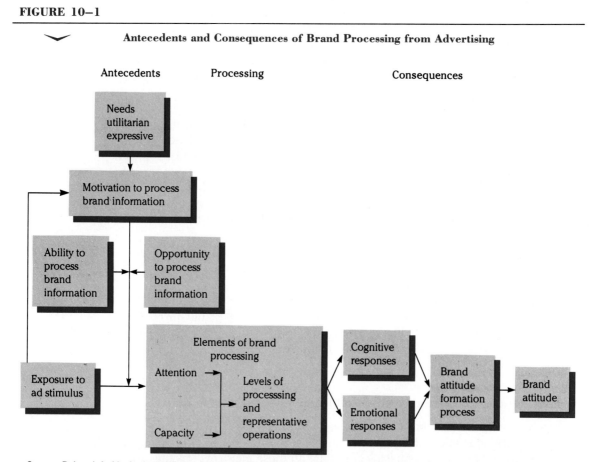

Antecedents and Consequences of Brand Processing from Advertising

Source: Deborah L. MacInnis and Bernard J. Jaworski, "Information Processing from Advertisements: Toward an Integrative Framework," *Journal of Marketing* 53 (October 1989), p. 3.

knowledge. Limits in these areas reduce the ability to elaborate. Opportunity concerns the situational environment at the time of exposure to the ad or to the elements of the advertisement itself that impact consumer information processing. For example, the advertisement may be shown during a distracting time in a television show, or music in the ad itself may distract the consumer.

Elaboration also relates to the level of involvement of the target consumer. High-involvement consumers are impacted almost completely by the message arguments. In contrast, low-involvement consumers are influenced by both arguments and peripheral cues. The ELM points out the importance of anticipating how much elaboration is likely to occur during message processing in developing persuasive advertisements. If elaboration is likely to be high, then more emphasis should be placed on compelling arguments to support the advocated position. In situations of expected low elaboration by consumers to the advertisement, other approaches that depend less on the degree of message processing are appropriate. These approaches include the use of a celebrity spokesperson or an emotional appeal.

Figure 10–1 provides a graphic overview of the ELM process. The antecedent conditions to advertising information processing are the need for a consumer benefit, the motivation, the ability to process information, the opportunity to process, and the advertising exposure itself. Information processing then occurs either through the central route or peripheral route to persuasion based on the degree of elaboration that is related to the attention to the advertisement and the capacity of the consumer to process information. Responses are then either cognitive or emotional with resulting attitude formation or change in the attitude toward the brand. The ELM provides a framework within which to evaluate specific approaches that may be used to present advertising messages. Related to these approaches are specific behavioral research findings that are useful in the development process of the advertisement message. We now turn our attention to some of these important findings.

Behavioral Research Findings for Advertising

Many relevant findings from behavioral research guide the development of advertising messages. These findings relate to (1) the characteristics of the message itself, (2) the attitudes toward the ad, and (3) characteristics of the consumer. Table 10–2 presents a summary of the most relevant conclusions to guide advertisers. These findings give more specific direction than the ELM for the actual development of advertising messages. They serve as a first floor to the foundation provided by the ELM. We have not reported all relevant behavioral findings in Table 10–2, but only the ones we think are most relevant to message development.

However, even more detailed guidelines are needed by developers of advertising messages in terms of the specifics in forming the messages. These "upper floors" of the ELM foundation building are addressed in the last two sections of this chapter. The next section of this chapter presents a framework for types of creative executions and examines when these different types of creative executions are appropriate. In the appendix to this chapter, we present even more specifics about what works and what does not work in advertising messages. These latter guidelines are mostly based on the collective wisdom and research of advertising practitioners.

TABLE 10–2

    Selected Behavioral Research Findings for Advertising

Characteristics of the Message

1. The more credible the source of the ad or the presenter in the ad, the more persuasive the ad. For example, certain celebrity presenters such as Bill Cosby have reputations as being credible.
2. Source credibility derives from expertise, celebrity status, gender fit with audience, physical attractiveness, likeability, and similarity with the target audience.
3. The quality of claims in an ad impacts the persuasive level of the ad. The most effective claims focus on (*a*) dimensions relevant to target consumers, (*b*) factual information, (*c*) verifiable information based on consumer search or experience, and (*d*) credible substantiation such as a test.
4. In low-involvement situations, the more claims made, the greater the persuasive impact of the ad. That is, the quantity of claims serves as a persuasive cue under the peripheral route in the ELM.
5. Two-sided messages (those including pros and cons) increase perceptions of an advertiser's truthfulness and believability relative to one-sided messages (those presenting only the pros).
6. In new-product introductions and in situations for a nonmarket leader brand, comparative ads (those that name another brand by name and make a direct comparison) outperform noncomparative ads, but this finding does not always hold.
7. Executional elements such as visuals, sounds, colors, and pace of the ad can impact its persuasive outcome, particularly ads designed to elicit emotional responses. Some of the detailed results related to these issues are discussed in the last section of this chapter.

Attitude toward the Ad

1. The ability of advertising to impact consumer attitudes toward a brand often depends on consumers' attitudes toward the ad itself.
2. In general, ads that are evaluated favorably can lead to more positive brand attitudes.

Characteristics of Consumers

1. Differences in consumer motivation can influence the effectiveness of a particular persuasion strategy. Highly involved consumers are more likely to respond to informational ads. Little involved consumers are more likely to respond to emotional ads.
2. Ads will be more persuasive with a moderate level of arousal in consumers than with either little or greatly aroused consumers.
3. The higher the relevant knowledge level of consumers, the more receptive they will be to informationally rich claims.
4. Existing attitudes impact the receptivity to persuasion from ads. In general, persuasive communication is more successful in creating attitudes than in changing them. Current attitudes allow for more effective counterargumentation with the message. Product experience is an important element in the formation of the currently held attitude.

Source: Adapted from a review prepared by James F. Engel, Rodger D. Blackwell, and Paul Miniard.

A USEFUL GUIDE TO CREATIVE ASPECTS

Creative aspects of advertising hold a veto power over the effectiveness of a campaign. Good decisions in other areas can be wasted without meaningful copy, themes, presentation, and so forth. The marketing manager is likely not to be involved directly in the formulation of creative plans. This aspect is typically performed by the advertising agency. The manager is required, however, to approve and suggest changes in its creative efforts. To properly carry out this function, he or she needs a guide as to what constitutes good advertising. The points to consider given here, based on the writings of Simon, have considerable practical usefulness.[5]

The analysis framework is based on developing links between product–market characteristics and advertising characteristics. To do this, one must first develop a classification scheme for both advertisements and products.

Alternative Advertising Approaches

The characteristics of ads that are important here relate to the way in which they attempt to activate buyers to action. The following list presents some of the activation methods classified by Simon.

1. *Information.* This type of ad presents straight facts. These facts are not presented in argumentative form, nor is the relevance of the facts explained. Classified and yellow pages ads are prime examples of information advertising, but many other examples exist, such as "round steak now 89 cents per pound," or "City Center Motors announces the arrival of the new models." Figure 10–2 presents an example of an information ad.

FIGURE 10–2

An Information Ad

2. *Argument or reason why.* This type of ad is structured in the form of a logical argument. The reasons utilized in the argument may be either facts or expected benefits to the consumer (social standing and so forth). Figure 10–3 presents an example of an argument ad.

3. *Motivation with psychological appeals.* This type of ad uses emotional appeals. It tries to enhance the appeal of the product by attaching a pleasant emotional connotation to it. The ad creates a mood. Selling points are then both explicit and implicit. Cosmetics, cigarette, and beer and liquor producers are heavy users of mood commercials. Figure 10–4 presents an example of this type of ad.

4. *Repeat assertion.* This type of ad constitutes the hard-sell approach to activation. The statements made in these ads, as well as the reasons why the statements hold, are usually unsupported by facts. Two examples of repeat assertion advertising are "Rolaids absorbs 20 times its weight in excess stomach acid" and "The little tablet is the more effective." The assumptions here are that people will believe a statement if they hear it enough and if they have no intrinsic interest in the product message. The advertiser is therefore just interested in getting across

FIGURE 10–3

An Argument Ad

the line to remember. Nonprescription drug producers are heavy users of this type of ad. Figure 10–5 presents an example of a repeat assertion ad.

5. *Command.* This type of ad orders or reminds us to do something. For example: "When you drink don't drive," "Give the United Way," or "Drink Coca-Cola." The assumption is that the audience is suggestible. Command ads probably work best for products that the audience knows well and thinks well of. Figure 10–6 presents an example of a command ad.

6. *Symbolic association.* This type of ad is characterized as a more subtle form of the repeat assertion ad. The intent is to get across one piece of information about the product. Here the product is linked to a person, a tune, or a situation that has particularly pleasant connotations. The product and the symbol then become highly interrelated. Can anyone look at a picture of the Rock of Gibraltar without thinking of what's-their-name? This type of appeal is obviously similar to emotional appeals. For example, beer is often associated with "good times with friends," a very emotional appeal. Both the emotion and the symbolic association

FIGURE 10–4

A Motivation-with-Psychological-Appeals Ad

are there. The first page of the color insert presents the classic Marlboro ad as an example of this approach.

7. *Imitation.* This type of ad attempts to present people and situations for the audience to imitate (using our product, of course). The assumption is that people will imitate those whom they wish to be like or whom they admire. Hence, we note the use of famous people in testimonials, status appeals, a group of young friends drinking beer, and so forth. Figure 10–7 shows this type of approach.

Information, argument, and motivation ads are all directed at the conscious, "reasoning" parts of the mind. The others are directed at more emotional parts of the mind. Table 10–3 presents a summary description of the seven activation methods.

Choosing an Approach for the Product

Simon also notes a number of dimensions on which products and their markets may be classified. The description of the market situation for a product by these considerations logically suggests how interest is to be activated. The designation

FIGURE 10–5

A Repeat Assertion Ad

of a product–market situation on each dimension logically suggests an activation procedure as follows.

1. *Industrial or consumer goods.* The information type and the argument type of ads are prevalent in industrial advertising. The complexity of the products, the dollar value of purchases, and the risks of choosing a faulty product all dictate ads that provide facts and present logical arguments. The second page of the color insert presents an example of an argument industrial ad.

For consumer goods, any one of the activation methods may still be appropriate. We must examine other dimensions before a more definitive answer can be reached. For consumer goods, then, we look at the following.

2. *What word best characterizes the product: style, mechanical, sensory, service, or hidden benefit?* If *style*, advertisers tend to use imitation, motivation, and symbolic association. For example, the advertising of fashion goods or beauty aids (see the third page of the color insert and Figure 10–7). If *mechanical*, advertisers tend to use information and argument. Note the use of statistical data in automobile and computer advertising (see Figure 10–8). If *sensory*, advertisers tend to use symbolic association, motivation, and imitation. These kinds of products appeal to all senses and need advertising that goes beyond just words. Note the use of well-known people in cosmetic ads. For example, Chaz's use of Tom

---

A Command Ad

FIGURE 10–7

An Imitation Ad

TABLE 10–3

Summary of Advertising Activation Methods

1. Information	Presents straight facts without the relevance of the facts being explained.
2. Argument or reason why	Structured in the form of a logical argument, using either facts or expected benefits.
3. Motivation with psychological appeals	Uses emotional appeals to try to enhance the appeal of the product by attaching pleasant emotional connotations to it.
4. Repeat assertion	Constitutes the hard-sell approach with the assumption that people will believe a statement if they hear it enough.
5. Command	Orders people to do something, assuming that the audience is suggestible.
6. Symbolic association	A subtle form of the repeat assertion ad that links the product to a person, music, or situation that has particularly pleasant connotations.
7. Imitation	Attempts to present people and situations for the audience to imitate, assuming that people will imitate people whom they wish to be like or admire.

Selleck and Cover Girl's use of Christie Brinkley are classics. If *service,* advertisers tend to use information and argument. People need to know that the service exists and rational reasons why they should partake of it (see Figure 10–9). If *hidden benefit,* advertisers tend to use information, argument, and motivation. Lots of products have hidden benefits; examples are nonprescription drugs, all kinds of insurance, and foods, to name just a few. Buyers must be informed of these benefits and persuaded that they are important either with argument or by appealing to emotion (see Figure 10–10).

3. *Is it a necessity, a convenience, or a luxury good?* For a luxury product, we would likely use symbolic association or imitation. Luxury products are designed to give prestige, so we must create the aura of prestige in the ads. Also, the farther away a product is from being a necessity, the more likely it is we will have to create a demand for the product class. Motivational methods are, then, likely to be useful (see Figure 10–11 for an example of a luxury-good ad). The more necessary a product, the more likely it is that activation methods other than motivation will be appropriate.

FIGURE 10–8

A "Mechanical" Product Ad Using an Argument Approach

4. *Stage of product class acceptance.* The newer the product class, the more people need information about it and reasons to buy it. We would then tend to use information, argument, and motivation (see Figure 10–12). As the product progresses through the life cycle, people become less interested in hearing information about it. Advertisers then turn to repeat assertion, imitation, symbolic association, or command.

5. *Stage of brand acceptance.* Even in an established product category, new brands must provide information, and therefore the early life-cycle methods are again appropriate (see Figure 10–13). The older brands utilize the later life-cycle methods.

6. *Price range.* If the item has a high price, advertisers tend to use information, argument, and motivation. People need reasons for spending so much (see Figure

FIGURE 10–9

A "Service" Product Ad Using an Argument Approach

10–14). The smaller the dollar amount, the more impulsive the purchase is, so symbolic association, command, and repeat assertion become more viable (see Figure 10–15).

7. *Closeness to competing brands in objective characteristics.* A brand with great physical differences from its competitors allows the advertiser to say a lot about the physical product (see Figure 10–16). The advertiser can therefore make use of information, argument, and motivation. Items that vary little from brand to brand (e.g., beer, cigarettes, tuxedos) must rely on other methods (see Figure 10–17).

8. *Repeatability of purchase.* Products with short repurchase cycles (e.g., soap or coffee) utilize symbolic association, command, repeat assertion, and imitation much more than those with long repurchase cycles (e.g., diamonds). Information and argument become old hat for the former but are critical for the latter. Note the difference between Figures 10–14 and 10–15.

9. *Method of consummating sale.* The more directly action-oriented the ad (e.g., mail-order ads, such as those for the Book-of-the-Month Club), the greater

---

FIGURE 10–10

A "Hidden Benefit" Highlighted by Using Argument and Motivational Approaches

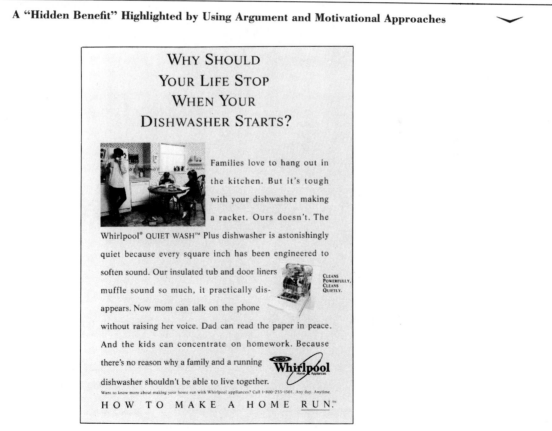

FIGURE 10–11

A Luxury Product Ad Using a Motivational Approach

Courtesy of Doyle Dane Bernbach Advertising Agency and General Wine and Spirits Company

the need for argument and motivation methods. These types of ads must do the complete selling job and therefore can use many activation methods (see Figure 10–18).

10. *Market share held by brands.* If a brand holds a dominant position in a market, it has a lot to gain by expanding the whole market. One would then use information, argument, or motivation—the methods we associated earlier with early stages of the product life cycle (see Figure 10–19).

Simon suggests that advertisers identify the most important product–market dimension and then select an activation method with this in mind. Think of the ads you have seen lately for, say, beer or watches. Pick a brand and work through Simon's procedure. We think you'll be impressed with the usefulness of the framework. Table 10–4 provides a summary of the relationship of the product–market situation and the choice of activation method for the creative execution.

Within any of these advertising approaches, there are millions of different ways to create the ad. The words, colors, and graphics of the ad can be used in infinite variety. Further, the advertiser can use such things as humor, a well-known

---

FIGURE 10–12

A Newer Product Class Based Product Ad Using Argument and Motivation Approaches

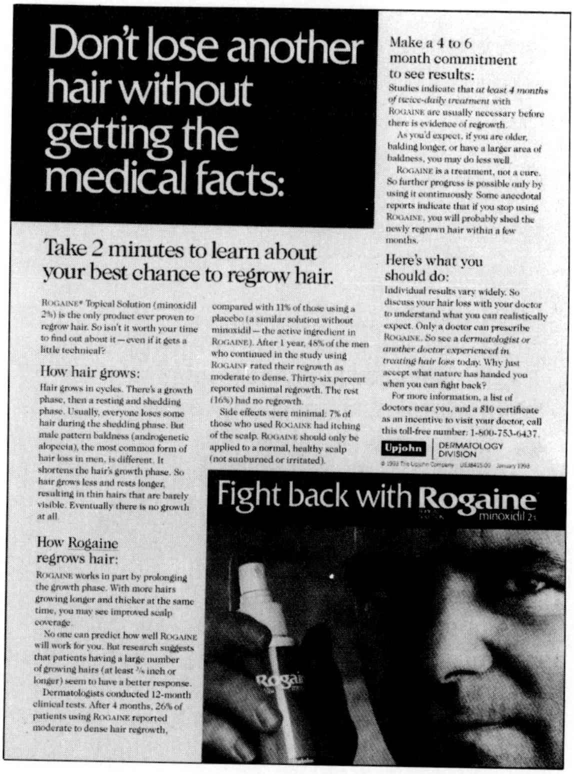

spokesperson, or a "slice of life" presentation (placing the advertising presentation in the context of a real-life situation). Thus, Simon's scheme can aid our understanding, but it does not reduce the need for creativity.

DESIGNING AND PRODUCING ADVERTISING MESSAGES

In this chapter so far, we have progressed (1) from the development of a copy platform, (2) to the application of the elaboration likelihood model (ELM) of consumer response to advertising, (3) to the stating of some useful behavioral findings for advertising, and (4) to the application of Simon's activation methods framework relative to the product–market situation to the development of advertising messages. A fifth level of knowledge in the development of advertising messages is the development of so-called creative rules of copywriting and artwork as applied to advertising. These creative rules are based on the research of prac-

FIGURE 10–13

A New Brand Using an Argument Approach

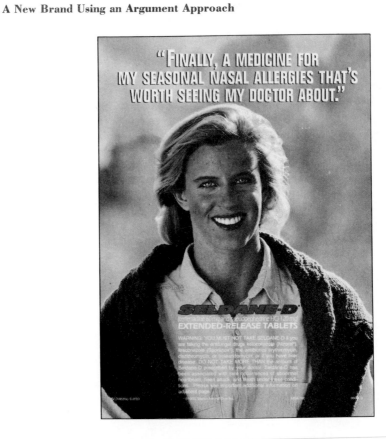

titioners and on their collected wisdom. This is a level of implementation detail that transcends the main focus of this book. Thus, we have placed some of these creative rules in the appendix to this chapter. Individuals who have created effective and memorable advertising copy have become legends in the field. One such legend is Stan Freberg, who is famous for his use of humor in ads. Promotion in Action 10–1 presents Freberg's view on the use of humor in ads.

The creative rules have both value and danger. On the positive side, much is known. David Ogilvy's books *Confessions of an Advertising Man* and *Ogilvy on Advertising* are typical of the research-based practitioner's creative rules. As Ogilvy noted:

> During a 10-hour train ride, I read the ads in three magazines. Most of them violated elementary principles which were discovered in years gone by—and set out in *Confessions.* The copywriters and art directors who created them are ignorant amateurs. What is this reason for the failure to study experience? Is it that advertising does not attract inquiring minds? Is this kind of scientific method beyond their grasp? Are they afraid that knowledge would impose some discipline on them—or expose their incompetences?[6]

FIGURE 10–14

A High-Priced Product Using an Argument Approach

On the other hand, the straightforward application of these types of creative rules has danger also. Creativity cannot be put into a straightjacket. As Harry W. McMahan, another successful practitioner, stated:

> Examples can help. Guidelines can help. But rules often lead the advertising novice astray. In our 20,000 commercials we can disprove almost any "rule." Why? Because . . . different product fields require different handling in communications and persuasion.[7]

We judge the creative rules in the chapter appendix to be useful for those interested in that level of detail. We also expect the reader to approach their use with care, for sometimes real creativity comes from breaking the so-called rules.

ANALYSIS OF THE MESSAGE

With all the millions of possible creative executions for an ad, the reader may conclude that it is impossible to differentiate a good advertisement from a poor

FIGURE 10–15

A Low-Priced Product Using a Repeat Assertion Approach

Symbolic-association ads, like this classic, attempt to link the product to positive feelings. Here, feelings of courage, tradition, and strength might be generated in the viewer.

For Bill Demby, the difference means getting another shot.

When Bill Demby was in Vietnam, he used to dream of coming home and playing a little basketball with the guys.

A dream that all but died when he lost both his legs to a Viet Cong rocket.

But then, a group of researchers discovered that a remarkable DuPont plastic could help make artificial limbs that were more resilient, more flexible, more like life itself.

Thanks to these efforts, Bill Demby is back. And some say, he hasn't lost a step.

At DuPont, we make the things that make a difference.

Better things for better living.

REG. U.S. PAT & TM OFF

This product argument ad also manages to make an emotional appeal for the superiority of the product.

EAUTIFUL
ESTĒE LAUDER

Perfumes are often promoted with style product ads, where the image conveys a sense of the product rather than specific information.

Clothing is often promoted with the imitation type approach.

one. Yet there comes a time when the advertiser must make such a decision so that time or space can be bought. In part, advertisers must decide on the basis of informed judgment, but they usually also make some use of copy tests (pretests).

Judgmental Analysis: Evaluation of Execution

An advertisement should be memorable in that it attracts and holds attention. It also must register its intended message and hence achieve its persuasive objective. The following questions are useful in assessing whether an ad is memorable and persuasive.

1. *Does the picture tell the story?* Given the large volume of competing advertising, no message has more than a fraction of a second to attract and hold the consumer's attention. Thus, the visual portion of the message must register the message without sole reliance on words.

2. *Are the words appropriate?* Do they communicate product benefits in terms that are meaningful to the target audience?

FIGURE 10–16

A Physically Different Product Using an Argument Approach

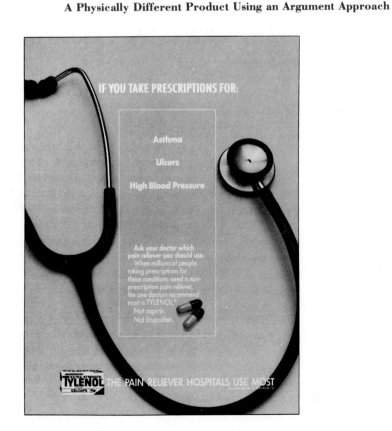

3. *Is one clear theme registered by the total advertisement?* Rarely will attention be held for a sufficient period to register more than one or two ideas, so the emphasis must be on a single-minded presentation of the message theme.

4. *Is the brand name registered?* Many times the brand name is not stressed. As a result, the reader or viewer fails to associate the message with the product.

5. *Is the tone appropriate?* In other words, is the style of message appropriate for the product? Demonstrations are best used with unique product attributes that can be illustrated. When this is not the case, the tone or impression left may interfere with the intended message. Humor is more appropriate when no unique product benefits are present; at other times, it may be entertaining but ineffective.

6. *Is the advertisement distinctive?* Does it stand out from the noise? The dangers of novelty have been stressed, but a message must have an element of distinctiveness to overcome mass media clutter.

FIGURE 10–17

A Product Not Very Different from Its Competitors Using a Motivation Approach

The Earth's Most Comfortable Shoes.
Our "worn to perfection" styles feature distressed oiled leathers and the flexible Comfort Curve sole.

Hush Puppies

For the Hush Puppies retailer nearest you, call 1-800-433-HUSH.

Figure 10–20 presents a magazine ad recently produced by Carnival Cruise Lines. Take a chance at answering the six judgmental analysis questions above as they apply to the Carnival ad. What do you conclude? Perhaps you, like most advertisers, would be reluctant to rely completely on your judgment alone to make evaluations of advertising messages. For this reason, advertisers use pretests (or copy tests, as they are most frequently referred to in the trade). These and other advertising testing procedures are discussed in Chapter 21. Just to complete the thought, the Carnival ad scored extremely well on copy testing procedures. Would you have judged this to be true a priori?

SUMMARY

This chapter has presented five steps in the development of advertising messages. First, it is necessary to establish a creative strategy or copy platform that includes statements about target audience, objective, advertising strategy, support, other considerations, and tone. The second step involves the understanding of consumer response based on the

FIGURE 10–18

A Direct Action Ad Using Argument and Motivation Approaches

FIGURE 10–19

A Dominant Brand Using an Argument Approach

TABLE 10–4

Choosing an Activation Method

Product/Market Situation	Activation Methods
Classification of Product	
Industrial	Information, argument
Consumer	Any activation method
Characteristic Word	
Style	Imitation, motivation, symbolic association
Mechanical	Information, argument
Sensory	Symbolic association, motivation, imitation
Service	Information, argument
Hidden benefit	Information, argument, motivation
Type of Good	
Luxury	Symbolic association, imitation
Convenience	Motivation
Necessity	Activation methods other than motivation
Stage of Product Class Acceptance	
New product class	Information, argument, motivation
Old product class	Repeat assertion, imitation, command, symbolic association
Stage of Brand Acceptance	
New brands	Information, argument, motivation
Old brands	Repeat assertion, imitation, command, symbolic association
Price Range	
High price	Information, argument, motivation
Low price	Symbolic association, command, repeat assertion
Closeness to Competing Brands in Objective Characteristics	
Large differences	Information, argument, motivation
Small differences	Repeat assertion, command, symbolic association, imitation
Repeatability of Purchase	
Short cycle	Symbolic association, command, imitation, repeat assertion
Long cycle	Information, argument, motivation
Method of Consummating Sale	
Direct action oriented	Argument, motivation
Market Share Held by Brand	
Dominant position	Information, argument, motivation

FIGURE 10–20

Carnival Cruise Lines Magazine and Television Advertisements

IF YOU'RE PASSING LIKE SHIPS IN THE NIGHT, IT'S TIME TO FIND EACH OTHER AT SEA.

When life's turning your loved one into a fondly remembered stranger, there's one way to get things back in perspective. Call your travel agent and reserve a Carnival® cruise. Just think of it. Experience playful days in the sun, charming tropical ports, exquisite food, dancing till dawn—sure to spark a new romance . . . or re-kindle an old one.

Let us pamper you. Every "Fun Ship"® is a magnificent resort—

with so many things to do. How about roulette after dinner? Or an exciting Las Vegas revue? On Carnival, you know virtually all your costs upfront—your air fare, meals, activities and entertainment are all included in one low price! And you can charge your entire vacation on your VISA card. It's your best vacation value.

So when life's getting just a little too hurried, discover what happens when you glimpse the moon from a floating island of light. Carnival. When you're ready to find each other . . . again.

See your travel agent for a 3, 4 or 7 day vacation from $395 per person, including air fare. Some restrictions apply. Prices higher in the West.

Experience the excitement of a Carnival vacation with our FREE 20 minute video. Send $3.50 for postage and handling to: Carnival Cruise Lines, Dept. 827, P.O. Box 9008, Opa Locka, FL 33054-9914.

▶ Carnival
THE MOST POPULAR CRUISE LINE IN THE WORLD™

VISA It's Everywhere You Want To Be.®

Registered in Liberia and the Bahamas.

Freberg: Humor's No Laughing Matter

Humorist, satirist, and advertising legend Stan Freberg was honored recently by the Smithsonian Institution when samples of his work were donated to the Center for Advertising History at the National Museum of American History in Washington. His quirky campaigns for Sunsweet prunes, Chun King Chinese food, Salada tea, and H.J. Heinz Co. soups were major contributions to advertising's creative revolution. Lately, he's labored for the Encyclopaedia Britannica from his offices in Beverly Hills, California.

While in Washington, Mr. Freberg spoke with *Advertising Age* Editor at Large Bob Garfield.

Advertising Age: David Ogilvy has denounced "creative showoffs" in advertising who would substitute entertainment value for persuasion. As a pioneer in entertaining advertising, how do you respond?

Mr. Freberg: David Ogilvy is absolutely right, if you substitute entertainment for persuasion. The client is not interested in how funny you can be, in how entertaining you can be. What he really wants to do is sell his product.

A lot of stuff looks like it's been done by art directors who are trying to win awards. . . . But Ogilvy is kvetching a little more than he needs to, probably.

Our [late] mutual friend from San Francisco, Howard Gossage, the man who first invited me into the advertising business, said to David Ogilvy, "What do you mean humor in advertising doesn't work? What about Freberg?" And Ogilvy said, "Oh, well. I didn't mean Freberg."

AA: So you worry about the gratuitous use of entertainment value, too?

Mr. Freberg: Boredom to me is the greatest sin of all, but it's now being edged out by people misusing entertainment and humor in an effort to keep you from zapping. Just to keep people from zapping you is not reason enough to do something that is totally irrelevant to what you're selling. . . . Nobody ever walked away from one of my commercials wondering what the hell the name of the product was.

Let me tell you a story. I walk into [a hotel] in Kansas City, Missouri, at one o'clock in the morning. I'm carrying my own luggage and I'm struggling with this luggage, and across the lobby the woman behind the desk yells, at the top of her lungs, "Today the pits, tomorrow the wrinkles! Sunsweet marches on!"

I say to this woman, "How many times did you see this commercial?" She said, "I only saw it once, but I was always hoping I'd see it again." I'm talking about 20 years after the Sunsweet thing was on the air.

AA: People associate you with humor in advertising, but you've also borrowed a page from Edward Bernays, the venerable press agent, and in many of your classic campaigns—I'm thinking of Kaiser aluminum foil and Salada tea—you've actively involved consumers, gotten them to respond to ads.

Mr. Freberg: Whenever possible. What I like doing is not only creating commercials that don't bore you to death, but commercials that can solve some problem that exists at the client's level.

[With Kaiser, they] didn't have any distribution for this foil because Reynolds had cornered the market. So I said, "What good is it to do funny commercials and put them on the air if people run down to the A&P and can't find it?" And that's when I came up with the campaign [which created a fictional Kaiser salesman who could sell product to "mean old grocers" and teetered on the edge of poverty. After the campaign, Kaiser won 43,000 new retail outlets].

Rosser Reeves and I were using different techniques to wind up in the same place—the same place that David Ogilvy has always ended up. It's not very complicated. It's salesmanship.

AA: You're doing spots for Britannica and MTM Enterprises but not a lot of other national campaigns. Why aren't you doing more work for higher-profile clients?

Mr. Freberg: Beats the heck out of me. I wish I was doing more work, but the fact is I kinda do what I want to do. I turn down people who come to me, for various reasons. They don't have enough money or I just don't believe in their product enough. I'm doing five [radio] commentaries a week on close to a hundred stations around America, and it takes a lot of time. But the fact is, people today in advertising hardly think about going outside of their own creative environment. . . .

Humor is such a fragile thing. Humor in advertising is like a gun in the hands of a child. You have to know how to do it. Otherwise it can blow up on you.

Source: *Advertising Age*, January 20, 1992, p. 52.

level of involvement and elaboration, as conceptualized by the ELM. Third, we outlined some useful behavioral generalization for advertising. These guidelines provide some direction to advertising specifics but should be taken only as directions, not firm conclusions for any particular ad. Fourth, the Simon activation framework took us deeper into the actual production aspects of advertisement. Finally, the appendix to the chapter presents creative rules for copywriting and art production. These rules should be applied with care.

The end result of the development of advertising messages should be rigorously compared against the six judgmental criteria presented in the last section of this chapter. In addition, research-based copy testing of the specific ad is often needed.

REVIEW AND DISCUSSION QUESTIONS

1. For the Habitrol ad in Figure 10–3, the Olympus camera ad in Figure 10–4, and the Estée Lauder ad in the color insert, prepare what you believe the associated copy platform could be. This requires you to reason and speculate based on the actual advertising execution.

2. For the same three ads, are the principles of the ELM applied properly? What ELM-based outcomes would you expect from these ads? Why? What type of elaboration would you expect? Why?

3. From magazines that interest you, select three ads that you consider to be the best and three that you consider to be the worst. Apply the judgmental criteria to these ads. What do you conclude? Also apply the Simon activation appropriateness approach to these ads. What do you conclude?

4. If you have been assigned the appendix to this chapter to read, apply the creative rules in the appendix to the Habitrol ad in Figure 10–3, the Olympus camera ad in Figure 10–4, and the Estée Lauder ad in the color insert. Also apply these rules to the six ads you selected in question 3. What do you conclude about the usefulness of these creative rules?

5. "All these detailed copy platforms, behavioral guidelines, and creative rules of copy writing do is prevent the creative people from really being creative." Comment.

NOTES

1. This approach and material, with slight adaptation, were provided by Professor Lawrence V. Johnson of the University of Kansas.

2. This section is based on an extensive presentation of this material in James F. Engel, Roger D. Blackwell, and Paul W. Miniard, *Consumer Behavior,* 7th ed. (Fort Worth, Texas: The Dryden Press, 1993), Chapter 15.

3. Christopher Puto and William D. Wells, "Informational and Transformational Advertising: The Differential Effects of Time," in *Advances in Consumer Research* 11, ed. Thomas C. Kinnear (Provo, Utah: Association for Consumer Research, 1984), pp. 638–43.

4. For a review of this literature see Engel et al., *Consumer Behavior,* Chapter 15.

5. This section is based on Julian L. Simon, *The Management of Advertising* (Englewood Cliffs, N.J.: Prentice Hall, 1971), pp. 169–206.

6. For the published insights of David Ogilvy, see David Ogilvy, *Confessions of an Advertising Man* (New York: Atheneum, 1963), and *Ogilvy on Advertising* (New York: Crown Publishers, 1983).

7. Harry W. McMahan, "Advertising: Some Things You Can't Teach—and Some You Can," *Advertising Age* (November 8, 1976), p. 56.

10

Designing and Producing the Mass Communications Message

The creative rules presented in this appendix are based on the research and practical experience of practitioners, especially David Ogilvy. Not all advertisers agree with all these rules. Indeed, some successful advertisements have been known to break some of them. New research will also from time to time change some of these rules. We do not present in this appendix all the points of disagreement about these rules. Thus, the reader should learn from these practitioners' research and experience but should also use the learning with wisdom and care.

PRINT ADVERTISING

The Headline

The headline is often considered to be "what would be said if only one or two lines of space were available for the message." It must put forth the main theme or appeal in a few words. Considered in this context, there is no reason to make it less than a powerful selling message.

Without doubt, the headline shoulders a large part of the task of attracting the reader's attention. It should tell the whole story, including the *brand name* and the *promise* to the buyer. Otherwise, the advertiser is wasting money. Research shows that four out of five readers never get farther than the headline. The illustration also aids in attracting and holding attention, but readership studies repeatedly demonstrate that the headline is the major component in attracting attention. If it is not powerful, many good prospects will never get far enough into the ad to read the message.

Classifications of Headlines   Headline information serves various purposes. It may provide news, state product claims, give advice, select prospects, arouse curiosity, or identify product or company name.

News   A news headline plays a role similar to its counterpart in the news story, for it often summarizes the point of highest interest in the copy. To command attention and arouse interest, such a headline must be pertinent and timely. It dispenses with cleverness and gimmicks and uses a direct, straight-selling approach. "Honda Number 1 in Consumer Satisfaction" is an example.

Product claim   Featuring a product claim can be a good attention-getter in that it appeals to the reader's self-interest. The claim should be significant and believable. A headline that says "This Tire Will Give You Good Mileage" would have less impact than one that says "This Tire Gives 30% More Mileage than Competitively Priced Tires." One might expect many brands of tires to give good mileage, but 30 percent more is something worth looking into.

Although many successful headlines make claims, the use of this approach has been somewhat weakened by advertising that makes irresponsible statements. You should proceed on the assumption that the reader will be dubious. To ensure believability, take care to provide ample supporting evidence in the copy.

Advice   Advice given in a headline may be followed by a promise of results from product use. Such a headline is "You Owe It to Yourself to Try Slimmo Reducing Tablets," with a secondary headline featuring a claim: "Use Slimmo 10 Days and Lose 10 Pounds." A properly conceived advice headline appeals to the reader's self-interest in that it is aimed at helping him or her solve a problem or prevent its occurrence.

Prospect selection   Because very few products are of interest to everyone, the advertisement should appeal only to potential customers. The headline is a principal device in the process of selecting prospects from among readers. Copy striving to reach everyone is usually so generalized that its effectiveness is lost. A headline that says "New Drug Aids Those Who Suffer from Asthma" would be a combination of news and selectivity. In other situations, the headline may be purely selective in purpose, as in the headline that says "Attention, June Graduates." The great majority of headlines are selective to some extent, regardless of emphasis.

Curiosity   Sometimes referred to as the provocative approach, the curiosity-oriented headline attempts to arouse interest by appealing to the unusual. The advertiser hopes that the reader will be stimulated to read the copy text to find the answer to a "riddle" that is posed.

The curiosity approach can be used when some aspect of the product is of such genuine and timely interest that the reader is predisposed to seek information. A headline that asks "Are You Protected from Atomic Pollutants?" would arouse interest on the part of many people and induce them to read the text for more information. Volkswagen has made effective use of this approach. In one of the most memorable advertisements in its campaigns, the headline read, "Lemon." Then the copy proceeded to explain the quality control procedures that prevent the customer from getting a "lemon."

The curiosity headline gives the copywriter great freedom to use his or her imagination, and its use can be tempting. However, some experts caution against the use of this approach in situations in which a direct-selling headline would be more appropriate. The curiosity type of headline too often is used for the sake of novelty alone, and, as was pointed out in Chapter 10, novelty without meaning is not creativity.

Product or company name   Occasionally the name of the product or company is used as the headline. This approach might be effective when the product is of such timely interest that the mere mention of the name is sufficient to arouse interest. During World War II, a headline reading "Tires" would have attracted real attention from consumers in the market of scarcity. Substantial interest among many ethnic and racial groups can be obtained today by featuring members of that specific group.

Some Guides for a Persuasive Headline   A fair amount of published research is available that delineates the characteristics of effective headlines. Although there is general agreement on certain of these characteristics, they can be violated successfully in many situations. There is a real difference, however, between violating a known criterion intentionally and violating it through ignorance.

Researchers at Marplan have found that confining the headline area to a small portion of the advertisement and using only one or two lines of type will produce the highest readership.[1] In addition, David Ogilvy mentions the following criteria:[2]

1. On the average, five times as many people read the headline as read the body copy. If you haven't done some selling in your headline, you have wasted 80 percent of your client's money.

2. Headlines should appeal to the reader's self-interest, by promising a benefit. This benefit should be the basic promise of the product.

3. Inject the maximum news into your headlines.

4. Include the brand name in every headline.

5. Write headlines that force the reader to read your subhead and body copy.

6. Don't worry about the length of the headline—12-word headlines get almost as much readership as 3-word headlines. Headlines in the 6- to 12-word group get the most coupon replies. Better a long headline that sells than a short one that is blind and dumb.

7. Never change typeface in the middle of the headline; it reduces readership.

8. Never use a headline that requires readership of body copy to be comprehensible.

9. Never use tricky or irrelevant headlines.

10. Use words to select your prospects—like MOTHER and VARICOSE VEINS.

11. Use words that have been found to contain emotional impact:

KISS	DARLING	INSULT	HAPPY
LOVE	ANGRY	MONEY	WORRY
MARRY	FIGHT	FAMILY	BABY

It is also generally accepted that the headline must be simple and easily understood. Moreover, it must join with the other message elements in presenting a unified and coherent message.

Copy

During construction of the headline, ideas flow toward the next step—writing the body copy. An idea put aside as inadequate for the headline often becomes a subhead, a copy-block lead line, or the lead for successive paragraphs. The copy reinforces the headline and delivers the sales message.

Whatever writing form the copywriter chooses to express the selling points, he or she will find that there is an ever increasing demand for facts. It is a naive copywriter who does not include hard information on the product and its benefits throughout the message.

Classification of Copy Approaches   It is useful to classify copy approaches by manner of presentation. In *direct-selling news copy,* for example, the message is presented in a straightforward manner similar to the informative content of newspaper articles. New-product messages are typical examples. In contrast, *implied suggestion* gives the reader an opportunity to draw conclusions from the facts that are presented. Usually the facts are obvious enough to direct the reader to a favorable conclusion about the product or service.

In *narrative description,* the copywriter starts with an account of some human experience that presents a problem and the solution in terms of favorable orientation toward a product. In a related copy type, the *story form,* human experience is also used in a straightforward account of product use by a purchaser. It may also involve an analogy between a storybook use and the product itself.

One effective approach is to use *monologue* and *dialogue.* The monologue is a single subject, such as a person (animals are also used as ad characters) reporting on personal reactions to certain goods and services. The dialogue presents a conversation between two persons (or animals) who elaborate on the merits of the product. This can often be in the form of a *testimonial message.* The testimonial implies that the reader can emulate or imitate the person giving the testimonial. It is also a means of stating authoritatively that certain benefits can be found in using a product or service by following the exemplary behavior of those featured.

Humor can be very effective if the entertainment value of the presentation has real selling appeal to those who are exposed to the message. Messages that deal with food, drinks, and entertainment generally find this an appropriate form. More will be said shortly about the use of humor. See also Promotion in Action 10–1.

Finally, some use can be made of the *comic strip* or *continuity* forms. These have found growing use because of the popularity of children's television programming and fictional characters, but its effectiveness is limited by mechanical problems in production of the comic strip.

Some Copy Problems

The use of humor   As mentioned above, considerable use is made of humor, but this should not be regarded as an index of its effectiveness. Many agree with Ogilvy's statement: "Humorous copy does not sell. It is never used by the great copywriters—only by amateurs."[3]

Others would not take such a strong stand, but research findings seem to support the conclusion that humorous commercials generally are less effective than their nonhumorous counterparts. The Schwerin Research Corporation reports that commercials featuring all humor (less than 4 percent of all advertisements) seldom prove to be as effective as other commercials. However, some use of humor, in general, will help the commercial to perform better than a commercial with no humor whatsoever. The conclusion, then, is that humor at its best is used sparingly.

The purpose of advertising is not to entertain. Few advertisements can entertain and sell simultaneously; both elements are combined only through use of great skill.

Answering competitors' claims   Perhaps it is human nature for an advertiser to react defensively when attacked by a competitor. Although direct competitive derogation is seen infrequently, many advertisers indirectly attack competitors with their own strong claims of superiority.

There is real danger in a direct counterattack. If a competitor makes the claim, for example, that its make of automobile is the "quietest on the road," it has in effect appropriated that claim for itself. If it is answered by a counterclaim stating that "we also are quiet," the earlier statement is reinforced. If an appeal is answered, it gains credence.

Direct-action copy   Much advertising copy is designed to activate those in the final stages of their decision-making process as they move toward purchase. Similarly, the copy may serve to lead those now preferring a brand to purchase it more frequently and in greater quantities.

Among the many direct-action approaches are samples, contests, coupons and price offers, premiums, and combinations of related products. Some of the objectives to be attained are:

1. To obtain new triers and convert them into regular users.
2. To introduce new or improved products.
3. To increase brand awareness or awareness of a new package.

4. To increase readership of advertising by using coupons as attention-attracting devices.

5. To stimulate reseller support.

Success with the direct-action approach is most likely where brand loyalty is low. A buyer may actively seek a special incentive to buy, such as a price reduction. In addition, the direct-action method can be highly effective when the product or service being advertised possesses no distinct competitive advantage. For this reason, coupons and other incentives are a basic competitive tool among manufacturers of soaps, breakfast foods, cake mixes, and other items where no single firm can claim uniqueness and where brand loyalty is not especially strong.

The direct-action or "forcing" approach must be used with caution. When all competitors use this type of stimulus, the result cannot help but have a diminishing effect for any individual firm. Moreover, the person may buy only for the incentive and return to a preferred brand later, in which case a costly promotion has failed.

Experience indicates that the forcing approach should seldom be used when strong appeals can be made to product superiority. The Scott Paper Company abandoned couponing for this reason and was successful in its stress on the product line itself and its unique advantages for the buyer. Moreover, a strong stimulus to buy will have a lasting effect through increasing market share only if the product clearly demonstrates its differentiation in use. Many new products have been successfully introduced by direct-action means, but sales of an existing product with no apparent superiority are not likely to be affected greatly.

The direct-action stimulus clearly has a legitimate role when it has been indicated through research that a significant number of buyers require an additional stimulus for purchase action. It should not be used simply as a competitive fad but should be based on consumer research.

Slogans   A slogan is a small group of words combined in unique fashion to embody the selling theme. In general, it will be short and to the point and feature the product name whenever possible. Through repetition, it may become associated with the product and its benefits, thereby provoking prompt recall of the advertising message.

Some slogans emphasize product performance, and the mention of the generic name is all that is needed to bring a powerful association to mind. Others are designed to emphasize product quality, such as the ageless slogan for Ivory Soap: "99 and 44/100 Percent Pure." A manufacturer may employ a sloan to minimize substitution of a competitor's product and stress confidence in quality. "You Can Be Sure If It's Westinghouse" became a well-known quality slogan.

Legal protection for slogans was granted in the Lanham Act of 1947. If the slogan is registered and certain additional requirements are met, legal protection is ensured. The detailed requirements of the act are explained in most basic marketing texts.

Some Guides for Persuasive Copy   Imagination, of course, must be disciplined to generate creative and persuasive copy. Although there is no universal set of steps to follow, there is substantial agreement with many of the following points mentioned by Ogilvy:

1. Don't expect people to read leisurely essays.
2. Go straight to the point; don't beat about the bush.
3. Avoid analogies—"just as, so too."
4. Avoid superlatives, generalizations, platitudes. Consumers discount them—and forget them.
5. Be specific and factual.
6. Be personal, enthusiastic, memorable—as if the reader were sitting next to you at a dinner party.
7. Don't be a dull bore.
8. Tell the truth—but make the truth fascinating.
9. Use testimonials. Celebrity testimonials are better than anonymous ones.
10. Don't be afraid to write long copy. Mail-order advertisers never use short copy—and they know exactly what results they get.
11. Make the captions under your photographs pregnant with brand names and sell.[4]

One could, of course disagree with some of these points. Some advertisers never use testimonials. Notice that several important basic criteria are set forth: Persuasive copy should be specific, interesting, believable, simple, and relevant.

If the copy surrounding an illustration or several illustrations does not make it apparent what the product's use or the benefit to the buyer may be, there must be a caption below the illustration. Research has generally found that the readership effect of a series of pictures with captions can be twice as great as body copy.

Nothing can lose a reader's attention more quickly than a general claim insufficiently supported by specific facts. "Chevrolet gets good gas mileage" is much less effective than "Chevrolet delivers 23.9 miles per gallon in the Mobile Gas Economy Run." Furthermore, the copy must contain relevant, meaningful information if it is to interest—not bore—the reader. Even interesting copy generally should not demand complex mental reasoning by the reader. It is much more effective if it focuses on a single theme.

The wording has much to do with the effect of the message on the recipient, for clumsy wording can violate the criterion of simplicity. Such words as *wonderful, powerful, time-saving,* and *finest* may lose their impact through overuse by advertisers, and the consumer is likely to reject them as being irrelevant. Good copy in most advertisements should amplify the headline, offer proof of what the headline claims, explain the product's advantages, and make clear what the reader is expected to do. It should in most cases end with an appeal to action, such as "visit your dealer now."

Visual Elements

The visualization of the basic theme is of such importance that one authority has suggested it be prepared before any other elements. According to this view, the most graphic, poignant, and appealing picture should be made of the theme; then the words are added. This is substantiated by a number of studies that demonstrate that the illustration is of critical importance in attracting and holding attention.

A number of methods can be used in creating the illustration: line drawings, cartoons, photographs, and artistic renderings of subjects. Photographs provide the most realism, but an artist's drawing may create a subtle mood or highlight an attribute of a product in use that may not be possible with photographs. In large part, the choice of the method will be made on a subjective basis by the creative team.

Classification of Visual Forms   Visual forms can be classified according to their features or techniques.

The product alone   Perhaps the simplest form of illustration is one in which the product is shown without background or setting. This method may prove powerful when the product has intrinsic characteristics that command attention. Precious jewels, high-priced automobiles, and similar distinctive items can attract attention without the use of background. At times, in fact, a background may distract from the product's impact.

The product in a setting   Not many products are of such distinction that they can be shown without background. The setting is chosen to show the product to advantage and, in many instances, the objective is to have the reader associate the quality of the setting with the product. In other situations, the setting may imply the pleasant and satisfying uses of the product.

The setting must be chosen carefully, for an incongruous background can lead to violation of the important criterion of believability. The low- or medium-priced car, for example, should not be shown in exclusive surroundings because the product would seldom be found in such an environment.

The product in use   This is perhaps the most widely used visualization. The power of suggestion is stimulated by this means because the reader immediately identifies with the product user and becomes the recipient of its benefits.

Benefits from product use   This method features the positive results derived from product use. It is hoped that readers will project themselves as ones who can benefit equally, especially if they have an acute need for the product.

Dramatizing need   Frequently, the need satisfied by a product is obvious, and visual treatment would be irrelevant. In other situations, the potential customer may realize that he or she has a need for the product when it has been illustrated. Moreover, effective visualization may dramatize the solution to an obvious and known need and thereby spur the reader to take action. Scouring pads, for example, are used mostly on pots and pans, but they also can be used to clean white-sidewall tires. The reader may have experienced difficulty in cleaning white sidewalls and may have never thought of scouring pads for this purpose. A dirty tire being made white can be a powerful illustration.

Explaining product uses   The illustration of a scouring pad in use dramatizes multiple product uses. Frequently, customers have limited market knowledge of product capabilities and may refuse to buy because they don't know how to use a product. If they do buy, they may use the product incorrectly and get poor results. The visual treatment can be helpful in showing details of methods of use or the procedures to be followed.

Featuring product details   Often the advertising theme will center around an improvement in some detail of the product or its operation. The detail may be dramatized by changing the pespective to make one part proportionately larger than others or by presenting the product from an unusual angle to call attention to that part. Other methods are to show a cross section of the product or print parts of it in color.

Dramatization of evidence   Evidence is often the lifeblood of effective advertising. Unfortunately, advertising too frequently has been handicapped by the use of unsupported claims. Many effective illustrations are created to support claims with factual evidence.

The comparison technique   This method may be used to point out certain product attributes that have competitive superiority. One variation is to show "before" and "after" pictures involving use of the product. The removal of carbon from engine valves after using a brand of gasoline for 6,000 miles is an example. Another method is to compare the results of using one product with the results obtained from another.

Dramatization of the headline   The headline and illustration are usually closely related, and the illustration can effectively strengthen the headline by communicating in a picture what the headline states in words.

The use of symbolism   The winged feet of Mercury symbolize speed; Uncle Sam signifies patriotism. Advertising may make effective use of symbols to associate the product or service with the basic idea conveyed. Notice how often the cross is used in advertising products with Christian religious significance.

Some Guides for Persuasive Visualization   Studies on the use of visual elements to attract and hold attention have disclosed that greatest effectiveness results when:

1. The illustration is placed in the upper part of the page instead of being positioned below the headline.

2. The illustration is the dominant element in the layout.

3. Photography is used instead of artwork.

4. People or things are pictured in proper proximity.

5. The colors used are vivid.

In addition, Ogilvy offers the following suggestions that can generally increase the probability of attracting and holding attention:

1. The average person now reads only four ads in a magazine; it is becoming increasingly difficult to find readers. That is why it is worth taking great pains to find a *great* illustration.

2. Put "story appeal" in your illustration.

3. Illustrations should portray reward.

4. To attract women, show babies and women.

5. To attract men, show men.

6. Avoid historical illustrations; they don't sell.

7. Use photographs in preference to drawings. They sell more.

8. Don't deface your illustration.

9. Use captions that are written the way people talk.

10. Don't use a lot of illustrations—they look cluttered and discourage a reader.

11. Don't crop important elements in your illustration.[5]

Some advertising artists would disagree with certain of these points; others would state different ones. Each would react according to personal experience and working knowledge.

The use of color   There is no question that using color adds to costs of space or time, printing, and production. Advertisers have found, however, that the extra cost is well rewarded for a number of reasons:

1. The attention-attracting and attention-holding power of the message may be increased sharply.

2. Contemporary social trends have encouraged experimentation in color in all phases of life, ranging from the factory to the home. Thus, people have become responsive to innovative color stimuli.

3. Most products look better in color, especially food.

4. Color can be used to create moods ranging from the somber apeal to the freshness of greens and blues.

5. Color can add an image of prestige to the advertisement, especially if most competing advertisements are in black and white.

6. Visual impressions can be retained in memory, hence resulting in greater message recall.

Numerous studies have demonstrated the attention-attracting power of color. It is, for example, the one outstanding factor in stimulating high readership of newspaper advertisements.

Skillful use of color also can set the mood for the advertisement. Connotations of various colors include:

RED: Anger, action, fire, heat, passion, excitement, danger
BLUE: Sadness, cool, truth, purity, formality
YELLOW: Cheerfulness, spring, dishonesty, light, optimism
ORANGE: Fire, heat, action, harvest, fall
GREEN: Calm, wet, spring, youth, nature, ignorance, immaturity
BLACK: Mystery, mourning, death, heaviness, elegance
WHITE: Cleanliness, purity, virginity

Color reproduction techniques have reached a high degree of refinement in magazines, and newspapers have made major improvements in its use. Increasing use has been made of preprinted inserts for newspapers, and real advances are seen daily in standard newspaper color procedures (run of press color). Inks have been standardized so that the advertiser can order certain colors and expect the same result anywhere the message is run. Moreover, production improvements have served to lower costs significantly, and the differential for the addition of color is now from 5 to 10 percent in newspapers. There is little doubt that it will be used in increasing amounts in a wide variety of newspaper ads.

RADIO AND TELEVISION

Copy and Visual Elements

The discussion to this point has been concerned with printed advertisements. It is to be expected that broadcast advertising differs in certain details. Radio has become perhaps the most informal of all media, and this informality has permeated its advertising requirements. Frequently the commercial is not written word for word but an outline is given to the announcer, who then provides words and style. Heavy use may also be made of humor and whimsy.

Ogilvy makes these suggestions for the television commercial:

1. It is easier to double the selling power of a commercial than to double the audience of a program.

2. Make your *pictures* tell the story. What you *show* is more important than what you *say*. If you can't *show* it, don't say it.

3. Try running your commercial with the sound turned off. If it doesn't sell without sound, it's a feeble commercial. Words and pictures must march together, reinforcing each other. The words in your titles must be identical with the words spoken.

4. In the best commercials the key idea is forcefully demonstrated. But in the poorest commercials there is little or no demonstration.

5. The best commercials are built around one or two simple ideas—*big* ideas. They are not a hodgepodge of confusing little ideas; that is why they are never created in committee. The best commercials flow smoothly, with few changes of scene.

6. The purpose of most commercials is to deliver the selling promise in the most persuasive and memorable way. State your promise at least twice in every commercial.

7. The average consumer sees 10,000 commercials a year. Make sure that she knows the name of the product being advertised in your commercial. Show the package loud and clear. Repeat the brand name as often as you can. Show the name in at least one title.

8. Good commercials rely on simple promises, potently demonstrated. But promises and demonstrations can be made tedious and indigestible by logorrhea [excessive talkativeness]. Don't drown your prospect in words.

9. Make the product itself the hero of the commercial.

10. In print advertising you must start by attracting the prospect's attention. But in television the prospect is *already* attending. Your problem is not to attract her attention, but to *hang on to it.*

11. *Start selling in your first frame.* Never warn the prospect that she is about to hear a "friendly word from our sponsor." Never start your commercial with an irrelevant analogy. Never start with an interrupting device.

12. Dr. Gallup reports that commercials which set up a consumer problem, then solve it with the product, then prove it, sell four times as much merchandise as commercials which simply preach about the product.

13. Dr. Gallup also reports that commercials with a news content are more effective than the average.

14. All products are not susceptible to the same commercial techniques. Sometimes there isn't any news; you cannot always use the problem-solution gambit; you cannot always demonstrate. Sometimes you must rely on *emotion* and *mood.* Commercials with a high content of emotion and mood can be very potent indeed.

15. To involve a person emotionally you should be human and *friendly.* People don't buy from salespersons who are bad mannered. Nor do they buy from phonies or liars. Do not strain their credulity. Be believable.

16. Movie screens are 40 feet across, but most TV screens are less than 2 feet across. Use close-up pictures instead of long shots. You have a small screen; get some impact on it.

17. You cannot bore people into buying your product. You can only *interest* them in buying it. Dr. Gallup reports that prospects are bored by "sermon" commercials, in which the announcer simply yaks about the product.

18. Television commercials are not for entertaining. They are for *selling*. Selling is a serious business. Good salespersons never sing. The *spoken* word is easier to understand than the sung word. Speech is less entertaining than song, but more persuasive. Persuasive commercials never sing.

19. The average consumer sees more than 200 commercials a week, 900 a month, 10,000 a year. For this reason you should give your commercial a touch of singularity. It should have a *burr* that will cling to the viewer's mind. But the burr must not be an irrelevance. And it must not steal attention away from the *promise*.

20. Whenever you write a commercial, bear in mind that it is likely to be seen by your children, your spouse, and your conscience.[6]

NOTES

1. "Basic Readership Factors," internal publication of Marplan Division of the Interpublic Group of Companies, Inc., New York.

2. David Ogilvy, "Raising Your Sights! 97 Tips for Copywriters, Art Directors, and TV Producers—Mostly Derived from Research," internal publication of Ogilvy, Benson & Mather, New York. Reproduced with permission.

3. Ibid.

4. Ibid.

5. Ibid.

6. Ibid.

C h a p t e r

11

Analysis of Mass Media Resources[1]

CONSUMERS AND MARKETERS RESPOND TO ADS IN MEDIA TYPES

Promotional managers have the choice of many types of media in preparing their media selection plans: the traditional media of newspapers, radio, television, outdoor, magazines, yellow pages, and direct mail—plus new media such as rental videotapes, movie theaters, high school classrooms, premium cable television channels (ones that you pay extra to view), grocery carts, checkout aisles, waiting lines at airports, and doctors' waiting rooms. How consumers and marketing professionals view the appropriateness of advertisements in these media is an important issue to those interested in promotional strategy. A recent study provided insight on the attitudes of consumers and marketing professionals about the "cluttering" of these media with advertisements. Some selected parts from the write-up of the study follow:

> Marketing executives are more annoyed than consumers by ads on non-traditional media such as videotapes, movie theaters, and TV monitors in doctors' offices and high school classrooms, according to an exclusive, two-pronged study by *Advertising Age* and the Roper Organization. And they are also more annoyed than the average consumer by magazine fragrance strips and commercials on premium pay cable TV channels.
>
> The findings indicate ad executives are getting fed up with the bad ads produced by their trade—and, importantly, that they're becoming more and more concerned about advertising clutter.
>
> The study also sheds light on the ad industry's overall attitude toward non-traditional media. In general, ad people gave higher approval ratings to traditional media such as network TV, basic cable, radio, and magazines than they did to alternative media.
>
> Ads that run via pay media such as videotapes, movie theaters, and premium pay cable channels were criticized most often by consumers and ad executives—but the annoyance numbers were much higher with latter group.
>
> The study was conducted by *Advertising Age* in conjunction with Roper in October. *Ad Age* telephoned a random sample of 400 marketing professionals; at the same time, Roper conducted the survey in face-to-face interviews with a random sample of 987 U.S. consumers

Some specific results are shown in the following table:

Media Type	Acceptable		Annoying		Don't Care	
	MP*	GP†	MP	GP	MP	GP
Magazines	96%	60%	1%	9%	2%	29%
Grocery carts	41	45	15	8	42	47
Movie theaters	25	36	65	31	9	29
TV in classrooms	23	30	62	27	12	30
Premium cable TV	22	29	59	32	15	28
Rental videos	19	30	69	37	10	29
TV in doctors' offices	41	35	36	26	20	33
TV at checkout aisles and airports	41	36	36	19	20	36

* MP = marketing professionals.
† GP = general public.

over age 18 in their homes. The margin of error is plus or minus 3 percentage points for the *Ad Age* survey and plus or minus 4 points for Roper's work.

A large number of consumers in the Roper poll said they "don't care one way or the other" about several types of advertising. Such neutral responses are considered good by some researchers—at least the ad isn't offending people, the thinking goes. But many research experts believe such ambivalence could be a harbinger of doom for the ad industry.

"People care less because there is too much advertising—they're just getting overwhelmed," PeopleTalk's Ms. Cohen said. "They are subject to so much that they tune it out."

Not surprisingly, the study found ad recall is better among industry executives than it is with the general population: 55.8 percent of marketing insiders could recall a specific advertising message from the previous 24 hours, versus 28 percent of consumers.

What is surprising is that 42.5 percent of the people who work in advertising couldn't recall an ad from the past 24 hours. And disheartening: Only 17 percent of all consumers were able to recall a specific brand name.

Taken as a whole, the numbers are nothing to write home about. The low general ad recall, coupled with the high annoyance levels in several media, could indicate a threat for the ad industry.

"It's important for us to move the acceptable number up," said Marcia Weiner, senior VP-associate director of strategic planning and research at DDB Needham Worldwide, Chicago, "When people feel negatively in a global way toward advertising, they feel less positive about a good ad or product."

Source: Adapted from Adrienne Ward Fawcett, *Advertising Age*, February 8, 1993, p. 33.

The ever changing world of mass media is well illustrated by the chapter opening feature. Many new media types are rapidly becoming available to promotional planners, and major changes are occurring in the traditional media. The investment of dollars in the mass media to reach the desired audience with a minimum of waste and a maximum of efficiency requires careful quantitative and qualitative analysis and selection of media vehicles. This is the topic of this chapter and the next.

EXPENDITURE TRENDS

In 1992, the total volume of advertising in the United States exceeded the $131 billion mark for the first time in history. As Table 11–1 indicates, newspapers are the leading media type, with $30.7 billion in expenditures, followed by television, with over $29.4 billion; direct mail, with about $25.4 billion; radio, with about $8.6 billion, the yellow pages, with about $9.3 billion; and magazines, with $7.0 billion. All media have increased in advertising expenditures over the last five years with two exceptions. Newspapers have declined slightly from $31.2 billion in 1988, and outdoor advertising declined from $1.06 billion in 1988 to $1.03 billion in 1992. The recession year of 1991 was the exception to the general growth pattern, with expenditures down in newspapers, magazines, and television, as well as in total.

It should be noted that the real increase in advertising volume is concealed by the increased cost of units of advertising. If inflation is taken out, there was about a 4 percent annual gain from 1968 to 1992. Additionally, we should note that the number of physical advertising units placed in various media has increased substantially.[2] Using 1968 as a base, the number of commercial placements on television has grown about 62 percent for spot television (local TV station buys), and about 46 percent for network television. The number of different brands advertised on television has grown about 50 percent during the same period, mostly in the spot market. In radio, spot commercial units are up about 60 percent, and network radio about 40 percent since 1968. Since 1973 magazine pages of advertising are up about 12 percent for national editions and 40 percent for special (regional or demographic) editions. Outdoor poster showings are up almost 40 percent since 1969, and newspaper advertising pages have increased by about 20 percent since 1960. This increase in units placed means that the fight to get consumers' attention is becoming more difficult. It is hard to get noticed.

The trend toward increased spending is expected to continue. Industry experts expect advertising expenditures to grow at 6 to 8 percent over the next few years.[3] Total yearly advertising expenditures are expected to reach over $175 billion by the year 2000. Advertising as a percentage of gross domestic product (GDP) declined from 2.20 percent in 1963 to a low of 1.97 percent in 1976. In 1992, this percentage had risen to about 2.4 percent.

NEWSPAPERS

Newspapers have long maintained first place among all media in terms of combined national and local advertising revenues. Newspapers are for the most part a local medium with daily circulation confined to the city of publication and immediately surrounding areas. There are notable exceptions to this local domi-

TABLE 11–1

Advertising Volume in the United States in 1992

Medium	Dollars (in millions)
Newspapers	
Total	$ 30,737
National	3,602
Local	27,135
Magazines	
Total	7,000
Weeklies	2,739
Women's	1,853
Monthlies	2,408
Farm Publications	231
Television	
Total	29,409
Network	9,549
Spot (national)	7.551
Syndication	2,070
Cable (national)	1,685
Spot (local)	8,079
Cable (nonnetwork)	475
Radio	
Total	8,654
Network	424
Spot (national)	1,505
Spot (local)	6,725
Direct Mail	25,391
Outdoor	
Total	1,031
National	610
Local	421
Business Papers	3,090
Yellow Pages	
Total	9,320
National	1,188
Local	8,132
Miscellaneous	
Total	16,427
National	12,124
Local	4,303
Total	
National	76,020
Local	55,270
Grand Total	$131,290

Source: *Advertising Age,* May 3, 1993, p. 4.

nance, including *The Wall Street Journal* and *USA Today.* The circulation of Sunday newspapers, however, frequently is much greater, often extending beyond state boundaries. There were 1,570 daily newspapers and 891 Sunday papers in the United States in 1993.[4]

The syndicated Sunday supplement is a distinct exception of the local flavor of newspaper editorial content. *Parade* and *Family Weekly* in effect are national sections inserted in more than 300 Sunday papers. Other supplements are local in editorial content and advertising. Some offer regional editions to permit insertion of advertising in a group of cities rather than purchase of the entire circulation.

Characteristics of Newspapers

Advantages   The use of newspapers as an advertising medium has the following advantages.

1. *Broad consumer acceptance and use.* Newspapers occupy a unique place in American life, according to studies. (See Table 11–2 for details.)

 a. Daily newspaper readership is high. Newspapers are read by 62 percent of all adults in the United States, and within the top 100 markets newspaper coverage includes 81 percent of the 99.1 million households.

TABLE 11–2

Newspaper Statistics

A. Cost and Coverage Cumulated by Top Market Groups

Market	Number of Papers	Number of Homes (000)	Total Circulation (000)	Daily Inch Rate, B/W	Cost per Page B/W
Top 10	78	29,082	14,011	$ 7,086	$ 826,510
Top 20	153	42,004	21,644	10,938	1,310,100
Top 30	209	50,988	26,603	13,755	1,655,960
Top 40	273	57,717	30,313	15,876	1,923,150
Top 50	346	62,841	33,711	17,936	2,181,300
Top 60	420	67,664	36,486	19,634	2,395,180
Top 70	431	71,342	38,850	21,046	2,573,150
Top 80	533	74,835	40,851	22,374	2,740,380
Top 90	590	77,840	42,639	23,481	2,879,890
Top 100	641	80,530	44,221	24,461	3,002,970

Daily newspapers in each market are included on the basis of circulation rank, until the combined circulations exceed 50% coverage of the market.

Source: *Marketer's Guide to Media,* Spring/Summer 1993; A. C. Nielsen *U.S. Television Household Estimates,* September 1992.

TABLE 11–2

Continued

B. Newspaper Readership (Average Weekday)

	Adults	Men	Women
Total	62%	64%	59%
Age			
18–24	51%	57%	46%
25–34	56	60	53
35–44	64	66	61
45–54	66	68	64
55–64	70	70	69
65+	66	67	65
Education			
Graduated from college	75%	78%	71%
Attended college	67	70	65
Graduated from high school	62	64	60
Attended high school	47	48	47
Did not attend high school	35	34	36
Household Income			
$50,000+	72%	75%	69%
$40,000+	71	74	67
$30,000+	69	72	66
$20,000–29,999	58	58	58
$10,000–19,999	52	52	52
<$10,000	42	37	44

Source: Simmons Market Research Bureau, 1993.

C. Newspaper Reach (Adults, Average Top 50 Markets)

	Net Reach of Leading Weekday Newspapers	
	Largest Circulation Newspaper	Top Two Newspapers in Circulation
Metro	47%	58%
ADI	35	45

Source: 1989 VNU/Scarborough and Simmons Top 50+ Newspaper Ratings Study-Metro and ADI Summary Reports.

D. Newspaper Readers per Copy

	Average Daily Paper		Sunday/Average Weekend Paper	
Age	Men	Women	Men	Women
18–24	.12	.10	.13	.12
25–34	.21	.19	.23	.23
35–44	.22	.21	.23	.22
45–54	.15	.15	.14	.15
55–64	.12	.13	.12	.13
65+	.14	.18	.14	.19
Total	.96	.96	.97	1.05

Sources: Audience—SMRB, 1992 M-6 and M-7 Volumes; Circulation—*Editor & Publisher International Yearbook*, 1993.

TABLE 11–2

Concluded

E. Newspaper Readership by Section

	Percent of Daily Newspaper Readers Who Read	
	Men	Women
All sections	64%	59%
Business	44	38
Classified	44	33
Comics	43	39
Editorial	46	42
Entertainment	43	43
Food or cooking	39	42
General news	53	48
Home	40	40
Radio–television	48	35
Sports	43	39
Other sections	43	41

Source: Simmons Market Research Bureau, 1993.

Source: The overall source for the content of this table and other tables in this chapter is, *1993 Leo Burnett Media Costs & Coverage.* Used with permission. Specific sources utilized by this guide are noted in each section of the tables.

b. Readership is 75 percent for college graduates and 35 percent for those who did not attend high school.

c. Newspaper reading increases with income. Of those making $40,000 plus, 71 percent read newspapers daily, compared to 42 percent of those earning less than $10,000.

d. Of the readers, most claim thorough readership. (See Table 11–2, part E.)

e. Because so many readers go through newspapers on a section-by-section basis, the average page has a 64 percent chance of being opened by men, and 59 percent by women. (See Table 11–2, part E.)

f. Weekend readership is also high.

2. *Short closing times.* Closing times refer to the deadline prior to publication by which advertising copy must be submitted. For daily newspapers, this period seldom exceeds 24 hours, thus giving the advertiser the opportunity to make last-minute changes. Closing dates for Sunday supplements, however, are generally much longer, usually ranging from four to six weeks.

3. *Improvements in color reproduction.* Standard newspaper color printing (ROP, or run of paper) has become widely available. Papers accounting for about 90 percent of total circulation offer black and white plus one ROP color; about

70 percent offer black and white and three ROP colors. Fine shadings and pastels are now possible but, because of the porosity of newspaper stock, truly fine color reproduction is difficult. The average costs for a full-page ad with black and three colors run about 31 percent above those for black and white.

Since high-quality color is so hard to achieve with ROP, use of preprinted color advertisements on a heavier stock of paper is increasing. This procedure, called Hi-Fi color, is available in about 90 percent of the markets and usually runs about $40 per 1,000 circulation above the cost of black and white. The chief disadvantage is that Hi-Fi methods require preprinting on a continuous roll of paper, and it is impossible to have the cuts coincide with the end of the copy. Creatively, this usually requires a wallpaper type of design. This problem may be eliminated, however, by the use of still another process, called Spectacolor, available in approximately 25 percent of the papers and costing little more than Hi-Fi. Preprinted inserts can be prepared either on ROP stock or rotogravure or other high-quality printing processes. These inserts are provided to papers, and the advertiser pays a special rate. Again the advantage is reproduction control.

4. *Increased geographic and market flexibility.* Newspapers are increasingly recognizing that one edition for a large market is not adequate to provide full local coverage. As a result, many papers now offer zone editions. The *Chicago Tribune,* for example, offers several zone variations and supplements corresponding to suburban areas. In addition, special-interest newspapers are becoming more established. Perhaps the most significant trend, however, is the growth of community and suburban newspapers and the further segmentation of large central-city newspapers. Also, a selling company called U.S. Suburban Press, Inc. (USSPI), has organized about 1,300 suburban papers in over 40 markets into a one-order/one-bill package, thus simplifying the buying process.

5. *Communication advantages.* The printed page is often believed to offer greater prestige and believability, perhaps based on the adage "Seeing is believing." There is no convincing research to verify this claim, but it is known that print induces superior retention of complex factual material when compared with oral presentation. Also, it is believed that print forces readers to become more involved in the subject matter by allowing them to grope to understand and to evaluate. Such involvement is less evident when material is presented in spoken form.

6. *Reseller support.* Newspapers are the most used of all media for the following kinds of reseller support:

a. Cooperative plans whereby dealers share costs.

b. Identification and promotion of the local dealer.

c. Promotion of quick action through coupons.

d. Other means to enlist dealer support.

Dealer enthusiasm for this use of advertising dollars often runs high.

Disadvantages   Newspapers also have disadvantages as an advertising medium, including the following.

1. *Rate differentials.* The gains in national advertising linage in newspapers have not been as rapid gains as those in local advertising. This lag is due in part to wide differentials between local and national (nonlocal) rates, in favor of local advertisers. As might be expected, rate differentials have been under fire. Defenders of the differentials in rates claim several justifications:

   a. National volume is not as dependable as local retail volume and therefore costs more to handle.

   b. The national competitor will have a large edge over the local counterpart and hence should be penalized.

   c. National advertisers are requesting more merchandising assistance in the form of special promotion to dealers, assistance in advertising plans, and other services.

   d. It costs more to handle national advertising. Newspapers claim that these costs are from 20 to 25 percent higher because the 15 percent discount is granted to agencies (this is the standard method of agency compensation), a cash discount is given, and representatives must be paid to solicit nonlocal advertising. The latter charge is also incurred for local advertising.

The first three of the claimed justifications have little basis in fact. The widespread use of newspapers by many national advertisers on a continuing basis largely removes the charge of lack of dependability; the national and local firms seldom are competitors, and in fact it is more common for the national advertiser to work in partnership with local dealers; and, finally, local advertisers seldom use an agency and therefore are prone to request more in the way of special services than the national firm. The payment of agency commissions, however, and the other costs are valid reasons for a nominal differential. The problem is that the usual differential is far in excess of this justifiable amount, and most newspapers at this point seem to be unwilling to change the status quo.[5]

2. *Costs of national coverage.* The costs of reaching a national market through newspapers can quickly become excessive. National coverage through this medium often requires an additional expenditure of 80 percent or more in comparison with network television and magazines. However, newspapers do provide better intensity of coverage of households.

3. *Short life.* Newspapers usually are not retained in the home for extensive periods of time. As a result, little opportunity exists for repeat exposure to advertisements. This disadvantage is shared by all media, however, with the exception of magazines.

4. *Reproduction problems.* Newspapers, of course, are printed on an absorbent paper stock, resulting in an inability to offer fine reproduction. In addition, the speed necessary to compose a daily newspaper prevents the detailed preparation and care in production that is possible when time pressures are not so great.

5. *Small "pass-along" audience.* Generally speaking, newspapers do not generate larger audiences through sharing of issues by purchasers often referred to as pass-along readership. The pass-along audience of magazines may be substantial.

Buying Newspaper Space

Newspaper rates are usually quoted in detail in volumes published periodically by the Standard Rate and Data Service (SRDS). The basic space unit for strictly local advertising is usually the column inch. The national rate, however, is quoted in terms of agate lines (14 lines represent a column inch). The newspaper page consists of six to nine columns, approximately 300 lines deep. The total number of lines is approximately 2,400. The tabloid page consists of about 1,000 lines with five or six columns.

Published rates vary if special treatment is specified. Color, of course, always carries a premium, as does location in a specific part of the paper. Unless otherwise specified, copy will be inserted on a run-of-paper basis.

For local advertising, gross space rates are usually converted to a common basis for purposes of comparison. The milline rate, widely used for this purpose, is calculated as follows:

$$\frac{\text{Line rate} \times 1,000,000}{\text{Circulation}}$$

Rates are compared, then, in terms of costs of the circulation that is achieved. Otherwise, an extremely low line rate might be deceptive if it fails to generate adequate circulation and advertising exposure. Also, milline rates are rarely used by national advertisers. They prefer to use a rating point measure, which is the reach of the paper times the frequency of insert, relative to cost.

Recently, newspapers have developed standard advertising units (SAUs) as a way of simplifying national advertising buys. The American Newspaper Publishers Association has been the leader in this action. There are 56 different SAUs. Most major newspapers have indicated a willingness to use such a system. SAUs represent different sizes of ads. Thus, a national advertiser could prepare one ad for insertion in over 1,300 newspapers and have rates quoted on this basis.

Also the Newspaper Advertising Bureau has developed a "Newsplan" program whereby national advertisers obtain discounts in newspapers. Eight of 10 newspapers are cooperating in this plan. Both SAUs and Newsplan await effective implementation for easy use by national advertisers.[6]

The Future of Newspapers

There can be little doubt that newspapers will continue to be vitally important as a local advertising medium. Two major trends will probably continue.

First, and most vital to the survival of the newspaper, is the development of increased technological sophistication. Most of the total newspaper copy in the United States is now printed on offset presses. The use of electronic technology is also increasing. Among the new systems is one that basically consists of a typesetting computer linked to a visual display monitor. It can be used for classified and display advertising as well as news copy. Previously entered copy can be recalled directly from memory files and can be paged.[7]

The second major trend is the segmentation and diversification of the newspaper industry with the growth of suburban and community newspapers and the publication of different sections of large central-city newspapers.

Chain-controlled newspapers are also expected to grow in importance unless the federal government decides otherwise. Other newspapers are expected to expand into national distribution, such as the *Christian Science Monitor*. However, there are logistical problems. For example, *The Wall Street Journal* transmits copy to local plants via satellite, as does the national edition of the *New York Times*. *USA Today* was started by Gannett as a national newspaper and continues to increase circulation, but it has failed to attract enough advertisers to show a profit.

Of special concern are newsprint shortages and rapidly increasing costs. For example, the price of newsprint has increased from $175 to about $600 per ton in 20 years. One solution to the problem that has been foreseen by many is broadcast of the local newspaper over two-way cable television. Hard copies could be made of items of particular interest through the use of a facsimile printer linked to the set. This appears to be a long time off. Since advertising revenue growth in newspapers has not kept up with inflation since 1989, there is tremendous pressure on newspapers to reduce costs.

Additional future concerns and prospects for newspapers include:

1. The acceptance of SAUs and associated growth in obtaining national advertising dollars.
2. Improvement in audience research. (See Chapter 12 for details.)
3. The potential display of newspaper pages on television screens in homes through cable hookups or direct transmission.

TELEVISION

The type of television under consideration makes a difference in any discussion; network program advertising differs substantially from advertising on local television stations. Recently, the dynamic growth of cable television has further complicated the discussion. We will center first on the characteristics of television in general and then on the use of network program advertising versus spot (local) announcements, and the nature of cable television.

In 1993 there were 1,681 operating television stations in the United States. The breakdown is as follows: 568 commercial VHF stations, 736 commercial UHF stations, 129 noncommercial VHF stations, and 248 noncommercial UHF stations. Most commercial stations are network affiliated, with only about 400 operating as independents.[8]

General Characteristics of Television

Advantages   The advantages of television as an advertising medium include the following.

1. *The combination of sight and sound.* Television, through its combination of sight and sound, provides audiences with a unique sense of participation and reality approximating face-to-face contact. As such, it commands full attention from viewers. The combination of sight and sound is also advantageous because of the creative flexibility offered to the advertiser. Full opportunity exists for product demonstration and the amplification of selling points with audio presentation. In addition, color telecasting has the advantages of greater emotional impact and presentation of appetite appeal. Of the more than 94.2 million U.S. households now equipped with television, about 98 percent have color sets. Of all television households, 67 percent have more than one set. Sixty-one percent of television households receive cable television programming.[9]

2. *Mass audience coverage.* Television is now in 95 percent of all the approximately 99.1 million U.S. households. Recent studies indicate that during an average day, 92 percent of these households will be exposed to television programming, and in the space of a week, this percentage reaches 98 percent. The average viewing time per day per television household is over 7 hours.[10] During an average week, the average television viewing time per television household is over 50 hours. Television is truly a mass medium. Table 11–3 presents a more detailed look at television viewing by providing data on some demographic characteristics of viewers by times of the day. Note that viewing is slightly less in higher income groups and among working women relative to other women.

TABLE 11–3

⌄   **Television Viewing**

A. Hours of TV Usage per Week

	7-Day 24-Hr. Total	Monday–Sunday		Monday–Friday	
		8:00– 11:00 P.M.	11:30 P.M.– 1:00 A.M.	10:00 A.M.– 4:30 P.M.	4:30– 7:30 P.M.
All Households	50.36	12.90	3.11	8.91	6.64
Households $60M+	45.36	12.88	2.95	6.75	5.74
Total Men	28.23	8.72	2.01	3.50	3.36
Men 18–49	25.16	7.76	2.02	2.87	2.66
Men $60M+ HH	21.50	7.59	1.68	1.89	3.32
Total Women	33.01	9.56	2.03	6.02	4.38
Women 18–49	28.35	8.29	1.94	4.94	3.37
Women $60M+ HH	24.15	8.07	1.54	3.68	3.03
Women Employed	26.71	8.65	1.91	3.39	3.08
Women with Children	29.70	8.29	1.97	5.80	3.53
Teens 12–17	21.92	6.46	1.32	3.25	3.34
Children 2–11	21.80	5.24	0.63	4.02	3.54

Source: A.C. Nielsen, *National Audience Demographics Report,* November 1992, February, May, July 1993.

TABLE 11–3

Concluded

B. Households Using Television (Percent of U.S. TV Homes)

	Percent of U.S. TV Homes				
	October–December 1991	January–March 1992	April–June 1992	July–September 1992	1991/92 Avg. Month
Monday–Friday					
7:00–10:00 A.M.(ET)	22%	22%	21%	21%	21%
10:00 A.M.–1:00 P.M.	24	26	23	25	25
1:00–4:30 P.M.	29	31	28	29	29
10:00 A.M.–4:30 P.M.	27	29	26	27	27
4:30–6:00 P.M.	40	41	36	35	38
Monday–Sunday					
7:00–8:00 P.M.	57%	59%	48%	47%	53%
8:00–9:00 P.M.	62	63	55	53	58
9:00–10:00 P.M.	64	64	59	57	61
10:00–11:00 P.M.	58	58	57	55	57
11:00 P.M.–12:00 Mid.	42	42	42	41	42
12:00 Mid.–1:00 A.M.	26	26	26	26	26

Source: A.C. Nielsen, *Households Using Television Summary Report,* 1991/1992.

3. *The psychology of attention.* The television viewer is in a sense a captive before his or her set. Most viewers give way to inertia and watch commercials rather than exert the effort to change the set to other program material. From this it can be inferred that they will be consciously exposed to a majority of advertising messages, with the result that at least one hurdle to promotional response is cleared. It must not be concluded, however, that exposure necessarily means favorable response. Response can be modified by the mechanisms of the viewer's selective perception and retention, discussed in earlier chapters. Low-involvement learning assigns television advertising even more power due to its ability to affect cognitive structure.

4. *Favorable consumer reaction.* Television is still a very popular medium with Americans. However, the percentage of households watching television over the last decade, especially network programming, has eroded. Using an index of 100 based on the percentage of households watching television in 1980–81, the prime time percentage of households watching fell to 63, and the day network to 68 in 1992–93.[11]

Disadvantages   Television also has certain disadvantages that affect its choice as an advertising medium.

1. *Negative evaluations.* There has been a growing tendency for programs to include more explicit sexual behavior and dialogue, more realistic violence,

and free use of curses and vulgarity. Some groups have organized boycotts of sponsors they believe are supporting these shows. In 1993 many sponsors indicated that they would seek to sponsor less violent, more family-oriented shows.

2. *Nonselectivity.* Although there may be growing selectivity among television watchers, it is still difficult to reach precisely a small market segment using television as the medium. Variations in program content and broadcast time will obviously achieve some selectivity, especially through children's programs, sports programs with masculine appeal, or late-night talk shows, but more precise segmentation in terms of age, income, and interest is practically impossible on broadcast television. Cable television (CATV) may eventually allow for such segmentation if it continues to develop, as many expect it will. This is discussed further in the section on the future of television.

3. *Fleeting impression.* The television message crosses the viewer's consciousness only momentarily and then is lost. If for some reason the message did not register, the promotional opportunity has been lost. The opportunity does exist for reexposure, however, through multiple commercials over a period of time.

4. *Commercial clutter.* Once a problem chiefly in spot (local) television, the common use of 30-second and 15-second commercials, along with participatory buying by advertisers, has resulted in a greater number of different commercial messages in each program. The competition in each commercial break combined with the shorter time used in developing and communicating the message has many advertisers worried about the persuasive effectiveness of the commercial—the fear of being lost in the crowd.[12]

5. *"Promo" clutter.* Another aspect of the general clutter problem relates to the networks' increased amount of hyping of their own shows. Again, getting one's message through to the consumer is made more difficult.

The Network Television Program

Over-the-air broadcast networks are dominant in television for the reason that they originate most of the popular programs. The networks are confederations of stations in which each one is compensated at the rate of 30 percent of the gross commercial rate for programs carried in its area. Although it is assumed that each station will air most network shows, the station is free to originate local programming if a greater profit can be made.

Several smaller networks also offer shows on a regional or selective programming basis. The Hughes Sports Network makes available to subscribing stations coverage of sports events not covered by the major networks. The Christian Broadcasting Network, with headquarters in Portsmouth, Virginia, includes several stations nationwide that operate on a nonprofit basis to broadcast a wide variety of religious programming. Metromedia owns six television stations that compete with the major networks in New York and several other large metropolitan areas. The Fox Network represents a very real attempt to forge a fourth major network with its own first-run programming. Fox has recently gained as much as 16 percent of prime-time television advertising revenue.[13] In addition, the big three networks' share of the evening viewership fell from 90 pecent in 1979 to less than 60 percent in 1992. The growing power of independent stations and cable programming is evident.

In addition, the use of transmission by satellite is done by Turner Broadcasting's WTBS Atlanta, WGN Chicago, and WWOR New York. They are transmitting their own shows to cable systems in other regions of the country and have earned the name "superstations." Further, Home Box Office (a division of Time, Inc.) and others transmit "pay" movies and other events via satellite to cable operators for sale to connected households.

Advantages of Purchasing Network Time   The advantages of network television programming as a medium for advertising include the following.

1. *Excellent time availability.* The networks have virtual control over the prime-time programming (8–11 P.M. New York time). Federal Communication Commission (FCC) rulings regarding access to prime time put some limitations on network programming during that period, but the advertiser who wishes to reach a truly vast, nationwide audience at one time must necessarily buy time from the networks during prime-time hours.

2. *Simplicity of arrangements.* The time purchase is greatly simplified when network television is used. The mechanics of purchasing spot time can become exceedingly cumbersome and costly.

Disadvantages of Purchasing Network Time   The disadvantages of network time also must be considered.

1. *Costs.* Network television advertising is precluded for many because of the costs, although local spot announcements often can be purchased in network service times. In addition, commitments must be made well in advance, and modifications can be made only with great difficulty.

2. *Availabilities.* Even if smaller companies could come up with the money to buy prime time on network television, they might find it quite difficult to find time available, especially on highly rated programs. This situation may have eased to some extent with the virtual end of sole sponsorship of any program by a single advertiser, but competition for the best programs still exists.

3. *Program mortality.* The rate of program mortality is traditionally high each season. There is no good way to determine in advance the probable success of a program, and too often time buys must be made on the basis of educated guesses. This is another reason why sponsorship of a single program has been largely replaced by time buying on a participating basis. The now-common network practice of program stunting, which uses specials and miniseries, has made the estimating process even more difficult.

4. *Variations in program popularity.* A program with a rating of 36 in one market (36 percent viewership) may produce a rating of only 10 in another market. The advertiser's market potential would match variations in program popularity only by accident, with the result that dollars can become allocated in such a way that potentials are not paralleled. A similar situation can result when program popularity does not parallel distribution. Occasionally, it is possible to purchase only part of the national coverage of a program, but this flexibility is the exception

rather than the rule. To help deal with this problem, the Lintas Campbell-Ewald advertising agency utilizes a computer-based time-sharing system to facilitate the analysis and auditing of alternative network television schedules on a market-by-market basis.

Buying Network Time

Network time is quoted at varying rates, depending on the time of the day and season of the year. Prime-time rates are most expensive, of course. Approximately 65 percent of all stations are members of the National Association of Broadcasters (NAB), which suggests that its members air commercials within the following guidelines:

1. *Commercials.* 9.5 to 12 minutes per hour in prime time and 16 minutes per hour in nonprime time. On children's weekend programs, 12 minutes per hour on weekdays and 10.5 minutes per hour on weekends.[14]

2. *Number of interruptions.*
   a. Prime time: two per 30-minute program, four per 60-minute program, and five per 60-minute variety show.
   b. Nonprime time: four per 30-minute period, one per 5-minute period, two per 10-minute program, and two per 15-minute program.
   c. Number of consecutive announcements: four for program interruptions and three per station break.

3. *Multiple-product announcements.* There is a 60-second minimum on multiple-product announcements unless they are so well integrated as to appear to the viewer as a single announcement. Local retailers are excluded from this rule. The NAB guidelines are usually followed, although the code has no legal standing due to court ruling.[15]

Because of the escalating costs of advertising, most television time is purchased on a participating plan by which program costs are shared by other advertisers. The 30-second commercial dominates, comprising 64 percent of all network advertising (up from 20 percent in 1970 and down from 74 percent in 1986). The average 30-second prime-time network television time slot in 1992 cost about $105,200, and daytime slots cost about $15,100. A 30-second slot on a top-rated prime-time series costs about $250,000, whereas low-rated slots averaged about $55,000. A 30-second slot on the 1993 Super Bowl cost $850,000. Obviously, these latter slots are not for the weak of budget. A widely used method of cost comparison is cost per 1,000 homes (CPM), which is based on the cost of the commercial time and the program ratings. Comparative numbers are presented in Table 11–6 at the end of the chapter.

Spot Announcements

Spot announcements are commercials shown on local stations, with the time purchased directly from the local stations involved. The network is not involved at all. Many of the disadvantages of network television can be overcome through use of spot announcements on local television stations purchased on a market-by-market (nonnetwork) basis. Time availabilities generally range from 10-second IDs (station identification breaks) to a full 60 seconds, although 30-second spots predominate.

Advantages of Spot Television   The use of spot announcements on television has some advantages for the advertiser.

1. *Geographic and time flexibility.* A key problem of purchasing network program time is the commitment to appear in nearly all markets where the program is aired even though market potentials may differ. Spot announcements are an effective alternative when the creative advantages of television are desired. Total costs are usually reduced through minimization of waste coverage.

2. *Reseller support.* Spot television also offers one of the advantages of newspapers in that it can be used effectively in cooperative advertising programs, for identification of local dealers, and in other ways to achieve dealer support.

Disadvantages of Spot Television   The disadvantages of spot announcements include the following.

1. *Chaotic buying procedures.* When local time is purchased, the buying situation can become chaotic. There is little uniformity in rates or in quantity discount plans. In addition, favored advertisers receive desirable time periods, and a personal relationship and difficult negotiations may be necessary to achieve the best time purchase. Firms representing many stations, such as the well-known Katz Agency, simplify these problems, but the difficulties remain so great that there is no shortcut to long experience in time buying.

2. *Commercial clutter.* An excess of commercials seems to be a problem for television in general, but the volume of nonprogram material appearing in station breaks is a real headache for the industry. Talent credits and announcements appear as trailers on network programs, several commercials are aired in the station break, and time must still be left for station identification and introduction of the next program. Not surprisingly, lower recall of brand advertising occurs when station-break commercials are used.

3. *Viewing at station-break periods.* It is well known that the number of viewers declines during station breaks. Some leave the room, and the attention of those who remain is frequently attracted elsewhere. The total audience and viewer attention at station breaks may not be optimum.

Buying Spot Time

The purchase of network time involves only one contact. Arrangements are considerably more difficult when local stations are used. The buyer either writes, teletypes, faxes, or telephones the station or its representative to request information on available time slots. These availabilities are then checked and communicated to the buyer, usually within 24 hours. The local stations sometimes guarantee protection in that advertisements for competing products normally will not be aired within 15 minutes of each other, but this practice is rapidly disappearing.

The listing of availabilities is always in writing, and a guarantee is given that the first buyer to make a request gets the time slot. Once the decision is made, the order is usually submitted by telephone and later verified in writing.

Costs are always quoted in a spot-by-spot basis, usually related to the time of day. Prime evening time usually carries the highest price and runs from 8 to 11 P.M. in all areas except the central time zone, where all classifications are one hour earlier. Stations affiliated with the network also quote fringe evening time from 6 to 7:30 P.M. and from 11 P.M. to 1 A.M. Daytime runs from sign-on to 5 P.M., Monday through Friday. In addition, it is common to quote a lower rate if the buyer is willing to run the risk that a competing buyer may later preempt the time spot. If one pays the full price, however, the buyer is guaranteed the time, and it is becoming increasingly common to reserve and hold desirable times over long periods by this means.

Most stations later verify, based on the program log, that the commercial actually was run. Following submission of this affidavit, the time bills become due. Third-party monitoring organizations such as Comtrac can be contracted to tape the broadcast to provide verification.

It is obvious that spot-time buying can be complex, and most agencies have specialists in this field. In addition, these complexities have been instrumental in the formation of specialized media-buying services. In order to manage the paperwork, many agencies are utilizing computers, their own and those of service companies such as Donavan Data Systems.

The Future of Television

Several specific issues promise to bring about changes in television programming and advertising: (1) the growth of cable television (CATV); (2) videocassette recorder/players; (3) the technological merging of television, computers, tele-phones, and cable; (4) changes in network programming; and (5) overcommercia-lization. These issues are discussed below.

CATV   The continued growth and sophistication of cable television may well have a dramatic effect on the television industry, dependent on the rulings and guidelines created by the FCC. The major function of CATV in its early days was to bring the regularly scheduled programs of commercial stations to areas beyond the range of their broadcast signals. Subscribers who formerly had poor reception and limited channel selection could, with cable hookups, receive clear pictures and a wide variety of channel selections. Now cable serves as an alternative to standard television by offering specialty channels such as movies, sports (ESPN, the sports network); Turner Broadcasting's 24-hour Cable Network News (CNN); and music. (See Table 11–4, part C.) In 1992, there were about 11,075 operating systems reaching about 57.3 million subscribers, or 61.5 percent of television households.[16]

Another attractive opportunity to CATV operators is pay television, which involves attaching to the subscriber's set a device that makes certain the pay TV broadcasts are impossible to view without the payment of a separate fee beyond the

TABLE 11–4

Cable Television Facts

A. NTI Sample: Cable Penetration by Market Divisions

	Cable	Pay Cable
Total U.S.	66%	28%
County Size		
A	64	30
B	68	30
C & D	65	24
Non-Adults		
None	64	23
Any	68	36
Age of HOH		
Under 50	67	32
50+	63	23
HH Income		
<$30M	57	21
$40M+	76	37
$50M+	78	39
Number of TVs		
1	57	20
2+	70	33

Source: NTI, *Cable TV: A Status Report,* May 1993.

B. Cable and Pay Cable Penetration

Year	Number* of Systems	Cable TV Homes†		Pay Cable Homes†	
		MM	Percent U.S.	MM	Percent U.S.
1960	640	.7	1.0	—	—
1970	2,490	4.5	7.5	—	—
1980	4,225	17.7	22.6	7.6	9.8
1985	6,600	39.9	46.2	22.7	26.4
1986	7,500	42.2	48.1	23.1	26.4
1987	7,900	45.0	50.5	23.7	26.8
1988	8,413	48.6	53.8	28.1	31.1
1989	9,010	52.6	57.1	28.6	31.1
1990	9,575	54.8	58.9	26.3	28.3
1991	10,704	55.8	60.6	25.9	28.1
1992	11,075	57.3	61.5	25.8	27.7

* January of each year.
† November of each year.

Sources: A.C. Nielsen, Cable Universe Estimates; November 1992 *Television & Cable Factbook,* 1992.

TABLE 11–4

Continued

C. Selected Satellite-Fed Cable Services

	Subscriber HH (000)	Cable Systems
Superstations		
WTBS	60,425	11,807
WGN	38,100	14,354
WWOR	13,500	2,100
WPIX	9,500	638
Pay Cable		
Home Box Office	19,900	9,100
Showtime	7,300	6,000
The Disney Channel	7,080	7,000
Cinnemax	6,100	5,700
Encore	3,900	1,100
Basic Cable		
CNN	61,738	11,636
ESPN	61,600	26,116*
USA Network	60,046	12,000
The Discovery Channel	59,533	9,756
TNT	58,950	9,069
Nickelodeon	59,900	9,616
The Family Channel	57,688	9,876
The Nashville Network	57,300	13,396
MTV	57,285	8,141
C-SPAN	57,200	4,218
Lifetime	57,000	5,865
Arts & Entertainment	56,088	8,400
The Weather Channel	53,381	4,925
Headline News	51,632	5,763
Nick-at-Nite	51,250	4,036
CNBC	48,300	4,000
VH-1	47,400	5,296
QVC Network	45,000	4,071
American Movie Classics	43,000	3,300
Black Entertainment Television	35,300	2,661
EWTN	31,000	1,025
Comedy Central	28,000	2,004
C-SPAN II	27,900	914
Mind Extension University	23,000	798
E! Entertainment Television	21,560	950
Home Shopping Network	20,800	1,474
VISN/ACTS	20,000	1,249
The Learning Channel	19,874	1,558
Country Music Television	18,900	4,880
The Travel Channel	17,500	735
Trinity Broadcasting Network	16,000	1,400
Silent Network	15,000	164
America's Disabled Channel	15,000	164
Nostalgia Television	14,700	740

TABLE 11–4

Continued

C. Satellite-Fed Cable Services

	Subscriber HH (000)	Cable Systems
Video Jukebox Network	13,000	104
Tetemundo	12,400	470
Home Shopping Network II	11,200	471
Univision	11,063	609
The Sci-Fi Channel	11,060	768
Bravo	10,500	475
Courtroom Television Network	8,000	600
QVC Fashion Channel	7,500	450

* Includes MMDS/SMATV systems.

Source: *CableVision,* June 7, 1993.

D. Top 20 Designated Metropolition Area (DMA) Cable Markets

DMA	Cable Homes	Percent of TV Homes
New York	4,263,040	64%
Los Angeles	2,935,890	59
Philadelphia	1,899,820	71
Chicago	1,680,850	55
Boston	1,526,750	73
San Francisco–Oakland–San Jose	1,512,170	67
Washington, DC	1,143,400	62
Detroit	1,068,250	62
Seattle–Tacoma	962,720	67
Tampa–St. Petersburg, Sarasota	927,780	67
Cleveland	918,450	63
Atlanta	915,580	61
Dallas–Ft. Worth	887,630	49
Pittsburgh	857,990	75
Miami–Ft. Lauderdale	851,470	66
Houston	769,890	51
Hartford & New Haven	763,150	83
San Diego	736,780	80
Orlando–Daytona–Melbourne	701,640	73
Sacramento–Stockton–Modesto	664,450	60

Source: A.C. Nielsen, *U.S. Television Household Estimates,* September 1993.

TABLE 11–4

Concluded

E. Top 10 Cable Markets

Market	Cable Penetration (% of TV Homes)
Palm Springs	87.7%
Honolulu	84.5
Hartford & New Haven	83.4
Monterey-Salinas	82.4
Santa Barbara–Santa Maria–San Luis Obispo	80.6
San Diego	79.9
Lafayette, IN	79.5
San Angelo	79.4
Victoria	79.4
Tuscaloosa	78.9

Source: A.C. Nielsen, *Cable Universe Estimates*, July 1993.

F. Top 20 VCR Markets

Market	VCR Penetration (% of TV Homes)
Anchorage	90.0%
Salt Lake City	84.5
San Francisco–Oakland–San Jose	84.5
San Diego	83.5
Elmira	83.0
Washington, DC	82.8
Charlottesville	82.6
Idaho Falls–Pocatello	82.6
Las Vegas	82.6
Santa Barbara–Santa Maria–San Luis Obispo	82.3
Sacramento–Stockton–Modesto	81.8
Chico–Redding	81.5
Bend, OR	81.4
Reno	81.4
Los Angeles	81.2
Portland, OR	81.2
Austin	81.0
Seattle–Tacoma	81.0
Denver	80.9
Medford–Klamath Falls	80.8
Total U.S.	77.2

Source: A.C. Nielsen, *NSI VCR Penetration Estimates*, July 1993.

monthly subscription charge. This system would make possible truly specialized programming since only those subscribers who specifically decide to watch a particular program and are willing to pay a fee to do so will be in the viewing audience. If commercial time is made available, the segmentation potential could be at least equal to that of the magazine. Even without pay television, more precise segmentation should be possible once CATV begins to produce its own programs. Pay cable reaches about 25.8 million subscribers in 50 states.

In 1993, the federal courts ruled that the regional Bell phone companies could compete for video services with the cable providers utilizing the phone lines. Thus, the television household could in the future be offered competitive "cablelike" programming services over their telephone lines by their regional Bell company. U.S. West and Warner Communications have already agreed to begin a test of such a service. In addition, Congress in 1992 passed a law to reregulate the cable television industry. This law effectively allowed regulators to set cable television rates and also provided that cable operators would have to pay fees to over-the-airwaves stations whose programming the cable operators provided in their basic service. Previously, no fees were paid to carry these channels.

The net result of the growth in CATV will be a fragmentation of the network and spot television audience, plus a decrease in audience size, with potential negative consequences on network and spot advertising revenues. However, for the cable networks to prosper and grow, they must also draw advertising revenues. To get these revenues, they must provide audience measurement numbers. Recently, ESPN and CNN both used A. C. Nielsen's Home Video Index to establish their audience sizes. The development of audience measurement techniques for CATV has been a major thrust of media researchers over the last few years. As noted in Table 11–1, total cable advertising revenues were about $2 billion in 1992.

Videocassette Recorders/Players The use of videocassettes is now common. Many companies are now marketing videocassette machines. The videocassette recorder releases viewers from the fixed time schedules for programs (time shifting). It greatly affects television viewing habits and causes great problems for those attempting to measure the size of audiences of television programs. A show may be watched at any time using this system, since the viewer can automatically record any program for future viewing even if he or she is not at home. Prerecorded videotapes of movies and sports events are also available at prices between $10 and $25, or rental in the $1 to $5 range. Recorded television shows also give the viewer the ability to speed through the commercials in the program. They are able to "zap" the commercials while recording or playing back tapes.

Technological Merging of TV, Computers, Telephones, and Cables Perhaps the most exciting likely future development centers around the capacity of known technology to provide television services beyond anything dreamed of just a few years ago. Viewers will have choices of hundreds of channels, will be able to interact with the programming, and will be able to select movies or programming to view when they wish to view it. Promotion in Action 11–1 provides insight into this brave new world as described by a student writing home to his mother. The

Television Technology Worth Writing Home About

Dear Mom,

I know what you mean. All this stuff about new TV and communication technology, 500 channels, information highways, video on demand—it's too much, too fast.

Most people figure the way they watch television and get information will probably change a lot over the next five or six years, but they can't grasp exactly how. It's hard even for somebody like you who's no stranger to computers, cable TV and portable phones. (By the way, do you still have that screen-saver program that looks like a tropical scene on your office PC?)

So, I talked to a lot of experts and executives about what's coming and how it may shape up for people like you and me. Maybe this will help.

For starters, yes, a lot has been happening. Just this Tuesday, Bell Atlantic, a phone company, won a lawsuit that gives it the right to sell TV programs like a cable company. Time Warner, which owns cable TV systems and cable channels such as HBO, is building a fiber-optic test system for 4,000 Orlando, Fla., customers. Fiber optics—hair-thin glass strands that transmit thousands of times more information than copper wires—will carry hundreds of channels, interactive TV and, at some point, telephone calls.

Tele-Communications Inc., the nation's largest cable company, will hook its first customers to a 500-channel system next year. Discovery Communications is about to start tests, in several communities, of technology that lets a viewer pay about $1 to watch a favorite TV show anytime, not just when it airs. Prodigy, the computer database service, is trying to become a service that you get on your television set by using a typical remote control.

It helps to keep in mind that all the companies and their tests are heading toward the same Holy Grail: a day when any viewer can easily get anything at anytime over the television.

"It ultimately means viewers have more control," says John Hendricks, president of Discovery Communications, which owns The Discovery Channel. "Television has always been appointment viewing and someone else was setting the appointment. In the future, the viewer will set the appointment."

That means, for instance, never again having to program the VCR to tape *Guiding Light*. You'll be able to call it up when you're free in the evening, maybe for a charge of 50 cents.

Or when you travel to Nashville to see your granddaughter, call up a weather report for that city. Or the next time an earthquake hits San Francisco and you're worried about your youngest son living there, you could sit in front of the TV and watch nothing but quake news from dawn to dusk.

You'll be able to use the TV for so much more. Say Dad wants to learn a little more German than just the days of the week. Since the TV will become two-way, he could tune in an interactive German language instruction video and actually respond to the lessons on the screen using the remote control.

Or if you two wanted to invest in a mutual fund, you could tap into a channel—maybe one operated by Prodigy—that would give you information on each of the 4,000 funds available, including ratings from magazines and newsletters.

Who knows what else may pop up. "Probably the very best things are going to be the things that we don't know what they are because somebody is going to invent them," says Joe Collins, president of Time Warner's cable division.

In fact, Collins said that while sitting next to CNN founder Ted Turner at an interview at USA TODAY. (No, Jane wasn't with him.) As an example, Collins noted that in cable TV's early days, Turner cooked up the unheard-of idea of a 24-hour news network. "Ted came to us and said how about that," Collins says, "and everybody said: 'It sounds like a bad idea.'"

Finally, the way things are evolving, you'll have more choices than ever. You'll be able to buy TV programs from at least one cable company, if not more. But you'll also probably be able to buy from the phone company or from a direct broadcast satellite company—though you'd have to buy a little satellite dish for that.

By the way, at some point you'll probably be able to choose whom you get phone service from—the phone company, the cable company or any of a handful of wireless-phone companies.

The technology to do all that is real. The reason things seem so confusing and jumbled now is that the technology is just starting to make its way into consumer tests. Companies like Bell Atlantic, TCI and AT&T don't yet have a clue what consumers really want out of this technology or how much they'll pay for it. They're just throwing it all against a wall to see what sticks.

But the situation will sort itself out pretty quickly because competition is going to be hot, hot, hot. Five years from now, any company that hasn't figured out how to make the new technology work the way consumers want it to work is going to be keeping company with IBM in the Old Behemoths Home.

Now, I know you had a few specific questions. So let's get to the first one: "My main thought is, how affordable will it be? And what if you have a large family? How can you keep teen-agers from running up the bill?"

Bringing up four boys brings on questions like that, huh?

Well, the dumb answer is that there is no consumer experience with super-TV systems, so everything about pricing is a guess.

Bell Atlantic, which thinks it could have such a system in Alexandria, Va., two years from now, says it believes it can deliver programming at lower cost than the local cable company. So prices could come down.

Discovery's Hendricks thinks monthly rates will fall—but people will spend more on television, buying special shows or sports broadcasts or information services. "We've almost proven that in focus groups," he says.

As for control over the teen-agers, many systems being tested give each family member a personal ID number that he or she has to punch in when ordering any pay-TV program or service. You could tell the cable operator that each son can spend up to $10 a month, then he's electronically cut off.

Another question: "How easy will it be to use? It doesn't bother me, but how about for somebody like your grandmother who's never been involved in the electronic age?"

The bottom line is that TV can only get easier. Now, you have to fumble with two or three remote controls, a *TV Guide* and a baffling VCR. A major push with the new technology is to make it as easy to use as a pinball game.

It helps, too, to know that 500 channels does not literally mean 500 channels of programming. It just refers to the capacity of the lines running into your TV. You may end up getting 60 cable channels like the three networks, CNN, Country Music Television. You would watch them just like you do today.

The rest of the capacity would be used to transmit special things you order, like movies or weather reports. You'd choose those by using your remote control to look through simple menus on the TV screen.

"We have models running today, and I can tell you that my 8-year-old son and my 78-year-old grandmother can use them with zero instructions," says Art Bushkin, president of Bell Atlantic's information services group.

Well, I'm out of space. I hope that helps. Now, when can you come here to baby-sit?

Love,
Me

Source: Kevin Maney, "Technology Worth Writing Home About," *USA Today*, August 26, 1993, pp. 1B and 2B.

implications of this technological capacity to advertisers is as yet not completely clear. However, it will likely complicate both the buying of television time and the measurement of television audiences.

Changes in Network Programming   All of the developments discussed above would have a bearing on network programming. The major trend created by the pressures of CATV, tape systems, and the choices created by the new technology would be toward more specialized programming, which would be necessary to fit into more selective viewing patterns. It has been predicted that the time spent watching television will continue to grow with increases in the number of television sets within each household. Since virtually each family member will have his or her own set, however, each will seek to watch a program conforming to his or her own interests. The decision will no longer have to be a compromsie of family interests. Television ratings on individual programs will drop as the audience becomes segmented, and eventually television programming may well become similar to that of radio. Due to a more highly segmented audience, the cost per thousand individuals will probably increase, but the cost per thousand prospects should remain about the same or decline. There will be movements in this direction for the next few years, but broadcasting as it is today will probably persist for quite some time. Eventually, however, broadcasting may come to be referred to as narrowcasting to a highly segmented audience.

Overcommercialization   Many individuals believe that overcommercialization is already a very serious problem, especially during station breaks and local programming. With the growing use of 15-second commercials, split 30s, participating sponsorship, and multiple-product announcements, the situation on network television has also rapidly grown more cluttered. Clutter will probably be reduced through a growth of new stations and multiset ownership, which fosters expansion of local programming to segment target audiences, commercials customized to local market needs, and local service programming. For a while, though, the advertiser is going to have to compete with a clutter of other commercials to gain viewers' attention.

Overall, the future of television is one of great changes brought on by technology. The impact on advertising will be great in the long run.

RADIO

Radio, once considered to be a dying medium following the rise of television, has come back to exert a dynamic and vigorous competitive challenge. To underscore the extent of change, it has become almost totally a local medium, whereas it was dominated by networks prior to the onset of television. Moreover, there are more than four times more stations on the air today than in 1945. Radio networks came to exist primarily to feed newscasts to local stations and a limited variety of additional programs. Recently, however, network radio has come back to attain high listening levels. (See Table 11–5, part C.) The number of networks has grown

TABLE 11-5

Radio Listening Facts

A. Percent Listening during Average Quarter Hour (Monday–Sunday)

	Men		Women		Teens
Daypart	18+	18–49	18+	18–49	12–17
6 A.M.–10 A.M.	20%	21%	20%	19%	12%
10 A.M.–3 P.M.	19	21	19	19	9
3 P.M.–7 P.M.	16	18	14	16	14
7 P.M.–12 Midnight	8	9	7	7	11
Avg. 6 A.M.–12 Midnight	16	17	15	15	11

Source: RADAR, Fall 1992. Copyright Statistical Research, Inc.

B. Percent Listening by Location (Monday–Sunday)

	In-Home			Out-of-Home Auto			Out-of-Home Nonauto		
Daypart	Men	Women	Teens	Men	Women	Teens	Men	Women	Teens
6 A.M.–10 A.M.	41%	62%	72%	33%	18%	17%	26%	20%	10%
10 A.M.–3 P.M.	26	40	48	30	21	26	44	39	22
3 P.M.–7 P.M.	26	39	59	23	34	25	31	27	15
7 P.M.–12 midnight	50	61	75	31	24	16	20	15	9
Avg. 6 A.M.–12 midnight	34	40	65	34	23	21	32	28	17

Source: RADAR, Fall 1992. Copyright Statistical Research, Inc.

C. Potential Radio Audience (Monday–Sunday, 6 A.M.–12 Midnight)

	Cumulative Audience			Avg. Qtr. Hour Audience		
	Men	Women	Adults	Men	Women	Adults
Total Radio						
Number (000)	85,694	92,013	177,707	14,035	14,057	28,092
Population percent	96%	95%	96%	16%	15%	15%
Network Radio						
Number (000)	70,346	72,193	142,539	8,443	7,766	16,209
Population percent	79%	74%	79%	9%	9%	9%

Source: RADAR, Fall 1992. Copyright Statistical Research, Inc.

from 4 in 1970 to 31 in 1993. In addition, FM radio, an unknown in 1945, has risen to over 95 percent penetration of U.S. homes and offers a new resource to the advertiser.

Characteristics of Radio

Advantages   Radio as an advertising medium has a number of advantages, including the following.

1. *The mass use of radio.* Of the over 577 million sets in use, 187 million are car radios, and 367 million are in homes or carried on the person. In 1992 there were 5,133 commercial AM stations, 5,801 commercial FM stations, and 1,933 noncommercial FM stations. There were radios in 96.6 million households. The availability of transistorized portable sets has enabled radio to become a medium that can be used anywhere. Within one week's time, radio will reach 96 percent of all people 12 and over in the United States. (See Table 11–5, part C, for details and other radio-listening facts.) In fact, during a single week, radio will reach well over 90 percent of all sex and age demographic segments of the United States.

2. *Selectivity.* Radio has become a selective medium because local stations have differentiated the program formats to appeal to various consumer segments. As a result, it is possible to reach nearly any class of consumer in most markets. Of course, geographic flexibility has long been a strength of radio, as is true of all local media.

3. *Speed and flexibility.* Of all media, radio has the shortest closing period, in that copy can be submitted up to air time. This flexibility has been capitalized on by many advertisers. For example, quite a few travel-related companies found the radio to be helpful in keeping their potential customers aware of the effects of the weather and encouraging them to still use their services.

4. *Low costs.* For an expenditure of about $100 in most markets, an advertiser can purchase air time. Of all media, radio's cost per time unit ranks among the lowest.

5. *Favorable psychological effect.* Although the evidence is not unequivocal, there is some basis to the claim that there may be less resistance to persuasion over radio because many activities are directed by spoken word. Radio has also been found to produce greater retention of simple material than print, especially among the least educated. Finally, radio is easily attended to with little psychological resistance, but this casual attention can be a disadvantage when radio serves as musical background for other activities.

6. *Reseller support.* Radio, along with newspapers and spot television, is also used on occasion with effective results to stimulate dealer cooperation and selling support.

Disadvantages   Counteracting the advantages of radio as an advertising medium are the following disadvantages.

1. *The nature of the message.* Of course, radio permits only audio presentation, a disadvantage for products requiring demonstration, the impact of color,

or the other features of visual media. Furthermore, the impression made is momentary, and, as with television, it is impossible to reexpose the prospect except through multiple commercials over a period of time.

2. *Chaotic buying.* Spot radio and spot television share the disadvantage of chaotic and nonstandardized rate structures and the bookkeeping problems connected with the purchase of time. Once again, however, large-station representations have simplified arrangements.

3. *Costs for national coverage.* As with all local media, the costs of national coverage can become substantial. Use can be made, of course, of network radio, and mass coverage is hereby achieved much more economically.

4. *Station fragmentation.* Unless substantial investments are made, it is difficult to achieve high levels of reach among mass audiences because of multiple-station fragmentation.

Spot and network radio rates are published by Standard Rate and Data Service. For stations subscribing to the code of the National Association of Broadcasters, 14 minutes of commercial time are permitted for each hour computed on a weekly basis, and the number of commercials is never to exceed 18 per hour or 5 per 15-minute segment. Many stations do not subscribe to the code, which is not binding, and offer a greater frequency of commercial time, much to the dismay of the advertising critics. This may be limited in the future by the Federal Communication Commission, which is now taking the position that licenses will not be renewed when stations broadcast commercials more than 18 minutes per hour for more than 10 percent of the broadcast day.

As with television, radio rates are differentiated into prime and secondary time. In radio, however, prime time covers the morning wake-up period and late afternoon drive-home time, when the most sets, especially car radios, are in use. The units of time available range from a few seconds to 60 seconds, thus affording great flexibility.

The cost per thousand homes reached is computed in a manner similar to that described for television. Although the accurate computation of network program ratings used to be difficult, RADAR (Radio All-Dimension Audience Research) was established in 1967 to help alleviate this problem, and the data on radio audiences available through RADAR are not too different from the Nielsen television ratings. Market-by-market audience information is also available from A. C. Nielsen. (See Chapter 12 for details.)

The Future of Radio

Radio may be characterized in the future by increasing network participation, more specialization, and further growth of AM and FM stereo. Network radio appears to be making somewhat of a comeback. CBS recently started the CBS Mystery Theater, and other old programs are growing increasingly popular when aired over local stations. Though this particular trend may be part of the overall mood of nostalgia, network radio is again exerting a greater influence through news and public affairs programming and giving advertisers more of a chance at national coverage.

Radio is one of the most segmented of the media. The ABC radio network is actually a combination of seven basic networks: contemporary, information, rock, talk, direction, entertainment, and FM. Almost every major market has an all-news station such as WBBM, Chicago, and some advertisers expect that eventually there will be nationally recognized frequencies where anyone in the major market areas of the country could turn for news, weather, or public affairs.

The growth and specialization of FM is expected to continue. AM-FM radios are already standard equipment on some automobiles, and the commercial production of radio sets that will handle only one band is expected to decrease rapidly. FM stereo is expected to achieve a much better market share over AM radio. This has caused a major thrust among some AM stations to broadcast in stereo. Regulations that prevented this have now been dropped.

It is also expected that cable television may draw some audience away from radio in two ways: (1) News cable networks will compete for some of radio's selective audience, and (2) music-oriented cable presentations (MTV, CMT, VH1, etc.) will also compete.

MAGAZINES

Magazines have long been a significant medium and continue to show vitality, in spite of problems with postage rate increases. Magazines today reach nearly all market segments and cover a variety of special interests such as boating and photography. Some mass circulation periodicals continue to exhibit health despite the problems they face. There are about 2,318 consumer/farm magazines and 4,662 business magazines.[17]

Characteristics of Magazines

Advantages   The advantages of magazines as an advertising medium include the following.

1. *High geographic and demographic selectivity.* Once a nonselective mass medium, consumer magazines have attained a high degree of geographic selectivity. It is now possible to purchase one or more of 145 regional or demographic editions of *Better Homes and Gardens,* 330 editions of *Time,* 81 editions of *TV Guide,* and 70 editions of *Reader's Digest.* Twelve different consumer magazines with circulations ranging from 1.8 to 18.8 million offer 50 or more regional and demographic editions. Of 76 of the best-known consumer magazines in the United States, only 24 do not have any regional or demographic editions. Small premiums are usually charged for regional or demographic advertising, but the increased efficiency of the advertisment in reaching prospects usually is worthwhile. The magazine also becomes more an option for advertisers, such as banking institutions, that serve only a limited regional market. Demographic flexibility has long been a major virtue of consumer magazines. Appeal can be made to distinct groups of buyers with special interests, and virtually any segment of the market

in terms of age, income, or other demographic variables can be reached with a minimum of waste circulation. The editorial content of the publication is also tailored to the interests of the audience being reached so that the advertising is usually received by the consumer in a receptive mood. Figure 11–1 presents a description of demographic editions of *Time.* One may also buy so-called magazine networks, which are groups of magazines. One example is the City News Urban group composed of *Newsweek, Time,* and *Sports Illustrated.*

2. *The receptivity of magazine audiences.* Magazine readers appear more receptive to advertising than do television viewers. Younger segments of the audience also find magazine advertising more believable than the commercials they see on television. In the business press area, readers often read ads to stay on top of new developments in products.

3. *Long life of a magazine issue.* Syndicated research indicates that there are between three and four adults readers for the average magazine issue and

FIGURE 11–1

Example of a Special Edition of a General Magazine

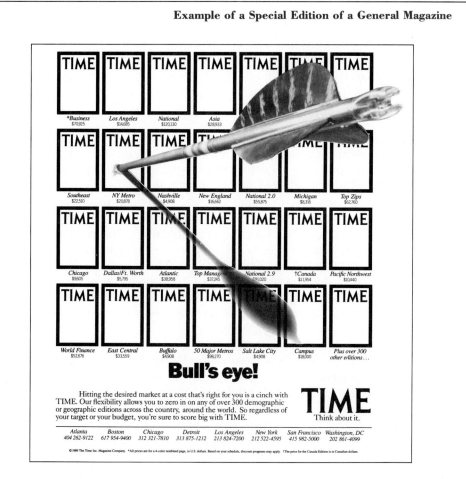

that the reader takes more than three days to read the magazine and devotes 60 to 90 minutes to doing so.[18]

Other advantages include (1) the selection of editorial content to match the nature of the advertising message and (2) the ability to reproduce ads in high-quality color.

The increased reading of magazines by those in upper income and educational levels is well established in survey findings and widely accepted as fact. The reach to prime prospects can be maximized by using the right publication for the purpose or, in some cases, a demographically selective edition of a popular magazine reaching many different groups of people.

Disadvantages   The disadvantages of magazines include (1) their inability to demonstrate the product in action, (2) their unintrusiveness relative to television and radio, (3) their limitation on geographic flexibility relative to television and radio, (4) their inability to display sound and motion, and (5) the lower levels of reach that go with repeated buys in a group of magazines compared to newspaper, television, and radio.

Magazines can also be expensive. For example, consider the cost of a four-color page in the following magazines in 1993: *National Geographic,* $142,951; *People,* $97,090; *Scientific American,* $31,300; *TV Guide,* $112,700; *Business Week,* $59,800; *Time,* $134,000; *Good Housekeeping,* $111,755; *Self,* $69,755; *Vogue,* $49,000; *Road & Track,* $48,775; and *Sports Illustrated,* $127,600.

The Future of Magazines

The immediate future should see the continued growth of special-interest and special-audience magazines and continued difficulties on the part of magazines for general readership. The growth of the special-interest magazine is reflected in the number of new magazines in this area. In the 1980s, more than 400 new special-audience consumer magazines were introduced, including the science magazines *Discover* and *Technology Illustrated,* and women's magazines *Vital, Everywoman,* and *Lears.* This trend has continued into the early 1990s. Figure 11–2 demonstrates how magazines compete for special-interest markets.

The result of this trend for the advertiser will be a higher cost per thousand readers because of decreasing circulation. This will be offset by the ability to isolate a narrow marketing segment for whom the commercial message would have relevance. Thus, the cost per thousand target audience member will likely decrease.

The magazine industry is not without its problems, basically in the form of rising postage, production, and labor costs. Partly due to inflation, production costs have risen steeply. Labor, paper, and ink costs have risen significantly. Magazines have continually passed these increases on to their readers and advertisers.

Finally, postal rates continue to climb, with the latest increase to take effect in 1993, and more expected in the next year or so. A growing number of new magazines such as Time-Life's *People,* their new general-interest magazine, may be designed chiefly for distribution through newsstands and retail outlets. Not only are postal costs thus avoided, but the cost of maintaining a subscription department can also be avoided. The main problem is building and maintaining a consistent circulation. Most magazines, however, have no real alternative to the U.S. Postal Service at this time, and it appears that higher postal rates will just have to be survived. Attempts by a confederation of magazines to have their own mail service are taking shape. Others such as *Better Homes & Gardens,* which uses private delivery services in 13 cities, seem committed to avoiding the U.S. Postal Service if possible. All of this has made the competition for shelf space at supermarket checkouts areas more intense.

OUTDOOR ADVERTISING

Outdoor advertising is the oldest of all the media; outdoor signs were found in Pompeii and elsewhere in ancient times. It still is an important medium for certain specific purposes, and outdoor service is offered in most cities and towns.

FIGURE 11–2

Intermagazine Competition

Approximately 220,000 standardized signs are available for use, and they had $1.03 billion in revenue in 1992.

Characteristics of Outdoor Advertising

Advantages   Several unique advantages are enjoyed by outdoor advertising.

1. *Flexibility.* Outdoor advertising can be readily tailored to create a truly national saturation campaign or to high spot in selected markets or even in parts of markets. The frequency of exposure can also be varied from market to market to adapt precisely to variations in potentials.

2. *A mobile audience.* The buyer views outdoor advertising while on the move, and many of those exposed will be purchasers of the product within a short time after viewing. This last-minute promotion thus may serve as a link between previous advertising messages and a probable purchase as a reminder of a need, or as the required trigger for a pending sale.

3. *Relative absence of competing advertisements.* For the most part, outdoor signs stand alone and are not subject to the competition of other messages. Thus, one source of distraction is removed, although it is apparent that outdoor surroundings substitute yet another and potentially more important source of distraction.

4. *Repeat exposure.* The opportunity for repeat exposure is great. It was found that a unit of sale reaches over 80 percent of all adults in the market in the first week. At the end of the month, 89.2 percent of the adults will have seen the message an average of 31 times.[19] These reach and frequency figures rise as income rises in that exposure to adults in high-income households is higher than average, and the average recall of message content is approximately 40 percent.[20] Thus, the advantages of repetition are clearly achieved.

Disadvantages   There are also certain disavantages to the use of outdoor advertising.

1. *Creative limitations.* The fleeting impression permitted by exposure to a mobile audience limits copy to a few words or a single powerful graphic. Thus, little more can be accomplished than a reminder or repetition of a brand name. When longer copy is required, outdoor ads cannot be used effectively.

2. *Mood of the viewer.* The consumer on the move is subject to many distractions, and prime attention is usually directed elsewhere. Furthermore, he or she may be faced with the inescapable irritations of heavy traffic, heat, and dirt, and thus the opportunity for a successful advertising impact is diluted.

3. *Public attack.* Outdoor advertising is under attack from many sources. The terms of the Highway Beautification Act authorize the federal government to require states to provide control of outdoor advertising and junkyards on interstate and primary highway systems. Title I of this act requires effective control of signs, displays, and devices within 660 feet of the right-of-way on interstate and primary systems. Other provisions restrict outdoor advertising in commercial areas and

check proliferation of signs. State and local restrictions also apply in many areas. The major effect of this act on the outdoor advertising industry, which actually supported its passage, has been the elimination of posters in small towns and the forced merger of small advertising production plants into larger ones to assure financial survival. The clutter of business signs, which is a major concern of environmentalists, is not an aspect of outdoor advertising, since the owners of the respective business establishments have these signs constructed on their own property.

The industry is not guiltless in the unwise placement of signs, but it maintains that violations of good taste and of a strict professional code are the actions of an irresponsible minority, and the majority are in agreement with the need to prevent abuse. To the credit of the industry, it has taken some positive action. A fairly extensive study was undertaken to assess the effects of the presence of billboards on people's reaction to the environment they see.[21] It was found that the majority of those who were vociferous about outlawing billboards were unaware when billboards were removed from a stretch of highway viewed in a laboratory. In addition, the presence or absence of billboards on the routes used did not prove to be critical in achieving "environmental quality"; the effect of removing utility poles had double the effect of removing billboards. However, it would be unwise to conclude on the basis of these limited results that consumers are indifferent to the presence or absence of billboards.

Purchasing Outdoor Space

Outdoor space is purchased directly from each outdoor sign company or from media-buying services specializing in outdoor, such as Out of Home Media Services, Inc. (OHMS). It gathers cost data and prepares estimates for any combination of markets, performs field inspections, and does the contracting.

Not all advertising agencies use OHMS because they may have complete departments equipped to handle outdoor contracts and billings. Space may also be purchased from any of the 700 individual outdoor companies, of course.

Space rates are published by OHMS. Quotations have always been made on the basis of the desired showing. A 100 showing, for example, is supposed to provide enough signs to reach 93 percent of the population an average of 21–22 times in a 30-day period; a 50 showing is supposed to provide sufficient signs to reach 85 percent an average of 10–11 times in this same period. A 100 showing may require only one or two signs in smaller areas, but costs for some of these signs can run as high as $30,000 per month in larger localities. The average cost of a regular panel in the top 10 markets is about $1,600 per month. Unfortunately, in practice, a 100 showing is usually what the plant operator says it is. This is one of the reasons why the advertisers are searching for other rating devices.

Although the quotation based on showings is still used most often, the Outdoor Advertising Association of America (OAAA) has been promoting among its members a new rating system based on gross rating points (GRP). The OAAA maintains that this new system will give advertisers a more accurate basis for comparing outdoor advertising with the other media. Gross rating points are calculated by considering the number of "impression-opportunities" on the average weekday, regardless of repeat exposures, as a percentage of the entire market. Therefore, if the locations of signs during a campaign allowed for 400,000 impression-opportunities (calculated by using government traffic reports) daily in a market of 500,000, the plan would deliver 80 gross rating points daily.

Standardized outdoor poster panels are approximately 12 feet high and 25 feet long with a copy area of roughly 10 by 23 feet. Copy is printed in 10 to 14 sections. Painted signs represent about 10 percent of all outdoor structures, although they account for more than 30 percent of total space billings. Recently, much smaller poster panels (8-sheet so-called junior panels) have made an impact on streets in large urban areas.

The Traffic Audit Bureau (TAB) is the auditing arm of the industry and is responsible for traffic counts underlying the published rates. Effective circulation is computed as the average daily traffic having a reasonable physical opportunity to see the panels. Total gross traffic is therefore reduced as follows to arrive at effective circulation: 50 percent of all pedestrians, 50 percent of all automobile passengers, and 25 percent of passengers on buses or other forms of mass transit. Thus, the 100 showing is based on effective circulation.

Several other organizations within the industry provide services to its members and to advertisers. The OAAA is the primary trade association; its members operate more than 90 percent of outdoor facilities in the country. One of the services of the OAAA is the Institute of Outdoor Advertising, a central source of information that also develops research, creative ideas, and methods for using the medium more effectively.

The Future of Outdoor Advertising

At least temporarily, outdoor advertising appears to have successfully withstood the attacks of the environmentalists. Its major problem is one it shares with most U.S. citizens—the probable extent of any future energy crisis. If auto traffic is significantly decreased in favor of public transportation, especially on trains and airplanes, outdoor advertising will be weakened. Continued growth is uncertain in the light of such developments. The attempt to develop small panels for urban use is one response to these potential problems. Also, great strides have been made in the development of electronic display panels.

TRANSIT ADVERTISING

A special type of outdoor media is transit media. Transit advertising has more than doubled its billings since 1969, and expectations were for an annual volume of about $130 million in 1993. Though it is still seen basically as a supplement to large advertising expenditures elsewhere, it is becoming an attractive option to many advertisers who have not used it previously.

Characteristics of Transit Advertising

Advantages   Among the advantages of transit advertising are the following.

1. *Opportune exposure.* Of those riding buses and subways, about half reported that their last use of transit was for shopping purposes. Moreover, 52 percent indicated some recall of inside-vehicle advertising, and more than 80 percent of those named specific products.[22] Thus, this type of advertising can serve as an effective last-minute stimulus to a purchase.

2. *Geographic selectivity.* As a strictly local medium, transit offers the advantage of placing dollars in proportion to local market potentials. It also is used to provide extra advertising weight when required.

3. *High consumer exposure.* Exposure figures vary, of course, from transit system to transit system. It is believed that at least 40 million Americans ride transit vehicles every month. The New York Transit Authority alone claims over 152 million rides monthly. A study of the Toronto transit system revealed that during one week, the unduplicated audience represents 52.4 percent of the total market and that, in the space of a month, the reach encompasses 67.5 percent of the market. The individuals making up this 67.5 percent coverage average 11 rides monthly.[23]

4. *Economy.* Transit advertising claims to be the least costly of all media. The cost per thousand inside-car exposures in the markets served averages between 15 and 20 cents, and for exterior exposure as little as 10 cents per thousand.

Disadvantages   Transit advertising also has some disadvantages.

1. *Weak coverage of portions of the population.* Although advertising is now available on the outside of vehicles, it is apparent that nonriders will not be exposed to the transit advertising on the inside of vehicles.

2. *Creative limitations.* The basic inside poster sizes are 11 by 28, 11 by 42, and 11 by 56 inches. Such small areas provide little opportunity for creative presentation other than short, reminder-type messages. Greater opportunities are presented by the use of outside displays, where it is possible to purchase the king-size poster, 2.5 by 12 feet. The standard exterior board is 30 by 144 inches. Exterior displays (30 by 144) are available on 400 New York City buses for about $60,000 monthly. Purchases may be made from either the individual companies or from centralized sources such as Metro Transit Advertising, a division of Metromedia.

The Future of Transit Advertising

The future of transit advertising is indeed bright. Any energy crisis that may prove hazardous to outdoor advertising can only add to the already healthy billings of transit advertising. The United States is growing increasingly conscious of its need for effective mass transit. Present systems are being enlarged, new ones such as Detroit's People Mover have been completed, and the use of mass transit is growing rapidly. As mass transit grows, so will transit advertising.

FIGURE 11–3

Intermedia Competition

Drivetime. Walktime. Anytime is radio time.

It's the age of the headset phenomenon. People listening as they jog, walk, ride the train, play or shop. Hearing only the sounds of their radio. Hearing your message with no distraction. Catch someone like that on the way to shop, and you can get immediate buying action. Some trick in today's economy.

Add this growing audience to radio's big drivetime audience: 85 percent of all commuters who go to work by car.

Radio is big at home, too.

Surprise. Almost 60 percent of all radio listening is done at home. And the average household has 5.5 radios. It's no wonder radio reaches more adults in a day than television, magazines or newspapers. Even busy working women listen to radio an average of almost four hours a day—that's more time than they give any other medium.

Radio hits all lifestyles.

Radio goes with more people, more places, than ever before.

Young, old and in-between. In their cars, their homes, even on top of their heads.

Don't let your potential customers walk on by. Get your message into the streets. Get it on radio. For more information, call (212) 599-6666. Or write Radio Advertising Bureau, 485 Lexington Avenue, New York, NY 10017.

RADIO Red hot because it works.

NEW MEDIA

This is an exciting time in the media business. Not only is there rapid change in the standard media discussed above, but also there are many new media available to advertisers. These include vidoe displays on grocery carts, rental videos, video channels in airports and doctors' offices, movie theaters, and television in the classroom. (See the chapter opener.) The value of these new media to advertisers will depend on the audience they deliver, and the availability of reliable audience measurement data. At this time not many advertising dollars have flown to these new media. Their value remains to be judged.

INTERMEDIA COMPARISON

The media types discussed in this chapter compete with each other vigorously for the advertiser's dollars. The basis on which they compete is essentially to sell their own advantages while trying to highlight other media's disadvantages. Figure

FIGURE 11–4

An Advertisement by Music Television (MTV) Attempting to Compete against Other Television Programs, Spot Radio, and Magazines

11–3 presents an example of intermedia competition at a trade association level (the Radio Advertising Bureau). Individual media vehicles also present themselves against other media types as well as against other vehicles in their class. Figure 11–4 presents an example of the latter type of activity.

One of the most fundamental bases on which media compete is cost. Table 11–6 presents a comparison of media costs prepared by the media department at the Leo Burnett advertising agency for the period 1975–1992. Care must be taken in interpreting these cost-per-thousand (CPM) numbers because they are calculated on a total audience basis. Also, outdoor audiences are measured in terms of total people while other audiences are measured in terms of adults, and television audiences are measured in terms of households, whereas magazine audiences are given by gross circulation, and so on. Of more interest to marketers is the CPM on target audience of the advertising program. Thus, for example, for a particular target audience, the CPM for a specific television time could be higher than for a particular magazine. The use of the CPM target audience concept will be discussed in Chapter 12. Keeping track of all this information about media is

TABLE 11–6

Media Cost Trends

A. Network Television, 1975 to 1992

	Avg. Cost/Commercial (:30)		CPM Homes	
	$000	Index	$	Index
Prime Time (Regular Programming)				
1975	$ 37.8	100	$ 2.88	100
1980	74.3	197	4.94	172
1985	115.5	306	8.06	280
1986	124.7	330	8.94	310
1987	128.6	340	10.13	352
1988	121.0	320	9.46	328
1989	139.6	369	11.26	391
1990	128.5	340	10.68	371
1991*	104.5	277	9.18	319
1992*	105.2	278	9.64	335
Daytime				
1975	$ 6.2	100	$ 1.35	100
1980	10.8	174	2.22	164
1985	16.4	265	3.48	258
1986	15.8	255	3.50	259
1987	14.8	239	3.11	230
1988	12.7	205	2.82	209
1989	13.6	219	2.98	221
1990	13.2	213	3.19	236
1991*	13.7	221	3.30	244
1992*	15.1	244	3.69	273

* Includes FOX

Source: A.C. Nielsen, *Household & Persons Cost Per Thousand,* November of each year.

B. Spot Television—1985 to 1992, Top 100 Markets

	Avg. Cost/Commercial (:30)		CPM Homes	
	$000	Index	$	Index
Prime Time				
1985	$74.3	100	$10.01	100
1986	71.5	96	9.57	96
1987	64.9	87	10.01	100
1988	74.5	100	11.06	110
1989	66.3	89	10.76	107
1990	68.5	92	11.44	114
1991	66.5	90	11.37	114
1992	74.2	100	11.60	116
Daytime				
1985	$10.0	100	$ 3.32	100
1986	10.2	102	3.44	104
1987	9.7	97	3.77	114
1988	10.2	102	3.98	120
1989	9.9	99	3.93	118
1990	9.4	94	4.05	122
1991	8.3	83	3.61	109
1992	9.0	90	3.89	117

Sources: *Media Market Guide*, 1st Quarter DMA Data each year; A.C. Nielsen, *DMA Planners Guide*, February each year; Nielsen U.S. Television Household Estimates.

C. Spot Radio—1988 to 1992, Top 50 Markets (Cost per Adult Rating Point, :60)

	Men		Women		Teens
	18–34	25–54	18–34	25–54	12–17
1988	$2,471	$3,992	$2,488	$3,748	$1,455
1989	2,690	4,062	2,576	3,745	1,627
1990	2,712	3,840	2,627	3,581	1,618
1991	2,547	3,537	2,499	3,412	1,753
1992	2,634	3,627	2,573	3,478	1,816

Source: *Media Market Guide*, 4th Quarter each year.

D. Consumer Magazines—1980 to 1992, 10 Selected Magazines

	Cost/Page 4 C		CPM-Circulation	
	$000	Index	$	Index
1980	$ 653.2	100	$ 7.34	100
1985	883.4	135	10.32	141
1986	906.5	139	10.92	149
1987	938.9	144	11.38	155
1988	974.2	149	11.88	162
1989	1,020.4	156	12.58	171
1990	1,060.1	162	13.40	183
1991	1,120.4	172	14.40	196
1992	1,168.9	179	15.44	210

Source: S.R.D.S., June 1980, 1988–1992, and September 1985–1987.

TABLE 11–6

Continued

E. Daily Newspapers, 1985 to 1992

	Inch Rate		Inch Cost/MM Circ.	
	$	Index	$	Index
1985	$24,050.21	100	$383.17	100
1986	25,149.88	105	402.39	105
1987	25,079.46	104	399.19	104
1988	28,624.36	119	456.57	119
1989	29,056.70	121	463.80	121
1990	30,279.40	126	485.80	127
1992	33,924.85	141	559.01	145
1992	33,632.90	139	559.02	145

Source: *Editor and Publisher Yearbook* 1992.

F. Syndicated Supplements, 1980 to 1992

	Cost/Page 4 C		CPM-Circulation	
	$000	Index	$	Index
1980	$235.1	100	$ 6.91	100
1985	426.2	181	11.58	168
1986	408.8	174	9.22	133
1987	439.9	187	9.65	140
1988	494.8	210	10.81	156
1989	542.9	231	11.33	164
1990	597.7	254	12.48	181
1991	657.8	280	12.70	184
1992	700.9	298	13.75	198

Parade and *U.S.A. Weekend* only.
Source: S.R.D.S., June of each year.

G. Outdoor—1980 to 1992, Top 300 Markets**

	Number of Panels	Monthly Cost* $000	CPM
1980	14,945	$2,679.9	$0.77
1985	13,098	4,121.0	1.15
1986	13,011	4,377.3	1.35
1987	13,025	4,770.2	1.40
1988	13,100	5,130.3	1.41
1989	13,051	5,240.7	1.53
1990	13,209	5,442.1	1.62
1991	10,990	5,297.9	1.38
1992	10,768	5,299.8	1.35

* 100 GRPs in all markets.
** Beginning in 1991, data based on 222 markets; not comparable to previous years.
Source: Institute of Outdoor Advertising.

a complex and time-consuming task. With the increasing importance of global marketing over the last decade, this task has become even more complex. Promotion in Action 11–2 describes some of the efforts that advertisers are undertaking to track media worldwide. It is an exciting time to be involved with the advertising aspects of media.

Tracking Worldwide Media Trends

Promotion in Action

11-2

The construction of an effective communications network is a key marketing success factor in the increasingly global business world. Advertising agencies are major links in this network. In order to effectively serve international clients, ad agencies need an intimate knowledge of the current media trends in various foreign countries.

The international advertising market has great untapped potential. Projections indicate that the volume of advertising in the United States will soon fall behind the volume generated by the rest of the world. And this volume is fairly concentrated. Fifteen countries (the United States, Japan, the United Kingdom, Germany, Canada, France, Brazil, Australia, Italy, the Netherlands, Spain, Switzerland, Sweden, Finland, and South Korea) accounted for more than 90 percent of all worldwide advertising expenditures as of 1985. These same countries also accounted for 61 percent of global gross domestic product. Anticipation of global trends among these countries, such as the dissolution of European trade barriers in 1992, will allow media professionals to more effectively serve their clients.

McCann-Erikson is one advertising agency that now tracks media data on a worldwide basis. One of the agency's major objectives is to determine which medium captures the largest share of ad expenditures. Its study examines television, radio, magazines, newspapers, and other media vehicles (cinema, outdoor, transit, direct, business-to-business, etc.). McCann-Erikson has found that newspapers hold the largest share in almost all of the countries studied, even the United States. Television accounts for a low share of ad expenditures in many of the European countries: 9 percent in West Germany, 5 percent in the Netherlands, 4 percent in Switzerland, 8 percent in Finland, and 17 percent in France. Several factors contribute to this trend: limited commercial TV availability, an extensive and well-established print industry, restricted TV commercialization policies, and stringent televison time-buying guidelines. Government ownership of broadcast facilities is common in these countries and accounts for many of these restrictions. Privatization is a relatively new development.

The other end of this limited commercial television environment is a well-developed magazine and newspaper industry. This condition indicates a high literacy rate. There are over 1,220 consumer publications in both Germany and the United Kingdom, and France and Italy each have over 900. At the other end of the spectrum, Brazil, with its low literacy rate, offers only 300 magazine titles while its struggling economy claims the lowest TV household penetration in the top 15 markets.

In amassing this and other media data, McCann-Erikson identified several key media trends:

1. The television medium will grow dramatically on both a household-coverage and usage basis. VCRs and the privatization of television channels will be major contributing factors.

2. Print media will also grow but at a slower pace. Improved economic conditions in Third World countries and subsequent improvements in education will increase literacy rates and increase the demand for print vehicles.

3. Advertising expenditures as a percentage of GDP will increase on a worldwide basis. Domestic markets will become saturated, and competitors will vie for limited supplies of advertising time and space.

4. The use of short-length (i.e., 15-second) TV commercials will increase globally. Although this practice is already common in other countries where air time has traditionally been scarce, U.S. advertisers, who are used to longer time slots, must find ways to communicate their message without sacrificing media and impact values.

5. Viewers' ability to bypass TV commercials is growing. The increasing use of remote controls and VCRs is reducing the number of commercials that television viewers actually watch, creating a new challenge for advertisers.

6. Major changes in political and economic structures will continue to encourage globalization. Eastern and Western Europe are prime arenas for these changes.

Pan-European media changes are expected to evolve more slowly than Pan-European marketing changes. Differences in language and culture will inhibit media's reach potential. One proposed solution is to segment Europe by language and cultural similarities instead of by national boundaries. This would cluster countries on the basis of broadcast and print-circulation delivery. Possible clusters include Austria-Germany-Switzerland, France-Belgium-Luxembourg-Switzerland, Italy-Switzerland, Great Britain-Ireland-Northern Ireland, and the Scandanavian countries.

Source: "Mediology: Our Global Link," *Marketing and Media Decisions,* May 1988, pp. 108–15.

SUMMARY

The purpose of this chapter has been to condense a wealth of material on media characteristics, advantages, disadvantages, possible uses, and other factors that must be understood before discussing the media selection process itself. Of greatest importance is the way in which each of the media discussed is adapting to the current environment because the changes have been great. Understanding these changes enables a marketer to discuss meaningfully the methods by which media should be analyzed and selected.

REVIEW AND DISCUSSION QUESTIONS

1. The differential between local and national line rates is said by many to be triggering an exodus of national advertisers from local newspapers. Given this fact, what reasons can be advanced for continuation of the differentials? Why, in your opinion, has there been so little change?

2. Contrast the milline rate and cost-per-thousand (CPM) formula. What advantage is gained by their use? What possible dangers can you see?

3. One of the most potentially important trends in the television medium is the merging of technology of TV, computers, telephones, and cable. What effects will this have on both local and national advertising in the future?

4. Advertisers are showing a growing concern with commercial clutter in television and radio broadcasts. If clutter is allowed to continue, what might be the effects in terms of the consumer, as well as on the advertising copy and format?

5. The FCC is authorized to refuse to renew local station licenses if they fail to operate within broad guidelines of public interest. What are the advantages and dangers of this policy? What factors should the FCC consider in deciding license renewal?

6. Under what conditions might a 60-second television commercial be worth twice the cost of a 30-second version?

7. In what sense is radio best described as narrowcasting? Is it a good predictor of the future of television?

8. In what sense can it be said that magazines are a highly flexible medium?

9. With a 100 showing, over 80 percent of all adults are reached with an average frequency of 31. What do these terms mean? Does this mean that outdoor advertising has unique advantages in terms of reach and frequency when compared with other media? What are the advantages of gross rating points (GRPs) as a substitute system of measurement?

10. For what types of products is transit advertising most suitable? Can it be used as a substitute medium for television and magazines?

NOTES

1. The authors wish to thank Mr. Bernard Guggenheim, vice president of Lintas Campbell-Ewald, for his assistance in the preparation of this chapter. Also, we wish to thank the Media Department at Leo Burnett Advertising for providing data and other assistance.

2. Based upon Bernard Guggenheim, "What the Research Shows about Actual Growth in Ad Volume," *Media Decisions*, March 1978, p. 90, and updates from various advertising agency media guides through 1993.

3. For example, see Pat Sloan and Melanie Wells, "Ad Leaders Offer Tepid Optimism for '93 Spending," *Advertising Age*, December 14, 1992, pp. 4 and 46, and "Myers Sees Spending Gain," *Advertising Age*, December 7, 1992, p. 41.

4. *1993 Editor and Publisher Yearbook.*

5. For a recent discussion of this long standing problem, see Christy Fisher and Joe Mandese, "4A's hits newspapers' national rates," *Advertising Age*, June 1, 1992, p. 40.

6. The Newspaper Association of America is promising to implement such a system effectively in 1993/94. See Christy Fisher, "NAA sets national ad-buy system," *Advertising Age*, March 1, 1993, p. 12.

7. For a detailed discussion see Christy Fisher, "Newspaper of Future Look to Go High-Tech as Experiments Abound," *Advertising Age*, October 5, 1992, pp. S-1 and S-8.

8. *Television Fact Book*, 1992.

9. *Leo Burnett 1993 Media Costs and Coverage*, p. 6.

10. *Leo Burnett 1993 Media Costs and Coverage*, p. 13.

11. *Leo Burnett 1993 Media Costs and Coverage*, p. 11.

12. For specific time allocated to advertising for various cable program channels see Joe Mandese, "TV CLUTTER: Who Has the Most, Who's Hurt the Worst," *Advertising Age,* May 4, 1992, p. 18.

13. Joe Mandese, "Fox Wins 16% Share of Prime-Time Sales," *Advertising Age,* May 24, 1993, p. 2.

14. For a discussion of the debate on this issue see Steven W. Colford, "Fine-tuning kids TV," *Advertising Age,* February 11, 1991, p. 35.

15. The Code Authority of the National Association of Broadcasters.

16. *Leo Burnett 1993 Media Cost and Coverage,* p. 15.

17. Ibid., p. 6.

18. Simmons Market Research Bureau at different years.

19. "Reach and Frequency of Exposure of Outdoor Posters," study conducted by W. R. Simmons and Associates Research, Inc., for the Institute of Outdoor Advertising, Inc.

20. "This Is Outdoor Advertising" (New York: Institute of Outdoor Advertising, Inc.).

21. "Measuring Human Response to the Urban Roadside," summary of a study conducted by Arthur D. Little, Inc.; published by the Outdoor Advertising Association of America.

22. "The Transit Millions," New York Transit Advertising Association.

23. "Toronto Transit Rider Study," p. 4.

Media Strategy

MOTEL 6'S MEDIA MIX HELPS DRIVE THE CUSTOMERS IN

A fittingly laid-back marketing campaign transformed Motel 6 from a backwoods joke to a king of the road. Motel 6 now rules the economy segment of the $51 billion, 2.8 million-room lodging industry. This chain of self-proclaimed "cheap" motels (the 6 originally stood for $6-a-night) was founded in Santa Barbara in 1962. For years, marketing was a foreign concept to the entire lodging industry, and the economy segment was slower to catch on than the rest. Word of mouth was the major advertising medium. Random billboards were sprinkled along some highways, and economy motels were listed in lodging directories. Little else was done to attract customers.

For 24 years, Motel 6 was quite content with this minimal effort. Tiny regional chains were no match for the lodging giant. But competitors recognized a good thing when they saw it. Other super-cheap national chains began to appear, Motel 6's market share nose-dived, and occupancy rates bottomed out at 66.7 percent. Major changes were needed to rescue the fallen giant.

Kohlberg Kravis Roberts & Co. (KKR) bought Motel 6 in 1985. It hired Joseph McCarthy, a long-time lodging business executive, as president and CEO. McCarthy hired Hugh Thrasher as executive VP of marketing and development. The two set up the company's first marketing department and hired the Dallas-based Richards Group as their advertising agency. The agency waited 10 months to begin advertising. Customers had some major gripes with the chain and the Richards Group "didn't want to bring people in until the product was fixed." Phones were installed to attract the important business traveler segment; local calls were free and, unlike many chains in the industry, Motel 6 levied no service charge for long-distance calls. A reservation center was established in Albuquerque, New Mexico, and an itinerary-planning service was also made available. The national pricing structure was adjusted to each city's economy. Prices now range from $31.50 (e.g., Washington, D.C.) to $17.95 a night (Odessa, Texas). This allowed Motel 6 to offer services such as "free" local calls and TV hookups while remaining "the lowest-priced national chain on any corner." A family rate was added, allowing children under 18 to stay for free, and a credit card policy was implemented. When the ads started, they focused on each improvement as it came off the assembly line. A new image was being created.

People over 50 make up about half of Motel 6's customer base; two-thirds of these were retired. The company refers to them as "inveterate coupon clippers who could easily afford a Hilton or a Hyatt." As McCarthy points out, "It's just that these people take the 'what do I really need' approach to travel." The group of 18- to 35-year-olds on a tight budget is another large part of the company's customer base. The business traveler group is also growing steadily. Half of this segment is self-employed; the other half is often on a per diem expense account. Motel 6 is just what they need to fit necessary travel into their tight budgets.

Money was tight when Motel 6 began its media campaign in 1986. With a total promotional budget of only $1 million, radio seemed the only way to go. And it went far—so far, in fact, that when the budget was increased over the next few years to $6 million and then to $8 million, the company saw no reason to change its basic media plan. The fact that most people arrive at Motel 6 by car, truck, or motorcycle was a major factor in this decision. The company estimates that three-quarters of these customers make a "through-the-windshield" decision on where to stay each night and arrive without a reservation. Radio has a good chance of reaching them at this critical decision point.

The chain increased its number of billboards to 775, but it still believes that radio is the most effective way to reach these travelers. They first tested their media strategy with spot buys and then expanded to network radio in 1988. In a typical year, Motel 6 spends about $1.5 to $2 million on spot radio, $9 to $10 million on network radio, and $300 to $400 thousand on billboards, for a total of about $11 to $12 million. More than 70 executions now air between 6:00 A.M. and 7:00 P.M. on most networks, including ABC, CBS, NBC, and TranStar. This covers the prime traveling hours, when Motel 6's target customers are on the road and seeking shelter.

Radio also created several unexpected advantages. Tom Bodett, the voice of Motel 6, has become something of a legend. Because people can't see Bodett, his ironic, real-folk voice becomes different things to different people. "Old people see him as a road-weary curmudgeon, younger people think he's one of them, and business people frequently say in focus groups they hear a harried salesman." TV or print ads would destroy these advantageous illusions. Competitors bewail the fact that they didn't find Bodett first, and their attempts at imitation fall short. Another key to the ads' success is that they tell people it's OK to be cheap, pointing out the fact that money saved on a motel bill can be more enjoyably spent on gifts and entertainment.

Source: "King of the Road," *Marketing & Media Decisions,* March 1989, pp. 80–86. Updated to 1993 with interviews with industry experts.

The main decisions in media strategy are the selection of media to utilize and the preparation of a media schedule. Media selection first involves a choice of *media class* or *type:* television versus radio versus magazines, and so on. Second, it involves the choice of specific *media vehicles* within the media class: "Monday Night Football" versus "60 Minutes," *Newsweek* versus *Time,* and so forth. Factors that are fundamental in media selection are (1) the requirements of creative strategy, (2) reaching the proper audience, (3) the requirements for reach versus frequency, (4) competitive factors, (5) cost efficiency, (6) qualitative factors, and (7) distribution requirements. Media scheduling deals with the geographical and seasonal placement of the advertisement in the media. To effectively select media and prepare a media schedule, the promotional planner needs to have access to accurate data about the audience delivered by the specific media vehicles available. This issue of media audience measurement is also discussed in this chapter. The Motel 6 illustration that began this chapter shows the potential competitive advantage to be gained by effectively selecting an appropriate media mix based on understanding the audience characteristics of the available media.

THE REQUIREMENTS OF CREATIVE STRATEGY

The advertising requirements for the product often can easily favor or eliminate certain media candidates. For example, it has been a long-standing agreement among broadcasters subscribing to the Code of the National Association of Broadcasters that liquor will not be advertised on radio or television. Moreover, the product may be so sensitive that good taste calls for its exclusion from certain media. The definition of good taste does change over time. For example, many personal care products are now advertised on television that were considered to be too sensitive for such exposure a decade or so ago.

The product personality also will dictate media choice. The promotion of expensive French perfumes in *Mad* would clearly be inappropriate. The match between product prospects and media audiences would be poor, of course, but of even greater importance, association of the product with the magazine could affect its image adversely.

Finally, the requirements of the message may dominate the media decision. An automobile advertisement featuring acceleration and passing power requires a medium that dramatizes action for maximum creative impact; where movement is required, television or sales films are the only possible choices. Color might be specified to provide a more realistic representation of an automobile and to strengthen emotional impact. The finest color reproduction is available in magazines, although acceptable color can be purchased in both television and newspapers. Finally, a requirement for sound eliminates substantially all media except radio and television (although some direct-mail promotions contain small recorded disks).

REACHING THE PROPER AUDIENCE

The pivotal consideration in media strategy is to select media vehicles that reach the target audience with a minimum of waste coverage. This is often referred to as *selectivity.* Computers make it possible to undertake selectivity analysis with considerable precision, conditional of course on the accuracy of available data. This means that the analyst must have a grasp of the nature, scope, and uses of available sources of audience data. Audience data are discussed in some detail here before focusing on their use in media planning.

Media Audience Data

If we set aside all practical considerations, most analysts agree that it would be useful to have at least six categories of data for media planning and evaluation. The essential categories are (1) *media distribution*—the number of copies of a newspaper or magazine in circulation, or the number of television sets or radio receivers available to carry the advertising, (2) *media audiences*—the number of people actually exposed to a medium, and (3) *advertising exposure*—the number of people exposed to the advertising units in the media. In addition, data are also useful on (4) *advertising perception*—the number of people aware of the message, (5) *advertising communication*—the number of people affected by advertising, and (6) *consumer response*—the number of people who make purchases.

The difficulty is that the roles of the medium and the message themselves intermix in categories 3 to 6. In these categories, it is difficult to determine whether people's awareness of the message is more attributable to layout, design, and wording than to the medium itself. Thus, only the first two stages focus on the medium itself, and media audience data are largely confined to these levels, as our discussion will be. A number of trade association and research supply companies are in the business of providing media audience data. The sections that follow discuss some of these organizations. We begin our discussion by examining the media distribution.

Media Distribution

Data in the media distribution category have long been available from such organizations as the Audit Bureau of Circulation (ABC). This organization is sponsored by national and local advertisers, advertising agencies, and publishers. It makes available sworn and audited statements of newspaper and magazine audiences. A publication must have at least 70 percent paid circulation (copies purchased at not less than one-half the established prices) to be eligible for membership and listing. Most publishers meeting this qualification are members of ABC.

Publications that distribute to special groups, perhaps on a free basis, are audited by the Business Publications Audit of Circulation (BPA). The functions performed by BPA closely parallel those of ABC.

The notion of total physical distribution of media vehicles quickly loses its significance when one moves out of the publications field. Although the Advertising Research Foundation has published its *National Survey of Television Sets in U.S. Households,* the most useful data on television and other media are confined largely to categories 1 and 2 above, with very little audience measurement data available on category 3.

These data are used primarily in providing a verified audit of circulation claims. The figures are sometimes used as a guarantee for the rates established in magazine space contracts, but the data are of little additional use in media planning decisions because there is usually a wide difference between physical distribution of the media and audience exposure to the media. Thus, we must examine media audiences as a more important concept in media planning.

Media Audiences

The term *media audiences* refers to the actual number of people exposed to a medium on both one-time and repeat bases. The methods of audience measurement are complex, as the discussion below indicates. In fact, the Advertising

Research Foundation (ARF), a nonprofit industry organization, is almost always studying this subject. Since the methods of audience measurement vary greatly with different media types, we will discuss this topic for each type of media.

Magazine Audiences   The accepted definition of the audience of a given magazine is the number of people claiming to *recall* looking into an average issue. This definition is supported by evidence indicating that those who look into a magazine tend to be exposed to most of its contents. It should be apparent, however, that survey research often encounters response distortion. For example, it is not unusual for a respondent to deny reading a magazine that would appear to place him or her in a bad light in an interviewer's eyes, or to claim readership of a prestigious publication.

It is obvious that methods used to measure actual readership must be designed to minimize response distortion. The most commonly used approach, the *editorial interest technique,* encompasses an attempt to make respondents believe that they are helping editors to evaluate the appeal of various editorial features. No attempt is made at the outset to determine whether or not the respondent actually read the issue. The question is usually reserved until the end and is often worded as follows: "Just for the record, now that we have been through this issue, would you say you definitely happened to read it before, or didn't read it, or aren't you sure?" Saving this question until the end of the interview and wording it carefully are effective devices to guarantee a minimum of overclaimed or underclaimed readership.

Another approach used to assess magazine readership is to interview different samples of respondents every day for a period of time regarding "yesterday's reading." Confining the interview to yesterday's reading is intended to prevent memory loss. Extension of the interviewing period also permits useful estimation of the total readership of a given magazine over time. It is well known, for example, that "issue life" (the time in which an issue continues to be read) may run into months.

Other advertisers believe that the best approach is the use of simple *direct questions* such as "Which magazines do you read?" The first step is to use benchmark studies using several techniques to determine the probability that claimed readership is accurate. From then on, it would be possible simply to ask respondents, "Do you read this magazine usually, regularly, quite often, seldom, or never?" and to modify the answers given by the probabilities of accuracy found from previous surveys. This approach offers an admirable degree of simplicity. Box A of Figure 12–1 contains five different versions of the questions often used in magazine research. The diversity of questions trying to measure the same thing is clear.

It is useful to distinguish four types of magazine readers (see Table 12–1). The classification relates to the source of the copy (whether purchased or picked up) and the location of reading (whether in home or out of home). We define:

1. Primary readers: A and B.
2. Pass-along readers: C and D.

3. Out-of-home readers: B and D.

4. In-home readers: A and C.

Readership can also be measured in terms of primary readers only (the person or household purchasing the magazine) or primary readers plus pass-along read-

FIGURE 12–1

Magazine Audience Research

Box A: Five Ways to Ask for Consumer Magazine Readership
1. Which of the magazines listed below have you read or looked into in the past month?
2. Which of these magazines do you read regularly; that is, at least three out of four issues?

Magazine	Read or Looked Into (Past Month)	Read Regularly (3 out of 4 Issues)
A	☐	☐
B	☐	☐
C	☐	☐
D	☐	☐
E	☐	☐
F	☐	☐
G	☐	☐
H	☐	☐
I	☐	☐
J	☐	☐

3. What magazines do you read regularly, that is, at least three out of four issues? (Please write in the names of the magazines.)

_____   _____   _____

_____   _____   _____

4. Next, the monthly publications. Next to each magazine, please check the box that describes how many different issues of the magazine, if any, you personally have *read or looked into* for the first time in the *last 4 months*.

Monthly Magazine	Do Not Read It	Read Now and Then, But Not in Last 4 months	In the Last 4 Months, I Have Read			
			1 Issue	2 Issues	3 Issues	4 Issues
A	( )	( )	( )	( )	( )	( )
B	( )	( )	( )	( )	( )	( )
C	( )	( )	( )	( )	( )	( )
D	( )	( )	( )	( )	( )	( )
E	( )	( )	( )	( )	( )	( )
F	( )	( )	( )	( )	( )	( )

5. For each of the magazines listed below, will you please check:
   (a) Whether or not *you personally* read the *most recent issue?*
   (b) Whether or not *you personally* read the *issue before that one?*

FIGURE 12–1

Concluded

	Did You Read the Most Recent Issue? (Please Check "Yes" or "No" For EACH)		Did You Read the Issue Before That One? (Please Check "Yes" or "No" For EACH)	
	Yes	No	Yes	No
A	☐	☐	☐	☐
B	☐	☐	☐	☐
C	☐	☐	☐	☐
D	☐	☐	☐	☐
E	☐	☐	☐	☐
F	☐	☐	☐	☐
G	☐	☐	☐	☐
H	☐	☐	☐	☐
I	☐	☐	☐	☐
J	☐	☐	☐	☐

ers. In practice, many agencies discount out-of-home and pass-along audiences.

Two major organizations are active in measuring total magazine readers, each using a different measure of reader. The first is the Simmons Market Research Bureau (SMRB). SMRB samples about 15,000 individuals annually. The readership measurement method is the "through-the-book editorial interest method." Respondents are shown logos of magazine titles and are asked to "pick out those you might have read or looked into during the last six months, either at home or at some place else." This is verified again later in the interview, after the respondent goes through a stripped-down version of each magazine.

SMRB also provides audience estimates for newspaper supplements, network television, and national newspapers. Also collected are usage patterns for products, brand loyalty, and some demographic and psychographic measures. A major competitor is Mediamark Research, Inc. (MRI). MRI draws a sample of about 30,000 individuals (15,000 in the spring and fall) and measures audience size with the "modified recent reading method." Here respondents are given a list of

TABLE 12–1

Classification of Magazine Readership

Source of Copy	Read in Home	Read out of Home
Purchased	A	B
Picked up	C	D

about 160 magazines and are asked to note the ones they have read during the most recent publication interval. This is done in two steps. First, a deck of cards containing magazines is sorted by the respondent to indicate those read in the last six months. The cards for the magazines read are then sorted to indicate those read in the last publication interval. With differences in the methods of audience measurement, and some differences in sampling procedures, it is little wonder that SMRB and MRI report different audience sizes. The result of this is a great controversy as to which is the correct estimate.

Recently the Lintas : USA advertising agency proposed an alternative method to the SMRB and MRI methods. The Lintas approach puts more emphasis on core readers of magazines and less on the total audience. This proposal and the currently most utilized methods of SMRB and MRI are controversial in the industry. The dynamic nature of the media audience measurement controversy is well illustrated in Promotion in Action 12–1, which discusses the Lintas proposal and reactions to it.

Promotion in Action

12–1

Arguing about Magazine Audiences: Who Counts?

The Magazine Publishers of America last week "applauded" but stopped short of endorsing Lintas : USA's proposal to change the way magazine audiences are measured.

Lintas' plan has stirred debate within the magazine industry over the need for new audience measurement techniques, putting pressure on the leading suppliers of such data, Mediamark Research Inc. and Simmons Market Research Bureau.

Bernie Guggenheim, Lintas' Detroit-based senior VP-director of media information services, traveled to New York to present the agency's ideas to the MPA on Nov. 4. The meeting followed an "open letter" to the magazine industry distributed last month by Lou Schultz, the agency's exec VP-director of media services, at the annual American Magazine Conference in Bermuda. At the time, he said Lintas is "officially putting total audience at the bottom of the spectrum" when evaluating a magazine's reach and efficiency.

A number of publishing industry executives are backing the call for new measurement tools. Most agree agencies should focus on core readers rather than total audience figures from MRI and Simmons.

Others say the methodology of MRI and Simmons is outdated and produces artificially inflated or otherwise off-the-mark counts.

"A tremendous amount of money is being spent using this information to evaluate magazines, and it's totally ludicrous," said Ron Galotti, publisher of *Vanity Fair.* "Syndicated research to me is a big farce at this stage of the game."

Simmons and MRI figures include readers who pay for a magazine as well as pass-along readers or others who read a magazine but didn't pay for it. But most publishers believe that with the growth of targeted marketing, their core readers are more valuable to advertisers than pass-along readers.

"The focus on total audience treats primary and secondary audiences as if they are equal, and there is a fair amount of research that exists that indicates they are not," Mr. Guggenheim told the MPA.

In a response sent to Messrs. Schultz and Guggenheim last week, Marian Confer, MPA VP-research director, said the research committee "applauds Lintas and Lou Schultz for taking the initiative . . . The magazine industry and Lintas share the same goals . . . we too would like more accurate data on issues of the quality of the reader."

But the letter suggested new audience measurement techniques are needed for all media, not just magazines. And it said the MPA couldn't help fund a new primary audience study since mass magazines that still compete with TV "would be unjustly penalized" because they depend on total audience figures.

Lintas has said it will contribute $15,000 toward developing a new primary audience survey and will ask other agencies, advertisers and media to do the same.

Donna Galotti, publisher of *Ladies' Home Journal* and a critic of syndicated research, said she will gladly contribute $15,000 on behalf of her magazine.

"What we need is a passive electronic measurement for magazine audiences," Ms. Confer said. "I'm convinced we'll have that within five years, and then Simmons and MRI will be kerplunk."

Such a "wearable passive meter" has been developed by Stephen Douglas, a media consultant, and Lee Weinblatt, president of Pre-Testing Co., a media research company.

But Mr. Douglas said the partners have had difficulty raising money to test the system.

Mr. Galotti of *Vanity Fair* believes the industry needs to come up with a uniform subscriber study to evaluate core readers.

"I have the best access to my readers, as does every other publisher in the business," he said.

Executives at Simmons and MRI defended their methods as the best available.

"Nobody has come up with a better way of doing it," said Alan Seraita, Simmons senior VP-director of magazine sales.

Alain Tessier, chairman-CEO of MRI, blamed agencies for "making demands upon audience research that are much larger than the designs of the survey."

Mr. Tessier pointed out that MRI produces primary audience figures, though Lintas' Mr. Guggenheim said even those counts are inflated and have to be forced down to fit with paid circulation figures.

Source: Scott Donaton, "MPA Hedges on Lintas Reader Study," *Advertising Age,* November 16, 1992, p. 18.

Newspaper Audiences   The measurement of newspaper audiences involves essentially the same procedures as those reported for magazines. For example, a reader is defined as someone who has read a part of the medium being analyzed, and the time period covered generally does not exceed one day.

The Audit Bureau of Circulation's Newspaper Audience Research Data Bank (NRDB) offers such data. NRDB is based on data provided by cooperating newspapers in the top 100 markets. The data are collected by the newspapers themselves and made available to NRDB. To be part of NRDB, the study must meet both methodological and format standards. In general, advertisers must rely on newspaper-collected audience data. A significant supplier of newspaper audience research data is the Scarborough Company, which provides both syndicated data (much like MRI does for magazines) and custom studies.

Television Audiences   Television audience data are frequently collected by means of a diary in which viewers record shows they have watched over a period of time. Several syndicated research services are widely used for this purpose, including American Research Bureau (ARB) for national audiences and Arbitron for local audiences. There is some use of coincidental telephone recall in which a sample of people is contacted by telephone during programs to establish listening or viewing patterns. Use is also made of the *audimeter,* which automatically records the number of television sets tuned to a particular channel.

The key problem with the audimeter is that it does not indicate the number of people watching a given television set, or the demographic characteristics of the audience. The response to these problems was the *people meter.* This is a device that is attached to the television set. It allows each member of a family to separately "log on" and "log off" television viewing time. The demographic characteristics of each family member are collected and viewing habits correlated with this demographic data. A. C. Nielsen is the leader in the development of people meters and maintains a people meter panel of 4,500 households. Nielsen abandoned diaries in favor of people meters in the late 1980s. Maintaining a people meter panel is very expensive. A. C. Nielsen has indicated that it may reduce the size of its people meter panel and augment it with the use of diaries. People meters do not measure visitors to the household as part of an audience, nor are they attached to television sets smaller than 5 inches. In addition, they do not measure actual commercial viewership.

Radio Audiences   A unique problem is presented by the fact that radios are used everywhere. Hence, diaries and audimeters have proven to be difficult as radio audience measurement procedures. However, Arbitron does use diaries for its industry-accepted local radio ratings. In the diary approach, each member of selected diary families is asked to complete a listing of each radio station they listened to in 15-minute intervals, plus indicate the location where they were listening. During the measurement period of a week, respondents are called twice to reinforce the proper completion of the diary. Thus, you may hear on your favorite local radio station a claim about its Arbitron rank in a particular time slot—listen for this.

Another approach is utilized for network radio audience measurement. RADAR (Radio's All Dimension Audience Research) is now the accepted measurement procedure for network audiences. In this measurement technique, two telephone panels are established, one in the spring and one in the fall. Each household is telephoned eight different times on consecutive days during the survey period and is questioned about radio listening habits for each quarter hour for the preceding 24 hours. Respondents also complete a standard questionnaire that gives such characteristics as age and sex. This permits a reporting of all radio listening and weekly cumulative audiences by subgroup within the population.

Audiences of Other Media   Other media such as outdoor and transit advertising provide no information regarding audience evaluation since the total audience of the medium and potential for advertising exposure coincide. Research measures for these media are discussed in the next section.

Audience Profiles

Up to this point, discussion has been confined to total audiences. Such data, however, are poor indications of the characteristics of the individuals reached. Today most media data are also classified in such terms as the classic segmentation access variables as age, income, occupation, sex, geographical location, and product purchases. It is commonplace for the media planner to receive many such reports. In fact, the volume of information has grown to the point that extensive computer storage facilities are a necessity. It was formerly necessary to consult research reports published by individual media when profile data were needed. This is no longer necessary because of the widespread use of the syndicated research services that report audience profiles for television and magazines, the two leading national media.

Ideally, it should be possible to estimate the third category of media data noted earlier, *advertising exposure* in the media (not simply media audiences), for all possible media. In addition, as was pointed out in Chapter 7, target markets can be accessed in terms that go far beyond the usual demographic classifications. However, media profiles have not as yet expanded to provide this depth of data. There is an obvious need to enrich the data base through provision of data on the activities, interests, and opinions (AIO scores) of media audiences.

Using Media Audiences Data

The central task of media selection is to achieve a media mix that reaches the target audience with a minimum of waste coverage and delivers exposure to the advertising unit in a proper frame of mind, apart from media content, so that the advertisement can perform its role. The most demanding task is to match the target market with media audience, and this obviously requires a good data base.

With available data and computer technology, it is possible to utilize a number of characteristics of both the target market and media audiences in media selection. Thus, there is little excuse for failure to use audience research in building a media schedule.

REACH AND FREQUENCY

Once determination is made of the extent to which a media schedule reaches the desired target market, it is important to determine both *reach* and *frequency. Reach* is the number of different target audience individuals or households exposed to the advertisement during a given period of time (often a four-week period is used). It is common to measure reach as a rating out of 100. Thus, for example, if a media schedule results in the exposure of 1 million out of 2 million in the target audience, the reach is said to be 50. *Frequency* is the average number of exposures to the advertisement per individual or household target audience member during the same time period. A very useful summary measure referred to as *gross rating points* (GRP) combines both of these considerations. GRP is the product of *reach times frequency.* GRP is widely used as an indication of advertising weight or tonnage generated by the media schedule. Essentially, GRPs represent the achieved communication objective. Buyers use them as a ready reference point to determine what a buy is worth.

It should be understood that there is a strategic trade-off among three factors: (1) the *cost* of a size (page versus half page) or length (15 seconds versus 30 seconds) of advertisement placed in a media vehicle, (2) the *reach* provided by the media vehicle, and (3) the *frequency* of exposure to a given target audience. Given a specific advertising budget, one of these three factors can be increased only by decreasing one or both of the other two factors. Media planners need to examine the GRP consequences of:

1. Increasing or decreasing the size or length of the advertisement in the selected media vehicles; this affects the amount of money available for the breadth of reach of the advertising campaign and the frequency of placement of the advertisement, as larger or longer ads consume more of the budget.

2. Increasing or decreasing frequency of the placement of the advertisement in the selected media; the basic question here is how often the target audience must be exposed to the advertisement in order to gain the audience's attention and interest, to change attitudes, or to stimulate action; the more dollars spent on the frequency objective, the less money there is available for broadening the reach of the advertising campaign or for larger or longer ads.

3. Increasing or decreasing the reach objective; this affects the funds available for the size or length of ads, and the frequency with which the ads may be placed in the selected media.

The strategic trade-off among these three factors is an iterative process. The media planner, with the assistance of specially designed computer software, tests different media plans in order to determine the one that best meets the campaign's objectives given the cost of media size and times, and the frequency needed with the desired reach.

An example of how GRP is calculated will promote understanding of these concepts. Table 12–2 represents the television viewing record over four weeks in 10 homes. Notice that all homes but home I were reached during the four weeks. This gives a reach rating of 90. There were 26 total exposures. If 26 is divided by the nine homes reached, this gives an average frequency of 2.9 exposures. GRP (reach times frequency) then is 261 (90 × 2.9).

The Problem of Audience Duplication

Reach was defined in the above example as the number of different homes exposed. A given media schedule could fail to achieve a reach objective by delivering multiple exposures to the same audience. For example, a specific television program may deliver much of the same audience as a particular magazine. Use of this television show and this magazine in a media schedule would increase frequency, but at the cost of reach. If intensive coverage of the same group is the objective, the duplication of audience would be appropriate, as it is desirable to select media that reach essentially the same people. An opposite strategy is required to maximize reach, that is, to find a media plan that minimizes this duplication. Therefore, *duplication* of audiences is an important factor to measure and understand. Media planners should know, as well as possible, the extent to which different media vehicles provide duplicate audiences. With this knowledge, they can make allowances for the duplication in their plans. In practice, the problem lies in estimating the extent of duplication present within a media schedule. Data for this purpose are far from ideal, although some estimates are provided by the various syndicated data services.

Using Reach, Frequency, and GRP Measures

The starting point is to establish a media objective, usually in terms of desired GRP levels. This is established once the strategic trade-off among size/length of advertisements, reach, and frequency has been established. For example, 100 gross rating points a week is a relatively heavy advertising schedule. In a highly competitive market, it is not unusual to invest at this level or even higher levels. The media planner must specify the media GRP levels desired. Then the media buyer can fit together an appropriate schedule.

TABLE 12–2

Reach and Frequency Patterns for 10 Television Homes over a Four-Week Period

Week	Message	A	B	C	D	E	F	G	H	I	J	Total Exposures
1	1	x				x			x			3
	2	x		x								2
	3		x		x		x	x				4
2	4			x							x	2
	5					x						1
	6					x						1
3	7	x					x	x				3
	8				x							1
	9		x		x							2
4	10				x	x		x				3
	11					x					x	2
	12		x								x	2
Total exposures		3	3	2	4	5	2	3	1	0	3	26

Source: Media Department, Ogilvy & Mather, Inc.

For example, the media plan for a certain food product called for at least 200 gross rating points and maximum reach using prime-time television commercials. The media plan depicted in Table 12–3 delivered 205 GRP with a reach of 78.6 percent of all television homes. Hence it was entirely satisfactory, all other things being equal. Notice, by the way, that an equivalent GRP level could also be generated with much lower reach and higher frequency. Therefore, it is necessary to specify both desired reach and GRP.

GRPs also provide guidance on which of several alternative plans would be most effective. Consider the data in Table 12–4, which shows the reach and frequency analysis for a luxury item targeted at men who own or intend to buy luxury items and who have incomes over $95,000. The best media plan includes

TABLE 12–3

⌣

Reach, Frequency, and GRP Levels Produced by a Media Plan for a Food Item

	Total Announcements	Average Rating per Announcement
Schedule—four weeks		
1 announcement per week on "60 Minutes"	4	20.0%
1 announcement every other week on "Murphy Brown"	2	18.8
1 announcement every other week on "Home Improvement"	2	25.0
1 announcement every other week on "Wide World of Sports"	2	18.7
Reach—78.6 percent of all TV homes	10	
Frequency—2.6		
GRP—205.0		

Frequency Distribution Number of Announcements	Percent of Homes	Cumulated Percent
0	21.4	—
1	21.6	21.6
2	22.4	44.0
3	15.4	59.4
4	10.0	69.4
5	4.8	74.2
6	2.9	77.1
7	1.2	78.3
8	0.2	78.5
9	0.1	78.6
10+	0.0	78.6

Source: Media Department, Ogilvy & Mather, Inc.

TABLE 12—4

Reach and Frequency Analysis for a Luxury Product

Plan 1	Plan 2	Plan 3
Spot *People*	Spot *People*	No Spot *People*
newsweeklies	newsweeklies	newsweeklies
no monthlies	monthlies	monthlies
Schedule (2×)	(1 ×)	
1 Spot *People*	1 Spot *People*	2 *Time*
		1 *Newsweek*
2 *Time*	1 *Time*	1 *U.S. News*
2 *Newsweek*	1 *Newsweek*	1 *New Yorker*
2 *U.S. News*	1 *U.S. News*	1 *Sports Illustrated*
2 *New Yorker*	1 *New Yorker*	1 *Business Week*
2 *Sports Illustrated*	1 *Sports Illustrated*	1 *Sunset*
2 *Business Week*	1 *Business Week*	1 *Esquire*
		1 *Fortune*
	1 *Sunset*	1 *National Geographic*
	1 *Esquire*	1 *Holiday*
	1 *Fortune*	1 *Harper's*
	1 *National Geographic*	1 *Atlantic*
	1 *Holiday*	1 *Reporter*
	1 *Harper's*	1 *Town & Country*
	1 *Atlantic*	1 *Status/Diplomat*
	1 *Reporter*	1 *Commentary*
	1 *Town & Country*	1 *Venture*
	1 *Status/Diplomat*	1 *Réalités*
	1 *Commentary*	2 *The Wall Street Journal*
	1 *Venture*	
	1 *Réalités*	
	2 *The Wall Street Journal*	

User Groups	Reach	Frequency	GRP
Plan 1			
Total men	37	2.9	107
Own luxury, intend to buy	46	3.2	149
Income of $95,000+	65	3.5	229
Plan 2			
Total men	53	2.0	103
Own luxury, intend to buy	61	2.3	142
Income of $95,000+	77	2.9	225
Plan 3			
Total men	53	2.2	115
Own luxury, intend to buy	60	2.5	154
Income of $95,000+	77	3.3	249

monthly magazines; this is especially evident when plans 1 and 2 are compared. Plan 3 is the preferred plan, as it delivers more GRPs for the target audience.

Finally, reach, frequency, and GRP measures can be an excellent guide to estimate budget levels through the built-up analysis discussed in Chapter 9. The data in Table 12–5, part A, for example, give a general indication of the reach and frequency levels achieved by from 100 to 300 GRP in a four-week period with

TABLE 12–5

Reach (R) and Frequency (F) Estimates and Costs at Various GRP Levels

A. Network TV Reach and Frequency (4-week period—households)

GRP Levels	Prime		M–F Daytime	
	Reach	Frequency	Reach	Frequency
100	55	1.8	38	2.6
150	66	2.3	43	3.5
200	73	2.7	48	4.2
250	77	3.2	52	4.8
300	79	3.8	55	5.5

Source: Leo Burnett Television Reach & Frequency System 1989. Reach based on averages for schedules for the average message-to-show ratio. Based on Nielsen People Meter Persons Cume Analysis 1987 and 1989.

B. Spot Television (costs cumulated by top market groups)

Markets	Percent U.S. TV HH*	Cost/HH* Rating Point			
		Prime Time	Day-time	Early Evening	Late Evening
Top 10	31	$ 5,234	$1,521	$1,722	$2,253
Top 20	45	7,280	2,148	2,479	3,294
Top 30	54	8.832	2,657	3,100	4,133
Top 40	61	9,686	2,959	3,461	4,644
Top 50	67	10,472	3,229	3,815	5,101
Top 60	72	11,070	3,434	4,072	5,442
Top 70	76	11,539	3,597	4,291	5,729
Top 80	80	11,971	3,752	4,482	5,977
Top 90	83	12,344	3,892	4,652	6,193
Top 100	86	12,709	4,027	4,813	6,410

* HH = Households.

Source: *Media Market Guide,* 4th Quarter projections.

a television schedule. To take just one illustration, 100 GRP in daytime network television will reach, on the average, 38 percent of all television homes with a frequency of 2.6 times in a four-week period. Suppose the objective of a media plan for a convenience food item calls for a 48 reach rating with a 4.2 frequency on network television using prime time placement. The 200 GRP level thus would be adequate. Table 12–5, part B, indicates that the gross cost for one GRP point in the top 100 markets on daytime television is $4,027. This would then yield a needed budget level of $805,400 (200 × $4,027).

Historically, reach and frequency were measures confined to television and magazine audiences. Now data sources and computer technology permit estimates across media and between various market segments. Therefore, these measures are finding widespread use in media planning.

COMPETITIVE CONSIDERATIONS

Competition can assume major significance in media decisions. At times, the advertising objective will call, for example, for maintenance of "share of voice." *Share of voice* is the dollar amount of advertising spent on a brand divided by the total dollar amount of advertising spent in this brand's product category. Thus, if we spent $5 million on our brand, and all the competitors in total spent $25 million (including our $5 million), our share of voice would be $5 ÷ $25 = 20 percent. This is especially likely in a situation in which the boundaries of a total market are more or less static and a number of competitors are offering essentially similar products.

The rationale underlying a share-of-voice objective is that market share will roughly parallel advertising share. In such situations, therefore, it is necessary to analyze market share, share of total advertising expenditures, and share of advertising messages actually reaching prospects. Consider the data in Figure 12–2. The first column depicts share of market for competing brands, and the next column reveals the best estimate of share of advertising spending for television. Brands A and B are spending in proportion to market share, whereas the management of Brand C apparently believes that a dominant position can be maintained with a smaller proportional investment. Brand D apparently is a new product and is spending to attain an anticipated share.

Obviously, the quality of the advertising and other factors will affect the figures, but the data are quite revealing. It would appear, for example, that the Brand A schedule will lead to an increase in share of voice as well as a probable gain in market share. Brand B probably will remain stable, but Brand C may be in trouble. All other things being equal, it will be difficult to maintain market share with spending levels that lag competition to this extent. Finally, Brand D should be watched closely because it should achieve significant market inroads.

It should be stressed that this example represents a situation in which competition is a major factor, and this is not always the case. Nonetheless, competition is relevant in the majority of instances.

The third column in Figure 12–2 may be somewhat more puzzling. It provides an estimate of the efficiency of spending and is not necessarily equivalent to total dollar levels. With available data sources providing information on media audience, program ratings, and so on, it is possible to estimate the probable advertising exposure delivered by each firm's media schedule. Here Brand A is highly efficient in that an 8 percent share of spending delivers 11 percent of total messages. Brand C, on the other hand, apparently is choosing media that do not reach its prospects in that it has attained only a 19 percent share as compared with a 25 percent dollar share. These figures become especially significant when they are related to the key segment, messages delivered to women, appearing in the fourth column.

COST CONSIDERATIONS

Space and time costs are always important factors in media selection. These data usually appear in the volumes published by the Standard Rate & Data Service (SRDS). However, in practice, network TV and radio costs must be obtained from the network. Spot television and radio costs in SRDS are guides but are of little value for real planning or buying since buys are negotiated in terms of price. Because of this problem of actual prices being different from SRDS, two other

FIGURE 12–2

Competitive Marketing and TV Advertising Shares of Nine Leading Brands

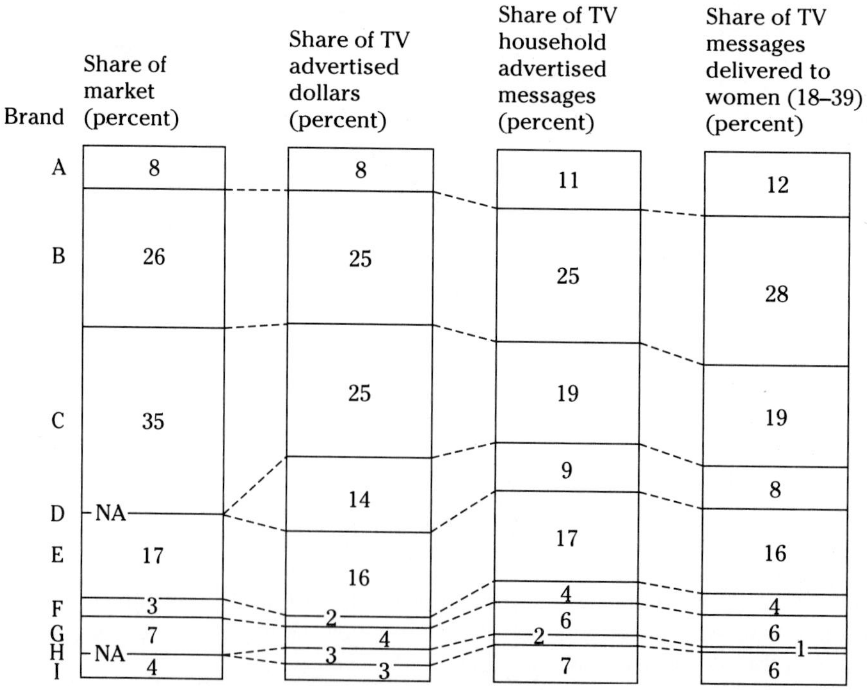

Brand	Share of market (percent)	Share of TV advertised dollars (percent)	Share of TV household advertised messages (percent)	Share of TV messages delivered to women (18–39) (percent)
A	8	8	11	12
B	26	25	25	28
C	35	25	19	19
D	NA	14	9	8
E	17	16	17	16
F	3	2	4	4
G	7	4	6	6
H	NA	3	2	1
I	4	3	7	6

services have developed. Conceptual Dynamics, Inc., publishes *Media Market Guide,* which among other things includes the cost for typical ad units by market. The second service is Spot Quotations And Data, Inc. (SQAD). This service provides real "street" prices for spot television in the top 51 markets. The measure provided by SQAD is the cost per household rating point (CPP) for a 30-second spot. SQAD averages the cost data from several unidentified agencies and combines them with the average of Nielsen and Arbitron audience measure for each market to give the CPP.

Recall from Chapter 11 that there are formulas (cost per thousand readers or homes, and the milline rate) that permit comparisons of the cost efficiency of various media. The logic of these formulas is that gross space costs must be refined by the audience reached per dollar spent before useful comparisons can be made across media.

The media planner then must obtain a CPM for the target audience for every media vehicle under consideration. The computer can be used to combine audience measurement data, target audience designation, and the cost of an insertion to generate such figures. Table 12–6 presents computer output from a run using Simmons's data for magazines. Note that the CPM target audience varies substantially depending on the target market specified. With computer technology, CPM target audience can easily be calculated for many different target audience designations. Most of these programs allow subjective weighting of audience data to take into account the media planner's judgments about growth trends since the

TABLE 12–6

Computer Output of CPM Target Audience Figures for Selected Magazines

			Total Adults			
Target Market: $25M + Age 18–34 Population—6,665 (000) Percent of Base—4.47			Reach			
Rank	Cost	Weight	(000)	Percent Covg.	Percent Comp.	CPM
1. *People*	13,475	111.20	1243	18.6	9.7	10.84
2. *Time*	24,705	60.00	1317	19.8	10.6	18.76
3. *Time*	24,705	55.00	1207	18.1	10.6	20.47
4. *Time*	24,705	50.00	1098	16.5	10.6	22.50
5. *Newsweek*	38,160	100.00	1687	25.3	9.5	22.62
6. *Playboy*	40,745	100.00	1684	25.3	10.6	24.20
7. *Time*	53,195	100.00	2196	32.9	10.6	24.22
8. *Sports Illustrated*	34,010	100.00	1147	17.2	9.1	29.65
9. *Business Week*	18,760	100.00	547	8.2	14.3	34.30
10. *Esquire*	14,000	100.00	408	6.1	8.8	34.31
11. *U.S. News & World Report*	26,420	100.00	691	10.4	8.2	38.23

TABLE 12–6

Concluded

Target Market:
$25M + Age 35–49
Population—6,635 (000)
Percent of Base—4.45

Rank	Cost	Weight	(000)	Percent Covg.	Percent Comp.	CPM
1. *Time*	24,705	60.00	1162	17.5	9.4	21.26
2. *Time*	24,705	55,00	1065	16.1	9.4	23.20
3. *People*	13,475	111.20	571	8.6	4.4	23.60
4. *Business Week*	18,760	100.00	753	11.3	19.6	24.91
5. *Time*	24,705	50.00	968	14.6	9.4	25.52
6. *Newsweek*	38,160	100.00	1438	21.7	8.1	26.54
7. *Time*	53,195	100.00	1937	29.2	9.4	27.46
8. *Sports Illustrated*	34,010	100.00	1144	17.2	9.0	29.73
9. *U.S. News & World Report*	26,420	100.00	733	11.0	8.7	36.04
10. *Esquire*	14,000	100.00	287	4.3	6.2	48.78
11. *Playboy*	40,745	100.00	831	12.5	5.2	49.03

Reach (spanning over the (000), Percent Covg., Percent Comp. columns)

Explanation of Output
1. For each run, a "target market" is defined by the user based on some demographic variable: for example, the first run specifies 18- to 34-year-olds earning $25,000 and over as the target.
2. "Population" refers to the number of U.S. adults in this target; for example, 6,665,000 adults are in the target market.
3. "Percent of base" refers to the ratio of population as defined in item (2) above to the total U.S. adult population; for example, 6,665,000 is 4.47 percent of the total U.S. adult population (over 18).
4. Cost refers to the four-color, full-page cost of a magazine.
5. "Reach (000)" refers to the number of target market readers of an average issue of a magazine in thousands.
6. Percent coverage (*Percent Covg.*) refers to the ratio of reach to population; for example, for *People* magazine, it is 1,243,000/6,665,000 = 18.6 percent.
7. Percent composition (*Percent Comp.*) refers to the ratio of target audience readers of a magazine to total readers of a magazine; for example, 9.7 percent of *People* readers are in the 18 to 34—$15,000-and-over target audience
8. "CPM" refers to cost per thousand target audience readers.
9. Weight allows the user to adjust the audience figures for a magazine. A weight of 100.0 means that the data on file are used as is in the calculations. *People* has been weighted up due to estimated expanded readership since the Simmons data were collected. Four different *Time* weights are presented. The 100.0 is the regular *Time* magazine. The other three weights for *Time* are for *Time Z*. This is so because Simmons surveys only measure readership on a national basis. Thus all special advertising editions of magazines (for example, *Time Z, Newsweek Executive, Business Week Industrial*) cannot be measured directly. What all publishers and users do in estimating readership is to simply take a percentage of the total readership when measuring demographic editions. *Time Z* is computed here by taking 50 percent, 55 percent, and 60 percent of regular *Time*. It was usual to use the 50 percent figure for $15,000 plus income and the 60 percent figure for $25,000 plus income.

audience data were collected (see weight of 111.20 for *People*) and to allow the analysis of special editions (note three different special versions of *Time* in the output; each is subjectively assessed in terms of weight).

As useful as the CPM formula can be, it is often abused. First, it may be assumed that costs are the dominant consideration in media selection, whereas any of the other considerations mentioned thus far could be of great importance, especially selectivity in reaching target markets. Furthermore, notice that the denominator of these formulas is circulation, readership, or viewership, none of which is modified to ascertain the number of prospects reached. A CPM of $2.83 could easily be a CPM for prospects of $20 because of inefficient coverage of the target market. Thus, formulas of this type should be used only when the denominator is refined to generate cost per thousand prospects reached as it is in Table 12–6.

Finally, it is difficult to interpret CPM figures under certain circumstances. CPM represents an average that treats all exposures the same, regardless of whether they are delivered to different people or represent increased frequency to the same people. As long as the repeated exposure is deemed to be of equal impact as the new exposure, CPM gives an advantage to a media vehicle that reaches a concentrated audience repeatedly. For example, it is possible to arrive at the same CPM with 10 percent of the people reached 10 times, 100 percent reached once, or 1 percent reached 100 times.

It can be concluded, therefore, that CPM must be used with caution. Cost efficiency is a useful criterion only when the other considerations mentioned in this chapter have also entered into the analysis. Even then it is only one criterion of an adequate media schedule, not the ultimate criterion, as many falsely assume.

QUALITATIVE MEDIA CHARACTERISTICS

The term *qualitative media characteristics* has come to assume several possible meanings. It is confined here to the role played by the medium or vehicle in the lives of the audience and with the positive or negative attitudes toward it and its advertising created by the medium or vehicle in its audience. This definition stresses the meaning of the medium to its readers, viewers, or listeners. Thus, editorial content of a newspaper or magazine, or "adult" content level of a television show, or music format of a radio station would all be examples of important qualitative media characteristics.

Qualitative values defy precise measurement and analysis, and existing data are sparse. Yet it should be clear that these characteristics form the mood in which advertising is received, and the resulting significance can exceed that of other factors that enter into media strategy. For instance, favorable attitudes toward a television personality can increase the effectiveness of advertising on that program. The recent decision of the Florida Orange Juice Council and Quaker State Motor Oil to drop Burt Reynolds as their advertising spokesperson and not advertise on his show, "Evening Shade," due to his well-publicized divorce is an example of these types of concerns.

As yet, no continuing data sources can be used to assess the qualitative media characteristics across media classes. Rather, the analyst must rely on isolated research reports and his or her own judgment. Judgment, moreover, frequently will suffice. It is intuitively obvious, for instance, that the editorial environment and subjective values of the reader of the *Atlantic Monthly* are such as to be incompatible with the advertising of washday detergents. In other situations, however, the qualitative considerations are not obvious, and the need exists for more and better data. Fortunately, in this situation also, there is no serious methodological barrier to needed research.

A prime illustration of avoiding certain media environments is the recent action by some advertisers to remove their sponsorship from television shows or a specific episode featuring too much violence. Numbered among these companies are Procter & Gamble, General Motors, General Foods, and McDonald's.

DISTRIBUTION REQUIREMENTS

Distribution geography and stimulation of reseller support are considerations that can easily become dominant in certain situations. *Distribution geography* refers to the density of distribution. Strictly national media would not be utilized if distribution were spotty across the country; local newspapers, radio, or television would represent a more economical media array. Promotional strategy also may call for heavy emphasis on dealer cooperative advertising, whereby the dealer places local advertising, paid for in part by the manufacturer. Media choices in these cases are confined to local media by necessity, for the market reached by national media usually would substantially exceed that of the dealer. An identical situation is present when the manufacturer places advertising over the dealer's name without cooperative sharing of costs.

Promotional strategy at times dictates heavy reliance on personal selling to gain retail distribution, and advertising may be used as a door opener. It is often very effective for the company salesperson to point out to the retailer that the product has been nationally advertised in a prestigious medium; the pulling power of the advertisement thus becomes secondary to its role as a selling point to dealers. The sponsorship of network television programs and placement of advertisements in large-circulation magazines are popular strategies for this purpose.

Finally, it is frequently appropriate to advertise in consumer media for the sole purpose of stimulating dealer efforts. Chrysler, for instance, sponsors television golf in part to serve as a rallying point for its dealers and as a stimulus for greater efforts on their part.

When all of the audience, cost, reach, frequency, and qualitative considerations are evaluated, the media planners must make the choice of a final media mix. The choice of media mix for Carnival Cruise Lines is presented in Promotion in Action 12–2.

SCHEDULING

Once the media to be used have been selected, it is necessary to determine the timing and allocation of advertising insertions. Of special importance are (1) scheduling by geographical region, (2) seasonal scheduling, (3) flighting (concentration of efforts in restricted time periods), and (4) scheduling within a chosen medium (size and location of insertions).

Geographical Scheduling

When the determination of geographical market potential was discussed in Chapter 9, the necessity to determine an index of relative sales possibilities on a market-

---

Carnival Utilizes Its Media Choices to Enhance Impact

Promotion in Action

12–2

A typical media mix for Carnival Cruise Lines is as follows:

Magazines	$ 67,600
National Sunday magazines	29,600
Network TV	13,168,100
Spot TV	1,249,000
Network radio	—
Spot radio	—
Outdoor	1,900
Network cable	289,900
Newspapers	11,487,600
National syndication	—
Total	$26,293,700

The use of television provides the capability for Carnival to show the "fun" nature of the product and to build primary demand. Network shows selected are those with high target audience composition (see Chapter 4 for target description). These shows include afternoon soap operas and network news programs.

More detailed descriptive advertisements are presented in the newspaper ads that appear in over 200 markets, especially in the Sunday travel sections. This medium allows Carnival to give information on schedules, itineraries, and prices. Tie-ins with specific travel agents are also possible with newspapers.

The magazines and the national magazines in Sunday papers selected include editorial-subject-relevant and target-audience-relevant ones such as *Cruise Travel*, *Travel-Holiday,* and *Modern Bride*. Magazines play a relatively minor reinforcing role in the Carnival media mix.

by-market basis was indicated. This index in turn serves as the foundation for geographic allocation of advertising dollars. The general principle is to allocate in proportion to market potential, all other things being equal. However, the "noise level" in major markets is higher than in smaller ones. Thus, more advertising weight relative to potential is usually placed in the larger markets.

Table 12–7 presents the geographical selectivity of the media plan for a convenience food item. Notice that allocations were made so that the schedule closely paralleled the index of brand use by county size.

The data in Table 12–7 provide only a very general indication of geographical selectivity. In addition, the agency utilized a computer program that permits media selection in proportion to market potential for each major metropolitan market. In this case, the projected percentage of sales in a given area became the target figure for total advertising impressions as well. Estimates were made of the necessary impressions for the entire fiscal year. These figures were then converted into gross rating points per week from which required dollar expenditure levels were estimated. In some cases, judgmental modifications were made when it was deemed advisable to ensure that certain markets should receive greater media weight than others. Finally, a computer printout compared original objectives for advertising impressions with actual media delivery. Some of the results were as follows:

Market	Target Impressions	Media Weight
Portland, Maine	1.7	1.5
Albany, New York	2.2	1.9
Milwaukee, Wisconsin	2.5	1.8
Los Angeles, California	11.2	11.9
Toledo, Ohio	0.9	1.1

Notice, first of all, that there was not an exact correspondence between target objectives and actual media weight, but the differences were so small as to be

TABLE 12–7

Geographical Selectivity of the Media Plan for a Convenience Food Item

County Size	Percentage in Sample Studied	Percentage of Users	Index of Brand Use (base 100)	Geographical Selectivity of Media Plan*
A	39.5	52.0	132	130
B	26.1	28.0	107	100
C	18.0	15.0	83	100
D	16.4	5.0	30	40

* Combination daytime television and three women's magazines.

negligible. Also, the media schedule was evaluated in terms of GRP delivered, not the number of dollars spent. The dollar figure is not necessarily a good measure of advertising message weight, which can be estimated only from audience ratings.

Seasonal Scheduling

Because many products show seasonal variations in demand, the advertiser is compelled to introduce appropriate modifications in the timing of advertising throughout the year. In some instances, media weight is placed immediately prior to a seasonal upsurge so that maximum sales are generated at the beginning of the season. The promotion of air conditioning or heating equipment is a good illustration. In other instances, funds are allocated so that increases or reductions coincide closely with sales patterns.

The convenience food example indicated some slight seasonal variations in sales of the product. As the following data indicate, the media plan coincided closely with seasonal patterns:

Quarter	Percentage of Sales		Percentage of Media Weight	
June	26 }	55	34 }	57
September	29 }		23 }	
December	24 }	45	22 }	43
March	21 }		21 }	

Flighting

Sometimes media planners are forced to concentrate dollar allocations in certain time periods while cutting back in other time periods. This is referred to as *flighting,* and it is done to avoid spending at an inadequate level throughout the year. The objective is to achieve higher reach and frequency levels in a more limited period with the hope that the impact generated will carry over in the remaining periods.

Consider, for example, the data in Figure 12–3. Substantially higher reach and frequency levels are generated when the advertising is concentrated in 26 weeks rather than spread over 52 weeks.

Flighting offers the following advantages:

1. Media rate and purchasing values such as better prices or discounts can be gained by concentrating ad dollars rather than spreading them.
2. There are communications values in concentrating advertising impact. A consumer awareness threshold that is impenetrable at light advertising levels can be crossed.
3. The availability of greater funds in shorter periods of time opens up new media strategy possibilities.

The first claimed advantage is rather apparent in that discounts increase in proportion to the concentration of dollars within a medium in a limited time period. Similarly, the third advantage can be a significant consideration in that a greater variety of media opportunities can often be presented. The second point, however, is more debatable. Obviously, a greater short-run impact can be made, but this may be at the sacrifice of continuing reinforcement during the interim periods. The net effect, therefore, can be the opposite of what is intended, especially if competitive efforts are strong.

Flighting is probably most useful when available funds are inadequate to sustain a continued effort at adequate levels. Indeed, at times it might be the only feasible strategy when it is considered that spending at an unduly low level may result in little or no impact in view of competitors' efforts.

Many different flighting patterns (sometimes called *pulses*) are available. One scheme for classifying these patterns is presented in Figure 12–4. But which pattern is best?

The most effective pattern depends on the advertising communication objectives in relation to the nature of the product, target customers, distribution channels, and other marketing factors. Consider the following cases:

A *retailer* wants to announce a preseason sale of skiing equipment. He or she recognizes that only certain people will be interested in the message and that the target buyers need to hear the message only once or twice to know whether they are interested. The objective is to maximize the reach of the message, not the repetition. The retailer decides to concentrate the messages on the days of the

FIGURE 12–3

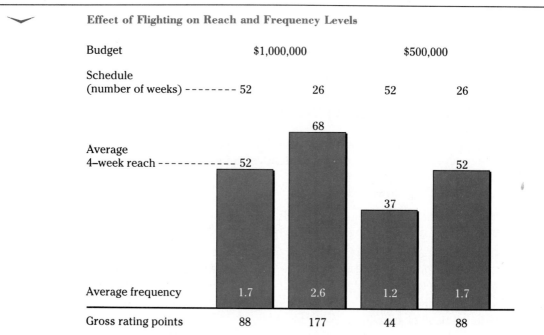

Effect of Flighting on Reach and Frequency Levels

		$1,000,000		$500,000	
Budget					
Schedule (number of weeks)	52	26	52	26
Average 4–week reach	52	68	37	52
Average frequency	1.7	2.6	1.2	1.7
Gross rating points	88	177	44	88

sale at a level rate but to vary the time of day to avoid the same audiences. Pattern (1) is used.

A *muffler manufacturer-distributor* wants to keep its name before the public yet does not want the advertising to be too continuous because only 3 to 5 percent of the cars on the road need a new muffler at any given time. The choice, therefore, is to use intermittent advertising. Furthermore, because Fridays are paydays for many potential buyers, it might be the best day to interest them in replacing a worn-out muffler. So the choice is made to sponsor a few messages on a midweek day and more messages on Friday. Pattern (12) is used.[1]

General rules should be used with care because promotion is a very situation-specific activity. A firm must be willing to experiment with its flighting pattern if it wants to determine the best one.

Scheduling within Media

Media scheduling necessitates specifying both the size of the space or time unit to be purchased and the location within the medium. These issues have been extensively researched, and it is now possible to advance a number of generalizations.

Size of the Advertisement   The numerous studies of size of the advertisement on the printed page have made it clear that doubling size will not double results. In fact, readership increases roughly in proportion to the square root of space

FIGURE 12—4

Classification of Advertising Timing Patterns

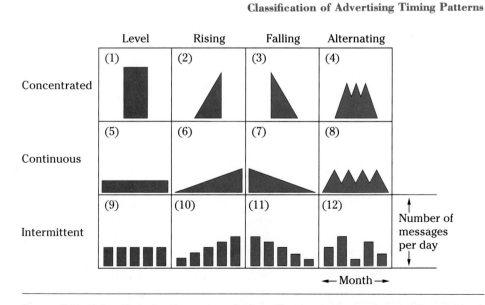

Source: Philip Kotler, *Marketing Management: Analysis, Planning, Implementation, and Control,* 7th ed. (Englewood Cliffs, N.J.: Prentice Hall, 1991), p. 613.

increase. This does not mean, of course, that a half page should necessarily be preferred over a full page. Size offers real advantages in greater power of attraction, more flexibility in layout arrangement, and greater opportunity for dramatic use of space elements. Moreover, the impact of larger space units on *attitude* may be greater, although existing evidence is not clear on this point.

The relative advantages of variations in the length of television or radio commercials defy generalization, although it is well known that longer commercials are often preferred for the reason that creative presentation is simplified when time pressures are not acute. The shorter commercial is usually more demanding to produce, but the rising costs of television time in particular have forced many advertisers to abandon the longer advertisement. The shorter commercial can be equally effective if proper care is taken to prepare a direct and convincing appeal. In fact, 30 seconds can be too much time for some messages, and the shorter 10-second commercial can be more effective. For example, this trade-off between effectiveness and cost has resulted in a trend toward shorter television commercials over the last few decades. At one time, the 60-second commercial was the norm, but through the late 1980s and early 1990s, the 30-second commercial is now the dominant form. As Table 12–8 indicates, the use of 15-second commercials has also become extensive.

Position of the Advertisement   From the numerous studies documenting the role of position on the page in printed media, the following generalizations have emerged:

1. It makes little difference whether the advertisement appears on the left- or right-hand page in either newspapers or magazines. The analysis of

TABLE 12–8

Television Commercial Length

| | Percent of Total Activity | | | | | |
| | Spot | | | Network | | |
	1990	1991	1992	1990	1991	1992
10 seconds	3.9%	4.2%	4.4%	0.1%	0.1%	0.2%
15 seconds	5.1	6.2	7.6	35.0	33.8	30.3
20 seconds	0.1	0.4	0.3	1.4	0.8	1.2
30 seconds	85.1	83.9	83.3	60.1	62.0	63.8
45 seconds	0.3	0.1	0.1	1.3	0.7	1.4
60 seconds	3.8	3.8	3.4	2.0	2.1	1.8
90+ seconds	1.7	1.3	0.8	0.2	0.5	1.4
Total	100.0%	100.0%	100.0%	100.0%	100.0%	100.0%

Source: Arbitron/BAR, *Commercial Length Summary Report,* 3rd Quarter each year.
Source: *Leo Burnett 1993 Media Costs and Coverage,* p. 12. Used with permission.

readership of the Million Market Newspapers, for example, presents this conclusion unmistakably. In fact, Starch has concluded from 40 years of research that the primary factor in readership is the advertisement it-self—what it says and how it says it.

2. In magazines, the greatest readership is usually attracted by covers and the first 10 percent of the pages, but beyond this the location of the advertisement is a minor issue.

3. Page traffic is high in nearly all parts of a newspaper, and position within the paper is of little significance.

4. Although position does not appear to be a crucial factor, some advantage accrues to the advertiser if the copy is located adjacent to compatible editorial features. Most newspapers and magazines attempt to ensure compatibility, and it can be specified by the advertiser for extra cost.

5. Thickness of the magazine has been found to exert only a slight effect on coupon returns and advertising recognition and recall.

6. A number of other generalizations result from a series of analyses of newspaper readership:
   a. Position in the gutter (the inside fold) is no different from position on the outer half of the page.
   b. Position on the page has little effect except when competing advertisements become especially numerous.
   c. There are known differences in readership of different editorial features such as general news and sports by sex and age.

It thus appears that position on the newspaper or magazine page and location within the issue are minor considerations. There can, of course, be significant exceptions to these generalizations, but the advertisement itself appears to be the determining factor in high readership or coupon return.

Position in broadcast advertising has been researched to a lesser degree, at least insofar as published literature shows. It is known from the meager published evidence, however, that commercials frequently perform better when inserted as part of a regular program than at the station break, which often becomes cluttered. Location within a program seems to be especially advantageous for longer commercials. Many also believe that commercials at the beginning and end of a program are placed at a disadvantage because of the clutter of program announcements, production and talent credits, and other distracting nonprogram material. If this disadvantage appears to be important, the sponsor purchasing time on a participating basis would do well to specify insertion within the program. Others believe that program commercial position is of no consequence, and not enough data exist to support either position.

SUMMARY

This chapter has investigated a number of factors that enter into media strategy, including requirements of creative strategy, audience selectivity, reach and frequency, competitive considerations, cost efficiency, qualitative factors, distribution requirements, and scheduling.

Clearly, it is impossible to present a conclusive set of steps leading to successful media selection in every problem. To do so would be to oversimplify relevant issues to an unrealistic degree. Media selection requires research thinking in that information must be sought at many points in the analytical procedure and utilized creatively and imaginatively. The considerations outlined above represent most of the major variables shaping the selection problem. A myriad of solutions is possible, depending entirely on these situational requirements.

REVIEW AND DISCUSSION QUESTIONS

1. The Tourism Bureau of France has hired you to prepare a media strategy for next year's advertising campaign to attract U.S. tourists to come to France. A media budget of $7.5 million has been allocated for this purpose. Prepare a media strategy for the bureau. Be sure to indicate (1) the dollar allocation across types of media (magazines, television, etc.); (2) the specific media vehicles you would recommend within the selected media types (*People, TV Guide,* "ABC National News," etc.); and (3) the scheduling of the placement of the ads. Also be explicit in your assumptions about target markets, data, and so on.

2. Prepare a media strategy for the introduction of a new subcompact car into the North American market by Chrysler, as per the preceding question.

3. The advertising agency for the Crummy Candy Company has submitted a media plan with the statement that "this plan is designed to achieve maximum frequency; reach is of little importance." The campaign is aimed at the market under 25 years of age, and the product being advertised is a popular chocolate bar that now has second place in market share in most local markets. Is frequency a desirable strategy for this type of product?

4. How can the media plan mentioned in question 3 be designed so as to achieve maximum frequency? What changes might be necessary if greater reach were desired?

5. Using the data in Table 12–6, select the magazine mix for the media plan for a new male/female cosmetic line that is targeted at the first target market presented in the figure. Now select a magazine mix for the other target group. Assume that you have $1 million to spend against the specific target group.

6. What data, analysis, and judgment likely went into the choice of Carnival Cruise Lines' media mix, as presented in Promotion in Action 12–2? Is this an appropriate media mix for Carnival?

NOTE

1. Philip Kotler, *Marketing Management: Analysis, Planning, Implementation, and Control,* 7th ed. (Englewood Cliffs, N.J.: Prentice Hall, 1991), p. 613.

e c t i o

5

SALES PROMOTION

We proceed from the discussion of advertising to another area of concern to the promotion manager, sales promotion. This area of activity involves channel management—methods of creating and managing demand for goods that generates flow through the channel from manufacturer to the ultimate consumer.

Chapter 13 continues the discussion of management program elements by considering problems inherent in gaining the support of independent resellers in the channels of distribution. By examining the tasks that resellers can be expected to perform given their objectives and limitations as independent businesses, we can suggest how manufacturers might stimulate reseller promotional activity or improve, supplement, or control reseller promotional efforts. Known as "push" strategies these strategies push products and services through the channel.

Chapter 14 discusses another form of sales promotion aimed directly at consumer and initiates the demand for a product or service. Known as "pull" strategies these strategies create the demand in the ultimate consumer that pulls product through the channel.

Working with Resellers: The Struggle for Channel Control

THE ECONOMY'S POWER SHIFT

Power in the economies of developed countries is rapidly shifting from manufacturers to distributors and retailers.

The phenomenal success of Wal-Mart, which made the late Sam Walton one of the world's richest men in less than 20 years, was based squarely on the chain's controlling the operations of its main suppliers. Wal-Mart, rather than the manufacturer—a Procter & Gamble, for instance—controls what should be produced, in what product mix, in what quantities, when it should be delivered, and to which stores. Similarly, in Japan, Ito-Yokado Co. controls the product mix, the manufacturing schedule, and the delivery of major supplies, such as Coca-Cola or beer, for its 4,300 7-Eleven stores.

In hardware, a few very large distributors—many of them owned by the independent retail stores they serve—actually design the products (or at least write the specifications for them), find a manufacturer, and lay down manufacturing schedules and delivery times. One example is Servistar, a Butler, Pennsylvania–based company, which buys for 4,500 stores across the United States and is owned by them.

The chains of hypermarkets that have come to dominate food retailing in France and Spain similarly control the product mix, manufacturing schedules, and delivery schedules of their main suppliers. And so do the discount chains that take a growing share of the U.S. market in office products. In the United States, the freestanding community hospital is no longer the principal customer for health-care products. Buying is now done by chains: for-profit ones, such as Humana; voluntary ones; and denominational ones, whether Catholic or Lutheran. They set the product specifications, find the manufacturer, negotiate price, and determine manufacturing schedules and delivery.

What Customers Want

Distributing is becoming increasingly concentrated; manufacturing, by contrast, is becoming increasingly splintered. Thirty years ago, three big automakers shared the U.S. market. Today the market is split among Detroit's Big Three, five Japanese firms, and two German firms. But 30 years ago, 85 percent of all retail car sales were done in single-site dealerships; even three-dealership chains were quite uncommon. Today a fairly small number of large chain-dealers—no more than 50 or 60–sell two fifths of all cars in the United States. Yesterday's dealer handled only one make. Today's chains may sell GM cars in one dealership, Toyotas in the dealership across the street, and BMWs in a dealership in the next town. They have little commitment to any one maker because they go by what their customers want.

These large distributors are becoming less and less dependent on manufacturers' brands. Thirty years ago, only two very big American retailers successfully sold their own private labels: Sears Roebuck and R. H. Macy. The largest American food retailer of that time, the Great Atlantic & Pacific Tea Company, tried to emulate these two. A&P's private labels were superior value. But the public refused to buy them, which all but destroyed A&P. Now private labels are flourishing.

What underlies this shift is information. Wal-Mart is built around information from the sales floor. Whenever a customer buys anything, the information goes directly—in "real time"—to the manufacturer's plant. It is automatically converted into a manufacturing schedule and into delivery instructions: when to ship, how to ship, and where to ship. Traditionally, 20 percent or 30 percent of the retail price went toward getting merchandise from the manufacturer's loading dock to the retailer's store—most of it for keeping inventory in *three* warehouses: the manufacturer's, the wholesaler's, and the retailer's. These costs are largely eliminated in the Wal-Mart system, which enables the company to undersell local competitors despite its generally high labor costs.

Source: Excerpted from Peter F. Drucker, "The Economy's Power Shift," *The Wall Street Journal*, September 24, 1992, p. A16.

THE STRUGGLE FOR MARKET ENTRY

As Drucker's appraisal indicates, manufacturers whose survival is based on their ability to get shelf space for their products from mass merchandisers face a considerable challenge. The shift of channel control to "power retailers" such as Wal-Mart, Kmart, Safeway, Kroger, and A&P is accelerating bidding wars in which powerful supermarket and mass merchandising organizations auction their retail shelf space to the highest bidder. The manufacturer that offers the lowest prices or grants the most generous promotional allowances gets the slot on the retailer's shelf. The cost to "buy" the slot is so high for many firms that they have little left in their budgets for other forms of promotion. This situation had gotten so serious that the president-CEO of Nabisco Foods Co., in a speech at the Food Marketing Institute show in 1989, said that the concentration of retail grocery trade power is intensifying so quickly that federal intervention may be necessary.[1]

Over the past three years, packaged food manufacturers have been fighting back by seeking distribution through superstores and deep discounters. This has hurt the traditional grocers so much that they are now seeking a peace treaty in their war with the manufacturers. Thus new forms of retail distribution, which better fill the needs of consumers, can rapidly change channel power relationships, as can be seen in Promotion in Action 13–1.

TECHNOLOGY AND THE POWER SHIFT

Certain resellers (a collective term for wholesalers and retailers) have increased their power in the channels of distribution relative to manufacturers because they have effectively utilized advances in information technology. Bar-code scanners,

Grocers Seek Peace Treaty in War with Manufacturers

Promotion in Action

13–1

The grocery store industry is bleeding—bright red, in fact. And at the [1992] Food Marketing Institute's (FMI) Supermarket Industry Convention . . . in Chicago, FMI trotted out its biggest guns, removed the firing mechanisms, threw up a white flag, and practically begged for a peace conference with manufacturers who are finding sweeter deals in the form of softer financial distribution resistance from other classes of trade—primarily superstores and deep discounters—that are stinging them severely in an already over-built, economically repressed marketplace.

In response, the grocery stores are offering warehouse club supersize packages, more services—including video departments—and more of the nutritionally right products from manufacturers that consumers are apparently asking for.

But most significant, grocers are asking for a peace conference with manufacturers. Mike Wright, chairman of Minneapolis-based Super Valu Stores and a longtime FMI friend and officer, called attention to the wrenching effect the deep discounters and superstores are having on traditional grocers.

He called for a restoration of "trust in this industry" through such a powwow with manufacturers, referring to coming to terms with each other on deals, items, prices, and terms, or slotting fees and promotional forward buying that have netted grocers big bucks from manufacturers, but now threatened by the new, less financially stressed distribution channels of discounters and superstores.

Where grocers once discounted superstore competition as insignificant, they are now at the point that Wright called them direct competitors, even in their bulk-purchase formats and asked manufacturers for equal access to the terms they have struck with the operators in this segment.

That calling for a peace process comes in the midst of absolutely horrid marketplace conditions for grocers. Their universe of 140,000 domestic stores is hindered by FMI research that shows decreases in average weekly grocery store expense per family and per person; same-store sales rates (sales at stores open long enough to have year-to-year comparisons); sales per labor hour (productivity per employee); and most other financial measures, nearly across the board.

In fact, about the only real positive news in an ailing economy for grocers is employment—the recession has made it easy to find employees, subsequently lowering turnover rates.

To support Wright's pleas and contentions, [Tim Hammonds, senior vice president of research at Washington based FMI] noted that superstores are further complicating the marketplace for grocers, with their increasing volumes and their particularly distressing—to grocers—propensity to attract shoppers more regularly, and at a phenomenal repeat rate.

Source: Excerpted from Howard Schlossberg, "Grocers Seek Peace Treaty in War with Manufacturers," *Marketing News*, June 8, 1992, pp. 16–17.

computerized inventory control systems, and microwave relays can collect and feed store information such as sales and product movement to headquarters at the speed of light. The power shift in favor of large resellers is based on the fact that they now have the ability to acquire and utilize market information that previously was available only to large manufacturers. Indeed, as Drucker notes, they use this information not only to design product specifications but also to arrange for product manufacture and distribution.

The new reality requires that producers of branded goods (and services) have a clear understanding of how the changes in manufacturer-reseller power relationships affect the task of promotion through the distributive channels. Without such an understanding, gaining meaningful promotional support from resellers will be increasingly difficult.

In this chapter, we try to analyze the promotional role that resellers play and attempt to provide some guidance as to manufacturer policy in an era of shifting power relationships.

THE PROMOTIONAL ROLE OF RESELLERS

The promotional strategy of a manufacturer is a blend of the elements of advertising, personal selling, and sales promotion aimed at attaining specific marketing objectives. Under certain product-market situations, the optimal blend of the promotional elements may allow only a small promotional role for resellers. For example, the selling of candy bars or razor blades may require heavy expenditures for consumer advertising and for gaining widespread availability and display at the point of sale. The manufacturer expects only that his or her myriad resellers stock the goods and keep them on display.

In contrast, the marketer of a new model of a top-of-the-line personal computer might require that an exclusive reseller in a given market call on potential business customers; provide leasing, training, and on-site repair services; and so forth. The promotional role of the reseller is considerably more complex under these circumstances.

In either case, the manufacturer concerned with gaining the needed support from the reseller organization must know what the role of these intermediaries is to be as a result of a given product-market strategy. Only with this information can the manufacturer evaluate the selling performance of wholesalers and retailers and consider ways to supplement or improve reseller performance.

The Impact of Manufacturer Promotional Strategy

Manufacturers often blame resellers for not being promotionally supportive. They do not realize that their own marketing strategies may discourage reseller effectiveness. For example, when manufacturers utilize multiple channels to reach various segments of the market, the manufacturers almost always increase the level of interchannel competition. One of the authors of this text, in a recent study, found that in the office furniture industry, many retailers resented manufacturer sales to end users on a direct basis or through architects and designers. Such resentments resulted in less enthusiastic support of these manufacturers' lines by retailers than of the lines of manufacturers who chose to sell only through the traditional dealer channel.[2]

In other situations, manufacturers who have created strong selective demand for their products may attempt to "pull" them through the channels with heavy investment in consumer advertising. Under this strategy, the reseller margins are slender and unless special promotional allowances are offered, the reseller will have little incentive to put much support behind the manufacturer's program other than to stock the item.

Manufacturers' pricing policies can also have an impact on the willingness and ability of resellers to engage in promotion of a specific brand or product. If the margin payment offered to the reseller does not cover the costs of doing the promotional job that the manufacturer requires, then the average reseller will cut back on his or her efforts.

Effects of Product Evolution

In addition to the effects of manufacturers' promotional strategy, we must also consider the changes in the promotional role of resellers as the product moves through its life cycle. Figure 13–1 illustrates some changes that occur as a hypothetical product moves through the key stages of its life cycle.

In the *introductory,* or *pioneering, stage,* the demand for the product with respect to price is generally more inelastic than in the later stages of development. However, the manufacturer must make a considerable investment in promotion in order to educate consumers about the existence and uses of the product. In the *competitive* stage of the cycle, the product is challenged by substitutes produced by other manufacturers. The selling task changes from stimulating primary demand to stimulating selective demand. Price becomes more important as cross-elasticity of demand (the sensitivity of demand for a product to changes in the prices of close substitutes) increases. The final phase of the cycle is the *mature,* or *commodity, stage.* When a product reaches the point at which market shares are relatively stabilized, where brand preference is low or nonexistent, and where price reductions will produce more profitable volume than will promotion, the product is said to have reached *maturity.* It has, indeed, become a commodity like salt, sugar, calcium chloride, or copper wire, and there is little need for promotion.

Introductory Stage   In the introductory stage of product marketing, a great deal of special selling effort is required to acquaint consumers with the new product type and to gain distribution at wholesale and retail levels. Some manufacturers sell directly to retailers in this stage, bypassing wholesalers until the need for special promotional effort has subsided. Other manufacturers use wholesalers but restrict distribution so that each wholesaler is willing to engage in the special selling required. Distribution at the retail level may also be on a highly selective basis to gain cooperation from individual retailers.

In those situations in which retail shelf space in supermarkets, mass merchandisers, and the like is needed, the role of the retailer is critical. Without "slotting" there is no availability to the market regardless of the attributes of the product. When introducing new products, manufacturers must direct most of their spending to trade promotion to gain reseller stocking and display.

Competitive Stage As products pass from the introductory stage to the competitive stage, manufacturers' promotional tasks change from building primary consumer demand and gaining access to trade channels to stimulating selective demand for their specific brands. When the product reaches this stage in its life cycle, manufacturers must recognize that wholesalers and retailers will require special incentives to continue promotional support. The reseller's task has changed from providing availability for a new product to routinely selling an established item. From the manufacturer's standpoint, unless selective demand for the product can be sustained through consumer advertising and sales promotion,

FIGURE 13–1

Promotional Strategy Changes over a Product Life Cycle

Product life cycle	Introductory stage	Competitive stage	Mature stage
Demand	Stimulate primary	Stimulate selective	Stimulate selective
Price	High	Lower	Lowest
Distribution	Sparse	Selective	Intensive
Consumer promotion	Educate consumers	Differentiate brand	Remind consumers
Trade promotion	Get resellers to stock and display	Gain reseller promotional support	Tie-in with reseller services

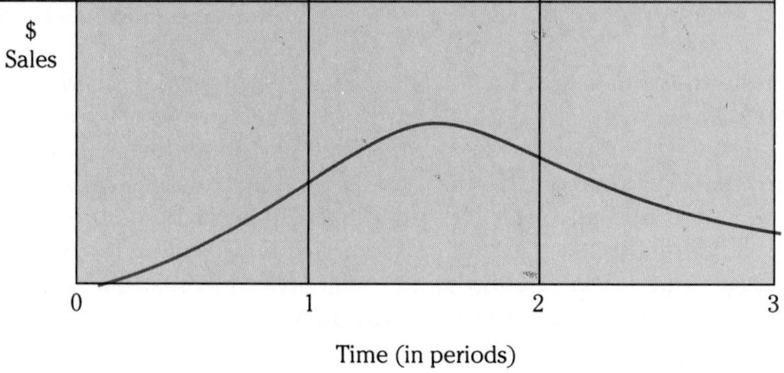

$ Sales

0   1   2   3

Time (in periods)

resellers will not continue to support it. For example, the new scanning technology will alert the retailer to a slowdown in shelf movement for a given product and thus make it a candidate for replacement. In the competitive stage, therefore, promotional spending is aimed at sustaining consumer demand to maintain shelf space and position. Of course, to stimulate reseller support, trade promotion must be continued but with less intensity than was the case in the introductory stage.

Mature Stage In the final stage of the life cycle, during which the product reaches maturity, brand preference weakens, physical variations among competing products narrow, and methods of production stabilize. In this stage, manufacturer strategy relies more on price than on nonprice means of promotion. As the price spread among competing brands in the same category narrows, the opportunities increase for wholesalers and retailers to sell on the basis of their own patronage appeals. Service, delivery, credit extension, and so forth become the reseller's important selling points. The manufacturer should use promotion to tie the product to the services offered by the resellers.

Implications of Reseller's Promotional Role

As we have said, when the selling role of wholesalers and retailers is at a minimum, they are usually concerned with little more than order taking. As elements of "push" strategy enter the mix, however, the aggregate selling resources of the reseller family become of considerable importance to the manufacturer's promotional program. This situation is especially prevalent when the product being sold is a higher-priced, high-involvement good such as a major household appliance. In this case, the reputation of the retailer may be of greater importance to the customer than the brand itself. Clearly, the rules of the game change when one is dealing with expensive, complex, and infrequently purchased products as contrasted with those that are relatively simple, low priced, and purchased frequently, such as packaged grocery products and health and beauty aids.

It is also important to note that the nature of the reseller's task can change from the normal order of requirements. If resellers are assigned some of the extraordinary selling activities required in the earlier stages of the maturity cycle, the manufacturer must be sure to offer extraordinary profit opportunities. On the other hand, if the product has matured, the manufacturer should recognize that the role of resellers in stimulating selective demand is limited. The wise manufacturer analyzes a promotional program to identify the selling task that *resellers might reasonably be expected to perform.* Only then is the manufacturer in a position to formulate policies for improving or supplementing reseller efforts.

When the manufacturer has a clear idea of the role its resellers can be expected to perform, given the overall promotional program, and when it understands the ways in which its other pricing, product, and distribution policies can influence wholesaler and retailer willingness and ability to sell, it can consider ways to improve or supplement reseller activities. With respect to *improving* the selling performance of wholesalers and retailers, the manufacturer can consider (1) training programs for reseller salespeople, (2) quotas for resellers, and (3) assistance to resellers with respect to their advertising and sales promotion efforts.

In terms of *supplementing* reseller activity, the manufacturer might consider (1) using missionary (specialty) salespeople, (2) providing display and selling aids, and (3) scheduling special sales and consumer deals.

Two means are suggested for *controlling* reseller activity: (1) the selection of resellers and (2) the vertical integration of reseller outlets through ownership or by means of contractual agreements.

IMPROVING RESELLER PERFORMANCE

Training Reseller Salespeople

One of the most effective methods by which manufacturers can improve reseller performance is to assume part of the responsibility for training wholesaler and retailer salespeople. One writer states bluntly, "Generally speaking you [the manufacturer] will benefit from your distributor relationships more or less in proportion to the effort you put into training the distributor's sales[people]."[3] A study made by the National Industrial Conference Board further affirmed the contention that training of dealer salespeople was profitable for manufacturers. It was found that well-trained reseller salespeople built goodwill for the manufacturer as well as for the dealer—by recommending the right product to satisfy the customer's needs and by keeping customers informed about the advantages and uses of new products. Moreover, well-trained dealers maintained more adequate inventories and had better service facilities than did untrained distributors. Finally, well-trained dealers required less of the manufacturer salespeople's time so that those persons could make more calls per day.[4]

Training at the Wholesale Level   Although the above generalizations about the value of training are valid for both wholesaler and retailer selling personnel, the objectives and scope of programs aimed at these two levels are different. The training programs at the wholesale level are intended to improve the salespeople's knowledge of the line and their selling techniques and often to train some to be management counselors for retailers. For example, one manufacturer of major household appliances has an extensive program to train the field representatives of its wholesale distributors. Courses held at the factory are given in such areas as product, business, and sales management; retail selling; handling used merchandise; service training; and general supervision of a sales territory. There is no charge for the courses, but the distributors must pay transportation and living expenses for their people in the program. Courses run for up to five and a half days, and the trainees are worked hard. Heavy emphasis is placed on visual aids, and after factory training, each distributor salesperson is equipped with a sound-film strip projector and a wide variety of training films. These films are made under factory supervision and are sold to distributors at production cost for use in their own training programs for retailer salespeople.

Thus, the objectives of a program to train wholesaler salespeople may be twofold—first, to provide them with knowledge about the product line and how it may be sold most effectively, and second, to prepare wholesaler salespeople to provide management assistance to retailers. This assistance may include training retailer sales personnel.

Regardless of the exact content of the manufacturer's training program, it is clear that a program for training wholesaler salespeople fills a gap that in many cases *cannot be filled by the wholesaler itself.* Because of either the pressures of day-to-day business or the lack of specialized sales management in smaller distributor organizations, many wholesalers will not or cannot do an adequate job of training, and the manufacturer can help perform this task. When the wholesaler does have training facilities and personnel, manufacturer assistance can make the program more effective and lighten the cost load.

Training at the Retail Level   Manufacturers' programs to train sales personnel at the retail level share many objectives with programs aimed at training wholesaler salespeople. Attempts are made to impart product knowledge to those who meet the public and to improve selling techniques. There are differences, however, because of the great dispersion at retail in terms of store size and location. A further complication is the stipulation of the Robinson-Patman Act requiring the manufacturer to offer promotional allowances or services (including those for training) to retailers on a "proportionally equal" basis. More is said about this requirement later in this chapter.

In spite of the difficulties in developing training programs for retailers, the manufacturer must take the initiative when high-quality retail selling is vital to success. For example, an association of mink breeders developed a promotional program encompassing both national advertising and point-of-sale activity. Unfortunately, the point-of-sale efforts were handicapped by a shortage of trained fur sales personnel. Moreover, even the larger retailers lacked the ability to develop a training program for their salespeople. To overcome this problem, the association developed a program to accomplish the following:

1. Make a retail sales force as competent in selling mink garments as they are in selling ordinary cloth garments.
2. Dispel doubts in the minds of sales personnel regarding the meaning and significance of the association label.
3. Remove the fear that surrounds the selling of fur garments.
4. Emphasize the association image of quality.

Nine stores agreed to participate in the first training session, which lasted three days and was held on the store premises. The association specialists conducted a class for the first 30 minutes of each day and then spent the rest of their time on the selling floor. The program was followed by the visit to each store from a "mystery shopper," who monitored sales procedures and offered suggestions for improvement.

In another situation, a manufacturer of fine English bone china distributed its line through 1,500 selected jewelry and department stores. Although serving a national market, the company sales volume could support only a relatively small appropriation of $400,000 for advertising and sales promotion. Research studies had shown that the retail salesperson was highly influential in the sale of china but were sadly lacking in product knowledge or awareness of the type of information consumers wanted from them. Moreover, retail sales personnel did not give the line much selling "push."

To improve the caliber of retail selling and to gain greater support for the product line, the manufacturer developed a program for training retail sales personnel. It consisted of a 20-minute sound film presented by manufacturer salespeople at meetings held for about 1,000 of their retail accounts. The film discussed fine china in general and was well received by sales personnel. To maintain continued contact with retail salespeople, the company developed a monthly sales bulletin providing product information, selling tips, and information about sales contests and informing retail salespeople of the national consumer advertising program.

These two examples of efforts to train retail sales personnel show that such a program is vital to the success of the manufacturer's promotional program when the product is such that the buyer must seek information and advice about it from the salesperson. In addition, it is clear that very few retailers have the means or the volition to initiate training programs for the sale of specific types of goods. Thus the manufacturer must assume the responsibility and the cost of training retail personnel if it desires an improvement in the quality and quantity of retail support. Moreover, this assumption of responsibility must be continuous because of the high rate of turnover of retail employees.

Quotas for Resellers

The establishment of quotas, if properly planned and administered, is a device that can improve reseller performance. Although the use of quotas to measure the performance of salespeople is quite common in a vertically integrated organization, the application of this technique to independent wholesalers and retailers is somewhat limited. One authority points out that

> not all sellers set quotas for their resellers. This results from one or more causes: failure to recognize that there is an underlying need to measure performance; difficulty in setting accurate quotas, especially where sales results may be far removed in time from sales effort, as for instance is often the case with the sale of costly industrial machinery; or lastly a realization of the inability to take any action if the quotas are not consistently met, as would be the case with the manufacturer whose product line would be of little importance to a reseller.[5]

An interview with officials of a home appliance manufacturer disclosed that quotas were used to measure the relative performance of independent wholesale distributors against sales branches. In addition, quotas were set for each sales division within the territory. Of course, in this situation, the manufacturer was granting exclusive agencies and could exert considerable influence in requiring distributors to meet quotas. Persistent failure to make the quota could well mean loss of franchise.

In cases in which the manufacturer's line is less important to resellers, the manufacturer's ability to encourage resellers to meet their quotas is weakened correspondingly. Even if the manufacturer cannot force distributors to meet quotas, however, the use of quotas to provide information on sales potentials can be a means to improve reseller performance. For example, the Atkins Saw Division of Borg-Warner Corporation offers its distributors a free market analysis of distributor territory. The purposes of this service are to aid distributors in accurate measurement of their sales performance, to help distributors establish quotas for retail dealers, and to get the resellers to work for a larger share of the available business.

Advertising and Sales Promotion Assistance

In addition to training reseller sales personnel and setting quotas for resellers, manufacturers can attempt to improve reseller efforts by assisting wholesalers and retailers in planning and executing their advertising and sales promotion programs. Such assistance may take the form of (1) cooperative advertising programs, (2) promotional allowances, (3) merchandising the advertising, (4) in-store promotions, and (5) contests and incentive payments for sales personnel.

Cooperative Advertising A program under which a manufacturer pays a portion of the reseller's local advertising costs is commonly called *cooperative advertising* (see Figure 13–2). Usually the manufacturer shares the cost of local reseller advertising on a 50–50 basis up to a certain limit, often a percentage of reseller purchases from the manufacturer. If, for example, the agreement specified a 50–50 share up to 4 percent of purchases, a retailer who had purchased $2,500 worth of goods from the manufacturer would be able to spend $200 on advertising them and would receive a $100 rebate from the manufacturer. Thus the net cost to the retailer would be $100.

An advantage of cooperative advertising to the reseller, in addition to the partial defrayal of the local advertising expense, is that under most programs the manufacturer furnishes a good assortment of advertising layouts and stereotype mats for reproduction in the local press.

There are also disadvantages for the reseller. First, there is a tendency to promote a line more than it deserves simply because the cost is being shared by the manufacturer. Moreover, the nature of the advertisements may stimulate selective demand for the manufacturer's brand without increasing the patronage appeal of the store. Finally, the expense and time needed to qualify for reimbursement may be discouraging. There are, however, independent agencies, such as the Advertising Checking Bureau of New York City, that can serve as a clearinghouse for co-op advertising documentation and manufacturer's payments.[6]

From the manufacturer's point of view, a well-planned cooperative advertising program can be useful. First, it involves the reseller financially. The wholesaler or retailer lays some money on the line to promote a given item. Even though the manufacturer matches the sum expended, the reseller has made an investment in promotion, and to protect its investment the wise reseller will make sure of three things: (1) that the stock of the item on hand is sufficient to back up the ad; (2) that the item (or items) receives adequate display at point of purchase and, perhaps, in the window; and (3) that the item (or items) advertised receives in-store selling support from the sales personnel. If a manufacturer's cooperative advertising program can get resellers to follow through in this manner, it is probably worth the trouble and cost of its administration.

For a more detailed view of a cooperative advertising program, we can look at one sponsored by the Palm Beach Company, a manufacturer of men's and women's summer-weight suits. In one year, for example, Palm Beach spent about $1 million for printed media advertising, with 60 percent of the budget for company advertising and 40 percent, or $400,000, for cooperative advertising with retailers. The bulk of the company advertising (80 percent) was placed in newspapers, with the remainder going to magazines and to trade advertising.

The cooperative advertising plan paid 50 percent of a retailer's cost for newspaper space, radio and TV commercial time, and billboard and car card space.

FIGURE 13–2

A Reseller-Oriented Promotion to Gain Dealer Use of Cooperative Advertising

2 column x 8"

Dealers could spend up to 4 percent of the net wholesale price of merchandise shipped to them, and they would be reimbursed up to a maximum of 2 percent.

Palm Beach required that the ads include proper product labels and descriptions and be devoted exclusively to the promotion of Palm Beach products.

The really interesting aspect of this program is the intensity with which the company promoted its cooperative program to the retail dealers. Strategy included the following:

1. A magazine-size booklet informing retailers of the Palm Beach line and promotional program for the coming year was mailed in the spring.

2. In addition, the retailer received a 17 × 25–inch cooperative advertising service book containing descriptive material, ad layouts, reproductions of available mats, and suggested radio scripts. Plates for four-color ads were also available at cost ($20 to $35) to retailers who wished to advertise in color.

3. The 50-person Palm Beach sales force devoted a major portion of its time talking to retailers about tying in their local promotion with the Palm Beach national campaign. The sales force also planned balanced promotional campaigns for retailers, including display, direct mail advertising, and newspaper advertising.

As a result of the program, Palm Beach reported that 65 percent of available cooperative advertising funds were used by retailers. Careful records were kept, and salespeople—as well as top executives—of the Palm Beach Company called on stores whose advertising usage was far below the potential permitted by their sales volume. Every attempt was made to convince those retailers to make full use of the cooperative advertising allowance.

The Palm Beach program illustrates a situation in which a high level of reseller support is vital in reaching the manufacturer's sales objectives. The manufacturer has placed a major emphasis on cooperative advertising to gain the reseller support required. Moreover, the program was carefully planned and coordinated with the national advertising campaign. To make certain that retailer participation in the program was as extensive as possible, the manufacturer engaged in considerable personal selling effort to get retailers to increase their advertising. Although there are these advantages to such a program, there also are real problems, which will be discussed later.

Promotional Allowances   In situations in which retail promotion is crucial to manufacturer success, payments may be made for types of reseller support other than media advertising. Such promotional allowances or payments are very often used to gain display at retail. Display is of great importance when the product sold is purchased on impulse or is unable to attract any "push" from retailers because of its limited contribution to overall retail profits.

The case history of Whitehall Laboratories, a well-known manufacturer of proprietary drugs, is a good illustration of the way one company attempted to improve reseller support for its products through the use of promotional allowances.[7] The company's line includes many well-known health and beauty aids, among which was the best-selling pain reliever Anacin. Whitehall spent several millions of dollars annually on national advertising. To supplement this heavy "pull" promotion, 100 salespersons called on retailers who carried health and beauty aids.

A research study had indicated that point-of-sale displays using about 2½ square feet of counter space were especially effective in increasing sales. The company embarked on a program to get as many retailers as possible to utilize the special display. The key to the program was an allowance to the retailer of 5 percent of its purchases if certain promotional activities were performed.

Whitehall faced two problems. First, competitors offered equivalent allowances (or in some cases, even higher allowances), and it was difficult to gain retailer support because of the tremendous demand for limited counter space. Second, most druggists took the 5 percent allowance, but not all followed through with the placement of the display. It was evident that some type of action was required to get drug retailers to participate in the display program and to make sure that they kept the display on the counter for as long as they were collecting the promotional allowance.

This case illustrates both the need of a manufacturer to gain display at retail and the difficulties faced in sustaining such support. The promotional allowance is one approach to gaining special retailer support, but to ensure its success, special payments have to be backed up by the manufacturer's sales force. In most cases, the competition for retailer display or advertising tie-in, as well as the general inertia of most retailers, required more than a mere payment. On the other hand, "push" (or the use of personal selling effort) by the manufacturer without special payment will not be as effective as "push" with a payment for special effort at retail.

Promotional allowances to the trade are not always used for promotion. Indeed, in the grocery industry it has been estimated that some retailing chains make up to one third of their profits from manufacturer promotional allowances meant for marketing. In addition, many chains stock up on manufacturer price specials, thus disrupting the manufacturer's production schedules and selling routines. In April 1992, Procter & Gamble changed its pricing policy in order to put an end to these abuses. P&G set lower wholesale prices on a wide range of products and at the same time cut back on the generous promotional allowances it offered to get retailers to stock up on its goods. See Promotion in Action 13–2.

By the fall of 1992, Colgate-Palmolive, Kraft General Foods, Chesebrough-Ponds, and Kimberly-Clark had followed suit. At the same time, P&G announced that it expected to save $175 million a year from its new pricing policy.[8]

Merchandising the Advertising   Have you ever gone into a store and asked to see a product that had been advertised recently on TV or in a magazine only to have been rebuffed by a salesperson who appeared not to know what you were talking about? Unfortunately, this experience is all too common. To prevent its recurrence, most manufacturers take considerable care to "merchandise the advertising." This is a process in which the manufacturer attempts to involve retailers

P&G Takes On the Supermarkets with Uniform Pricing

Using its enormous clout in the marketplace, the Procter & Gamble Company is taking a bold step to simplify the Byzantine system of American grocery pricing. Though the move could reduce the wild swings in consumer food prices, replacing them with what the industry calls "everyday low prices," it could also squeeze supermarket profit margins.

Throwing out its old price list on nearly half of its products over the last few months, Procter & Gamble has set lower wholesale prices on goods ranging from Jif peanut butter to Cascade dishwashing soap. But the savings have not made supermarkets happy. Procter & Gamble has also slashed the generous discounts it used to persuade grocers to stock up on its goods.

In the view of Procter & Gamble and many other packaged goods manufacturers, grocers have abused these so-called promotional allowances by stockpiling products on special—wreaking havoc with manufacturers' production schedules in the process. Over the last 10 years, grocers have spent millions of dollars to build warehouses solely to stock excess inventories of goods bought on special. Such buying practices have allowed them to go perhaps six months or more before reordering a product.

This Doesn't Happen Every Day

How Procter & Gamble's new pricing strategy might work for Dawn dishwashing liquid.

Old Pricing Strategy	New Pricing Strategy
Highlights:	Highlights:
Retailer buys 380 cases at the full suggested retail price of $1.56 a bottle, and 620 at the discount price of $0.82 a bottle.	Suggested retail price is cut by 22%, to $1.21.
Retailer only gives consumers a full discount on 500 cases.	Trade allowance, or discount given to retailers, is cut to $0.11 a bottle.
	Every bottle sold to retailers is discounted to $1.10.
Procter & Gamble sells:	Procter & Gamble sells:
380 cases for $14,227 ($1.56/bottle)	1,000 cases for $26,400 ($1.10/bottle, or $1.21 − discount)
620 cases for $12,202 ($1.56 − $0.74 allowance)	Gross: $26,400
Gross: $26,429	
Retailer sells:	Retailer sells:
500 cases for $11,880 (0.99/bottle)	1,000 cases for $31,680 (Averaging $1.32/bottle)
120 cases for $3,715 ($1.29/bottle)*	Gross: $31,680
380 cases for $17,237 ($1.89/bottle)†	
Gross: $32,832	
Consumer pays:	Consumer pays:
$1.37 (average price)	$1.32 (average price)

The bottom line: Procter & Gamble gets $29 *less;* the retailer gets $1,152 *less;* the consumer gets $0.05 *more.*

* The feature price, or the suggested promotional price.
† Suggested retail price plus 20% markup.

Sources: Kidder, Peabody and Jay Freedman, Lincoln Capital Management.

By removing the incentive for grocers to overstock, Procter & Gamble hopes to even out the retailers' order flow and its own production cycles. And it hopes that giving shoppers consistently lower prices will breed brand loyalty, making consumers less sensitive to the recurrent sales that have diluted such loyalties in recent years.

Not surprisingly, the program is being closely watched and quietly tested by many of Procter's rivals, including Kraft General Foods, the nation's largest food company. And the advertising industry is giddy over the prospect that a reduction in promotional spending might bring more money its way.

But the move could hurt supermarket chains, which have come to rely on promotional payments from manufacturers for profits. Though trade allowances were originally designed to give grocers flexibility in marketing a product, allowing them to decide, for instance, whether to discount or to spend on advertising to help move more product, many have simply pocketed the money. Analysts believe that some chains make up to a third of their profits from trade payments meant for marketing.

"There is a growing public discussion of the fact that the manufacturer sees very little of its promotional dollar reach the hands of the consumer," said Patrick L. Kiernan, senior vice president of the Grocery Manufacturers of America, Inc., a group of large food processors. The trade allowance is "the drug of choice in our industry," he added. "It has not helped the efficiency of the system."

Source: Excerpted from Eben Shapiro, "P&G Takes On the Supermarkets with Uniform Pricing," *The New York Times,* April 26, 1992, p. F5.

in the national ad campaign by making sure that they are aware of the campaign schedule and contents, and by having the manufacturer's sales force make sure that retailers are stocking and displaying the products being advertised. The manufacturer also provides retailers with in-store and window displays that tie in to the national campaign and arranges for special cooperative advertising or promotional allowances. The manufacturer provides product selling-point information to salespersons, and so forth. The goal is to create synergy in that the effect of the coordinated efforts of both the manufacturer and the retailer will be greater than if each party worked alone. If when you enter a store to see an advertised item and find that it is on display and that the salesperson is knowledgeable about its features, the advertising has been effectively "merchandised."

An approach to gain reseller support that does not use cooperative advertising or promotional allowances is shown in Figure 13–3. It is essentially a strategy in which the manufacturer attempts to create strong selective demand for the brand by means of a pull strategy using consumer advertising. The trade advertising that you see in this figure exhorts the retailer to merchandise the advertising with heavy in-store support to take full advantage of the manufacturer's efforts.

FIGURE 13–3

A Reseller-Oriented Sales Promotion Aimed at Merchandising the Advertising
of the Manufacturer

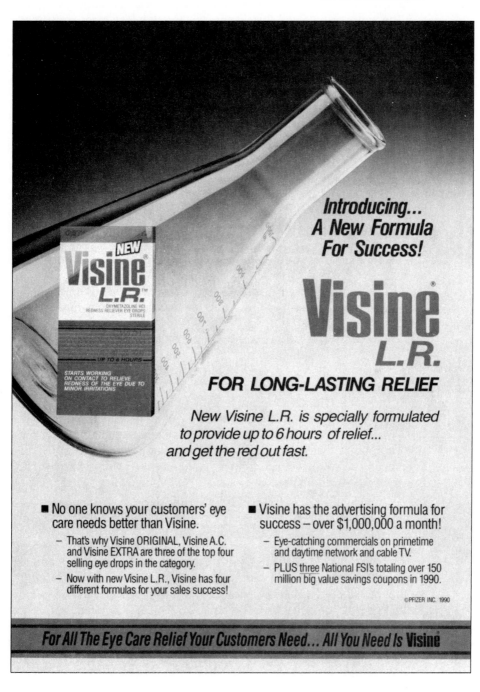

In-Store Promotions   Other types of manufacturer programs to improve reseller demand-stimulation efforts may be aimed at achieving limited objectives over a short period of time. An in-store promotion developed by a manufacturer of nickel (widely used in the manufacture of stainless steel) is a good example.

The sponsor believed that if demand for stainless steel consumer products could be increased, the derived demand for nickel would be stimulated. A program was planned around department stores because research indicated that they had the most powerful influence on consumer buying habits in the major market areas. The objectives of the program were (1) to spotlight stainless steel in the large stores, (2) to generate sales enthusiasm among retail sales personnel, and (3) to increase demand for stainless steel products and thus the derived demand for nickel.

The promotion was timed for February and was first run with 32 participating stores. Four-color, two-page ads were inserted in two leading shelter magazines in addition to local newspaper ads featuring the name of the cooperating department stores in each of 32 market cities. The stores ran 103 newspaper ads featuring stainless steel, and many devoted key window space to the display of stainless steel items. Several steel manufacturers supported the nickel producer's national advertising effort.

Retailer cooperation was gained by offering the campaign to each store on an exclusive basis in its area. Nominal cooperative advertising allowances were granted, and each retailer was provided with a complete promotional kit. Sales training sessions developed for retail personnel featured a nine-minute training film produced for this purpose.

The results were so favorable that the in-store promotion was continued for three more years. Modifications in the program were minor, but retailer and industry participation increased greatly in each succeeding year.

A similar type of effort on behalf of Hilton Hotels was the Hilton "Follow the Sun"campaign.[9] Tie-ins were made with airlines and with the leading retailers in 15 target areas. The campaign sought to relate the Hilton Hotels' vacation and honeymoon facilities to the bridal promotions of the retailers. The promotion was built around a contest in which registrants might win a free honeymoon in the Caribbean or Hawaii. The participating stores were given a format around which to develop their bridal promotions and also benefited from the store traffic generated by the chance to win a free honeymoon.

Regardless of the method used by the manufacturer, in-store promotion must offer the retailer a quid pro quo or it will not succeed. Few retailers will put themselves out to support a specific manufacturer unless doing so promises a reasonable payoff (see Figure 13–4.) Although an in-store promotion does offer a retailer a profit potential worthy of its effort, it must still be carefully planned by the manufacturer, and the execution of the program must be guided through to the end if best results are to be obtained. Once a manufacturer has concluded a successful in-store promotion on a modest scale, it is easier to expand the number of participants the next time it is run. Retailers have an effective grapevine that informs them on how their counterparts in other markets did with a specific promotion.

FIGURE 13–4

A Reseller-Oriented Sales Promotion Aimed at Getting In-Store Display

Contests and Incentives   To stimulate or improve the selling effort at retail, manufacturers may devise contests or provide special incentives for retail sales personnel. A contest or incentive plan is generally a part of a larger program and is aimed at motivating salespeople to participate in the selling campaign with enthusiasm. In the bone china case, for example, communication with the salesperson was established through the monthly sales bulletins. Shortly after the bulletin was first issued, it was used to announce a monthly contest based on the theme "How I Made a Bone China Sale." Prizes were awarded to salespeople who sent in the best letters each month. The grand prize was a trip to England. Retail salesperson participation in the contest, which served to focus attention on the overall promotional campaign aimed at gaining retailer support, was unusually high.

Contests or incentive payments developed by the manufacturer can get out of hand. If used too frequently, contests can cause the salesperson to be more concerned with a payoff for good sales performance than with the merits of the product line itself. Salespeople begin to sell items because *they*, rather than the customers, will profit most from the transaction. This attitude, which may give the manufacturer a temporary increase in volume, does not necessarily provide a lasting benefit unless the product itself is superior. Too many manufacturers use incentive payments and contests to push products that are inferior to those offered by competitors.

Moreover, contests and incentive payments for retail sales personnel may conflict with the desires and objectives of retail management. Some retailers refuse to allow their employees to participate in manufacturer-sponsored contests or to accept incentive payments from manufacturers because they want to maintain control over their own selling activities. For a manufacturer's program of contests or incentives to succeed, it must have the approval of retail management. The program should basically serve as an attention getter to interest salespeople in the product line and the overall promotional campaign. Finally, it should be viewed as a short-run effort to support the overall program, not as a long-run substitute for product attractiveness or utility.

Legal Problems and Other Issues

The manufacturer's use of cooperative advertising programs, promotional allowances, and other forms of assistance is not without its problems. Especially serious are restrictions imposed by law. Sections 2d and 2e of the Robinson-Patman Act have perhaps the most relevance to promotional allowances and services as granted by sellers to resellers.[10]

These sections of the act define, in rather loose terms, the conditions under which nondiscriminatory payments or services can be made to members of a reseller group. Such payments or services are legal if they are granted on a "proportionally equal" basis. That is, their dollar value must be in proportion to the size of the reseller's purchases from the seller. For example, a reseller buying $10,000 worth of goods a year from a manufacturer is entitled to 10 times the value of payments or services (received from the manufacturer) as the reseller whose purchases totaled only $1,000.

Moreover, the seller's program must allow participation by all interested resellers. The nature of the seller's promotional strategy must not exclude competing resellers on the basis of size, geographical location, or other characteristics.

Revised guidelines issued in 1969 required, among other things, that (1) all competing customers, whether wholesalers or retailers, must be informed of the availability of a co-op plan; (2) the plan must be "functionally available" to all competing resellers on proportionally equal terms and must include more than one way for resellers to participate; and (3) the advertising media cannot quote higher rates than are actually charged to allow customers to claim greater payments than they are entitled to under the co-op plan.

New Guidelines Released

In 1990, the Federal Trade Commission released new guidelines that revised the 21-year-old rules governing the use of promotional allowances, including cooperative advertising. The new guidelines make it less risky for a manufacturer to refuse to grant co-op ad allowances to a discount reseller who upsets the manufacturer's pattern of distribution. Another change deals with the concept of *proportionately equal.* In the past, this meant that differences in allowances granted to competing resellers had to be proportionately equal to the dollar volume of purchases by the resellers. That is, if one reseller bought $1,000 worth of goods from the manufacturer and another bought $500 worth of goods, the first reseller could receive promotional support from the manufacturer that cost twice as much as that granted the second reseller. Under the new rules, a new concept, *value to seller,* would modify the proportional rule. This means that a reseller offering exceptional opportunity for promotion or for market entry would be allowed to receive value-based promotional allowances that exceeded those allowed under the former cost-based proportionally equal rule.[11]

These changes are further discussed in Chapter 19. They will cause a great deal of debate and could lead to new tests of the Robinson-Patman Act itself.

SUPPLEMENTING RESELLER PERFORMANCE

In those situations in which *improving* the quality or quantity of reseller performance of selling activity does not succeed in reaching manufacturer promotional objectives, more direct action must be taken to *supplement* reseller effort. The manufacturer must assume some of the responsibility for selling and sales promotion at wholesale and retail levels. The utilization of missionary salespeople is one method of gaining greater activity at reseller levels in the channel of distribution. The provision of selling aids and the offer of consumer deals (or price deals) are other methods.

Missionary (Specialty) Selling

The use of manufacturer salespeople to supplement the personal selling activities of resellers is known as *missionary,* or *specialty, selling.* In the sale of consumer goods, missionary salespeople are employed by manufacturers to contact both wholesalers and retailers. They check wholesalers periodically to determine if they have adequate stock. They call on retailers to inform them of new products, to arrange window and in-store displays, to provide advice on selling, to answer questions posed by the retailer, and, in general, to build goodwill. If they take orders for merchandise, they usually turn such orders over to wholesalers for filling.

In the sale of industrial goods, missionary salespeople train distributor sales-people, demonstrate effective selling techniques by accompanying distributor salespeople on their calls, secure introductory orders from users, and assist distrib-utor salespeople in closing those sales that demand greater technical knowledge or selling skill than the distributor salesperson has.

On the other hand, the use of missionary salespeople is probably not wise when other elements of the promotional program are weak. Missionary selling is an expensive undertaking for any manufacturer, and its use to cover up deficiencies in the product or in the distribution, pricing, or promotion strategies can be an unnecessary financial burden. In addition, excessive dependency on missionary selling can generate wholesaler resentment. When missionaries assume tasks such as routine order taking or delivery that could be performed by wholesaler salespersons, the wholesaler may believe that it is just a short step to his or her total circumvention. Even if circumvention is not the issue, wholesalers may resent the missionary salespeople infringing on the time of their sales force and preventing the most effective allocation of their salespeople's time.

There is little doubt that the correct use of missionary or specialty selling can improve or supplement reseller selling efforts. The problems that arise with their use, however, are often caused by using missionaries to *supplant* reseller efforts where supplementation would suffice, or by poor management of the missionary selling effort. The net result of improper use of missionary selling, regardless of its cause, can be less reseller promotional support rather than more.

Display and Selling Aids

Manufacturers' provision of display material for point-of-purchase use, mailing pieces for reseller distribution, dealer identification signs, and similar incentives are other ways to supplement reseller efforts. A manufacturer uses these promo-tional devices to stimulate demand for the product and to get an increased share of the dealer's promotional effort placed at the manufacturer's disposal. (Promo-tion in Action 13–3 details the success of displays.)

The manufacturer usually has great difficulty, however, in getting resellers to utilize these display materials and selling aids. Based on the volume of material distributed to resellers, it appears that manufacturer response to nonuse of material is to double the quantity made available. Because resellers often do not know

Fox Z. Doodle Display Sells Cheese Snacks

To launch Doodle O's cheese snacks . . . , Borden Inc. shunned expensive television and print advertising and created instead 25,000 cardboard cutouts of an orange fox wearing sunglasses. The cartoonish mascot, dubbed Fox Z. Doodle, was part of a merchandise display that held 200 sample-size packages of the circular snacks. The gimmick was so effective that the displays had to be refilled daily, instead of on a weekly basis as planned.

The Doodle O's success story shows just how susceptible consumers are to the storehouse of merchandising tactics nearly every retailer relies on. Shoppers may come into a store with a shopping list, but they are more likely to grab a product off an eye-catching display than to scout out a brand on the shelves. And while manufacturers are paying retailers more and more for the privilege of mounting special displays, the cost can be well worth it.

How Product Displays Stack Up (Based on supermarket sales during the 13 weeks ended Sept. 13)

	% of Units Sold on Display	Increase in Unit Sales Due to Displays	Weeks on Display
Frozen dinners	3.5%	245%	5.8
Laundry detergent	9.4	207	6.7
Salty snacks	16.4	172	12.5
Carbonated soft drinks	20.8	138	12.9
Canned soup	1.7	101	2.6
Internal analgesics	4.2	96	7.2
Refrigerated orange juice	2.1	89	2.2
Deodorants	5.3	67	6.5
Toothpaste	10.0	64	8.6
Dog food	3.1	64	5.8
Disposable diapers	2.7	62	2.1

Source: Information Resources Inc.

Stacking laundry detergent on special displays increased supermarket sales of the product 207 percent during the 13 weeks ended September 13, [1992] according to Information Resources Inc.'s InfoScan service. In the same period, displays for frozen dinners were even more effective, resulting in a 245 percent sales increase. Meanwhile, displays helped increase sales of soft drinks by 138 percent. Other products that fly off displays: snack foods, apple juice, and cereal.

Source: Excerpted from Kathleen Deveny, "Displays Pay Off for Grocery Marketers," *The Wall Street Journal,* October 15, 1992, p. B1.

what to do with this great flood of material, it is not uncommon to find much of it in the refuse box in unopened cartons.

Several approaches are available to the manufacturer who requires some degree of product display or other cooperation from retailers. The payment of promotional allowances for display, the use of the sales force to obtain display and in-store promotion, and the practice of charging resellers a total payment for materials may help gain better point-of-sale display or selling effort.

Perhaps the most effective approach is that of pretesting dealer aids. An executive of General Foods reported the following:

> We made several field surveys . . . on the use to which our point-of-sale material was being put, and we reached some disappointing conclusions. We learned, for example, that on several campaigns last year, only half the material shipped out to the field was being used effectively. . . . It had not been checked with the field to predetermine its acceptance. We now have a continuous program . . . for periodic surveys of the grocery stores regularly contacted by our salesmen. . . . This system afforded us an accurate picture of the types and amounts of material which could best be used in these stores. . . . We are convinced that it is a waste of time, effort, and money to send point-of-purchase material to the field if we cannot demonstrate how it will work for the benefit of the store operator.[12]

The Whitehall case noted earlier illustrates the difficulties of using promotional allowances to gain point-of-sale display. Because research had indicated that a new type of display increased sales as much as 150 percent in those stores where it was used for a 60-day period, Whitehall developed a bonus plan for its salespeople. This plan could result in a salary increase of as much as one third for those salespeople who were able to get the stores in their territories to utilize the new point-of-sale displays. The extent of the payment to salespeople indicates the value of display to the company. This situation is of special interest because Whitehall was spending over $5 million annually, or 20 percent of sales, on national advertising. It appears, therefore, that even with extensive "pull," point-of-sale display is an important element of strategy.

Consumer Deals (Price Deals)

When the manufacturer wishes to blend price promotion into its promotional mix to increase sales at retail, it may offer the buyer a temporary price reduction. Such reductions are known as *consumer deals* or, more explicitly, *price deals.* Consumer deals differ from deals to the trade in that consumer deals attempt to create "pull," while trade incentives are aimed at getting reseller "push." Regardless of the target, a price deal is an attempt to exploit price sensitivity of demand. A study of the Chicago market provided the following information about price deals:

1. Off-season price reductions seem to be more profitable than in-season price reductions.

2. A high frequency of price promotions tends to make consumers overly price conscious.

☑ CHECK US OUT

CRAWFORD
CARGO MATES

CARGO RETAINING BAR

☑ **SERVICE**
- 100% FILL RATE
- 48 HOUR SHIPPING
- EDI READY
- PROVEN PERFORMANCE

☑ **ONE STOP SHOPPING**
- BROAD PRODUCT MIX
- CONSOLIDATE ORDERS
  SHIP WITH STORAGE
  & ORGANIZATION
    - SAVE FREIGHT
    - ONE INVOICE

☑ **QUALITY**
- HIGHEST STANDARDS
  IN THE CATEGORY
  AS DOCUMENTED BY
  INDEPENDENT TEST LABS

☑ **PACKAGING**
- BILINGUAL INSTRUCTIONS
  ENGLISH/SPANISH
- SPACE SAVING
  CLAMSHELLS
- IN USE ILLUSTRATIONS
  CONSUMER FRIENDLY

☑ **PRICE**
- HIGHEST VALUE
- LOWEST COST
- FAST TURNS
- HIGH GROSS MARGINS

☑ **CRAWFORD**

CRAWFORD PRODUCTS, INC
301 WINTER ST.
P.O. BOX 1215
WEST HANOVER, MA 02339

1-800-225-5832 (OUTSIDE MA)
617-826-8141 FAX: 617-826-4671

This company is marketing their product line to a reseller to gain in-store display and merchandising.

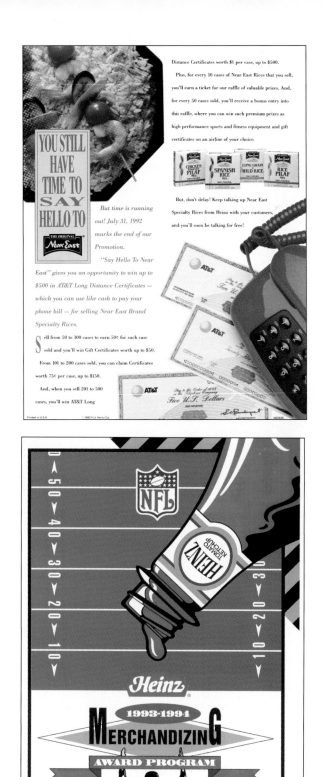

Heinz uses a number of programs to entice its resellers to feature its products.

CHOOSE ONE AWARD WHEN YOU BUILD A 10+ CASE DISPLAY OF HEINZ CHILI SAUCE
AND / OR HEINZ SEAFOOD COCKTAIL SAUCE IN ADDITION TO YOUR HEINZ HOMESTYLE GRAVY DISPLAY.

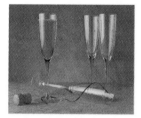

CHAMPAGNE FLUTES

*Enjoy the sparkle of your favorite
champagne in these handblown flutes.
This set of four is patterned after the
classic stemware designed for French
champagne. Made in Hungary
exclusively for Williams-Sonoma.*

SCROLL WINE RACK

*Display eight of your favorite wines
in this handwrought solid iron rack.
Attractive and functional design is
reminiscent of turn-of-the-century
French cafe furniture.*

CUISINART MINI PREP PROCESSOR

*This petite processor performs like the
larger models, yet requires no more
counter space than a half-gallon carton
of milk. Has a patented blade for chop-
ping small items like herbs and onions.*

CORNING THERMAL CARAFE

*You will always have something
hot to drink with this stainless steel
carafe. Keeps beverages hot up to
8 hours. Push button opens and
closes the spout.*

THE POWER OF SEIKO.

LET IT ENERGIZE YOUR:

- Sales Awards Programs
- Dealer Loaders
- Business Gifts
- Premiums
- Incentives
- Recognition Events
- Personalized Programs

AND REMEMBER: NOT EVERY SEIKO IS FOR YOUR WRIST.

YES, please have a salesperson contact me.
I am planning a program in ☐ 30 days.
☐ 60 days. ☐ 90 days.
☐ Yes, please send me a free Seiko Premium
Catalog including men's and ladies' watches
and clocks for future programs.

Name _____
Company _____ Title _____
Address _____
City _____ State _____ Zip _____
Telephone _____ / _____

Return to: SMM 9/92
    National Sales Manager
    Incentives and Awards
    Seiko Time
    1111 Macarthur Blvd.
    Mahwah, New Jersey 07430
    **For more information
    call 1-800-545-2783
    or fax your order to (201) 529-1248.**

SEIKO
THE FUTURE OF TIME

Circle No. 150 on Reader Service Card

A secondary market for many products is for use as sales premiums and incentives.

3. Deals do not seem to be a good way to counter new brands offered by competitors, and they are not necessarily more effective if accompanied by product or package innovations.

4. Price dealing is more effective for new brands than for established ones, and it is almost always more effective if kept in proper balance with advertising.

Study of Coupons Pits Manufacturers against Grocers

Promotion in Action

13-4

The following article appeared in *The Wall Street Journal* in May 1992:

CHICAGO—When does a penny add up to a $75 million dispute? When grocers and manufacturers disagree over how much it costs to process cents-off coupons.

For the past nine years, coupon-issuing companies have paid an average of eight cents to supermarkets and other retailers for handling each piece of discount paper turned in by consumers. Now a study by Arthur Anderson & Co., the accounting firm, indicates that a more realistic fee would be seven cents. The auditors' field work included videotaping check-out clerks at supermarkets to determine the average time spent per coupon: 6.8 seconds.

Last year, U.S. consumer redeemed an estimated 7.5 billion coupons for savings of an estimated $4 billion.

A hefty $75 million   One cent for every coupon redeemed thus would add up to a hefty $75 million. Big savings for manufacturers? A heavy hit to supermarket chains' bottom lines? Not so fast.

The survey results are scheduled to be made public today. But already, organizations representing manufacturers and grocers are putting different spins on those results. The Grocery Manufacturers of America Inc. applauds the survey as confirming that "the cost of handling coupons has fallen" by three-quarters of a cent since 1983. That, of course, means the group's members could save millions of dollars annually if grocers go along with the new figure. Last year, manufacturers paid distributors $596.8 million in fees for coupon handling.

Supermarkets' position   However, that possible savings may be wishful thinking. The Food Marketing Institute, which speaks for the supermarket trade, issued a news release saying that fee increases imposed by coupon clearinghouses after auditors had completed their work can't be ignored. The fee hike and lengthened payment periods for retailers, the supermarket organization argues, "leaves the situation now virtually identical with the cost estimate from the previous study."

Because of price-fixing laws, both sides are careful not to speculate on what their memberships might do with the new survey. But if a major manufacturer, such as Procter & Gamble, decides to start paying seven cents and a big supermarket chain balks, chaos could result.

The supermarket industry estimates that about 292 billion coupons are issued each year, resulting in a redemption rate of about 2.5 percent.

Source: "A Study of Coupons Pits Manufacturers against Grocers," Richard Gibson, *The Wall Street Journal,* May 15, 1992, p. B4.

5. No brand—not even a well-established, nondealing luxury brand—is invulnerable to price-deal competition if it has basic marketing problems, and price-deal promotion is never a cure for marketing problems.

6. When special promotional campaigns fall short of expectations, the manufacturer will do better to question its own planning and policy making than to blame the failure on "intractable" retailers.[13]

The last point above has special relevance to the stimulation of reseller performance because the use of price deals to buyers may hinder rather than help reseller cooperation. (See Promotion in Action 13–4 for a discussion of coupons.) Poor scheduling, inadequate trade incentives, excessive frequency of deals, and the like may cause wholesalers and retailers to rebel. Interviews with several retailers indicated, for example, that the pressure on grocery retailers to shift inventories back to the manufacturers has been increased in part by the extra confusion and expense caused by a multiplication of deal merchandise.[14]

CONTROLLING RESELLER PERFORMANCE

The control of reseller promotional performance is considerably more difficult for the manufacturer than is control of its own sales force. First, the chain of command that exists in an integrated organization is replaced with a relatively unstructured network of communication connecting the manufacturer with independent intermediaries. Through this network flows a series of suggestions and persuasion rather than commands. (Of course, the greater the selective demand for the products of a given manufacturer, the greater the weight the suggestions will carry with resellers.) Second, resellers are both geographically dispersed and operationally diverse. No two wholesalers (or retailers) are really alike because each serves the market in a unique manner in terms of location, assortments carried, and demand-stimulation mix used. The manufacturer's loss of direct authority due to passing the title of goods sold to the resellers plus reseller dispersion and diversity makes manufacturer control of reseller activities a most difficult undertaking under ordinary circumstances.

The degree of control over reseller performance that manufacturers can exert reflects the importance of the manufacturer's line to the individual wholesaler or retailer. When the manufacturer engages in highly selective or exclusive agency distribution and has limited market coverage to make its line more important to its selected resellers, some degree of control over these resellers may be expected.

Adapting to the New Environment

When a manufacturer requires the broad market coverage and strong promotional efforts offered by mass merchandisers, selectivity of distribution is not a feasible way to gain influence in the channel. This leaves the other alternative: Make the line as important as possible by developing a strong consumer franchise.

Recent evidence supports the view that the most effective way for manufacturers to resist the demands of mass-market resellers for slotting allowances and other "excessive" promotional payments is to build a strong selective demand for their brands through product quality and consumer promotion. Campbell Soup, for example, has a long-standing policy of not paying for slotting or shelf space.

Campbell Soup's director of promotion has stated, "We use good marketing programs to show why customers should stock our products, regardless of the size of the category or our position in it. We try to show that we are not flooding the market with products arbitrarily, and we do consumer research and product testing to back that up."[15]

CPC International, whose product line includes such strong brands as Skippy peanut butter and Mazola oil, has also turned down requests for payment.[16]

In other cases in which the will to resist is lacking or the brand franchise is weaker, manufacturers are trying to work out a compromise with their retail distributors. At the Pillsbury Company, the vice president of marketing reported that company strategy is to work with retailers to gain access to stores' scanning data. By analyzing space allocations and pricing points, Pillsbury can help retailers merchandise categories and increase profit per linear foot in a category. By doing so, Pillsbury gains leverage over how retailers stock and allocate their shelf space.[17]

To aid manufacturers and retailers in this type of analysis, computer shelf-management programs are becoming available (See Figure 13–5). Apollo Space

FIGURE 13–5

Effective Shelf Management Means More Profitable Sales

Management Systems and Space Man are two examples of such programs. Although such systems are helpful in the short run, practices that will eventually increase manufacturer channel influence are improving product quality noticeably, reducing the frequency of price promotions, and communicating the selling points of the brands more effectively to the consumer.

Selected Resellers

A *control process* consists of formulating standards of performance, measuring performance, comparing actual results with the standards, and then taking action to correct substandard performances. If resellers are selected wholesalers or retailers for the line of a given manufacturer, the basis for control may be in the franchise agreement. In situations in which the manufacturer's franchise is extremely valuable (as in the sale of automobiles), the reseller may contract to supply data on sales volume, inventory levels, and general operating expenses. Such information may be used by the manufacturer to measure reseller performance against a variety of standards. Commonly used criteria include share of market, sales growth over time, and reaching goals or quotas. In addition, attention may be given to size of sales force, expenditures of advertising and sales promotion, and similar items.

Once arrangements have been made to monitor the reseller's performance in a quantitative sense (hopefully within the franchise agreement), attention can be paid to the qualitative nature of reseller performance. This aspect of reseller control does not usually require a contractual arrangement. A perceptive manufacturer's salesperson can report on how resellers are using promotional materials furnished by the manufacturer and whether resellers have effective training programs for their sales personnel. Moreover, the manufacturer or an independent agency, such as the Advertising Checking Bureau, can audit the reseller's media advertising for control of cooperative advertising payments or to measure the support being given to the manufacturer's line. Similar checking may measure reseller activity in setting up point-of-sale display or in sponsoring demonstrations or special selling events.

Nonselected Resellers

When broad distribution through many resellers is required, the manufacturer's problem of control is intensified. There is a limit to what the manufacturer may expect from any one reseller in terms of furnishing data or following a specific recommendation to improve performance. The manufacturer becomes less concerned with the measurement and control of individual reseller performance and concentrates instead on the group performance of its resellers.

The manufacturer may attempt to classify the many resellers carrying its line by type of institution, location, size, ownership, and other criteria. Then a distribution cost analysis may be made to show the relative profitability to the manufacturer of different groups of resellers. One such study, made by a manufacturer of major electrical appliances, indicated the relative profitability of sales made through diverse channels of distribution and retail outlets. Thus, given a situation in which many resellers are used, measurement of reseller performance may help the manufacturer control *its utilization of specific groups of resellers* rather than the performance of individual resellers.

Some devices for the measurement and control of selected resellers can also be used with broad, intensive distribution. For example, a manufacturer's salespeople may arrange for retailer use of point-of-sale displays and then check back to see if displays have been properly placed. Such a program was seen in the case of Whitehall.

Manufacturers may also take elaborate steps to check on cooperative advertising efforts of resellers. Members of a special department or outside agencies can be used to supplement internal efforts.

Knowledge of the levels of reseller inventories is vital to many manufacturers who engage in intensive distribution through many resellers. Unable to use their salespeople to take shelf and storeroom counts of goods, the manufacturer may avail itself of the services of an independent research agency to collect data on how rapidly products are moving off the retailer's shelves.[18] Without such information, the manufacturer might mistake an inventory accumulation by resellers for steady or rising consumer demand for the line.

Vertical Integration

Because of the limits on the control that manufacturers can exert over independent intermediaries, many producers have chosen to vertically integrate their channels of distribution through ownership of either all or part of the channel intermediaries. Through ownership, the manufacturer gains maximum control over the manner in which its goods are physically distributed and promoted in all of the channel stages.

Vertical Integration by Means of Ownership   This can be a very expensive undertaking. Not only are the capital commitments enormous, but unless the producer's product line is broad and sales volume is high, unit distribution costs will generally be greater in this arrangement than with traditional channels. For those firms engaging in vertical integration by means of ownership, the higher costs of physical distribution are accepted as a trade-off against the higher levels of promotional activity and customer service that can be provided by closely controlled resellers. Firms such as Sherwin-Williams (paints), Hart, Schaffner and Marx (men's clothing), Goodyear (tires), and Florsheim (shoes), among others, have found that vertical integration has been an effective channel strategy.

Vertical Integration by Negotiation (Distribution Programming)   The vast majority of firms that do not have the economic capability to own their own resellers find themselves in an increasingly severe competitive struggle with their more integrated rivals. To counteract the advantages associated with vertical integration by ownership and to avoid having to make the needed financial commitments, many of these firms are adopting a strategy of *distribution programming,* in which an integrated marketing system is developed by contractual agreements between a manufacturer and members of the reseller organization.[19]

Development of a planned, professionally managed distribution system utilizing independent resellers enables manufacturers to increase the effectiveness and efficiency of their distribution activities. Distribution programming requires manufacturer-reseller agreement on a comprehensive set of policies for the promotion of a product through the channel. These policies are formulated by a joint effort between the manufacturer and the individual reseller in an attempt to negotiate a relationship giving both parties some of the advantages of vertical integration without the need for the manufacturer to purchase resellers.

Planned vertical marketing systems are rapidly displacing conventional marketing channels as the dominant mode of distribution in the U.S. economy. Planned systems are taking over because they avoid the loose relationships, autonomous behavior, and diseconomies associated with traditional channels of distribution. In addition, they do not require the capital investments associated with ownership systems. Yet these planned systems, which are professionally managed and centrally programmed networks preengineered to achieve operating economies and maximum market impact, can compete effectively with systems that are vertically integrated through partial or complete ownership of channel intermediaries.

Formulating a strategy   The first step in formulating a strategy of distribution programming is careful analysis of marketing goals and requirements of the manufacturer and the needs of retail (and wholesale) resellers. These goals and requirements are outlined in Table 13–1. Note that they can be stated in quantitative terms, thus eliminating the danger of misunderstanding during subsequent negotiations between a manufacturer and individual resellers.

After the completion of the analysis, specific distribution policies can be formulated. Although quite numerous, the policy alternatives generally fall into three major categories: (1) those that offer "price" concessions to resellers, (2) those that provide financial assistance to them, and (3) those that provide some form of protection for resellers.

Using the mix of distribution policy alternatives available, and based on the prior analysis of goals and requirements, a programmed merchandise agreement must be developed for each type of outlet used in the pattern of distribution. This agreement, the result of joint deliberation between the manufacturer and a reseller, is essentially a comprehensive plan to distribute and promote the producer's product line for a period of six months or longer. An outline of such an agreement is found in Table 13–2. Its completeness is of special interest.

Subsidiary plans   After a clear delineation of quantitatively measurable goals, the agreement focuses on plans for inventory requirements, merchandise presentation, personal selling, and advertising and sales promotion. Finally, the responsibilities of both parties are enumerated, together with a schedule of dates on which certain performances are due.

Programmed merchandising agreements are fairly widespread in the following product categories: garden supplies, major appliances, traffic appliances, bedding, sportswear, cosmetics, and housewares. Manufacturers that use programmed merchandising include General Electric (on major and traffic appliances), Baumritter (on its line of Ethan Allen furniture in nonfranchised outlets), Sealy (on its Posturepedic line of mattresses), Scott (on its lawn-care products), and Villager (on its dress and sportswear lines).

SUMMARY

Manufacturers' policies developed from diverse marketing strategies influence the role of resellers in the overall promotional program. Since personal selling activities make up the largest portion of promotional activity at wholesale and retail levels (with the exception of self-service stores), the maximum use of reseller potential can be made when the manufacturer emphasizes a push strategy. Regardless of the selling activity expected, if the *quality* of the selling performance by wholesalers and retailers is less than is desired by the manufacturer, the manufacturer may lend assistance to *improve* reseller performance.

TABLE 13–1

A Frame of Reference for Distribution Programming

Manufacturer's Marketing Goals	Retailer's Requirements
Based on a careful analysis of:	"Compensation" expected for required support
Corporate capability	(stated in terms of):
Competition	Managerial aspirations
Demand	Trade preferences
Cost-volume relationships	Financial goals
Legal considerations	Rate of inventory turnover
Reseller capability	Rate of return on investment
and stated in terms of:	Gross margin (dollars and percent)
Sales (dollars and units)	Contributions to overhead (dollars and percent)
Market share	Gross margin and contribution to overhead per
Contribution to overhead	dollar invested in inventory
Rate of return on investment	Gross margin and contribution to overhead per
Customer attitude, preference, and "readiness-	unit of space
to-buy" indices	Nonfinancial goals
Manufacturer's Channel Requirements	Distribution Policies
Reseller support needed to achieve marketing goals	Price concessions
(stated in terms of):	Financial assistance
Coverage ratio	Protective provisions
Amount and location of display space	
Level and composition of inventory investment	
Service capability and standards	
Advertising, sales promotion, and personal selling	
support	
Market development activities	

Source: From *Vertical Marketing Systems,* edited by Louis P. Bucklin. Copyright © 1970 by Scott, Foresman and Company. Reprinted by permission of the publisher.

Training programs for reseller salespersons seem to be one effective way in which manufacturers can upgrade the wholesaler personal selling effort. Such assistance is especially desirable when the product sold requires demonstration, installation, or a high degree of technical competence on the part of the reseller salesperson. Training is not recommended in cases in which the volume potential of the manufacturer's line is small in relation to the costs involved in setting up a suitable program.

Providing market information beyond what the reseller unit can gather for itself seems to help it allocate its selling efforts more effectively. Such information can point out where sales opportunities are not being exploited and how the reseller's performance measures up against that of other members of the reseller organization.

TABLE 13–2

Outline of a Programmed Merchandising Agreement

1. Merchandising Goals
   a. Planned sales
   b. Planned initial markup percentage
   c. Planned reductions, including planned markdowns, shortages, and discounts
   d. Planned gross margin
   e. Planned expense ratio (optional)
   f. Planned profit margin (optional)
2. Inventory Plan
   a. Planned rate of inventory turnover
   b. Planned merchandise assortments, including basic or model stock plans
   c. Formalized "never out" lists
   d. Desired mix of promotional versus regular merchandise
3. Merchandise Presentation Plan
   a. Recommended store fixtures
   b. Space allocation plan
   c. Visual merchandising plan
   d. Needed promotional materials, including point-of-purchase displays, consumer literature, and price signs
4. Personal Selling Plan
   a. Recommended sales presentations
   b. Sales training plan
   c. Special incentive arrangements, including "spiffs," salesmen's contests, and related activities
5. Advertising and Sales Promotion Plan
   a. Advertising and sales promotion budget
   b. Media schedule
   c. Copy themes for major campaigns and promotions
   d. Special sales events
6. Responsibilities and Due Dates
   a. Supplier's responsibilities in connection with the plan
   b. Retailer's responsibilities in connection with the plan

Source: From *Vertical Marketing Systems,* edited by Louis P. Bucklin. Copyright © 1970 by Scott, Foresman and Company. Reprinted by permission of the publisher.

If the *quantity* of reseller effort is less than is deemed necessary to achieve manufacturer objectives, assistance may be provided in the form of missionary salespeople. These manufacturer efforts have as their objective the *supplementation* of reseller activity. When carefully supervised, such assistance can greatly increase the extent of sales effort aimed at wholesaler customers.

Under appropriate conditions, cooperative advertising programs are a very effective form of advertising assistance. They are especially helpful when, as with selected distribution, it is necessary to identify local retail sources of supply. Further, by getting distributors to invest their own funds in the local promotion of the manufacturer's brand, cooperative advertising programs may predispose resellers to carry better assortments of stock and to push the products advertised.

Manufacturer contributions that help resellers to do a better selling job themselves or encourage reseller promotion, such as display material or special deals, must be carefully integrated into the overall strategy, with special attention being paid to making these aids or deals fit the requirements of the resellers.

The manufacturer must be careful not to attempt to supplement wholesaler performance when efforts to improve it would suffice. Otherwise, the manufacturer will incur unnecessarily large promotional costs. Conversely, if additional selling effort is needed at the wholesale or retail level, manufacturer programs to improve the quality of current reseller performance will probably not fill the gap.

Manufacturer efforts to supplement or improve reseller performance may grow to take over functions typically considered to be reseller functions. Such shifting should not be permitted by the manufacturer unless analysis and experimentation indicate that efforts to supplement or improve reseller performance will not do the job. The manufacturer's assumption of tasks historically performed by wholesalers and retailers may suggest that it is considering their ultimate circumvention. The reseller that harbors such a suspicion is not likely to offer its selling support willingly.

The control of promotional activities by the manufacturer is much easier when control is under the manufacturer's direct supervision. The same is true with manufacturer control of the sales force. Control becomes more difficult when the effort is that of independent intermediaries who have purchased the manufacturer's product line for resale. Regardless of the degree of difficulty involved, the control process in either case is identical and consists of setting standards, measuring performance in light of these standards, and taking corrective action when actual performance is substandard.

The extent of control over resellers is a function of the importance of the manufacturer's line to them. Thus efforts to create selective demand through advertising or to reduce intrachannel rivalry by means of selective distribution should result in heightened manufacturer ability to control reseller efforts. If resellers are uncooperative for one reason or another, the manufacturer may use independent specialists to check on their performance. The manufacturer can always control its own channel strategy by careful selection of resellers, even if it cannot control their individual performance.

If a level of control is needed beyond that which can be expected from independent channel intermediaries, the manufacturer may engage in partial or complete ownership of its resellers. Because of the long-term financial commitments associated with vertical integration through ownership, an increasingly utilized alternative is vertical marketing integration by means of contractual relationships between manufacturers and individual resellers. The resulting distribution system provides many of the advantages of a system owned by the manufacturer without requiring a heavy investment in ownership. It also preserves the independence of the intermediary and allows the intermediary to provide the distributive economies that result from carrying the lines of several manufacturing sources.

REVIEW AND DISCUSSION QUESTIONS

1. As a manufacturer of high-speed cutting tools that are sold to the auto industry, you are very dissatisfied with the amount of promotional support that you are getting from your industrial distributors. Why might it be a mistake to place all of the blame on the distributors for the lack of support? What should your first step be in trying to rectify this lack of promotional effort on the part of your distributors?

2. The Johnson Company manufacturers car telephones. When the product first came into being, Johnson set up a group of exclusive dealers in 30 key territories. These dealers received generous margins and were expected to engage in a great deal of "push" effort at the retail level. Recently, Johnson has noticed that similar products are showing up in a variety of outlets, including discount houses, and are being heavily advertised at a price much lower than that of its product. What is going on here? Is this normal? What should Johnson do?

3. ABC Food Products is trying to get distribution through the leading supermarket chains for its new frozen dessert, Koolcake. Formerly, a new product introduction required some free goods and special promotional allowances. Now ABC has been asked by one chain for an up-front payment of $2,500 per store for handling the new product. What is happening? Can ABC do anything to gain distribution without paying the slotting allowance?

4. Radio Ham, a manufacturer of amateur radio transmitting equipment, is complaining that the salespeople at the retail level do not know how to sell its products. It insists that the retailers train their personnel better. The retailers are telling Radio Ham that they have 200 other manufacturers to worry about and that Radio Ham will just have to do the best it can with what the retailers offer.

   Suggest a course of action for Radio Ham that might help ameliorate the problem. Why does the responsibility to take the initiative fall largely on Radio Ham in such a situation?

5. Imagine that you are a consultant to the Nadir Radio and TV Company, which manufactures radios and TV sets for sale to the public through a network of selected dealers. Nadir has been dissatisfied with the support it receives from its dealers. You are recommending increased use of cooperative advertising as a means to improve the extent and quality of reseller promotion. Explain how co-op advertising can be helpful to Nadir.

6. Your boss has asked for your opinion as to increasing control over retail distribution and promotion by means of distribution programming. How would you explain distribution programming, and what would you tell the boss about the pros and cons of its implementation?

NOTES

1. Judann Dagnoli and Julie Liesse Erickson, "Grocery Retailers Get Tougher," *Advertising Age,* May 15, 1989, p. 4.

2. Martin R. Warshaw, C. Merle Crawford, and Robert M. Tank, "Resolving Channel Conflicts in the Office Furniture Industry," *Business Marketing* 70 (March 1985), pp. 106–16.

3. Carl C. Gauk, "Training the Distributor's Salesmen," *Development of Dealer and Distributor Cooperation for Greater Sales,* Marketing Series no. 80 (New York: American Management Association), p. 4.

4. E. F. Higgins and J. F. Forgarty, Jr., *Training Dealers*, Studies in Business Policy no. 48 (New York: The Conference Board) p. 4.

5. Harry L. Hansen, *Marketing: Text and Cases*, 4th ed. (Homewood, Ill.: Richard D. Irwin, 1977), p. 475.

6. Robert D. Wilcox, "Co-op Advertising: Getting Your Money's Worth," *Sales & Marketing Management* 143, no. 5 (May 1991), pp. 64–68.

7. Hansen, *Marketing*, p. 475.

8. Eben Shapiro, "P&G Sees Big Savings in Price Plan," *New York Times*, October 14, 1992, p. C4.

9. Hansen, *Marketing*, pp. 615–17.

10. Public Law no. 92, 74th Cong., H.R. 8442, June 19, 1936.

11. Isadore Barmash, "FTC Plans Rule Change on Co-op Ads," *New York Times*, February 13, 1989, p. D13.

12. W. P. Lillard, "Point-of-Purchase Promotion," *Proceedings, 6th Annual Advertising and Sales Promotion Conference*, Ohio State University Publications, College of Commerce Conference Series No. C-65, pp. 55–57.

13. Charles L. Hinkle, "The Strategy of Price Deals," *Harvard Business Review* 43 (July-August 1965), pp. 75–85.

14. Ibid., p. 82.

15. Rebecca Fannin, "Bring a Bag of Money," *Marketing & Media Decisions* 22 (June 1987), pp. 38–45.

16. Ibid., p. 45.

17. Ibid.

18. The A. C. Nielsen Company's retail store audit is the best known of these approaches.

19. This section is based on an excellent article by Bert McCammon, Jr., "Perspectives for Distribution Programing," in *Vertical Marketing Systems*, ed. Louis P. Bucklin (Glenview, Ill.: Scott, Foresman, 1970), pp. 32–50.

Management of Consumer Sales Promotion

CBS AND KMART TEAM TO DELIVER SAMPLE PACKS TO CONSUMERS

Contrary to reports that the CBS–Kmart marketing partnership is winding down, the No. 1 TV network and second-largest retailer are teaming up this fall for a new series of promotions that will run at least into 1994.

The effort, dubbed the "CBS–Kmart Premiere Value Pack," will be the first product sampling program ever launched by a major TV network.

Recently, CBS shifted the focus of its fall promotion to a major effort tying in with Nabisco Biscuit Co. brands. The partnership fueled speculation that the relationship between CBS and Kmart was waning.

Although Nabisco is the focal point of the promotion, Kmart's 2,300 stores will play a supporting role. The retailer will provide signage and in-store displays of the CBS/Nabisco promotion, dubbed "America's Favorites."

Nabisco and Planters LifeSavers Co. are also the first brands to sign on to the separate CBS/Kmart value pack sample promotion.

CBS executives declined to comment on the project. But in a joint letter sent to key promotion industry executives last week, CBS Senior VP-Marketing and Communications George Schweitzer and Kmart VP-Sales Promotion Dave Schuvie invited marketers to participate.

Under the program, 2 million sample packs will be distributed in Kmart stores. Kmart will promote the sample packs in-store and via its Sept. 13 circular, which will reach 68 million consumers.

Sample packs will be distributed to the first 2 million customers redeeming coupons found inside the Kmart circulars, industry executives say.

The sample packs will have program graphics promoting CBS' prime-time shows, and the network will air 100 gross rating points of promotion time during the fall premiere week to generate viewer awareness.

Marketers participating in the value pack will pay between $120,000 and $280,000, depending on whether they place a sample item, a coupon or a combination of the two in the packs.

Although it's unclear how many products will participate, CBS and Kmart are guaranteeing category exclusivity.

CBS and Kmart are expected to launch at least two more promotion efforts during the 1992–93 season that are designed to promote traffic in Kmart stores and viewing of CBS shows.

It's unclear whether those projects will also involve advertiser tie-ins, but CBS has been trying to develop a family of marketing partnerships.

Teaming Kmart and Nabisco this fall is one example; CBS also teamed Kmart with Coca-Cola Co., Visa International and Walt Disney Co. in its 1991–92 promotion and often mixes complementary advertisers in its mall tour promotions.

Source: Joe Mandeso, "New Promos Fuel CBS–Kmart Linkup," *Advertising Age*, May 25, 1992, pp. 1 and 51.

Sales promotion has been defined by the American Marketing Association as encompassing "those marketing activities, other than personal selling, advertising, and publicity that stimulate consumer purchasing and dealer effectiveness,"[1] and "as media and nonmedia marketing pressure applied for a predetermined, limited period of time at the consumer, retailer, or wholesaler in order to stimulate trial, increased consumer demand or improved product availability."[2]

These activities occupy a gray area between advertising and personal selling, possessing characteristics of each promotional tool. For example, if a premium were to be offered to induce buyers to try a new product and the offer was made in an advertisement in a national magazine, how would you classify the activity? A well-accepted view is that the premium offer would be a sales promotion because of its nonrecurrent nature and because it was aimed at stimulating consumer demand *in the short run*. The communication of the offer itself in the national medium would be advertising.

We see in the CBS–Kmart example in the chapter opener the utilization of two specific consumer promotion techniques: coupons and samples of products. In an integrated marketing communications program, these consumer promotions are often utilized with the trade promotion activities discussed in Chapter 13. Note also that this campaign is integrated with advertising activity and tied to a channel institution in order to have synergistic impact. This chapter presents a discussion of various consumer promotion techniques.

SCOPE AND IMPORTANCE OF CONSUMER SALES PROMOTION

Consumer sales promotion has been one of the most exciting areas in the promotional strategy field over the last decade. No text can truly capture this dynamic. Consumer sales promotion includes product sampling, coupons, cents-off offers, refunds and rebates, contests and sweepstakes, and premiums.

Figure 14–1 conceptualizes the relationship between the consumer promotion techniques to be discussed in this chapter and the trade-directed promotional activity discussed in Chapter 13. They are all designed to affect the end consumer, either directly (pull) or indirectly through the actions of the channel members (push).

Expenditure on consumer promotion reached a high of $30 billion in 1985 but declined to $25 billion by 1988. Expenditures jumped to $27 billion in 1989, fell to $25 billion in 1990, and have risen to $26 billion in 1991 and to $28 billion in 1992.[3]

Sales promotions are becoming such a popular marketing tool that some packaged goods giants are beginning to worry about the long-term effect they may have on brand loyalty.[4] The intense competition for retail shelf space and the desire on the part of brand managers to show quick gains in market share have had a snowball effect on promotional campaigns. Companies keep offering more coupons, bigger rebates, and more valuable sweepstakes prizes in an effort to draw customers from the competition.

This marketing approach neglects the brand images that some manufacturers have spent decades developing through advertising. "It's much easier to just give people a cents-off coupon so they'll buy your product instead of the next guy's,"

FIGURE 14–1

Relationship between Consumer and Channel Directed Promotion

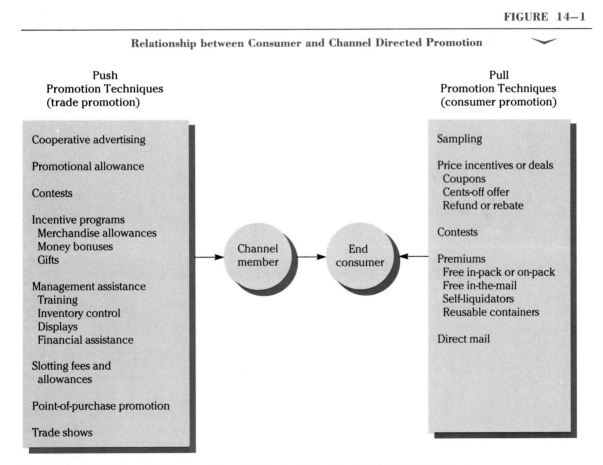

Source: Adapted from Thomas C. Kinnear and Kenneth L. Bernhardt, *Principles of Marketing*, 3rd ed. (Glenview, Ill.: Scott Foresman/Little Brown, 1990), p. 522.

says David Hurwitt, marketing vice president at General Foods Corp. "Then he'll give even more cents off next month, you respond, and the war goes on."

Advertisers are disturbed by this trend toward more expensive promotions. They are also worried that consumers are starting to take promotions for granted. When automakers offer rebates, their sales go up; when the rebate ends, sales drop while potential car buyers wait for the next round of rebates to start.

Companies also fear that heavy couponing, which represents a significant proportion of all sales promotion, is evaporating brand loyalty and turning retail brands into commodities. Some customers may not buy their usual brand if they don't have cents-off coupons for it. Marketers have also noticed an increasing tendency among shoppers who don't use coupons to simply buy the cheapest brand in the store.

Experts believe that to avoid these problems, companies will have to adjust the way promotions are being used. They say that promotions should be a part of an integrated marketing plan, supporting and enhancing product image and advertising.

One of the reasons that this potential excessive use of consumer promotions exists is that brand managers who are looking to have quick success are aware that promotions can produce quick jumps in market share. According to Lou Houk, vice president of the Chicago sales promotion agency Frankel & Co., these marketers concentrate on getting immediate results instead of thinking about long-term strategy.

"New brand managers come in and say, 'What can I do to make a mark?'" explains Houk. "They can't fool around with the advertising too much because of bureaucracy and because the system is already in place. But they know if they put a consumer promotion together, all of a sudden market share will move."

Sales promotions are also usually cheaper than advertising, and their results are more easily identifiable. For example, a major national TV advertising campaign may target 50 percent of the households in the country at a minimum cost of $2 million. A promotional campaign using coupon inserts can reach as many households for only $1.25 million, and the effectiveness of the campaign can easily be determined by the number of coupons redeemed.

In any given year, the range of consumer promotions utilized by consumer goods companies is approximately as follows:[5] coupons, 91 to 95 percent; sampling new products, 60 to 78 percent; sampling established products, 35 to 75 percent; refunds and rebates, 80 to 85 percent; cents-off, 65 to 78 percent; contests, 30 to 55 percent; sweepstakes, 65 to 78 percent; and premium offers, 55 to 82 percent.

CONSUMER PROMOTION ALTERNATIVES

The remainder of this chapter discusses the major consumer promotion techniques listed in Figure 14–1.

Sampling

Consumer sampling is an effective but rather costly means of introducing a new product. As a technique, it is probably used more by large firms that produce broad lines of packaged consumer food or health-and-beauty items and engage in extensive advertising and personal selling on a national basis. When used as part of a coordinated promotional campaign to introduce a new product, the catalytic effect of sampling on trial usage and subsequent repurchase can be sufficiently strong to more than defray the expense of sampling.

Distribution   The physical distribution of the sample either to resellers for redistribution to consumers or directly to consumers is a formidable task. Mail, house-to-house private delivery, distribution at point of purchase, and inclusion in the package of another product are some of the ways suggested to get the sample into the hands of the prospective customer.

There is little doubt that providing a free sample can break through the noise level and stimulate a higher rate of trial than can other promotional efforts. Such trial is not gained without the expenditure of a good deal of money, and unless the trials translate into repurchase, the sampling promotion cannot be deemed a success. Repurchase data may not be available for several weeks after initial distribution of samples and even if repurchase rates are high, it is difficult to determine how much influence the sampling promotion had on market results. What might be in order at this point would be a postintroduction market survey to determine how consumers were influenced to buy. Agree shampoo reached a leadership position in the market within six months of introduction and eventually obtained over a 20 percent share of the market by using mass sampling. Over 31 million samples were distributed.

Promotion in Action 14–1 illustrates some of the logistical dynamics and power of sampling.

Sampling Corporation of America Gears up for Halloween

Promotion in Action

14-1

Sampling Corporation of America strives to "distribute samples and coupons in an environment that will maximize their usage and reinforce the brand name and existence." The Glenview, Illinois–based promotion company has conducted a special Halloween program for the past eight years. In honor of the holiday, millions of schoolchildren are given costumes, paper jack-o'-lanterns, and bright orange, black, and white plastic bags stuffed with coupons and product samples. Treats for their parents? Sampling and its customers think so.

The eye-catching orange, white, and black plastic bags feature a variety of Halloween figures intermingled with the logos of the participating brands. The real treats are inside: reflective safety stickers (for the kids to put on their costumes while trick-or-treating); a safety poster; a booklet for parents containing safety tips and ideas for simple costumes, makeup, and party games; and, of course, the coupons and product samples. Product samples usually include candy, snacks, an aseptically packaged juice box, and sometimes toothpaste.

Sampling Corporation distributes these Halloween bags free to local schools and school districts. Most schools hand out the sampling bags in conjunction with a safety speech given by a teacher or police officer. The National Safety Council lends its support as well. Bob O'Brien, director, public relations for the Chicago-based council, asserted that "our community safety department looked over the materials and made a number of recommendations on the safety advice. The idea of getting the message into the parents' hands is very valuable and we just don't have the horsepower to get into those households." This tie-in with holiday safety lends credibility to Sampling Corporation's program.

Do parents actually take the time to examine the bag's contents and read through the booklet? According to Cincinnati's Burke Market Research, the answer for most families is yes. For one participating brand, both brand awareness and total advertising awareness increased by 40 percentage points—mainly due to unaided awareness. Brand usage increased 35 percentage points and actual purchases of the brand increased by 20 percentage points. The packages' coupons were a great success as well, with 17 percent of consumers using them and 65 percent planning to do so in the future.

According to Stephen Kaplan, executive vice president, Sampling "can do something that major brands can't do for themselves. We can get products and coupons home to parents through the schools." An increasing number of well-known companies are using Sampling to do just that. Eighty percent of each year's participants are repeat customers. This year's samples include Kraft Handi-Snacks, Candilicious, and Del Monte Fruit Cup.

Best Foods, marketer of Karo corn syrup, found Sampling's program to be a great fit with its own marketing strategy. For several years, Karo had been trying to convince parents that Karo is a good medium for Halloween makeup; it's safer than masks, fun, and inexpensive. Jim Coyle, director-promotion planning for Best Foods, admitted, "It would have been difficult to communicate that usage [as makeup] directly to the user. We felt that if kids were sold [on the makeup idea], then they'd take it home to mom and dad." Sampling's Halloween promotion provided a great vehicle.

Sampling's growth is another mark of its success. The company now distributes its Halloween sample bags to 10 million 6- to 12-year-olds, covering half the country's households with children in that age group. A similar program is being developed for summer safety. Sampling's revenues of $5.5 million for the 1992 fiscal year are up $450,000 from 1986. Revenues for 1995 are projected at $8 million.

Source: "Promo Dresses Up for Halloween," *Advertising Age,* November 16, 1987, pp. S-12–14. Updated to 1992 by discussion with industry experts.

Purpose of Sampling   In other situations, sampling may not do the job. Customers will either disregard the sample or use it without switching their patronage. There can be many explanations for such a failure, but the first hypothesis that should be investigated is that the consumer could find no demonstrable difference in the new product that would motivate him or her to buy it. Sampling is most effective when the key attributes setting the new product apart from its competitors are difficult to describe adequately in print or visual media. Scent, taste, consistency, balance, and the like are selling points that can be effectively communicated by sampling.

On occasion, sampling will be used for other reasons. There have been some attempts to revive the sales of a slumping product, but the distribution of the sample rarely reverses the downturn. The cause most often lies in some marketing deficiency that should be remedied first. Also, some large firms use sampling as a defensive weapon to blunt the attempts of competitors to introduce new products through this means. Procter & Gamble, in particular, has utilized this strategy for decades, and its continuing domination in many product classes attests to the influence of its marketing muscle.

Generally, the advertiser will not undertake the sampling effort but will retain one of the variety of service firms in this field. One of the largest is the Reuben H. Donnelley Corporation, which distributes samples through mass mailings, handouts, or door drops. It also is possible to confine distribution to more selective audiences through Welcome Wagon and other specialized service firms.

Price Incentives

The use of a short-term reduction in price to encourage trial use of a new product or to stimulate demand for an established product is referred to as offering a *consumer deal.* Such deals are most frequently communicated to consumers by means of coupons and cents-off promotions. Figure 14–2 illustrates a deal in which the consumer can obtain a price reduction by presenting the coupons to the retailer at time of purchase. The coupon and cents-off promotions are used to stimulate further consumer response in the short run.

A somewhat different approach is shown in Figure 14–3. Here we see a price reduction of two thirds of the retail value of the item being offered to those customers who will send the coupon together with payment directly to the manufacturer.

The objective of all of these sales promotions is to increase product trial among prospective customers. The best results are obtained in those product categories in which the rate of repurchase due to brand loyalty is low. Where brand loyalty is high, small price differences are unlikely to overcome the perceived advantage of remaining with a preferred brand. In the first place, brand switching is often seen as having a high degree of perceived risk, with the result that the psychological cost of trying an unknown brand is too high. Furthermore, a price-induced trial may last for only one purchase, and basic brand preferences may remain unchanged. Usually when loyalty is high, relatively large price reductions will be required.

There is always the danger that offering consumer deals will become the standard competitive tool, in which case no competitor really benefits. All engage in it for mostly defensive reasons, and the consumer will wisely adopt the strategy of purchasing the brand that offers the best deal at that time. No competitor really can gain differential advantage under these circumstances.

The consumer deal will most likely succeed under these conditions:

1. When the manufacturer has used the price incentive only infrequently and at widely spaced intervals.

2. When the manufacturer avoids dealing as a strategy to force the retailer to stock in hopes of offsetting acceptance of a price offer by a competing brand.

3. When the brand is relatively new.

4. When deals are not used as a substitute for advertising.

At all costs, deals should be avoided as a cure-all for declining sales. An ever present tendency is to resort to the price incentive when the real problem lies elsewhere in deficiencies in the marketing mix. Careful analysis must be undertaken before embarking on this strategy—to ascertain that there is a favorable probability of increasing brand loyalty. Often this requires an actual market test. Great care must also be taken to maintain normal advertising support, and the trade must be approached in such a way that its cooperation is both solicited and maintained. The result otherwise may be a financially abortive strategy or, even worse, the triggering of unnecessary and ruinous competitive warfare.

FIGURE 14–2

A Consumer Cents-Off Deal Implemented by a Coupon Included in a Magazine Advertisement for Redemption by the Retailer

**A Consumer-Oriented Price Reduction Deal Implemented by a Coupon in a Magazine
with Redemption and Delivery of Merchandise by the Manufacturer**

THIS PAGE IS WORTH $4.00

Take $4.00 from the regular $5.95* price of Hanes Alive® support pantyhose. And what do you get?

A darn good bargain for only $1.95. Why are we doing this? Because we believe that once you wear Alive, you'll find they look so good and make your legs feel so much better, that you'll never want to wear anything else. And that's what we're counting on.

How to get it.

We'll send you our most popular color, Barely There,* (same as in photograph) in our most popular style. Just fill in the form below and send it with check or money order for $1.95 payable to HANES HOSIERY, INC. P.O. Box 847, Rural Hall, N.C. 27045. Allow 4 to 8 weeks for delivery.

Orders cannot be filled for women under 4' 10" and 95 lbs. or over 5' 10" and 170 lbs.

NAME _____

ADDRESS_____

CITY_____ STATE_____

PHONE #_____ ZIP_____

HEIGHT Ft _____ In _____

WEIGHT _____
            H46

Please do not send cash through mail. Offer valid with use of this form only and must include zip code. Limit one per family. Duplicates voided by computer. Offer expires June 30, 1978. Void where prohibited or otherwise restricted.
*Suggested retail price.

Hanes Alive Support.
Some women are more alive than others.

©1974 Hanes Hosiery Inc

Concerns about reducing brand equity and brand loyalty have resulted in some manufacturers attempting to replace excessive dealing with everyday low prices (EDLP). Procter & Gamble has been the most active in implementing this concept at both the trade and consumer levels. Refer back to Promotion in Action 13–2 (p. 359) for an extensive discussion of this approach at the trade level. At this time, the EDLP approach has not resulted in a decrease in money spent in aggregate on consumer sales promotion. Indeed, there has been expenditure growth over the last two years, as noted earlier.

Couponing

The use of coupons as a means of sales promotion is very closely associated with price incentives. In fact, coupons are the major medium by which the manufacturer offers the consumer a price deal. If redeemed at a retail store, the coupon is used by the retailer and the wholesaler to gain reimbursement from the manufacturer.

The use of coupons as a means of consumer sales promotion has increased dramatically over the last few decades and shows all signs of continuing to do so, despite ongoing forecasts of coupon saturation. In 1962, 5.3 billion coupons were distributed. This number grew to 90.6 billion in 1980, 163.2 billion in 1984, 221.7 billion in 1988, 292 billion in 1991, and about 330 billion in 1992. In 1991 and 1992, consumers redeemed about 7.5 billion and 8.3 billion coupons, respectively. The average face value of redeemed coupons was 54 cents in 1991 and 59 cents in 1992.[6]

The popularity of coupons is based on several advantages associated with their use. First, the use of coupons limits the price reduction to those customers who are sensitive to the price deal. All of the other customers continue to pay the regular price. Second, coupons enable the manufacturer to specify the time frame for the promotion. This enables coordination with other activities in the promotional mix. In addition, the time limit induces more immediate response from consumers. Third, since many products are losing their distinctiveness, the coupon offer may give the manufacturer something with which to develop a selective demand for a brand.

Distribution   Coupons are distributed to consumers in a variety of ways. Free-standing inserts (FSIs), which are leaflets of coupons inserted into a newspaper, constituted 79.6 percent of distribution in 1991, down from 79.9 percent in 1990. Newspapers remained steady from 1990 to 1991 at 5.3 percent of 1991 coupons, and magazines did the same at 2.3 percent. Direct mail accounted for 5 percent in 1990 and 4 percent in 1991. Coupons on or in packages represented 3.5 percent in 1990 and 3.8 percent in 1991. One significant trend in coupon distribution has been the in-store distribution of coupons at the shelf or at the checkout. This category of distribution was very small a decade ago but now represents about 5 percent of distribution, up from 3.9 percent in 1990.[7] Redemption rates vary substantially by type of distribution. FSI redemption rates are about 3 percent, while direct mail redemption rates are about 5 percent, in-package about 13 percent, on-package about 33 percent, and in-store approaches almost 100 percent.[8]

Cost The cost of using a specific medium must, of course, be considered in relation to both the coverage offered and the redemptions expected. In addition, the financial liability associated with redemption of coupons seems to occur with differing time lags, depending on the medium used. Nielsen research indicates that "newspaper offers redeem faster than either pop-up or on-page magazine coupons; and pop-up magazine offers come in faster than on-page magazine coupons."[9]

In order to compare various coupon plans and distribution alternatives, many companies calculate the estimated cost per redeemed coupon. Since the redemption rates and distribution costs vary by method, each method will have a different cost per coupon. Table 14–1 presents a procedure for calculating these costs.

On average, cost per coupon redeemed is estimated to be newspapers run-of-paper solo, 55 cents; newspaper co-op, 37 cents; Sunday supplements, 75 cents; magazine on-page, 72 cents; magazine pop-up, 78 cents; and direct mail, 59 cents.

Although the couponing that we have been discussing in this chapter is consumer-oriented promotion, it is obvious that those strategies that require redemption at point of purchase cannot be executed without the cooperation of the retailers and wholesalers in the channel of distribution. The process of receipt of the coupons, their redemption, and subsequent submission to the manufacturer for repayment is costly. Although most retailers receive a payment of about 8 cents per coupon handled, many complain that coupons cause more delay, expense, and general trouble than they are worth. The wise manufacturer makes certain that it

TABLE 14–1

	Cost per Coupon Redeemed: An Illustration
1. Distribution cost 10,000,000 circulation × $8/M	$ 80,000
2. Redemptions at 3.1%	310,000
3. Redemption cost 310,000 redemptions × $.25 face value	$ 77,500
4. Handling cost 310,000 redemptions × $.08	$ 24,800
5. Total program cost Items 1 + 3 + 4	$182,300
6. Cost per coupon redeemed Cost divided by redemptions	58.8¢
7. Actual product sold on redemption (misredemption estimated at 20%) 310,000 × 80%	248,000
8. Cost per product moved Program cost divided by product sold	73.5¢

Source: Updated to 1993 by the authors from Louis J. Haugh, "How Coupons Measure Up," *Advertising Age,* June 8, 1981, p. 58. Reprinted with permission. Copyright Crain Communications, Inc. all rights reserved.

doesn't overdo the use of coupons and that resellers are adequately compensated for their efforts when a coupon deal is used.

On the other hand, very often retailers are found to have engaged in misredemption practices in which customers are given some monetary benefit when they have not bought the product. This is a cost that must be considered—see Table 14–1.

The cost to manufacturers for the misredemption and the fraudulent redemption of coupons is estimated to be about $1 billion per year. Promotion in Action 14–2 describes four types of scams that are all too common in the coupon business.

Premiums

A *premium* is the offer of some type of merchandise or service either free or at a bargain price to induce purchase of another product or service offering. Although premium promotions vary greatly, their principal purpose is quite specific: to

---

Promotion in Action

14–2

The Coupon Scams

The Fake Storefront

A scam artist rents space cheap, sets up a store, then starts sending in coupons to manufacturers for payment. Pretty soon the store's shelves are bare, but the "owner" is still sending in coupons he has obtained illegally.

Stuffing the Ballot Box

A retailer legitimately obtains cash from clearinghouses and manufacturers for all the coupons handed in by shoppers. But he boosts his take illegally by sending in extra coupons purchased at steep discounts from various sources, such as unscrupulous printers.

Playing the Middleman

An ambitious operator can make money supplying other operators—by collecting coupons by the pound and selling them to retailers, buying and selling proofs of purchase, or counterfeiting coupons and proofs of purchase.

The Redemption Scam

Manufacturers offer big cash rebates on large items to shoppers who mail in forms, together with proofs of purchase—receipts, labels, or box tops. A con artist uses the rebate forms and proofs of purchase, either real or counterfeit, to illicitly collect the refunds without buying the products.

Source: Coupon Information Center; U.S. Postal Service; and "Coupon Scams Are Clipping Companies," *Business Week*, June 15, 1992, p. 110.

induce consumers to change the brands or amount purchased. The goal may be to switch consumers from their present brand to that of the promoter in order to gain trial use, with hopes of repeat purchase. Or the goal may be to induce present customers to increase their use of the brand or to purchase it in larger-sized packages. Premium promotions are effective in that they appeal to the very human desire to get a bargain. Their widespread use is shown in industry figures indicating that firms engaged in the supply and distribution of premiums grossed over $18 billion annually. However, the overuse of premiums is a concern in some industries.

Effective promotion planners do not first choose a premium and then develop their creative strategy—they develop their creative strategy and then choose a premium that "fits" their overall program. Several recent cases exemplify this principle. Using a two-page spread in a Sunday newspaper supplement, Carnation's Friskies pet food offered dog and cat owners five cents-off coupons and a "$36 value" pet-care grooming kit for only $9.95 with proofs of purchase. Kimberly Clark's Huggies diapers came up with yet another unique infant premium—the first national premium offer of a tape cassette of "personalized" lullabies produced by Playskool. A Valassis freestanding ad offered a $1 Huggies coupon and a free personalized tape for 24 proofs of purchase. Another example was a character premium that has become a nationally recognized symbol: the California Raisins. The popular three-inch raisin figures were available for just 99¢ with a proof of purchase from any package of California raisins.[10]

Premiums may be classified in terms of whether they are offered free or are to some extent self-liquidating (see Figure 14–4). In the latter case, the customer pays an extra amount that covers the manufacturer's out-of-pocket costs. Recent evidence indicates that with self-liquidating premium offers, consumers are less concerned with the amount they are required to pay than with whether or not they will be getting a bargain. One of the most successful self-liquidating premium offers was the Kool Cigarette promotion that offered a sailboat for $88 with the enclosure of 10 empty packages as proof of purchase. Over 20,000 customers ordered this premium.

Free premiums may range from toys offered for cereal box tops to towels packed in boxes of detergent. The item offered is carefully selected and often pretested to ensure that it will be sufficiently appealing to induce purchase. In most cases, the premium offered is not directly related to the main product, as would be the case in a combination offer promotion. The ratio of free to self-liquidating premiums is about 55 percent to 45 percent.

Delivery and Redemption of Premiums   Premium promotions differ by mode of delivery or redemption. The most widely used mode is the "free-in-the-mail" approach. The offer is communicated to the consumer by coupons or by media advertising. Requests for the free premium are mailed to the manufacturer or to a premium redemption specialist where they are processed and deliveries are arranged. This process is quite expensive.

The alternative strategy of placing the premium in or on the package of the basic product simplifies premium delivery and stimulates interest at point of sale.

The on-packaging premium has become increasingly popular as technology has enabled the use of blister or bubble packaging. With a blister pack, for example, the premium can be placed next to the main product without fear of detachment and loss. Yet the plastic packaging material allows the premium to be seen at point of purchase, thus stimulating consumer reaction. Of course, the use of the in- or on-pack modes of delivery requires the support of the resellers. They must buy the promotional packs and display them so that they will be available when the national advertising communicates the promotion to the public. Closely associated with on-pack promotion is the use of the package itself as a premium. This topic will be discussed in the section on packaging.

The use of premiums is effective in gaining short-run trial use. However, unless the product offers a distinctive advantage to the consumer, trial use will not translate into repeat purchase. In that case, the premium promotion is simply

---

FIGURE 14—4

Example of a Self-Liquidating Premium Offer

providing a temporary boost to product sales. A better strategy would be to divert some of the promotional resources to product development activities.

Packages as Premiums   Packages can be used as premiums. Instant coffee packed in containers that can be used as servers, cookies packed in jars that can be reused, and the like are examples of how packages themselves can be used as a form of premium promotion.

Contests and Sweepstakes

Promotional activities that involve consumers in the advertising and merchandising activities of the manufacturer by gaining their participation in games of skill or chance are known respectively as *contests* (see Figure 14–5) and *sweepstakes* (see Figure 14–6). In comparison to other means of sales promotion, contests and sweepstakes are considered to be potentially as strong as the strongest premium offer (in-pack) and stronger than the weakest premium offer (self-liquidating).

A contest requires that the participant apply a skill in creating an idea, a concept, or an end product. Contests have been based on suggesting the best name for a new product or new uses for established products, or, as in the case of the Pillsbury Bake-Off Contest, on creating and utilizing recipes to produce outstanding baked goods. In contrast, sweepstakes are games of chance in which each participant has an equal chance of winning a prize from a rather extensive and expensive list of rewards. Care must be taken to prevent the sweepstakes from being considered a lottery, which is illegal in many states. Judicial review has indicated that the requirement that a sweepstakes entrant buy the manufacturer's product is not a "consideration" that would make the event a lottery. Even so, most firms that use sweepstakes allow contestants to use facsimiles of the box top or coupon as well as the real thing.

Contests and sweepstakes have many advantages, including their ability to gain a high degree of consumer involvement in the manufacturer's advertising and merchandising program. In addition, they can help gain support from resellers and often add excitement or interest to a lagging product or advertising theme.

A well-conceived and well-run contest can have major benefit to the marketer. Consider the case of Eagle Food Centers.[11] Based in Milan, Illinois, Eagle Food Centers ran a highly successful campaign from April 15 to June 3. This campaign, "The Search for Eagle Kids," invited customers with children between the ages of 5 and 12 to describe why their child was the "perfect Eagle Kid" in 50 words or less. The prize for each of the 10 winning Eagle Kids was a $1,000 savings bond and an opportunity to appear in an Eagle print ad and TV commercial.

The Eagle Kid contest directly appealed to parents in Eagle stores' retail area, which included 105 stores in Illinois, Indiana, and Iowa. Colorful signs and point-of-purchase displays supported the contest in-store. Window displays and "aisle danglers" featured cartoons depicting potential Eagle Kids. Each region designated special "Kid Days" when all children who visited Eagle stores received Eagle Kids balloons, buttons, bumper stickers, shoelaces, license plates, and refreshments.

FIGURE 14–5

Example of a Contest Promotion

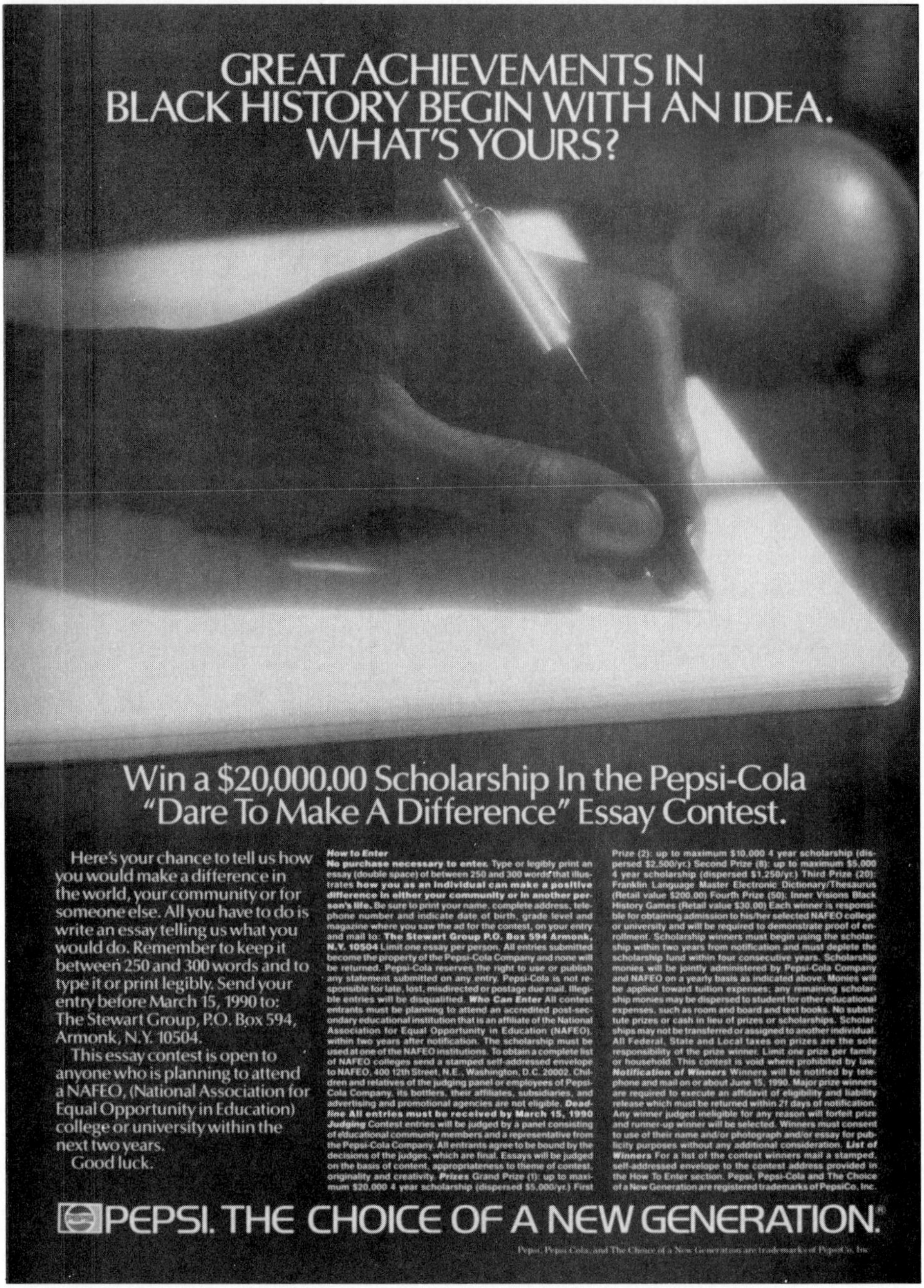

"Kid Days" promoted the contest while generating awareness and support for local stores.

Customers were definitely aware. Phone calls poured in asking for additional information and inside advice on what type of photograph to send. Ray Myers, Eagle's ad vice president, stressed that the Eagle Kids campaign was not a beauty contest: "We tried to avoid 'professional' children, hoping to give recognition to kids who represented a true cross-mix of our customers' families."

The contest was a great success. Eagle Foods received over 2,500 entries during the eight-week contest. The 10 winners were chosen throughout Eagle's marketing area. The end result was a diverse collection of children. The winning ad featured the Eagle Kids riding on a school bus while a voice-over described how children represent our future. Only subtle references were made to the Eagle promotion. According to Myers, Eagle Foods is "convinced this type of marketing effort helps us broaden our customer base and strengthens our positioning of the new Eagle Foods among this very important market segment." Jonathan Blum, general manager at Ogilvy & Mather Public Relations, Chicago, believes that the success of the Eagle Foods contest and other similar marketing campaigns by

FIGURE 14-6

Example of a Sweepstakes Promotion

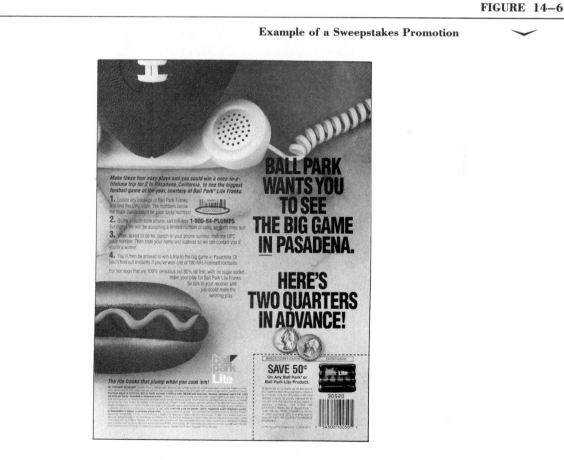

grocery retailers makes creative, family-oriented promotions a good bet for the future.

Sweepstakes are increasingly popular vehicles for increasing consumer loyalty and creating excitement in the marketplace.[12] A significant segment of the market believes that advertisements and cents-off coupons pale in comparison to free trips and automobiles. According to Charles Visich, a former marketing consultant and present senior vice president at Southland Corp., product promotion has turned into a giant lottery: "People are developing a pot-of-gold-at-the-end-of-the-rainbow mentality." Jeff Conner, product manager for Heinz Ketchup, remarked, "The prizes are getting larger because people are desensitized to the small things. If you want to get their attention, you have to offer them something exciting."

The growing popularity and social acceptance of state lotteries gets credit for a lot of "contest fever." According to Visich, "Whenever somebody wins $23 million, it makes people who have never won anything think twice. The winners are glamorized on television. Society is telling us it's okay to participate." And thousands of consumers do participate in sweepstakes each year.

Sweepstakes have several advantages from a marketing point of view. As Visich points out, "The value of a 50-cent coupon is known in advance. But if I offer a trip to Hawaii, the incentive is much more exciting." Mailboxes full of junk mail and the seemingly endless parade of television commercials make it hard for manufacturers to make their products stand out. But Joe Namath offering tickets to a major football game is an attention-getter.

Companies often choose prizes for their promotional sweepstakes that tie in with their products. Pine-Sol disinfectant, which is marketed as a complete household cleaner, came up with the idea of giving away a free house. Pine-Sol's "Whole House" Sweepstakes awarded $250,000 in mortgage payments to its lucky winner. GE Lighting offered a free family vacation to Walt Disney World to see *Illumni-Nations,* GE's magnificent light display at Disney's Epcot Center. Prizes like these attract consumer attention.

A supermarket survey conducted by the Point-of-Purchase Advertising Institute found that two thirds of all purchase decisions are made by customers in the store. This indicates that strong in-store display support is crucial for product success. As a result, separate sweepstakes are often set up for store employees to encourage more elaborate point-of-purchase displays. Although some companies require nothing more from employees than a mail-in card, others require photos of attractive displays. According to John Beh, national sales manager for GE Lighting, "Offering a contest where store managers can be rewarded for building special in-store displays drives additional volume." Prizes are sometimes given as reductions in merchandise costs so that the entire winning store gets credit.

Manufacturers win other benefits by going the sweepstakes route. An average of 3.2 percent of all supermarket coupons is redeemed today. Thousands enter sweepstakes, yet few are big winners. And sweepstakes are less expensive than giving stores straight cash merchandising allowances. Some prizes that have commercial tie-ins promoting a specific airline or hotel are special bargains. As one supermarket executive remarked. "That trip may be worth $5,000, but it may not cost the sponsor a dime. Think of the advertising impact to seeing the words

'Disney World' in 23,000 supermarkets nationwide. That has great commercial value." Even the manufacturers are lured by the offer of "something for nothing."

The use of contests and sweepstakes is not without its hazards. The folklore of marketing has many stories of contests and sweepstakes gone bad. Promotion in Action 14–3 speaks clearly to this issue. Great care in planning, testing, and implementing the details is needed for successful promotions.

Coke's Olympic Promotion Comes Up Flat

Promotion in Action

14–3

Coca-Cola USA's "Medals & Millions" Olympics joint promotion with CBS could turn into a loser if the company doesn't find a winner.

As of Friday, five days after CBS' Olympics coverage ended, not a single grand-prize winner had emerged. And some industry observers believe it behooves Coca-Cola to find one.

"From a credibility standpoint, you want to find a way to give away the top [prizes], at least," said Maxwell Anderson, president of Promotion Activators, who suggested Coca-Cola hold a second drawing if the winnings go unclaimed.

"It's bad that no one won during the Olympics," said Tom Pirko, president of Bevmark, an industry consultancy. "If there's no winner by the April 30 [deadline], then Coke is the loser . . . The sooner Coke announces winners, the better, or else they lose the value of the Olympic tie-in."

Mr. Pirko said this could be the equivalent of Coca-Cola's ill-fated 1990 MagiCan promotion, when some of the cans containing cash and coupons malfunctioned, and the effort was aborted.

The watch-and-win promotion was created in-house and offered consumers a chance for a $1 million grand prize each night of CBS' 16-day Winter Olympics coverage from Albertville, France. To win, consumers needed to match numbers printed on game pieces with numbers broadcast by the network.

Coca-Cola began distributing 170 million game pieces nationwide on Coca-Cola soft drinks in January, and the company has credited the promotion with boosting January sales from January 1990 levels.

CBS ran extensive on-air promos announcing the game and credits the contest with contributing to its high Olympics ratings.

Coca-Cola spokesman Randy Donaldson said the company is eager to give away the money. Consumers have until April 30 to claim the grand prizes, but Coca-Cola won't run additional advertising to promote the winning numbers, Mr. Donaldson said.

Instead, it will mail a list of winning numbers to consumers who request it by calling a special 800 phone number listed on the game pieces.

Mr. Donaldson said Coca-Cola so far has received 50,000 requests for the numbers and will start to mail that information this week.

"Somehow they should let the public know they are still eligible because the TV commercials said 'during' the CBS coverage," said Hellen Berry, senior VP-marketing at Beverage Marketing Corp., another industry consultancy. "And then they should publicize that there is an 800 number."

Coca-Cola has a different promotion on tap for its tie-in to NBC's Summer Olympics telecast, and efforts are expected to center on a premium offer and include music to appeal to a younger age group.

Source: Alison Farley, "Where's the Winner?" *Advertising Age,* March 2, 1992, pp. 3 and 29.

SUMMARY

This chapter has discussed some of those marketing activities encompassed by the term *consumer sales promotion.* The growing importance of these activities was described, and special attention was paid to such promotional alternatives as sampling, price incentives, couponing, premiums, and contests and sweepstakes.

REVIEW AND DISCUSSION QUESTIONS

1. For the CBS–Kmart, Sampling Corporation, and Eagle Food Centers examples of consumer sales promotions in this chapter indicate:
   a. The likely objectives of the promotion.
   b. The rationale for selecting the specific consumer promotion type.
   c. The role consumer sales promotion played relative to other promotional tools.
   d. How the effectiveness of the consumer sales promotion could be evaluated.

2. How should trade promotion (see Chapter 13) and consumer sales promotion be integrated into a promotional plan?

3. Coke's difficulty with a consumer contest, illustrated in Promotion in Action 14–3, is not unusual. Many firms have such contests go bad. How could these types of difficulties be anticipated and avoided?

4. Do consumer sales promotions diminish brand equity and loyalty? Comment.

5. From newspapers, FSIs in newspapers, and magazines, select an example of each of the types of consumer sales promotions discussed in this chapter. Critically evaluate these promotions.

6. Suppose that Bristol Myers is planning to introduce a new allergy tablet that does not have the side effect of causing drowsiness. What consumer sales promotions and trade promotions would you use to support this entry? Be specific.

NOTES

1. American Marketing Association, *Marketing Definitions: A Glossary of Marketing Terms* (Chicago: American Marketing Association, 1960), p. 20.

2. Peter D. Bennett, *Dictionary of Marketing Terms* (Chicago: American Marketing Association, 1988), p. 179.

3. Donnelly Marketing, *15th Annual Survey of Promotional Procedures.*

4. This section is adapted from *Business Month,* July 1987, pp. 44–46.

5. Donnelly Marketing 15th Annual Survey of Promotional Practices, and same publication at other years.

6. "A New Look at Coupons," *the Nielsen Researcher* 1 (1976), p. 2, updated to 1992 from the same source and from Scott Hume, "Coupon Use Jumps 10% as Distribution Soars," *Advertising Age,* October 5, 1992, pp. 3 and 42.

7. Ibid.

8. Ibid.

9. Ibid.

10. This section is based on "Premium Positioning," *Marketing & Media Decisions*, May 1989, p. 112.

11. This section is based on "Creative Campaigns Can Hit Baby Boomers Where They Live," *Marketing News*, October 10, 1988, p. 14.

12. This section is based on "Sweepstakes Fever," *Forbes*, October 3, 1988, pp. 164–66.

Section

6

PERSONAL SELLING

In following the stages in promotional strategy outlined in Chapter 4, we have given considerable attention to the management of mass communication efforts. This part continues the discussion of management of program elements by considering the problems inherent in managing the firm's personal selling resources. These resources provide for face-to-face contact with potential customers to inform them of new product or service offerings and to persuade them to buy.

Although personal selling is used at every level in business, from the manufacturer to the retailer, this section is primarily concerned with manufacturers' use of a sales force to seek out new business by contacting end users or resellers. Many of the points discussed are applicable at all levels of the distribution channel.

Chapter 15 deals with personal selling as a special form of interpersonal communication and with the nature of the selling task. Chapter 16 discusses the management aspects of building, training, deploying, and motivating a sales force.

Chapter

15

Strategic Interpersonal Communications

WHY ARE OREOS TOPS IN FOOD SALES?

What really makes the Oreo America's favorite cookie? No, not the ridged chocolate lids or the vanilla cream between them, but the best customer-focused sales organization in the packaged goods industry. Last year Neo Inc., a sales consultancy in Shelton, Connecticut, asked 1,014 retail managers and buyers which salespeople served them best, and Nabisco Biscuit, which makes Oreos, came out on top.

While other companies are just beginning to organize their selling around their clients, the $2.8 billion operation that also cooks up Fig Newtons, Ritz crackers, and Triscuits has been at it since the mid-1980s. Nabisco Biscuit's salespeople think like their customers. And this has helped to double the business's operating profits over three years to an estimated $440 million in 1991. Says Ellen Marram, 45, the president and CEO: "We train our sales people to be extensions of the store. Their jobs are not only to get the product onto the shelves but to get it out of the store and into people's homes."

While its parent, RJR Nabisco, was hacking away at operating expenses following history's largest leveraged buyout three years ago, Nabisco Biscuit increased spending more than 20 percent to build its sales organization and strengthen its customer service. To give salespeople more time to work closely with store managers, Nabisco added 400 merchandisers, who build store displays and keep the cracker boxes neat on the shelves.

Unlike most food companies, Nabisco runs a "direct store delivery" operation. There's no dropping shipments at central warehouses for retailers to pick up and cart to their stores. Company rigs show up at the back doors of 105,000 stores about three times a week, and then Nabisco's 2,800 sales reps manhandle the products from the storage areas onto the shelf or display rack.

All sales reps carry hand-held computers to collect sales data for individual stores, and two thirds of them use their own laptops to help retail buyers configure their shelf space most productively. The computer feeds a salesperson, who, of course, tells the store manager the answers to such questions as, Which store in Wichita sells Chips Ahoy! cookies more profitably—Dillon's, where you face the cookie display as you start down the aisle, or the grocer who stashes the cookies on a shelf halfway down? Answer: Dillon's, because the display attracts impulse buyers.

Source: Excerpted from Patricia Sellers, "How to Remake Your Sales Force," *Fortune,* May 4, 1992, p. 100.

PERSONAL SELLING IN THE PROMOTIONAL MIX

Personal selling, properly done, can have high promotional impact because it usually targets only one person at a time and offers immediate feedback of objections and reactions. Its value to the firm is underscored by the fact that more is spent on personal selling by all businesses in total than on other promotional efforts. In fact, it is estimated that many firms spend twice as much on personal selling as on advertising.

Although the use of personal selling is widespread in the aggregate, its importance in relation to other promotional tools varies widely with individual firms. In some situations, promotional goals are best met with advertising or sales promotion. In this chapter, we are most concerned with firms in which the overall marketing strategy requires heavy reliance on personal selling and the use of sales personnel to seek out buyers. Such firms are usually manufacturing companies, although many wholesalers and retailers use their salespeople to locate and cultivate new customers.

We must not forget, however, that most salespersons are employed at the retail level. Unfortunately, selling skills of retail salespersons range widely from top-notch to nonexistent. We hope that what we have to say in these chapters will be of use in improving retail selling effectiveness from the viewpoint of a promotional manager of a retail organization or of a manufacturer dependent on the selling skills of the company's retail resellers.

Designing a Personal Selling Strategy

Five major sets of questions must be answered in order to design an effective personal selling strategy:[1]

1. How can the personal selling effort best be adapted to the product-market environment in which the firm operates? How can personal selling be most effectively combined with the other elements of the firm's marketing and promotional strategies over the product (service) life cycle?

2. How can potential customers best be approached, pursuaded to buy, and serviced?

3. How should the sales force be organized to call on and manage a variety of customers as effectively and as efficiently as possible?

4. What level of performance can be expected of each member of the sales force in the next planning period?

5. How should the sales force be deployed? How should sales territories be defined, and how should each salesperson's time be allocated within each territory?

We will attempt to answer the first three questions in this chapter and in Chapter 16. The last two questions will be considered in Chapter 21.

The Influence of Communication Tasks

Personal selling is essentially a communication process. The communication tasks facing the firm determine how and to what extent personal selling will be used in the promotional strategy mix. Table 15–1 illustrates when personal selling should play a major role in the mix. It indicates that personal selling can do the promotional job best given the need to communicate about complex product or service offerings, when channel systems cannot do the job by themselves, when price is subject to negotiation, and when advertising cannot reach targets or provide sufficient information about the offerings.

The Influence of the Product-Market Situation

To illustrate how the role of personal selling changes with various product-market situations (thus addressing the question of the competitive environment), three

TABLE 15–1

When the Sales Force Is a Major Part of the Promotional Mix

Mix Area	Characteristics
Product or service	Complex products requiring customer application assistance (e.g., computers, pollution control systems, steam turbines).
	Major purchase decisions, such as food items purchased by supermarket chains.
	Features and performance of the product requiring personal demonstration and trial by the customer (e.g., private aircraft).
Channels	Channel system relatively short and direct to end users.
	Product and service training and assistance needed by channel intermediaries.
	Personal selling is needed in "pushing" product through channel.
	Channel intermediaries available to perform personal selling function for supplier with limited resources and experience (e.g., brokers or manufacturer's agents).
Price	Final price negotiated between buyer and seller (e.g., appliances, automobiles, real estate).
	Selling price and/or quantity purchased enable an adequate margin to support selling expenses (traditional department store compared to discount house).
Advertising	Advertising media do not provide effective link with market targets.
	Information needed by buyer cannot be provided entirely through advertising and sales promotion (e.g., life insurance).
	Number and dispersion of customers will not enable acceptable advertising economies.

Source: David W. Cravens, Gerald E. Hills, and Robert B. Woodruff, *Marketing Decision Making: Concepts and Strategy* (Homewood, Ill.: Richard D. Irwin, 1980), p. 384. Reprinted by permission of Richard D. Irwin, Inc.

short case histories are presented in this section. They detail the experiences of a manufacturer of proprietary drugs, a manufacturer of personal computers, and a provider of specialized welding services.

Proprietary Drug Manufacturer   A manufacturer wants to launch a new cough remedy through retail drugstores. Market research indicates that the market is geographically dispersed and that a large percentage of present users of similar remedies are potential buyers for the new product, which has several unique features. Cost analysis indicates that national advertising by means of newspapers, radio, and TV spots will provide the most economical coverage of the market. Accordingly, $2 million is appropriated for consumer advertising, $500,000 for trade promotion, and $200,000 for personal selling. Why the disparity in amounts? What is the role assigned to personal selling?

The answer to the first question is that for the product type and the large and dispersed market, advertising and trade promotion can stimulate demand more economically than personal selling. Proprietary health aids that have hidden qualities may appeal to strong human emotions involved with health and well-being, thus making advertising especially effective. Moreover, the sales potential of the product promises sufficient revenues to sustain a costly advertising campaign. This situation is ideally suited to an emphasis on advertising in the promotional mix.

Personal selling effort is utilized, however, at three different levels in the channel: manufacturer, wholesaler, and retailer.

The manufacturer has salespeople who call on large wholesalers and chain drug retailers. The advertising aimed at the household buyer meanwhile is creating a "pull" effect, and the primary task of the salesperson is to make certain that resellers have adequate stock. The selling task here is essentially order taking. But salespeople spend considerable time ensuring that wholesaler and retailer point-of-sale efforts are coordinated with the national advertising campaign.

The budget does not allow very much personal selling activity by the manufacturer, so the available effort is directed to customers who appear to offer the greatest potential. The great bulk of the orders is received by mail from interested wholesalers and retailers.

At the wholesale level, a different type of personal selling activity is taking place. The wholesaler sales force makes routine calls on members of the wholesaler's customer group. These salespeople carry catalogs and price lists describing thousands of items. Their essential function is order taking. If, however, the demand for the new patent medicine is being felt at retail and these salespeople are aware of the manufacturer's promotional plans, they may engage in some promotional selling aimed at getting the retailer to carry special stocks and to provide in-store promotional tie-ins.

Personal selling at the retail level is represented by the retail clerk or the pharmacist, who may suggest the brand to customers asking for that type of remedy. Since the product is being highly advertised, customers will probably ask for the remedy by name, thus reducing the personal selling task at retail to one of order filling. Retailer support, in this instance, is largely confined to providing ample display and counter space for the product.

Computer Manufacturer   After several years of research and development, a California manufacturer of personal computers developed a powerful portable computer. Due to limited production capacity and the desire to give consumers a great deal of personal attention at the point of sale, the manufacturer decided to have only a few hundred dealers carry the line. A modest advertising campaign directed to the trade as well as to end users was planned. The bulk of promotional effort, however, was to be in the form of personal selling at both the manufacturer and retailer levels.

The manufacturer must develop a highly skilled group of salespeople whose principal task is to get several hundred of the best computer retailers in the country to stock, display, demonstrate, and sell the new computer. This will not be an easy task because the product type is totally different in a technical sense from anything previously made. The cost of the new product will be relatively high, and the demand is unknown. In this situation, the manufacturer salesperson must be an order getter. Creativity and aggressiveness are necessary if the salesperson is to succeed in gaining the best quality retailers in each market area.

Selling effort at retail is also very important. A potential customer for the new computer must be given a very thorough demonstration of how it operates. The retail salesperson must have knowledge of the product and persuasive ability to make the sale. The manufacturer's margin payment to the retailer must, therefore, include payment for the superior selling effort required.

Over time, as the product moves along its life cycle and enters a more mature stage, the personal selling task will change along with other elements of the marketing mix. The product itself will be better known by potential customers, distribution will be more intensive, price will be reduced, and the promotional mix will include a larger amount of consumer advertising and less personal selling effort. See Figure 15–1.

From the manufacturer's standpoint, the need then will be to gain more sales from present retail outlets rather than to increase the coverage of the market. The selling task will become more routine, with greater emphasis on order taking and service. Similarly, at retail, the requirement for a creative selling job will have lessened. At all levels in the product channel, personal selling will give way to greater reliance on consumer advertising and price promotion.

Electron Beam Welding Service   A small company offers an electron beam welding service to industry. The electron beam technology, developed in the aircraft industry, had not gained widespread acceptance in the manufacture of industrial goods and consumer products, although it offered many advantages over conventional welding techniques.

The company hired a manufacturers' representative on an expenses-plus-commission basis to contact potential accounts within the market area. After two years, the owners found, much to their dismay, that the sales representative was not producing enough business to cover expenses. A reappraisal of promotional strategy was in order.

If the owners of this small company had analyzed their present customers in terms of information needs, they would have found that some required much more information than others. For example, buyers who had previously used the process or who had a relatively small job to be welded did not require much selling effort. On the other hand, those who were unfamiliar with the nature of electron beam welding or who had large and expensive jobs to complete required a great deal of information about the technical capability of the supplier, the price, and the delivery date for the finished work. In one case, it took six months of inquiry and negotiation to close a sale.

From this type of analysis, it would appear that although a manufacturers' representative might handle the routine buying situations, he or she would have neither the expertise nor the time to deal with more complex situations. Given such a set of circumstances, the owners of the welding service would either have to hire a salesperson of their own to engage in the complex selling task or, if such an addition were not economically feasible, they would have to assume the responsibility themselves.

Implications of the Cases   The three situations discussed above illustrate briefly how product and market influences affect the role played by personal selling in

FIGURE 15–1

As Computers Become Better Known to Consumers, Superstores Develop

the promotional strategy mix. In the consumer market, as products mature, the role of personal selling is diminished and advertising becomes more important. In the industrial market, as the product moves through its life cycle, personal selling is generally a more important element in the promotional mix than is advertising. However, as the information requirements of industrial customers vary, so do the extent and nature of the personal selling task.

WHAT DO SALESPEOPLE DO?

As the case histories indicate, there can be wide variations in environmental or strategic conditions that influence the role of personal selling in a given firm. Regardless of these variations, the work to be done by salespeople can be identified and described. For example, the salesperson must seek out or meet prospective buyers, discover customer needs and attitudes, and help customers to buy the product or service best suited to their needs. In helping the customer to buy, the salesperson must be prepared to supply generous quantities of information about product or service characteristics. The salesperson must also persuade the buyer that a particular offering is best suited to the buyer's needs and must act decisively to overcome buyer uncertainty by sensing how and when to close the sale. Follow-up after the sale is also important to ensure that buyers receive the fullest utility from the purchase and to prevent dissonance by assuring customers that they have made the correct choice.

Thus the essential tasks of personal selling consist of (1) locating and/or meeting prospective customers, (2) discovering customer needs and attitudes, (3) recommending a product package to fill those needs, (4) developing a sales presentation aimed at informing the customer of product attributes and persuading the customer to buy the recommended package, (5) closing the sale, and (6) following up to ensure total satisfaction with the purchase.

Of course, all salespeople do not place equal emphasis on the various components of the selling task. This may be the result of inadequate performance or simply because the selling strategy requires a different presentation. It is essential that the selling task be clearly defined so the salesperson understands the nature of the job to be performed. This definition must attempt to have as much of the salesperson's time as possible devoted to face-to-face or telephone selling. Unfortunately, as seen in Promotion in Action 15–1, studies indicate that less than half of an average salesperson's time is spent on these critical activities.

Salesmanship

Salesmanship is a direct, face-to-face, seller-to-buyer influence that can communicate the facts necessary for making a buying decision; or it can utilize the psychology of persuasion to encourage a buying decision. Another way of looking at salesmanship is to consider it as a set of skills that can make personal selling effort more effective. Because these skills are important in noncommercial as well as commercial settings, it is worthwhile to examine the subject in detail. (Promo-

Salespeople Spend Half Their Time Not Selling

Salespeople spend less than 50 percent of their working time actually selling, according to a special report from the Dartnell Corp., a Chicago–based business publisher. More than 50 percent of a sales representative's average workweek is not spent selling, but rather traveling, waiting, or doing paperwork.

The report compares results from a Dartnell survey entitled "How Salespeople Spend Their Time," which tallied responses from more than 300 sales representatives in a variety of industries, and *The 26th Sales Force Compensation Survey*, which asked more than 250 managers how reps spend their time.

Respondents estimated the amount of time a salesperson spent in the following categories:

Total hours worked per week: Sales reps said they work 48.9 hours a week, and managers said reps work 47 hours a week.

Hours spent on selling activities: Reps said they spend 22.5 hours selling; managers said the figure was 23.5 hours.

Hours spent on nonselling activities: Reps said they spend 26.4 hours a week not selling; managers said the number was 23.5 hours.

Selling activities were broken down into face-to-face and telephone contact. Salespeople said they spend 12.6 hours a week selling face-to-face and almost 10 hours on the phone. Managers said reps spend about 14 hours on face-to-face sales and 9.4 hours on telephone sales.

Nonselling activities included traveling/waiting, service calls, and administrative duties such as paperwork. Sales reps and managers agreed that about 10 hours a week are spent on travel/waiting and about 6 hours on service calls. Administrative work was the one nonselling area where managers and sales reps had different conclusions. Reps estimated they spent more time on administrative work (10 hours per week) than managers estimated they did (6.6 hours).

Otherwise, the results of the two surveys matched closely, but suggested that both groups need to find ways to help salespeople use their time more effectively for selling.

"Effective time management and planning are already key issues for salespeople," says salesmanship editor Frances Berman. "Although they put in 9- to 10-hour days during the week, and possibly several hours on the weekend, salespeople still spend at least half their time on non-selling activities. More efficient planning and self-management could go a long way in reducing non-selling hours, making selling hours more productive and increasing sales."

The Dartnell Corp. is a leading producer and distributor of business information and training materials, including books, manuals, newsletters, audiocassettes, and films and videos. In 1992, the company will celebrate 75 years as a source of sales training materials and information. Dartnell has offices in Chicago, Boston, London, and Sydney, Australia.

Source: "Salespeople Spend Half Their Time Not Selling," *American Salesman*, March 1992, pp. 19–20.

tion in Action 15–2 tells the story of one person with the golden touch of sales-manship.)

All of us are continuously selling our ideas and ourselves to others. In trying to land a job or gain the attention of a member of the opposite sex, we are engaged in selling.

Effective selling either in a commercial or noncommercial context requires a very clear understanding of the nature of interpersonal communication when one party is attempting to influence the response of another.

Buyer-Seller Interactions

There are a variety of influences on the way the buyer receives and interprets messages sent by the seller. The seller's appearance, personality, and level of knowledge about the product or service offered all have an effect. Buyer knowledge of the seller's company and familiarity with the seller on a personal basis also play a part in how the seller's message is received, and whether or not it is acted on. Even the buyer's immediate state of mind or of health can have a major influence on the buyer-seller communication process.

Given the large number of operative variables, research has been undertaken to provide insights into formulating an effective sales approach. In the life insurance industry, for example, it was found that prospects who bought insurance knew more about the salespeople and their companies, and felt more positively toward them, than prospects who did not buy. In addition, the greater the similarity

---

The Golden Touch

Promotion in Action

15-2

Salesmanship is a people game, and great salesmanship is largely a matter of *feel*. Some people have it; some don't.

Nicholas Barsan has the touch. The top performer of 1986 among the 75,000 U.S. real estate brokers affiliated with Century 21, dashing, dark-browed Barsan, 47, was born in Romania. He emigrated to the United States in 1968 and owned a wholesale food company and then a restaurant before he began selling property four years ago. In 1986, he moved $27 million of homes in Jackson Heights, Queens, netting $1.1 million in commissions. In this solidly middle-class New York City neighborhood, the average home sells for $225,000, so a fellow has to work to do that kind of volume.

Though a millionaire, Barsan still knocks urgently on strangers' doors, hungry for new business. He still hands out key chains and car window scrapers imprinted with his name, lest anyone forget it. But Barsan knows he can sell more homes with less effort by dealing again with customers he has already satisfied. So he calls on the people who bought their homes from him. "You ready to sell yet?" he asks. A third of Barsan's sales are to repeat customers.

Source: Excerpted from Monci Jo Williams, "America's Best Salesmen," *Fortune*, October 26, 1987, p. 124. Used by permission.

between the salesperson and the prospect, in terms of physical, demographic, and personality characteristics, the greater the likelihood that a sale would occur.

Such findings may be useful when the number of potential customers is small, the sale involves a large outlay, and there is a possibility of matching salespeople and prospects. It is doubtful the strategy would be viable with large numbers of prospects, low-value unit sales, and limited ability to match sellers and buyers.

Different Selling Situations

Selling situations differ in degree of difficulty—a selling strategy developed for one situation may not be suitable for another. For example, we may classify selling goals as (1) order getting, (2) order taking, and (3) supporting.

The *order getter* engages in creative selling and aggressively undertakes a campaign to seek out potential buyers and make a sale. *Order takers,* on the other hand, operate on a more relaxed basis. They make routine calls on customers to maintain a continuing relationship. Their approach is a low-pressure one designed to enable them to live well with their customer group for a long time. It is a mistake to compare order takers unfavorably with order getters, for their goals are different. However, if a salesperson who is supposed to be an order getter performs as an order taker, management must step in to remind him or her of the need for creative and aggressive selling.

In the *support* category, selling activities are not aimed at getting or taking an order; missionary selling, technical support, and assistance in management or promotion fall into this group. These indirect selling activities build goodwill for the seller and help the order-oriented salespeople to close the sale.

It is obvious that the salesperson's task varies with the assigned role. But the position of the seller in the channel also has a profound effect on the nature of the selling job. Manufacturer salespeople selling to wholesalers or end users play a role different than that of wholesaler salespeople selling to retailers, or of retail salespeople selling to shoppers who come to their stores. And market characteristics, as well as the product itself, influence the basic selling task.

It is important, however, to recognize that the skill level required of the salesperson varies considerably over the range of selling situations. The quality of sales ability required in order getting is considerably higher than that required to take orders or provide service after the sale, although the latter activities also call for proper performance.

STEPS OF A SALE

Many authors who have written on the subject of salesmanship indicate discrete steps or stages. Although in reality the selling process is continuous, with considerable overlapping of the steps, it is useful to consider the steps one at a time. In addition, we will consider those steps described by Beach and others in writings that have endured the test of time.[2] The steps include (1) prospecting, (2) the preapproach, (3) the approach, (4) the presentation, (5) meeting objections, (6) the close, and (7) the follow-up.

Prospecting

In this, the first stage of the selling process, the salesperson attempts to locate prospective customers who are likely to have a need or desire for the products or services offered. In addition, the prospect must also be qualified to buy, that is, have the authority to enter into a purchase agreement and be financially able to pay for the purchase. The goal of prospecting, therefore, is to locate individuals who have needs that can be satisfied by the products and services offered by the salesperson and his or her company. The prospecting process is continuous because enough likely candidates must be provided to fully utilize the salesperson's time.

The systems that are used in prospecting are varied and numerous. One approach is termed the *snowball technique:* Every prospect, regardless of whether she or he has made a purchase, is asked to recommend one or two additional prospects. Leads may also be elicited through advertisements containing coupons requesting further information about the product/service offering or from direct mail activities in which prepaid postcards are enclosed for the same purpose. These responses, then, provide leads for salespersons. When all else fails, the salesperson may adopt the *cold canvass* approach—he or she calls on a series of individuals, knowing little more about them than their name and address. The cold canvass approach is the least productive in terms of time and effort spent. If *planned* prospecting and selling are not taking up all of a salesperson's time, however, the marginal cost of cold canvassing is low, and the benefits will generally exceed the costs.

Preapproach

Once a prospect has been identified and qualified, the problem facing the salesperson is how to approach the prospect with the greatest effectiveness. Analysis of information gathered about the prospect's purchase behavior in the past, about the nature of current needs, and about alternatives offered by competitors can lead to the development of an approach strategy. These preliminaries constitute the preapproach step.

The Approach

This is the most easily identified step in the selling process: it occurs when the seller first meets the buyer. Unfortunately, too many selling processes start at this step without sufficient prospecting or preapproach effort. The approach must be carefully planned, especially if the salesperson is meeting the prospect for the first time. The goal of the approach is to secure the prospect's interest and attention. If this goal is not met, the selling process stops. The best the salesperson can do is exit politely so he or she can try again another day.

Approaches vary from the most widely used and least effective one of presenting a business card to the prospect or the prospect's secretary to the more imaginative approaches in which the salesperson uses product samples, premiums, or intriguing opening statements to capture the prospect's interest. Careful prospecting and preapproach planning should provide ideas for strategies most likely to succeed with a given prospect.

The salesperson will know very quickly whether an approach is succeeding. If the prospect invites the salesperson to have a seat or to continue with the presentation, the approach has worked. A polite suggestion that the salesperson leave because the prospect is very busy indicates that the salesperson will have to try again another time or with another prospect.

The Presentation

The objective of this step is to create in the prospect's mind a desire for the product or service offered. To achieve this, the salesperson must communicate as complete a story as possible about the product attributes and the benefits that the prospect will derive from it. The salesperson must gain the prospect's confidence as a prelude to effecting a change in the prospect's behavior. The seller must always be aware of the dyadic relationship in which he or she is involved. The seller must be the influencer; the prospect is the one who must act. To avoid making a decision, most prospects will raise objections as the presentation continues or will attempt to sidetrack the seller with extraneous remarks. The skilled salesperson will know how to anticipate and overcome objections and will be able to steer the discussion back to the topic at hand.

Some sellers use "canned" presentations—those that have been carefully developed and memorized. This approach has the advantage of completeness because the presentation has been pretested to make sure it covers the principal selling points. It lacks the spontaneity and flexibility of a noncanned approach, and thus its use is not recommended except in rather standardized selling situations in which relatively unskilled salespersons are being used.

Meeting Objections

Closely allied with the presentation step is that of meeting objections. Indeed, one could make a good case for combining this step with the preceding one. But because this skill is so important to the salesperson, we will look at it a little more closely. Objections can be handled most effectively if the salesperson knows what the true purpose of the objection is. For example, the prospect might object to some aspect of the product's physical design as a device to cover up the fact that he or she cannot afford to make the purchase at this time. In this case, even if the salesperson overcomes the stated objection, the sale will not materialize. Perhaps continued probing by the seller would uncover the true nature of the problem. Then a discussion about the possibility of extended terms or a leasing agreement might be fruitful.

In other cases, the best way to handle objections is to treat them as requests for clarification or for additional information. The prepared salesperson will anticipate objections and be prepared for them. Indeed, in such cases, overcoming an objection may impress the prospect and help to close the sale.

Closing the Sale

This is the step in which the goal of the salesperson is to obtain action, preferably a commitment on the part of the prospect to become a buyer. The skill of closing is perhaps the most important that a salesperson can possess but is also the most difficult to master. A seller who cannot close has been described as a "conversationalist." Part of the skill of closing is knowing when the prospect is ready to buy. When the prospect's questions pertain to delivery dates or credit terms, the time to close is at hand. The salesperson who is uncertain that the time is right might attempt a "trial" close that can be pushed to a complete close if the prospect appears willing to act or withdrawn if the prospect requires more information or more persuasion. Closing techniques differ widely, ranging from those that simply ask for the order to those that involve a promise to alter the offering to suit the specific needs of the buyer in order to gain the sale.

Closing is a skill, and preplanning the presentation and carefully monitoring the verbal and body language of the prospect can help the salesperson to develop that sixth sense that is so crucial to successful selling. (See Promotion in Action 15–3 for one salesperson's view of the sales process.)

See the People

Promotion in Action

15-3

When I started selling life insurance almost 20 years ago, the name of the game was to see as many people as possible.

There was an old adage that the three most important rules in selling were:

- See the people.
- See the people.
- See the people.

In the 1950s, the typical life insurance salesperson saw five outside appointments a day. In the 1970s, the typical salesperson saw three a day.

Sales managers and long-time sales reps did not view the decline in appointments as a favorable sign.

During the past five years as a sales management consultant and sales trainer, I have found that more salespeople resist getting out and making calls. They tell me that direct mail, advertising, and other business development techniques will generate sales.

It is rare, however, to find either a sales rep or manager who is actually happy with the number of sales that result from such methods alone. These additional resources should complement selling, not replace it.

I also remember from my early days that a sales rep could expect after a proper sales presentation to close one of every three prospects. This ratio was generally applied to most industries.

Today I hear that one of every four or five sales is the norm for many industries. Has something changed in the past 20 years? Is there something different in the buying and selling process, or are salespeople just selling less?

The more likely answer is that the reason for the increase in the ratio for closing sales is the same as the decrease in the number of actual sales calls made.

Any analysis of closing ratios requires careful consideration of the way sales are being made. Two critical factors are whether salespeople today are practicing good sales techniques and whether they are making the effort to close sales.

Another change over the years that appears to have affected closing ratios is the compensation for sales reps. More of them receive good base salaries plus a commission, rather than a base amount to meet minimum basic living expenses, in addition to commissions for actual sales.

I agree with this change because it creates a more professional atmosphere between buyer and seller.

On the other hand, when salespeople are paid even though a prospect does not buy, what system does the employer have to monitor actual sales performance and hold salespeople accountable when they are to blame for lost sales?

Even when salespeople are paid commission on top of a good base salary, there is no incentive against inferior performance short of termination.

Minimum call and presentation standards always seem to work. Give sales reps standards to exceed, and hold them accountable. Teach them good sales techniques that include closing the sale, and sales will begin to increase.

There is really no other way to sell. Over the years I have developed my own rules of selling. The old rules still apply; I have only added to them:

- See the people.
- Close the sale.
- Hold the salesperson accountable.

Source: Excerpted from Alan Test, "The Old Ways of Selling Still Work Best," *Marketing News*, May 25, 1992, p. 4.

Follow-Up

Many salespeople end their selling efforts when the order is signed. This is a very serious shortcoming because the after-sale, or follow-up, stage is so valuable for removing any feeling of dissonance the buyer may have and for making sure that the buyer is receiving full utility from the purchase. Follow-up is the ideal time to suggest add-on sales of accessory equipment or maintenance items. The buyer is relaxed, committed, and thus fairly receptive to proposals to increase the investment and gain more advantages from the initial buy.

Even if no further business occurs during the follow-up, the salesperson's effort will be repaid many times over by uncovering problems that might have made future sales difficult and by cementing a relationship that will make future sales much more likely.

SUMMARY

This chapter begins by listing five major sets of questions to ask when designing a personal selling strategy. It then considers personal selling as a communication process, discusses the influence of the product-market situation (with three case histories illustrating the different roles of personal selling), and examines salesmanship as a set of skills used by salespeople to improve their effectiveness.

Some variables in the buyer-seller relationship are the seller's appearance and knowledge, and the buyer's familiarity with the seller. Also, the degree of difficulty of selling situations is based on whether the salesperson is an order getter, an order taker, or a support person.

The steps in the selling process as enumerated by Beach and others have stood the test of time: (1) prospecting, (2) the preapproach, (3) the approach, (4) the presentation, (5) meeting objections, (6) closing the sale, and (7) follow-up.

REVIEW AND DISCUSSION QUESTIONS

1. You are a promotion consultant trying to help a client develop a campaign for her product line. She does not have a clear idea of how personal selling differs from advertising as a communication process. How would you explain the differences to her?

2. You have just graduated from business school and are interested in a sales position. You have interviewed several companies and are impressed by the different emphasis that some companies place on personal selling as compared with others. How do you explain these differences?

3. In your search for a selling job, you are finding that different positions call for different types of selling activities or place different degrees of emphasis on various aspects of the selling task. How do you explain these differences? How do you find a job that places emphasis on what you like to do?

4. You have accepted a position and have been quite happy for a number of years. You especially enjoy the challenge of explaining how the products work and how they can save money for the user. Lately you are finding that everyone knows about your product, and you are facing stiffer and stiffer price competition. What is going on here? Is your firm in trouble? Should you seek another position?

5. John Jones is an excellent salesman who knows his product and his customers' needs. He does not do as well as Jim Smith, who is newer to the company and does not have Jones's breadth or depth of knowledge about the product or the market. In a discussion with his sales manager, Mary Worth, the suggestion is raised that Jones improve his closing technique. What is a closing technique? Is it hard to learn? Can one practice closing?

6. Fred Star is a fine auto salesman. He always stays in close touch with his customers after he sells them a car. He says that he must allay any hints of "cognitive dissonance" (anxiety after the sale) on the part of his customers. What is he talking about? What does one do to reduce the effects of this psychological state?

NOTES

1. Adapted from Gilbert A. Churchill, Jr., Neil M. Ford, and Orville C. Walker, Jr., *Sales Force Management,* 3rd ed. (Homewood, Ill.: Richard D. Irwin, Inc., 1990), p. 20.

2. Frederick A. Russell, Frank H. Beach, and Richard Buskirk, *Selling: Principles and Practices,* 11th ed. (New York: McGraw-Hill, 1982).

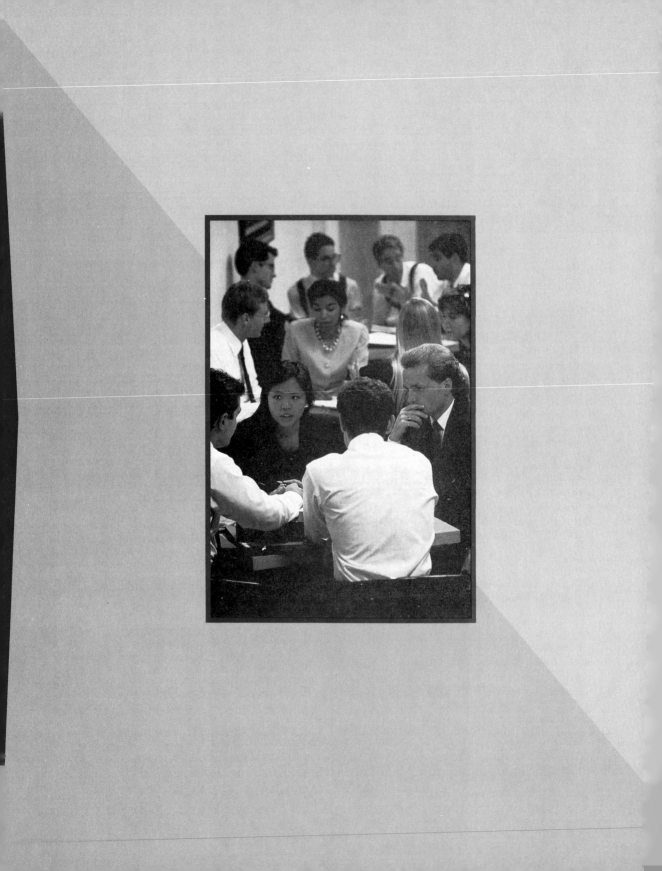

Chapter 16

Managing Personal
Selling Efforts

AMERITECH SALES TRAINING: AN UPSIDE-DOWN APPROACH

"The way we were teaching was exactly the opposite of the way people learn," said Sam Bulmer, manager of training for Ameritech Information Systems. "We made our training and our sales results better by literally turning things upside down."

What Ameritech turned upside down is the traditional "tell, show, do" pattern of instructional design. In this familiar model, the trainer explains the new concept to the learner, demonstrates applications of the concept, and finally gives the learner an opportunity to try it.

In moving away from the traditional, Ameritech sought a new technique that emphasized the primacy of experience. The design it ultimately adopted starts with experience and is called "do and debrief."

Learning begins with assignments that require action, teamwork, and commitment. Participants learn by experiencing success and failure.

Explanations and demonstrations follow the action and are part of the debriefing phase of the training process. They help learners solve problems or meet needs raised by the experience of doing the assignments. This imitates the natural process of learning.

This approach has been extremely effective. Do and debrief is the cornerstone of Keystone for Sales Success, the company's flagship sales training program.

A needs analysis showed that Ameritech account execs needed to score better in technical knowledge of products and services, ability to analyze customer needs, avoidance of high-pressure sales techniques, and the ability to carry out promises.

"Our relationship to customers is particularly critical," Bulmer said. "Ameritech sells solutions to problems, so we are more interested in the customer's perception of our services than just making the sale. Our account executives need to sell intangible services which are part of the technical solution."

Ameritech's new approach "accomplishes in two days what traditionally would have taken six," Bulmer said. "The do and debrief approach is better operationally. It takes less time and makes training more efficient. This in turn makes it cheaper though that was not our intent."

Source: Excerpted from Jim Cusimano, "Ameritech Sales Training Turns Tradition Upside Down," *Marketing News,* September 14, 1992, p. 34. Used by permission.

This chapter deals with the management aspects of personal selling. Building and maintaining a sales force are complex tasks. The vignette above describes what Ameritech has done to bolster sales training to target the information systems market. Note the planning and effort needed to accomplish this task.

This chapter covers the recruitment, selection, training, and assignment of sales personnel, as well as their compensation and motivation. Included in Chapter 21 will be coverage of the evaluation and control of sales force efforts.

BUILDING THE SALES FORCE

The creation of an effective selling organization must begin with a clear understanding of the nature of the selling task. The processes of recruitment, selection, and training will vary with the sales assignment. A job that involves calling on wholesalers to determine their stock needs and the promotion of a commodity-type product line is different from one in which the salesperson deals with diverse types of customers or products.

Those in the company responsible for recruiting, selecting, and training salespeople need a clear grasp of overall promotional strategy. The overall strategy determines the *kind* of selling required. The kind of selling, in turn, determines the personal qualifications needed by members of the sales force, as well as the methods of training, compensation, and motivation that are used.

Job Description and Recruitment

Before recruiting activities can take place, the nature of the selling task must be clearly delineated. Management must prepare a carefully thought-out and fully updated job description for every position on the sales force. An example of a job description for a farm machinery salesperson is given in Figure 16–1.

Once the specific kind of selling job to be filled has been determined, the search for a likely employee can begin. Currently employed salespeople, college students, and persons in business currently holding nonselling jobs are the prime prospects for sales jobs. The recruitment process, however, is a difficult one, for personal selling is not as attractive a career choice to many of the more talented or better-educated people as other alternatives. Many view a sales career in terms of long hours, frequent travel, and constant discouragement. The growing recognition of the value of the sales force as a resource of the firm has resulted in attempts by management to improve salespeople's working conditions and financial remuneration and to provide them with security for the future. Unfortunately, it takes time to change career images, and personal selling is still handicapped by the stigma of "hucksterism" and recollections of Arthur Miller's play *Death of a Salesman.*

Sales Force Attrition
The problem of turnover also makes recruitment difficult. Undeniably, not all people who attempt a career in selling are successful. Those who are poor producers either become discouraged and drop out or are eventually

FIGURE 16–1

Job Description, Sales Representative—Office Systems

Job Title: Sales representative

Establishment—Department: Marketing BD Sales

Function

   Promotes and consummates the sale of office systems and related equipment, paper, accessories, and other supplies within an assigned geographic territory, for the Business Division.

Major Activities:

   A. Establishes and maintains close liaison between the company and customers within an assigned geographic territory, for the ultimate purpose of selling Business Division products.

   B. Establishes and maintains a working rapport with customers by providing expertise in the analysis of systems problems and the application of BD products and services to the solution of these problems.

   C. Provides service to customers by recommending changes in operating procedures, assisting them in planning for office systems applications, recommending equipment purchases and supervising their installation, suggesting methods of quality control, and checking to determine that equipment and systems function properly.

   D. Provides accurate and timely information on office products and demonstrates to customers the benefits derived from utilizing these products in his or her business. Keeps customers and prospects updated on new products and office systems.

   E. Assists customers in achieving the high quality capabilities of the company's office products.

   F. Prepares a variety of reports and correspondence including data reports on activities, expenses, market acceptance of office products, product problems, market needs, etc.

   G. Studies customers systems needs and formulates written proposals to satisfy these with the general philosophies established by BD. Outlines systems recommendations incorporating products in customer proposals, cites advantages and operating cost reductions resulting from the proposed system.

   H. Maintains a thorough familiarity of the products of other manufacturers in order to deal with questions posed by customers and prospects in daily activities.

   I. Participates in and/or originates customer seminars and education programs by instructing customers and their personnel in the capabilities of office systems and the proper application and operation of BD products. Provides information and assistance at trade shows and exhibits to interested persons.

   J. Keeps abreast of the new developments and trends in office equipment and systems in order to be capable of understanding customer needs and to be better prepared to provide workable solutions to customer systems requirements.

   K. Handles product complaints and makes recommendations to the marketing center regarding goodwill replacements of products.

   L. Advises district, and/or regional, and/or BD management of any information pertinent to BD activities, gathered as a result of observations made in the field. Reports include new systems applications, activities of other manufacturers, equipment modifications and improvements, customer needs, etc.

   M. Follows up on all sales leads as quickly as possible. Makes new calls on potential customers to stimulate interest in BD products.

   N. Plans activities in a manner that provides for adequate territory coverage. Allocates time on the basis of maximum potential yield and/or priorities established by the district sales manager.

FIGURE 16–1

Concluded

Scope of the Position:

A. Accountability

1. Reports to the district sales manager of the marketing center to which assigned. May direct the activities of less experienced sales representatives assigned to assist on a project basis or for training and development purposes.

2. Responsible for reviewing unusual complex and/or sensitive problems, proposals, or controversial matters with supervision prior to taking any action. Manages the assigned territory with considerable independence.

3. The assigned territory is in the middle range in relation to others in the region in overall dollar accountability, and/or customers have complex installations with sophisticated systems and product applications with which the sales representative must be familiar.

4. Responsible for having a thorough knowledge of all BD products and services and is capable of effectively analyzing, from a systems viewpoint, customers' problems and needs in developing new business by demonstrating the capabilities of Business Systems products to satisfy these needs.

5. Is capable of independently meeting expected sales goals for all categories of products in the assigned territories.

6. Responsible for submitting knowledgeable reports on emerging trends in the marketplace, market needs, and ideas for new products that demonstrate a thorough understanding of the company's position in the marketplace and the direction it must pursue to maintain and improve this position.

7. Shows increasing expertise and professionalism in customer contracts, diagnosis of customer needs, analysis of systems, preparation and presentation of proposals for new systems based on sound economic evaluations.

8. Is expected to exhibit maturity and competence in running the assigned territory with a minimum of direction. Has demonstrated the ability of developing large accounts, multiple sales, etc.

B. Innovation

1. Has a thorough understanding of the capabilities of other manufacturers' product and effectively uses this information to serve customers' needs.

2. Demonstrates originality and creativity in solving systems problems and meeting needs of the market.

3. Responsible for consistently aiding customers by disseminating information on new methods, systems, and techniques that are applicable to their operations.

Job Knowledge:

A. Has a college degree or the equivalent in applicable training and experience.

B. Requires completion of the basic BD training program.

C. Requires a thorough knowledge of all billing, credit, and distribution procedures, paperwork, and policies and is capable of resolving complex problems in these areas with a minimum of confusion, frustration, and inconvenience for all parties concerned.

D. This level of activity is generally achieved with four years' selling experience, or the equivalent, with the assigned products where the individual is subjected to all types of problems and challenges covering the entire product line.

Source: Gilbert A. Churchill, Jr., Neil M. Ford, and Orville C. Walker, Jr., *Sales Force Management*, 3rd ed. (Homewood, Ill.: Richard D. Irwin, 1990), pp. 418–19.

terminated by their employers. Successful salespeople, on the other hand, may shift to other companies to improve their positions or rise to a position in sales management in the same company. Regardless of the cause of turnover, the net result is that openings in sales are frequent. Attrition because of failure or success means that the recruitment task must be continuous and closely attuned to the future needs of the selling organization. For example, if a company with a 200-member sales force loses 20 people a year, it must replace its entire sales force every 10 years!

Selecting Salespeople

Assuming that a continuing supply of applicants is available, the next step is selection. This phase is of great importance because success here can have a great impact on the effectiveness of the selling organization. Selection of qualified and motivated people results in more and higher-quality selling activity. It also reduces separation, either voluntary or involuntary. This in turn means less turnover and lower expense incurred by the firm.

Three tools are useful in the selection process: (1) the personal history statement, (2) psychological tests, and (3) the personal interview.

Personal History Statement   The personal history statement or application form is designed to elicit information about the prospective employee useful for initial screening. Conventional practice is to cover such areas as:

1. *Personal data*—age, height, and weight.
2. *Education*—including a résumé of the applicant's educational background, with data on performance, extent of self-support, and extracurricular activities.
3. *Experience*—prior employers, types of jobs held, and reasons for leaving.
4. *References from several sources*—former teachers, employers, and current acquaintances who can provide information about specific traits or abilities.
5. *Personality and motivation*—general questions about interests in hobbies, organizations, sports, and so on. The applicant may also be asked to explain why he or she is interested in selling as a career and why he or she chose the specific company as a possible employer.

A great deal of information about the prospective employee can be gathered by means of a well-designed personal history form. Not only the specific information but also its mode of presentation can give insight as to the type of candidate. If used as a preliminary screening device, the questionnaire must be designed to get the type of information *relevant* to the nature of the job. In addition, analysis and interpretation of the application form must be carried out by persons who are skilled in psychology, aware of the nature of the job, and involved in the design of the application form.

Psychological Tests   Perhaps the most controversial tools used in selecting salespeople are psychological tests. These devices are used to supplement the information gained from personal history forms and from the interview. It would, however, be unwise to view them as a substitute for the other selection options.

These tests are designed to provide insights about the applicant's intelligence, personality, and interests. Intelligence tests are perhaps the least criticized of all the tests in terms of reliability and validity. The problem is not with intelligence tests themselves but with the relation of a given level of intelligence to probable success in the sales position. It is clear that a minimum level of intelligence is required of salespeople and that perhaps higher levels are needed for successful performance in more technically oriented selling tasks. However, too high a level of intelligence for a given selling job may result in boredom and subsequent job dissatisfaction.

The successful use of intelligence tests is predicated on screening out extremely low and high performers for further investigation. If some relationship can be found between a range of intelligence and success in a particular type of selling job, then, of course, the tests assume predictive value.

Tests of personality, interests, and aptitudes appear to have greater relevance than intelligence tests. These tests deal with human traits that are important in a sales situation. Unfortunately, they are not easily validated—that is, shown to be successful in predicting success in a given situation. Tests are designed to predict, but often it is not clear just what they are predicting. The user must analyze the nature of the selling job in terms of the personality traits most likely to lead to success. Then the employer must construct a test to measure the existence of such traits or use a standardized test of some sort and engage in sufficient experimentation to validate the test or, more likely, the battery of tests. The goal is to be able to predict which persons from a group of applicants are most likely to succeed in a given selling situation. It is quite clear that this goal requires not only personnel skilled in psychological testing procedures but also time, money, and a sales force of sufficient size and turnover rate to provide opportunities for validation experiments. Smaller firms may utilize the services of testing consultants. It must be reemphasized, however, that without validation in terms of the particular selling task, testing should be considered only a small part of the selection procedure.

The Personal Interview   Another approach to selection is the personal interview. The interview is a flexible device and may be used for such diverse purposes as initial screening, as in college campus recruitment, or for final investigation prior to hiring.

The purposes of the interview include discovering traits not uncovered by the application or by testing, probing to find out more about interest and motivation, and evaluating such characteristics as personal appearance and oral expression. The interview may either be structured through a questionnaire or be unstructured, depending on the preference of management. Regardless of the type of interview used, management must provide well-defined criteria that can be used to evaluate the person being interviewed as well as to validate the interviewing process. This provision of criteria is especially important when selecting salespeople because interviewers often have many ill-founded preconceptions about the personality attributes of a good salesperson.

In order to prevent interviewer biases or preconceptions from lessening the effectiveness of the interview as a selection device, many firms have the applicants appraised personally by several interviewers. Regardless of the method, the personal interview can be a useful tool if it can be validated against later sales success. Such validation, in turn, requires a standardized approach. Traits that are important to the selling task at hand must be identified, and all the interviewers must agree on how the existence of these traits is to be discovered and measured.

Training Salespeople

The third component in building a successful sales force is training. After recruitment and selection of new additions to the sales staff, effort must be expended to prepare these people to assume their selling responsibilities. However, training must not be limited to new personnel—it is a continuing process encompassing all members of the sales force, old as well as new.

Training programs vary widely from firm to firm, and the type and extent of training required is a function of several factors, including:

1. The complexity of the product line and product applications.
2. The nature of the market in terms of buyer sophistication.
3. The pressure of competition and the resulting need for nonsales service.
4. The level of knowledge and the degree of the sales experience of the trainee.

Goals of Training   Regardless of the type of program required in a specific situation, the objectives of a training program for newly selected salespeople are quite clear: to make the salesperson more productive, to enable the salesperson to reach a sales norm more rapidly, and to reduce the rate of sales force turnover.

In terms of increasing selling productivity, training can:

1. Provide the product knowledge necessary for all beginning salespeople.
2. Introduce new products and new applications of old products to regular members of the sales force.
3. Point out opportunities in which the existing line can be used to satisfy customer needs.
4. Emphasize nonselling activities (e.g., information gathering) aimed at improving customer relations or cultivating selected accounts.
5. Increase salespeople's productivity by showing them how to utilize their time more effectively and how to engage in personal expense control.

Sales trainers are currently being asked to go well beyond developing and delivering basic skills programs for new hires to the sales staff. According to one expert, trainers must develop more sophisticated applications of product knowledge and market knowledge to respond to market changes, evolving technology, and strategic shifts such as a change in market targets. The goal of training should be to equip salespeople to function as an integral part of the customer's business. Experts say that the customer has supplanted the product or service as the driving force in sales.[1]

It takes considerable time for a new seller to become familiar with a territory. Not only is the learning process time consuming, but also several months often must pass before the new person has the feel for the territory and can develop sales volume consistent with sales potential. The training program must be viewed as a means of supplementing the role of experience in the learning process. Its goal is to shorten the time span required between introduction of a new salesperson to a territory and his or her attainment of a satisfactory level of sales volume.

Because of the considerable expense involved in building a sales force, each salesperson represents a large investment of the firm's resources. When salespeople leave for one reason or another, the investment is lost. In addition, the replacement of an experienced salesperson by a new recruit results in a lag in sales volume until the new seller becomes experienced. Thus turnover, although inevitable, is expensive.

Training, both initial and continuing, may be viewed as an additional investment made to reduce the rate of turnover and thus the related costs and losses of revenue. Proper training may help the individual salesperson to be more successful by teaching him or her new sales techniques and approaches. Perhaps of even greater importance is the supportive role that training plays by indicating to the salesperson the concern of the company for his or her success. Thus it has a motivational role that may be as important to the building of a successful selling organization as its informational role.

Assignment of Sales Personnel

After recruitment, selection, and initial training at the home or district office, the new salesperson is assigned to a territory where he or she will come into contact with current or prospective buyers. In some situations, the salesperson will be assigned to a senior salesperson who will provide guidance and instruction. In other situations, the new seller may explore the territory alone, although under the general supervision and tutoring of the sales manager in the district.

The importance of proper assignment cannot be fully understood without considering the concept of *territory*. Although the term has a geographic meaning, it would be a mistake for a sales manager to think of a territory only in terms of its geographic boundaries. These boundaries are important in that they affect the distances that salespeople must cover and provide a basis for collecting data used in estimating sales potential or measuring sales performance. More important, the territory should be considered in terms of its customer content. The number and type of firms and their needs for various types of goods and services are the territorial attributes that are important in making assignments. Envisioning the sales territory as a set of actual or potential customers helps achieve the true goal of assignment, which is to match the selling resources available as effectively as possible with the buying needs of the target group of customers.

To achieve this goal, the assignment of new sales personnel must be well planned. Assigning a territory to an individual whose training and experience are insufficient to satisfy customer needs results in customer dissatisfaction and salesperson frustration. To avoid such problems, many companies design their sales territories around clusters of customers with similar needs for information and service. The actual location of the customer is of secondary importance as long as there are transportation services that can minimize travel times.

When the skill level required of salespeople varies greatly among the firms in the cluster or even within each individual firm, assignment of new salespeople may be facilitated by providing them with backup support. Thus when new salespeople encounter selling situations that require more skill and experience than they can offer, more experienced senior salespeople can be called in from the district or home office.

Regardless of how the assignment task is handled by sales management, it is important that managers recognize that it is not an easy task for a new person to begin selling effectively without continued support and ongoing training. Carefully matching the skill levels of new salespeople with customer needs and providing backup support when necessary can help a company avoid excessive rates of turnover among new employees and can maintain high levels of customer satisfaction while new salespeople are learning the skills of their trade.

Carnival Cruise Lines Example   Carnival Cruise Lines provides an interesting example of how one company assigns new additions to its sales force. Because of the prospective acquisition of three new cruise ships in 1990, Carnival decided to increase the size of its sales force by 10 in 1989 and to assign these persons to the territories on the basis of the current travel agent base. Inasmuch as 99 percent of all cruise sales were made through travel agents, Carnival had concentrated on being "user friendly" to agents. In line with this policy, past experience indicated that an agent base of between 500 and 550 per representative was a "comfortable" number. Representatives were expected to make approximately 30 calls a week, varying call frequency with the potential of the agent to produce sales. Not being able to make 30 calls a week was taken as a signal that some reallocation of effort might be required. See Figure 16–2.

A second consideration was the market share held by Carnival in each territory. These data were collected by Cruise Line International Association, which monitors sales of 40 cruise companies worldwide. Carnival's showing as average or lower than average in market share was considered another signal that corrective action might be needed. Third, the ratio of sales per 1,000 of population in a territory was examined to see how well that territory was performing compared to other territories. Management stated that the key to success was "to be sensitive to market expansion opportunities." For example, 20 percent of business was repeat in 1985; it was 30 percent in 1988. These data indicate a tendency to concentrate on reselling present customers. What will be needed to fill the growing capacity, however, is not such concentration but market expansion to attract new customers.[2]

SALES FORCE MANAGEMENT: COMPENSATION AND MOTIVATION

In the actual management of an ongoing sales organization, it is assumed that the sales force has an acceptable rate of turnover and that new people are being added to fill vacancies caused by terminations, territorial growth, or a combination of both factors. It is also assumed that a training program for the newcomers is available, as well as a continuing program of retraining for the more seasoned members of the sales force. Given this type of situation, the next aspect of sales force management to be considered is compensation.

Compensating Salespeople

Company policies that determine the level of payment received by salespeople have an important influence on the effectiveness of the sales force. Policies that are fair—that recognize variations in territorial sales potentials and reward individuals for a job well done—attract a better caliber of applicant and help keep more productive sellers satisfied. Thus well-designed and executed compensation plans can help to upgrade the quality of the selling force while reducing the

---

FIGURE 16–2

Promotion of Carnival Sales Reps to Travel Agents in Trade Press

turnover rate. This latter benefit means that the costs of recruitment and selection are lessened and the investment in training is utilized more effectively. (Promotion in Action 16–1 discusses the "risk" factor with regard to compensation.)

The goals of a good compensation plan have been stated in various terms, but most agree that the purpose is to gain the cooperation of the employees and further the interests of the employer. This is not an easy objective to achieve because individual self-interest on the part of a salesperson does not always coincide with the goals of the firm. Thus the most effective compensation plans are designed to provide an incentive for performing the activities the employer deems most profitable. These activities include making sales, of course, as well as providing service, cultivating new accounts, gathering market intelligence, and so on. The difficulty encountered in devising a good compensation plan is caused by the diverse nature of the typical selling job in terms of tasks to be performed as well as the breadth and heterogeneity of the product line or customer list. The complexity of the problem becomes especially evident when the dynamics of product-line development, customer turnover, and competition are added to this situation.

The starting point for appraising or redesigning a compensation plan is the all-important job analysis. A particular selling task must be analyzed in terms of

Adjusting the "Risk" Factor

Promotion in Action

16–1

There are certain considerations to be made [when undertaking the development of a sales compensation plan] that will affect the mechanics of plan design. First is the "leverage" or balance between base salary and commission. The basic consideration here is the amount of risk the salesperson will assume. The more risk, the more generous the commission, since salespeople are paid from performance revenues (sales), as opposed to just being an operating expense.

Base salary is just that, the amount paid as salary. This can be a weekly or monthly draw with a quota or simply a guarantee. The commission kicks in once salespeople meet quota. Leverage is usually expressed as a ratio, such as 24/76 (24 percent of target compensation as salary, 76 percent as commission).

There are some practical considerations concerning the selection of the sales commission leverage ratio, the primary one being your particular sales environment. The length of your sales cycle, difficulty of sale, sales volume required, and resources available all affect the perceived "appropriateness" of the leverage ratio.

For example, if you have mature marketing and lead generation programs in place, dollar volume per sale is large, and the sales cycle is moderate, then a high leverage is appropriate (that is, the majority of salespeople's compensation is commission). On the other hand, if your sales support is lacking, your lead generation nonexistent, and marketing merely a term in your business plan, then a low leverage point is appropriate, due to the amount of nondirect sales work and sales infrastructure development that has to be done by the salesperson.

Source: Excerpted from Jeffrey P. Geibel, "Developing a Compensation Plan That Attracts Top Talent," *Sales & Marketing Management,* June 1992, p. 162. Used by permission.

the components of the task which, when performed well, lead to success. These are the components the compensation plan must spotlight to get more and better performance from the sales force. Second, an income analysis of the salespeople involved must be made. Will the compensation plan proposed provide competitive levels of income to members of the sales force? Will any members of the force receive a reduced income if the plan becomes operative?

A new compensation plan should not cause major short-term changes in the income of participants. Instead, it should change the rewards for performance of certain activities or for the sale of certain products over a period of time so that changes are evolutionary rather than sudden.

After a careful job analysis, including a definition of objectives for the compensation plan, a tentative approach can be developed and discussed with the salespeople. This step provides an opportunity for feedback—a chance to pick up new ideas from the sales force as well as to hear their criticisms. It also allows management to explain the way in which the plan will operate and to anticipate and assuage fears salespersons may have about the proposed plan's impact on their well-being. The plan proposed may be modified in view of the salespeople's suggestions and fears.

After preliminary analyses, the plan is ready to be tested. A test can be simulated by utilizing past sales records to see what earnings would have been if the new plan had been in force. Or the new plan can be put into effect in specific territories representing a range of competitive conditions and employee skill and experience. The second approach is preferred because it is impossible to tell how salespeople will react to a new plan until they actually work under it. Information from the actual test run can be used to improve the plan further and to indicate whether or not it should be fully implemented.

Components of Compensation   The methods of compensation are (1) base salary, (2) commission, and (3) bonus.

Base salary   The base salary is payment for certain routine activities performed by the sales force. It is a means of control by which management can require that a route be covered or that certain types of supporting activities be performed through guaranteed income. It also provides a cushion against large fluctuations in employees' income caused by conditions beyond their control. Hence, the greater the routinized selling activity or the larger the fluctuation in sales volume, the more the reliance is likely to be placed on base salary in the compensation mix.

Commission   A commission or percentage payment associated with the sale of certain items in the line is used by management to direct the sales effort to specific items (or customers). Rates of commission may be periodically adjusted to reflect changes in product or customer profitability or in the market environment. The role of the commission form of compensation is determined by the incentive requirements and the stability of sales volume. Customer needs for nonselling services place limits on the degree of sales incentive that management can blend into the compensation mix. With too much emphasis on incentive compensation, the salesperson becomes a "high-spotter," spending time with larger accounts and neglecting smaller ones.

Bonus   Bonus compensation is a more diffused type of incentive payment. Generally, bonuses are paid for exceeding a predetermined quota, although they may represent some allocation of profits based on performance and length of service. A bonus is a means of letting a salesperson share in the progress of the firm without making the payment as directly related to performance as is the case with a commission. The bonus may be very important in compensating technical representatives who back up salespeople by solving customer problems but who do not actually make sales.

An actual compensation plan may call for any combination of the three components. The nature of the selling task and the requirements of the market that determine the role of personal selling suggest the emphasis to be placed on salary, commission, and bonus payments.

Objectives of a Good Compensation Plan   The following have been suggested as four general objectives of a compensation plan:

1. To attract and hold good salespeople.
2. To stimulate the sales organization to produce the maximum attainable volume of profitable sales.
3. To control selling expense, especially where there are major fluctuations in sales volume.
4. To ensure full attention to customer needs through complete performance of the sales job.

Although the general objectives are common to all compensation programs, the relative importance of each one may change with respect to different firms or to individual firms in different stages of development. For example, the small firm just starting out may find that expense control is the most important objective of its compensation plan. On the other hand, a more established firm might find that competition requires a compensation plan that motivates the firm's salespeople to the complete fulfillment of customer needs.

In addition to the general objectives, individualized goals may be designed to achieve specific company marketing and sales objectives. The following goals have been suggested:

1. To encourage solicitation of new accounts and development of new sources of revenue.
2. To encourage full-line selling.
3. To stimulate the sale of more profitable products.
4. To hold a salesperson responsible for the profit contribution on sales where she or he can influence margins.

The specific objectives listed above are by no means exhaustive. Neither are they common to all plans for compensating salespeople. A truly effective program contains the means to reach goals common to all firms. In addition, it will be tailored to reach specific objectives that are an outgrowth of the resources, competition, and promotional strategy of the individual firm.

Carnival Cruise Lines Example   Carnival Cruise Lines uses a very effective approach to compensation. Its sales representatives have no caps on their earnings. They have realistic quotas and have direct input into the quota-setting process. Every effort is made to protect the present representative if an additional one is assigned to the territory. The company seeks to maintain its credibility with the representatives by keeping all promises it makes. A company executive stated that the key attributes of all successful Carnival representatives are intelligence, flexibility, the ability to listen, and hunger. The Carnival sales force has the least turnover in the industry; its members are loyal and have extraordinary esprit de corps.[3]

However, Carnival, like most companies that depend on resellers, finds that the same selling enthusiasm that characterizes its sales force is not always found among travel agents. Carnival's top person in sales and marketing states his views in Promotion in Action 16–2.

Motivating Salespeople

The very nature of the selling job requires that special attention be paid to the proper motivation of personnel. The seller who works alone and away from home faces considerable discouragement in daily routine. The depressing effects of loneliness and rejection usually require some type of supportive action from management. For some personalities, the selling task may be sufficiently intriguing to require little more in the way of motivation than a good incentive compensation plan and a new list of prospects. Such salespeople are rare, however, and the average member of the sales force requires some motivating efforts in addition to that provided by regular monetary compensation. The human traits of laziness and procrastination are as present among sellers as any other group in society, and managers have learned from experience that effort expended to overcome human inertia pays off in increased sales productivity.

The types of motivating action that might be taken by management are varied. Essentially, they may be classified as (1) additional incentive compensation, (2) career advancement, and (3) contests or other types of special sales stimulation promotions. See Figure 16–3.

Additional Compensation   This attempt at providing added motivation for the salesperson is predicated on the belief that monetary rewards are the most meaningful. The payment of special compensation in addition to the regular plan may be used to motivate salespeople to reach special short-run objectives in terms of sales volume, customer coverage, or product emphasis. Monetary rewards have the advantage of being direct, easily understood by employees, and readily administered. The question is simply this: Do they motivate salespeople to sell as well as other rewards such as those discussed below?

Carnival Exec Says Travel Agents Don't Know How to Sell

The following is part of an interview with Bob Dickinson, Carnival Cruise Lines' senior vice president of sales and marketing by Alan Fredericks, editor-in-chief of *Travel Weekly.*

TW: You are widely regarded as the most outspoken cruise line executive on the need to improve travel agents' selling skills. How do you respond when some suggest that you are overly critical?

Dickinson: Let me start this way. I was in the business 15 years before it really dawned on me that agents don't know how to sell. So that's more of an indictment on the supply side.

I think the first time I talked about it was at the ASTA world congress in Houston in 1987.

We had gone through reports from our Mystery Vacationer program, where our people visit agencies, and we found that not only did many agents not know how to sell, some of the things that they were doing were just bizarre.

So I continued to tell the story. Then about two years ago, when I was starting to get the "kill the messenger" response, I decided to document it.

I frequently speak to groups of agents. I took those opportunities to ask them how many prospects come into their office, how many prospects call in, how many sales they close.

We did elaborate analyses, and based on a wide range of agencies, we found that average closing rates ranged from 3 percent to 15 percent.

At the same time, we looked at a much smaller but a growing group of agencies that have put together some of the platform planks, if you will, to convert at least a portion of their agencies from a ticket agency to a retail vacation store.

We tracked the closure rates of some of those folks, and they were closing 45 percent to 60 percent. The productivity was four to six times greater than for the other agencies.

TW: What is it that the more successful group is doing differently that makes them so much more productive?

Dickinson: Five things.

One, they are knowledgeable in selling techniques and have frequent sales training.

Two, they like to sell.

Three, they sell a limited number of suppliers, and that allows them to become more informed about the products.

Four, a significant part of their compensation is on the basis of either piecework or incentives. If they sell, they make more; if they don't, they don't make as much.

And five, if they are full-service agencies, they separate selling people from service people so the people with the high closing rates for vacations aren't handling corporate accounts and doing a lot of ticketing.

If you look at those five things in the average group, you find the absolute converse of what the more successful agencies do.

They don't know the selling techniques. They're fearful of selling, specifically the fear of rejection. Their compensation is on the basis of salary or some mystical year-end bonus that is too ill-defined. They sell everything to everybody and don't know in depth about enough products.

And they say they don't have the time to sell because the phone is ringing and it's a commercial account, and the order taking is taking precedence.

Source: Excerpted from an interview by Alan Fredericks, "Dickinson Prescribes Strategies for Boosting Sales Productivity," *Travel Weekly,* January 13, 1992, pp. 1, 33–35.

Career Advancement   In this approach, the better sales performers are offered transfers to more lucrative territories or are invited to join the ranks of sales management. Thus the income advantage of job betterment is combined with the prestige of a rise in the organizational hierarchy. The motivating appeal of job advancement is less immediate in its impact than a direct monetary payment. But the reward, if achieved, has longer-lasting benefits to the salesperson. The problem, of course, is the lack of immediacy of payoff.

Special Activities   Somewhere between the immediate and somewhat prosaic approach of direct monetary payoffs and the longer-run approach involving job advancement lies a range of special activities including contests and other types of special sales promotions aimed at increasing sales personnel motivation. Contests are especially popular among sales managers for this purpose. They view contests as a means to elicit extra effort to achieve short-run goals by means somewhat more dramatic than purely monetary payments. Contests may liven the competitive spirit of the salespeople, may involve wives and children, and may promise rewards such as travel or vacations with pay, which may have more general appeal than mere money.

Numerous dangers are inherent in the use of contests as motivators, however. Like any other form of stimulation aimed at getting extra effort in the short run, contests may lose their impact with continued use. The nature of some contests

FIGURE 16–3

Recognition for Top Sales People

and other events may alienate the more serious and professionally oriented members of the sales force. Moreover, contests by their very nature engender rivalry among members of the sales organization and may thereby break down a close group relationship built over a long period of time. They must be used with care and never as a substitute for effective activity in the other aspects of sales force management discussed earlier.

Methods of Communication

Because salespeople work at a distance from the home office and are usually on their own a great deal, management has a special problem in establishing lines of communication to them. Written messages going out to the field and reports from the field flowing in are found in almost all sales situations, but there is a serious question as to the effect of this type of communication on employee morale or motivation. Certainly, a note from a superior congratulating a salesperson on a job well done will give the salesperson a feeling of being recognized and appreciated, but a routine written pep talk too often has little or no effect on motivation.

Recognition of the shortcomings of written communication has led many sales managers to use the telephone instead of the memo. Of course, personal contact is the best method of communication between salespeople and their managers. Traditionally, the sales manager has attempted to build a personal relationship with the individual salespeople. In fact, a psychiatrist, highly experienced in these matters, has indicated that sellers often view their sales manager as a parent figure and are quite disturbed emotionally when separated from this superior by transfer or promotion.

Organizational Variables and Their Impact on Sales

Policies and procedures that determine the patterns of organization of sales force management can have an important influence on sales force motivation.[4] For example, in the years preceding World War II, most sales organizations were highly formalized, highly centralized structures. Salespersons were considered as objects to be moved around the territories like chess pieces on a chess board, given their sales quotas, and discarded if they failed to produce. In reaction to this type of treatment, the concept of *human relations* developed in the postwar era. Scholars in this area stressed the importance of interpersonal relationships and the motivation of workers, including salespersons. "Management became less authoritarian and more participative. Sales executives began to realize that salespeople are individuals with emotions, personalities, expectations, and self-concepts."[5]

At present, organizational theorists recognize that neither of these extremes is effective in optimizing worker productivity and profitability. Effective management today requires a balance between the formalized hierarchical organizational structure and the human relations approach. The organization is regarded as a total system, and decision-making theory is stressed. See Table 16–1 for a summary of contrasts between traditional and current models in organization theory.

Research has indicated that closeness of supervision, span of control, influence over standards, frequency of communication, opportunity rate (opportunity to be promoted to sales management), recognition rate, compensation rate, and earnings opportunity ratio (ratio of total financial rewards of the highest paid salesperson to the total rewards of the average salesperson) all influence sales force morale and motivation.[6]

It is beyond the scope of this text to explore this area in greater detail, but in reading Promotion in Action 16–3, you should recognize that effective selling is an extremely complex activity. It is one that calls for bright, motivated salespeople and effective sales management. The high cost of personal selling and the inroads of competition mean that the days when a salesperson can be placed in a territory without any guidance or support are gone. To succeed takes a team effort with all eyes focused on the customer.

SUMMARY

This chapter considers personal selling as a special form of interpersonal communication. Inasmuch as the salesperson is the key element in the communication process, the nature of his or her task is examined in some detail. In addition, the process by which a sales force is built into an effective promotional resource is examined. Furthermore, attention is paid to the compensation and motivation of the individuals who make up the selling organization.

In this chapter, the sales force is treated in the same manner as advertising—as a "controllable." This implies that the type, amount, and direction of all promotional efforts are subject to variation in the short run by marketing management.

TABLE 16–1

⌣   **Two Models of Organizational Theory**

Traditional	Current
1. More likely to be production oriented.	1. More likely to be marketing oriented.
2. Internally oriented.	2. Oriented toward external environment.
3. Highly formalized and inflexible.	3. Less formalized; more flexible.
4. Centralized authority.	4. Decentralized authority.
5. More levels of supervision and shorter span of control.	5. Fewer levels of supervision and broader span of control.
6. Major concern is toward the system; system becomes an end in itself.	6. Management relies on the workers rather than on the system; system is only a means to an end.
7. Orientation is toward how the job is done.	7. Results oriented: *Did* you get the job done?

Source: William J. Stanton and Richard H. Buskirk, *Management of the Sales Force*, 6th ed. (Homewood, Ill., Richard D. Irwin, 1983).

This view of personal selling as a promotional input subject to control in the short run is generally sustainable. However, a really effective selling organization cannot be built overnight. Thus, although short-run control is possible in terms of type of effort, extent of effort, or direction of effort, the truly qualitative aspect of the effort depends on a continuing process of recruitment, selection, training, supervision, and control. Good management is vital at each of these stages if the firm is to get the best payoff possible from its personal selling effort.

REVIEW AND DISCUSSION QUESTIONS

1. You want to hire three salespersons for your small software company. Outline a written job description and explain why a complete written job description is the foundation on which a sales force is built.

What Makes a Top Performer?

Promotion in Action

16-3

What does it take to make it in selling today? A recently published survey by Learning International says that for salespeople, skills far beyond those involved in making a presentation are needed; for sales managers, it's the ability to plan and support their field people as never before. And, according to LI, most of us aren't making the grade.

For its survey, LI, a Stamford, Connecticut, training company, asked 3,200 managers, colleagues, and customers to judge 495 salespeople and sales managers they had worked with or with whom they had had recent business dealings. The respondents were asked to rate the subjects' effectiveness and for those they rated highly, to state what was special about their performance.

What makes a salesperson outstanding from the viewpoint of customers and others? Foremost is the ability or orchestrate events and bring together a selling team—the salesperson and whatever support people are needed to make the sale. Second is the ability to counsel clients based on a deep knowledge of the way they operate and what their product and service needs are.

To earn top status, the respondents said, a salesperson must also be skilled at problem solving and providing customer service, both being the secret for building long-term relationships. LI researchers add that learning these skills is in itself a long-term affair—most of the people who "won" the survey had been in sales at least five years.

Sales managers who were identified as most effective excel at the following:

1. Correctly analyzing customers' individual needs, developing sales goals that meet their company's own goals, and establishing territories for the people under them.

2. Mentoring their field people by skillful coaching and giving constructive criticism and full support.

3. Being strong communicators, not only with the field sales force but with upper management as well.

Source: "Short Takes," *Sales and Marketing Management*, May 1989, p. 23. Used by permission.

2. Seven persons have applied for the jobs described in your job description (Question 1). You are now setting up a schedule for personal interviews. What dangers must you avoid when interviewing the applicants?

3. Of the seven persons interviewed (Question 2), you are really interested in four of them but you want to be very careful in your selection. You are considering sending these applicants for psychological testing. What are the benefits and dangers of such a move?

4. You have hired three persons for the sales force and now must start to train them to perform in the field. What should be the goals of such a training program? Can sales training ever cease?

5. Imagine that two years have passed since you started your company and your sales force has grown to 20 persons. Your services are well-known in the market area, and the nature of the selling task is changing. You are considering a change in the compensation plan to reflect these different conditions. What guidelines should you consider when proposing a new plan of compensation?

6. The compensation plan discussed above has been implemented and has resulted in a drop in sales force morale and in motivation. Is this normal? What can you do to alleviate the causes underlying these symptoms of salesperson dissatisfaction?

NOTES

1. Dick Schaaf and Tom Cothran, "Sales Training in the Era of the Customers," *Training: Sales Training Supplement,* February 1988, pp. 3–4.

2. Personal interviews (May 1989), and Fay Rice, "How Carnival Stacks the Decks," *Fortune,* January 16, 1989, pp. 108–16.

3. Ibid.

4. This section borrows heavily from William J. Stanton and Richard H. Buskirk, *Management of the Sales Force,* 6th ed. (Homewood, Ill.: Richard D. Irwin, 1983), pp. 46–47.

5. Ibid.

6. Gilbert A. Churchill, Jr., Neil M. Ford, and Orville C. Walker, Jr., *Sales Force Management,* 3rd ed. (Homewood, Ill.: Richard D. Irwin, 1990), pp. 418–19.

Section

7

OTHER FORMS OF
PROMOTIONAL STRATEGY

We turn in this section to the two remaining elements of the promotional mix: (1) direct marketing and (2) public relations, publicity, and corporate advertising.

Direct marketing, often referred to as *database marketing,* has come into ascendency as one of the most widely used promotional strategies. As you will discover, its strength lies in the direct, personalized relationship with an identified customer. More and more marketers are finding that this is a primary way to attract new customers and to maintain their loyalty.

Public relations, publicity, and corporate advertising, on the other hand, have a different function—to build internal and external support for the organization, its policies, and its directions. While this category of communications often is referred to as *supplemental communications,* you will discover the important role it plays in setting the climate for an organization and building a firm basis of public acceptance.

C h a p t e r

17

Direct Marketing

TICKET TO GOOD TIMES

Confronted with increasing social and regulatory pressures in the beer industry, Miller Brewing Company needed new channels for reaching Miller loyals and competitors' customers. A revolutionary direct response advertising campaign was successfully launched, focusing on adult beer drinkers aged 21–34 in the Atlanta area.

Miller successfully tested an affinity card offering beer drinkers a variety of value-added benefits. Offers to Miller Time card holders included, among others, free T-shirts, discounts to local music events, and coupons good for Miller beer at retail locations.

Miller wanted to build a database of names to increase traffic at the retail level, as well as to acquire new retail placements. How was its target reached? The multimedia campaign used spot TV, cable TV, and direct response TV, focusing on sports and music programming as well as late-night shows. It used Atlanta's top two rock/pop radio stations and advertised in *Creative Loafing* (circulation 110,000), Atlanta's top entertainment and nightlife newspaper. Mailings were sent to names gathered from these sources.

Source: "Ticket to Good Times," *Direct Marketing*, November 1992, p. 36. Reproduced by special permission.

What you have just read illustrates the growing importance of direct marketing—"an interactive system of marketing which uses one or more advertising media to effect a measurable response and/or transaction at any location,"[1] Its most important tool is the *consumer database,* the all-important list of buyers and prospects who receive precisely targeted appeals. And it embodies the philosophy of *individualized marketing,* defined in this way by Rapp and Collins: "a very personal form of marketing that recognizes, acknowledges, appreciates, and serves the interests and needs of selected groups of consumers whose individual identities are or become known to the advertiser [marketer]."[2]

Growing numbers of consumers have come to prefer in-home shopping and buying. Therefore, direct marketing is increasingly used to bypass the retail shopping outlet. But it is also used as a valuable complement to more traditional channels because it enables the marketer to segment precisely and to reach consumers in multiple buying contexts.

In this chapter, you will see how direct marketing (now increasingly referred to as *database marketing*) has emerged as one of the most valued promotional strategies in most of the developed countries of the world.

THE UNIQUE NATURE OF DIRECT MARKETING

Direct marketing offers the powerful benefit of providing an ongoing relationship between company and customer. As eminent marketing commentator Philip Kotler put it,

> Now is the time for really remembering those customers of yours, the nuances, what and when they bought, what they're interested in, keeping up with their needs, and showing your continued interest in them.[3]

The personalized nature of the exchange process offers real benefits for potential customers. The following are the main reasons why it is proving so popular:

1. A greater desire for shopping convenience and service, reflecting changed lifestyles resulting from the increased number of working wives and the greater priority placed on leisure.
2. The growth of *cocooning*—a term coined by Faith Popcorn to capture the growing trend to turn "inward" and center life around the home and family.[4]
3. Growing distaste for shopping in overcrowded stores and malls—congested parking lots, uninformed salespeople, long lines, and so on. Promotion in Action 17–1 will give you a feeling for why so many shoppers are avoiding public shopping.
4. Greater willingness to pay by credit card, thus facilitating non-face-to-face transactions.

There are equally strong benefits for the company. No longer is the marketer adrift in the competitive sea, dependent entirely on ability to attract attention of an unknown and unidentified customer in the mass market. The following are some bottom-line features that make direct marketing especially attractive:[5]

1. *It goes directly to an identified person or household.* It does not go to a general audience, as does most media advertising.
2. *The goal is some type of action.* That action can take the form of replying by return mail, sending a coupon, making a telephone call, and so on.
3. *Because the goal is specific action, results can be measured with precision.*
4. *It is interactive.* It involves a direct exchange of information and response between two parties.
5. *It makes use of a customer database.* A computerized record is kept of each customer's background, purchase patterns, interests, and so on.

This provides an excellent source for targeting future marketing efforts with precision.

The Persuasive Impact of Direct Marketing

One fundamental principle of direct marketing is this: Direct marketing usually achieves the greatest results when consumers are in the later stages of their decision process. The primary intent is to elicit a buying (or giving) response, and effectiveness is measured in terms of return on investment (ROI).

Every direct marketing effort is measured against the demanding criterion of ROI. This means that direct marketing ordinarily has not been used when the primary objectives are to build awareness, change beliefs, and change attitudes. This premise is being rethought, however.[6] Consider these words by industry executive Malcolm Karlin:

> Getting results is important, but what you have to do is to be true to your product and brand. "Safe" techniques traditionally employed by direct marketers . . . diminish brand respect over the long haul.[7]

Some firms, such as Xerox Corporation, are gauging shifts in consumer attitudes toward products before and after direct mail to evaluate changes in consumer perceptions.[8] If this becomes a trend, the role for direct marketing will broaden.

Shoppers' Blues: The Thrill Is Gone

Promotion in Action

17–1

Marlene Dash would appear to be a marketer's dream come true. The corporate manager likes to dress smartly, both on and off the job. She owns a condominium in Chicago and takes pride in furnishing it well.

Yet Ms. Dash, in her mid-30s, loathes shopping. Lousy service and poor selections at many stores have turned a once-favorite pastime into what she calls a "frustrating" experience. These days she would rather exercise, visit friends, or read."If you don't make it reasonably easy for me," she says, "I'm not going to waste my time."

Ms. Dash is far from alone. Shopping has become such a chore that more people hate browsing in stores than hate doing housework, according to the "American Way of Buying" survey conducted by *The Wall Street Journal.* Nearly a third of the 2,064 people interviewed by Peter D. Hart Research Associates said they "Do not enjoy at all" window shopping or browsing.

That feeling is amply confirmed by the spectacular growth of catalog companies that have stolen sales from retail stores for much of this decade. Yankelovich, Clancy, Shulman, a market research firm in Westport, Connecticut, warns clients that Americans' love affair with shopping is on the rocks: More than half the women it has surveyed in recent years, and an even larger percentage of men, say shopping for clothes is a hassle.

But underlying these complaints is a more far-reaching change: For many shoppers, the thrill is gone.

Source: Francine Schwadel, "Shoppers' Blues: The Thrill Is Gone," *The Wall Street Journal,* October 13, 1989, p. B1. Reproduced by special permission.

A Growth Industry

As Figure 17–1 indicates, 1991 in-home sales generated by direct marketing topped $210 billion in the United States, the fastest growth of any ad medium. Furthermore, there is rapid growth outside the United States, especially in such countries as Spain, Germany, the Netherlands, and Japan. See Table 17–1.

The magnitude of direct marketing is further underscored by the fact that the estimated total expenditure on all direct response media in the United States

FIGURE 17–1

Charting U.S. Direct Marketing Growth

A. Charting U.S. Mail-Order Sales Growth

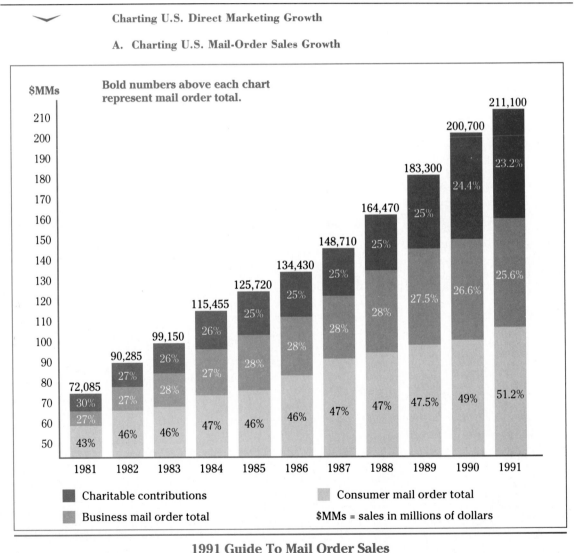

1991 Guide To Mail Order Sales

TABLE 17–1

Direct Marketing Growth Worldwide, 1991

Country	% of Retail Sales	Growth %
Spain	0.05%	26.1%
Germany	4.70	22.0
Netherlands	1.60	13.9
Japan	1.20	13.0
Australia	5.00	11.0
Italy	0.50	10.2
Canada	—	10.0

Source: "International Mail Order Marketing Statistics," *Direct Marketing,* October 1992, p. 29. Reproduced by special permission.

equals two thirds of all advertising, direct and nondirect.[9] Furthermore, direct marketing is also used to raise funds for all sorts of nonprofit organizations. Almost $50 billion was raised in this way in 1991.[10] Direct mail and telemarketing are the leading methods, each accounting for more than 40 percent of total expenditures, with the remainder being accounted for by interactive video and other methods.

FIGURE 17–1

Concluded

B. Ad Mail: The Fastest-Growing Medium (% of Total Ad Expenditures)

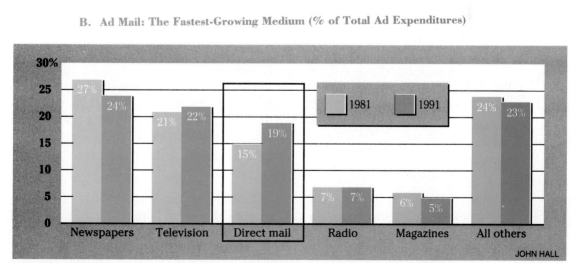

Sources: "Mail Order Top 250+," *Direct Marketing,* July 1992, p. 20; and Harry J. Buckel, "Economics, Efficiency Spur Shift to Ad Mail," *Advertising Age,* August 31, 1992, p. M-3. Reproduced by special permission.

THE DATABASE: THE KEY TO DIRECT MARKETING SUCCESS

Whatever the objective, the unquestioned key to direct marketing success is locating and identifying likely prospects and building a responsive database. Assume that you are the marketing manager for a company offering a new series of video games. At this point, retail distribution does not seem to be the best strategy, and a decision has been made to try direct marketing. How do you build a database?

Two possibilities are available: (1) existing lists (an in-house list or names purchased from a list broker) and (2) geodemography.

Existing Lists

If you have sold video games before and have retained customer names, this in-house list is your logical starting point. Generally such lists are computerized and can be segmented by recency of purchase (purchase in the last few months or so), frequency, dollar amount, and type of products purchased.

Another possibility is to try existing lists available from a list broker. A starting point might be the purchase of names of people who have bought similar (or even identical) products through other sources. What do you think of this option?

> CAPCOM USA list contains 532,434 names at $85/M. These consumers own a Nintendo Entertainment System or a Nintendo Game Boy, and have spent between $35 and $55 on software for their systems.[11]

By "$85/M," this broker is saying that the list can be purchased for $85 per 1,000 names. There is good reason to think that these people might be prospects because of their usage of Nintendo products.

Another alternative is to approach a list broker for a *compiled list.* These lists are composed of names collected from a variety of sources such as census, home buying, car registration lists, and so on. It may be possible to infer interest from purchasers of collateral products or other related behaviors.

Before using any list, it is essential to test a sample of names prior to a full-scale rollout. The most common sample size for tests of this type includes 5,000 names. Testing the CAPCOM list requires a total direct-cost investment of $425 (5,000 at $85/M) plus printing and mailing. The entire list should be purchased only if sales response to the test sample gives a positive return on investment. Precise testing is a unique advantage of direct marketing.

Geodemography[12]

The United States is geographically divided into more than 250,000 census tract block groups containing an average of 361 household units. These block groups are the heart of geodemographic segmentation systems such as PRIZM offered by Claritas, ACORN by CACI, and VISION by National Decision Systems.[13]

The starting point is to enter detailed characteristics of present customers into a database. These characteristics are then correlated with the clusters in one of the geodemography computer programs. This identifies names of others whose profile matches current customers. The assumption is that they will be more prone to respond to advertising, through either targeted mass media or direct marketing, than people in general.

The new Buick Roadmaster station wagon was launched in April 1991 through use of magazines targeted at specific ZIP codes.[14] Ads in such magazines as *Newsweek* were aimed at 4,940 of the country's more than 40,000 ZIP codes, mostly in upscale suburbs in the Northeast and Midwest. The ads featured a personally addressed ink-jet card inviting the prospect to send for more information on the car.

DIRECT MARKETING STRATEGIES

Telemarketing

Telemarketing has two phases: inbound (calls from the consumer) and outbound (sales calls direct to the consumer). There is no clear indication of the dollar magnitude of each, although it is estimated that they are about equal in dollar volume.

Inbound Telemarketing   Avon Products, Inc., formerly sold its line of cosmetics and perfumes largely through direct sales visits to customers' homes. A new program called Avon Select was introduced in 1991 and allowed customers to order either through a representative as before or by mail, telephone, or FAX. By 1992, the company was mailing catalogs and offers to 10 million homes with an average response rate of 11 percent.[15] Successful case histories such as this one abound both in the United States and abroad.[16] See Figure 17–2.

Many telemarketers also are making use of *audiotex*.[17] A computerized answering machine takes the incoming 800-number call that can be stimulated by ads in any medium. The machine asks questions and automatically records answers. In addition, full buyer information is collected. The answering machine dramatically lowers the cost per call when it is compared with the use of an operator.

One of the most effective uses of inbound telemarketing is for aftersale service. Nintendo of America, for example, receives about 50,000 inbound toll-free calls per week.[18] These calls are, of course, an ideal source of names for ongoing direct marketing of Nintendo products.

Outbound Telemarketing   Telephone sales are becoming prevalent in both consumer goods and industrial marketing firms. A vast majority of Fortune 500 companies (one of which is Avon Products, Inc., mentioned earlier) make at least some use of telephone sales. Some sales representatives now take initiative by telephone, inviting those who received a catalog to place an order. This has done wonders to improve customer response and retention.[19]

Telecommunication technologies have sharply increased telemarketing productivity.[20] Automated telemarketing systems, for example, predict when a sales agent will be available and automatically dial the next prospect. In addition, orders are logged directly into the computer mainframe. Even more advanced is the voice response unit, a robot that translates elements from data-entry screens into a spoken voice, accompanied by automated recording of orders placed by touch-tone phones. There is not much left for humans to do in such systems.

If you are going to use outbound telemarketing, here are some suggestions:

1. *Best results are achieved when the sales offer is a timely response to changing events.* "Mr. Smith, the stock market has jumped 18 points in the last week, and bonds have slipped. We would like to show you how to increase your yield by switching to mutual funds now."

2. *You must know your prospect.* The author of this chapter lived in a brick home for years and received frequent calls from aluminum siding dealers. Nothing could scare them off—from sarcasm to threats. The best outcomes often come from previous customers when your call is based on firsthand knowledge of their previous buying behavior. "Mr. Jones, your Acura Leg-

---

FIGURE 17–2

Avon Select

end now is five years old, and I would like to personally invite you to see the new model."

3. *Call at convenient times.* Does anyone appreciate being interrupted at dinner to hear about a new stock offering?

4. State your offer and benefit at the outset. You will have only a short interval to capture and hold the prospect's attention, and there is little room for delay.

Coping with Growing Backlash

More and more firms are making use of computerized, prerecorded presentations. Industry sources estimate that 7 million Americans each day receive an automated telephone sales pitch from around 190,000 solicitors.[21]

Apparently this tactic has had some success, but there is increasing evidence that a growing backlash may make it less attractive. According to Lorna Christie, director of ethics and consumer affairs at the Direct Marketing Association, "People are more annoyed about receiving unsolicited calls than [receiving unsolicited] mail."[22]

It hardly seems necessary to stress that telemarketing is successful over the long haul only when it is based in responsible professionalism. Everything we said about professional sales techniques in Chapter 15 also applies here. All too often, untrained people produce more alienation than sales. Telephone solicitation is a legitimate activity that can provide real consumer benefit if it is done responsibly. Unfortunately, the frequency of discourtesy and abuse may be tainting the field for everyone.

Direct Mail

You open your mail, and your eye is stopped by an 8½-by-11-inch mailer with a mason jar on the cover full of red peppers. The copy asks, "Would you rather eat a jar of hot peppers or take your children shopping for six hours straight?" It goes on to say, "Finally, shopping without the struggle. A new kind of place for moms and kids is opening in Merrilville [Indiana]." It ends with a Sears logo and an announcement of its power-format kids' store, Kids & More.[23] See Figure 17–3.

This was a test mailing for a new department that offers everything for kids under one roof, complete with entertainment and diversion. Targeted at mothers with children under the age of 12, it has proven to be so successful in terms of generating traffic and new name acquisition that newspaper advertising expenditures have been reduced.[24]

As you no doubt are aware, direct mail is big business. Why is this method so successful? You may be surprised to discover that about two thirds of the public enjoys opening their mail (including advertising). In fact, this has been found to be one of the most enjoyable activities of the day.[25]

The evidence overwhelmingly indicates that direct-mail ads are read. There have been numerous confirming studies published in such sources as *Direct Marketing*. Also, the author of this chapter has worked for years with nonprofit organizations using direct mail for fund-raising. All of this research (which unfortunately is proprietary) indicates the same conclusion.

Then what about all the complaints about junk mail? We do not deny that much of the stuff received daily falls exactly into that category and winds up in the trash can. Brad Edmondson issues a very appropriate challenge in Promotion in Action 17–2.

The Direct-Mail Letter

Read the letter in Figure 17–4 carefully. Is this a good letter? No one can say for sure just by looking at it because the ultimate proof lies in the return on investment that it generates. But there are some guidelines that will help you.

The first question always should be, Is the recipient a likely prospect? This takes us back to choosing a mailing list, which always must be a central consideration. The second question is this: Does the offer provide a real benefit for the person who reads the letter?

FIGURE 17–3

A New Kind of Place for Moms and Kids

Kids & More at Sears
Paramus Park

Bulk Rate
U.S. Postage
PAID
Berwyn, IL
Permit No. 73

```
*****CAR-RTE SORT ** CR01
AAA          K-AA
SAMPLE A. SAMPLE
1234 ANY STREET
BOX 55555  R1
ANYTOWN, US 12345-1234
```

Would you rather
eat a jar of hot peppers
or take your children
shopping for six hours straight?

If your answers are positive, then and only then should you look into the details of the execution. Although no one has a precise formula, letters are tested in the same manner as lists. Does changing the headline, for example, stimulate greater buying response? Perhaps three different headlines will be compared in terms of ROI. Such comparison can be made with any part of the letter. The outcome is that any direct marketer can learn quickly what works and what does not.

Some of the most commonly used guidelines are given by Bob Stone in Table 17–2. Read them carefully and then compare them to the following evaluation of the letter from GTE Sprint in Figure 17–4:

1. The benefit is stated right at the outset—you will save money by using Sprint.

2. Specific details are given on what you will get, and these are backed up with comparative rates as proof.

3. You are told that you may have higher rates if you do not act.

4. The benefit is clearly restated in the P.S., as it should be.

5. Action is incited by the offer of a free hour of long-distance calling.

You will notice that "direct" is different from what you might have learned in creative writing class. Copy is clear and concise. Paragraphs are short. "Action" words are used. There is good reason for this: The reader's attention span is

---

Death to Junk Mail

Promotion in Action

17-2

Mail that misses its target is junk. Now there is a way to cut junk mail without cutting profits, but few businesses are doing it. Why?

Last year, the Equifax Corporation pioneered a "consensual database" called Buyer's Market. Consumers completed a questionnaire indicating the types of offers they wanted to receive in the mail. Those who wanted to know about reading material and lingerie would receive those types of third-class mail, and nothing else.

Buyer's Market was a financial flop, but the concept deserves serious attention. Some industry figures are now proposing that a nonprofit consortium be formed to give consumers a way to self-select their mail for free. The result would be a better image for the industry and a drastic reduction in junk mail.

Direct marketers have long known that through careful targeting of mailing lists, you can mail fewer letters and make a higher profit. Consensual databases take the process a step further by eliminating people who say they don't want to be bothered.

The principle here is that when consumers say no, they mean no. But the problem is that salespeople are trained not to take no for an answer. "There's a paternalistic attitude in the industry," says Mary J. Culnan, a professor at Georgetown University. "Marketers think they know what people really want, and they are going to put mail in your mailbox whether you want it or not."

Source: Brad Edmondson, "Death to Junk Mail," *American Demographics*, September 1992, p. 2. Reproduced by special permission.

FIGURE 17–4

A Direct-Mail Offer

GTE *SPRINT*

GTE Sprint Communications Corporation
500 Airport Boulevard. Suite 415
Burlingame CA 94014

Choose new Sprint® Direct
Dial Service by

and you'll get a FREE
HOUR OF LONG DISTANCE
CALLING!

Mr. Anyone
Street Address
Illinois

Dear Mr. Anyone:

   Illinois Bell will be sending you a letter and ballot soon asking you to choose your long distance telephone service.+

   That's why I'm writing to you now...to offer some important reasons why we think GTE Sprint is your best choice.

   First, you save as much as 30% over AT&T any time of the day, any day of the week on your calls to anywhere outside Illinois, and on calls to places like Peoria and Rockford within Illinois, too.

   Here are examples of how much GTE Sprint could save you on calls made from the Chicago area:

Long Distance Calls from the Chicago Area to:	Time of Day	Minutes	Monthly Usage	AT&T	Sprint	% Savings
Los Angeles	Day	20	$75 - $149.99	$7.97	$6.83	14%
Peoria	Eve	3	$20 - $ 74.99	$ .81	$ .66	19%
Phoenix*	Night	15	$75 - $149.99	$3.45	$2.10	39%

See rate chart on Sprint Order Form for more information

   Second, Sprint knows you want to hear and be heard clearly. That's why we spent $1.5 billion modernizing our network -- just to make sure you get the high quality you deserve.

   Third, GTE Sprint's personal service representatives are available to receive your call, toll-free, 24 hours a day. That means you can always get

   + By order of the Federal Communications Commission, Illinois
      Bell must randomly assign a long distance company to any
      customer who does not make a choice.

limited, and therefore you must get the benefit across quickly and succinctly. We agree that long copy can be used if there is consumer interest. Still, writing a direct-mail letter is different from writing a book or personal letter.

Curbing Abuses

Consumers in many quarters are increasingly voicing concern over junk mail abuse. In particular, a 1988 study by American Express Company revealed that

FIGURE 17–4

Concluded

your service questions answered any time of the day or night, any day of the week.

Plus, with Sprint you'll continue to dial the same easy way you're used to dialing with AT&T, and you can use any type of phone -- pushbutton or rotary dial.

So what does Sprint Direct Dial Service add up to? The best value you can get: savings + quality + service + convenience.

Because we want you to discover for yourself all the good things we already know about Sprint, here's our special offer:

Sign up for Sprint now and get the best value in long distance...plus a free hour of long distance calling!

To choose Sprint, simply sign and send in the enclosed Sprint Order Form. Or call 1-800-521-4949, ext. 870. We'll notify your local phone company that you've chosen Sprint as your long distance phone company.

Then, when you receive your local phone company's letter and ballot, check "GTE Sprint" to make doubly sure they hear your choice of Sprint loud and clear!

Whichever way you choose Sprint, you'll get your free hour of long distance calling!

We know you'll be pleased with GTE Sprint. Now, more than ever, it's your best value in long distance service.

Sincerely,

Barbara B Press

Barbara B. Press
Director, Residential Services

P.S. Remember, if you do not select a long distance company, your local phone company has been ordered by the FCC to select one for you. Act now. Take a few minutes to read the enclosed brochure. Then mail your Sprint Order Form or call us at 1-800-521-4949, ext. 870.

> No-Risk Sprint Guarantee
>
> If, for any reason during your first 90 days of saving with Sprint, you decide to switch your long distance service back to AT&T, we'll cover any switching fee charged by your local phone company. (Confirmation of switch back to AT&T required. Offer subject to regulatory approval. Void where prohibited.)

90 percent of those surveyed believe that companies should disclose more about how they use their mailing lists. Also, 80 percent stated that information collected for one purpose should not be used for another.[26]

It should be pointed out that all direct marketers are required by law to protect the wishes of all persons who do not want their name sold for any purpose whatsoever (see Chapter 19). We doubt, however, that such provisions are well known.

It seems clear that matters are reaching a point of diminishing returns. Our only conclusion is that too many direct marketers are disregarding return on investment and are basing their strategy on wishful thinking. If we have reached saturation, this will be clearly reflected in negative return on investment, and nothing is a better corrective.

Catalog Marketing

The Crate & Barrel Company has been a catalog success for more than 10 years. Single and married women in the 25–49 age range are targeted with an array of contemporary housewares, cookware, linen, and giftware with emphasis on the $20–$50 price range. The company's mail-order response rate from September 1991 through January 1992 was an extraordinary 3 percent, triggering a 10 percent sales increase for 1991.[27]

Nearly all of the leading mail-order marketers listed in Table 17–1 use some

---

TABLE 17–2

⌄

Making Direct Mail Work for You

Promise a benefit in your headline or first paragraph—your most important benefit. You simply cannot go wrong by leading off with the most important benefits to the reader.

Immediately enlarge on your most important benefit. Many writers come up with a great lead and then fail to follow through. Try hard to elaborate on your most important benefit right away, and you'll build interest faster.

Tell the reader specifically what the benefit is. It's amazing how many letters lack details on such basic product features as size, color, weight, and sales terms. Perhaps by being so close to the proposition, the writer assumes that the reader knows all about it—a dangerous assumption!

Back up your statements with proof and endorsements. If you can back up your own statements with third-party testimonials or a list of satisfied users, everything you say becomes more believable.

Tell the reader what might be lost unless action is taken. Here's a good spot in your letter to overcome human inertia—imply what might be lost if action is postponed.

Rephrase your prominent benefits in your closing offer. The stronger the recall of the benefits, the easier it will be for the reader to justify an affirmative decision.

Incite action, NOW. This is the spot where you can win or lose the battle to inertia. So wind up with a call for action and a logical reason for acting now.

Source: Bob Stone, *Successful Direct Marketing Methods*, 3rd ed. (Lincolnwood, Ill.: Crain Books, 1984), pp. 272–73. Reproduced by special permission.

type of catalog. Catalog selling has also caught on worldwide and is by no means an American phenomenon. In fact, global catalog company sales in 1991 broke down this way: the United States, 49 percent; Europe, 40 percent; and other countries, 11 percent.[28]

Catalogs offer multiple advantages, especially convenience and availability of hard-to-find merchandise. The marketing opportunities are bright indeed, as you will discover in Promotion in Action 17–3.

Direct-Action Advertising

When advertising media are used to stimulate a direct buying response, the primary characteristic is an appeal to have the consumer call an 800 number or to return a coupon. Figure 17–5 shows a fund-raising appeal with a coupon keyed to show the magazine in which it appeared and the date of the issue.

Direct response television also can be effective, especially through the use of cable TV on the local level.[29] For example, Black & Decker's household product group successfully experimented with two-minute commercials, as did Allstate Enterprises. The latter attempted to show in two minutes how a consumer could get travel and insurance benefits.

The usual form of response is a toll-free number, although handling arrangements can also be made with the carrying station for a fee as high as 30 percent of the selling price.

Most Americans, as well as increasing numbers of Europeans, also have access to home shopping channels through cable TV. Home shopping channels have grown slowly since their onset, but the potential is great:

> Shop-at-home TV has become more than a billion-dollar business with a loyal, repeat-buying, nearly cult-like following in its viewership, with the potential to reach nearly every home that has a TV set and a cable hookup.[30]

A Report Card on the Direct-Mail Catalog Industry

L. L. Bean and Lands' End topped *Consumer Reports* magazine's October 1991 catalog survey. The survey found that nearly 90 percent of respondents had placed at least one catalog order in the previous year, with nearly 40 percent placing eight or more. In the magazine's previous survey five years ago, only 25 percent of respondents reported eight or more annual purchases.

As 800 numbers have become more prevalent for ordering, *Consumer Reports* said companies have improved customer service. Most respondents said they liked getting catalogs, but of the 20 percent who didn't, more than one third worried about the books' environmental impact. Only 7 percent, though, complained about postage and shipping costs.

Source: "Bean, Lands' End Top Consumer Survey," *Direct Marketing*, November 1991, p. 8. Reproduced by special permission.

One of the ways to generate greater profitability is to feature higher-margin specialty items similar to those offered in catalogs. The J. C. Penney Company, for example, began an "electronic catalog" home shopping network in 1989 and reached 6.5 million homes in a short time.[31]

Interactive Electronic Media

The burgeoning growth of information technology is a tantalizing frontier for direct marketers.[32] Yet one of the promising early developments, videotex, has been slow to ignite. Videotex is an electronic shopping medium that interactively links buyer and seller. Anything that can be typed on a computer keyboard can be transmitted to the home screen and copied if the TV set has facsimile capability.

About $2.5 billion has been spent on videotex technology in the past decade, but it only reaches 1.5 to 2.0 million customers (compared with 0.5 million in 1986), with $400 million generated yearly in revenues.[33] At least in part, the slow growth is due to the fact that only 20 to 25 percent of American homes have a personal computer.

FIGURE 17–5

Fund-Raising through Direct Mail

Sponsor a Child for Only $14 a Month.

At last! Here is a $14 sponsorship program for Americans who are unable to send $20, $22, or $24 a month to help a needy child.

And yet, this is a full sponsorship program because for $14 a month you will receive:
• a 3 1/2" x 5" photograph of the child you are helping.
• two personal letters and an updated photo from your child each year.
• a complete Sponsorship Kit with your child's case history and a special report about the country where your child lives.
• issues of our newsletter, "Sponsorship News."

All this for only $14 a month?

Yes — because Children International believes that many Americans would like to help a needy child. And so we searched for ways to reduce the cost — without reducing the help that goes to the child you sponsor.

For example, your child does not write each month, but two letters a year from your child keep you in contact and, of course, you can write to your child as often as you wish.

And to minimize overseas costs, our field workers are citizens of the countries where they serve. Many volunteer their time, working directly with families, orphanages and schools.

You can make a difference!

$14 a month may not seem like much help to many Americans, but to a poor family living on an income of $1.50 or $2.00 a day, your sponsorship can help make all the difference in the world.

Will you sponsor a child? Your $14 a month will help provide so much:
• emergency food, clothing and medical care.
• a chance to attend school.
• help for the child's family and community, with counseling on housing, agriculture, nutrition, and other vital areas to help them become self-sufficient.

A child needs your love!

Here is how you can sponsor a child immediately for only $14 a month:

1. Fill out the coupon and tell us if you want to sponsor a boy or a girl, and check the country of your choice.

2. Or mark the "Emergency List" box and we will assign a child to you who most urgently needs to have a sponsor.

3. Send your first $14 monthly payment in right now with the coupon to Children International.

Then, in just a few days, you will receive your child's name, photograph and case history.

May we hear from you? We believe that our Sponsorship Program protects the dignity of the child and the family and at the same time provides Americans with a positive and beautiful way to help a needy youngster.

Carlos lives in a one-room shack with a dirt floor and no furniture. He needs nutritious food, medicine, clothing and an education. Won't you help a child like Carlos?

Sponsorship Application

☐ Yes, I wish to sponsor a child. Enclosed is my first payment of $14. Please assign me a ☐ Boy ☐ Girl ☐ Either.

Country preference: ☐ India ☐ The Philippines ☐ Thailand ☐ Chile ☐ Honduras ☐ Dominican Republic ☐ Colombia ☐ Guatemala ☐ Ecuador ☐ Special Holy Land child program

☐ OR, choose a child who most needs my help from your EMERGENCY LIST.

NAME _____

ADDRESS _____

CITY _____

STATE _____ ZIP _____

☐ Please send me more information about sponsoring a child.
☐ I can't sponsor a child now, but wish to make a contribution of $_____

Please forward your U.S. tax-deductible check, made payable to:

Children International®
Joseph Gripkey, Chief Executive
2000 East Red Bridge Road • Box 419413
Kansas City, Missouri 64141

A worldwide organization serving children since 1936. Financial report readily available upon request.

In France, on the other hand, videotex is connected with the telephone system. Statistics show that videotex screens are used by 60 percent (5.5 million) of telephone subscribers in France, where it is viewed as a substitute for yellow- and white-pages telephone directories.[34]

An alternative is interactive cable. In addition to offering its electronic catalog, the J. C. Penney Company has tested Telaction, which permits the buyer to communicate with a TV monitor by using a touch-tone telephone. This allows pictures and prices to appear on the screen, and the consumer can respond instantly.

The imminent widespread adoption of fiber-optic telephone technology is a major breakthrough. This could well represent the launching of unheard-of-data-base marketing possibilities. Be prepared for what appears to be a very promising future for interactive electronic media.

In-Home Personal Selling

House-to-house personal selling annually accounts for about 2 percent of all general merchandise sales, but this number is declining. Two companies known for their large field selling force, Fuller Brush Company and Mary Kay Cosmetics, Inc., have been forced to change directions. Both are using other media such as retail stores, telemarketing, or direct mail to make primary contacts. Skyrocketing costs and reduced availability of women at home during the daytime are the primary reasons.

MANAGING THE DIRECT MARKETING PROCESS

Three remaining issues of direct marketing warrant discussion: (1) integrated strategies, (2) measurement of effectiveness, and (3) management of the database.

Integrated Strategies

The Allen-Edmonds Company has established a significant niche in the men's dress shoe market, and its product is becoming well known as the "Rolls Royce" of shoes.[35] The company relies on ads in *Business Week, Fortune, The Wall Street Journal,* and other publications to generate awareness and interest. But it also provides a catalog at $3.00 per prospect that shows the full line of shoes and gives addresses of the nearest retailers where they can be purchased. This kind of database marketing helps build an unprecedented level of customer loyalty, a figure that approaches 100 percent.

This example illustrates a simple point: No element of the promotional mix stands completely on its own—there is a synergistic effect. Direct marketing impact is greater when advertising, sales promotion, and other elements are combined in one unified, coordinated strategy.

Measurement of Effectiveness

There are three important factors to measure when assessing direct marketing effectiveness: (1) percentage response rate, (2) mailing list attrition, and (3) return on investment. There is no escaping the accountability provided when these numbers are made available daily. This can make life uncomfortable for some, but it is an inescapable way of life for direct marketers.

Percentage Response Rate   It may come as a surprise to discover that profit can be made even when only a very small percentage of the total who receive a mailing place an order. A 2 percent rate usually will be acceptable, although we prefer to see a higher figure.

It is usually disturbing to realize that 98 percent of your prospects can ignore you even though you are making money on your efforts. Rates of 5 percent or less, however, probably must be accepted as a good measure of reality unless you are working with a high-quality list composed of very interested people. In these instances, response rates of 10 percent or more might be expected.

Mailing List Attrition   Buying response rates measure only one aspect of effectiveness—immediate sales. But we are equally, if not more, interested in customer loyalty. For example, an offer could generate a 10 percent or more initial return but fail to stimulate repurchase. In that case, the *attrition rate* is too high.

Reduction of attrition rates is always a valid goal. This is measured simply as the percentage of repeat customers for any given period, usually a year. If this figure is 75 percent or more, your communication is having good impact on loyalty.

Return on Investment   ROI, of course, is the single most important measurement in direct marketing. It is computed as the ratio of revenue produced divided by total costs. This is done for each individual effort—a mailing, a direct response ad, and so on.

Assume, for example, that a mailing produces an ROI of 3.9 percent. Although you are making money, this could be quite insufficient if your cost of capital is 8 percent. This tells us that this piece did not pull as it should and falls short of financial expectations.

Managing the Database

The direct marketer's greatest asset is the database. The basic component, of course, is each customer's name and buying record. The following are some of the most essential facts to store in the customer file:

Source—how the name was acquired (from an ad, letter, etc.).

Personal information—how the person is to be addressed (first name, etc.).

Any demographic or psychographic data you might have.

Date and size of first purchase.

Motivation—the type of appeal to which the customer responded.

Every purchase recorded by dollar size.

Management is not especially interested in each customer record per se, but managers make considerable use of summary reports. Some of the reports that find greatest use are:

1. *Monthly sales and ROI figures given by each specific appeal, medium, and creative package*—this is how to find out what is really working.

2. *List growth and attrition*—are we attracting new customers and holding those that we have?

3. *Purchase size*—upgrading size of purchase is always a realistic objective.

The database provides for no end of segmentation possibilities. For example, assume that your telemarketing is showing a high ROI. Call up all who have bought by telephone in the past three months and appeal once again. Do the same if a particular type of direct mail or catalog works. Similarly, you can isolate customers who have responded to certain direct-mail appeals and press ahead with a related campaign.

Another good practice is to purge from the active mailing list those individuals who have not purchased at all during the past year. Make sure, however, that the names are not lost. It frequently is possible to reactivate lapsed customers at a later time.

Again, we remind you that the successful direct marketer lives with these numbers. The reports reveal the dynamics of buying behavior and suggest no end of strategic possibilities that seldom are possible without a database.

SUMMARY

This chapter focuses on marketing activities that are designed to produce some form of measurable direct buying response. Direct marketing is growing in importance as consumers find ways to circumvent the inconvenience of retail purchasing.

The list of names of prospects and buyers, referred to as the database, is the key to successful direct marketing. Several ways to build a database, including use of in-house lists, lists from other sources such as list brokers, and geodemography, are discussed.

REVIEW AND DISCUSSION QUESTIONS

1. "No way am I going to put my ad in a mailbox. It will get lost in that clutter and never be read. I'll stick with print ads as I always have." What is your comment?

2. Take an inventory of your mailbox during a given week. What have you received in the way of ads? Would you say that most who have written to you have a good idea of your background and interests? What, if anything, captures and holds your attention? What lessons can be learned from this?

3. Would you recommend telemarketing for an agency raising funds for drought relief? What types of people should be called? What are the odds of success?

4. Would TV ads or a 30- or 60-minute TV special be a better strategy for drought relief fund-raising? Why or why not?

5. You are the advertising manager for a high-fashion clothing designer that owns a highly exclusive store on the North Shore of Chicago. The store sells only its own creations. Would you consider any type of direct marketing? If so, what would you recommend?

6. In view of a growing backlash against some types of telemarketing, would you advise a stock broker to use this medium to find new customers? What would you suggest be done by this firm to avoid annoying those who are reached?

NOTES

1. "Direct Marketing—What Is It?" *Direct Marketing,* June 1985, p. 20.

2. Stan Rapp and Tom Collins, *The Great Marketing Turnaround—The Age of the Individual and How to Profit from It* (Englewood Cliffs, N.J.: Prentice Hall, 1990), p. 37.

3. Thomas E. Caruso, "Kotler: Future Marketers Will Focus on Customer Data Base to Compete Globally," *Marketing News,* June 8, 1992, p. 21.

4. Faith Popcorn, *The Popcorn Report* (New York: Doubleday, 1991).

5. A helpful and widely quoted booklet is: Vin Jenkins, *The Concept of Direct Marketing* (Melbourne, Australia: Australia Post, 1984).

6. Jim Kobs, "Action Blends with Image-Building," *Advertising Age,* November 9, 1988, p. 78.

7. Alison Fahey, "A Question of Image," *Advertising Age,* September 25, 1989, p. S-6.

8. Ibid.

9. *Direct Marketing,* September 1989, p. 4.

10. "Mail Order Top 250+," *Direct Marketing,* July 1992, p. 20.

11. *Direct Marketing,* June 1991. p. 64.

12. See Dwight J. Shelton, "Birds of a Geodemographic Feather Flock Together," *Marketing News,* August 28, 1987, p. 13. For an excellent description of how geodemography is applied to fund-raising strategy, see Daniel F. Hansler and Don L. Riggin, "Geo-Demographics: Targeting the Market," *Fund Raising Management,* December 1989, p. 35–43.

13. Hansler and Riggin, "Geo-Demographics."

14. Raymond Serafin and Cleveland Horton, "Buick Ads Target ZIP Codes," *Advertising Age,* April 1, 1991, pp. 1 and 34.

15. Janet A. Smith, "Channel Wars," *Direct Marketing,* April 1992, pp. 33–37.

16. "Internationally Speaking," *Direct Marketing,* December 1988, pp. 36–40.

17. For a brief description of how audiotex works, see *Direct Marketing,* April 1989, p. 96.

18. "The Power of Nintendo," *Direct Marketing,* September 1989, pp. 24–29.

19. Smith, "Channel Wars," p. 33–37.

20. Robert Lewis, "Tempting Telecommunications Technologies," *Direct Marketing,* February 1991, pp. 55–57.

21. John Osbon, "Abuses Draw Congress' Fire," *Advertising Age,* September 25, 1989, p. S-8.

22. Ibid.

23. Ray L. Velkers, "Sears' Kids Strategy Matures," *Direct Marketing*, December 1990, pp. 32ff.

24. Ibid.

25. The results were found in a nationwide Roper study quoted by Joseph Campana, "Chrysler Mail Campaign Gets Leads, Supports Dealers" (speech given at Direct Marketing Association of Detroit, October 6, 1983).

26. Osbon, "Abuses Draw Congress' Fire," p. 5–8.

27. "Growing Catalog Keeps on Glowing," *Direct Marketing*, November 1992, p. 45–46.

28. Nicholas di Talamo, "Getting U.S. Catalogs into Europe," *Direct Marketing*, December 1992, p. 21.

29. Linda Cecere, "TV Availabilities Put Squeeze on Marketers," *Advertising Age*, October 17, 1985, p. 19.

30. Howard Schlossberg, "Picture Still Looks Bright for TV Shopping Networks," *Marketing News*, October 23, 1989, p. 8.

31. Ibid.

32. See Janet A. Smith, "The New Frontier," *Direct Marketing*, May 1991, pp. 24–27.

33. Michael J. Major, "Videotex Never Really Left, But It's Not All Here," *Marketing News*, November 12, 1990, p. 2.

34. Ibid.

35. Mollie Neal, "If the Shoe Fits . . . Market it," *Direct Marketing*, January 1992, pp. 19–22.

18

Public Relations, Corporate Advertising, and Publicity

SEARS' PUBLIC RELATIONS DEBACLE

Faced with serious public relations problems, companies tend either to stand up and take the heat or duck and deflect the blame. After being accused by California's Consumer Affairs Department of systematically overcharging for car repairs, Sears, Roebuck & Company initially tried to duck, according to crisis-management experts, who added that such a response could potentially alienate customers and make it more difficult for the company to retain its reputation for trustworthiness.

"Their first response was absolutely atrocious," said Gerald C. Meyers, a consultant in Bloomfield Hills, Michigan, who teaches courses on crisis management at Carnegie Mellon University.

Sears' first response to the accusation was to call them politically motivated and to deny any fraud. It accused the California department of trying to gain support at a time when it was threatened by severe budget cuts. Using lawyers as its primary spokesmen, it held to that position for several days as the crisis intensified and spread. California consumer regulators said they would seek to close all 72 Sears auto centers in the state, and the California Attorney General's office said it was considering filing a civil suit seeking monetary damages.

The New Jersey Division of Consumer Affairs said all six of the Sears auto centers it visited during a recent undercover investigaton recommended unnecessary repairs. The Attorney General is examining the results to prepare for possible legal action.

Nationwide news reports, meanwhile, concentrated for days on the findings of the undercover California investigators, who said Sears routinely overcharged for work, made unnecessary repairs and charged for work that was never done.

It is unclear how the crisis will affect Sears' business. But Sears has sought to contain any damage with newspaper advertisements, in the form of a letter from Edward A. Brennan, the company's chairman, that strike a more contrite tone and pledge that the retailer will satisfy all its customers.

"With over two million automotive customers serviced last year in California alone, mistakes may have occurred," said the advertisement, which began appearing in newspapers around the country. . . . "However, Sears wants you to know that we would never intentionally violate the trust customers have shown in our company for 105 years."

Charles Ruder, Sears' vice president for public affairs, said the company's response to the allegations had been proper under the circumstances. But he said the company had been caught off guard by California regulators' decision to go public with the charges . . . , and he said the company made a conscious decision . . . to shift from a response based on legal issues to one addressing the concerns of customers.

"We are emphasizing that the key is trust and integrity and that if mistakes were made we will rectify them," Mr. Ruder said. "In a business where trust is important, we wanted to make sure we got that across."

But public relations and crisis management consultants said it would be difficult for the company to recover from its initial mishandling of the problem. "They turned off their customers," Mr. Meyers said. "They turned public opinion against them. They apparently thought the lawyers would take care of it and that they'd be a success in a court of law, but in a situation like this that should be way down your list of priorities."

Source: Excerpted from Richard W. Stevenson, "Sears' Crisis: How Did It Do?" *The New York Times*, June 17, 1992, pp. C-1 and C-4. Used by permission.

Public relations is a promotional management function that "uses two-way communication to mesh the needs and interests of an institution or person with the needs and interests of the various publics with which that institution must communicate."[1] Its purpose can be to inform various publics about certain aspects of corporate policy or to cushion the effects of a corporate crisis.

The Sears story that you just read is an example of a public relations disaster caused by management's flawed first-response strategy. Instead of taking actions to reinforce the company's image of trust and integrity, management ducked and tried to deflect the blame. In contrast, the manner in which Johnson & Johnson

---

TABLE 18–1

Representative Objectives for the Public Relations Function to Target Markets

To Ultimate Consumers

Disseminate information on the production and distribution of new or existing products.
Disseminate information on ways to use new or existing products.

To Company Employees

Offer training programs to stimulate more effective contact with the public.
Encourage pride in the company and its products.

To Suppliers

Provide research information for use in new products.
Report on company trends and practices for the purpose of building a continuing team relationship.

To Stockholders

Disseminate information on: (1) company prospects, (2) past and present profitability, (3) future plans, (4) management changes and capabilities, and (5) company financial needs.

To the Community at Large

Promote public causes such as community fund-raising drives.
Disseminate information on all aspects of company operations with the purpose of building a sense of unity between company and community.

handled the 1982 crisis in Chicago in which seven persons died from poisoned Tylenol is a classic example of a successful reactive response to a crisis situation with the aid of a good public relations plan.

Public relations programs can also be proactive. Carnival Cruise Lines, for example, keeps its channels of communication open to several publics. Its public relations efforts played an important role in reducing internal anxieties about the acquisition of Holland America Lines. With respect to external publics, its PR activities have ranged from informing the travel industry about a joint venture in European cruise travel with Club Mediterranee to reducing public fears about the safety of its ships during hurricane Andrew.

The very term *public relations* means that a person or institution is engaged in persuasive communications with certain publics. These "publics" are analogous to what marketing strategists would call *target markets*. Table 18–1 illustrates the variety of target markets at which public relations messages might be directed and suggests representative objectives for public relations campaigns. As can be seen, some of the target publics, such as company employees, are internal to the firm while others, such as the stockholders, are external.

INTERNAL COMMUNICATIONS

Internal communication is designed to let employees know what management is thinking, as well as to facilitate communication in the reverse direction. At one time, organizations were small enough so that this could be done easily on a

TABLE 18–2

Media for Internal Public Relations

Medium	Principal Advantages
Employee publications	Treats subjects in depth; visually attractive
Manuals and booklets	Flexible; complete in details
Newsletters	Easily prepared; low-cost coverage
Posters	Colorful; dramatic; attention-getting
Bulletin boards and information racks	Timely; strategically placed
Exhibits and displays	Highly flexible; attention-getting
Closed-circuit television and teleconferencing	Dramatic; attention-compelling; involves audience; good for training
Motion pictures and videotapes	Flexible; good for demonstration
Grapevines	Informal; timely
Speeches and meetings	Two-way communication; treats problems in depth
Advisory groups	Two-way communication; takes advantage of expertise

Source: S. Watson Dunn, *Public Relations: A Contemporary Approach* (Homewood, Ill.: Richard D. Irwin, 1986), p. 295.

face-to-face basis, but this is no longer possible in most situations, and the need often exists for a formal communication program designed for purposes such as distributing information and building morale. Failure to provide such a program can have devastating effects on productivity, morale, and turnover.

Because the details of internal communication programs are beyond the scope of this book, only brief reference is made to the variety of media that can be utilized for this purpose. These are itemized in Table 18–2.

An example of the use of internal communications is the program by which the Atlanta Gas Light Company introduced its new corporate symbol to employees.[2] Following a series of mergers, the company was faced with difficult communications and public relations problems caused by the use of three different names in different parts of the state of Georgia. A need existed to design a company symbol that was so distinctive and identifiable that it would immediately identify the "gas company," no matter where or when it was seen. Once the new symbol was designed and adopted, it was necessary to inform employees of the program and to indicate how they could assist in building a more distinct public image. This took the form of stories in company magazines, letters to supervisors, and personal visits by top executives of the company to key executives and operating staff.

EXTERNAL COMMUNICATIONS

As a part of the promotional plan, public relations is most concerned with external communications designed to enhance the image of the organization in the minds of its various publics—ultimate consumers, suppliers, stockholders, and the community at large. The image is the overall reputation or *personality* achieved by the organization in its public interface.

Image is of great importance for overall promotional strategy because it is the attitudinal background against which all organizational offerings are evaluated. If it is defective, a considerable competitive handicap results.

There is no denying that many, if not most, business firms are facing a growing public credibility crisis. This has been caused, in part, by the attacks from consumerists, government, and other critics. It is also true, however, that public antipathy has been aroused by numerous examples of product failure, outright deception, and various other forms of irresponsibility.

Some firms by and large ignore their public image. Many others, however, are quite sensitive to their public interface and make wise use of corporate advertising, customer relations programs, and publicity. Table 18–3 illustrates the rich variety of media opportunities available for this purpose. Of special importance in the external campaign are (1) organizational symbols, (2) corporate advertising, (3) customer relations programs, and (4) publicity.

Organizational Symbols

Organizational symbols and names are significant in identifying the organization and differentiating it from competitors. Each symbol in Figure 18–1 is a type of shorthand stimulus that calls to mind a constellation of meanings every time it is seen.

Concern over corporate image has prompted a rash of symbol changes in recent years. In part, this has been brought about by mergers, as was the case with the Atlanta Gas Light Company. In other situations, management believed that established symbols projected an image that was no longer in keeping with the current environment or current organizational activity.

The symbol must identify the organization at a glance, or it has failed its intended purpose. Most of those illustrated in Figure 18–1 meet this criterion well.

Recent research indicates that using the corporate symbol as a logo together with the company or product name has a significant influence on consumers' attitudes. Promotion in Action 18–1 shows that the use of a logo together with a name enhanced the score for trustworthiness and quality for Buick, Nike, Visa, and Delta. In the case of Wendy's, the score decreased.

Corporate Advertising

Corporate advertising differs from the types of advertising discussed previously in that it is aimed at benefiting the corporation as a whole rather than specific products or services. Although its purpose is to build awareness and favorable attitudes toward the whole firm, the problems of message design and media selection are quite similar to those faced in product or service advertising.

According to *Public Relation Journal*'s 20th annual corporate advertising survey, $1.47 billion was spent on corporate advertising in the United States in 1990, an increase of 4 percent from the previous year.[3]

TABLE 18–3

Media for External Public Relations

Medium	Principal Advantages	Principal Limitations
Newspapers	Community prestige; intense coverage; control by audience; selectivity; staffing by professionals	Short life; hasty reading; poor reproduction of visuals
Magazines	Selectivity; long life; credibility of source; good reproduction	Lack of area flexibility; lack of immediacy; duplication of audiences
Television	Strong personal impact; mass coverage; believability; prestige; high memorability	Fleeting exposure; little audience segmentation; time limitation; emphasis on entertainment
Radio	Immediacy; selectivity; mobility	Fleeting nature of messages; audience fragmentation
Direct media	Selectivity; flexibility; personalizing	High cost per contact; difficulty in compiling mailing list; poor image
Special events and displays	Targeted to special audiences; attention-compelling	High cost per contact; requires specialized help in arranging

Source: S. Watson Dunn, *Public Relations: A Contemporary Approach* (Homewood, Ill.: Richard D. Irwin, 1986), p. 333.

FIGURE 18–1

Organizational Image Symbols

What's in a Logo?

What's in a name? Never mind, it's what's in a logo that matters. According to a survey by the Schechter Group, a New York corporate-identity consultant, consumer attitudes about brands and the companies marketing them are significantly influenced by logo design, color, and other components.

The Logo Value survey, conducted in July [1992] to measure whether logos enhance or detract from consumer perceptions, seeks to help marketers determine whether their logos are mighty Marlboro men or embarrassing Edsels.

The survey showed that 55 percent of the national brand and company logos exposed to consumers elicited different responses, either better or worse, than the brand and company names alone when presented plain, sans logos. Surprisingly, it found that logos even influenced consumer attitudes about long-established brands and companies like Buick automobiles and Delta Air Lines, as well as newer ones like Nike sneakers and Wendy's fast food (see the figure).

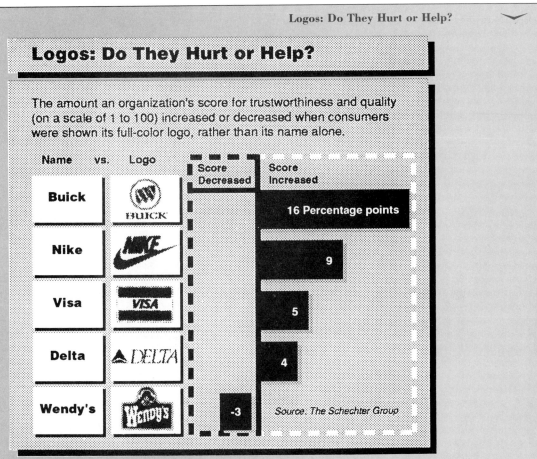

Logos: Do They Hurt or Help?

The amount an organization's score for trustworthiness and quality (on a scale of 1 to 100) increased or decreased when consumers were shown its full-color logo, rather than its name alone.

Name vs. Logo	Score Decreased	Score Increased
Buick		16 Percentage points
Nike		9
Visa		5
Delta		4
Wendy's	-3	

Source: The Schechter Group

The New York Times

Source: Stuart Elliot, "Symbols That Win, or Lose, Consumer's Seal of Approval," *The New York Times*, September 16, 1992, p. C19; and the Schecter Group. Used by permission.

"I would expect that the unadorned name would essentially communicate the same as the dressed-up name," Alvin S. Schechter, chief executive of the Schechter Group, said in an interview in a midtown Manhattan cafeteria, surrounded by logos emblazoned on beverage cans and bottles, snackchip bags, and candy wrappers.

"Whether I say Lexus, or show you the Lexus flag, it's the same product," he added.

"The bottom line is that the logo does affect the image," he continued, "illogically, perhaps. My reputation shouldn't be based on my tie or the cut of my suit, but appearance and perception do influence image."

"When it comes to a logo, I think people have felt it's a soft measurement," Mr. Schecter said. "They sense it's outdated, or they sense that they need a new look." He added that he hoped the data from his survey, now in its second year, could serve "as diagnostic information that allows companies to make their decisions."

For instance, he noted that according to the survey, Lexus, Toyota's luxury car line, "has been in the market a very short time, yet its imagery performance is almost as good as Cadillac's," a far older competitor.

Of 24 logos tested in the July [1992] survey—ranging from those of Apple Computer to MasterCard to Wendy's International—in 17 cases the full logos elicited more positive response than the names alone. These included Quaker State motor oil, Cadillac, General Mills, and Buick.

In six cases, the logos scored less than the names by themselves. Those cases included Mastercard, Burger King, Wendy's, and Texas Instruments.

And in one case, Apple Computer, there was no difference between the name-only image and the full-logo image, maybe because, after all, an apple is just an Apple.

One big contributor to how a logo affected perceptions, Mr. Schechter said, was, unexpectedly, color.

"It was amazing," he added, that Visa's colors—blue, white, and gold—enabled that credit card to outscore its rival, Mastercard—red and yellow—by 61 percent to 58 percent.

More predictably, Mr. Schechter continued, pictorial or character logos were "looked at with more affection than abstract trademarks." For example, among the top-performing packaged-goods logos was Pillsbury's pudgy doughboy.

Separately, consumers were also shown the logos only, minus the names, to gauge familiarity. The three most recognized: the Apple Computer apple, by 96 percent, followed by the Burger King stylized hamburger bun and the Pillsbury doughboy, each with 95 percent recognition.

Source: Excerpted from Stuart Elliot, "Symbols That Win, or Lose, Consumers' Seal of Approval," *The New York Times,* September 16, 1992, p. C19.

As noted in Table 18–4 the biggest spending increases were for syndicated television, national spot radio, cable TV, and network TV. New large-volume advertisers included giant retailers who were having all kinds of difficulties caused by leveraged buyouts and mergers. Association spending was dominated by associations of automobile dealers.

It has been suggested that corporate advertising may be divided into three major categories: issue or advocacy advertising, financial- or investor-relations advertising, and general corporate image building.[4]

Issue or Advocacy Advertising   When a company is faced with legislative or social activity deemed to be threatening, issue advertising is one way to present the company's side of the argument. The tobacco companies, for example, faced with increasing public pressure to limit smoking, have been engaged in heavy advertising to present the case for less government regulation. The Mobil Company has used, with great effect, the op-ed page of *The New York Times* to defend itself against charges of excess profits and lack of interest in environmental protection. Huntsman Chemical Corporation uses advocacy advertising to present scientific findings showing that plastic is kinder to the environment than is paper; the ad is seen in Figure 18–2.

TABLE 18–4

Top 10 Corporate Ad Spenders across Nine Media, 1990 (Ranked by Total Media Dollars, $ Thousands)

Corporations	Nine-Media Total	Magazines	Newspapers Incl. Sunday Magazines	Outdoor	Network Television	Spot Television	Syndicated Television	Cable TV Networks	Network Radio	National Spot Radio
1. General Motors Corp.	154,509	25,554	3,862	41	105,934	11,832	1,121	3,213	2,132	820
2. American Telephone & Telegraph Co.	59,545	7,294	596	—	35,572	7,937	1,581	5,062	796	706
3. Sears Roebuck & Co.	50,504	4,159	14,425	4	25,273	867	1,857	1,168	2,475	277
4. Ford Motor Co.	46,025	19,905	431	176	19,367	123	634	286	4,399	704
5. Chrysler Corp.	41,201	8,543	590	2	23,120	1,072	943	688	17	6,226
6. May Department Stores Co.	32,621	22	30,618	—	—	1,961	—	—	—	20
7. Campeau Corp.	31,070	53	27,655	—	—	3,361	—	—	—	—
8. United Telecommunications Inc.	25,114	32	—	—	22,052	865	1,864	302	—	—
9. RH Macy & Co. Inc.	24,822	182	23,525	—	—	1,115	—	—	—	—
10. Dayton-Hudson Corp.	24,522	—	14,618	—	291	9,585	—	24	—	5
Top 10 total	489,931	65,744	116,318	223	231,609	38,719	7,999	10,742	9,819	8,758
Total: all others	982,707	440,210	116,332	5,955	243,983	118,694	5,325	19,779	13,407	19,022
Report total (all companies reporting)	1,475,326	507,114	233,659	6,178	475,592	157,493	13,324	30,522	23,226	28,219
Associations										
1. General Motors Corp. Dealers Assn.	269,840	—	20,169	119	1,027	245,573	—	22	—	2,931
2. Ford Auto Dealers Assn.	168,972	—	18,399	877	3	146,546	—	—	—	3,148
3. Chrysler Corp. Dealers Assn.	91,675	27	2,626	59	89	80,811	—	—	—	8,063
4. Toyota Auto Dealers Assn.	89,426	—	3,821	245	—	84,581	—	—	—	778
5. Honda Dealers Assn.	54,948	—	2,987	8	—	50,682	—	—	—	1,271
6. Nat'l Dairy Promo. & Research Board	54,924	14,045	—	—	25,856	4,455	4,067	6,502	—	—
7. Toyo Kogyo Co. Auto Dealers Assn.	49,657	—	1,922	—	—	47,736	—	—	—	—
8. National Live Stock & Meat Board	32,388	10,194	439	5	12,623	2,024	—	1,177	5,718	208
9. Hyundai Dealers Assn.	28,008	—	1,328	—	—	26,680	—	—	—	—
10. Mitsubishi Auto Dealers Assn.	26,942	—	668	—	—	26,235	—	—	—	39
Top 10 total	866,779	24,266	52,359	1,311	39,598	715,322	4,066	7,701	5,718	16,437
Total: all others	455,859	79,308	59,455	3,455	73,301	174,929	7,090	8,050	22,992	27,280
Report total (all companies reporting)	1,337,818	103,574	117,089	4,904	112,898	898,368	11,156	16,433	28,711	44,685

Source: Paul H. Alvarez, "Corporate Advertising Survey: Magazines, TV Top '90 Media Lists," *Public Relations Journal,* September 1991, pp. 18–19.

Financial-Relations Advertising   This type of advertising strives to create awareness of and stimulate interest in a company or corporation among security analysts and potential investors. Many smaller companies find that corporate advertising of this type is their only means to attract the attention of their various publics and to build a favorable image among members of the financial community.

One of the few pieces of concrete evidence of a link between corporate advertising and stock prices comes from the W. R. Grace 1980 television advertising campaign: their "Look into Grace" series. The commercials highlighted the company's excellent business and financial attributes and then asked, "Shouldn't you look into Grace?" After the commercials ran for 13 weeks in test markets, conventional studies of attitude and awareness indicated that familiarity and approval were at significantly higher levels than before the campaign.[5]

Another area of increased PR activity is among banks, insurance companies, and brokerage firms that have had to face a series of damaging events such as bad loans, insider trading, or too heavy reliance on junk bonds. Promotion in Action 18–2 illustrates how one PR firm is tapping this market.

FIGURE 18–2

An Example of Advocacy Advertising

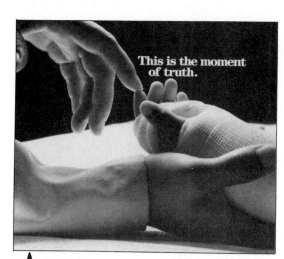

Image Building   Corporate advertising can be used to establish a company's identity or to change an image held by its various publics (see Promotion in Action 18–3). The campaigns of GTE, TRW, and ITT are examples of efforts by companies that through acquisitions have gained many brand names. Consumer advertising of these brands does little to establish corporate identity or to create a desired image. One corporate campaign is described as follows:

> GTE's ads present the company's technological achievements in telecommunications as surprising innovations. This leads to the response, "Gee! No, GTE" and creates a link that (1) ensures association of the corporate name with the innovation and (2) works to eliminate the memory block inherent in perception of an acronym.[6]

A PR Firm's Big Push into Finance

Promotion in Action

18–2

As banks and insurance companies struggle to overcome their bad loans and brokerage firms cope with insider trading and all three fight to expand into each other's business, some public relations experts think the time is ripe for a new push into the financial-services industry.

At Burson-Marsteller, which says it has surpassed Hill & Knowlton as the world's largest public relations agency, this opportunity has led to a hiring binge that has doubled the size of its financial group, to 10 people.

The new additions include four highly paid senior executives with decades of public relations experience at the Chase Manhattan Bank, Morgan Stanley & Company, Salomon Brothers, and the First Boston Corporation—the types of blue-chip companies that public relations firms crave as clients.

While public relations firms and the public relations staffs of larger companies are little known to the public, they often play a crucial role in developing a company's image. Seemingly innocuous assignments, like promoting a company's products or services, can lead to press coverage that attracts new business or raises the company's stock price. In times of crisis, public relations firms advise their clients on how to deal with journalists and how much they should disclose.

Although Burson officials say it is too soon to gloat about increased billings, they are confident that their moves will open more doors with new clients in the financial field.

"A lot of banks have cut staff, but they still have just as much work to be done," said Frasier P. Seitel, who joined Burson [in 1992] as a senior counselor and had been head of public relations at Chase Manhattan.

"There is a limit to how much the remaining staff at the banks can double up, so I think prospects are good for outside providers like us."

[Paul A. Holmes, editor of *InsidePR,* a monthly newsletter about public relations,] said banks in particular needed good advice. At the same time that they are seeking to expand in the insurance business and to open branches across the country, he noted, banks have seen their image tarnished by heavy loan losses, layoffs caused by mergers, and a poor record of lending in low-income neighborhoods.

Source: Excerpted from Michael Quint, "A PR Firm's Big Push into Finance," *The New York Times,* June 8, 1992, p. C5.

On the other hand, when a company runs into problems such as those of the Manville Corporation, whose image had been sullied because of problems with asbestos, a TV blitz of $7 million was used to convey a corrective message. Another type of company image advertising is that in which the goal is to inform the public of the corporation's good citizenship. See Figure 18–3, in which Raytheon informs

---

Promotion in Action

18–3

What Is a Corporate Image?

In nutritional circles, it's said that you are what you eat. As a corporate entity, you are what people think you are.

According to a recent report from the Opinion Research Corporation (ORC), corporate image is a major part of what sells a company and its products. In the study, 97 percent of the responding senior and middle managers acknowledged that image accounts for a significant measure of the successes and failures of their organizations.

This study reflects the acknowledgment in the corporate community that people do business with a given firm or buy its products for more than the quality of the goods and services. The collective knowledge of customers, stockholders, bankers, brokerage houses, dealers, distributors, and the media regarding a company can affect its sales, earnings, valuation, ability to obtain loans, and ability to attract quality employees.

Corporate image is defined as the perceived sum of the entire organization, its objectives, and plans. It encompasses the company's products, services, management style, communications activities, and actions around the world.

Many firms focus little attention on their corporate image until it has been severely damaged. Often, this recognition comes too late to remedy the situation.

Building a positive corporate image requires skillful long-term planning. Management cannot limit its focus to the next few weeks or months. Plans to ensure a positive corporate image should create an impression that will last for years.

Benefits of a Strong Image

Products have lives. According to A. C. Nielsen, 30 brands that are currently leaders in their respective categories will lose their positions in less than two years. A strong corporate image can extend product lives and can also buoy a firm through the inevitable sales valleys by providing:

- A complete awareness among managers of the firm's long-range goals.
- More clearly defined corporate objectives and direction.
- Improved insights into competitive positions and market conditions.
- Improved internal and external communications.
- A positive accounting to customers of the firm's position in the industry and the marketplace.
- Improved understanding of the organization within the financial community.
- Better understanding of the company, its objectives, and its direction by employees, suppliers, directors, and the media.

Source: Excerpted from G. A. Marken, "Corporate Image—We All Have One, but Few Work to Protect and Project It," *Public Relations Quarterly* 35, no. 1 (Spring 1990), pp. 21–23.

readers of its "can-do" spirit while basking in the glow of the success of its Patriot missile in the Gulf War.

Customer Relations Programs

Over the past decade, a growing interest in consumerism has motivated corporations to respond more effectively to customer needs and complaints. Many firms have established customer relations programs. When Ford Motor Company recognized that consumers were favoring Japanese cars because of their perceived high quality, it introduced a companywide quality assurance program. The fact that quality was now receiving top attention from all Ford employees was communicated to the public in ads like the one in Figure 18–4. Lockheed in its ad emphasizes that its research-and-development (R&D) program enables it to deliver technology that is both reliable and affordable.

FIGURE 18–3

An Example of Corporate Image Advertising

SEND US MORE CHALLENGES.

There's a spirit in our company. A belief that when you work harder, work smarter and work as a team, there isn't a challenge that can't be met.

It's the Raytheon Spirit.

It's a "can-do" spirit that's part of every Raytheon company, and it produces results:

• To help clean the air we breathe, our United Engineers & Constructors subsidiary is assisting utilities to meet strict, new clean air regulations cost effectively.

• To help detect deadly windshear near airports, Raytheon has developed Terminal Doppler Weather Radar. Now air traffic controllers can warn pilots away from these threats.

• To help meet tougher automotive emission standards, our Badger Company has been selected to license the Mobil Benzene Reduction Process (MBR) which will help reduce the concentration of this compound in gasoline.

• To help train U.S. Air Force pilots, Beech Aircraft is producing the Jayhawk T-1A, a military version of its successful Beechjet 400A.

• To help the troops of Desert Storm defend against Scud missiles, the people of Raytheon worked around the clock and delivered over 500 Patriot missiles to the Gulf before the first Scuds were ever launched.

Not all our challenges are as dramatic as these. But one way or another, they all lead to better products and better services.

At Amana, we're turning out more energy efficient appliances. At our Cedarapids subsidiary, we're developing technology and equipment to make the rebuilding of our infrastructure more affordable. And, in defense electronics, we're continuing to excel in producing and upgrading proven tactical defensive systems for the military.

There are strong advantages to being a company that can handle so many different challenges in so many different fields. We are able to share brainpower and technologies across the company. And we are able to increase efficiencies while decreasing costs.

The advantages all add up to improvements to our bottom line. Every year, for the past seven years, Raytheon has reported record sales and record earnings.

We thrive on challenges. Send us more.

Raytheon

WE THRIVE ON CHALLENGES

Amana Refrigeration, Inc. • The Badger Company, Inc. • Beech Aircraft Corporation • Caloric Corporation • Cedarapids, Inc. • D.C. Heath and Company
Raytheon Europe • Raytheon Marine Company • Raytheon Service Company • Seiscor Technologies • Semiconductor Division • Sorensen Company
Speed Queen Company • Switchcraft, Inc. • United Engineers & Constructors International, Inc.

Courtesy Raytheon

PUBLICITY[7]

Publicity is the provision of information designed to further the interests of an individual or organization in such a manner that the media use the information without charge because they deem it of great interest to their audiences. The principal types of publicity are business feature articles, news releases, financial news, new-product information, background editorial material, and emergency publicity. Regardless of how well this material is prepared, without the cooperation of the press little information will reach the public. Given that there are over 100,000 editors in the United States and Canada, it is no small job for public relations people to keep the information going to the large number of persons who control the flow of publicity.

Fortunately, the attitude of the press toward publicity is improving. To the surprise of several experts, a large proportion of editors queried stated that they found 50 percent of the publicity material received to be valuable for immediate or future use, and more than one fourth of the editors said they would like to

FIGURE 18–4

Two Customer Relations Corporate Advertisements

FIGURE 18–4

Concluded

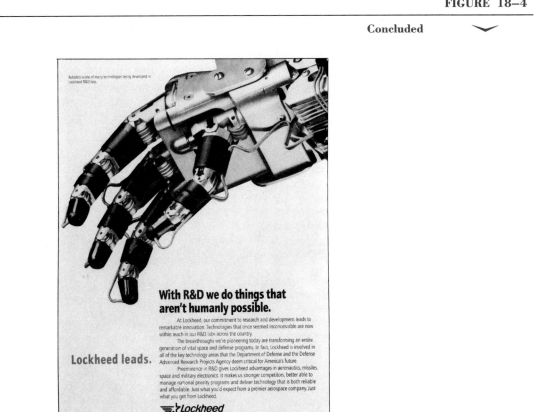

receive more.[8] On the other hand, the press is critical of the dissemination by business of irrelevant or poorly written news releases, or of releases that are little more than thinly disguised advertisements.

The wise public relations professional learns the press's editorial needs, policies, audiences, and operating problems. At the same time, the astute editor recognizes how publicity can be an important source of newsworthy information for his or her newspaper or magazine, or television or radio station.

The main avenue of communication with the media is through personal contact with editors, publishers, and feature writers of the print media—including wire services and syndicates, and news directors of radio and television stations. By making themselves available to the media, public relations people can increase the opportunities to have their material printed or broadcast. On rare occasions, the public relations people arrange a press conference. The purpose of such a conference should be the announcement of something very important, such as a new-product introduction, a new pricing policy, a new acquisition, or a new chief executive. Press conferences called for inconsequential matters will result in lack of response when something of real importance occurs.

Other publicity methods include mailing press releases, giving press previews of new models or new facilities, and holding press-management luncheons where special reports can be given and the press can query the top corporate officers. At the luncheons, press kits containing mimeographed news releases, photographs, biographies, and background materials can also be distributed.

CASE HISTORIES OF TWO PUBLIC RELATIONS CAMPAIGNS

The following two case histories illustrate the basics of strategy and execution in public relations programs. The first concerns the Perrier corporate response in reaction to the findings of impurities in its sparkling water; the second, the proactive campaign to announce the acquisition of the travel and tourism business of Holland America Lines by Carnival Cruise Lines.

A Reactive Public Relations Strategy for Rescuing Perrier[9]

In early 1990, routine purity testing in North Carolina found traces of benzene in samples of Perrier sparkling water. The concentration of benzene was very small (12.3 to 19.9 parts per billion) and posed a negligible health risk. However, fearing the reaction of the health lobby against benzene, a known carcinogen, The Perrier Group of America on February 9 removed 72 million bottles of Perrier water products from distribution in North America. By February 14, every Perrier brand was withdrawn worldwide even though potential consumer concern about the minute impurities in Perrier was much less in Europe and Asia than in North America.

As a partial result of the Tylenol tragedy of 1982, when seven persons died in Chicago after taking poisoned Tylenol capsules, The Perrier Group UK, based in London, developed a crisis management strategy and organized a crisis management team. This strategy was implemented upon learning of the American test results with local confirmatory testing, informing of appropriate governmental authorities, working with resellers, activating telephone information hot lines, and developing informative press releases.

Unfortunately, before the results of the new testing became known, confused signals emanated from headquarters in Paris. A spokesperson for the company hypothesized that the benzene could have come from a greasy rag used to wipe the bottling machinery. This statement turned out to be false, but its dissemination by the press further tarnished Perrier's reputation for purity.

Another misjudgment occurred after the results of local testing became known. For example, when test results in the United Kingdom verified the presence of benzene, Perrier UK was prepared to withdraw all products from store shelves. Headquarters executives in France vetoed the plan, stating that they wanted a single announcement to come during a Paris press conference to be held later in the day. This event turned into a shambles, as Perrier had expected only French reporters and had not realized that the problem had evoked wordwide interest. Hundreds of journalists besieged the headquarters, causing massive jams and frayed tempers.

A company spokesperson reiterated the hypothesis that the benzene came from attempts to clean the bottling machinery and denied rumors that the company had been sabotaged. The company's 75-year-old chief, Gustave Leven, announced a worldwide recall to protect Perrier's reputation for purity. Later in the month, Perrier came to the conclusion that benzene had gotten into the product from failure to clean the filters that remove naturally occurring impurities in the source water.

Plotting a Comeback Fortunately for Perrier, its competitors did not take advantage of its plight. Because of either a lack of resources or fear of harming the category, the other sellers of bottled water kept quiet, thus allowing Perrier to regroup. Using Perrier's tremendous clout with retailers because of the profitability of the line, the CEO of Perrier Group of America sent letters to 550 retail CEOs and indicated that to get back on track Perrier would soon be supplying pure product and would support the return with an increase in the marketing budget from $6 million to $25 million, of which $16 million would go to consumer advertising and the balance into trade promotions and special events. Perrier estimated that the cost of the glitch worldwide would exceed $30 million after taxes.

Burson-Marsteller, the PR agency that handled the Tylenol comeback, was hired to measure public attitudes toward the product in its key markets: the United States, Canada, France, and the United Kingdom. After a 10-day print and radio campaign in which Perrier admitted its mistakes and stated that the problem had been solved, research indicated that 85 percent of Perrier customers would buy the product again. Perrier returned to U.S. shelves on April 26, 1990, and six weeks later was available in 90 percent of its former outlets.

What Was Learned from the Crisis? Although some Perrier groups had a crisis management strategy in place, management communications at headquarters in Paris broke down so that conflicting messages about the company's handling of the crisis were sent. These confused the public and unnecessarily damaged Perrier's reputation.

It has been suggested by experts in crisis management that in the case of multinational corporations a central crisis management team (CMT) should be established, as well as satellite CMTs in overseas subsidiaries. These CMTs should be linked with direct communications so that a unified effort can be coordinated on a worldwide basis, taking into account the special needs, if any, of the various country markets. In addition, every effort should be made to avoid the dissemination of information that only adds to consumer confusion.

It also appears that the best course of action for a company, especially one that causes its own problems, is to accept full blame immediately and to indicate how the difficulty will be resolved. Any attempts to evade responsibility almost always cause a greater degree of consumer displeasure.

FIGURE 18–5

An Example of an In-House Newsletter

Carnival Capers

Volume 15/No. 12   Carnival Cruise Lines   December, 1989

A Time For Thanks

The holiday period is the time of year when, traditionally, we take stock of things: where we've been, where we are, and where we're going.

We've come a long way from our inaugural voyage in 1972 when we ran aground. (The drink of the day was MARDI GRAS on the rocks!) 1989 has given us much to be thankful for:

- The acquisition of Holland America Line/Westours and Windstar Sail Cruises
- The terrific cooperation and "can do" spirit of their personnel — whether it's savvy senior management or a personable Alaskan tour guide
- The unique opportunity our sales force now has to provide you and your clients with a broad spectrum of non-competing vacation alternatives including our sparkling new Carnival Crystal Palace Resort & Casino on the Bahamian Riviera
- The outstanding support of tens of thousands of travel agents like yourself who bask in the glow of high

customer satisfaction from our array of vacation products

- Our new corporate offices — an entire 10-story building devoted to making Carnival as "user friendly" as possible for you to book us and work with us. Our state-of-the-art telephone and computer technology offers you what we believe to be the best service standard in the industry. (Our new address is shown at the bottom.)

We look to 1990 with keen anticipation. We eagerly await the inaugural of our newest SuperLiner ms FANTASY on March 2. (We even became an owner of the shipyard to insure that this splendid new vessel would be completed to our high standards.)

The FANTASY gives us a 25% increase in capacity ... the ability for you to have an additional 200,000 happy, satisfied customers.

All of us at Carnival Cruise Lines thank you for your past business and pledge to work hard to earn your continued support.

Availability

Individual
- Mid-December on: Excellent for HOLIDAY, JUBILEE, CELEBRATION and FESTIVALE 7-day cruises, and CARNIVALE and MARDI GRAS 3- and 4-day cruises.
- Christmas on: excellent for TROPICALE 7-day cruises.

Group
- Excellent winter and spring group space available on all Carnival Cruise Lines' "Fun Ships."

**Note: Now is the time to begin booking individual and groups for the following exciting new products:
- 3- and 4-day cruises on the world's newest "Fun Ship" — the FANTASY.
- The January 7th TROPICALE and the March 25th JUBILEE special 13-day transcanal cruises.
- TROPICALE 7-day cruises from San Juan beginning January 20th.
- JUBILEE 7-day cruises from Los Angeles to the Mexican Riviera beginning April 8th.

Mystery Vacationers

$1,000 Winners	$10 Winners
David Huff AVENUES TO TRAVEL, LTD. Broken Arrow, OK	Kate Ricci AMBASSADOR TRAVEL Altamonte Springs, FL
Jeanne Stephen LIBERTY TRAVEL Rockaway, NJ	Adele Kaehler ROSENBLUTH TRAVEL AGENCY, INC. Bala Cynwyd, PA
Donna Munson TEMPO TRAVEL Parma, OH	

Winter Cruise-A-Thon

Space is still available at Travel Trade's 6th Annual Leisure Travel Conference and Winter Cruise-A-Thon in Fort Lauderdale on January 11-14, 1990. For information and reservations, call Travel Trade Publications at (212) 883-1110.

Back Of The Front

On the back of this month's Carnival Capers please find a quick reference guide for the products of Carnival Cruise Lines and Holland America Line/Westours, Inc.

Crystal Palace

Enclosed in this month's Carnival Capers please find the winter issue of Carnival's Crystal Palace Resort & Casino newsletter. The lead article features our newly created specialty suites including the Galactic Fantasy suite with a tariff of $25,000 a night. (Fully commissionable!)

Season's Greetings

A Proactive Public Relations Strategy at Carnival Cruise Lines[10]

As noted previously, Carnival Cruise Lines acquired the cruise, hotel, and land tour businesses of Holland America Lines in January 1989. To illustrate how a large corporation handles the communications to its various publics given an event of this magnitude, we present a brief case history illustrating how public relations served to fill needs that could not have been filled by the other elements of the promotional mix.

External Publics   The day-to-day task of public relations at Carnival is to communicate with three external publics.

The first public is the trade press (*Travel Weekly, Travel Agent, Travel Trade*, and so forth). This audience is important because 99 percent of tour business originates with travel agents, and the trade press is an important communicator to the agents. In addition to the trade press, Carnival publishes in-house newsletters such as *Carnival Capers* (illustrated in Figure 18–5) and *Carnivalgrams*, which are mailed directly to agents together with releases for agents who publish their own in-house newsletters. In addition, the company publishes *Currents* magazine, which is distributed to past Carnival passengers and the travel agent community. This publication is aimed at creating top-of-mind awareness to Carnival passengers without bypassing the travel agents.

The second public is composed of travel editors and free-lance travel writers. These people develop materials that are printed in newspaper travel sections, general audience magazines, and travel guides.

The third public is the financial community. As a publicly held company with shares traded on the American Stock Exchange (ASE), Carnival must conform to SEC regulations by informing the financial community of any company happenings that have the potential to influence the price of the company's stock. Carnival uses, among others, the services of PR Newswire, which can alert the financial community on very short notice. Pertinent information is also sent by facsimile machine directly to the ASE.

Internal Publics   This category includes all of the land-based employees (headquarters staff and sales representatives) as well as those operating the various ships at sea.

The Acquisition of Holland America Lines   On November 11, 1988, an agreement in principle was reached whereby Carnival would purchase the travel and tourism activities of Holland America Lines. A letter of intent had been signed and the proposed transaction was subject to the signing of a formal agreement, approval by directors and shareholders of each company, and the waiting period required under current antitrust legislation.

This information had to be communicated to all concerned publics. Special attention had to be paid to the financial community and the employees of both companies. Carnival did not want its employees or those of Holland America to be caught by surprise. A PR release was prepared (see Figure 18–6) and sent to

FIGURE 18–6

Carnival Cruise Lines Public Relations Releases

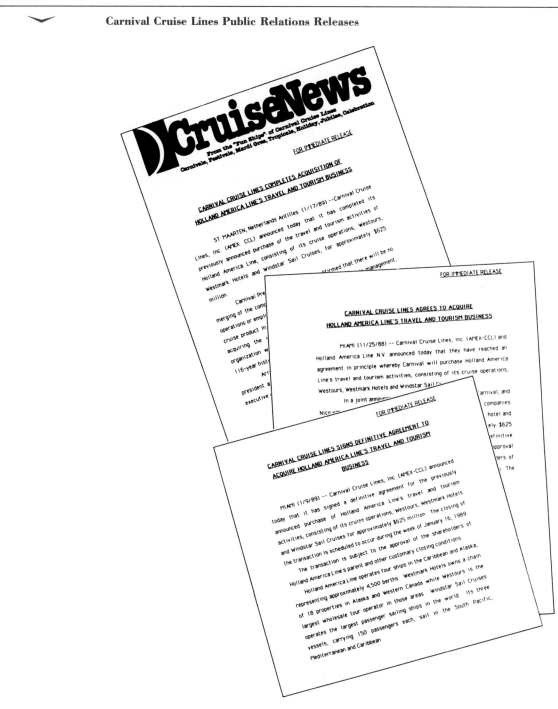

the external publics. A letter explaining the impact of the acquisition was developed and was sent to all employees so that they would receive it at the same time the public announcement was made. Arrangements were made with Holland America management in Seattle to inform their employees in the same manner.

Access to the company president by the press was arranged. Network TV coverage (NBC's "Today Show") and local Miami TV coverage were facilitated, and a special video news release was developed. In addition, meetings were arranged between the chairman and president of Carnival and the top executives of Holland America Lines and several of the ship captains to explain the plans that Carnival had for improving the performance of the acquired businesses.

On January 9, 1989, a second release was prepared announcing the signing of a definitive agreement. On January 17, 1989, the third release was developed informing the various publics that the acquisition had been completed (see Figure 18–6).

The Commissioning of the *Fantasy*   In early 1990, the newest addition to the Carnival fleet, the *Fantasy,* was commissioned in Helsinki, Finland, where it was built. The first lady of Finland christened the ship, and the ceremony was beamed by satellite to Cable News Network and to local Miami TV stations. The *Fantasy* began cruising in the spring of 1990, and Carnival wanted as much publicity as possible about the new ship coming on line.

Other Public Relations Activities   Carnival is a principal benefactor of the National Foundation for the Advancement in Arts, which provides support for newcomers in all areas of the arts. To raise funds for the Foundation, Carnival donated a three-day cruise to Nassau (Arts Fest at Sea) in January 1990, with all proceeds going to the foundation.

The company also supports the New World Symphony Orchestra (Miami) led by Michael Tilson Thomas, which gives talented young musicians (ages 18 to 30) a chance to get a start in a symphony orchestra.

THE IMAGE OF PUBLIC RELATIONS

It is clear that much can be done to improve organization image through external public relations. Unfortunately, public relations is often undertaken as "window dressing" to gloss over and distort the true facts. The result is that the public relations industry itself has a bad image in many quarters, a reputation that is frequently quite deserved. Organizational accountability demands credibility in dealing with the public. To use the vernacular, anything less than this is rightly termed a *corporate ripoff.*

SUMMARY

This chapter examines public relations, corporate advertising, and publicity as supplemental forms of communication. It notes the manner in which an organization can address its various publics, both internal and external, and public relations program. It also discusses corporate advertising and compares issue and advocacy advertising.

The chapter concludes with two case studies of successful campaigns showing how a total program utilizes all of the tools discussed previously and blends them into a communications mix that helps a company overcome adversity or handle a complex merger.

REVIEW AND DISCUSSION QUESTIONS

1. Your company has just experienced a disaster in that a leak in some piping at a large factory has spread poisonous gas over the countryside, injuring many people. You are in charge of public relations and must make immediate recommendations to the top management. Develop a short action plan based on lessons learned from the public relations debacle at Sears.

2. Compare and contrast internal versus external public relations. Explain how management in the Perrier situation utilized both of these activities to reach its goals.

3. The Todt Corporation, a large manufacturer of agricultural chemicals used for insecticides, has been besieged by activists who claim that the corporation's products are causing cancer in humans. The activists have no real evidence to support their claims, but they are raising a lot of public concern. The Todt Corporation has hired you to initiate a program of corporate advertising. What would you do in this situation?

4. How does public relations differ from publicity? How does one go about getting publicity?

5. What role does corporate imagery play in today's competitive environment? How does one go about developing a corporate image?

6. What role do you see for public relations activities in the decade ahead? Would you be interested in a career in public relations? Why or why not?

NOTES

1. S. Watson Dunn, *Public Relations: A Contemporary Approach* (Homewood, Ill.: Richard D. Irwin, 1986), p. 50.

2. Bertrand R. Canfield and H. Frazier Moore, *Public Relations: Principles, Cases, and Problems,* 7th ed. (Homewood, Ill.: Richard D. Irwin, 1977), pp. 70–75.

3. Paul H. Alvarez, "Corporate Advertising Survey: Magazines, TV Top 90 Media Lists," *Public Relations Journal* 47, no. 9 (September 1991), pp. 14–19.

4. Thomas F. Garbett, "When to Advertise Your Company," *Harvard Business Review* 60 (March-April 1982), p. 100.

5. Ibid., p. 103.

6. Ibid.

7. This section borrows heavily from Canfield and Moore, *Public Relations,* Chapter 7.

8. Ibid., p. 136.

9. Gary Kurzbard and George J. Siomokos, "Crafting a Damage Control Plan: Lessons from Perrier," *Journal of Business Strategy* 13, no. 2 (March/April 1992), pp. 39–43; "Management Brief: When the Bubble Burst," *Economist,* August 3, 1991, pp. 67–68; Patricia Sellers, "Perrier Plots Its Comeback," *Fortune,* April 23, 1990, pp. 277–78.

10. Based on personal interviews, May 1989, mail and phone interviews, Fall 1992.

COORDINATION AND CONTROL

In this penultimate section, we address critical issues the inform and shape the promotional process, from its inception to the evaluation of its success.

Chapter 19 addresses a key issue that defines much of the activity in the arena of promotion and advertising, the legal environment. As the name implies, the environment of laws and regulations, in a sense, defines the playing field for all that promotion managers do. Therefore, we summarize the chief constraints that you must know to stay within the boundaries of the playing field.

Chapter 20 covers the important subjects of organizational structures and the use of specialized agencies. The two primary types of organizational structure—the functional and product—are examined. In addition, since few companies have the resources to design and implement full promotional programs, we explore the strategic use of firms that specialize in direct marketing, media buying, creative design, and marketing research, with special emphasis on the workings of advertising agencies.

The tools of marketing research find considerable use in advertising strategy. Chapter 21 analyzes research procedures used to pretest the message before it is placed in the media, and the methods used to analyze the actual sales and communication effectiveness of the campaign.

19

Adaptation to the
Legal Environment

ARE AD AGENCIES RESPONSIBLE FOR FALSE CLAIMS
OF CLIENTS?

An apparently unprecedented ruling that an agency can be forced to pay damages in connection with false claims made in a client's advertising caught the agency involved off guard and sent lawyers scrambling to assess its potentially chilling effects.

"We were really surprised," Elizabeth Mason, president of Friedman Benjamin Inc., said in her first interview since the ruling on Friday by United States District Judge Kimba M. Wood in New York.

"We felt we took every precaution possible to make sure our claims were substantiated," she added, referring to the content of the ads that were the subject of the ruling, for the Ultra Glide razor and blades made by Wilkinson Sword Inc. "I don't know what else we could have done."

The ruling followed an order by Judge Wood in October that Wilkinson Sword pay $953,000 in damages to the Gillette Company, whose Atra Plus blades were deemed inferior in the ads. Her latest ruling was that Friedman Benjamin was just as liable and should be included in the damage award.

The ruling was particularly significant because of its timing, coming as consumers are being inundated by comparative advertising campaigns that go beyond traditional chest-thumping self-promotion to make tough, frequently disparaging references to rival products.

Many of those campaigns have wound up in court as the bickering combatants fail to reach agreement on whether the disputed ads ought to be discontinued. The most publicized recent case involved two brewing powerhouses, Anheuser-Busch Inc. and the Coors Brewing Company, squabbling over commercials for Anheuser's Natural Light beer that belittled the process used to make Coors Light beer.

"I think you'll see agencies forced to make a much more rigid review of the ad copy they're producing, particularly if it's comparative advertising," said Thomas Morrison, a lawyer specializing in advertising law at Patterson, Belknap, Webb & Tyler in New York.

William J. Marlow, a lawyer at Loeb & Loeb in New York, said that in the Wilkinson case, which involved claims run in television advertising in 1989, the ruling by Judge Wood "presents a potentially grave situation" for agencies.

Source: Excerpted from Stuart Elliot, "Wilkinson Damage Award Has Agencies Agencies Scrambling," *The New York Times,* August 26, 1992, p. C17.

WARNING! Disregarding the contents of this chapter may be harmful to your well-being. The legal environment in which you will operate during the decade of the 90s is in a state of flux, and unless you know what you are doing, you and your firm could be in big trouble. You must know how the law will impinge on your freedom to act as a manager of promotion. As a brief example of what has been taking place in recent years, please consider the following news headlines:

"State Regulations Restrict TV Advertising by Lawyers"

"FCC Adopts Rules to Curb Telemarketing"

"Agencies Feel Legal Heat on Competitive Claims"

"Proposed Food Labeling Rules May Paralyze Food Marketers"

"Sweepstakes, Contests and Games Run into Legal Disputes"

As you can see, lots of things are happening. Our goal in this chapter is to describe the legal environment as we see it today and to clarify the changes that are taking place with respect to new law and the interpretation of established law.

In addition, we want you to be aware of two major points: (1) The legal environment is in a state of constant change, and (2) ignorance of the law is no defense when you are charged with a violation.

Filling the Regulatory Vacuum   Federally imposed legal constraints on marketing in general and promotion in particular multiplied during the decade of the 70s. The high-water mark of federal regulation was reached in the early 1980s. The Reagan administration had the general goal to deregulate business activity whenever possible, and Congress went along. Budgets of regulatory agencies were cut, and the regulators were told to concentrate on important cases and to stop harassing business about "minor" problems. Ironically, the regulatory vacuum that grew at the federal level has been filled to an increasing extent by regulatory activity at state and local levels of government.

Because of the growing dispersion of regulation, the federal government has been under increasing pressure to regain control. This pressure is being exerted in part by big business, which finds that it is easier to comply with one set of federal rules than with those of 50 states and hundreds of smaller governmental units. Under the Bush administration, many attempts at the federal level to increase regulation of promotion and other business activities were made or were proposed for the future. Only a moratorium on new regulations imposed by the Bush administration because of pre-election political demands temporarily slowed a trend toward increasing governmental restrictions on business. Given the election of President Clinton it is only a matter of time before the pendulum swings back and the rules and regulations again proliferate. It is almost certain that marketers will be facing more rather than less regulation by federal, state, and local governments during the remainder of the 1990s.

Although a review in this text of the major laws and regulations influencing promotion is necessary, the coverage cannot be exhaustive. Our goal is to provide enough detail to allow you to sense the current state of governmental and self-regulatory policies and to determine whether a proposed promotional campaign meets the requirements set by Congress and the various federal, state, and local regulatory agencies.[1]

PERTINENT LEGISLATION

Federal Legislation

Although laws and regulations to control promotional activities exist at federal, state, and local levels of government, the constitutional underpinnings of our judicial system give first precedence to federal statutes and federal administrative law. Thus in our discussion of pertinent legislation, activities at the federal level will dominate. However, when state or local regulatory efforts are of considerable importance, they will be noted.

A review of history indicates that prior to the 20th century, the doctrine of "let the buyer beware" prevailed, with little or no buyer protection against false and deceptive methods of sale. Post office fraud laws were passed in 1872 to curb the use of the mails to defraud, but not until the passage of the Pure Food and Drug Act in 1906 and the Federal Trade Commission Act in 1914 did effective legal curbs exist. Unfortunately, the Food and Drug Act had limited applicability in that it required only that a correct description of contents be printed on the packages of patent drug items. This statute was superseded by the Federal Food, Drug, and Cosmetic Act of 1938, which will be noted later in this chapter.

The Federal Trade Commission Act Unlike the first Pure Food and Drug Act, the Federal Trade Commission (FTC) Act of 1914 was the first truly effective legislation aimed at curbing promotional abuses and preventing unfair methods of competition. Thus, in one law, Congress provided for both consumer protection and antitrust surveillance.

The FTC Act set up a commission of five members and a staff of approximately 1,500 persons, divided among three bureaus: Competition, Consumer Protection, and Economics. An organizational chart is shown in Figure 19–1. The FTC's initial concern under Section 5 of the act was to prohibit unfair methods of competition in interstate commerce where the effect was to injure competition. The prevention of deceptive methods of promotion was only a secondary objective. However, over the years, as strengthened by several key Supreme Court decisions, the FTC increased its activities against false and misleading promotional activities.

The Robinson-Patman Act In 1936, Congress passed this amendment to the Clayton Act designed to give the FTC broad powers to control discriminatory pricing practices. We will discuss the ramifications of this statute in some detail later in this text.

The Wheeler-Lea Amendment This statute, passed in 1938, significantly broadened the powers of the FTC.[2] Its contents are noted in Table 19–1. Following the Wheeler-Lea Amendment, a series of congressional actions have required certain

FIGURE 19–1

The Federal Trade Commission

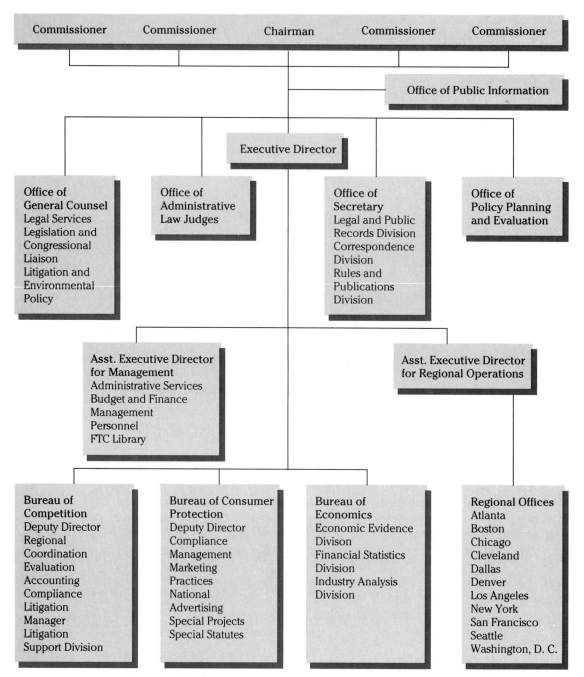

FEDERAL TRADE COMMISSION

| Commissioner | Commissioner | Chairman | Commissioner | Commissioner |

Office of Public Information

Executive Director

Office of General Counsel
Legal Services
Legislation and Congressional Liaison
Litigation and Environmental Policy

Office of Administrative Law Judges

Office of Secretary
Legal and Public Records Division
Correspondence Division
Rules and Publications Division

Office of Policy Planning and Evaluation

Asst. Executive Director for Management
Administrative Services
Budget and Finance
Management
Personnel
FTC Library

Asst. Executive Director for Regional Operations

Bureau of Competition
Deputy Director
Regional Coordination
Evaluation
Accounting
Compliance
Litigation Manager
Litigation Support Division

Bureau of Consumer Protection
Deputy Director
Compliance
Management
Marketing Practices
National Advertising
Special Projects
Special Statutes

Bureau of Economics
Economic Evidence Divison
Financial Statistics Division
Industry Analysis Division

Regional Offices
Atlanta
Boston
Chicago
Cleveland
Dallas
Denver
Los Angeles
New York
San Francisco
Seattle
Washington, D. C.

Source: "Your Federal Trade Commission, What It Is and What It Does," Federal Trade Commission (U.S. Government Printing Office, 1977).

TABLE 19–1

Major Federal Legislation Affecting Promotion

1906 Pure Food and Drug Act

Requires the correct description of contents on the package of drug items.

1914 Federal Trade Commission Act

Prohibits unfair methods of competition in interstate commerce where the effect is to injure competition.

1936 Robinson-Patman Act

Empowers the FTC to control discriminatory pricing practices, including advertising.

1938 Wheeler-Lea Amendment

Provides that intent to defraud no longer needs to be proven.
"Unfair methods of competition" is expanded to encompass deceptive acts or practices.
The FTC receives jurisdiction over false advertising of food, drugs, and cosmetics.
The FTC is empowered to issue cease and desist orders.
The FTC is permitted to issue injunctions to halt improper food, drug, or cosmetic advertising when it appears that the public may be harmed.

1938 Federal Food, Drug, and Cosmetic Act

Empowers the FDA to investigate and litigate concerning advertising claims on the label or package of food, drug, and cosmetic items.

1946 The Lanham Act (The Trademark Act)

Gives the seller the exclusive right to use a trademark that it owns in a given line of trade. Section 43(a) offers federal protection to businesses against many forms of unfair competition.

1962 Amendment to FDA Act

Authorizes the FDA to establish comprehensive procedures for premarketing approval of claims and labels for prescription drugs.
Provides for full disclosure of side effects and complications possibly associated with prescription drugs.

1966 Amendment to FDA Act

Gives the FDA power to seize shipment of goods on receiving evidence that its regulations have been violated.
Authorizes the FTC to institute its own court actions if the Justice Department does not act within 10 days of an FTC request.
Increases penalties for violations of cease and desist orders.
Permits the FTC to obtain preliminary injunctions against unfair or deceptive advertising.
Grants all federal regulatory agencies far-reaching information-gathering powers.

1975 Magnuson-Moss Warranty—FTC Improvement Act

Clarifies and strengthens product warranties.
Broadens the jurisdiction of the FTC and extends its rule-making authority.

1980 FTC Improvement Act

Requires FTC to submit proposed rules to Congress that would require a majority vote by both houses to become effective. (A recent Supreme Court decision has made this requirement questionable.)
Unfairness can no longer be used as a basis for rules restricting advertising.

1988 Trademark Law Revision Act

Prevents advertisers from misrepresenting the qualities or characteristics of "another person's goods, services, or commercial activities." Law effective as of November 1989.

industries to provide special disclosures of information on their labels and in their advertisements to prevent consumer deception. Six laws are of special note because of the increased power they have given the FTC to control the promotional activities of firms in these industries. The names of these laws indicate the nature of their applicability:

Wool Products Act (1939)
Fur Products Labeling Act (1951)
Textile Fiber Products Act (1958)
Fair Packaging and Labeling Act (1966)
Truth in Lending Act (1969)
Fair Credit Reporting Act (1970)

FTC Monitoring   The FTC staff continually monitors all forms of interstate promotion. For example, television networks are required to submit typed scripts covering one broadcasting week each month. The FTC also processes a substantial number of complaints from individuals yearly.

The FTC holds a preliminary investigation if action appears to be required. Minor complaints may be turned over to the Division of Stipulation for an informal, nonpublicized settlement. But more serious cases result in a formal complaint issued by the Bureau of Litigation upon the approval of the full commission.[3] A respondent has 30 days to answer a formal complaint, after which a hearing is held before an examiner. The examiner's decision may be appealed to the FTC by either side, and, in turn, commission decisions may be appealed through the federal courts. The FTC may issue a consent order whereby actions are enjoined but the respondent admits no guilt. A guilty judgment after formal proceedings, however, culminates in a cease and desist order. Consent orders and cease and desist orders are both binding.

The FTC of its own volition or at the request of an industry group occasionally calls a trade conference to establish a code of fair practice. The codes thus established may cover activities the commission deems to be illegal, such as the use of a fictitious list price or following unethical practices that are technically within the law.

The Alaska Pipeline Bill   In late 1973, the FTC was further strengthened by passage of legislation appended to the Alaska Pipeline Bill. The law authorized the FTC to institute its own court actions if the Justice Department does not act within 10 days on an FTC request, to increase penalties for violations of cease and desist orders from $5,000 to $10,000, and to obtain preliminary injunctions against unfair or deceptive advertising. In addition, the bill grants all federal regulatory agencies, including the FTC, far-reaching information-gathering powers.[4]

The Magnuson-Moss Warranty—Federal Trade Commission Improvement Act   This law, passed in 1975, has two parts. The first deals with ways to clarify and strengthen product warranties to improve consumer protection. The second part is of special interest to managers of promotion because it broadens the jurisdiction of the FTC and expands its rule-making authority.

Certain changes are clear, such as the derivation of expanded powers for the FTC from statute rather than judicial review. The impact of other changes is less clear. For example, Magnuson-Moss provided the FTC with rule-making authority, permitting it to establish trade regulation rules that specify unfair or deceptive acts or practices that are prohibited. The term *unfair,* however, was neither defined nor clarified.[5]

FTC Improvement Act   In 1980, because of criticism of the FTC's rule-making activities, the second FTC Improvement Act was passed.[6] The first part of the act required the FTC to submit proposed rules to Congress, where a majority vote in both houses is required to become effective. Subsequently, the FTC issued a rule that would have required used-car dealers to disclose defects in the cars for sale. In 1982, both houses of Congress vetoed the rule, but the Supreme Court held that this method of restricting the authority of the FTC was unconstitutional. (The rule was never issued, however.) In 1983, a rule regulating funeral homes was submitted to Congress and became effective when Congress refused to act.

FTC Rule-Making   An important function of the FTC is that of making rules to govern the promotion of selected products and services. For example, an FTC ruling as of September 1, 1989, swept away hundreds of state and local laws that regulated the sale of eyeglasses.[7] This ruling pits thousands of self-employed optometrists against the growing number of optical chains that dispense eyeglasses quickly and at generally reduced prices. Although Congress cannot exercise veto power over an FTC rule such as this one, too many rules that upset entrenched interests can cause Congress to put the brakes on the FTC by threatening to cut its budget.

Another constraint on the FTC's rule-making authority is that unfairness cannot be used as the basis for a rule restricting advertising. The vagueness of the definition of *unfair* and concern for the protection of commercial speech under the first Amendment caused Congress to limit the FTC's activities in this area.

The Lanham Act   Also known as the Trademark Act, this act, passed in 1946, allows manufacturers to register their brand names and trademarks and thus gain a monopoly in their use. Section 43(a) of the Lanham Act has been the basis of several suits by brand owners who claimed that the value of their brand had been damaged by misleading comparative advertising by competitors.

The Federal Food, Drug, and Cosmetic Act   The Pure Food and Drug Act of 1906 was supplanted in 1938 by the Federal Food, Drug, and Cosmetic Act. The Food and Drug Administration (FDA) is empowered to investigate and litigate advertising claims appearing on the label or package of food, drug, and cosmetic items. The FTC monitors all *other* forms of advertising for these products.

As a result of increasing pressures for more effective efforts to protect the consumer, the Hazardous Substance Labeling Act was passed in 1960. This law requires special disclosure on the label of household products that have toxic, corrosive, irritant, or similar characteristics. In 1962, still more regulatory power was granted the FDA with the amendment of the 1938 act to give the FDA authority to establish comprehensive procedures providing for premarketing approval of claims and labels for prescription drugs, as well as provisions that assure that advertising is consistent with permissible labeling claims. This legislation was especially aimed at gaining the full disclosure of side effects and complications that might be associated with prescription drugs.

The Fair Packaging and Labeling Act (1966)   This act granted the FDA additional powers to require disclosure of information on labels of food, drug, and cosmetic products and to regulate packaging procedures that might tend to confuse consumers or make product comparisons difficult.

The FDA has the power to seize shipments of goods upon receipt of evidence that its regulations have been violated. Notable examples of seizure in recent years include shipments of frozen orange juice allegedly containing misrepresentation of contents and shipments of coffee containing false price information. Of course, in situations where consumer health is endangered, the FDA has recalled entire batches of products, as it did when botulism appeared to exist in canned tuna, mushrooms, and soups.

For many years, the FDA and the FTC were antagonists because of the overlapping nature of their jurisdictions. In recent years, however, the two agencies have become close collaborators rather than rivals. With its vast scientific resources, the FDA tests product efficacy. Although the FDA's control is limited to what goes on the label (with the exception of prescription drugs, where it also controls advertised claims), the results of its experimentation are used by the FTC as the basis of its charges of misrepresentation or fraud.

In 1962, with the advent of the new legislation, the FDA undertook a study of the effectiveness of all prescription drugs then on the market. Findings announced 10 years later resulted in removal from the market of several products that were deemed ineffective. At that time, the FDA began a similar study of over-the-counter products such as analgesics and antacids.

The FDA is a potent force in the regulation of product development and promotion by members of the food, drug, and cosmetics industries. One example of the FDA's ability to influence events is the end of the fish-oil supplement craze. Touted as helpful in combating high cholesterol and triglyceride levels, the fish-oil category reached sales of $45 to $48 million in 1987, with the major brands spending about $10 million in measured media. The FDA, however, questioned the use of fish-oil supplements by the general public. In mid-1988, it sent a letter to some 100 fish-oil marketers stating that they were making advertising claims that they could not substantiate. The letter asked that the claims cease under threat of legal action. Category advertising dropped to $2 million in 1988, with sales down to $35 million.[8]

In November 1992, the FDA, in conjunction with the U.S. Department of Agriculture, was to put into effect sweeping new regulations governing food label-

Who knows what lurks behind the doors of an occupant list mailing?

This is an occupant. Does it look like your customer? It must, because so many direct marketing programs are anonymous. They target occupants. Or their cousins, the *Residents*.

At Metromail, we like people. People with names. People we know something about, so we can tell you if they're good prospects for your brand. Or if they're not. That's why we have so many databases filled with so much information about people. And their families.

Far too often marketers all but ignore the people at an address and target the occupants. Maybe that's because when the people move out, the *occupants* are still there.

Some marketers even think that they can transform *occupants* into people. One look and you'll know that you can't.

One call and you'll know that we can. Metromail Consumer Product Services. 708/932-3600

Metromail
AN R.R. DONNELLEY & SONS COMPANY
Consumer Product Services
Transforming information into opportunities.

Accurate and well-selected mailing lists are key to any direct-mail effort.

The Trouble With FSI's Is That They Give An Incentive To Users Who Don't Need One.

Betty's COOKIES

Betty's COOKIES 30¢ off

If someone is already consuming your product happily at full price, chances are you want to leave well enough alone.

But FSI's don't know how to discriminate. Instead of building market share by getting you new customers, the FSI is busy handing discounts to your current users.

Waste like this doesn't make sense, when you could be expanding your franchise with Checkout Coupon.® Positioned at the Point of Scan,℠ Checkout Coupon issues an

© 1992 Catalina Marketing Corporation.

Wasted distribution to the regular full-price user makes FSI's more expensive than meets the eye. The greater the waste, the higher the cost.

incentive only when a shopper purchases a product you've specified in advance, such as a competitive brand.

The Checkout Coupon system reaches over 65 million shoppers nationwide. Now there's some food for thought. Call Catalina Marketing, 721 East Ball Road, Anaheim, California 92805. (800) 955-9770.

CHECKOUT COUPON ║║║║®

Circle No. 101 on Reader Service Card

It is critical that marketers find efficient ways of reaching consumers with the appropriate incentive offer.

Far below the surface of the Gulf of Mexico, one of the first treasures of its kind can be found. It's an artificial reef, created from a former Phillips Petroleum production platform.

And while you can't see it, this reef has attracted the attention of hundreds of species of fish. As a result, this is something that has also been attracting the attention of many commercial as well as recreational fishermen.

Although we left this underwater paradise years ago, we took with us an unforgettable picture of life that will remain deep within us all. And it is one which will endure for generations to come. To us, that's what it means to be the performance company.

PHILLIPS PETROLEUM COMPANY 66

To understand our concern for the environment, sometimes you have to look beneath the surface.

To find out more about environmental innovations from Phillips, write to: Rigs to Reefs, Phillips Petroleum Company, 16 D-2 Phillips Building, Bartlesville, OK 74004.

Corporate advertising is often intended to address concerns about the company's products.

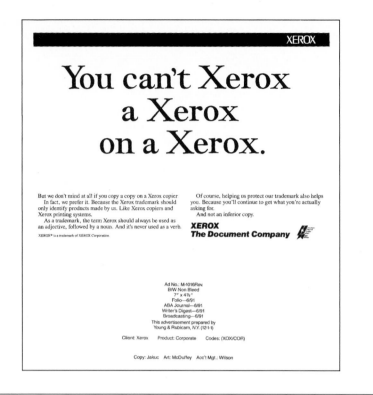

Other kinds of corporate advertising are intended to protect the company's assets, such as its name.

ing embodied in the 1990 Nutrition Labeling and Education Act. The FDA proposal restricted the use of descriptive terms and health claims commonly used in food marketing and required that labels indicate, in addition to fat, protein, and other nutrient content, what desirable daily intakes of these ingredients should be. The Department of Agriculture, which has jurisdiction over the labeling of meat and poultry products, wanted labels that simply indicated fat, protein, and nutrient content.[9] See Figure 19–2.

This conflict was resolved largely in favor of the more comprehensive FDA rules by President Bush in early December 1992. Industry will have 17 months to comply, but many labels meeting the new requirements were expected to appear by mid-1993.

The Federal Communications Commission   Since the passage of the Telephone Consumer Protection Act of 1991, marketers who use telephones have to follow a complex series of rules set out by the FCC. Some details of the act and the resultant rules are illustrated in Promotion in Action 19–1.

FIGURE 19–2

An Example of Excellent Nutritional Labeling

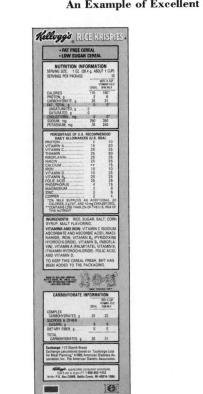

FCC Adopts Rules to Curb Telemarketing

[1992] The Federal Communications Commission adopted rules to help consumers avoid calls from pesky telemarketers and to regulate the use of automatic dialers, prerecorded messages, and facsimile machines.

Under the rules, telemarketing companies will be required to maintain an in-house list of residential telephone subscribers who don't want to be called. And it banned telemarketing calls to homes before 8 A.M. and after 9 P.M.

Critics charged that the agency didn't go far enough in establishing rules to carry out the Telephone Consumer Protection Act of 1991. They argue that the lawmakers intended for the FCC to develop a nationwide database of consumers who don't want to be bothered by so-called cold calls from stock brokers, long-distance carriers, and other salespeople who work the phones to drum up business.

"The FCC chose the path of least resistance, a do-not-call list run by the companies making the calls," said Representative Edward J. Markey (D., Mass.), chairman of the House telecommunications subcommittee. "This is like putting a fox in charge to keep other foxes out of the chicken coop." Representative Markey, who sponsored the legislation in the House, also faulted the FCC for not setting up a procedure for notifying customers of their new rights to curb the number of unwanted calls.

Instead of a directive for marketers or others to notify citizens directly, the agency said it would issue a "consumer alert" to consumer groups and state consumer protection agencies as well as industry associations and local telephone companies.

The Direct Marketing Association, the nation's leading trade association for telemarketers, had worried that the law would result in stricter rules, but expressed enthusiasm over the agency's action. "The DMA is pleased the FCC, after a careful examination of regulatory options, has chosen not to mandate a government-administered national database" of consumers who don't want marketing calls, said Richard Barton, the association's senior vice president for government affairs.

The FCC suggested that when consumers get unsolicited calls and don't want to be bothered again, they state clearly that they don't want further calls. The marketer is then required to record the request on in-house, regional, or industry-based calling lists. If a consumer continues to receive unwanted calls, he [or she] can take the telemarketer to state court for damages of up to $500.

The FCC took a hard line on telemarketing calls that could pose a health or safety hazard. It barred automatic dialer calls as well as recorded messages to emergency phones, health-care facilities and numbers for which the call recipient may be charged.

The law doesn't apply to nonprofit and public organizations or political fund-raising.

But the new rules have other loopholes through which annoying calls can slip. The rules prohibiting recorded-message calls to homes, for instance, exempt calls from market research organizations and political pollsters. Debt collection calls also are protected.

The rules could help trim fax traffic by banning unsolicited "junk fax" advertisements and require that fax transmissions clearly indicate the sender's name and fax number.

The new rules [went] into effect December 20, 1992.

Source: Excerpted from Mary Lou Carnevale, "FCC Adopts Rules to Curb Telemarketing," *The Wall Street Journal,* September 18, 1992, pp. B1 and B10.

State and Local Regulations

Given the early inadequacies of federal regulation of promotion, *Printer's Ink* magazine in 1911 proposed a "model statute" for the regulation of promotion at the state level. At present, a substantial majority of the states have adopted this statute in whole or in modified form and thus spell out very clearly what practices constitute deceptive advertising. These statutes have changed over time to reflect changing values and practices.

The variety of local laws regulating promotion defy description. Some of these laws parallel the *Printer's Ink* model, and others regulate house-to-house selling, advertising appeals, and the use of such media as billboards and signs.

The important aspect of state and local regulation is that given the reduction in resources allocated to the federal agencies, state and local regulators have taken up the slack in many situations. For example, in a California case, *People v. Western Airlines,* the court ruled that the state's deceptive advertising law applies to the airline's fare promotions. In *Committee on Children's Television v. General Foods,* parents were permitted to sue General Foods, Safeway Stores, and involved ad agencies for damages caused by encouraging the purchase of sugared cereals. Campbell Soup Co. agreed to abide by advertising guidelines in nine states to settle a dispute over health claims made in the company's "Soup Is Good Food" campaign.[10] Actions such as these noted above bear out the thoughts of one writer, who states, "Thus, while the regulation of advertising continues, the venues for control have changed."[11] Table 19–2 illustrates the diversity of the challenges facing advertisers in recent years.

Self-Regulation

In 1971, the advertising industry in cooperation with the Council of Better Business Bureaus (CBBB) established an ambitious program of self-regulation. The goal of the program was to enable the members of the industry to respond more effectively to public complaints about national advertising. The coverage of the program was broad, and, in addition to matters of truth and accuracy, it also covered matters of taste and social responsibility.

The mechanics of the program, which are quite complicated, are illustrated in Figure 19–3. It can be seen that complaints about advertising are received by the Council's National Advertising Division (NAD), which evaluates them. At this point, either the complaint is dismissed or the advertiser is requested to provide substantiation of its claims. Once again, the complaint may be dismissed or, if the substantiation is not acceptable, the advertiser can be requested to discontinue its message. If the advertiser agrees to cease and desist, the case is terminated. If not, the matter can be appealed to the National Advertising Review Board (NARB) by either the advertiser or the NAD.

The NARB is composed of a chairperson and 50 members representing various segments of the advertising industry and the public at large. In response to an appeal, the chairperson may appoint a five-person panel to consider the case. If the panel finds in favor of the advertiser, the case is closed. If the panel finds that the ad in question is misleading, the advertiser is requested to modify or terminate use of the message. Refusal on the part of the advertiser to obey the findings of the panel results in referral of the complaint to the appropriate governmental agencies, and the findings of the NAD and NARB panel are made public. Figure 19–4 illustrates the responses of five companies to challenges from the NAD.

Local Advertising Review Program   Because a great deal of advertising and sales promotion is local and cannot be effectively reviewed by a national organization, the American Advertising Federation (AAF) and the Council of Better Business Bureaus (CBBB) have approved an industry self-regulation program that operates at the local level. This local advertising review program (LARP) has as its goal improving truthfulness and accuracy of advertising and enhancing public confidence through voluntary means. At the heart of this program is a local advertising review committee (LARC) composed of equal numbers of groups affiliated with local advertisers, representatives of local advertising agencies, and the general public. The local advertising review process is shown in Figure 19–5.

TABLE 19–2

⌄   **Who's Challenging Advertising Claims**

Complainant	Forum	Product	Complaint	Status
American Home Products	Federal district court	Johnson & Johnson's Tylenol	Ads imply that ibuprofen causes stomach irritation	In discovery
Center for Science in the Public Interest	New York and Texas attorneys general	Kraft's Cheez Whiz	Ads say the pasteurized processed cheese is real cheese	Under investigation
	New York attorney general	McDonald's Chicken McNuggets	Ads say 100% chicken without saying product is fried in animal fat	Under investigation
General Foods' Oscar Mayer Subsidiary	Better Business Bureau	Sara Lee's Bryan's bacon and bologna	Ads say products are No. 1 in the South	Advertising modified
New York Attorney General	Internal investigation	VLI's Today contraceptive sponge	Ads say the sponge has no side effects	Advertising modified

Although the FTC stance toward deceptive or fraudulent advertising was considerably narrowed under the Reagan administration to handle "only the blatant cases," large national advertisers have not been let off the hook. Consumers and companies are seeking relief through the National Advertising Division (NAD) of the Council of Better Business Bureaus, Inc., as well as through the courts. Ironically, those large advertisers who welcomed the reining in of what appeared to them to be a too-active FTC are now having to face private challenges to their advertising claims that are even more difficult and costly to overcome than were those emanating from the public sector.

Source: *Business Week,* December 2, 1985, and National Advertising Division (NAD) of the Council of Better Business Bureaus, a self-regulatory group.

FIGURE 19-3

A Flow Diagram of the National Advertising Division (NAD) and National Advertising Review Board (NARB) Self-Regulatory Process

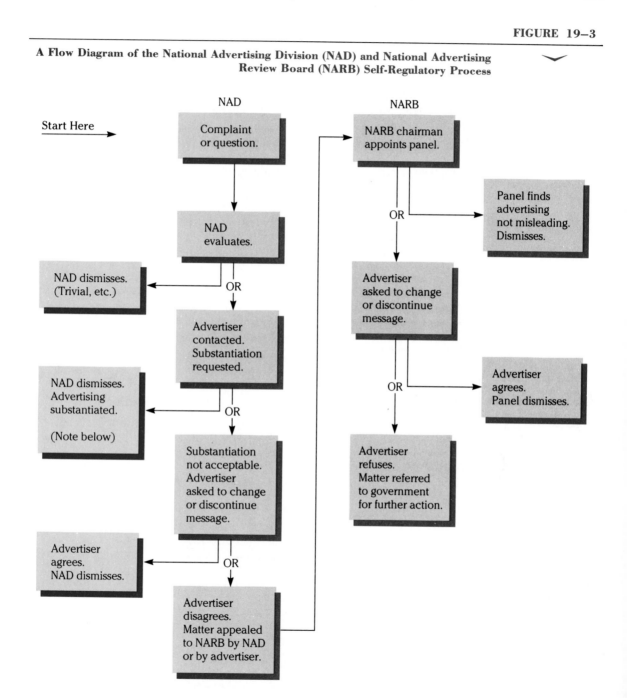

IMPORTANT AREAS OF REGULATION

Although the vigor or regulatory activity by the federal government with respect to the promotional activities of business has diminished over the past decade, there is certainly more regulation today than there was 30 years ago. The special message sent to Congress by President John F. Kennedy in 1962 entitled "Strengthening of Programs for Protection of Consumer Interests"[12] can be said to have marked the beginning of an era. Certainly the years since the early 1960s have been marked with legislation and administrative actions aimed at promoting a fuller realization of the rights of consumers. In his special message, Kennedy enumerated six basic rights as outlined in an earlier chapter.

As noted in the preceding sections, the Federal Trade Commission and the Food and Drug Administration are the major, but by no means the only, recipients of power to regulate promotional activity by business. We will discuss briefly some of the regulatory efforts of these two agencies and the philosophy underlying their actions.

FIGURE 19–4

An Example of the Public Reporting of National Advertiser Participation in the NAD/NARB Self-Regulatory Process

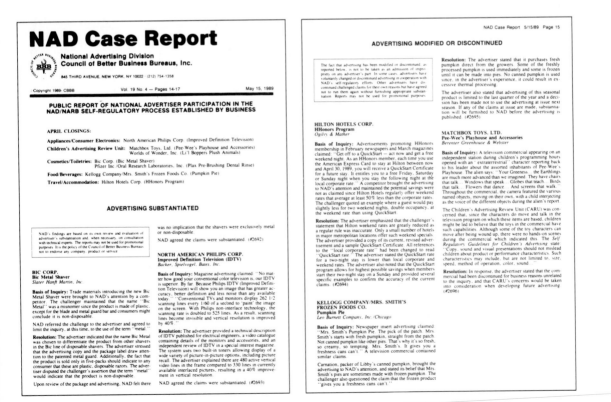

Content of Advertisements

A large proportion of present and proposed regulation involves restricting or controlling the content of the advertisement. These questions of content include whether or not the advertisement is truthful, in good taste, respects the reader's right to privacy, and so forth. The FTC has been especially concerned with cases of deception, and the legislative branch of the federal government has passed laws that actually forbid the advertising of certain products in selected media.

Figure 19–6 illustrates the various steps taken by the FTC in handing misleading or deceptive advertising.

Misleading Representation   Many of the complaints issued by the FTC have been aimed at stopping such overt deceptions as representing foreign merchandise to be of domestic origin, or claiming in the absence of proof that a wheat germ oil improves heart action. A more important issue from the viewpoint of the mass

FIGURE 19–5

The Local Advertising Review Process

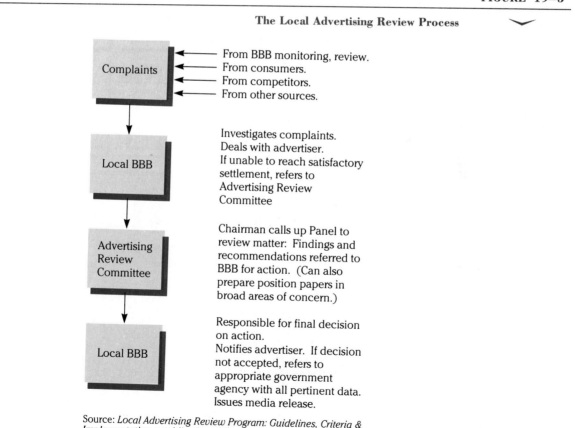

Complaints
— From BBB monitoring, review.
— From consumers.
— From competitors.
— From other sources.

Local BBB
Investigates complaints.
Deals with advertiser.
If unable to reach satisfactory settlement, refers to Advertising Review Committee

Advertising Review Committee
Chairman calls up Panel to review matter: Findings and recommendations referred to BBB for action. (Can also prepare position papers in broad areas of concern.)

Local BBB
Responsible for final decision on action.
Notifies advertiser. If decision not accepted, refers to appropriate government agency with all pertinent data.
Issues media release.

Source: *Local Advertising Review Program: Guidelines, Criteria & Implementation,* a publication of the American Advertising Federation and the Council of Better Business Bureaus, Inc., undated, p. 6.

FIGURE 19–6

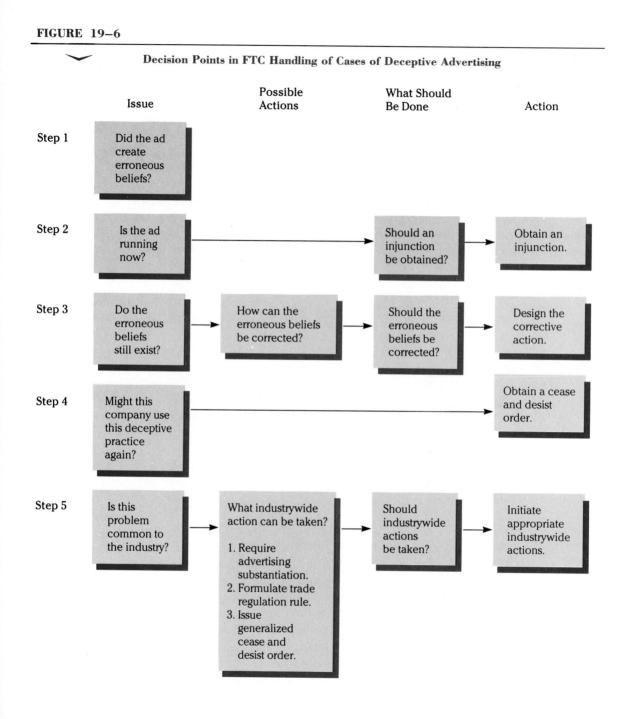

Decision Points in FTC Handling of Cases of Deceptive Advertising

communicator, however, has arisen from a series of complaints issued by the FTC pertaining to how products are represented in television commercials.

The so-called sandpaper case stands as a landmark. The Ted Bates Advertising Agency claimed in a series of television commercials that Palmolive Rapid Shave would soften sandpaper sufficiently to permit shaving the sand grains from the paper. To illustrate this claim on television, a sheet of plexiglass covered with sand was substituted for sandpaper. The commission held that such a representation was false and misleading, but the respondents answered that the technical requirements of television present such difficulties that substitutes often must be made for materials used in commercials. They went on to point out that there was no intent to deceive and that such substitution in no way misrepresented product qualities. The FTC ruled as follows, however:

> The argument . . . would seem to be based on the wholly untenable assumption that the primary or dominant function of television is to sell goods, and that the commission should not make any ruling which would impair the ability of sponsors and agencies to use television with maximum effectiveness as a sales or advertising medium. . . . Stripped of polite verbiage, the argument boils down to this: "Where truth and television salesmanship collide, the former must give way to the latter." This is obviously an indefensible proposition.

As a result of this decision, *both the client and the agency were prohibited from making any type of deceptive claim in the future.* Notice that the order issued was so broad as to prohibit the future deception, although criteria defining deception were not in existence. The courts held that such a broad order was improper and remanded the case to the FTC to reconsider. A revised order was later issued. The commission was upheld by the federal courts with a final decision that the sandpaper mock-up used was deceptive. This finding does not mean that mock-ups and other artificial devices are prohibited; rather, it constrains the advertiser from using demonstrations that are likely to be mislead. For another example of a ruling on misrepresentation, see Promotion in Action 19–2.

Deception   The courts have traditionally held that advertising must be written so as not to deceive "the trusting as well as the suspicious, the casual as well as the vigilant, the naive as well as the sophisticated." In the sandpaper case, the product did not remove grains from sandpaper in the manner claimed in the television commercial. Doubts have been expressed, however, as to whether such a presentation really misrepresents product features in such a manner as to be harmful to the consumer. The problem is, of course, to define where puffing (see below) stops and misrepresentation begins.

Since the sandpaper case, the FTC has handled several similar situations. In one case, the FTC accepted an assurance of voluntary compliance from Lever Brothers Company, Inc., to discontinue certain TV commercials advertising its laundry detergent All. The TV spots in question showed an actor wearing a stained shirt being immersed in water up to his chin. As the water rose, the actor added the detergent and expounded on its efficacy. As the water receded, the actor showed off his stain-free shirt. The FTC ascertained that the shirt had been washed in the interim by means of a standard washing machine and had not been cleaned by the immersion process.

The FTC accepted voluntary compliance, forestalling a more formal procedure, because it held that the commercial in question was of a "fanciful or spoofing" variety. The FTC held, however, that even these types of commercials can be misleading and suggested that any advertiser in doubt as to whether its commercial had the capacity to deceive should apply to the FTC for an advisory ruling prior to disseminating the commercial for broadcast.

Puffing   Making exaggerated claims for a product or service (referred to as *puffing*) is often the defense to a complaint of false or misleading advertising. For example, in cases involving misrepresentation and in those involving breach of warranty, the courts may accept puffing as a valid defense. However, legal writers have noted a move away from accepting puffery as a defense. Recent court decisions indicate that it is not possible to know in advance whether statements will be held to be puffery, and therefore advertisers should use exaggerated claims and statements only after careful consideration of the possible consequences.[13]

Promotion in Action

19-2

Volvo and Agency Pay for Faking "Bearfoot" Ad

Volvo Cars of North America and Scali McCabe Sloves, the ad agency that made the faked "Bearfoot" ad for the Swedish car maker, settled charges by the Federal Trade Commission, with each agreeing to pay $150,000.

But, as is typical in such settlements, neither party admitted violating any law. And neither the car company, a unit of AB Volvo, nor Scali admitted knowing the cars in the ad were tampered with.

The ad in question showed a huge-tire "monster" pickup truck driving over the top of a row of cars, crushing the roofs of every vehicle but a Volvo station wagon. A settlement last October with Texas's attorney general disclosed that the ad was rigged: The roof of the Volvo was reinforced with lumber and steel, while the pillars of the other cars in the ad were severed or weakened.

As a result of that settlement, Volvo ran public apologies for the ad in a number of major newspapers. Scali, a unit of WPP Group, resigned the $40 million Volvo account shortly afterward.

The FTC settlement prohibits Volvo and Scali from any similar misrepresentations in the future. Volvo, which maintained that the cars in the ad were faked without its knowledge, said, "We are pleased that this matter has been resolved and we can put it behind us."

Scali said, "The FTC did not find that Scali knew of or condoned any alteration of, or tampering with cars used in the commercial." The agency declined to comment further.

Some critics charged that the FTC settlement didn't go far enough. Dan White, who blew the whistle to the Texas attorney general's office, said he was "appalled and furious" over the agreement. "Clearly the settlement is nothing, particularly for a case this strong."

Source: "Volvo, Scali Settle with FTC," Joanne Lipman, *The Wall Street Journal*, August 22, 1991, p. B3.

Comparative Advertising and the Lanham Act   With more and more companies engaging in comparative advertising, it is not surprising that some companies are striking back with legal claims against competitors who employ unsubstantiated claims or whose advertising deprecates the qualities of competitors' offerings. Although encouraging direct product comparisons, the FTC has generally not gotten involved with business-to-business advertising. In this area, a new law of comparative advertising was developed around section 43(a) of the Lanham Act (1946), which proscribes false description or representation. The plaintiff in several lawsuits proved that a competitor's false statements were likely to deceive a substantial portion of the intended audience.[14] In addition, new rulings indicate that the advertising agency can also be held legally responsible, as you saw in the feature at the beginning of this chapter regarding Wilkinson Sword.

In November 1989, the little-noticed Trademark Revision Act of 1988 became effective. This statute makes it much easier for victims of what has been termed *attack advertising* to sue. Under the old Lanham Act, advertisers were prohibited from misrepresenting their own products. The new act prevents them from misrepresenting the qualities of another person's goods, services, or commercial activities.[15]

The Consent Order   Another important action against misleading advertising is the consent order. Several years ago, the FTC issued an order prohibiting the Colgate-Palmolive Company and its advertising agency from using "deceptive tests, experiments, or demonstrations to sell its products." The FTC specifically challenged the truthfulness of a water demonstration in a TV commercial for Baggies, the company's brand of plastic bags.

It should be noted that consent orders differ from orders in litigated cases only in that they do not constitute a finding, nor do respondents admit to violating the law. The consent orders are fully as binding in forbidding respondents to engage in practices prohibited by the order. Consent orders cannot be appealed to the courts. Sixty days after their issuance, they become enforceable with fines up to $10,000 per violation.

The Fairness Doctrine   When the FTC was founded in 1914, Congress guaranteed it the power to proceed against "unfair methods of competition." In 1938, the Wheeler Lea Amendment extended the powers of the FTC beyond unfair methods of competition to "unfair or deceptive acts or practices." This was the first legislative attempt to extend the jurisdiction of the FTC from manufacturers and competitors to include consumer protection.

The Magnuson-Morse Act (1975) supported what has been termed the *fairness doctrine* and its extension to rule development for consumer protection. The FTC wasted little time in exercising its new powers and proceeded to develop rules to regulate the advertising of ophthalmic goods (1978), vocational schools (1978), the funeral industry (1979), credit (1979), and used cars (1979). In addition, in February 1978, the FTC issued a staff report that recommended that advertising on television aimed at young children be restricted sharply.

The public outcry against limitations on commercial freedom of expression and the requirements to use "balancing" messages was so intense that in 1980 Congress passed the FTC Improvement Act, which put the use of the fairness doctrine on hold until 1984, when the limits on children's advertising were dropped. In 1987, Congress abolished the fairness doctrine completely. Since that time, it has attempted to reinstate the fairness doctrine but with little success given the veto power of Republican presidents. It is unclear, as of the time of this writing (July 1993), what President Clinton would do if faced with a renewed attempt on the part of Congress to reinstate the fairness doctrine.

Advertising to Children   The current situation with respect to this topic is that the FTC still retains control over some of the technical details of commercial production. Given the lack of FTC control over other aspects of the problem, the three major TV networks have developed a set of guidelines to which advertisers must adhere (see Figure 19–7). Unfortunately, nonnetwork stations are consider-

Promotion in Action

19–3

ABC Retreats on Bid to Relax Ad Guidelines

The ABC network just months ago mounted a bold bid to dump tired old advertising restrictions. It proposed ditching long-standing rules including those forbidding doctors from plugging products and banning actors from popping pills in pain-reliever commercials.

Yet this week, bowing to pressure from advertisers and some industry groups, ABC abruptly backed off its gutsy initiative. It quietly issued revised guidelines that are as strict as any of the old rules—and are even tougher, in some cases. Some advertisers howled that if ABC didn't regulate them, the government would do the job instead. "And certainly, self-regulation is preferable," an ABC spokeswoman says.

The new guidelines mark an embarrassing retreat. As recently has September, one ABC executive declared that the old rules were "fossils," hopelessly out of date given today's sophisticated TV audiences. The other two major networks, which have similar rules, were widely expected to follow in their rival's footsteps. The three networks establish their own rules regulating what advertisers can and cannot do in ads.

In reversing course, ABC has retained quaint restrictions—beer ads, for example, can't show people actually drinking beer—that seem out of step at a time when network programming is rife with drinking, drug abuse, and sexual escapades.

"Restrictions are good if they make sense," says Martin Puris, chief executive officer of ad agency Ammirati & Puris, which creates ads for the likes of BMW and Arrow Shirt. "But I'm watching 25 minutes of guys drinking and smoking—and my commercial can't have them doing either? What sense does that make? It's hypocrisy."

ABC had considered a proposal that would have allowed the sound—though not the sight—of beer drinking in commercials; now both remain forbidden fare. The network deleted another proposal that would have permitted commercials touting fortune-telling, astrology, card-game lessons, and craps courses for the first time. ABC also has decided to stick with the so-called man-in-white rule, which bans doctors or actors portraying them from endorsing products. And it kept intact the rule against pill-popping.

Source: Excerpted from Joanne Lipman, "ABC Retreats on Bid to Relax Ad Guidelines," *The Wall Street Journal,* March 13, 1992, pp. B1 and B4.

ably more lax than the networks, and advertisers are increasingly taking advantage of the situation.[16]

Interestingly, the ABC network, which had previously pressed for the dumping of what it termed "tired old advertising restrictions," backed off, bowing to pressure from advertisers and some industry groups. For more details, see Promotion in Action 19–3.

FIGURE 19–7

Network Guidelines for Children's Advertising

A Sampling of Guidelines
Each of the major television networks has its own set of guidelines for children's advertising although the basics are very similar. A few rules such as the requirement of a static "island" shot at the end, are written in stone; others however, occasionally can be negotiated.

Many of the rules below apply specifically to toys. The networks also have special guidelines for kids' food commercials and for kids' commercials that offer premiums.

	ABC	CBS	NBC
Must not overglamorize product	✓	✓	✓
No exhortative language, such as "Ask Mom to buy . . ."	✓	✓	
No realistic war settings	✓		✓
Generally no celebrity endorsements	✓	Case-by-case	✓
Can't use "only" or "just" in regard to price	✓	✓	✓
Show only two toys per child or maximum of six per commercial	✓		✓
Five-second "island" showing product against plain background at end of spot	✓	✓	✓ (4 to 5)
Animation restricted to one-third of a commercial	✓		✓
Generally no comparative or superiority claims	Case-by-case	Handle w/care	✓
No costumes or props not available with the toy	✓		✓
No child or toy can appear in animated segments	✓		✓
Three-second establishing shot of toy in relation to child	✓	✓ (2.5 to 3)	
No shots under one second in length		✓	
Must show distance a toy can travel before stopping on its own		✓	

Source: Joanne Lipman, "Double Standard for Kids' TV Ads," *The Wall Street Journal,* June 10, 1988, p. 25.

Obscenity and Bad Taste   It is difficult to define what is obscene or what is in bad taste. Generally, advertisers and the media have policed themselves to avoid advertising that might prove to be illegal or offensive, given present-day community standards. Because of many complaints about "sexually provocative" direct-mail advertisements, Congress in 1967 passed a law entitled "Prohibition of Pandering Advertisements in the Mails." This law allows a householder to file a notice with the local postmaster requesting that certain advertisements not be delivered to his or her address. When notified by the postal authorities, the advertiser must remove the householder's name from the mailing list and make certain that no future mailings are sent to that address. A U.S. Supreme Court decision of May 1970 upheld the 1967 law and interpreted it so broadly that a citizen of the United States has the right to prevent a direct-mail advertiser from sending anything at all one does not wish to receive.

Type of Product Advertised

Social conventions prevent certain types of products from being advertised. For example, hard liquor is not yet advertised on television, and only in recent years have women been seen in printed media advertisements for liquor. Social objection to advertising is diminishing, with the result that more freedom is being exercised not only with respect to what is being advertised but also with respect to how it is presented.

The most important restriction on the promotion of a product in the history of advertising occurred on January 1, 1971. After that date, the FTC was empowered to ban the advertising of cigarettes on radio and television.

The amount of revenue lost by the broadcast industry has been enormous, and although some of the funds used for broadcast advertising have been shifted to other media, in total the cigarette industry has drastically cut back on advertising expenditures. In addition to the ban on broadcast advertising, the legislation also required that the cigarette label contain the statement "Warning: The Surgeon General has determined that cigarette smoking is dangerous to your health."

The FTC also acquired the authority to monitor the cigarette industry's other advertising activities to see if a large buildup of promotion in nonbroadcast media would occur. As noted above, no such buildup occurred, and this part of the law has remained inoperative.

Vertical Cooperative Advertising

Advertising in which the manufacturer shares the cost with resellers is called *vertical cooperative* or *co-op* advertising. This type of promotion is big business; an estimated $11 billion in co-op money was available in 1987; with about 40 percent of that amount going unspent. Manufacturers and retailers are both looking for ways to get more of it into circulation.[17]

Because payments for co-op advertising may be used as disguised price discrimination, an illegal practice under the Robinson-Patman Act, the FTC is quite vigilant in monitoring co-op programs to ensure their legality. The rules of the game were spelled out in a 1969 policy statement of promotional allowance and cooperative advertising that has been updated over the years.

In August 1990, new nonbinding guidelines took effect which indicate that manufacturers may make co-op payments to retailers at amounts either equal to the retailer's co-op ad expenditure or based on number of unit sales (which could be a considerably higher amount.[18] In addition, the new rules make it less risky for a manufacturer to bypass a reseller that undercuts the manufacturer's suggested minimum resale prices. One point is certain: The proposed use of cooperative advertising requires careful study of the legal guidelines associated with the Robinson-Patman Act, which change with the political climate.

Advertising and Competition

For over 20 years, the prevailing wisdom among economists and governmental regulators has been that a positive relationship exists between advertising levels and rising industrial concentration, primarily in consumer goods industries. Based in part on this thinking, the U.S. Supreme Court in 1967 upheld the FTC's order that Procter & Gamble divest itself of the Clorox Company, which it had acquired 10 years earlier. One of the principal considerations involved in this decision was that the huge advertising outlays of Procter & Gamble and the promotional expertise it had at its disposal substantially reduced competition in the liquid bleach industry.

Flushed with success, the FTC in 1971 accused four major cereal manufacturers of having a joint market monopoly. Kellogg, General Mills, General Foods, and Quaker Oats were alleged to have engaged in "actions or inactions" over a period of 35 years that had resulted in a highly concentrated, noncompetitive market for ready-to-eat cereals. The FTC stated that this had been accomplished by "proliferation of brands and trademark promotion, artificial differentiation of products, unfair methods of competition in advertising and promotion, and acquisition of competitors."

After 10 years of extremely costly litigation, the FTC was not able to set new legal precedents through the application of antitrust law to oligopolies, and the case was dropped at the behest of the Reagan administration in 1982. In retrospect, it appears that competition in the cereal industry was vigorous and effective and that the consumer has not suffered because of the promotional resources and skills of the members of the industry. Indeed, the whole notion that advertising can be harmful to competition has been questioned by recently published empirical studies that indicate no relationship between levels of advertising expenditures and increased concentration or decreased consumer welfare.[19] In spite of this evidence, however, heavy advertisers with dominant market shares must be wary of the potential for antitrust action.

Remedial Alternatives

Various remedies for consumer protection may be classified into three categories: prevention, restitution, and punishment. Examples of preventive remedies would be the FTC's Code of Conduct, or Trade Regulation Rules, and the disclosure-of-information requirements in written consumer warranties as mandated by the Magnuson-Morse Act. An example of restitution would be corrective advertising, and of punishment would be fines or imprisonment.

Prevention   One type of preventive remedy is *advertising substantiation,* a program developed by the FTC in 1971. The goal of this program is to ensure that advertisers use only those claims for their product or service offerings that can be supported by fact. Since the inception of the program, companies in a variety of industries have been required either to submit proof of stated claims or to terminate or modify the advertising message in question.

Restitution   For several years under the program for advertising substantiation, complaints were settled either by furnishing acceptable proof of claims or by signing a consent decree under which the advertiser agreed to modify or terminate the claim. In some cases, as part of a consent decree, the FTC required that the advertiser devote a portion of its future advertising to what has been termed *corrective advertising*. In such advertising, the consumer had to be informed as to the true status of the product or service, and any misleading claims had to be corrected or modified.

In 1975, the FTC found that claims made for Listerine mouthwash by its manufacturer, Warner-Lambert Company, were false. The company had advertised for almost 50 years that Listerine could prevent common colds or lessen their severity. These claims could not be substantiated, and the FTC required that their use be terminated. In addition, Warner-Lambert was ordered to insert in the next $10 million of its advertising the statement "Contrary to prior advertising, Listerine will not help prevent colds or sore throats or lessen their severity."

Warner-Lambert tested the findings of the FTC and its authority to order corrective advertising in the federal courts. In two cases brought before the Court of Appeals for the District of Columbia Circuit in 1977, the FTC was upheld both on its original finding that the advertising claims were false and on its authority to order corrective advertising. The corrective statement, however, was modified slightly in that Warner-Lambert was allowed to drop the phrase "Contrary to prior advertising" from the statement.[20]

Warner-Lambert took the case to the Supreme Court, which in 1978 refused to review the findings of the appeals court. Thus the powers of the FTC in both the areas of claim substantiation and corrective advertising have been upheld. Whether these powers have been effectively utilized in recent years is another question (see Table 19–3).

Promotion in Action 19–4 suggests that many pharmaceutical advertisers are violating FDA regulations and may be subject to legal action as discussed previously.

In a recent exhaustive study of the current state of corrective advertising, William Wilkie and his colleagues have come to the following conclusions:

1. Although the FTC's power to order corrective advertising as a remedy is

TABLE 19–3

The FTC Attacks Fraudulent Medical Claims

Washington—With two commissioners holding out for even sterner action, the Federal Trade Commission has added a therapeutic pain reliever to its list of medical treatments, the performances of which have failed to live up to advertising claims.

The FTC's proposed consent agreement with Biopractic Group Inc., Riegelsville, Penn., has resulted from a series of claims for Therapeutic Mineral Ice, a product that allegedly would reduce pain and inflammation from muscle sprains, arthritis, rheumatism, and other maladies.

Biopractic ads falsely claimed that various doctors, medical centers, and athletic teams—including the U.S. and Soviet Olympic track squads—had said Therapeutic Mineral Ice was effective, the commission said, and that it stimulated the brain to produce beta-endorphin, which is a pain-relieving hormone.

Mineral Ice was sold through drug and health-food stores and chiropractors for $14.95 a 16-oz. container.

The commission's attempt to rein in more unsubstantiated ad claims represents another battle in its war on fraudulent medical aids and treatments that in recent months has included vitamins, hair restorers, diet aids, food supplements, and a toothpaste.

Under terms of the proposed agreement, Biopractic must have adequate subtantiation for its ad claims and, to repeat its beta-endorphin claims, must meet standards of the Food and Drug Administration and present evidence from two well-controlled clinical tests.

Commissioners Patricia Bailey and Michael Pertschuk dissented from the majority opinion, arguing that the consent order should have been stronger.

They also felt that the commission's order, by suggesting that Biopractic in the future might be able to substantiate its claims, was overly lenient.

"There is no expectation whatsoever that what [Biopractic] said can be substantiated," a commission staff member said. "We don't believe they can be backed up, and we didn't think the commission was doing the public a service by leaving the door open to the future possibility . . . that they could come back and substantiate their claims."

Source: "FTC Ices Therapeutic Product Claim," *Advertising Age*, October 8, 1984. Reprinted with permission. Copyright Crain Communications, Inc. All rights reserved.

TABLE 19–4

The Five Legal Criteria for Corrective Advertising

Issue	Requirement for the Order
1. Orientation	The remedy must be prospective rather than retrospective in nature
2. Goal	The remedy must be nonpunitive in nature.
3. Substance	The remedy must bear a reasonable relation to the violation in question
4. Scope	The remedy must not infringe on the First Amendment rights of the firm.
5. Form	The remedy should be in the least burdensome form necessary to achieve an effective code.

Source: William L. Wilkie, Dennis L. McNeill, and Michael B. Mazis, " 'Marketing's Scarlet Letter': The Theory and Practice of Corrective Advertising," *Journal of Marketing* 48 (Spring 1984), p. 15, published by the American Marketing Association.

not under question, it is significantly limited by certain legal criteria (see Table 19–4).

2. While it appears that corrective advertising has the potential to yield consumer benefits, past campaigns have been weak in consumer communications. Postcampaign research indicated that consumer impressions were not changed. This result is not surprising, given the fact that consumer effectiveness was not a prime concern of the FTC in the cases studied.

3. Such factors as the philosophical change in the FTC under a new administration, lack of a systematic FTC program, wide variations in terms of requirements, and the large role played by consent negotiations between

---

Promotion in Action

19–4

Rx for Pharmaceutical Advertisers: Clean Up Your Act

Medical journals are considered some of the most reliable sources of information around. Yet the pharmaceutical ads they carry are rife with inaccuracies, misleading claims, and advice that could be downright dangerous, a new study claims.

The study found that an overwhelming 92 percent of 109 ads analyzed appeared to violate Food and Drug Administration regulations, which require ads to fully disclose side effects or inappropriate uses. Researchers from the University of California at Los Angeles asked physicians and pharmacists to analyze the ads, and found that 28 percent of the campaigns would have been rejected altogether, while an additional 69 percent needed revisions. The results will be released today in the current issue of *Annals of Internal Medicine*.

"It's dangerous, and it's a pervasive problem," warns UCLA Professor Michael S. Wilkes, the study's lead author. Too often, he says, "doctors have no way to learn about many of these drugs other than the ads"—and what they're learning is perilously wrong.

Reviewers found, for example, that 44 percent of the ads would lead physicians to prescribe a drug incorrectly if they had no other information. A number of ads didn't stress dangerous side effects and didn't include enough safety information. Many wrongly indicated that a drug was recommended for the elderly or other patients for whom it was inappropriate.

Often, expensive drugs were touted as the best choice, when far cheaper versions would be equally effective, Dr. Wilkes says.

The study doesn't single out inaccurate pharmaceutical ads. But Dr. Wilkes says offenses were committed by major pharmaceutical companies "across the board," not just a renegade few. The most common offenders, he added, included antibiotics, hypertension drugs, antidepressants, sleeping pills, and birth-control products. The ads were culled from 1990 issues of 10 major journals, including the *New England Journal of Medicine,* the *American Journal of Psychiatry,* and *Obstetrics and Gynecology*.

The results suggest a sweeping overhaul is needed in the huge pharmaceutical advertising business. Medical journals rigorously screen the articles they print, yet the paid ads they accept are rarely scrutinized. The journals can't afford to reject too many ads, as they depend on them for survival: Pharmaceutical companies poured $352 million into medical publications in 1991, Wilkes says.

Source: Excerpted from Joanne Lipman, "Drug Ads Rife with Errors, Study Claims," *The Wall Street Journal,* June 1, 1992, pp. B1 and B3.

the FTC and the respondent company have all served to weaken the role of corrective advertising.[21]

It is obvious that, given the above findings, changes in the FTC philosophy and the approach to corrective advertising will be needed for a more effective remedy in the future for the problems that misleading advertising creates for consumers.

Other remedies classified under the heading of restitution include those that require advertisers to make affirmative disclosure about their products or services indicating the weak points of their offerings as well as the strong ones. Refunds to customers who have been misled and subsequently harmed, limitations of contracts, and cooling-off periods for consumers who buy from door-to-door salespeople are additional forms of restitution for consumer protection.

Punishment   The final category of remedies includes punishment. The FTC has the authority to levy fines of up to $10,000 per violation of a cease and desist order. A defendant who refuses to obey an injunction may be found in contempt of court and sentenced to jail. Although the punishment remedy has been used sparingly in the past, it is an effective alternative that can be applied if attempts to protect the consumer through prevention and restitution remedies fail.

Regulation of Personal Selling[22]

To this point, the discussion has dealt with the regulation of advertising. However, personal selling activities also come under the surveillance of federal, state, and local laws. In the following sections, we will deal with a few of the major areas that should be of concern to promotion managers who are developing personal selling strategies.

Combinations and Conspiracies   The first of the major antitrust laws, the Sherman Act of 1890 prohibits combining or conspiring to restrain trade in interstate commerce. Because the courts have held that almost all commerce in the United States is interstate due to the inevitable movement of product and promotion over state lines, the applicability of the Sherman Act is extremely broad. The law prohibits, for example, agreements between two or more competing firms that provide for the division of a geographic market so that they are not rivals. Another example is the use of agreements by which competing companies set prices at specified levels. The most famous series of cases in this latter area occurred in the 1960s when several large electrical equipment manufacturers were found guilty of setting prices on electric power-generating equipment by means of a bidding formula.

Tie-in or Requirements Contracts   Certain contracts that require tie-in sales are deemed to be illegal under the Clayton Act of 1914 if the effect may be to restrict competition or to create a monopoly. For example, a manufacturer of laser printers cannot require that purchasers use only its brand of paper and toner if such a requirement might damage other sellers of similar supplies.

Sales policies that require buyers to deal exclusively with the supplier can also run afoul of the law. Please note that tie-in or requirements contracts are prohibited when their effect *may be* to restrict competition and create a monopoly. Thus even sellers with small market shares must be careful not to ignore these restrictions because the requirements for a successful prosecution under the Clayton Act are less stringent than under the Sherman Act.

Price Discrimination   The Robinson-Patman Act of 1936, discussed earlier in this chapter, prohibits the sale of goods of similar grade or quality to competing buyers at different prices when the effect may be to restrict competition or create a monopoly. When such effects have been determined to exist, the seller may utilize several defenses. These include (1) the fact that the price differentials reflect differences in cost in manufacture, selling, or delivery; (2) that the price differential was granted in "good faith" to meet the lower price of a competitor; and (3) a severe change had occurred in the market or marketability of the goods.

Brokerage Allowances   The Robinson-Patman Act also states that customers who buy directly from the seller without the use of brokers may not receive a payment or price reduction to reflect the nonuse of a broker. This is an idiosyncrasy of Robinson-Patman, which is really more an attempt to redress an imbalance of economic power between large and small firms than a pure antitrust law.

Promotional Allowances and Payments   Salespersons must be vigilant when offering promotional payments and/or allowances to customers who are competing with one another. The Robinson-Patman Act specifies that the value of such payments or allowances should be proportionally equal to the purchases made by each buyer. Thus, a customer buying $10,000 worth of goods in a year is entitled to twice the value in allowances and services as a customer purchasing $5,000 worth of product per year. In addition, all competing customers must be informed of the availability of the allowances or services.

Other Legislation   In addition to its regulation of advertising, the FTC act covers personal selling and sales promotion activities. It outlaws various means of "consumer deception," although it never exactly defines that term. Misrepresentation, "bait-and-switch" techniques, statements of salespersons that cannot be verified, or promises that cannot be kept can be in violations of the FTC Act. The Truth-in-Lending legislation means that all credit terms must be fully disclosed to the buyer. In addition, "cooling-off" legislation allows buyers of goods sold door-to-door to cancel purchases of $25 or more within three days after the sale.

Local laws that regulate personal selling and sales promotion are increasing in number. Of special concern are abuses by door-to-door salespersons, which have resulted in local "green river" laws that prevent salespersons from calling on homes without the permission of the occupants. Laws require persons in certain businesses to obtain licenses before they can sell within the area bounded by the local authority. These licenses can be required for door-to-door selling, panhandling, and sidewalk food service, and more professional businesses such as real estate and insurance agencies, which sell high-value products and services to the public.

SUMMARY

The purpose of this chapter is to provide a brief description of the current state of the legal environment in which marketers must operate. In addition, the chapter reviews some of the more pressing legal restrictions on promotion. The following are some of the key areas that are considered.

Pertinent federal legislation and its development over the years is examined. Special attention is paid to the role of federal agencies in reaction to excesses that occurred during the deregulatory decade of the 80s. The move of the states into areas of regulation vacated by the federal government is also noted.

Of special concern is the future of the FTC and the FDA. Will these agencies receive the funding they need to fulfill their responsibilities? Can the Food and Drug Administration regain its control over the drug industry? Widespread cheating in the area of generic drugs with hints of payoffs to FDA personnel has clouded the reputation of this embattled agency.

We then turn to self-regulatory agencies and consider the roles of the National Advertising Division (NAD) of the Better Business Bureaus and the National Advertising Review Board (NARD) and its extension to the local level, the LARB. Questions are raised as to the effectiveness of these entities and whether or not their activities can moderate regulation of promotion by governmental agencies at all levels.

Additional topics in this chapter include the fairness doctrine, advertising to children, co-op advertising, and the effects of promotion on competition. The chapter concludes with coverage of the various remedies available to a firm that has been found guilty of misleading the consumer, and with a discussion of the regulation of personal selling.

In this chapter, we cover some but not all of the issues you will face in the near term. Only a solid understanding of what has happened in the past will allow you to chart your course for the future. Be alert, have competent legal counsel, and, above all, be concerned with the well-being of the consumer. Experience has shown that this is the best orientation to guarantee success over the long run.

REVIEW AND DISCUSSION QUESTIONS

1. Imagine that you are the product manager of Healthbran, an oat bran–based breakfast cereal. You want to make some health claims for your cereal in the current advertising. Given the new role being played by the state attorneys general regarding health claims, what actions should you take to make sure that you will not run into trouble?

2. You are a young person in a marketing position at a large consumer goods company, and you are trying to decide among two candidates for the House of Representatives. One candidate supports the fairness doctrine; the other does not. What questions might you put to these candidates to help you to understand the issue more clearly?

3. Suppose that a competitor has been demeaning the quality of your brand in his or her advertising. What recourse do you have to stop the advertising and perhaps even to collect damages for the harm done to the image of your brand?

4. You have been called before the National Advertising Division (NAD) because it has received some complaints about your advertising. Specifically, you are charged with using a comparative price that was not realistic. What materials must you bring to the hearing? What are your rights if the NAD rules against you? Briefly outline the steps available to you in this self-regulatory process.

5. You are a toy manufacturer and want to advertise your product line to children on Saturday-morning TV. What guidelines must you consider if you plan to buy time on the three major networks? Is there any difference in the requirements if you advertise on cable TV? Explain.

6. Imagine that you are an administrative law judge faced with the prospect of issuing a punitive ruling in the case of a manufacturer of a cough syrup who made false claims for the efficacy of the product. What remedies might you propose to assure that the consumer is protected and the manufacturer is properly penalized?

NOTES

1. For a more detailed background on legislation see, Ray O. Werner, *Legal and Economic Regulation in Marketing* (New York: Quorum Books, 1989); Dean Keith Fueroghne, *"But the People in Legal Said . . .": A Guide to Current Legal Issues in Advertising* (Homewood, Ill.: Dow Jones-Irwin, 1989); Louis W. Stern and Thomas L. Eovaldi, *Legal Aspects of Marketing Strategy: Antitrust and Consumer Protection Issues* (Englewood Cliffs, N.J.: Prentice Hall, 1984), Chapters 7 and 8; and Joe Welch, *Marketing Law* (Tulsa, Okla.: Petroleum Publishing Company, 1980).

2. Public Law 447, approved March 21, 1938, 75 Cong., 3d Sess., U.S. Stat. L., vol 52.

3. The issuance of a formal complaint may not be necessary in situations specified in the Magnuson-Moss Act of 1975 (discussed later in the chapter).

4. Public Law 93-153 (1973).

5. Public Law 93-637 (1975).

6. Federal Trade Commission 1980, *Improvement Act of 1980,* Public Law 96-2532.

7. Michael deCourcy Hinds, "Optical Industry Braces for Change under Deregulation," *The New York Times,* April 22, 1989, p. 16.

8. Patricia Winters, "Fish-Oil Sales Founder," *Advertising Age,* January 2, 1989, p. 9.

9. Bruce Ingersoll, "Food Concerns, Public in Limbo over Labeling," *The Wall Street Journal,* November 11, 1992, pp. B1 and B8.

10. Richard Koenig, "Campbell Soup Agrees to Ad Guidelines in Nine States to Settle Dispute over Claims," *The Wall Street Journal,* May 11, 1989, p. B4.

11. Thomas J. McGrew, "The Shift in Advertising Oversight," *Ad Forum,* December 1984, p. 21.

12. *Congressional Record,* March 15, 1962, pp. 108, 3813–17.

13. Joshua Honigwachs, "Is It Safe to Call Something Safe? The Law of Puffery in Advertising," *Journal of Public Policy & Marketing* 6 (1987), pp. 157–70.

14. Steven A. Meyerowitz, "The Developing Law of Comparative Advertising," *Business Marketing* 70, no. 8 (August 1985), pp. 81–86.

15. Jeffrey A. Trachtenberg, "New Law Ads Risk to Comparative Ads," *The Wall Street Journal,* May 1, 1989, p. B6.

16. Joanne Lipman, "Double Standards for Kids' TV Ads," *The Wall Street Journal,* June 10, 1988, p. 25.

17. Leslie Brennan, "How Retailers Are Putting It All Together," *Sales & Marketing Management* 140 (May 1988), p. 62.

18. "FTC Revises Co-op Ad Rules," *Advertising Age,* August 20, 1990, p. 61.

19. E. Woodrow Eckard, Jr., "Advertising, Concentration Changes, and Consumer Welfare," *Review of Economics & Statistics* (Netherlands) 70 (May 1988), pp. 340–43.

20. *Warner-Lambert Co.* v. *Federal Trade Commission,* CCH P61,563 A-D.C., August 1977), and CCH P61, 646 (CA-D.C., September 1977).

21. William L. Wilkie, Dennis L. McNeill, and Michael B. Mazis, " 'Marketing's Scarlet Letter': The Theory and Practice of Corrective Advertising," *Journal of Marketing* 48 (Spring 1984), p. 26.

22. This section borrows heavily from Robin Peterson, *Personal Selling: An Introduction* (New York: John Wiley, 1976), Chapter 14.

c h a p t e r

20

Working with the Advertising and Promotion Industry

THE AMEX/CHIAT DIVORCE: A WARNING TO AD AGENCIES

What ails the ad agency business today was never more painfully clear than the stunning, abrupt dismissal by American Express of Chiat/Day/Mojo.

Industry analysts were quick to pin blame on Chiat's "creative" direction. "Impersonal" was the conventional critique. "Insufficiently emotional" was another typical gibe.

But the problem was not Chiat's creativity; using a credit card as an airplane tail or an elevator door are creative ideas by any subjective measure. The problem was that Chiat could not grasp the issues shaping the card marketer's *business problems.* The finest creativity in the world is lost without a strategic compass. Everybody knows that. Or do they?

In fairness, the blame is not entirely Chiat's. AmEx apparently did not fully understand the source of its own problems, either. AmEx incorrectly assumed that its business problems were firmly rooted in its *advertising*, that by changing its advertised image it could regain lost market share.

This AmEx assessment would be endearingly quaint if it weren't so nearly disastrous. Fortunately, AmEx managed to stumble into the solution to its real problem: the declining loyalty of its retail and service establishments. Quite by accident, AmEx discovered that its Ogilvy & Mather–created test campaign, intended to mend fences with trade factors, was also being well received by consumers. The commercials glamorize restaurateurs and merchants who take the American Express card, in an effort to smooth over trade complaints that costs of accepting the card are too high. AmEx has found a *strategy* that works; creativity for its own sake is in remission.

The problem runs deeper than a simple shift in dollars from advertising to promotion marketing. Yet for years, advertising executives have railed against the incredibly expanding promotion industry for spoiling their party. The Chiat-AmEx Ogilvy episode instead suggests that ad agencies could learn a thing or two from their promotional counterparts that has little to do with the scourge of coupons, contests, and sweepstakes. AmEx, ironically, backed into a strategy that promotion agencies have been advancing for years—building the consumer franchise by marketing to the trade. It is a given in the promotion world that trade and consumer marketing efforts must overlap.

The AmEx revelation may well inspire a new ad strategy for the major package-goods companies. It may not be long before we see brand advertising that simultaneously idealizes the shopping experience at various chains, independents, and even corner grocery stores—just as the Ogilvy AmEx ads glamorize its retail and service establishments. This strategy would advance the store image-building objectives of the supermarket trade in harmony with the brand image-bulding goals of package-goods companies. If ad agencies wait much longer, creating such an ad campaign will no longer be their job.

Source: Excerpted from John Bissell, "What Ails Ad Agencies?" *Advertising Age,* November 16, 1992, p. 22.

Anyone in the United States with goods or services to sell to the public is free to promote those offerings to prospective consumers. Advertising, direct mail, and various other types of sales promotion are readily available and can be utilized by the owner of a one-person company or by a large corporation. In most cases, however, the promoter lacks the skills necessary to undertake the promotional campaign and thus seeks the assistance of various members of the advertising and promotion industry. This chapter will be concerned with those institutions that are available to carry out the various promotional functions, with special emphasis on the advertising agency. As you can see from the opening feature, advertising agencies are in a state of flux as brand promotion by mass media is being threatened by increases in trade promotion. In addition, mergers (many across national borders), a recession-induced slowdown in all promotional expenditures, and the weakening position of network TV are greatly affecting many members of the promotion industry.

We will discuss these changes later in the chapter, but first we must take a brief look at how businesses organize to perform the promotional functions. This

FIGURE 20–1

A Functional Organization

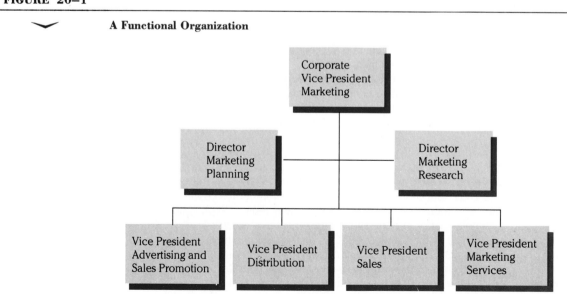

is important because the nature of the resulting structures can affect the firm's interface with members of the promotion industry.

ORGANIZATIONAL STRUCTURES

The firm's marketing function (and hence promotion) can be organized in two basic ways: the functional organization and the product organization.

The Functional Organization

The most traditional form is the functional structure illustrated in Figure 20–1. This is seen most often in a single-product firm existing in a stable industry. Here the need is more for efficiency than innovation or adaptability, and this type of structure lends itself well to tight, centrally directed management. This organizational pattern has the disadvantage that decisions are made by several functional managers who may or may not work together. Equally important, innovation

FIGURE 20–2

A Product Organization

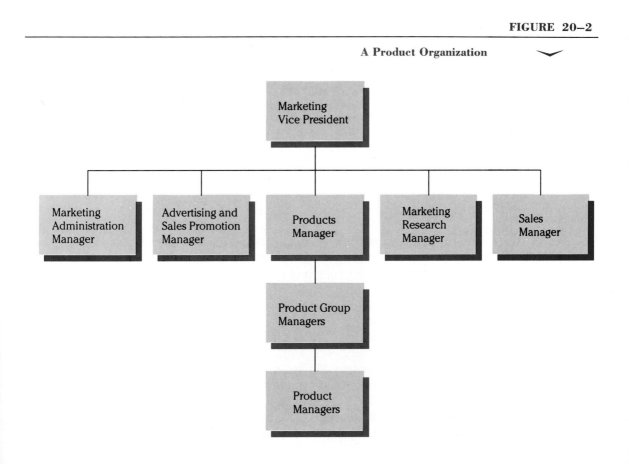

definitely is restricted. Usually levels of approval are required for each action. They tend inevitably to dampen initiative. The ability to adapt to competitive change is thus restricted. This factor, in itself, is leading to the decline of this type of structure.

The Product Organization

Over three quarters of the *Fortune* 500 companies are organized to place the product or brand manager in the central position of the organizational structure (Figure 20–2). This manager is given responsibility for profit performance and (we hope) sufficient authority to draw on the functional resources needed to achieve planned goals.

The brand manager must accomplish six tasks:

1. Developing a long-range and competitive strategy for the product.
2. Preparing an annual marketing plan and sales forecast.
3. Working with advertising and merchandising agencies to develop copy, programs, and campaigns.
4. Stimulating interest in and support of the product among the sales force and distributors.
5. Gathering continuous intelligence on the product's performance, customer and dealer attitudes, and new problems and opportunities.
6. Initiating product improvements to meet changing market needs.[1]

You can see from this list how the product manager interacts with external promotional resources such as the advertising agency and sales promotion specialists.

Difficulties with the Product Management Form of Organization

Although the product management form of organization can undoubtedly facilitate participative management, given sufficient commitment from the top executives, it is not without its difficulties. First, product managers are often not given sufficient authority to carry out their responsibilities. If this is so, their task becomes one of persuasion and cajoling to gain support from others in the firm.

Second, the area of concern of product managers is so broad that they rarely develop expertise in any one area. They are thus at the mercy of experts within or without the firm who claim to know more about the subject at issue than they do.

Third, the product management mode tends to be more expensive than other types of organization. Each product is set up as a small business with a number of people on the management team. This team is duplicated for each product. To overcome this problem, Procter & Gamble decided to eliminate the position of advertising manager for most but not all of its 90 brands in late 1987. The company instituted the position of "category" manager to take the place of several advertising (product) managers. Two years later, it appeared that the brands that kept their advertising managers did better than those that were under category managers. The category managers could not devote the needed attention to the individual brands, especially when interacting with the advertising agencies. Procter & Gamble is reversing its policy, and at least 15 associate advertising managers were recently promoted to advertising manager. It thus appears that managers at the product level are here to stay, even if they are expensive.[2]

Finally, the turnover rate among product managers is high. The good ones get promoted and the poor ones leave. Thus it is hard to get continuity of management at the product manager level for periods of time exceeding two or three years.

Making the Functional Organization Work in Practice

Although less desirable from the perspective of adaptability, participative management, and innovation than the product management organization, the strictly functional organization can be made workable. The key is to have someone who is responsible for profit performance and who is backed with authority. Where this person is placed in a formal organization chart is relatively unimportant because the volatile competitive scene is forcing bureaucracies to give way to *adhocracies.* This means that regardless of the constraints of the organizational structure, improvisations are made to coordinate the resources necessary to accomplish the marketing task.

Peter Drucker puts his finger squarely on the issue:

> Innovative organization builds a kind of nervous system next to the bony skeleton of the formal organization. Where the traditional organization is focused on the logic of the work, there is an additional relationship focused on the dynamics of ideas.[3]

We must stress that none of this will work, regardless of the structural shape, without the proper commitment of top management to innovation and excellence.

THE ADVERTISING AGENCY

Recognizing that they are unlikely to possess the range of services needed to mount a complex promotional campaign, firms of all sizes use advertising agencies. The agency originated as a broker of space for advertising media in the late 1800s, but it has changed dramatically since that beginning.

Organization of the Advertising Agency

Most full-service advertising agencies are organized around five basic functions, as illustrated in Figure 20–3. The most important of these in terms of the allocated share of personnel and budget is the creative function. The people in this area develop the ideas and modes of presentation that make the advertisement.

A second important area is media, where strategies are planned and executed for placing advertising. The media department is responsible for the timing and geographic coverage of the advertising as well as for buying space in print media and time on broadcast media to ensure the most effective use of the promotional budget.

Closely allied with the media function is the operations area, which, in addition to handling the internal business of the agency, is responsible for billing clients and making payments to the various media. The traffic area (a subfunction under operations) physically handles and distributes the advertising copy, art, film, and other components of the advertising compaign within the agency and to the various media.

The research area is responsible for gathering and analyzing data to enable the agency to answer a variety of questions such as which is the most effective advertising theme, the best media mix, the most appropriate budget, and so forth.

Finally, the account management function is responsible for agency-client relations. In the daily task of producing advertising, the account executive on the agency side and the product manager on the client side are the parties who work together closely. The account executive works with the client (usually the product manager) to develop an effective marketing and promotion strategy. He or she

FIGURE 20–3

Organizational Chart of a Typical Advertising Agency

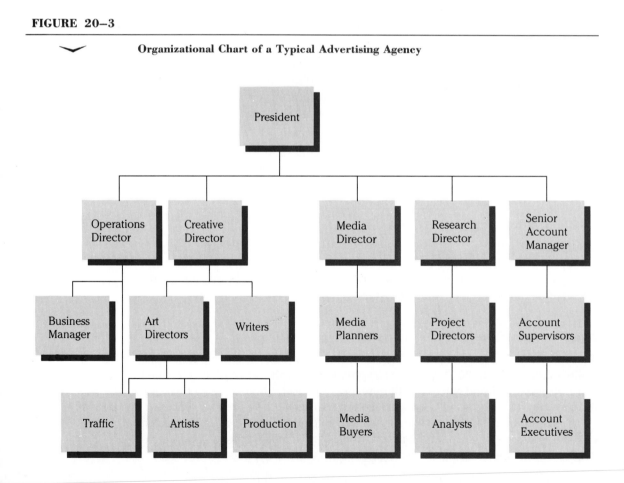

then communicates the requirements of this strategy to the creative staff, the media planners, and others in the various support groups of the agency as needed.

Large Advertising Organizations   Table 20–1 presents a list of the 50 largest advertising agencies ranked in terms of their "equity gross income." Gross income includes the sum of commissions on media billings, the markup on materials and services (usually 17.65 percent), and fee income. The changes in corporate restructuring that have occurred in recent years have blurred the distinction between agencies and holding companies. For example, Leo Burnett Co., a large Chicago-based agency, directs its foreign units through an international holding company. Thus in this table only those organizations that own 50 percent or more of themselves can quality for a "top 50" ranking. Each of these is then ranked on 100 percent of its equity gross income. The portion not owned can be claimed by another agency on the "top 50" list.

An ad placed by a large agency to promote its services is shown in Figure 20–2, but this is only a small part of its new-business efforts. There is continual volatility and turnover in this industry because of aggressive solicitation packages. Often complete campaigns are prepared on a speculative basis to woo a potential client from its present agency (see Promotion in Action 20–1).

Because the agency had its beginnings as a media broker, the media themselves have long established a process of agency recognition before space or time orders will be honored. This recognition is presently based on proof that the agency has sufficient financial resources to pay space or time charges of its client defaults on payment. On occasion, proof might also be requested to demonstrate that the agency offers adequate personnel and facilities to provide proper client service. Generally, this approval is given pretty much automatically.

Until the 1950s, however, the approval process was much more controversial. This was due to a stringent requirement that the agency must accept compensation only through the 15 percent commission offered on space or time costs. In other words, agencies could not rebate any portion of this commission, thus preventing agencies from engaging in any kind of flexible pricing policies with their clients. A consent decree signed by five media associations and several associations of advertising agencies in the 1950s ended all prohibitions on commission rebates.

Principles of the Agency-Client Relationship

Through trial and error, four basic principles were established to serve as the foundation of the agency-client relationship. The first three are obvious and non-controversial, but the fourth has become a major issue:

1. *Client approval of expenditures*—The agency is obligated to obtain prior approval for all expenditures made on the client's behalf. Without question, this is good business practice.

2. *Client obligation for payment*—The client is obliged to pay its space, time, and service bills promptly. The agency itself must pay all space and time billings even if client payment is not in hand. If the client is remiss in its obligations, it causes an unwarranted drain on the agency's cash flow.

TABLE 20–1

World's Top 50 Advertising Organizations (Ranked by Equity Gross Income)

Rank '91	Rank '90	Advertising Organizations, Headquarters	U.S.–based Agency Brands Included	Worldwide Gross Income 1991	1990	% Change	Worldwide Capitalized Volume 1991	1990	% Change
1	1	WPP Group, London	Ogilvy & Mather Worldwide; Thomson-Leeds; Cole & Weber; Ogilvy & Mather Direct;Ogilvy & Mather Yellow Pages; A. Eicoff & Co.; J. Walter Thompson Co.; J. Walter Thompson Direct; J. Walter Thompson Healthcare; Thompson Recruitment; Brouillard Communications; Scali, McCabe, Sloves; Fallon McElligott; Morton Goldberg Associates; The Martin Agency; Stenrich Group	$2,661.8	$2,715.0	–2.0	$17,915.8	$18,095.0	–1.0
2	2	Interpublic Group of Cos., New York	McCann-Erickson Worldwide; McCann Direct; McCann Healthcare; Lintas: Worldwide; Lintas: Marketing Communications; Dailey & Associates; Fahlgren Martin; GS&B: Lintas: Long, Haymes & Carr; Lowe Group; Lowe & Partners; Laurence, Charles, Free & Lawson	1,798.9	1,735.6	3.6	12,100.8	11,684.9	3.6
3	3	Saatchi & Saatchi Co., New York/London	Saatchi & Saatchi Advertising Worldwide; Cadwell Davis Partners; Conill Advertising; Cliff Freeman & Partners; Klemtner Advertising; Rumrill-Hoyt; Team One; Backer Spielvogel Bates Worldwide; AC&R Advertising; Kobs & Draft; Campbell-Mithun-Esty	1,705.5	1,700.5	0.3	11,663.4	11,637.4	0.2
4	4	Omnicom Group, New York	BBDO Worldwide; Baxter, Gurian & Mazzei; Frank, J. Corbett Inc.; Doremus & Co.; Lavey/Wolff/Swift; Tracy-Locke; DDB Needham Worldwide; Bernard Hodes Group; Kallir, Phillips, Ross; Rainoldi Kerzner Radcliffe; Rapp Collins Marcoa	1,471.2	1,349.0	9.1	10,442.9	9,813.2	6.4
5	5	Dentsu, Tokyo	Dentsu America	1,451.0	1,254.8	15.6	10,680.1	9,671.6	10.4
6	6	Young & Rubicam, New York	Young & Rubicam; Cato Johnson Worldwide; Chapman Direct; Sudler & Hennessey; Wunderman Worldwide	1,057.1	1,073.6	–1.5	7,840.1	8,000.7	–2.0

		Agency	Subsidiaries						
7	7	**Euro RSCG**, Paris	Della Femina, McNamee; Lally, McFarland & Pantello; Messner Vetere Berger Carey Schmetterer; Tatham/RSCG	**1,016.3**	1,071.4	−5.1	6,955.7	6,894.8	0.9
8	8	**Grey Advertising**, New York	Grey Advertising; Gross Townsend Frank Hoffman	**659.3**	617.0	6.9	4,437.4	4,135.2	7.3
9	9	**Hakuhodo**, Tokyo	Hakuhodo Advertising America	**655.6**	586.3	11.8	4,686.7	4,529.4	3.5
10	10	**Foote, Cone & Belding Communications**, Chicago	Foote, Cone & Belding Communications; FC8 Direct/U.S.; IMPACT; VICOM/FCB; Wahlstrom & Co.	**616.0**	543.4	13.4	4,651.0	4,390.1	5.9
11	12	**Leo Burnett Co.**, Chicago	Leo Burnett Co.	**576.6**	531.8	8.4	3,890.6	3,585.4	8.5
12	11	**D'Arcy Masius Benton & Bowles**, New York	D'Arcy Masius Benton & Bowles; Medicus Intercon International, Clarion Marketing & Communication	**534.6**	532.5	0.4	4,509.3	4,406.7	2.3
13	13	**Publicis-FCB Communications**, Paris	Publicis	**512.8**	438.1	17.0	3,433.7	2,962.7	15.9
14	14	**BDDP Worldwide**, Boulogne, France	Wells Rich Greene BDDP	**277.0**	236.0	17.4	1,941.3	1,625.4	19.4
15	15	**Bozell, Jacobs, Kenyon & Eckhardt**, New York	Bozell; Poppe Tyson	**221.0**	213.4	3.6	1,660.0	1,570.0	5.7
16	17	**Tokyu Agency**, Tokyo	NA	**176.9**	170.3	3.9	1,482.4	1,387.0	6.9
17	19	**Daiko Advertising**, Osaka, Japan	NA	**174.3**	159.5	9.3	1,278.1	1,199.3	6.6
18	16	**N W Ayer**, New York	N W Ayer	**171.3**	185.9	−7.9	1,361.1	1,469.2	−7.4
19	20	**Asatsu**, Tokyo	Asatsu America	**166.2**	140.7	18.1	1,194.0	1,018.0	17.3
20	24	**Dai-Ichi Kikaku Co.**, Tokyo	Kresser Craig D.I.K.	**159.9**	133.8	19.5	1,113.1	916.2	21.5
21	22	**TBWA Advertising**, New York	TBWA Advertising	**144.8**	137.8	5.1	1,001.9	919.0	9.0
22	21	**Chiat/Day/Mojo**, Venice, Calif.	Chiat/Day/Mojo; Anderson & Lembke	**141.1**	139.2	1.4	1,022.6	1,006.7	1.6
23	25	**Dentsu, Young & Rubicam Partnerships**, New York	Lord, Dentsu & Partners; Bowes Dentsu & Partners	**129.2**	128.0	1.0	935.9	924.9	1.2
24	23	**Ketchum Communications**, Pittsburgh	Ketchum Communications	**127.2**	134.2	−5.2	978.8	1,030.4	−5.0
25	18	**Lopex**, London	Warwick Baker & Fiore	**124.0**	163.3	−24.1	818.4	1,077.9	−24.1
26	28	**Yomiko Advertising**, Tokyo	NA	**110.8**	102.9	7.7	889.6	795.6	11.8
27	27	**I&S Corp.**, Tokyo	NA	**106.1**	104.1	1.9	849.0	833.0	1.9
28	26	**Ross Roy Group**, Bloomfield Hills, Mich.	Ross Roy Inc;; Calet, Hirsch & Spector; Griswold	**105.1**	106.0	−0.9	700.5	707.0	−0.9
29	32	**Cheil Communications**, Seoul	NA	**101.6**	73.1	39.1	315.8	274.1	15.2
30	29	**Asahi Advertising**, Tokyo	NA	**96.7**	88.9	8.8	582.1	522.7	11.4
31	30	**Man Nen Sha**, Osaka, Japan	NA	**91.1**	87.0	4.7	588.0	566.0	3.9
32	31	**Gold Greenlees Trott**, London	Babbit & Reiman Advertising; GSD&M; Martin-Williams Advertising	**87.0**	86.3	0.8	629.4	628.0	0.2
33	34	**FCA Group**, Suresnes, France	Bloom FCA	**79.0**	66.1	19.7	615.5	510.7	20.5

TABLE 20–1

Concluded

Rank '91	Rank '90	Advertising Organizations, Headquarters	U.S.-based Agency Brands Included	Worldwide Gross Income 1991	1990	% Change	Worldwide Capitalized Volume 1991	1990	% Change
34	38	**Sogei,** Tokyo	NA	**68.4**	57.8	18.3	433.0	364.6	18.7
35	35	**Armando Testa Group Worldwide,** Milan	NA	**67.1**	64.3	4.3	515.0	481.8	6.9
36	33	**Clemenger/BBDO,** Melbourne	NA	**66.0**	67.1	-1.7	391.2	399.0	-2.0
37	40	**TMP Worldwide,** New York	TMP Worldwide	**65.3**	55.8	17.0	435.3	371.9	17.0
38	36	**Nihon Keizaisha Advertising,** Tokyo	NA	**63.6**	62.5	1.8	389.8	366.3	6.4
39	37	**GGK International,** Zurich	NA	**61.3**	61.9	-1.0	398.2	377.5	5.5
40	39	**Orikomi Advertising,** Tokyo	NA	**58.7**	57.5	2.0	487.6	440.0	10.8
41	41	**Earle Palmer Brown Cos.,** Bethesda, Md.	Earle Palmer Brown Cos.	**57.2**	54.1	5.7	454.7	415.6	9.4
42	44	**Hill, Holliday, Connors, Cosmopulos,** Boston	Hill, Holliday, Connors, Cosmopulos	**55.0**	50.1	9.9	367.0	333.9	9.9
43	45	**Chuo Senko Advertising Co.,** Tokyo	NA	**52.8**	50.0	5.8	382.9	369.2	3.7
44	50	**DIMAC Direct,** Bridgeton, Mo.	DIMAC Direct	**52.5**	44.9	16.9	138.8	107.8	28.8
45	43	**CDP Europe,** London	NA	**51.0**	50.5	1.1	378.6	354.2	6.9
46	46	**Admarketing,** Los Angeles	Admarketing	**50.8**	48.5	4.6	317.2	277.2	14.4
47	42	**W.B. Doner & Co.,** Southfield, Mich.	W. B. Doner & Co.	**49.8**	51.4	-3.1	395.3	395.4	-0.0
48	49	**Hal Riney & Partners,** San Francisco	Hal Riney & Partners	**48.8**	45.0	8.3	325.0	300.0	8.3
49	47	**Ally & Gargano,** New York	Ally & Gargano; Dugan/Farley Communications	**44.6**	46.6	-4.4	363.7	383.1	-5.1
50	48	**Oricom,** Seoul	NA	**43.8**	46.2	-5.1	147.9	174.0	-15.0

Notes: Gross income and billings are in millions of U.S. dollars. Rank for 1990 reflects advertising organization's current composition. The U.S.-based agency brands, in boldface, present only among multi-tiered holding companies, are major divisions. Companies in the Top 50 hold minority equity in each other as follows: Foote, Cone & Belding Communications owns 49% of the Publicis-FCB Communications; Omnicom Group owns 46.67% of Clemenger/BBDO; Young & Rubicam and Dentsu each own 50% of Dentsu, Young & Rubicam Partnerships; Dai-ichi Kikaku Co. owns 10.69% of FCA Group.

Source: *Advertising Age,* April 13, 1992, p. S24.

Agencies Return to Self-Promotion

Sensing that the worst of the recession might be over, ad agencies are starting to practice what they preach. After a year or more of silence, some of Madison Avenue's best-known names—and the least-known, too—are springing for ad space to toot their own horns.

Big agencies such as Wells Rich Greene BDDP, New York, and Foote, Cone & Belding, Chicago, have taken out newspaper ads to tout themselves to prospective clients. WPP Group's J. Walter Thompson has been running a campaign in the trade press all spring, proclaiming itself the "home run agency." Small agencies, too, have been ponying up thousands of dollars in tough times to squeeze extra mileage out of a favorite campaign or put their name on the map.

But Madison Avenue's self-congratulatory mood poses some real risks. Too often the backslapping ads are cumbersome and uninspired efforts, and glaring gaffes can be an embarrassment rather than a way to lure new business. By advertising themselves, agencies also are drawing attention to the fact that they had stopped for most of the recession—even as they exhorted clients to buck up and keep spending.

The self-promotions, moreover, could leave some clients miffed and wondering why the shops aren't devoting more time to the advertising they are paid to create. "I can't imagine a client caring one iota about what you say about yourself," says Jack Sansolo, vice chairman of Boston agency Hill, Holliday, Connors, Cosmopulos, which lately has avoided joining other ad agencies in advertising their own talents. "It's more important what you say about the clients."

Perhaps agencies have shied away from self-promotion because of what happened to McCabe & Co., one of the few agencies that went that route last year. The much-derided effort ran in newspapers and heralded the formation of Ed McCabe's new shop. The ad drew hoots and potshots from competitors for its headline, "A Time Whose Agency Has Come," and illustration of Noah's Ark, with dark clouds looming overhead and a horde of clients lined up to enter.

J. Walter Thompson ran a much-admired flight of baseball-themed house ads this spring in the trade press and plans to resume them in late summer. "Every home run starts with a pitch," says one, with nine baseballs representing the client categories—including fast food, liquor, and athletic footwear—that the agency has open.

But even that effort was tinged with embarrassment. One headline contained the statement "Some home runs clear the benches, ours clears the shelves." A fight clears the benches; but a home run clears the fences—and one letter to *Advertising Age* pointed out the malapropism.

Ad agencies always counsel their clients to spend their way out of recessionary times. But they themselves are remarkably frugal when it comes to house ads. Billings for most agency campaigns are tiny, barely running above the $100,000 mark. And spending has been practically nil until recently. Both

Advertising Age and *Adweek* were once plump with ads for agencies and other media companies. But *Advertising Age*'s adpages shrank 30 percent from 1985 to 1991, according to *Media Industry Newsletter. Adweek*'s pages shrank 63 percent in the same period.

Both trades have detected an uptick in the first quarter of 1992. *Ad Age*'s pages were up 9.6 percent to 601 in the first quarter while *Adweek*'s were up 13.4 percent to 220.

Source: Excerpted from Laura Bird, "Hits and Misses Mark the Return of Ad Agencies to Self-Promotion," *The Wall Street Journal,* May 22, 1992, p. B4.

3. *Forwarding of cash discounts*—Most media offer cash discounts for prompt payments. The agency is obligated to forward this discount to the client.

4. *Avoidance of a relationship with competitors*—Traditionally, the agency was forced to refrain from handling a directly competitive client. In return,

FIGURE 20–4

The Advertising Agencies Advertise

the client was expected not to retain other agencies simultaneously. This may have worked in a simpler era when company mergers and multiple product lines were less common, but it is raising no end of problems at the present time. What should be done when one major firm is taken over by another and winds up having competitive brands? Or when a merger results in several agencies with the same corporate account?

As one step in providing some clarity, the American Association of Advertising Agencies stated that the "ideal agency-client policy on account conflicts is one which is based on individual product categories rather than the total product line of any given client."[4] This would prohibit any single agency from handling directly competitive brands but would permit it to handle noncompetitive brands from clients who have product lines that are competitive with those that are in the agency.

In an interesting study, Herbert Zeltner found that 60 percent of 150 top managers in client and agency organizations believe that conflicts will increase sharply in the next few years, especially given the plethora of corporate mergers and takeovers.[5] About the only consensus was that brands competing haed-to-head should not be in one agency. There was little agreement, however, on where to draw the line after that point. The need is to define exactly what is meant by *conflict*. The urgency of the problem makes it pretty certain that this must be done soon.

Promotion in Action 20–2 offers a discussion of client loyalty to advertising agencies.

Agency Compensation

Rapid changes are taking place in agency compensation methods. The plans used are (1) the commission system and (2) the fee system. It also is common to use these two in combination.

The Commission System   Most media are commissionable in that the agency is paid 15 percent when it places an order for time or space. The 15 percent sum is entirely arbitrary when viewed from the agency perspective. It may or may not cover the costs of actual services provided. All costs of planning, designing, preparing, and placing ads are to be covered by the commission. Other services such as marketing research, direct marketing, sales promotion, and publicity are usually billed as an extra charge. Direct marketing and sales promotion methods do not qualify as commissionable because they are specially designed for the client.

According to a 1986 study, fewer and fewer advertisers and their agencies are using the 15 percent media commission. Less than half (43 percent) of major media users responding to the survey said that they use the 15 percent commission. This percentage is down from 52 percent in 1983. Smaller advertisers are shifting to the fee system, and the larger ones tend to use a commission rate other than 15 percent.[6]

Because a sizable number of advertisers are still using the commission system,

Promotion in Action

20-2

How Loyal Are Agency Clients?

Given half a chance, ad executives will wax eloquent about their loyal clients. J. Walter Thompson brags about the 90 years it has served Lever Bros., and the 70 years it has spent with Kraft, while Leo Burnett boasts of its 42-year honeymoon with Kellogg.

But as for the average client? *Loyal* is perhaps the last word that should come to mind, surprising new research suggests.

In the past five years at the 50 biggest ad agencies, a stunning 67 percent of clients have parted ways, concludes a study by Sanders Consulting Group of Richmond, Virginia.

"There's very little loyalty to agencies any more," observes R. Quigg Lawrence, the senior consultant who conducted the study. "Long-term relationships in many cases seem to have gone by the boards."

The study has already prompted criticism from ad executives. Several who learned about it from this newspaper [*The Wall Street Journal*] warned that it is simplistic: To measure loyalty, the consulting firm merely compared agencies' client rosters from February 1987 and February 1992, finding that two thirds of the clients had moved on.

Critics point out that the research wrongly gives equal weight to all clients, from the puniest to the largest, and fails to consider new business wins. Others insist the results are exaggerated, as many of the clients deemed "lost" were in fact one-time projects or tiny start-up ventures that failed.

"It's mean-spirited . . . highly biased and inaccurate," rails Jay Chiat, chairman of Chiat/Day/Mojo, which tied with WPP Group's Thompson for the dubious distinction of worst loyalty record. According to the study, 86 percent of the clients on Chiat's 1987 roster had left by 1992. What the study doesn't note is that in 1990, Chiat sold its San Francisco office, accounting for 15 of its supposedly "lost" clients. Others, like Drexel Burnham Lambert, went out of business.

Still, even most ad agency executives interviewed say that, whatever its shortcomings, the study points up an urgent problem facing the ad business today. The protracted recession has made clients quick to jump ship and to blame their ad agencies for their own problems. Ad agencies have made the situation worse by trying to raid rivals' most coveted clients in a desperate bid for new business.

"The environment for clients and ad agencies has become unstable" over the past five years, says Paul Kurnit, president of Griffin Bacal. He pins only part of the blame on the economy. Other culprits in his view: clients' increasing reliance on promotions other than advertising, and ad agency mergers, which made clients feel "that agencies were less dedicated and loyal to their business." According to the study, Griffin no longer handles four of the five clients listed on its 1987 roster.

Not surprisingly, the agency that fared best of all was Leo Burnett, which had a loss rate of just 24 percent, or 6 out of 25 clients listed in 1987. Burnett is legendary in the ad business for catering to clients, and for growing with new assignments from existing clients rather than by accumulating new clients.

"The priority always has to be growing existing business" and keeping current clients happy, says Ed Wax, Saatchi's chairman and chief executive officer. "That's your heart and soul."

Source: Excerpted from Joanne Lipman, "Study Shows Clients Jump Ship Quickly," *The Wall Street Journal*, May 21, 1992, p. B4.

we will discuss it in some detail. Then we will examine why the divergences and accommodations are taking place.

Pros and cons of the commission system   The commission system is defended by some advocates on the basis of its ease of understanding and administration. Moreover, they claim that the fixed amount of 15 percent avoids price competition among agencies. The argument is that an idea is difficult to evaluate in cost terms, and agency competition in terms of price is thus impossible. Finally, they hold that the agency is rewarded in proportion to the use made of its ideas—the more the space or time purchased, the greater the commission in total dollars.

Most of these arguments for the commission system dissolve on close analysis. The critical weakness is that a 15 percent commission may not be related to services performed by the agencies. It might result in overpayment or underpayment. Consider this example: The 15 percent system would seem to indicate that an ad running in a magazine charging $35,000 per page for advertising requires seven times the effort to produce as an ad running in a magazine charging just $5,000 per page for advertising. But this is just not so.

Another important weakness is that the commission system has provided an excuse for some agencies to avoid using accounting systems to justify their charges. To many advertisers, especially manufacturers, the absence of cost accounting is unthinkable.

Industry adjustments   General Motors (GM) Corporation's divisions have gone to a sliding scale form of compensation to reflect more closely agency costs of producing advertising. The GM agency receives the traditional 15 percent only on the first $50 million of billings. A sliding scale takes effect over $50 million, with the agency earning progressively lower commissions with additional expenditures.[7]

In addition to being a poor reflection of actual costs, the commission system has another bias. Unfortunately, it tempts agencies to place dollars in commissionable rather than noncommissionable media regardless of what mix will best achieve the client's promotional goals. In an attempt to overcome this bias and to see all of the promotional options available, Procter & Gamble, the nation's second largest national advertiser, changed its compensation structure starting with the 1990 fiscal year. Under its new policy, in addition to paying the 15 percent to traditional measured media, P&G will extend the commission to cover all of the other forms of sales promotion available, ranging from mall events to ads on shopping carts.[8]

The Fee System   In this arrangement, the agency is compensated only by a fee based on costs plus an appropriate markup, with all commissions either rebated directly or deducted from the fee. There are benefits to both parties. From the client's perspective, the nature and extent of services to be utilized are negotiated, thus assuring that unnecessary expenditure is avoided. There always is the possibility that a commission represents overcharges. The agency also benefits in that cash flow is regularized. Moreover, there is greater incentive to recommend the noncommissionable media and to provide additional services. There is assurance (not provided by the commission system) that compensation will be adequate.

This system requires precise cost accounting. Agency staff must keep accurate time records that become the basis for client charges. But such data should always be collected, no matter what the compensation system, to provide a picture of account profitability.

There has been a substantial shift toward the fee system during the past decade. The reasons for this shift include (1) inflation in media prices, which generated windfall earnings for many agencies; (2) increased cost consciousness among advertisers; and (3) increased performance in-house of work formerly done by agencies.[9]

The Current Situation   Given the increased acceptability of the fee system by advertising agencies and the continued use of the commission system, albeit with certain variations and adjustments, it seems that for the foreseeable future, the advertiser and the agency will use the combination of compensation methods that best suits the needs of the situation. The very large advertisers will press for some type of sliding scale commission or reduced commission plus bonus if certain goals are reached. Or, as in the Procter & Gamble situation, they will pay commissions on some sales promotion activities that were formerly noncommissionable. For small advertisers, say those with billings under $3 million, agencies will probably negotiate a fee or a commission with a guaranteed minimum so that they will be certain of a profit after developing a campaign to meet the advertiser's goals. Promotion in Action 20–3 describes how one company, Quaker Oats, has developed a new compensation plan that combines a minimum guaranteed payment with a sliding scale compensation plan. See Figure 20–5.

The House Agency

Over the past several years, the trade press has reported that some large advertisers have removed their accounts from advertising agencies and have developed their own *house agency* to manage them. The motivation for this move has been the belief that the house agency could handle the account more effectively than a large independent organization serving many clients. Even more common has been the practice of the advertiser's taking over the media planning and buying function from the independent ad agency. These firms believed that they could economize on the cost of buying media.

The latest available data indicate that although the numbers of accounts lost to house agencies have been increasing, the volume of billings involved favors independent agencies. Data for 1984 indicated that American Association of Advertising Agencies (AAAA) members lost 68 accounts with billings of $35.5 million. During the same year, they picked up 38 accounts with billings of $85.9 million.[10]

What appears to be affecting this shifting is the recognition that the economies of going in-house are not usually as great as expected. In addition, advertisers are discovering that independent agencies can offer a large staff with wide experience and objectivity. Even in those cases where there are some economies of media buying in-house, the advertiser discovers that these can be offset quickly by the loss of some of the other benefits offered by independent agencies. On the other hand, some advertisers appear to be pleased with their house agency operations and show no interest in shifting back to an independent agency.

Development of a Productive Working Relationship

Good working relationships between client and agency do not just happen—a real dedication to this end is required (see Promotion in Action 20–4). Experience has established some important guidelines.[11]

Maintain a Top-Level Liaison Top-level executives from both parties must communicate regularly to air issues arising as part of day-to-day operations. Most junior staff do not have sufficient background or status to modify operating policies or to put out fires. Minor misunderstandings can easily develop into major difficulties.

FIGURE 20–5

Quaker Oats Uses a Sliding Scale Commission Plan to Pay for Ads Like This

Quaker Oats "Guarantees" Agency Pay

Quaker Oats Co. is instituting a new agency compensation plan that recognizes the realities of today's package-goods marketing environment.

Two key elements of the compensation plan are a "guaranteed" commission level and a sliding scale of commissions based on a brand's ad budget. The plan was finalized last week and is retroactive to July 1, the start of Quaker's fiscal year.

The guarantee addresses the agency business's toughest problem, particularly in this recessionary climate: unpredictability.

At the beginning of the fiscal year, each Quaker brand will set an ad budget. The agency on that brand is guaranteed a comission based on 90 percent of the original budget—no matter how actual spending is cut during the year.

"What it does is address the problem agencies have forecasting our spending and allocating manpower appropriately," said Clark Hine, vice president of advertising and marketing communications. "The reality of today's business environment is that with one call a client may cancel his ad budget for the rest of the year.

"With this, we've said that we will forgo a certain amount of flexibility in order to guarantee our agencies a known stream of revenues. In return, we expect them to provide adequate manpower, high-quality staffing, and continuity on our account."

The second part of the new plan revises Quaker's historic 15 percent commission rate. Now, an agency will get 15 percent for the first $10 million of an account's billings; 13 percent for every dollar between $10 million and $20 million; and 10 percent on any spending above $20 million.

"This sliding scale is based on the recognition that, generally speaking, the larger an account is, the more profitable it is," Mr. Hine said. "It doesn't take a heck of a lot more work to manage a small brand than a larger brand. We're taking the windfall profits out of the big brand by paying a lower commission on the last dollars spend, but paying a full 15 percent on the first $10 million."

According to current spending levels, only two Quaker brands are in the $20 million-and-up range: Gatorade, and the family of Quaker Oatmeal products, which Mr. Hine said will be treated as a single brand.

The $30 million Gatorade business is handled by Bayer Bess Vanderwarker, Chicago. Bayer Bess's estimated $60 million in Quaker billings includes Cap'n Crunch cereal (a $12 million brand last year), Cycle dog food (estimated at about $8 million to $10 million this year) and various smaller brands.

The Quaker Oatmeal business, with measured spending of about $25 million last year, is at Jordan, McGrath, Case & Taylor, New York. Jordan handles about $60 million in Quaker billings, including Aunt Jemima products ($11 million last year), Life cereal (a $10 million brand last year), Quaker Oat Squares ($11 million last year), and Quaker 100% Natural cereal ($4 million last year).

Less affected by the sliding scale commissions are Quaker's three other main agencies: Goldberg Moser O'Neill, San Francisco, agency for Golden

Grain's $5 million to $8 million account; J. Walter Thompson USA Chicago, whose main assignment is the $10 million account for Kibbles 'n Bits 'n Bits 'n Bits dog food; and Berry-Brown, Dallas, which handles smaller brands and Hispanic advertising. Goldberg last year worked on a similar system as a pilot test.

The final, less structured part of the Quaker plan is "a more formal and more rigorous system to give our agencies feedback on their performance," Mr. Hine said. "Because we're taking the uncertainty out of their revenue stream, we want to make sure they service each brand properly."

He added that though service hasn't been a problem with Quaker's agencies specifically, "Generally, we think it's a problem."

"Now, our agencies won't have to hedge their bets out of fear that a brand's budget will go from $10 million to $7 million," he said. "We want the best people an agency has to offer and want to keep those people involved in our business over time. We don't want our relationship with our agencies to be affected in any way by variation in our spending levels."

Mr. Hine said the Quaker agencies have responded very positively to the plan. "We're taking their biggest problem out of the equation," he said.

Each Quaker division president—breakfast, pet food, Golden Grain, frozen foods, and grocery specialities—signed off on the compensation plan.

"We made the decision that we wanted this to be a Quaker policy working across all our divisions; getting all of us into the same boat took some time," Mr. Hine said.

Although the bulk of Quaker's annual U.S. ad spending, about $200 million, will fall under the compensation plan, Mr. Hine said some smaller brands and new products will continue to use a free payment system.

Source: Julie Liesse, "Quaker 'Guarantees' Agency Pay," *Advertising Age,* October 28, 1991, p. 4.

Evaluate Promotion in a Marketing Context   When sales drop, the blame all too quickly (and perhaps legitimately) is aimed directly at advertising. Then a quite common next step is to fire the agency—and repeat the entire process a year or two later. But advertising cannot maintain market share for long when the product lags competitively, prices are out of line, distribution is insufficient, and so on.

Part of the problem here is the inappropriate use of sales objectives. Although sales are a valid objective under certain conditions (see Chapter 9), advertising generally should be evaluated in terms of legitimate communications goals. These, in turn, must be agreed on by all parties in advance. Now we are in a position to see if the agency has accomplished what it set out to do.

Do Not Abandon a Campaign Prematurely   One of the greatest pressures is to stop a productive compaign because executives (or their wives or husbands) are tired of seeing the ads. Every agency has its stories that seem funny when retold of how trivial preferences have led to the abandonment of a great campaign. It is necessary to recognize that everyone involved with a company quickly gets sick of the advertising because of sheer familiarity. But please note—*you are not typical of the average consumer.* Abandonment is appropriate only when there is a downturn in productivity.

Do Not Be Carried Away by Creative Execution   Many years ago, David Ogilvy said, "Don't ask for great ads; insist instead on great campaigns,"[12] Anyone can argue with details of execution and overlook the most important consideration in the process—*consumer benefit must be communicated clearly and memorably.* Nothing else really matters. Fortunately, this issue can be clarified by pretesting the advertising by using such methods as focus groups (see Chapter 21).

Emancipate the Agency from Fear   Some companies are known as "agency hoppers," making a change every year or two. What kind of output can they expect from an agency? They certainly will not get innovation. Why undertake the risk? Give them what they want! And that most likely will be mediocrity.

Also it is important to note that all agencies will fail at times. So evaluation should be based on the overall batting average. Any group will do its best when it realizes that a misstep will not necessarily be fatal.

We are not saying that an unproductive agency should be tolerated. That would make no sense. But it also must be recognized that an agency change is not necessarily a lasting solution. No one has a surefire formula; all mature marketing people are fully aware of this point and will take steps to make sure that the charge of poor agency performance has been verified before taking such drastic action.

Simplify Approval   The author of this chapter will never forget the travesty of a client "nitpicking to death" a campaign that pretested well and looked promising. First one client executive and then another added personal touches until the final output was nothing more than you would expect from a committee—bland advertising that had lost its cutting edge. The coup de grace was added by the chairman of the board when a member of his family was added as one of the actors in a commercial.

Remember our earlier insistence that authority and responsibility be placed as close to the firing line as possible. The client's marketing or brand manager should have the final say without further dilution. This also means, of course, that he or she will be held accountable for what happens.

Permit the Agency to Make a Profit   The operating margin is sufficiently small that most agencies will cut costs and avoid utilizing top talent if a client demands too much for what it pays. With no incentive to offer its best, the agency most likely will resign the account. It, too, has a right to make a reasonable return on investment.

Can This Marriage Be Saved?

One of the most talked-about topics in advertising is the state of relationships between agencies and their clients. And an annual survey on the subject found that agencies might think about subscribing to the *Ladies' Home Journal* to study its monthly installments of "Can This Marriage Be Saved?"

A preview of the 1992 Salz Survey of Advertiser-Agency Relations showed some surprising disparities in attitudes between parties that are ostensibly partners. For instance, 63 percent of the advertisers surveyed said they thought there was "more teamwork" in their relationships. By contrast, only 28 percent of the agencies gave the same response. Asked if money has become more of an issue in their relationships, 46 percent of the advertisers said yes—while 90 percent of the agencies did.

And asked whether changes in their relationships are related to pressures and frustrations brought on by the recession, almost four times as many agencies as advertisers said yes. Among agencies, 38 percent said yes and 60 percent said no. Among advertisers, the division was far sharper: 10 percent yes, 87 percent no.

"By virtue of the fact they hold the pursestrings, the advertisers set the tone of their relationships," said Nancy L. Salz, president of Nancy L. Salz Consulting, a New York company whose clients include Apple Computer, the Advertising Council, the Association of National Advertisers, Kraft General Foods, Pepsico, and Philip Morris. Salz Consulting will soon issue its seventh annual survey on the vagaries of the often fractious interaction between agencies and their clients.

"If they say what's happening is not related to the recession she added, "They're sending a message that more agencies than I'd expect haven't heard."

In other words, agencies that say their problems with clients are temporary in nature, products of a sour economy, could be rudely surprised by clients who consider these problems far more substantial or systemic.

Of course, agencies and advertisers did find common ground on some issues, but none that would give agencies reason to celebrate. Asked if their relationships are "more tense" than before, 40 percent of the advertisers said yes, a response given by 55 percent of the agencies.

And when 46 percent of advertisers replied that when troubled with the quality of their agencies' creative work they ask for assistance from other agencies more readily than in the past, 40 percent of the agencies said they had noticed their clients' growing impatience.

The responses by clients to the survey, which canvassed the nation's top 200 advertisers (and all but 1 of the 100 largest agencies), indicate they are coming to regard their advertising "as more of a commodity," Ms. Salz said, a trend that portends ill for agencies if they are relegated to the status of "vendors or suppliers" rather than partners.

Agencies need to feel they are in partnerships she added, as evidenced by what she called a "startling" response to one important question: Agencies were 40 percent more likely to report that they were able to do their "best work" for clients when there was more teamwork in their relationships than when there was not.

And it could only benefit advertisers to encourage such partnerships, Ms. Salz continued, rather than continually change agencies, "for a bottom-line reason: The better the agency knows the business, the better the chances of getting outstanding advertising."

Source: Stuart Elliot, "Agency-Client Study Shows a Marriage on the Rocks," *The New York Times*, June 1, 1992, p. C8.

USING SPECIALIZED SERVICES

Although full-service agencies still account for the bulk of the advertising business, over the years specialized firms have developed to offer limited services on a more in-depth and concentrated basis. These include (1) direct marketing agencies, (2) media-buying services, (3) creative boutiques, and (4) market research firms.

Direct Marketing Agencies

Direct marketing using such strategies as telemarketing, interactive video, and direct mail is not commissionable. Hence, it found its way into the full-service agencies only recently, largely by way of mergers. Nevertheless, numerous direct marketing shops have developed high skill and are worthy of consideration. Because direct marketing is growing dramatically, these agencies are getting increased use.

Media-Buying Services

The media-buying service initially appeared in the mid-1960s to provide help for smaller advertising agencies. A period of rapid growth has ensued, largely due to the growing complexity of media buying—brought about by the proliferation of specialized media to reach highly segmented markets. Today these organizations serve both agencies and clients, who determine their own media strategies so that the sole role of the media-buying service is to execute the plan in optimum fashion. Historically, there has been a concentration in broadcast media, but this is rapidly changing. Compensation plans vary, but most consist of some type of fee averaging from 3 to 5 percent.

The media-buying service has provoked controversy, much of it stemming from the traditional advertising agency, which has seen some departure of clients. Growth of media-buying services has continued unabated, however, and it would appear that continued media proliferation will make for a bright future for skilled media buyers.

Creative Boutiques

The success of the media-buying service has encouraged the formation of specialized agencies whose sole function is to provide assistance in creative planning and execution. Media buying and other activities are left to the client. Compensation is a negotiated fee. The greatest use to this point has been for new-product development, print advertisements, and television commercials. Perhaps the most significant advantage is concentration of talent within one group, which can be focused as needed on specific projects. The number of such groups has increased over the past decade, but their growth seems to be leveling off, indicated by the fact that several leading full-service agencies are unbundling (charging separately for specific services) and are willing to provide creative services for a fee if that is all that the client desires.

Market Research Firms

The significant role of marketing research has been stressed in this text, and expenditures for this purpose have increased dramatically during the past decade. The demands for technical expertise in this function have grown commensurately. Only a few advertisers have in-house capability for this purpose, and most make use of outside research agencies. These specialized organizations can provide services such as the following: interviewing and field supervision, sampling design, questionnaire construction, data analysis, and specialized store audits.

MARKET CHANGES AND THE ADVERTISING INDUSTRY

As we approach the midpoint of last decade of this century, advertisers as well as advertising agencies face an uncertain future. The mass markets of the past have been fragmented into hundreds of smaller markets, and advertisers have been seeking new ways to communicate with them.

As new-product introductions increase and brands proliferate, the consumer is paying less attention to commercials on network television. Thus the advertiser seeking to persuade members of targeted market segments to buy his or her product is using an assortment of promotional tools that include in-store announcements, ads on shopping carts, couponing, direct mail, discounting, and rebates. The growth rates of billings and profits of many agencies have been cut in half because many of these promotional functions are noncommissionable or are handled outside the agency.

Another factor affecting the advertising industry is the increased economic power of retailers vis-à-vis manufacturers. This power shift, discussed in greater detail in Chapter 13, is largely the result of bar-code scanner technology, which provides the retailer with information on product movement that formerly was available only to the manufacturer. Armed with this information, retailers have been selling their shelf space to the highest bidder and requiring "slotting allowances" of up to $4,000 per store to get a new product on the shelves. These expenses come out of the manufacturer's total promotional appropriation and thus leave that much less for media advertising.

In a recent year, for example, Campbell Soup put 80 percent of the marketing budget for its dry-soup division into advertising inside stores. To give its agencies an incentive to use alternative media in their marketing plans, Campbell decided to pay them a commission for in-store ads. But the commission was less than 15 percent because Campbell was doing its own research and ad placement—work ad agencies used to do routinely.[13] See Figure 20–6.

The Future of the Advertising Agency

Given current market trends, it is likely that the advertising agency of the future will emphasize ancillary services to a greater extent. At the time of this writing, some major agencies stated that the provision of such services accounts for 30 percent of their corporate revenues. It is possible that in the not-too-distant future, over half of agency revenue will come not from media advertising but from providing other forms of sales promotion and from the sale of ancillary services such as market research.

On the other hand, some industry watchers who are more optimistic believe that the current stagnation in industry growth will be short-lived. Current evidence in support of this optimism has been a modest but discernible shifting of resources. Some large advertisers have backed off from price cutting and other promotions aimed at short-term gains and increased investment in consumer advertising to bolster brand images over the long run.[14]

Other observers of the advertising scene believe that the current stagnation will be replaced by a new surge of creativity. It is their prediction that smaller agencies will be the source of creative people of the stature of Leo Burnett and Bill Bernbach, who touched off the creative revolutions of the past, and that this new burst of creativity will get the advertising agency business back on a fast-growth track.

SUMMARY

This chapter covers the important subjects of organizational structures and the use of specialized agencies. No matter how brilliant the strategy, everything can be sidetracked unless the organization, in its entirety, takes on a marketing orientation. Top management, in particular, must establish the climate and provide a vision.

Given that the goal of the firm is to create customers, it must have a pervasive commitment to innovation, quality, and excellence. A philosophy of participative management will allow these commitments to permeate the rank and file of the enterprise and increase employee productivity and accountability.

Two types of organizational structure—functional and product—are examined. Because product management organization has become so dominant, promotional management was discussed in that context. The great advantages of flexibility and innovation more than compensates for the disadvantages of the product organization.

Few companies have the resources necessary to design and implement a full promotional program. For this reason, companies make considerable use of advertising agencies and various other agencies specializing in direct marketing, media buying, creative design, and marketing research. The advertising agency is described fully in terms of its functions, compensation, and effective use.

Finally, the changes in the market that threaten the future of the advertising agency are discussed. The fragmentation of the market, the proliferation of new products, the seeking of new ways to communicate with consumers, and the shift in market power in favor of large retailers all mean that the era of the ever increasing use of the mass media (especially network TV) is ending. Agencies that adapt to change most successfully will focus on improving their creative efforts and will seek to make up lost advertising revenues by the sale of ancillary services.

REVIEW AND DISCUSSION QUESTIONS

1. You have just taken control of a small service business employing 20 people. The business is not doing well, and you want to instill in the employees the theme that the purpose of a business is to "create a customer." How do you get this philosophy to permeate organizational ranks and become a reality?

2. The XYZ Corporation is currently organized on functional lines. The CEO has asked you to write a memo to him on the pros and cons of switching to a product form of organization. What key factors will you include in your communication?

3. Jane Hill, the product manager of Krispy Bits dog food, has found herself at a disadvantage in that she does not have the necessary experience or expertise to appraise the research designs that she is getting from the company's marketing research people. What can she do, if anything, to minimize this disadvantage?

4. Imagine that you are seeking new business for your ad agency. The prospective client you are in contact with has the potential for $25 million a year in billings. Your agency has always used the 15 percent commission, but the prospective client states that she is interested only in a negotiated fee basis of compensation. How would you handle this situation.

5. Your full-service ad agency is being buffeted by clients who want to handle various parts of the advertising task in-house. This leaves you, in many cases, with the less profitable aspects of the business. What are the pressures for change? What can your agency do, if anything, to survive?

6. You are on the verge of signing a new client for your ad agency. In addition to the standard contract, the client wants a brief and simply worded statement of guidelines for developing and maintaining an effective working relationship between his company and your agency. What key guidelines would you include in the statement?

NOTES

1. Philip Kotler, *Marketing Management: Analysis, Planning, Implementation and Control,* 7th ed. (Englewood Cliffs, N.J.: Prentice Hall, 1991), pp. 691–92.

2. Laurie Freeman, "P&G Keen Again on Ad Managers," *Advertising Age,* September 25, 1989, p. 6.

3. Peter F. Drucker, *An Introductory View of Management* (New York: Harper & Row, 1977), p. 536.

4. *The Ideal Agency-Client Policy on Account Conflicts* (New York: American Association of Advertising Agencies, 1973).

5. Herbert Zeltner, "Client Agency Conflicts," *Advertising Age,* March 5, 1984, pp. M64–M68.

6. "Survey Shows Advertisers Quitting Traditional Commission System," *Marketing News,* June 20, 1986, p. 13.

7. Laurie Freeman, "Big Issue for 1988: Compensation," *Advertising Age,* November 23, 1987, pp. 1, 60–61.

8. Editorial, "P&G Levels the Playing Field," *Advertising Age,* February 27, 1989, p. 16.

9. Michael Cooper, "Agency Compensation: Fees vs. Commissions: A Conversation with Al Achenbaum," *Marketing & Media Decisions,* Fall 1984, pp. 109–206.

10. Stewart Alter, "Balance of Ad Trade Follows Full-Line Shops," *Advertising Age,* December 2, 1985, p. 102.

11. We have benefited from many sources including David Ogilvy, *Ogilvy on Advertising* (New York: Crown, 1983), and *Confessions of an Advertising Man* (New York: Dell, 1963); and Kenneth Roman and Jane Maas, *How to Advertise* (New York: St. Martin's, 1976).

12. Ogilvy, *Confessions of an Advertising Man,* p. 92.

13. Randall Rothenberg, "Changes in Consumer Markets Hurting Advertising Industry," *The New York Times,* October 3, 1989, pp. 1 and 45.

14. Stuart Elliott, "Some Leading Clients Favor a Shift in Selling Strategies," *The New York Times,* October 12, 1992, p. C7.

21

Measurement of Promotional Effectiveness

AHOY TO NAVY PROMOTIONAL EFFECTIVENESS MEASUREMENT

The U.S. Navy expends significant funds each year to attract young men and women to "join the Navy." The Navy implements an integrated promotional effort in order to attain its recruiting objectives. This effort includes an *advertising program,* a recruiting *sales force,* and special *sales promotion* offers such as college tuition dollar credits. The measurement of the effectiveness of this promotional effort is a significant concern to the Navy. Thus, market researchers conducted a study to evaluate the marketing effectiveness of the U.S. Navy recruiting program and to quantify the relationship between the promotional effort and enlistment achievements. This was done by estimating the impact of changes in the advertising budget, the size of the Navy recruiting force, and sales promotion offers on Navy enlistment contracts for various categories of recruits. The study reported here was based on a one-year controlled experiment in which levels of Navy recruiters and advertising were systematically varied. The evaluation of sales promotion offers was left to other studies.

Researchers chose the area of dominant influence (ADI) as their analysis unit for the experiment. An ADI is a geographical area that receives its television signal from a central city or town. Electronic media-rating services assign individual counties to an ADI based on media-use patterns of sampled households. ADIs allow researchers to execute and measure changes in electronic advertising throughout the experiment. Twenty-six of the more than 200 ADIs in the United States were chosen as experimental markets because of their relative insularity. An additional 17 markets were chosen as control cells. Treatment conditions (a given level of advertising and a given sales recruiting force size) were assigned to each of the 26 treatment markets. A number of characteristics differed across these markets: demographic, socioeconomic, levels of total military enlistment per capita, and the Navy's share of total military enlistment. Since the Navy Recruiting Command believed the last two variables were major factors in the effectiveness of marketing efforts, the market research team ensured that markets exposed to treatment conditions covered a wide variety of "total enlistment" and "the Navy's share of total enlistment" levels. Markets were classified in terms of these variables and were randomly assigned to treatment conditions. Treatment conditions included combinations of increasing or decreasing advertising by 50 percent or 100 percent, increasing or decreasing the number of recruiters by 20 percent, leaving advertising at prestudy levels, and leaving the number of recruiters at prestudy levels. Control conditions were created in the markets that maintained prestudy levels of both advertising and recruiters.

Detailed data were collected on the 42 chosen markets and were divided into four broad categories: enlistment contracts, recruiters, advertising, and environmental variables. Monthly data were compiled for both Navy contracts and total Department of Defense contracts. This information was further sorted into the following categories: high school and non–high school, females, blacks, and two different mental groups. Navy recruiter data were collected on the basis of both applied person months and total recruiters present during each month. This information was divided into two groups: that for recruiters who were established in the recruiting function and that for recruiters who were in the first four months or last six months of their tour (when researchers hypothesize they are less effective). Advertising deliveries, measured by both gross impressions (GRPs) and dollars, were collected for each ADI and were categorized according to national print (further classified as magazines, newspapers, and direct mail), national electronic media (identified as TV and radio), local, and joint campaigns for all of the armed services. Four environmental variables were also taken into account: percentage of unemployment, median family income, percentage of black population, and urbanization (the percentage of 17- to 21-year-old males who reside in counties with populations over 150,000). These variables served as blocking factors in the field experiment. The experimental markets used, the structure of the assignment of treatment conditions, and the control markets used are noted in the diagram below.

AD + 100%		Davenport-Rock Island	
AD + 50%	Tulsa Roanoke Syracuse	Washington Indianapolis Richmond	Boston St. Louis Charleston–Huntington
AD Same	Baltimore Cheyenne, WY Laurel, MS	Providence Terre Haute Springfield, IL*	Harrisburg South Bend Grand Junction, CO
AD −50%	Wilkes Barre Phoenix Odessa-Midland	Chicago Pittsburgh Columbus, OH	Dallas Louisville Lansing
AD −100%		Johnstown–Altoona	
	Recruiters −20%	Recruiters Same	Recruiters +20%

*Additional control markets:

Nashville	Des Moines	Waco
Los Angeles	Youngstown	Sioux City
Charlotte	West Palm Beach	McAllen
Greenville	Chattanooga	Anniston
Knoxville	Huntsville	

Analysis of the data collected led to a number of conclusions. The number of recruiters did have a significant impact on enlistment. A recruiter's effectiveness was dependent on the recruiter's tenure. Only certain types of advertising expenditures were effective, with a wide variation in the degree of media impact. Socioeconomic factors also had major impacts on enlistment. And in addition to increasing Navy enlistment, the Navy's marketing efforts expanded the total market for all military enlistment.

Source: Vincent P. Carroll, Ambar G. Rao, Hau L. Lee, Arthur Shapiro, and Barry L. Bayus, "The Navy Enlistment Marketing Equipment," *Marketing Science* (Fall 1985), pp. 352–74, as presented in Thomas C. Kinnear and James R. Taylor, *Marketing Research: An Applied Approach,* 4th ed. (New York: McGraw-Hill, 1991).

This chapter will consider ways to measure the effectiveness of all promotion elements. The first part will outline the prerequisites necessary to promotional effectiveness measurement. The second part will cover various approaches to measure the effectiveness of advertising, the third part will discuss the measurement of the effectiveness of consumer sales promotion and trade promotion, and the fourth part of the chapter will discuss means of evaluating and controlling the performance of the sales force. The importance of implementing an approach to the measurement of promotional effectiveness is clearly illustrated in the Navy example that began the chapter. After observing the results of its market test, the Navy recruiting director would clearly have a usable understanding of the impact of its advertising and sales force expenditures.

PREREQUISITES FOR THE MEASUREMENT OF EFFECTIVENESS

Certain prerequisites must be in place within an organization before a useful program for the measurement of promotional effectiveness can be implemented. The first is that an explicit *objective must be stated* for each element of the promotion mix and for the integrated campaign as a whole. In Chapter 8 we discussed the establishment of promotional objectives in detail. What should be clearly understood here is that it is impossible to assess the effectiveness of an aspect of promotion or of the whole campaign unless an objective is established against which to compare the actual results of the promotion. Let us remind ourselves of the nature of a well-stated objective. Promotional objectives should specify:

1. *What* is to be accomplished, for example, awareness of the product or trial purchase.

2. *How much* of this is be accomplished, for example, 75 percent awareness or 20 percent trial.

3. The *target market* or *segment* within which it is to be accomplished, for example, college students or women 18–25.

4. The time period within which the objective is to be accomplished, for example, by June 30, 1995.

It is only against these types of well-stated objectives that one can implement a competent program to measure promotional effectiveness.

The second prerequisite is that the organization must have a willingness to spend time and money on *marketing research* directed at measuring the effectiveness of promotion. There are now methodologies that can reasonably be applied to the question of promotional effectiveness. The major constraint is the willingness of management to believe in the importance of and commit resources to the accomplishment of this task.

MEASURING ADVERTISING EFFECTIVENESS

The measurement advertising effectiveness has been studied for many years, with the result that a whole industry of advertising measurement companies is available to the promotional manager. Some of these suppliers are discussed below.

Pretesting and Posttesting Advertising

This chapter evaluates measures that are useful both in *pretesting* a message and in assessing its effectiveness following its placement in the media, as part of the whole advertising plan (*posttesting*). A persistent question is whether advertising effectiveness can be measured. The response in the past was mixed, but about 73 percent of advertisers use some type of effectiveness measurement.[1] Some believe that creativity and copy testing are incompatible. This position has little merit because creative imagination can produce *ineffective* copy. In reality, many artists and copywriters do not want to be held accountable for the productivity of their output. Part of the difficulty is that some managers use copy tests as a "report card." A better approach is to give artists and writers copy-testing results with the option to use them as they see fit and to reveal or not to reveal the results as they choose.

We believe, on balance, that the arguments for copy testing outweigh the arguments against it. The objective is not to find a definitive measure of communication success. The presently available methodology will not justify such a goal. Rather, all that can be provided is a good indication of whether or not copy will be comprehended and responded to as intended. Although this does not guarantee production of a good advertisement, it *substantially lowers the risk of failure.* At the very least, copy tests, if properly used, will differentiate a poor message from a good one. What they cannot do definitively at present is distinguish a *good* message from a *great* one. This type of fine discrimination awaits further methodological development.

AN IDEAL COPY-TESTING PROCEDURE: PACT

Of course, the reliability and validity of any copy-testing procedure need to be demonstrated. *Reliability* means that the procedure is free of random error. That is, the measure is consistent and accurate. *Validity* refers to the procedure being free of both random and systematic error. Validity addresses the question of bias and deals with the question "Are we measuring what we think we are measuring?" Thus, a reliable test would provide consistent results every time an ad is tested.

A valid test would provide predictive power to the performance of the ad in the market. Unfortunately, all too many suppliers of copy-testing services do not provide measures concerning these issues. Thus, a set of principles aimed at improving copy testing has been established. These principles are called *PACT* (*Positioning Advertising Copy Testing*). These nine principles state that a "good" copy testing system:[2]

1. Provides measurements that are relevant to the objectives of the advertising.
2. Requires agreement about how the results will be used in advance of each specific test.
3. Provides multiple measurements because single measurements are generally inadequate to assess the performance of an ad.
4. Is based on a model of human response to communication—the reception of a stimulus, the comprehension of the stimulus, and the response to the stimulus.
5. Allows for consideration of whether the advertising stimulus should be exposed more than once.
6. Recognizes that the more finished a piece of copy is, the more soundly it can be evaluated and requires, as a minimum, that alternative executions be tested in the same degree of finish.
7. Provides controls to avoid the biasing effects of the exposure context.
8. Takes into account basic considerations of sample definition.
9. Demonstrates reliability and validity empirically.

These are important recommendations that should be followed. In doing so, the reliability and validity of copy testing would improve greatly.

Table 21–1 is a classification of the most widely used advertising measurement methods, classified first into those most useful in measuring response to the *advertisement* itself or its contents (awareness, comprehension, liking, and so on). The second classification differentiates actual impact of the message on *product* awareness, attitude, or usage. These data can be gathered under either *laboratory* conditions in which the respondents are aware they are being measured or *real-world* conditions, in which there is no awareness of the measurement process. In virtually all the testing procedures listed in Table 21–1, the results for the specific advertisement being tested are compared against (1) the *norms* for all ads in that testing procedure and (2) often against the norms for that particular product class and media environment.

CELL I: ADVERTISING-RELATED LABORATORY MEASURES FOR PRETESTING

In the category of advertising-related laboratory measures are those that yield data on attention, comprehension, retention, or response to the message itself in a laboratory-type research situation, as opposed to measures under real-world conditions. A variety of approaches that primarily measure the ability of a stimulus to attract and hold attention is discussed. The usefulness of what are fundamentally copy-testing procedures is greatest in pretesting advertisements.

1. The Consumer Jury

Consumers are frequently asked to analyze an advertisement and rate its probable success on the assumption that if laypeople are superior to the advertising expert in their conscious opinions as to the effectiveness of an advertisement, it is only because they are better judges of what influences them than is an outsider. Typically, 50 to 100 consumers from the target audience are interviewed, either individually or in small groups.

The dominant approach here is to utilize some type of *rating scale* to elicit intensity of preference for each stimulus. No attempt is made to provide a ranking.

TABLE 21–1

Classification of Advertising Effectiveness Measures

	Advertising-Related Test (reception or response to the message itself and its contents)	Product-Related Test (impact of message on product awareness, liking, intention to buy, or use)
	Cell I	Cell II

Laboratory Measures (respondent aware of testing and measurement process)	Pretesting Procedures
	1. Consumer jury
	2. Portfolio tests
	3. Readability tests
	4. Physiological measures
	    Eye camera
	    Tachistoscope
	    GSR/PDR
		Pretesting Procedures
		1. Theater tests
		2. Trailer tests
		3. Laboratory stores

	Cell III	Cell IV
Real-World Measures (respondent unaware of testing and measurement process)	Pretesting Procedures 1. Dummy advertising vehicles 2. Inquiry tests 3. On-the-air tests Posttesting Procedures 1. Recognition tests 2. Recall tests 3. Association measures 4. Combination measures	Pretesting and Posttesting Procedures 1. Pre- and posttests 2. Sales tests 3. Minimarket tests

Source: Adapted from the classification schema utilized by Professor Ivan Ross at the University of Minnesota.

In one example, advertisements were developed to influence public attitudes toward the Prudential Insurance Company and to cause people to think better of the company than of the insurance industry in general. Twenty-five attitude-scale statements were developed, focusing on aspects of the company and its operation. Respondents were asked to rate on a 10-point scale the degree to which the statements applied to most life insurance companies and then to the company whose advertisements they were viewing in disguised form, with company identity blocked out. The effectiveness of the advertisement was judged on the basis of the extent to which it induced a change in the rating of the company to make it more favorable than that for the industry. Meaningful differences were produced, and it was possible to isolate the most effective creative treatment.

The advantages of the scale are (1) that it provides a basis to isolate dimensions of opinion; (2) that the technique is standardized and suceptible to comparison over time; (3) that it is reliable and replicable; (4) that full allowance is made for individual frames of reference; and (5) that problems of question-phrasing are eased. Also, norms giving average results by product class or even for previous ads for the same brand can be calculated. Almost all major copy-testing services give norm scores. Furthermore, determination of degrees of intensity of feeling provides a basis for ranking alternatives and assessing how well each performs against predetermined norms. Finally, the wording of questions reduces the danger that the individual will "play expert" and distort his or her reported opinion.

Consumer jury measures are widely used. However, many experts believe that the artificiality of the questioning procedure introduces bias so that the ratings can have questionable validity. For this reason, more use is now made of the other measures discussed in this section as well as the real-world measures to be discussed later.

2. Focus Groups

A common variant of the consumer jury is obtaining consumer qualitative reactions to ads in a focus group interview. A focus group involves a moderator who conducts a loosely structured interview with 6 to 12 target consumers simultaneously. The moderator works from an interview plan but does not force structure on the discussion among the members of the focus group. The discussion usually starts with a broad discussion of the product category, and then the moderator gently directs the discussion to the brand of concern and then to the specifics of the advertising being tested. Typically, sample ads are shown to the focus group. The reactions of the members of the group in their discussion of the ad are then summarized.

The data so generated are qualitative. No attempt is made to count the number in the group who prefer one ad over another. Thus, drawing definitive conclusions from focus groups is dangerous. Some advertisers mistakenly believe that focus group results represent the whole market. Focus groups can be useful in giving creative directions to ads, insights into consumer motivations in the product category and their reaction to types of ads, and helping to identify ads that deserve further testing by more quantitative procedures.

3. Portfolio Tests

The portfolio test method requires the exposure of a group of respondents to a portfolio consisting of both *test* and *control* advertisements. The test ad is the one whose impact the advertiser wants to measure; control ads are ones for which the testing company has response scores based on extensive testing over some period of time. Control ads allow the advertiser to calibrate the effectiveness of a test ad based on its score relative to the control ads' scores. In addition, the control ads allow the tester to identify a subject who is not attending to the advertisement assessment task. This identification is based on scores for the control ads that are far out of the norm for those ads. The principal criterion of effectiveness is playback of the content following exposure. The test advertisement that induces the highest recall of content presumably will be most effective in capturing and holding attention.

Portfolio tests are widely used, but attacks have been directed at the pretest use of this device. Critics contend that recall scores can vary from alternative to alternative for several reasons:

1. Variations can occur due to interviewing errors or memory defects, although this can be true of *any* research.
2. Differences may arise as a result of the consumer's interest in the products being promoted.
3. Recall scores may not be appropriate measures for low-involvement learning situations; recognition is a better measure in these circumstances.

For the portfolio method to perform as claimed, scores on recall of the control advertisements should vary less from test to test than scores on the stimuli under analysis. However, it appears that product interest dominates all other factors. Apparently interest in the product seems to affect memory of the advertisements viewed and thereby obscures real differences between the stimuli.

Regardless of the danger of memory distortion, this test serves its purpose well if recall data correlate with readership scores following investment of funds in the campaign. Each user must be satisfied that the predictive power of this device is sufficient to warrant the costs of research.

4. Readability Tests

Procedures are available to permit analysis of the readability of copy without consumer interviewing. The foremost method was developed by Rudolph Flesch, whose formula is in wide use.[3] The Flesch formula focuses on the human interest appeal in the material, the length of sentences, and the familiarity of words. These factors are found to correlate with the ability of persons with varying educational backgrounds to comprehend written material.

Readability of advertising copy is assessed by determining the average number of syllables per 100 words. These factors are then substituted into the Flesch formula, and the results are compared with predetermined norms for the target audience. It is usually found that copy is understood most easily when sentences are short, words are concrete and familiar, and frequent personal references are made. Mechanical rules should not be observed to the extent that copy becomes stilted or unoriginal. The Flesch method is only a means to check communication efficiency, and gross errors in understanding can be detected and avoided. It should always be used, however, in connection with other pretest procedures.

5. Physiological Measures

Also within the advertising-related laboratory methods is a series of physiological measurement procedures.

The Eye Camera   For many years, it has been possible to track eye movements over advertising copy with the eye camera. The route that a person's eyes follow is then superimposed on the layout to determine which parts appear to capture and hold attention and whether or not various elements are perceived in the order intended by the creative person.

Eye camera results provide a guide in designing a layout so that the eye follows the intended path, but the findings contain a large degree of ambiguity. In the first place, exposure is undertaken in highly unnatural conditions, and it is questionable whether resulting eye movement patterns are what they would be when the consumer is not looking into a large apparatus. Furthermore, eye attraction does not necessarily reflect the person's thoughts or indicate success in capturing attention. Lingering at one point may also indicate difficulty in comprehension. For these reasons, the eye camera has never achieved wide usage. For it to be used widely, its validity must be proven.

The Tachistoscope   This laboratory device is basically a slide projector with attachments that allows the presentation of stimuli under varying conditions of speed and illumination. The tachistoscope has come to be a useful tool for many advertising researchers, especially in magazine and outdoor advertising. The Leo Burnett agency, for example, uses it to assess the rate at which an advertisement conveys information. The speed of response is recorded for various elements of an advertisement (illustration, product, and brand), and it has been found that high readership scores correlate with speed of recognition of the elements under analysis. Response to visualization seems to be especially important.

GSR/PDR   Galvanic skin response (GSR) and pupil dilation response (PDR) measure different aspects of attention attraction. GSR measures first the decline in electrical resistance of the skin to a pasage of current and second changes in the potential difference between two areas of body surface. When GSR rises, it is believed to be an accurate indicator of *arousal* in response to a stimulus.

PDR, on the other hand, measures minute differences in pupil size and appears to be a sensitive measure of the amount of information or load processed within the central nervous system in response to an incoming stimulus. At one time, it was widely claimed that PDR measured emotional response, and several published studies purported to document that it could isolate attitudinal reaction to marketing stimuli. The weight of current evidence, however, makes this interpretation highly questionable.

A series of studies was undertaken using both GSR and PDR with a variety of audio and print stimuli.[4] It was found fairly consistently that good short-term and long-term retention occurs when both GSR and PDR are high in response to an advertisement.

CELL II: PRODUCT-RELATED LABORATORY MEASURES FOR PRETESTING

Some techniques can be utilized under laboratory conditions to determine the effects of the message on consumer attitudes toward the product or service itself—such as awareness, attitude shift, and changes in buying intentions. Included in this category are the threater tests, trailer tests, and laboratory stores. These methods are fundamentally pretesting procedures.

1. Theater Tests

Theater tests are a means to assess changes in stated consumer product preference after exposure to advertisements. Typically, tickets are mailed to about 350 to 1,000 respondent households, to yield a sample of 250 to 600. Respondents are also recruited by telephone and mall intercept. ARS and ASI Market Research, Inc., offer these types of test. The research format is essentially the same for all testing sessions: people are invited to view new televison shows with commercials inserted in the usual place. A drawing is held before the showing, and each consumer is offered a choice of various products as gifts. Product choices are noted, and then the show and commercials are viewed. Another drawing and offer of gifts is held after exposure, and changes in stated brand preference are noted. Written comments are also solicited on the programs and the commercials.

Theater tests may tap a dimension of response that enables reasonably accurate prediction of advertising success, and for this reason it is in wide use. Respondents are presumably unaware that they are rating advertisements, and the tendency toward "buyer expertise" may thus be eliminated.

2. Trailer Tests

Respondents may be brought to a central location, often a portable trailer or van set up in a shopping center, where they are shown several advertisements with or without surrounding editorial material or programming. Usually a comparative evaluation is made of two or more executions of the same theme. Respondents are told that the product can be made to different formulations and are shown copy describing each. Then they are asked to choose between the two formulations; questioning reveals what the commercial communicates. Although the technique is artificial, many believe that it is a useful way to measure *comprehension* of the copy. Furthermore, it is quite inexpensive.

3. Laboratory Stores

The laboratory store is a variation on the theater technique described above. Respondents are exposed to advertising under various types of conditions and are then permitted to shop in a small store. Usually coupons or chits that can be redeemed for actual merchandise are provided. In this way, actual product movement in response to advertising can be monitored.

CELL III: ADVERTISING-RELATED MEASUREMENT UNDER REAL-WORLD CONDITIONS FOR PRETESTING AND POSTTESTING

Procedures used in the second major category of technique depicted in Table 21–1, real-world measures, usually involve exposure under real-world conditions such as would normally be encountered in the consumer's home. Most researchers believe that the greater realism provided enhances the validity of the resulting data. This section discusses the fairly extensive group of real-world measurements of response to or liking of the message itself. Some measurements are usually used to pretest the message prior to investment in time or space; others are usually used to posttest following airing or viewing. We begin our discussion by examining pretesting procedures.

Pretesting Procedures

1. Dummy Advertising Vehicles   Many testing organizations use a dummy magazine for pretesting purposes; such tests can result in accurate predictions of response. Editorial features of lasting interest are permanent items in this magazine; the only variations in the five yearly editions are test advertisements. Each printing is distributed to a random sample of homes in various geographical areas. Readers are told that the publisher is interested in evaluations of editorial content and are instructed to read the magazine in a normal fashion. A return interview focuses on both the editorial content and advertisements. Each advertisement is scored on recall, extent of copy readership, and whether or not the advertisement induces product interest.

The use of dummy vehicles is subject to the same criticisms as the portfolio test, but this procedure possesses the distinct advantage that advertisements are tested under completely natural surroundings—normal exposure in the home. *Recall* of content under such circumstances is likely to produce a more realistic indication of advertising success.

2. Inquiry Tests   Inquiry tests measure advertising effectiveness on the basis of return of coupons (from advertisements inviting readers to send for information) run under normal conditions in printed media. Different creative treatments may be compared in several ways: (1) by running coupons in successive issues of the same medium, (2) by running them simultaneously in issues of different media, and (3) by taking advantage of "split-run" privileges offered by some media whereby alternate copies carry different versions of the message. The split-run procedure is more widely used because all variables other than creative differences between stimuli are held constant.

The inquiry tests can focus on a number of creative variations: (1) one advertisement versus a completely different version, (2) variations in type or other elements of the same appeal, (3) summed inquiries compared over the total run of two or more campaigns, and (4) the effectiveness of different media when the same advertisement is run in each.

The advantages are apparent in that no interviews are required, and quantitative analysis of data usually presents no problems. As a result, the costs are not excessive. This approach, however, suffers from crucial limitations. First, the presence of a coupon attracts attention to the copy for this reason alone, and true differences in creative treatment can be obscured. Second, many people may read the copy and not return the coupon. Certain people are more prone to take this action than others, and "volunteer bias" can greatly overstate or understate the true effectiveness. One must constantly be aware that pretesting copy is very different from testing individual elements. Finally, coupon return bears no special relationship to advertising effectiveness because changes in attitude and in awareness, the communication of copy points, and a host of additional responses are not tested. It must be concluded that the disadvantages far outweigh the advantages of the coupon-return method for most purposes. The inquiry test should be used only when coupon return is the objective of the advertisement. When this is so, it is a completely valid measure of response.

3. On-the-Air Tests   Some research services measure response to advertisements that are inserted into actual television or radio programs in certain test markets. The "on-the-air" test is an example. The advantages and disadvantages are identical to those encountered in the use of dummy vehicles. In television, some of the best-known services used are Burke Marketing Services' Day-After Recall (DAR), Gallup and Robinson's Total Prime Time (TPT), and Information Resources Inc.'s Behavior Scan.[5]

DAR tests   DAR tests typically involve about 200 respondents who are contacted by telephone in any of 34 available cities and who claim to have watched a specific television show the night before. Measures are taken in both *unaided* and *aided* recall fashion. To begin with, respondents are asked if they remember seeing a commercial for a product in the product class of interest. If they do not, then they are asked if they remember a commercial for the specific test brand. Those who recall the ad in either fashion are asked what they recall about the specific copy points of the ad.

Total prime time   TPT is a service of Gallup and Robinson (G&R) that can test commercials that appear in prime time. They survey about 700 men and 700 women in the Philadelphia area. Qualified respondents are those who have watched at least 30 minutes of network prime time the previous night. Another approach that is used is G&R's In-View. Here respondents are called in advance and are invited to watch the show in which the test ad will appear. About 150 men and 150 women are used in In-View, all from the Philadelphia area.

Measures taken for both TPT and In-View include:

1. Proved commercial registration (PCR—the percentage of these who can recall (from company or brand cues) and accurately describe the ad.

2. Idea communication—the percentage of recallers who can recall specific sales points in the ad.

3. Favorable attitude—percentage of favorable comments about the brand offered by the respondent.

BehaviorScan Information Resources Inc. (IRI) developed BehaviorScan, which collects information that relates consumer purchases to television-viewing choices. By tracking family purchases at the grocery store through the electronic scanner system and placing meters on TV sets to monitor the selection of programs and TV commercials, IRI has developed a useful advertising research tool. BehaviorScan can also test various commercials by broadcasting them to selected homes and then monitoring grocery purchases to see if the ad induced the family to buy the product.

One of the most useful benefits of such a system is the collection of historical data. IRI puts such data into a software program and sells it to consumer product companies. For instance, brand managers at Colgate-Palmolive Co. used the software package to decide whether to market a new detergent using the developed advertising campaign. The company saved eight weeks and 35 percent of the cost of regular test marketing by avoiding test marketing research and using the information package sold by IRI instead. Other firms offer similar services, often using cable television.

Posttesting Procedures

The following real-world tests of advertisements are usually performed on a post-test basis.

1. Recognition Tests The readership of printed advertisements has long been assessed using a standard technique called *recognition measurement,* which was developed by Daniel Starch. In 1992, Starch Inra Hooper, Inc., measured about 100,000 ads in more than 100 magazines and newspapers. The Starch method is described in detail because other related procedures are quite similar.

The nature of the Starch method The Starch organization annually surveys approximately 30,000 advertisements in nearly 1,000 consumer and farm magazines, business publications, and newspapers. A national sample consisting of interviews in 20 to 30 geographical areas is chosen for each study. Although the sample is not a random selection, attempts are made to parallel the circulation makeup of each medium under analysis.

Interviewers are assigned a given number of readers over 18 years of age with certain demographic characteristics in terms of income and location. Studies usually include from 100 to 200 interviews per sex, and the quota for each interviewer is fairly small. The interview is conducted in the respondent's home. The interviewer commences by asking whether or not the particular periodical had been read prior to the interview. If the answer is affirmative, the issue is opened at a page specified in advance to guarantee that the fatigue resulting from the interview will not unduly bias advertising appearing at the back of the issue. The respondent is then asked, for each advertisement, "Did you see or read any part of the advertisement?" If the answer is yes, he or she is asked to indicate exactly what parts of the layout and copy were seen or read.

Four principal readership scores for the sample are reported:

1. *Noted*—the percentage of readers who remember seeing the advertisement.

2. *Seen-associated*—the percentage of readers who recall seeing or reading any part of the advertisement identifying the product or brand.

3. *Read most*—the percentage of readers who reported reading at least one-half of the advertisement.

4. *Signature*—the percentage of readers who remember seeing the brand name or logo.

Several additional scores are also calculated and reported:

1. *Readers per dollar*—the number of readers attracted by the advertisement for each dollar invested in space.

2. *Cost ratios*—the relationship between readers per dollar and the median readers per dollar for all half-page or larger advertisements in the issue. A "noted cost ratio" of 121, for example, means that the copy exceeded the par for the issue by 21 percent.

3. *Ranks*—the numerical ordering of all advertisements from highest to lowest by readers per dollar.

Data are available on the readership of component parts of each layout, such as secondary illustrations, the company signature, or various copy blocks. Figure 21–1 presents an ad with readership scores placed on it. The Starch method is a syndicated service, and other organizations offer similar services. In addition, individual advertisers and research consultants frequently conduct private specialized readership studies.

Analysis of the recognition method   The recognition method, especially the Starch approach, is by far the most widely used means of measuring advertising readership. However, a growing number of criticisms of the technique have been published in recent years. These criticisms for the most part are based on significant methodological questions. The potential research pitfalls that have been reported involve (1) the problem of false claiming, (2) the reproducibility of recognition scores, and (3) sensitivity to interviewer variations.

The problem of false claiming   The interview is conducted informally, with the respondent simply being asked to indicate whether or not he or she remembers seeing a given advertisement. It has been feared that the respondent could consciously or unconsciously give a completely false reply because no means exists to check its accuracy. Research has brought this problem into sharper perspective.

The Advertising Research Foundation undertook the Print Advertisement Research Methods (PARM) study. The analysis of recognition by the PARM staff showed a surprising tendency for scores to remain stable over time. In other words, the scores showed little variation as the interval between the date of the claimed readership of the magazine and the date of the interview increased. If the recognition score truly measures memory, the scores should exhibit a reliable tendency to decline over time. For example, the recognition of meaningful data was 97 percent after 20 minutes, as compared with 75 percent after two days. The failure of Starch scores to show this pattern indicates the possibility that factors other than memory are dictating research findings and distorting results.

The PARM study indicated that interest in the product leads to substantial overclaiming of readership. In addition, the PARM study found that recognition

FIGURE 21-1

Starch Results for Toyota Ad

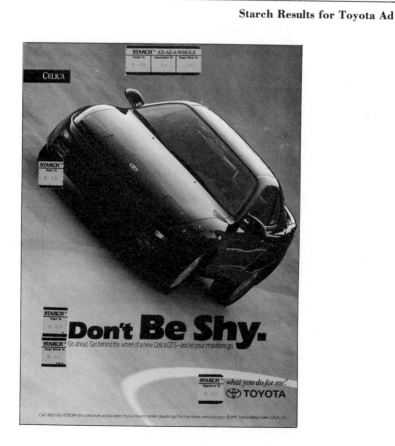

of advertisements is significantly higher among owners of the advertised product. These results taken together suggest the strong possibility that product interest markedly distorts memory and leads to false advertising readership claims. Perhaps all that can be done in the absence of further research is to utilize some type of controlled recognition procedure. In one of the most promising approaches, false advertisements are used to detect overclaiming, and respondents indicate the certainty with which they remember seeing and reading an advertisement. Over-claiming can be detected fairly reliably.

Reproducibility of recognition scores   The Starch organization, of course, uses a small national sample chosen by nonrandom means. Questions have arisen concerning the representativeness of this sample and the degree to which scores would differ if more rigorous sampling were used. The PARM study utilized a much larger randomly chosen sample so that these questions could be answered.

It was found that the average noted score in PARM interviews was 21.7 percent, as compared with the 26.4 percent average score reported by Starch. Although there is a small absolute difference, the correlation was found to exceed 0.85 (1.00 is perfect). As a result of this close agreement, concern over the sampling procedure has abated.

Sensitivity to interviewer variations   Starch interviewers are trained not to point or to direct the respondent's replies in any way. Presumably such gestures could introduce bias. The PARM study analyzed the sensitivity of data to interviewer variations by using both experienced and inexperienced interviewers. Separate tabulation of results showed no significant differences in the noted scores produced by each group.

Using recognition scores   Given the many unanswered issues about methods, what uses can be made of recognition data? Certainly the approach can be helpful in three ways:

1. Readership scores are at least a rough indication of success in attracting and holding attention because it goes without saying that an advertisement must be perceived before advertising objectives are realized.
2. The relative attention-gaining power of variations in creative treatment can be assessed from one campaign to the next or within the same campaign by controlled experiments.
3. The attention-gaining power of competitors' campaigns can be measured.

These data are most useful if an entire campaign is analyzed rather than each advertisement one at a time. It is possible, for example, that the individual score can be biased by an unrepresentative sample for a given issue or other random variations. These variations become neutralized when many stimuli are compared over time. Perhaps the least effective use of recognition scores is to test the attention-gaining power of minor components within an advertisement. It is asking far too much of any reader to remember one's behavior in such minute detail.

Finally, these scores should not be projected to the entire market. The sample is not random, and for that reason no such projection can be made with measurable accuracy.

2. Recall Tests   Recall measures assess the impression of advertisements on the reader's memory according to the extent and accuracy of answers given, without exposure to the stimulus.

Unaided recall   The purest measure of memory relies on no aids whatsoever. The respondent might be asked, for example, "What advertisements have you seen lately?" Such a question is obviously difficult to answer because few respondents will retain such sharp recollections of advertising exposure that much detail will be recalled. Also, it is quite difficult to measure the impact of a specific campaign in this fashion because answers will vary over a wide range of products. For these reasons, unaided recall is seldom relied on as the only measure.

Aided recall   A practically limitless variety of means can be used to jog the respondent's memory and thereby sharpen recall. One might be asked, "What automobile advertisements do you remember seeing in yesterday's paper?" or "What brand of coffee do you remember hearing about recently?" The recall of a specific brand is a strong indication of the strength of the advertising impression.

The Gallup-Robinson impact test   The Gallup-Robinson test, perhaps the best known of the aided recall measures, is offered as a syndicated service. Basically, the technique involves five steps:

1. The person interviewed must recall and describe correctly at least one editorial feature in the publication under analysis.
2. The respondent is then handed a group of cards on which are printed the names of advertised brands that appear in the issue, as well as some that do not. The respondent is asked to indicate which of these products are advertised in the issue.
3. For each advertised brand the respondent recalls from the issue, she or he is interrogated in depth to assess the strength and accuracy of recall.
4. The issue is then opened to each advertisement the respondent recalls. The respondent is asked whether this is the advertisement he or she has in mind and if it is the first time he or she has seen it. If the respondent has not seen it before, the data are discarded in order to arrive at a "proven name registration" figure.
5. Information is gathered on the age, sex, education, and other details of the background of each person interviewed.

The interviewing usually commences on the day after the magazine appears. Responses are edited thoroughly to ascertain that the recall is genuine. The final score, *proven name registration* (*PNR*) is adjusted by size of the appeal, color, placement on the page, and the number of competing advertisements in the issue.

The PARM study referred to earlier also analyzed the Gallup-Robinson approach. The correlation between scores produced by the PARM staff and Gallup-Robinson was 0.82 for women and 0.61 for men. Therefore, this technique was found not to be as fully reproducible as the Starch approach.

Gallup-Robinson scores were found to show the expected pattern of drop-off as time between reading the issue and the interview increased. For this reason if no other, it is quite likely that two different interviewing organizations would produce different results, for only by accident would all respondents be in exactly the same stages of memory decay. The PARM study also detected that the Gallup-Robinson measure is highly sensitive to interviewer skill. The more inexperienced interviewer produced scores that differed significantly from those of the interviewer with greater experience, thus underscoring the need for rigorous training and tight field control.

It has been concluded that the PARM test in general verified that the Gallup-Robinson test truly measures memory, as its proponents claim, with a minimum of distortion from other factors (unlike the Starch measure).

Evaluation of recall tests   It is apparent that unaided and aided recall both offer minimum cues to stimulate memory, and it may be that memory is *understimulated*. The triple-associates tests (described below) and identification tests, of course, minimize this difficulty.

Understimulation of memory may not seem to be a problem. Consider the situation, however, when the advertised product is a convenience good and the objective is merely to register the name repetitively over a long period, or the situation involves low-involvement learning. In all probability, the respondent will not recall seeing the advertisement, but the objective still could have been attained. The point is that recall favors the distinctive appeals, especially those that are highly entertaining, and other high-involvement products. The danger arises when one assumes that a low score always implies failure to attract and hold attention.

Recall and position in the issue   It has frequently been believed that the position of the advertisement in the issue affects recall. For instance, it seems reasonable to expect that the advertisement close to the editorial section will be favored. It has been found, however, that the environment and location of the stimulus were not factors in recall scores. The content of copy and the visualization seem to be the dominant factors.

Finally, it cannot be assumed that the true "impact" of the advertisement has been isolated. This observation is pertinent because the Gallup-Robinson method is frequently referred to as "impact" measurement. If *impact* means the stimulation of buying behavior or successful attainment of other advertising objectives, aided recall in no definitive way is an indication of success. All that can be said is that high recall scores reflect that a strong conscious impression was made and that attention was successfully attracted and held.

3. Association Measures   A time-honored measure of message recall is the *triple-associates test*. Respondents are asked the following type of question: "Which brand of gasoline is advertised as offering 'more miles per gallon'?" Two associates or factors are inherent in such a question: (1) the generic product (gasoline) and (2) the advertising theme ("more miles per gallon"). The third element, the brand name, is to be supplied by the respondent. The percentage of correct answers is thus a measure of the extent to which advertising has correctly registered a theme.

The triple-associates test can easily be modified to suit individual situations as long as it is confined to measurement of registration of a theme or a very abbreviated message. The communication of longer copy or advertising elements cannot be measured effectively with this technique. Also, registration of theme must not be taken as implying that advertising objectives have been achieved. All that can be said is that the advertisement communicated.

4. Combination Measures   It seems safe to observe that a recognition test *over-stimulates* readers or viewers and that recall measurement *understimulates* them. It is possible, however, to combine these measures to capitalize on the strengths of each.

A controlled combination   One of the authors combined the recognition and recall procedures by removing test advertisements from their editorial surroundings, exposing consumers to the copy for a controlled interval, and asking for playback of copy and other features following exposures. Respondents were first qualified as being readers of the issue in which the advertisements appeared, and they were then exposed to five advertisements, one by one, for a short controlled interval. The advertisement was then removed from sight, and the respondent was asked to state whether or not he or she recalled seeing the advertisement. If the reply was affirmative, the respondent was asked to state in detail the major features, copy points, illustrations, and other components. Finally, one of the five stimuli was an advertisement scheduled for appearance one month following the date of the interview, and it was used to detect false recognition claims. The extent of false claiming was found to be minimal. This procedure minimizes the overstimulation inherent in the Starch method. The interval of exposure appeared to be long enough to jog the memory but not long enough to permit further reading of the advertisement and false claiming. Furthermore, the recall phase verified the accuracy of recognition claims. Thus this type of measure seems to be a more accurate indication of readership than either recognition or recall measures used separately.

CELL IV: PRODUCT-RELATED MEASURES UNDER REAL-WORLD CONDITIONS FOR PRETESTING AND POSTTESTING

The most sophisticated and demanding of the various measurement approaches is field measurement of the effects of advertising. Sales test techniques, in particular, generally require considerable time and expense and hence are utilized mostly for purposes of posttesting the effects of an entire campaign. However, all of these procedures may be used on a pretest basis if one is willing to invest in a local tryout of a campaign (e.g., test market a number of creative executions). The pre- and posttests (to be described) are indeed widely used in the measurement of effectiveness.

Pretesting and Posttesting Procedures

1. Pre- and Posttests   When it is not possible to establish a clear-cut sales objective for advertising, the objectives usually are stated in terms of stimulation of awareness, attitude shift, or changes in preference. Whether or not the advertising has been effective requires measurement of changes in response of the initial attitude. Therefore, persons in a market segment will be tested before (pre) and after (post) exposure to the advertising.

A case study of pre- and postmeasurement   We will first analyze a case in which communication effectiveness was measured simply. Then the issues and problems related to the technique will be examined.

A pain reliever   The manufacturer of a leading brand of pain reliever had previously focused advertising on the theme of "fast relief." Because leading competitors were also doing this, it was decided that a new advertising objective should be (1) to hold the present level of awareness of the headache-relief theme (35 percent) and (2) to increase awareness of the cold-relief message from 15 percent to 25 percent in six months. This strategy was undertaken in test markets. The results indicated that the headache message registration actually declined 2 percent at the outset but overall penetration of cold relief reached 28 percent at the conclusion, thereby exceeding expectation.

The case example outlined above has several important aspects: (1) a measurement of message penetration at the beginning of a period, (2) a clear-cut communication goal, (3) another measurement either during or at the end of the campaign period, and (4) an assessment of ensuing changes.

In general, this case is a representative illustration of research-oriented advertising management. The following are some associated problems that may not be apparent to the reader.

1. What is the nature of the sample studied at the beginning of the period? Is it representative? If it is intended to focus on prospects, where is such a list obtained? It may not be possible to draw a random sample because of these problems, and, of course, the effect of nonrandomness is the inability to project the results to the universe being studied.

2. Were the people studied either in the interim or at the end of the campaign period the same as those chosen in the beginning? If so, the distinct possibility exists that the process of measurement may seriously bias later replies. The fact that respondents are asked for their opinions frequently causes them to think more deeply and change their opinions at a later time.

3. If the same people were not measured at a later point, were the samples studied clearly matched as to age, income, and other demographic variables?

Even more to the point, is it known that the later samples studied possessed the same beginning attitudes as the sample used previously? Differences in any of these respects may vitiate the results.

4. Is it known what attitude changes would have occurred in the interim without advertising? Even when there is no intervening advertising, some percent of respondents will change their attitudes or brand preferences because of changes in the environment. In the same sense, it is essential to determine what nonviewers or nonreaders would have done before concluding that any changes are a result of advertising.

Until the above questions can be answered satisfactorily, conclusions cannot be drawn about the validity of the research. Basically, the only way in which these problems can be overcome is through utilization of an experimental design where attempts are made to control all the variables but one—in this case, the advertising used.

Experimental designs for ad tests In a *controlled experiment,* the researcher intervenes to control for as many extraneous variables as possible. The independent variables (the ads) are exposed only to those the researcher wishes, and the results of exposure or nonexposure to the ads are measured (attitudes, preference, purchase, etc.). This allows for causal relationships between the ads and the results to be made. Usually it is necessary to use a test group and a control group. One group is exposed to the advertising and the other is not. The design is represented thus:

A Simplified Experimental Design	Experimental Group	Control Group
Premeasurement	Yes	Yes
Exposure to advertising	Yes	No
Postmeasurement	Yes	Yes

Changes that would have occurred in any event, without the exposure to advertising, presumably will be detected as differences between the pre- and postmeasurements in the control group. This change is subtracted from that noted in the experimental group, and the residual is the change attributable to advertising exposure.

However, the simple design above, sometimes called the *before-and-after with control group design,* may be grossly inadequate for this type of problem. As mentioned before, the simple fact of asking people for their opinions is known to change opinions later, and a very real source of bias is thus introduced by using the same experimental subjects for before-and-after measurement. One way to control for this factor is to use a four-group, six-study design, as illustrated in Table 21–2.

The use of four groups allows detection of the possible biasing effect of premeasurement. If, for instance, the effect introduced by advertising in the first experimental group is much greater than that in the second group receiving no premeasure, it is quite probable that the premeasurement biased later responses.

In that case, the premeasurement of the first group under each heading would be compared with the postmeasurement of the groups receiving no premeasure.

No doubt the four-group, six-study design represents the ideal means to isolate the communication effectiveness of advertising. It would be a mistake, however, to fail to point out the difficulties arising when one attempts to use this "textbook ideal" research method:

1. Is it possible to establish *equivalent* test and control groups, especially when two or more of each kind are used to create the necessary four groups? Unless the answer here is yes, the research becomes questionable.

2. Is it possible to find equivalent groups, one of which is not exposed to the advertising? It may not be possible when a saturation campaign is being used. The individuals not exposed may be very different from those who are, and it may be exceedingly difficult to find typical groups of consumers who would qualify for this particular purpose.

3. Is the information gained worth the cost? The more elaborate the design, the greater the research costs. The basic issue, then, is the return for the investment relative to less ideal designs, and this question is exceptionally difficult to answer.

The problem of finding equivalent groups becomes somewhat less crucial when the numbers in each are large. Difference in various dimensions may then be offset by the force of large numbers. The second problem also may be overcome when the campaign is confined to a select group of media. For instance, assume that dollars are invested in one television program. It may then be possible to find equivalent exposed and unexposed groups, but it must never be forgotten that those who watch the program may still differ from nonviewers in psychological outlook and other characteristics. Finally, the last question is the most difficult of all. Little more than advance hunches regarding the return for an investment in research is possible until more is known about the strengths and weaknesses of various research methods.

It should now be apparent that the case study above suffers from possible sources of bias, yet the application of experimental design also presents real problems. The issue, then, once again revolves around the uses to which the

TABLE 21–2

A Four-Group, Six-Study Design

	Experimental Groups		Control Groups	
	1	2	1	2
Premeasurement	Yes	No	Yes	No
Exposure to advertising	Yes	Yes	No	No
Postmeasurement	Yes	Yes	Yes	Yes

research is put. Measurement without a control group provides a useful but rough indication of progress, and the strengths and weaknesses of the campaign can be pinpointed. If management uses these data with caution and fully recognizes that others factors in addition to advertising could be introducing change, the return of information for a minimum research expenditure can be worthwhile. It is another matter, however, for management to take the results of uncontrolled research as a definitive indication of success or failure. The abandonment or continuation of a campaign theme involving millions of dollars should not rest on such a foundation. In this instance, experimental design procedures should be utilized. There are problems in methodology and possible sources of bias in experimental research, too, but the chances for error resulting from the research methods used or uncontrolled factors are substantially reduced.

2. Sales Tests   The question of whether the influence of advertising on sales can be measured has prompted much discussion in recent years, both pro and con. Consider, for example, the somewhat negative point of view in the following quotation:

> In essence, current sales figures are not the final yardstick of advertising performance unless one or more of these factors are present:
>
> 1. Advertising is the single variable.
> 2. Advertising is the dominant force in the marketing mix.
> 3. The proposition calls for immediate payout (such as in mail-order or retail advertising).
> 4. These conditions seldom prevail among so-called nationally advertised products.[6]

The point is that advertising is usually only one variable in the marketing mix, and it must pull together with the product, price, and distribution channel to produce sales. The contention is that the communication aspects of advertising are usually the only measurable results. As was noted in Chapter 8, this focus on communication has come to be referred to as DAGMAR (*d*efining *a*dvertising *g*oals, *m*easuring *a*dvertising *r*esults).

DAGMAR, however, is referred to by some as a *philosophy of despair*. The argument is that communication goals are being substituted for the more relevant objectives of sales and profit and that communication comes from many sources other than advertising. Moreover, communication does not necessarily mean sales or profit, and examples are reported where one medium produced greater awareness or response but fewer sales or results than another. Therefore, some advocate testing the influence of advertising on sales and attaining profit objectives rather than on communication objectives.

It is useful to distinguish two distinct situations. The first is where one can directly attribute a sale to an ad. This is generally true in direct action ads, such as the Book-of-the-Month Club ad in Figure 21–2. A sales objective is relevant here, and results are easily measured by the level of sales obtained. However,

FIGURE 21–2

An Ad for Which Direct Tracing Is Possible

The Story of Civilization for 20^{00}

The Story of Civilization by Will and Ariel Durant. 11 Volumes

[Publisher's list price **248^{55}**]

You simply agree to buy four books during a year.

Book-of-the-Month Club® offers new members *The Story of Civilization* at extraordinary savings. It's your opportunity to obtain all 11 volumes for just $20—a set exactly like the one sold in bookstores for $248.55. To own it is to have at your fingertips a reference work of undisputed authority. To read it is to enjoy history made live with unfailing excitement and power. In fact, more than seven million Durant books have been distributed by the Club in American homes! It's hard to imagine a more valuable set of books for your home library, especially if there are students in the family.

Bookstore Quality at Book Club Savings

You conveniently shop at home at tremendous savings. Example: if you took *The Story of Civilization* for $20.00, bought six books and two Book-Dividends, you could save an average of $240—*including* postage and handling. And these are true savings, because every book is exactly like the one sold in the bookstores... the same size, paper, type and binding. Book-of-the-Month Club never sells small-size, cheap "book club editions."

Book-Dividends

Every book you buy earns credits which entitle you to select Book-Dividends at hard-to-believe savings. You enjoy savings of *at least 70%* on a wide selection of valuable books—from reference works to Rembrandt—when you remain a Club member after the trial period.

Additional Benefits

A distinguished collection of specially produced record albums—from Billie Holiday to Vladimir Horowitz...a wide variety of beautiful gifts and games... the best of children's books...a Club charge account with no service or interest charges...and much more...all made available *exclusively* to members.

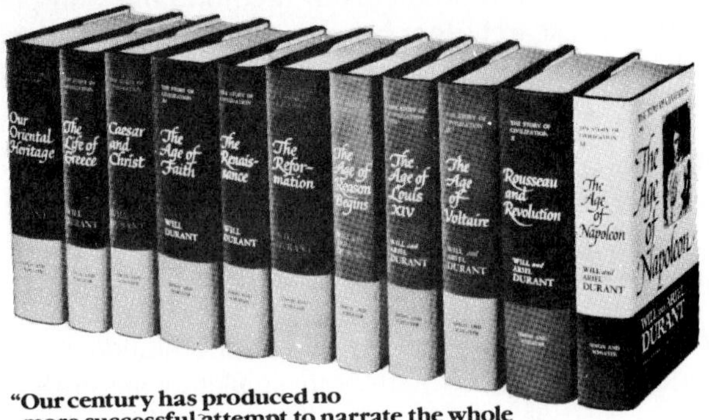

"Our century has produced no more successful attempt to narrate the whole common story of mankind"–CLIFTON FADIMAN

I. Our Oriental Heritage. Ancient Egypt and the Near East. The Far East, early to modern times.

II. The Life of Greece. Explores all facets of Greek life from prehistoric times to the Roman conquest.

III. Caesar and Christ. The rise of Rome and Christianity and the collapse of classic civilization.

IV. The Age of Faith. Christian, Islamic and Judaic civilizations, 325 to 1300, including the Crusades.

V. The Renaissance. Italy's golden age, 1304 to 1576. A turbulent world of intrigue and great art.

VI. The Reformation. Europe's religious conflicts, from two centuries before Luther to Calvin.

VII. The Age of Reason Begins. Europe, 1558-1646. The age of Shakespeare, Rembrandt, Galileo.

VIII. The Age of Louis XIV. The brilliant era of the "Sun King," Milton, Cromwell, Peter the Great.

IX. The Age of Voltaire. Europe from 1715 to 1756. The world of Frederick the Great, Wesley, Bach.

X. Rousseau and Revolution. Europe from the Seven Years' War to the storming of the Bastille.

XI. The Age of Napoleon. France's domination of European history, from the fevers of the French Revolution to Napoleon's defeat at Waterloo. A history of European civilization from 1789 to 1815.

BOOK-OF-THE-MONTH CLUB

Some of the benefits of Membership.

You receive the *Book-of-the-Month Club News*, a literary magazine, 15 times a year (about every 3½ weeks). Each issue reviews a Main Selection plus scores of Alternates.

If you want the *Main Selection* do nothing. It will be shipped to you automatically. If you want one or more Alternate books—or no book at all—indicate your decision on the reply form always enclosed and return it by the date specified.

Return Privilege. If the *News* is delayed and you receive the *Main Selection* without having had 10 days to notify us, you may return it at our expense.

Cancellations. Your membership is cancelable at any time after you have bought 4 additional books. Simply notify Book-of-the-Month Club.

Book-of-the-Month Club, Inc.
Camp Hill, Pennsylvania 17012   8-A8-2

Please enroll me as a member of Book-of-the-Month Club and send me THE STORY OF CIVILIZATION. Bill me $20 for all eleven volumes, plus shipping charges. I agree to buy 4 books during the coming year.   62

Mr.
Mrs.
Miss ....
                    (Please print plainly)

Address .... Apt. ....

City ....

State .... Zip ....

AMERICA'S BOOKSTORE®
Since 1926, 320 million books in 14 million homes.

the more general situation is where direct tracing of sales results to ads is *not* possible. Here a legitimate controversy exists.

The controversy over whether the influence of advertising in attainment of sales objectives is measurable has been briefly described above. The authors do not take sides in the argument but believe it is pertinent to inquire into the possible ways in which the sales effectiveness of promotional dollars might be measured. These include the three discussed below: (1) direct questioning, (2) experimental designs, and (3) minimarket tests.

Direct questioning of buyers   On occasion, it is fruitful to question buyers directly to define the factors that lead them to make a purchasing decision. For example, heavy television advertising for the *Living Bible* was undertaken in several test markets during the Christmas season. Direct questioning of buyers at point of purchase demonstrated high recall of television advertisements, although word of mouth was found to be the dominant influence on the decision.

The difficulties of direct questioning should be apparent. First, most people have great difficulty recalling the circumstances surrounding a decision. It is possible, of course, to minimize this difficulty by progressively taking the respondent back in time and asking him or her to restate the situation as completely as possible. For example, one may associate the purchase of a new automobile with a particular time of year, with particular family discussions, or with other events. Questioning can help one to recall the situation so that the influences on one's decision may come into sharper focus.

Even if the purchasing environment is clear in the respondent's memory, it still is doubtful that the role of advertising will be revealed. It seems to be natural for many to deny being influenced by advertising. This would presumably be admitting in some way to not being rational in buying. Moreover, advertising often works in virtually undetectable ways. Awareness might have been stimulated years before, and it is impossible for the buyer to restate this influence by introspection. These problems are potent barriers indeed. For this reason, introspection by the buyer is seldom relied on to any great extent.

Experimental designs for sales tests   There is no satisfactory substitute for an experimental design to isolate the influence of advertising from the influence of other elements in the marketing mix. The application of experimental design to this problem, however, is complex, and the problems to be faced are many. They include (1) selecting the appropriate design, (2) selecting test and control markets, and (3) analyzing these results.

The appropriate design for sales testing   The before-and-after with control group experimental design is applicable for sales testing. This design uses several test cities and control cities. The procedure was described earlier in this chapter in the section on experimental design for ad tests, and is well illustrated in the Navy market experiment that began this chapter. Sales usually are measured by auditing the inventories of a sample of stores, perhaps using the A. C. Nielsen store audit or a similar service. There is no need in this case for the more complex four-group, six-study design (see Table 21–2) because no interviews are being made. As a result, there is little chance that premeasurement of sales will bias the results. A sales test usually runs from six months to a year to permit time for advertising influence to be exerted. Several test and control markets should be used to minimize the danger that the markets chosen are later found to differ in some important aspect.

Selecting test and control markets[7]   Every attempt must be made to assure that the markets chosen closely mirror the total market. In addition, the test and control areas must not differ in the following respects.

1. *Size*—Usually population areas from 100,000 to 300,000 are used. The areas must be large enough to encompass a variety of economic activities, yet not be so great that measurement and analysis of results are unduly costly.

2. *Population factors*—Areas with distinct and unique ethnic characteristics usually should be avoided. Milwaukee, Wisconsin, with its German stock, would be an unlikely area to test advertising for French wines. The more representative the area, the less likely it is to be rendered atypical by local disturbances such as strikes or layoffs. A one-industry town would be severely shocked by such an occurrence.

3. *Distribution*—The product must be readily available in retail outlets. If possible, retailers and wholesalers should not be informed of the test in order to prevent unusual sales activity on their part that would severely bias the results.

4. *Competitive considerations*—Competition in the test and control areas should not deviate from that usually faced in the entire market. The competitive climate during the test must be carefully monitored because any changes may render the test invalid.

5. *Media*—Full advertising media facilities must be available for use, or comparable media must be available in the test and control areas, and the media should not overlap with other markets (no "leaking").

Analysis of results   If the results of an experiment are those shown in Table 21–3, the results in the test city must be adjusted by the percentages for the control city to show the effect of advertising. Notice that the control city showed a definite decline in sales. If conditions were similar in both areas, it is necessary to calculate what would have happened in the test city without advertising. A 10 percent decline in the test city would have given dollar sales of $360, whereas in reality the sales were $480. Therefore, $360 must be subtracted from $480 to give a net increase of $120. Thus, the actual net increase is 30 percent in dollar sales and 31.7 percent in unit sales. The actual meaning of these changes must be assessed, using appropriate statistical tests.

These results are predicated on the assumption that all other things are equal in the test and control cities. Again we must emphasize that variation in any factor, such as competition or retailers' efforts, present in the test cities and not in the control cities (or vice versa) will confound the experiment. If it appears that factors have not varied, however, the data should give a reasonably accurate measure of the influence of advertising on sales.

Multivariable experimental design   In the above example, only one variable has been measured—the advertising campaign in the test areas. It is possible to study more than one variable at a time and in so doing to reduce the cost of repetitive individual experiments. The Navy experiment was a multivariable design—advertising and sales force.

Multivariable designs are elaborate, and the difficulties of controlling variables are compounded. The data must be analyzed by analysis of variance, a statistical technique that permits delineation of the significance of sales differences resulting from individual variables or from variables in combination. In addition, sales frequently are lost in areas where advertising is reduced; costs become high when test advertising proves to be ineffective; and it is costly to undertake the necessary rigorous analysis and interpretation of data. As a result, experimental designs, especially of such great complexity, are usually the province of the large advertiser. This is not to say, however, that such designs cannot be tailored to the marketing research budgets of the smaller firm.

Even though the difficulties to be faced are great, there is no doubt that proper experimental procedures will permit measurement of the sales power of advertising. Many top marketing companies use experiments regularly. In one experiment for Du Pont, for instance, industrial advertising was undertaken in all but two states, which then served as the control, and changes in effectiveness were assessed in both sections. Similar examples are reported by others. The use of new technology such as IRI's BehaviorScan and Nielsen's ERIN help in this process.

3. Minimarket Tests   There are ways to undertake full-scale experiments without the time and expense necessary for the market tests discussed above. One way is use of the so-called *minimarket*. Minimarkets, or control markets, are cities in which a marketing research firm has paid retailers to guarantee that they will carry

TABLE 21–3

Comparison of Test City and Control City Sales Returns

City	Sales before Test Advertising (Feb. 1– Mar. 31)	Sales during Test Advertising (April 1– May 31)	Percentage Increase or Decrease	Adjusted Percentage Increase or Decrease
Control City A				
Dollars	$300	$270	−10.0	
Units	300	250	−16.7	—
Test City X				
Dollars	$400	$480	+20.0	30.0
Units	400	$460	+15.0	31.7

Note: For purposes of simplification, only one test city and one control city have been used in this example. In actual practice, at least three test cities and three control cities are used.

a product that the research firm designates. These cities, which tend to be smaller and more isolated, include Akron, Duluth, Erie, Lubbock, Mobile, Boise, and Colorado Springs. The leading research services providing this type of procedure include IRI, Nielsen, and AdTel, a part of SAMI/Burke Marketing Services. AdTel utilizes a dual-cable CATV system and two balanced scanner panels of 1,000 households each. Because it is possible to control all variables except the one being tested over television, a precise measurement of effects is possible.

MEASURING CONSUMER AND TRADE PROMOTION EFFECTIVENESS

Measuring the effectiveness of consumer and trade sales promotion is subject to the same difficulties as measuring the effectiveness of advertising. That is, these techniques are used in the presence of other marketing activities, and especially are almost always used in conjunction with advertising. Also, because the objective of consumer and trade promotion is almost always to actualize a sale, the focus of the measurement of the effectiveness is on sales. Typically, then, the promotion manager is measuring sales promotion impacts in real-world contexts where the interest is on sales. Thus, promotional effectiveness measurement usually utilizes the same types of procedures as in Cell IV of Table 21–1: pre- and posttests, sales tests, and minimarket tests. The same types of control and analysis are appropriate.[8]

Thus, the most common approaches utilized in the measurement of the effectiveness of consumer and trade promotions are as follows.

1. *Time series measurement of sales before and after the promotion, without control group.* This approach attempts to find a sudden increase in sales as a result of the promotion. It does, however, suffer from lack of control of other influences on sales.

2. *The experimental and control group design with pre-promotion and post-promotion measures of sales effectiveness.* This design controls for other influences on sales. It is the same type of design as outlined in Table 21–3.

3. *Statistical analysis of historical data.* Here regression procedures are used to try to find relationships between promotions and sales. Since the data utilized are typically nonexperimental, the factors that influence sales other than the promotion must be accounted for statistically.[9]

MEASUREMENT OF SALES FORCE EFFECTIVENESS

Personal selling efforts must also be carefully evaluated if maximum effectiveness is to be achieved. Just as for advertising, consumer sales promotion, and trade promotion, the development of standards of sales performance of all companies must be closely related to the specific sales objectives previously planned. In the evaluation of the sales force, the evaluation process may differ from firm to firm because of the unique circumstances faced in terms of market potential, customer and product mix, competition, and qualitative characteristics of the sales force. These issues set the evaluation of the sales force apart from the evaluation of advertising and promotion.

Standards for Measurement of Performance

Promotion in Action 21–1 describes an increase in personal selling efforts by Carnival Cruise Lines. Just how should Carnival measure the effectiveness of this increase? In doing so, it is important to set both quantitative and qualitative standards in the evaluation of the sales force.

Quantitative Standards   The most commonly used standards are quantitative and are based on single ratios or combinations of ratios. Those expressed in

---

Carnival Cruise Lines

Promotion in Action

21–1

Carnival Cruise Lines, the largest operator in the cruise industry, had 60 sales representatives calling on 35,000 travel agents to stimulate almost $600 million in sales. Two developments were destined to impact the size of the sales force and the way it would operate in the future.

The first development was the purchase of Holland America Line's travel and tourism business, which included four ships that operate in the Caribbean and Alaska, Westours, Westmark Hotels, and Windstar Sail Cruises. Holland America's 34 sales representatives called on 6,000 "core" agents who provided the bulk of the Holland America business.

Second, Carnival had three large cruise ships under construction, with capacities of 2,050 berths each (based on two berths per cabin). The first ship was scheduled to begin cruising in the early 1990s, with the two other ships to follow approximately a year apart.

Carnival thus faced the problem of increasing the size of its sales force to maintain its revenue growth rate and to provide customers for the 75 percent increase in capacity coming on line over the next three years. In addition, Carnival management had to coordinate the operations of the Carnival sales force with those of the Holland America sales force.

Role of the Representatives

Carnival representatives have the challenge of developing the leisure-vacation business and converting it into a Carnival cruise. Competition is land-based resorts, sightseeing, and so forth. Carnival's strategy is to target middle-America and to sell the idea of the ship as the destination with ports of call being bonuses. The ships are designed to provide a range of activities such as dining and dancing, casino gambling, deck activities, health spas, and so on. The Carnival package includes round-trip airfare from anywhere in the country as well as meals and entertainment while at sea. Those in the industry consider the package to be an outstanding value.

Working with Holland America Lines

Coordinating the efforts of the 34 Holland America sales representatives with the Carnival sales force was the second challenge facing management. At the time of the acquisition in early 1989, Holland America representatives called on many of the agents covered by the Carnival sales force. In fact, about 8,000 of the 35,000 agents gave Holland America some business. Carnival sales management developed a new incentive plan for Holland America representatives that made them responsible for bringing in 80 percent of the planned revenue goals for Holland America with the Carnival representatives being responsible for the other 20 percent. It was further stipulated that Carnival representatives would not cover the Holland America core agents as long as the Holland America sales force did its job. Sales efforts of both sales forces would be backed up by print and electronic media ad campaigns, sales promotion, the Carnival Agency Sales Service Department, and a newly developed Alaska Help Desk for travel agents representing Holland America.

In addition, the company holds about 100 sales receptions a year in various regions of the country. At these receptions, local travel agents are greeted by their sales representatives and, perhaps, a Carnival executive. They are wined, dined, and entertained while being given a pep talk about the advantages of selling customers on Carnival or Holland America cruises.

The evaluation of the effectiveness of all this sales force activity was a crucial issue for Carnival's management.

Source: Personal interviews and Faye Rice, "How Carnival Stacks the Decks," *Fortune*, January 16, 1989, pp. 108–16.

quantitative form, however, are the easiest to calculate and to explain to salespersons. This latter factor is most important, especially when the performance standard is being used for incentive purposes as well as for control. Some ratios or measures commonly used include:

1. Sales volume as a percentage of sales potential.
2. Selling expense as a percentage of sales volume.
3. Number of customers sold as a percentage of total number of potential customers.
4. Call frequency ratio, or total calls made divided by total number of accounts and prospects covered.

There are other measures in addition to these, such as average cost per call and average order size, which can be part of the appraisal. The correct choice of measures to use in combination is best set by the sales manager to meet the needs of a specific situation.

Profit contribution standards Most writers on the subject agree that the key measurement for setting standards is sales volume achieved in relation to sales potential. After all, the main objective of the sales force is to make sales, and without such sales, considerations of profitability cannot begin. However, more and more, the norms of sales performance are being combined with those of expense control so that profitability standards may be set. Perhaps the best way to control and appraise sellers' performance is by applying the techniques of distribution cost analysis. In this manner, not only can relative profit contributions of individual salespersons be measured but also standards can be set by which to judge such diverse factors as gross profits, product mix sold, customer mix, direct selling expenses, and the amount of sales promotion assistance going into the territory.

Distribution cost analysis   In very simple terms, a distribution cost analysis would be used to determine the gross margin contribution of each salesperson. This computation based on sales volume less cost of goods sold would give some idea of the *initial* profitability of the product mix being sold. From gross margin would be subtracted those expenses that can be allocated to the salespersons on a causal or benefit basis. This means that only those items that are *caused* by that person's activity or that *benefit* him or her in terms of reaching goals (direct-mail advertising, for example) should be charged against a personal gross margin contribution. The residual is the contribution to general overhead (not allocated to the territory) and to profit. This amount, often termed the *contribution margin,* is an excellent measure of the *relative* performance of individual salespersons. But, equally important, the technique allows the development of both revenue and cost standards based on actual as well as desired performance.

The contribution margin can also be used as part of a return-on-investment (ROI) analysis. For example, if a certain territory produced a contribution margin of $80,000 on sales of $1 million and if $500,000 of company assets had been employed in support of the territory, the following ROI calculations could be made:

$$\frac{\text{Contribution: \$80,000}}{\text{Sales: \$1,000,000}} \times \frac{\text{Sales: \$1,000,000}}{\text{Investment: \$500,000}} = 16 \text{ percent ROI}$$

The use of two fractions rather than one (contributions over investment) is to illustrate that the ROI is a function of both the profitability of the sales volume and the turnover rate. Thus, ROI can be improved in a given territory by increasing sales with investment held constant, by increasing profitability of sales, or by reducing the investment needed to sustain the present level of sales.

By indicating the relative ROIs of various territories, the analysis can be used to appraise how well the various salespersons are doing, given the assets at their disposal.

Qualitative Criteria   The setting of quantitative performance standards, whether based on revenue, cost, or other considerations, has as its major shortcoming the inability to measure activities and traits that may pay off for the salespersons in the long run. To make certain that these qualities are not overlooked in the appraisal process, many firms use a more subjective approach in order to develop norms of performance standards related to the qualitative aspect of the salesperson's job. In some cases, the sales manager or supervisor uses personal judgment in appraising how well the salesperson displays the desired traits. In other cases, a more formalized merit-rating checklist may be used.

Comparing Sellers' Performance to Standards

It is inevitable that some attempts will be made to appraise sellers' performance. Appraisals are needed to indicate where performance is substandard and to provide evidence to support salary adjustments or promotions. Appraisal also provides a good check on how well the sales force building process—selection and training—is being carried out. Last, but very important, is the beneficial effect that a well-administered appraisal program has on seller morale and motivation. Consider the following situation where the standards are unclear to the sales force:

> The senior management of a premium wine producer could not understand its sales force's insensitivity to the company's annual sales goal, which was measured in cases of wine. Although the sales staff worked hard to influence distributors' salespersons, the number of cases actually sold seemed to be of secondary interest. To the company, however, it was critical: The purchase of grapes, glass bottles, corks, and other costly product components were based on the annual case goals. Unfortunately, the winery had not set individual goals for its representatives. As a result, they were more oriented to customer relations than to the sale of a "hard number" of wine cases. Such omissions are not uncommon. Assigning specific, quantifiable goals with associated cash rewards for achievement would provide clear direction to salespersons and their managers. Any number of specific goals could be applied.[10]

The difficulties encountered are numerous. The selling task itself is quite complex, and short-run effort by salespersons may not have immediate results. In addition, some of the results may not be measurable or may not be separable as a consequence of joint effort.

The appraisal process begins with a rather mechanical step. It is the comparison of the actual performances of salespersons or groups of salespersons with the performance standards previously developed. Data on actual performance may come from an analysis of company records or from special reports required of salespersons. Once the data are collected, the evaluation process can begin.

A brief example may be helpful here. Baker and Kent are two salespersons whose sales to date are $93,000 and $98,000, respectively. Their performances are to be measured primarily on the basis of sales in relation to sales potential, the latter being expressed as a quota figure, as follows:

	Sales to Date (in $000)				Percentage of Quota to Date	
	This Year	Last Year	Increase or Decrease	Quota in ($000)	This Year	Last Year
Baker	$93	$ 80	+16	$170	55%	47%
Kent	98	104	−6	200	49	52

If performance is measured on sales alone, it might appear that Kent is outperforming Baker. In terms of quota, however, Baker is performing better. Indeed if the trends from last year are considered, Kent appears to be slipping while Baker is improving.

Although the relatively sparse data presented above can provide for some important analysis, it cannot answer all of the questions required for a complete performance evaluation. For example, the appraiser would need to know the relative profitability in the short run of the sales volume recorded. An analysis of gross margins less allocable expenses would provide the needed answers.

Current-period seller activities that may have payoffs in the future require the use of different standards of performance. Evaluation may take place on the basis of effort expended to gain new accounts or to cultivate old ones. Regardless of the approach, the objective is to gain some feel for the way in which the salesperson is performing the non-order-seeking portion of the job.

In addition to the quantitative evaluation of the salesperson's performance, there is the appraisal of qualitative factors such as attitude, judgment, and appearance. Here the appraiser may use some sort of rating scale. It is good policy to have several people involved in subjective evaluation of salespersons to avoid bias on the part of those engaged in the rating process.

It cannot be stressed too strongly that the criteria, both quantitative and qualitative, used as the bases for appraisal must be consistent with the seller's task as *communicated by the written job description.* The selling job differs widely from firm to firm, and the appraisal process must be custom-made to fit the specific needs and goals of the individual selling organization.

Corrective Action

If the preliminary stages of the *control process* have been handled correctly, the sales manager should have a good idea of the relative performance of the salespersons under her or his supervision. The concept of relative performance is based on performance compared with predetermined standards. In those cases in which individual performances are well below the norms, the sales manager or supervisor can take corrective action. The philosophy underlying this action is that a better use of the resources (sellers) under one's control will increase the contribution of the sales organization to the goals of the firm. This objective might also provide the basis for remedial action where performances are substandard. Essentially, this involves helping the salesperson to utilize his or her most valuable resource—time—more effectively. After this type of remedial action has been undertaken, a second approach may be considered—the direction of activity to areas of greater opportunity.

Time-and-Duty Analysis   This approach to better use of a salesperson's time is an adaptation of the time-and-motion studies used by industrial engineers in the factory. With respect to time utilization by sales personnel, several generalizations can be made. First, a measurable relationship exists between selling time and sales volume. In addition, the actual amount of selling time available to a salesperson in a typical day is very limited. Travel, waiting, small talk, customer service, and report writing all steal time from creative selling. A rule of thumb in some industries is that a sales representative spends about half of his or her time in contact with the customer and the other half in traveling. Second, through careful training and scheduling, management can increase the time available for essential activities at the expense of nonessential ones. Indeed, the essential activities that management wants performed should be scrutinized carefully to see if they are, in fact, essential. For example, many companies ask their salespersons to aid in collecting past due accounts in their territories. If this is really an essential activity, no further question need be raised. In many cases, however, it would be better to use trained credit and collection personnel for collection activity, thus freeing the salespersons to concentrate on the selling task. Third, in addition to increasing the selling time available, it is vital that time be used effectively. For example, many sales managers find that when their sales representatives use genuine sales arguments or reasons to buy in their presentations to prospects, sales result with greater frequency than if the product is merely mentioned.

Of course, changing the selling approach is only one of the ways in which selling time can be made more productive. The point is that management will be in a better position to correct substandard performance if it knows how much selling time is available and how it is being used. Time-and-duty analysis is one way to get this information.

Routing   If about half of the salesperson's time is spent in contact with the customer (perhaps with one sixth of the time used for promotional selling and one third of the time engaged in nonselling activity), the other half is spent in traveling. This travel time bears a very high hourly cost. If sales managers make careful routing and travel plans in situations in which such control is feasible, the savings in time can be substantial. In any event, travel time can be made more productive by having the salesperson use a car phone, by having sales training tapes available, or by simply having the salesperson use the travel time to plan ahead mentally for the next call.

REALLOCATION OF EFFORT

Changing the nature of the seller's task or reducing travel time to allow more opportunity for creative selling is in a very real sense a reallocation of resources. When time is the scarce item, attempts are made to provide more of it for selling and to improve the utilization of that which is available. This attempt to optimize the performance of each individual salesperson in each territory may be only one approach by the sales manager to improve overall performance of the sales force. (See Promotion in Action 21–2 for a discussion of the "X" factor.) Certainly, corrective action should begin at the individual level, but time utilization is only a part of the story. The chances of success are also conditioned strongly by the sales targets chosen. If individuals are using their selling time effectively yet their performance is substandard, perhaps their effort should be reallocated to different products or to different customers. Further analysis of product types sold and customer classes covered may suggest whether the product mix or customer mix can be changed to improve the performance of the subpar salespersons.

However, the sales manager has one other alternative to consider. Briefly, that is whether to reallocate selling resources among the various territories that make up the market. Economic analysis provides the conceptual ideal for allocation of selling effort among territories. The rule for an *optimum* allocation is that the level of selling expenditures in each territory should be such that the incremental receipts per dollar of selling effort should be equal among all territories.

Although this standard cannot be applied precisely to the reallocation of selling effort, a simplified version may be usable. This is the rule that for an optimal allocation, the variable cost of personal selling should be equal to sales

---

Sales Management and the "X" Factor

Most sales professionals spend 80 percent to 90 percent of their time prospecting and qualifying. Selling is something they do only after a long cycle of "little sales." In fact, some sales reps never even write an order.

In pharmaceutical sales, for example, sales reps attempt to persuade a physician to write prescriptions for their products, and if the physician does (and the prescription is correspondingly filled at a local pharmacy), a wholesale drug order is the eventual result. The salesperson isn't really in this loop at all—except indirectly. For these salespeople, results are often calculated by a third party, sometimes in another territory, city, or ZIP code altogether. And if you're in capital equipment sales, sometimes you make only one or two sales a year.

The X Factor

If you're a sales manager who deals with this type of selling situation, what is it that you actually manage? The answer—and this is true, to a greater or lesser degree, for all sales managers—is that you manage the selling process. In other words, you manage your salespeople as they work their way through your industry's generally accepted selling cycle. Often, you manage to a certain "activity" level. The life insurance rookie, for example, must make "X" number of phone calls to generate "X" number of appointments to generate "X" number of sales. Managing the part of that process that involves the actual sale is only a small piece of the pie.

This only serves to reinforce the importance of setting goals and objectives as part of the sales process. Your actual sales numbers will never be met if you only manage to quota. The pharmaceutical sales manager, for example, must set realistic numbers for daily face-to-face calls with physicians. If the industry average is 6.6 calls per day, maybe you should make your goal 7.5 calls. The point is that while it may be fun to swap war stories about that "big sale," there's a lot of very unglamorous and unavoidable hard work that has to happen before you ever get to those great closing numbers.

Source: Excerpted from Jack Falvey, "The Progress of the Process," *Sales & Marketing Management*, September 1992, p. 12.

in each territory. For example, take two territories, A and B. An input of $2,000 in sales effort to each territory results in sales of $5,000 in A and $20,000 in B, for a total of $25,000. Obviously, the response function of B is more favorable than that of A. Shifting inputs from A to B should result in a net increase in sales with no increase in selling costs.

The marketing or sales manager must know how much of a shift in selling expenditures among the territories is necessary to achieve the optimum allocation. A mathematical method for answering the question can be constructed based on two assumptions: (1) that relationships between total variable selling costs and sales in each territory are known from past experience and (2) that underlying factors that determined the relationship in the past have not changed significantly.

SUMMARY

This chapter has examined the assumptions, strengths, and weaknesses of the various approaches for measuring advertising effectiveness, promotional effectiveness, and sales force effectiveness. The use of some of these approaches, however, does not shed light on the actual response by the buyer. This may seem to be an obvious point, but frequently it is forgotten by users of research. A high Starch score, for instance, may be a favorable indication of success, but high readership does not necessarily imply a strong response, nor does it indicate a rising sales curve. Thus, some more sophisticated approaches utilize experiments to evaluate the effectiveness of advertising and sales promotion, and even the sales force.

Given the state of the art, it is essential to advance a strong warning against the quest for certainty. Everyone has a tendency to assume that a quantitative finding is absolute—something on which to rely. The manager who relies on research data religiously without a skeptical, questioning attitude is falling prey to the false god of certainty. Such reliance may lead the manager to make wrong conclusions that can be costly. Moreover, an unquestioning attitude implies intellectual inflexibility, which has no place in promotional evaluation today.

The evaluation and control of sales force efforts requires the development of performance goals and standards. Actual performance is then compared with these predetermined guidelines, and management appraisals are made on how well individual and group performance met the norms. The final step in the process is taking corrective action by changing the extent and (or) direction of the sales effort and improving its quality.

The short-run goal of the evaluation and control process is to meet the firm's revenue and sales targets more effectively by improving the productivity and morale of the sales force. The long-run and more general objective of the evaluation and control process is to ensure that the sales force is the proper size and is trained and directed to make an optimum contribution to the overall long-term profitability of the enterprise.

REVIEW AND DISCUSSION QUESTIONS

1. Are measures of attracting and holding attention necessary to evaluate advertising success?

2. What are the major types of advertising response that can be measured? Critically evaluate each.

3. What is the basis of the argument that claims that advertising effectiveness should be measured (a) in terms of communication of the message and (b) in terms of sales?

4. Describe an experimental design to measure the effectiveness of alternative sampling plans (free product in the mail) for a new product.

5. Imagine that you are the sales manager of a small sales force of 10 persons that sells computer services to law firms. Each salesperson has a geographic area to cover, but these areas differ in size and sales potential. Outline the basic steps that you would take to set up a system of evaluation and control of these efforts.

6. You are trying to develop a compensation system for the members of your company's sales force. You are especially concerned with rewarding those salespersons for activities that contribute greatly to the firm's profitability on a yearly basis. How would you go about measuring the relative profit contributions made by each salesperson?

NOTES

1. Thomas C. Kinnear and Ann R. Root, *1988 Survey of Marketing Research,* (Chicago: American Marketing Association, 1989), p. 44.

2. "21 Ad Agencies Endorse Copy Testing Principles," *Marketing News,* February 19, 1982, pp. 1 and 9; see also the complete PACT statement in the *Journal of Advertising* 2, no. 4 (1982), pp. 4–29.

3. Rudolph Flesch, *The Art of Readable Writing* (New York: Harper & Row, 1974).

4. Unpublished research studies under the supervision of James F. Engel.

5. This whole section is based on Thomas C. Kinnear and James R. Taylor, *Marketing Research: An Applied Approach,* 4th edition (New York: McGraw-Hill, 1991), Chapter 24.

6. Russell H. Colley, *Defining Advertising Goals* (New York: Association of National Advertisers, Inc., 1961), pp. 10 and 12.

7. For a detailed discussion of experimentation, test marketing, and minimarkets, see Thomas C. Kinnear and James R. Taylor, *Marketing Research: An Applied Approach,* 4th edition (New York: McGraw-Hill, 1991), Chapters 9, 20, and 23.

8. For an advanced discussion of the specifics of the analytical approaches used, see Robert C. Blattberg and Scott A. Neslin, *Sales Promotion: Concepts, Methods, and Strategies* (Englewood Cliffs, N.J.: Prentice Hall, Inc., 1990), Chapters 6, 7, 8, and 9.

9. These types of procedures are beyond the scope of this book. The interested reader should consult Blattberg and Neslin, *Sales Promotion,* Chapter 7, and any reference book on the analysis of covariance.

10. Excerpted from Stockton B. Colt, Jr., "Improving Sales Productivity: Four Case Studies," *Sales & Marketing Management,* May 1989, p. 10. Used by permission.

Section

9

EPILOGUE

The man [person] who knows right from wrong and has good judgment and common sense is happier than the man [person] who is immensely rich! For such wisdom is far more valuable than precious jewels. Nothing else compares with it. Have two goals: wisdom—that is, knowing and doing right—and common sense. Don't let them slip away, for they will fill you with living energy, and are a feather in your cap.

Proverbs 3 : 13–15, 21–22, *Living Bible*

From the perspective of the profit-making (or nonprofit) enterprise, promotional strategy is a valid and defensible activity. But can the same be said from the perspective of society as a whole?

At one time ethical, economic, and social considerations were a central concern in texts and courses. Unfortunately, a sampling of the current literature and of course content in business schools shows that this concern has died away. Have we fallen into the trap of "Anything goes as long as I can make a buck"? This seems to be the case in all too many quarters.

In this concluding section, we address serious issues that the responsible manager cannot evade. Ultimately, most of these issues can be resolved only by a personal sense of right and wrong.

Economic and
Social Dimensions

HERE COME THE B-29s

With Asia's $90 billion-a-year cigarette market in their sights, U.S. tobacco firms are moving hungrily into markets from Tokyo to Thailand. U.S. government pressure and slick advertising first opened regional doors for the likes of Philip Morris, RJ Reynolds, and British American Tobacco Co. (BAT), but now these firms are using good-old American marketing know-how to challenge local marketers on their home fields.

Executives attacked Asian markets wtih the same enthusiasm as their predecessors attacked markets back home during the 50s and 60s. Western models and lifestyles create glamorous standards to emulate, and Asian smokers can't get enough.

This success has created a furor among domestic manufacturers that annually are losing more of their markets to imports. Hirayama Takaeshi, director of Tokyo's Institute of Oncology, compares foreign cigarette promotion to *"the old B-29 bombings" of World War II* [italics added].

Source: Mike Levin, "U.S. Tobacco Firms Push Eagerly into Asian Market," *Advertising Age,* January 21, 1991, p. 2. Reproduced by special permission.

The over-55 age group will remember the devastating B-29 attacks over Tokyo and other Japanese cities at the end of World War II. This siege culminated in the atomic destruction of two major cities, Hiroshima and Nagasaki. Now America is once again attacking Japan (and vice versa), this time with an entirely different set of weapons. Not surprisingly, Asian governments are retaliating with cries of outrage and tough local ad restrictions.

The objections are twofold: (1) The invading marketers are promoting a habit that has far-reaching negative health, social, and economic impacts; and (2) local firms and interests are being hurt by the invasion. What is your opinion? First, does advertising have the power to induce people to behave in ways that are nonbeneficial? And, second, does this kind of competition ultimately have a negative economic effect?

We have thrown you right into the center of arguments that have raged for decades. Advertising, of course, draws the most fire because of its visibility. Therefore, it receives the most attention in this chapter as we address the macro effects of promotion on consumer behavior, new-product introduction and prices, and competition and market structure.

The purpose of this chapter is to expose you to the essence of the moral and ethical dilemmas that have surfaced. These issues may seem remote to you at this stage, but they will not be for long. Today's business is increasingly being held accountable for all that it does. Let the words of Peter Drucker sink in:

> This new concept of social responsibility no longer asks what the limitations on business are, or what business should be doing for those under its immediate authority. It demands that business take responsibility for social problems, social issues, social and political goals, and that it become the keeper of society's conscience and the solver of society's problems.[1]

ADVERTISING AND MASS MARKETING: BENEFIT OR VILLAIN?

Advertising and mass marketing are judged and vindicated in reference to some fundamental underlying premises derived, at least in part, from classical economic theory:[2]

1. The role of advertising is purely to inform and motivate, not to cause us to think or act in ways purely dictated by the marketer's intent, whether it be noble or venal.

2. The advertising message gives the consumer truthful information without the inherent potential of deception by omission.

3. Advertising has a positive social impact by motivating people to work and to prioritize their lives in ways that contribute to improved standards of living.

In this section, we will explore these premises one by one with the goal of providing you a balanced picture of the pros and cons that have arisen through decades of critical scrutiny. No doubt you will conclude, as we do, that the "jury is still out" on many of the most critical issues. Indeed, there may be no final verdict. The challenge is for you to form your own opinion and to act responsibly on what you believe.

Advertising: Informative or Persuasive?

Our first premise reads as follows: The role of advertising is purely to inform and motivate, not to cause us to think or act in ways purely dictated by the marketer's intent, whether it be noble or venal. In other words, the consumer must maintain full sovereignty and not be manipulated to act in a way that would be inconsistent with his or her best interests.

Paul Farris and Mark Albion suggest that there are two schools of thought: (1) the traditional premise of classical economics that the consumer is in control (Advertising = Information), and (2) a diametrically opposed perspective that the advertiser is in control (Advertising = Market power).[3] For a compact summary of these perspectives and the resulting implications, see Table 22–1.

What you hold to be true in this important respect affects your assumptions regarding the impact of advertising on (1) consumer behavior; (2) freedom of competitive market entry and survival, and (3) the functioning of price in the marketplace.

TABLE 22–1

Two Schools of Thought on Advertising's Role in the Economy

Advertising = Market Power		Advertising = Information
Advertising affects consumer preferences and tastes, changes product attributes, and differentiates the product from competitive offerings.	**Advertising**	Advertising informs consumers about product attributes and does not change the way they value those attributes.
Consumers become brand loyal and less price sensitive, and perceive fewer substitutes for advertised brands	**Consumer Buying Behavior**	Consumers become more price sensitive and buy best "value." Only the relationship between price and quality affects elasticity for a given product.
Potential entrants must overcome established brand loyalty and spend relatively more on advertising.	**Barriers to Entry**	Advertising makes entry possible for new brands because it can communicate product attributes to consumers.
Firms are insulated from market competition and potential rivals; concentration increases, leaving firms with more discretionary power.	**Industry Structure and Market Power**	Consumers can compare competitive offerings easily and competitive rivalry is increased. Efficient firms remain, and as the inefficient leave, new entrants appear; the effect on concentration is ambiguous.
Firms can charge higher prices and are not as likely to compete on quality or price dimensions. Innovation may be reduced.	**Market Conduct**	More informed consumers put pressures on firms to lower prices and improve quality. Innovation is facilitated via new entrants.
High prices and excessive profits accrue to advertisers and give them even more incentive to advertise their products. Output is restricted compared to conditions of perfect competition.	**Market Performance**	Industry prices are decreased. The effect on profits due to increased competition and increased efficiency is ambiguous.

Source: Paul W. Farris and Mark S. Albion, "The Impact of Advertising on the Price of Consumer Products," *Journal of Marketing* 44 (Summer 1980). Reproduced by special permission.

The Impact of Advertising on Consumer Behavior   Promotion in Action 22–1 presents two sides of a long-running controversy over the role that advertising and mass marketing should perform in a properly working society.

On the one hand, you read that the central role of marketing communication in classic economic theory is to inform:

> There is a need in all market transactions to inform. With such information, markets are made more nearly perfect; the sovereignty of the consumer is served; and the latter learns where and by whom he is served.[4]

Persuasive advertising, on the other hand, has traditionally been viewed as intrusive and manipulative. John Kenneth Galbraith comes right to the point:

> From the standpoint of strict economic orthodoxy, advertising verges dangerously on the subversive . . . . So long as wants are original with the consumer, their satisfaction serves the highest of human purposes . . . . But the foregoing holds only if wants cannot be created, cultivated, shaped, deepened or otherwise induced. Heaven forbid that wants should have their source in the producers of the product or service.[5]

In reality, it is difficult to dichotomize between information and persuasion. Promotion, in its essence, performs both functions, because relevant information undeniably leads to changes in beliefs, attitudes, and behavior. Whether this is good or bad, of course, depends entirely on your evaluation of the outcomes.

We feel that the root of this controversy lies in widespread distrust of the motives and integrity of marketers. Certainly there is some basis for such distrust,

---

Promotion in Action

22–1

Advertising: Inform or Persuade?

Point*

The traditional defense of advertising and selling is that they offer benefits to the consumer by providing information that is useful in buying decisions. As consumer economist Hans Thorelli put it, "Informed customers are protected consumers—more than that, they are liberated consumers.

Counterpoint†

Whatever advertising's direct effect in stimulating sales and making people buy more goods, it fully merits its reputation as an emblem of fraudulence. I do not mean fraudulence in the sense the Federal Trade Commission would recognize . . . . I take as emblematic the old McDonald's slogan, "We do it all for you." That, of course, is a lie . . . . [Advertising] does not seek to improve the lives of consumers except as a means to the end of sales.

* Source: George J. Stigler, "The Economics of Information," *Journal of Political Economy* 60 (1961), pp. 213ff. Hans Thorelli, "The Future for Consumer Information Systems," in *Advances in Consumer Research* Vol. 8, ed. Jerry C. Olson (Ann Arbor, Mich.: Association for Consumer Research, 1980), pp. 222–32.
† Source: Michael Schudson, {i} *Advertising: The Uneasy Persuasion* (New York: Basic Books, 1984), p. 10.

and we will have more to say about this shortly. Where we get uneasy is with charges such as this one leveled by Quentin J. Schultze:

> Advertisers cajole, persuade, encourage, mystify, obfuscate, embellish, exaggerate, urge, wheedle, and admonish. They tell stories, create cosmic dilemmas, build clever arguments, and anthropomorphise products, and depict social relations . . . . Advertisers do these things principally to serve the clients.[6]

Schultze is entitled to his opinion, but it is, after all, only opinion.

We suspect that many critics have some unspoken premises: (1) The only truly helpful information relates to price, performance, and other objective data; (2) the more information we have, the better; and (3) marketing efforts appeal to the "irrational." But who can make such judgment calls?

Here is the determining principle: The consumer must have access to information that is relevant in terms of the evaluative criteria used in purchase. When that information is truthfully and fairly presented, changes in attitude and behavior are quite likely. Each consumer makes the judgment as to what is relevant, and the economic system acts responsibly when that need is met without quibbling over an indefinable line between information and persuasion.

Freedom of Competitive Market Entry and Survival   The defenders of advertising have traditionally argued that economical access to a mass market is an absolute necessity if there is to be ongoing innovation and new-product development. This, in turn, will be lost if the marketers assume undue power and interfere with consumer sovereignty.

There is little doubt that advertising provides a much-needed boost to entrepreneurial behavior. There also is a strong incentive to produce better-quality products. To see what happens when modern marketing is nonexistent, one need only turn to those economies that have recently moved away from their Marxist roots. Where previously there was little or no concern about consumers, matters changed dramatically. Branded and advertised products no longer can get away with shoddy quality that so characterized nonidentified, state-manufactured products. The consumer, of course, is the primary beneficiary.

In other words, it can be argued that mass promotion facilitates and strengthens competition, although this is disputed by some. For opposing points of view, see Promotion in Action 22–2.

Critics argue that advertising reduces competition. If this contention is true, there should be high levels of advertising in those industries in which leading firms have a large market share, and vice versa. This would happen for two reasons: (1) Larger advertisers would have the power to keep new competitors out, and (2) the sheer economic requirements for survival would discourage potential market entrants. New competitors would have difficulty in gaining a foothold, and the outcome would be monopoly power.

The advocates of mass marketing contend that market shares of existing firms would stabilize if this incentive for innovation did not exist. The evidence on this issue is mixed.[7] Although there are high levels of advertising for some products (e.g., and soaps and cigarettes) there are not high levels for many others.

Furthermore, there is no permanence of market share in those situations where high levels of advertising do exist. Data have consistently shown that the top firms in one decade often are in quite a different position in the next. It takes more than sheer marketing firepower to survive, as the managements of such firms as General Motors and Sears have demonstrated.

It cannot be denied that the heavy marketing investment necessary for survival is a deterrent to entry. But advertising should not bear this burden alone. It is more realistic to conclude that the requirements of large-scale operation are the fundamental deterrents to entry, and advertising is just one component.

To sum up, it is not possible to make a convincing case that mass promotion, in and of itself, creates entry barriers and promotes monopoly positions. Entry is always an uphill battle when such large investments are needed, but Wal-Mart, Intel, Mitsubishi Electronics, and others have proven that it can be done.

Furthermore, you would have to look long and hard to find any firm with a guaranteed monopolistic market position. Can you name any?

The Functioning of Price in the Marketplace   Price competition occupies a historic center place in classical economic theory. For a system to function properly, there must be no impediments to price competition. If advertising, in turn, gives power to the marketer, then price competition will be inhibited.

Marketers have traditionally contended that advertising lowers prices because of the advantages of economies of scale. The critics counter, however, that advertisers gain such a consumer edge that price competition no longer is necessary. Representatives of both sides speak for themselves in Promotion in Action 22–3.

Promotion in Action

22–2

Is Advertising a Barrier to Competitive Entry?

Point*

[speaking to the issue of advertising, entry barriers, and monopoly power] That competition is both vigorous and intensive among companies already in the market is clearly apparent from the marked increases in the number of products available and the significant changes that continue to take place in the market shares in most industries.

Counterpoint†

The second most disturbing feature is advertising . . . lies in the area of monopoly power it has placed in the hands of the most substantial spenders (that is, investors in advertising). The national advertising outlay is not evenly divided among contenders for customers. It bulks with a very heavy weight at the top. It appears difficult, if not impossible, today to launch a new brand of food or drug without the outlay of as much as $10 million. If this is true, then what we face is a fantastic tax upon freedom of market entry.

* Source: Jules Backman, *Advertising and Competition* (New York: New York University Press, 1967), p. 8.
† Source: Colston E. Warne, "Advertising—A Critic's View," *Journal of Marketing* 26 (October 1962), p. 12.

Some light is shed on this issue from the economic literature. As Vincent Norris discovered, it is necessary to distinguish between national advertising by manufacturers and local retail advertising.[8] The weight of the evidence, mostly from the 1970s and earlier decades, leads to this conclusion: Advertising has the tendency to stimulate competition and to lower prices at the retail level,[9] whereas it may reduce price competition at the manufacturer level.[10]

Before we accept these conclusions, however, we must recognize that the competitive dynamics have changed. Until the mid-1970s, the differences in price between heavily advertised and nonadvertised goods were not large. In most cases, major industries were characterized by *oligopoly*—a few competitors producing similar products. Because price reductions were promptly met, nonprice competition usually prevailed.

But what a change in the 1990s! Few companies have freedom from voracious price competition. How common it is even in the oligopolistic airline industry for

---

Does Advertising Lower Prices?

Point*

The theory of the relationship between advertising and prices can be briefly summarized as follows:

1. There is not enough evidence available to judge whether for the economy as a whole advertising results is a net increase or decrease in manufacturers' selling prices.

2. If advertising is found to cause manufacturers' selling prices to increase, the magnitude of the price rise will be more than offset by the power of advertising to reduce distribution margins. Accordingly, on balance, advertising tends to reduce final consumer prices.

3. Advertising cuts distribution margins on advertised brands for two reasons: *first,* advertising causes goods to turn over rapidly so that they can be sold profitably with smaller markups, and, *second,* advertising creates product identity—which, in differentiated products, permits the public to compare prices between stores, thus setting a limit on the retailer's freedom to mark up.

Counterpoint†

Obviously, to the extent that partisan advertising alone creates brand loyalty, it creates a noncompetitive market situation. It is little wonder in recent years that we have seen a flight from price competition into promotional rivalry . . . . Not only the small company but the middle-sized company stands a decreasing chance to survive in a period when market survival depends upon the magnitude of promotional outlays rather than upon efficient production reflected in lower prices.

* Source: Robert L. Steiner, "Does Advertising Lower Prices?" in *Advertising's Role in Society,* ed. John S. Wright and John E. Mertes (New York: West Publishing Company, 1974), pp. 215–16.
† Source: Colston E. Warne, "Advertising—A Critic's View," *Journal of Marketing* 26 (October 1962), p. 12.

a smaller competitor such as Southwest Airlines to trigger a price war. And this is commonplace wherever one turns.

In other words, price competition is dominant today, and this leads to the unmistakable conclusion that advertising power does *not* inhibit price competition in today's marketplace. Furthermore, there are no signs that change is on the horizon.

Advertising: Truthful or Deceptive?

Here is the second basic foundational premise on which to judge the impact of mass communication in marketing: The advertising message gives the consumer truthful information without the inherent potential of deception by omission.

This premise has been given its fullest expression in the "Consumer Bill of Rights," first proposed in 1962 by the late President John F. Kennedy. The following two rights define the domain for legitimate, socially responsible marketing communication:[11]

> *The right to be informed*—provision of facts necessary for an informed choice; protection against fraudulent, deceitful, or misleading claims.
>
> *The right to be heard (redress)*—assurance that consumer interests receive full and sympathetic consideration in formulation and implementation of regulatory policy, and prompt and fair restitution.

In other words, the consumer has the right to receive commercial communication giving relevant and truthful information accompanied by genuine feedback when something goes wrong. Once again, attack and counterattack characterize the literature on this important issue.

The Issue of Deception   Nothing interferes more with the consumer's legitimate rights than deception. When it is practiced, consumers often make choices they would have avoided if the full truth had been known.

As you may recall from Chapter 4, deception in advertising occurs if a message in any way creates a false brief or perception about product features or expected performance. This definition places explicit emphasis on perceptions.

There are three types of deception. The first and most obvious is an outright lie, a statement that can be falsified by objective information. The second is claim-fact discrepancy, in which a claimed benefit must be qualified if it is to be understood (e.g., "50 percent off everything on our shelves [if you come in between midnight and 3 A.M.]). The third and most insidious occurs when information processing leaves an erroneous impression about a product or service even though there has been no outright lie. A flagrant example is use of a credible spokesperson to motivate the consumer to trust an unworthy product.

The record of the free enterprise system on deception is spotty, and there always has been a need for regulation. During the 1960s and 1970s, there was considerable crackdown by the federal government. Unfortunately, this regulation abated under the Reagan and Bush administrations, apparently in the belief that the free enterprise system will provide correctives if it is left alone.

This seems to reflect an unfounded optimism about human nature. For example, *Business Week* noted that Procter & Gamble is a "once-cautious giant hound in the FDA [Food and Drug Administration] obedience school."[12] For the interesting story of what happened here, read Promotion in Action 22–4.

We prefer a somewhat more rigorous regulatory atmosphere that supplies a consistent "well-lighted street." When the odds of getting caught are high, the deterrent is more real.

Redress   There is no question that consumer dissatisfaction levels are increasing, and calls for *quality assurance* ring loud and clear. As one consumer researcher put it, we are seeing an "almost Naderistic feel of the '60s in a fight-back trend that is making consumers more conscious about getting ripped off." (Ralph Nader spearheaded the consumerism movement, which began in the 1960s.)[13]

As you have read in earlier chapters, there are ample legal remedies providing for redress across a variety of abuses. The solution lies in top management recognition that quality and customer satisfaction are basic commitments of every responsible business enterprise.

A Mixed Scorecard   On balance, we believe that a better than passing grade can be given to the economic system from the perspective of consumer welfare and interest. Yet sufficient examples of excesses and abuses, including many not mentioned here, exist, which have given rise to the new consumerism movement mentioned above. Pressures have been strong indeed to correct such abuses as deception, defective products, and inadequate information.

The response of business to consumerism, on the whole, has been positive,

---

Proctor & Gamble on a Short Leash

Promotion in Action

22-4

For months, the Food and Drug Administration had been writing letters to Procter & Gamble Co., complaining that it was misleading to use the word *fresh* on Citrus Hill packages because the orange juice is made from concentrate. And despite a long day of meetings between agency and company representatives [in the spring of 1991] P&G still would not back down and remove the offending word.

Finally, at about 10:30 P.M. one evening in April [1991], P&G's people stalked out, apparently convinced that the FDA wouldn't take action. They were wrong. Within days, the FDA flexed its regulatory muscle by seizing a shipment of Citrus Hill. An embarrassed P&G quickly agreed to alter the labels. And just a few weeks later, the FDA forced it to take the words *no cholesterol* and a small heart off packaging for Crisco corn oil.

These high-profile incidents are only the latest in a strong of setbacks the consumer-products giant has suffered recently at the FDA. It has run into obstacles partly because many of its products and claims are ground-breaking. It has also, by its own admission, mishandled some issues.

Source: John Carey and Zachary Schiller, "Procter & Gamble: On a Short Leash," *Business Week*, July 22, 1991, p. 76. Reproduced by special permission.

but the record is mixed. Our point is that promotion can and does perform a socially responsible and valid role when it is managed and conditioned by a genuine consumer orientation. Unfortunately, exceptions often speak so loudly that the public is understandably skeptical.

The Enhancement of Standards of Living

Our third foundation premise states: Advertising has a positive social impact by motivating people to work and to prioritize their lives in ways that contribute to improved standards of living. The debate on this issue is twofold: (1) Is mass promotion, as presently practiced, a needed stimulus in this respect? and (2) Is an enhanced standard of living a valid social goal? Take time to read Promotion in Action 22–5.

The Need for Persuasion to Enhance Living Standards   The rationale is that motivational influences are not sufficient to induce people to work, to produce, and to distribute the necessary goods. Some stimulus is required to influence them to attain higher incomes and to spend what they make on a rising inventory of goods and services. Critics, on the other hand, express concern over the ways in which marketers exploit this motivation to further their ends.[14]

Promotion in Action

22–5

Does Advertising Have Beneficial Effects on Standards of Living?

Point*

Apart from what a specific advertising campaign does for a specific product, there is a broader combined effect of the thousands of advertising exhortations that confront every consumer in America each day, a constant reminder of material goods and services not yet possessed. That effect at the level of individual motivation is felt as a constant impetus toward more consumption, toward acquisition, toward upward mobility. At the collective level, it is felt in the economic drive to produce and to innovate which fuels our economic systems.

Counterpoint†

Advertising exploits the human condition. Realizing that people are naturally covetous, that they form identities from the purchase and display of products and services, advertisers portray various styles of life and visions of reality, hoping to create and maintain meaningful images of people. They show us how to improve our social relationships, how to reduce our anxieties, and how to realize our most personal dreams. All of these things can be accomplished, they suggest, through buying and using particular products.

* Source: Leo Bogart, "Where Does Advertising Research Go from Here?" *Journal of Advertising Research* 9 (March 1969), p. 10.
† Source: Quentin J. Schultze, "Poets for Hire: The Ethics of Consumer Advertising," *Media Development* (1987), p. 3.

We agree with Marsha Richins that no evidence conclusively documents advertising to be a primary causative factor in upward mobility.[15] There is no question, however, that it is a major contributing factor, given (1) the nature of humans as acquisitive beings and (2) the presence (or absence) of environmental conditions that favor economic development.

After a lifetime of study, the eminent historians Will and Ariel Durant came to this conclusion:

> The first biological lesson of history is that life is competition. Competition is not only the life of trade, it is the trade of life—peaceful when food abounds, violent when the mouths outrun the food . . . . We are acquisitive, greedy, and pugnacious because our blood remembers millenniums through which our forebears had to change and fight and kill in order to survive, and had to eat their gastric capacity for fear that they should not soon capture another feast.[16]

If this view is correct, we are constrained by human nature to live a self-centered life, according to the dictates of ego. Thus materialistic striving is a symptom of basic human nature that, admittedly, is fueled and channeled by promotion. (This, by the way, is the Judeo-Christian view, which proceeds from the premise that we are incomplete within ourselves, that we are sinners who cannot change apart from repentance, faith, and total commitment to God.)

The socioeconomic climate also is a major determinant. Taking North America as an example, we know the European settlers were forced to conquer a hostile environment. The Protestant work ethic was perpetuated and reinforced through the doctrine of individual effort inherent in the Protestant religion. In addition, a unique orientation toward the future resulted from a conscious revolt against the traditions of parent countries. Finally, individual initiative proved fruitful because of bountiful natural resources. Advertising is not required, therefore, as a primary incentive for work and achievement. It is our contention that striving toward improvement of living standards is intrinsic in humans.

But there is no question that this motivation is reinforced by advertising and directed toward specific products and services. Therefore, promotional efforts do exert an effect on national income. Yet it is entirely likely, as Michael Schudson[17] and others argue, that the combined effect of promotional efforts strengthens and intensifies materialistic strivings. This leads us to the next issue.

Is a High Standard of Living a Valid Social Goal? This premise is being challenged on two bases: (1) historical precedent and (2) environmentalism.

Historical precedent Historians Will and Ariel Durant, along with others, see the materialism of today as symptomatic of a society in the last stages of decay:

> Caught in the relaxing interval between one moral code and the next, an unmoored generation surrenders itself to luxury, corruption, and a restless disorder of family and morals, in all but a remnant clinging desperately to the old restraints and ways. Few souls feel any longer that "it is beautiful and honorable to die for one's country." A failure of leadership may allow a state to weaken itself with internal

strife. At the end of the process a decisive defeat in war may bring a final blow, or barbarian invasion from without may combine with barbarism welling up from within to bring the civilization to a close.[18]

Historians are not alone in expressing their doubts about the materialistic course of free enterprise societies. There was widespread conviction, especially in the aftermath of the Vietnam War, that the business system was accentuating the very forces bringing society to its knees. Could advertising promote a short-term gain at the expense of long-term cataclysm?

Environmentalism   The world began to awaken in the early 1970s to the reality that its basic resources are not inexhaustible. In Western societies, such resources as air and water had come to be viewed as a common property to be used by all, with the cost to be borne by society.

These concerns became a rallying point of the environmentalism movement. Environmentalists broaden societal consensus beyond consumer satisfaction and focus it as well on *life quality*. They reject a marketing concept that centers only on meeting materialistic desires and strongly advocate the addition of societal and ecological considerations. Every indication is that these voices will continue to grow in the 1990s.[19]

Is There a Solution?   Some serious issues are raised here. But let's be honest: Is it probable that a social consensus will emerge calling for restrictions on the individual consumer and the free enterprise system? We think this is highly un-likely.

Kennedy's original "Consumer Bill of Rights" included the right to choose; this includes, as the late Clare Griffin argued, "freedom for people to do foolish things."[20] If this right is removed or substantially altered, a step has been taken backward from a free enterprise system.

Certainly the world has had an object lesson documenting that Marxist social-ism has failed to produce the economic utopia envisioned by its founders. The crumbling systems of Eastern Europe vividly underscore that only a limited ruling class prospered while the general public lived in deprivation and social needs were unmet. If this is what we mean by restriction of free enterprise, it is not likely that anyone will freely embrace it.

Those who advocate radical change in the freedom of choice (and their numbers are declining) proceed on an all-important but unarticulated premise that humans enter the world with no inherent predisposition to become self-centered and materialistic. The assumption is that self-centeredness is implanted and shaped by the environment.[21] If this is true, the logical solution lies in radical reform.

Others, including Will and Ariel Durant, take quite a different view of human nature, labeling us as "acquisitive, greedy, and pugnacious,"[22] This, of course, is also the Judeo-Christian position that contends that people must change before the world will change. The Durants were not in the least bit optimistic that social surgery would solve the problem. Consider their words: "Nothing is clearer in history than the adoption by successful rebels of the methods they were accustomed to condemn in the forces they deposed."[23]

We agree with John Kenneth Galbraith's current position, that "perhaps this is not a socially perfect design for an economic system. It is, however, the one with and by which we live."[24] An economic system, after all, is only a reflection of the people who populate it. The ultimate solution to the real problems is responsible social action based on strong ethical and moral convictions.

STRENGTHENING THE FREE ENTERPRISE SYSTEM

It is our contention that there is nothing inherent in a profit-motivated free enterprise system that demands a narrow selfishness and lack of identification with the broader concerns of mankind. The key is to adopt a proper attitude with respect to social and ethical responsibility.

This requires an individual commitment to *ethical responsibility*—determination of how things should be and pursuit of morally justified courses of action. The question is no longer whether changes will occur in business practice but how these changes will occur and what form they will take.

Organizational Mission

Financial Accountability   A firm, especially if it is incorporated, outlives any individual set of managers. Present management must of necessity be oriented toward long-term financial survival. It cannot afford to extract a short-term monetary gain from shoddy merchandise or poor service because it must rely on repeat sales. In this sense, the firm profits when the consumers' interests are served.

Accountability to Consumers   We have talked about *consumer rights* without defining the term. The word *right* implies that an individual, oneself or others, is entitled to something. Consider the definition put forward by business ethicist Manuel Velasquez:

> Rights are powerful devices whose main purpose is that of enabling the individual to choose freely whether to pursue certain interests or activities and of protecting those choices.[25]

Do consumers have rights? An affirmative answer by any of us carries with it a commitment to put consumer interests first, over and above monetary or political considerations. This can require some costly choices. Consumerism as a movement has arisen because management has often been guilty of one-way communication with the buyer; it is not listening to feedback.

Accountability to Society as a Whole   "It is increasingly recognized that business must divert some of its profits to help solve social problems." These were the sentiments of the president of Hunt-Wesson Foods in a speech made to an industry group.[26]

Hunt-Wesson has acted on its convictions in many ways, such as financing improved medical care facilities in the inner city. It is only one of a number of firms that recognize a broader social responsibility beyond that of financial returns. Indeed, survival—the basic goal of any enterprise—may demand expenditures and efforts of this type.

Phasing Accountability into Strategy   Most organizations now assign rewards to individual managers on the basis of sales performance, regardless of how much publicity they give to social responsibility. This is accentuated in the product form of organization, which decentralizes corporate and divisional responsibilities. When this happens, there is a tendency to centralize ethical concerns, if they exist at all, at the headquarters level. Often there is no diffusion to the levels at which decisions really are made and implemented.

The solution is for top management to initiate appropriate social and ethical considerations, to make compliance a part of the reward and punishment system, and to provide staff help in implementation at decentralized levels. IBM's Guidelines for Business Conduct are worthy of your consideration (see Table 22–2).

Cooperative Efforts

Because social and ethical responsibilities will never be met completely by individual organizations, a need exists for cooperative efforts. Certainly as a very minimum, an industry should provide a means for curbing false advertising, as well as other practices that are deceptive or unethical. The Advertising Code of American Business is a good starting point (see Table 22–3).

TABLE 22–2

Summarized Portions of IBM's Business Conduct Guidelines

- Avoid misrepresentation.
- Refrain from using IBM's size unfairly.
- Treat everyone fairly.
- Avoid reciprocal dealing.
- Report violations of procurement laws.
- Avoid disparaging competitors.
- Avoid premature disclosure of unannounced products.
- Refrain from further selling after competitor has the firm order.
- Contact with the competition must be legal and proper.
- Avoid making improper use of confidential information.
- Do not obtain information by improper means.
- Avoid violations of patents and copyrights.
- Do not give or accept bribes.

Source: BUSINESS CONDUCT GUIDELINES, International Business Machines Corporation, Armonk, NY, September 1993.

Unfortunately, there are numerous codes of practice that represent nothing more than unenforced platitudes. Such superficial efforts, often undertaken to keep government at bay, do more harm than good in the final analysis, because they give businesses a false sense of "having done something."

It is sometimes said that it goes against the grain of free enterprise to make cooperative codes of ethics compulsory, and to an extent we must agree. Nevertheless, it must not be overlooked that the mass media are intended for public use and are not the sole province of the advertiser. The government can present a convincing case for expanded activity to protect the public interest if self-regulation does not suffice. As never before, the advertising industry is faced with a challenge in this respect that cannot be ignored.

Cooperative efforts have taken the following forms: (1) Better Business Bureaus, (2) policing by advertising media, (3) cooperative improvement efforts, and (4) industry public service.

Better Business Bureaus Local Better Business organizations are sponsored by business firms to eliminate unfair methods of competition. They work with the national Better Business Bureau, which, among other things, publishes *Dos and Don'ts in Advertising Copy* to help advertisers steer clear of legal and ethical hurdles.

Individual customers or business firms initiate complaints to Better Business Bureau offices, and the action taken varies from publicity to legal action. The

TABLE 22–3

The Advertising Code of American Business

1. **Truth.** Advertising shall tell the truth, and shall reveal significant facts, the concealment of which would mislead the public.
2. **Responsibility.** Advertising agencies and advertisers shall be willing to provide substantiation of claims made.
3. **Taste and Decency.** Advertising shall be free of statements, illustrations, or implications which are offensive to good taste or public decency.
4. **Disparagement.** Advertising shall offer merchandise or service on its merits, and refrain from attacking competitors unfairly or disparaging their products, services, or methods of doing business.
5. **Bait Advertising.** Advertising shall offer only merchandise or services which are available for purchase at the advertised price.
6. **Guarantees and Warranties.** Advertising of guarantees and warranties shall be explicit. Advertising of any guarantee or warranty shall clearly and conspicuously disclose its nature and extent, the manner in which the guarantor or warrantor will perform and the identity of the guarantor or warrantor.
7. **Price Claims.** Advertising shall avoid price or savings claims which are false or misleading, or which do not offer provable bargains or savings.
8. **Unprovable Claims.** Advertising shall avoid the use of exaggerated or unprovable claims.
9. **Testimonials.** Advertising containing testimonials shall be limited to those of competent witnesses who are reflecting a real and honest choice.

volume of advertisements and sales claims investigated each year by the Better Business Bureau is said to substantially exceed that processed by governmental enforcement agencies.

Policing by Advertising Media   The media also have taken some positive steps in the form of industry self-regulation. Magazines and newspapers frequently turn down advertising that in their opinion violates good taste or is deceptive in its claims.

Most of the larger television and radio stations belong to the National Association of Broadcasters (NAB). The NAB issues a seal of approval to stations subscribing to its Code of Good Practice. This code is fairly rigorous in its provisions; it bans, for example, payoffs, rigged quiz shows, and deception regarding product characteristics. This is not to say that all areas of public responsibility are comprehended in this code. There have been numerous attempts to establish the NAB as a more definitive voice within the industry, and support for such an action may be growing.

Cooperative Improvement Efforts   Industry associations of various types attempt to induce their members to adhere to ethical codes. The Proprietary Drug Association of America, for instance, enforces a code of ethics for its members, which handle more than 80 percent of all packaged medicines sold in the United States. Similarly, the Toilet Goods Association operates a board of standards to which members submit advertising copy. The board ensures that the copy is consistent with provisions of the Food, Drug, and Cosmetic Act and other legislation.

One encouraging cooperative effort is the National Advertising Review Board (NARB) sponsored by the Council of Better Business Bureaus and other organizations. Its national advertising division receives and evaluates complaints against advertising. If an agreement cannot be reached, complaints are referred to the NARB for study by a panel.

Some have contended that NARB efforts have been too few and that its machinery grinds too slowly. There may be merit to this criticism, but hasty judgments also would be unwise. Further assessment of the NARB record must await longer service.

Industry public service   Some members of the business community have long been sensitive to their role in serving the public sector of the economy. The War Advertising Council was the first formal manifestation of this awareness; it was set up during World War II under the sponsorship of advertisers, agencies, media, and trade associations. The primary purpose was to stimulate the sale of war bonds, and this objective plus others was given a real assist by the industry. This organization was later superseded by the Advertising Council.

The variety of public causes supported by the Advertising Council is impressive. Among the better known organizations and social issues given backing are (1) higher education, (2) the American Red Cross, (3) United Community, (4) the Radio Free Europe Fund, (5) the Youth Fitness program, and (6) the Smokey the

Bear campaign to prevent forest fires. Costs are underwritten by advertisers, media, and agencies.

The Individual Manager

If the spirit of social and ethical responsibility discussed here is to be made operative, the commitment of individual managers to this end is required. This commitment, however, often requires a type of personal courage and sacrifice that many are not prepared to give because too many obstacles must be faced.

Evidence is mounting that today's competitive atmosphere is generating serious pressures to compromise personal ethics.[27] Corporate decision makers are facing a real dilemma.[28] It is not surprising that businesses are signing up for "Ethics 101."[29]

Most managers encounter conflict when they discover that their youthful ideals and goals run counter to business operations that seem to be low on principle and high on expediency. This conflict is most severe for managers aged 34 to 42, and it often is manifested by an unwillingness to take on new problems and a desire to minimize the total demands of a job on one's life.

What choices do we have? Some managers see no problem with subtle deception and other forms of legal but basically immoral business behavior. Others conclude that they will do what is necessary for themselves, regardless of the consequences, as long as they do not get caught. So much for ethics!

Fortunately, there are increasing examples of managers who dare to be different. Creative people in advertising agencies are demanding factual backup of advertising claims from their clients. Younger managers are not hesitating to voice their dissatisfaction with insulting advertising. Executives at all levels are refusing to give in when forced to behave illegally or unethically.

The authors are personally familiar with a number of executives who have successfully taken their stands. Others, unfortunately, have taken their stands and paid the price of dismissal, but their personal integrity remains intact.

Ultimately everyone must come to grips with the eternal question of whether or not there are standards of truth that can govern behavior. Some say no—that truth is illusive and behavior should be based on the whims of the moment. Others place their roots deeply in religious or moral conviction and guide their lives accordingly.

Those who have found themselves—who have a workable philosophy of life—have a place to stand, from which they can dare to be different. Those who have not come to this point have little choice but to cave in when the pressures become great. Society as a whole has a right to expect more.

SUMMARY

This chapter is devoted to a critical analysis of the economic and social role of promotion. The criticisms of this economic activity are far reaching, and the pros and cons are discussed in terms of their effects on prices, competition, consumer choice, and standards of living.

For the most part, the claimed social benefits of promotion are based on the premise that a high and rising standard of living is a valid goal. Once this premise is disavowed, the issues become more sharply focused because the materialistic society of today's Western world may be sowing the seeds of its own destruction. It is pointed out, however, that the economic system is merely a reflection of the basic motivations of its members, and the ultimate solution lies outside of business itself.

Nevertheless, there is much that can be done through a philosophy of business management that stresses not only financial accountability to owners and stockholders but also accountability to consumers and to society as a whole. Some suggestions are given that center on the corporate mission, collective activities, and the role of the individual manager.

REVIEW AND DISCUSSION QUESTIONS

1. A well-known student of consumer affairs made the following statement to a group of home economists at a national meeting: "One of the greatest problems consumers face is lack of adequate information in making a purchase decision. They lack the know-how to be rational buyers, and business is not about to do anything to help them. The only hope is for government and other agencies to step in and give the consumer the information she needs." Comment.

2. Many proposals are advanced to reform the practice of advertising. Some have as their intent the elimination or reduction of the volume of advertising and hence a reduction of the socially detrimental effects of undue materialism. In your opinion, will this type of reform be a meaningful step in solving the basic underlying problems?

3. William Lazer has argued that marketing should work toward the end of helping the consumer to accept self-indulgence, luxurious surroundings, and nonutilitarian products. Do you agree?

4. The president of Hunt-Wesson Foods proposes that business must divert some of its profits to help solve social problems. However, this may serve to reduce the financial rewards to stockholders, thus giving rise to what might become a conflict of interest. Can this conflict be resolved?

5. In what sense are many criticisms of promotion really a criticism of poor management?

NOTES

1. Peter F. Drucker, *An Introductory View of Management* (New York: Harper & Row, 1977), p. 271.

2. For further background, see Kim B. Rotzoll and James E. Haefner, *Advertisig in Contemporary Society,* 2nd ed. (Cincinnati, Ohio: South-Western, 1990), pp. 162–68.

3. Paul W. Farris and Mark S. Albion, "The Impact of Advertising on the Price of Consumer Products," *Journal of Marketing,* 44 (Summer 1980).

4. John Kenneth Galbraith, "Economics and Advertising: Exercise in Denial," *Advertising Age,* November 9, 1988, p. 81.

5. Ibid.

6. Quentin J. Schultze, "Poets for Hire: The Ethics of Consumer Advertising," *Media Development* 3 (1987), p. 11.

7. For a review of this evidence see Rotzoll and Haefner, *Advertising in Contemporary Society,* pp. 91–92.

8. Vincent P. Norris, "The Economic Effects of Advertising: A Review of the Literature," in *Current Issues and Research in Advertising,* vol. 7, ed. Claude Martin and James Leigh (Ann Arbor, Mich.: Division of Research, School of Business Administration, University of Michigan, 1984), p. 105.

9. Ibid.

10. William S. Comanor and Thomas A. Wilson, *Advertising and Market Power* (Cambridge, Mass.: Harvard University Press, 1974); and J. J. Lambin, *Competition and Market Conduct in Oligopoly Over Time* (Amsterdam: North Holland, 1976).

11. Robert J. Lampman, "JFK's Four Consumer Rights: A Retrospective View," in *The Frontier of Consumer Interest,* ed. E. Scott Maynes (Columbia, Mo.: University of Missouri, American Council on Consumer Interests, 1988), pp. 19–36.

12. John Carey and Zachary Schiller, "Procter & Gamble: On a Short Leash," *Business Week,* July 22, 1991, p. 76.

13. For a detailed review of consumerism and its implications, see James F. Engel, Roger D. Blackwell, and Paul W. Miniard, *Consumer Behavior,* 7th ed. (Forth Worth, Tex.: Dryden Press, 1993), Chapter 24.

14. See Richard W. Pollay, "Quality of Life in the Padded Sell: Common Criticisms of Advertising's Cultural Character and International Public Policies," in *Current Issues and Research in Advertising,* vol. 9, ed. Claude Martin and James Leigh (Ann Arbor, Mich.: Division of Research, School of Business Administration, Unviersity of Michigan, 1986), pp. 173–250.

15. Marsha L. Richins, "Media, Materialism, and Human Happiness," in *Advances in Consumer Research* vol. 14, ed. Melanie Wallendorf and Paul Anderson (Provo, Utah: Association for Consumer Research, 1987), pp. 352–56.

16. Will and Ariel Durant, *The Lessons of History* (New York: Simon & Schuster, 1968), p. 19.

17. Ibid, p. 93.

18. For an interesting review, see Ronald Grover, "Fighting Back: The Resurgence of Social Activism," *Business Week,* May 22, 1989, pp. 34–35.

19. Michael Schudson, *Advertising: The Uneasy Persuasion* (New York: Basic Books, 1984).

20. Clare E. Griffin, *The New Face of Capitalism* (Ann Arbor, Mich.: University of Michigan Graduate School of Business, 1961), p. 18.

21. This is the essential premise of B. F. Skinner, *Beyond Freedom and Dignity* (New York: Alfred A. Knopf, 1971).

22. Durant and Durant, *The Lessons of History,* p. 9.

23. Ibid., p. 34.

24. Galbraith, "Economics and Advertising," p. 81.

25. Manuel G. Valesquez, as quoted in Van B. Weigel, *Business Ethics and Transitional Economies,* unpublished manuscript, Eastern College, 1991, p. 187.

26. Quoted in *Advertising Age,* February 23, 1970, p. 191.

27. Geoffrey P. Lantos, "An Ethical Base for Decision Making" (unpublished manuscript, Fall 1986).

28. Daniel E. Maltby, "The One-Minute Ethicist," *Christianity Today,* February 19, 1988, pp. 26–29.

29. John A. Byrne, "Businesses Are Signing Up for Ethics 101," *Business Week,* February 15, 1988, pp. 56–57.

30. *Sales Management,* May 1, 1969, p. 20.

Index

Credits

Chapter 1

pg. 2, Courtesy Heuer Time & Electronics Corporation; pg. 5, Courtesy Heuer Time & Electronics Corporation; pg. 11, Courtesy Speidel Division of Textron Inc.; pg. 17, Courtesy Nissan Motor Corporation USA; pg. 19, Courtesy Van Den Bergh Foods Company.

Chapter 2

pg. 29, Sharon Hoogstraten; pg. 30, Courtesy Italian Government Travel Office; pg. 36, Courtesy Michelin Tire Corporation; pg. 37, Courtesy S.C. Johnson & Son, Inc., Courtesy Miller Brewing Company; pg. 38, Courtesy Swatch Watch USA; pg. 39, Courtesy The Procter & Gamble Company; pg. 41, Courtesy The Hertz Corporation; pg. 42, Reprinted with permission of CPC International Inc. Knorr is a registered trademark of Knorr-Naehrmittel Ag.

Chapter 3

pg. 50, ITAR-TASS/Sovfoto; pg. 56, Illustration by Richard Westgard for *Marketing News*, January 17, 1991. *Marketing News* is published by the American Marketing Association.; pg. 58, Courtesy Chrysler Corporation; pg. 59, Courtesy Hiram Walker & Sons; pg. 60, Courtesy William Grant & Sons, Inc.; pg. 61, Courtesy Chrysler Corporation, Courtesy Pentax Corporation; pg. 62, Courtesy Thomas J. Lipton Company; pg. 65, Courtesy The Gillette Company; pg. 67, Courtesy Grosvenor Canada; pg. 70, Courtesy DuPont, Courtesy J.E. Seagram Corporation.

Chapter 4

pg. 76, Courtesy Sterling Winthrop Inc.; pg. 89, Courtesy Royal Viking Line, Courtesy Princess Cruises, Courtesy Norwegian Cruise Line; pg. 91, Courtesy Carnival Cruise Lines.

Chapter 5

pg. 96, Courtesy Saturn Corporation; pg. 98, Courtesy Saturn Corporation; pg. 101, Courtesy Kraft General Foods, Inc.; pg. 110, Courtesy Hiram Walker & Sons.

Chapter 6

pg. 116, Steven Rothfeld; pg. 123, Courtesy Lufthansa German·Airlines USA; pg. 124, Courtesy 3M; pg. 129, Courtesy Campbell Soup Company; pg. 130, Courtesy Rhone-Poulenc Rorer Pharmaceuticals, Inc.; pg. 135, Courtesy Mitsubishi Motor Sales of America, Inc.

Chapter 7

pg. 144, Courtesy Van Den Bergh Foods Company; pg. 155, Courtesy Johnson & Johnson, Courtesy Midas International Corporation; pg. 158, Copyright (1993) Mazda Motor of America, Inc. Used by permission, Courtesy Bristol Meyers Squibb; pg. 165, Courtesy The Procter & Gamble Company, Courtesy Volvo Cars of North America.

Chapter 8

pg. 172, Sharon Hoogstraten; pg. 175, Courtesy Bristol Meyers Squibb.

Chapter 9

pg. 188, Ron Chapple/FPG International.

Chapter 10

pg. 218, Sharon Hoogstraten; pg. 228, Courtesy CIBA-GEIGY Corporation; pg. 229, Courtesy Olympus Corporation; pg. 230, Courtesy The Coca-Cola Company. Coca-Cola and the Dynamic Ribbon device are registered trademarks of The Coca-Cola Company.; pg. 231, Courtesy Anheuser-Busch Companies; pg. 232, Courtesy Helene Curtis Industries, Inc.; pg. 233, Courtesy Chinon America, Inc.; pg. 234, Courtesy Roadway Services; pg. 235, Courtesy Whirlpool Corporation; pg. 236, Courtesy The House of Seagram; pg. 237,

Courtesy The Upjohn Company; pg. 238, Courtesy Marion Merrell Dow; pg. 239, Courtesy Cunard Line Ltd.; pg. 240, Courtesy The Pepsi-Cola Company; pg. 241, Courtesy McNeil Consumer Products Company; pg. 242, Courtesy Hush Puppies Company; pg. 243, Courtesy Green Mountain Coffee, Inc.; pg. 244, Photo Courtesy of Hewlett-Packard Company; pg. 246, Courtesy Carnival Cruise Lines.

Chapter 11
pg. 264, Sharon Hoogstraten; pg. 295, Courtesy of Time Magazine; pg. 297, Courtesy Gruner & Jahr USA; pg. 302, Courtesy Radio Advertising Bureau, Inc.; pg. 303, Courtesy MTV.

Chapter 12
pg. 312, Courtesy The Richards Group for Motel 6.

Chapter 13
pg. 344, Courtesy The Southland Corporation and Ito-Yokado Co., Ltd.; pg. 356, Courtesy Palm Beach Company; pg. 361, Courtesy Visine-Pfizer, Inc.; pg. 363, Courtesy RTC/Beverage Marketing Group; pg. 371, Courtesy Heinz USA.

Chapter 14
pg. 380, Courtesy NBC; pg. 388, Courtesy Royal Crown Cola Company; pg. 389, Courtesy Hanes Hosiery, Inc.; pg. 394, Courtesy King Arthur Flour; pg. 396, Courtesy PepsiCo, Inc.; pg. 397, Courtesy Hygrade Food Products Corporation.

Chapter 15
pg. 404, Courtesy Nabisco Foods Company; pg. 410, Courtesy CompUSA.

Chapter 16
pg. 420, Jeff Smith/The Image Bank; pg. 430, Courtesy Carnival Cruise Lines; pg. 436, Courtesy Mary Kay Cosmetics, Inc.

Chapter 17
pg. 442, Courtesy Miller Brewing Company; pg. 450, Courtesy Avon Products, Inc.; pg. 452, Courtesy Ogilvy & Mather; pg. 458, Courtesy Holy Land Christian Mission International.

Chapter 18
pg. 464, Sharon Hoogstraten; pg. 470, Courtesy The Schechter Group, Inc.; pg. 474, Courtesy Phillips Petroleum/photography by Jeffrey L. Rottman, Peter Arnold, Inc.; pg. 477, Courtesy Raytheon Company; pg. 478, Courtesy Ford Motor Company; pg. 479, Courtesy Lockheed Corporation; pg. 482, Courtesy Carnival Cruise Lines; pg. 484, Courtesy Carnival Cruise Lines.

Chapter 19
pg. 488, Sharon Hoogstraten; pg. 502, Courtesy National Advertising Division—Council of Better Business Bureaus, Inc.

Chapter 20
pg. 520, Sharon Hoogstraten; pg. 532, Courtesy DMB&B; pg. 537, Reprinted with permission of The Quaker Oats Company.

Chapter 21
pg. 548, Courtesy Navy Recruiting Command; pg. 563, Courtesy Starch INRA Hooper and Toyota Motor Sales USA; pg. 572, Courtesy Book-of-the-Month Club.

Chapter 22
pg. 588, Don Smetzer/Tony Stone Images.

Color Insert 1
pg. 1, Courtesy The Perrier Group; pgs. 2&3, Courtesy Speidel Division of Textron Inc.; pg. 4, Courtesy Elite Foods, Inc.

Color Insert 2
pg. 2, Courtesy DuPont; pg. 3, Courtesy Estee Lauder; pg. 4, Courtesy Nautica.

Color Insert 3
pg. 1, Courtesy Crawford Products, Inc.; pgs. 2&3, Courtesy Heinz USA; pg. 4, Courtesy Seiko Time.

Color Insert 4
pg. 1, Courtesy Metromail; pg. 2, Courtesy Catalina Marketing Corporation; pg. 3, Courtesy Phillips Petroleum Company; pg. 4, Courtesy Xerox Corporation, Courtesy Rollerblade, Inc.